P9-EDC-487

The Prehistory of the Mind

The Prehistory of the Mind

The cognitive origins of art, religion and science

with 70 illustrations

THAMES AND HUDSON

For my children Hannah, Nicholas and Heather

First published in the United States of America in 1996 by Thames and Hudson Inc., 500 Fifth Avenue, New York, New York 10110

Library of Congress Catalog Card Number 96-60367
ISBN 0-500-05081-3

Printed and bound in Slovenia

Contents

Preface

IT TOOK MILLIONS of years for the human mind to evolve. It is the product of a long, gradual process with no predestined goal or direction. During the final 2.5 million years of this process, our ancestors left traces of their behaviour such as their stone tools, food debris and paintings on cave walls. They only left written records towards the very end of this period, starting a mere 5,000 years ago. Consequently to understand the evolution of the mind we must look at our *prehistory*, for it was during that time that the distinguishing features of the human mind arose, features such as language and an advanced intelligence. To gain an understanding of the mind leads on to an appreciation of what it means to be human. I hope, therefore, that *The Prehistory of the Mind* will be of interest not just to archaeologists and psychologists, but to any moderately inquisitive and reflective reader.

I have tried to write a book that makes the evidence from prehistory accessible to readers who may never previously have heard of an australopithecine or a handaxe. But this book also tries to put forward a new theory for the evolution of the mind. The academic audience who must judge this theory will need to see it supported at a level of detail that is perhaps tedious for the general reader. I cater for those scholars with extensive notes to provide additional support for claims made within the text. These will also be of value to students trying to get to grips with the complexities of the archaeological record and human evolution.

Although the evolution of the mind was a slow, gradual process, there were nevertheless key events which acted as turning points for how the mind evolved. Similarly the evolution of this book has been a gradual process, but one for which I can see three defining events. Without these it would either not have been written, or, like the mind, have remained in a rather primitive state. After having my initial interest in prehistoric cognition stimulated by reading the work of the American archaeologist Thomas Wynn, the first of these defining events was in 1988 while I was a Research Fellow at Trinity Hall in Cambridge. At lunch one day the Master of the college, Sir John Lyons, casually asked me whether I had ever read *The Modularity of Mind* by Jerry Fodor. I hadn't, but did so immediately. And thus an idea about the prehistory of the mind was sown within my mind, although it remained there with little growth for the following six years. Then – the second event – one evening in April 1994, after having left Cambridge and joined the staff at Reading University, I had dinner with Leda Cosmides, John Tooby and Michael Jochim in a beach restaurant in Santa Barbara, California. Leda and John bombarded me with their ideas about an evolutionary psychology, and gave me a list of books to read, each of which became critical to the development of my work. Finally, a few months later, I chatted with a colleague of mine, Mark Lake, as we ate at a motorway service station somewhere on the M6 in the middle of the night while driving to my excavations in Scotland. We talked about archaeology, the mind and computers and I realized that it was time to get the prehistory of the mind out of my mind and on to paper.

The opportunity to do so was granted by my colleagues in the Department of Archaeology at Reading University who allowed me to take a period of research leave, between January and March 1995, during which the first draft of this book was written. I am grateful to my Reading colleagues not only for this period of leave but for having provided such a pleasant and stimulating environment for developing my version of cognitive archaeology since joining them in 1992. Richard Bradley, Dick Byrne and Clive Gamble kindly read that draft and provided many perceptive criticisms and words of encouragement.

While re-writing the book many people provided me with new references, their unpublished papers and simply their time – often no more than a few words in conversation which, unknown to them, were of such value to me. Others have been most helpful in my research on ancient minds during my time in Cambridge and Reading. I would particularly like to thank: Leslie Aiello, Ofer Bar-Yosef, Pascal Boyer, Bob Chapman, Michael Corballis, Leda Cosmides, Nyree Finlay, Bill Finlayson, Robert Foley, Chris Knight, Alexander Marshack, Gilbert Marshall, Paul Mellars, Richard Mithen, Steven Pinker, Camilla Powers, Colin Renfrew, Chris Scarre, Rick Schulting, John Shea, Stephen Shennan, James Steele, Chris Stringer and Thomas Wynn. Throughout that time, Mark Lake has been a sounding board for my ideas and to him I am particularly grateful. I also owe a debt to the editorial staff at Thames and Hudson for their help during the final stages of writing. And I would like to thank Margaret Mathews and Aaron Watson for the line drawings.

Most of the writing for this book was undertaken on the dining room table at home in the midst of the hurly-burly of my family life. Consequently my biggest thanks must go to my wife, Sue, and to my children for suffering the piles of books and my constant tapping at the wordprocessor. It is indeed to my children, Hannah, Nicholas and Heather, that I dedicate this book as thanks for having such lively and thoroughly modern young minds.

1 Why ask an archaeologist about the human mind?

THE HUMAN MIND is intangible, an abstraction. In spite of more than a century of systematic study by psychologists and philosophers, it eludes definition and adequate description, let alone explanation. Stone tools, pieces of broken bone and carved figurines – the stuff of archaeology – have other qualities. They can be weighed and measured, illustrated in books and put on display. They are nothing at all like the mind – except for the profound sense of mystery that surrounds them. So why ask an archaeologist about the human mind?

People are intrigued by various aspects of the mind. What is intelligence? What is consciousness? How can the human mind create art, undertake science and believe in religious ideologies when not a trace of these are found in the chimpanzee, our closest living relative?[1] Again one might wonder: how can archaeologists with their ancient artifacts help answer such questions?

Rather than approach an archaeologist, one is likely to turn to a psychologist: it is the psychologist who studies the mind, often by using ingenious laboratory experiments. Psychologists explore the mental development of children, malfunctions of the brain and whether chimpanzees can acquire language. From this research they may offer answers to the types of questions posed above.

Or perhaps one would try a philosopher. The nature of the mind and its relation to the brain – the mind-body problem – has been a persistent issue in philosophy for over a century. Some philosophers have looked for empirical evidence, others have simply brought their considerable intellects to bear on the subject.

There are other specialists one might approach. Perhaps a neurologist who can look at what actually goes on in the brain; perhaps a primatologist with specialized knowledge of chimpanzees in natural, rather than laboratory, settings; perhaps a biological anthropologist who examines fossils to study how the brain has changed in size and shape during the course of human evolution, or a social anthropologist who studies the nature of thought in non-Western societies; perhaps a computer scientist who creates artificial intelligence?

The list of whom we might turn to for answers about the human mind is indeed long. Maybe it should be longer still with the addition of artists, athletes and actors – those who use their minds for particularly impressive feats of concentration and imagination. Of course the sensible answer is that we should ask all of these: almost all disciplines can contribute towards an understanding of the human mind.

But what has archaeology got to offer? More specifically, the archaeology to be considered in this book, that of prehistoric hunter-gatherers? This stretches from the first appearance of stone tools 2.5 million years ago to the appearance of agriculture after 10,000 years ago. The answer is quite simple: we can only ever understand the present by knowing the past. Archaeology may therefore not only be able to contribute, it may hold the key to an understanding of the modern mind.

Creationists believe that the mind sprang suddenly into existence fully formed. In their view it is a product of divine creation.[2] They are wrong: the mind has a long evolutionary history and can be explained without recourse to supernatural powers. The importance of understanding the evolutionary history of the mind is one reason why many psychologists study the chimpanzee, our closest living relative. Numerous studies have compared the chimpanzee and human mind, notably with regard to linguistic capacities. Yet such studies have ultimately proved unsatisfactory, because while the chimpanzee is indeed our closest living relative, it is not very close at all. We shared a common ancestor about 6 million years ago. After that date the evolutionary lineages leading to modern apes and humans diverged. A full 6 million years of evolution therefore separates the minds of modern humans and chimpanzees.

It is that period of 6 million years which holds the key to an understanding of the modern mind. We need to look at the minds of our many ancestors[3] during that time, including the 4.5-million-year-old ancestor known as *Australopithecus ramidus*; the 2-million-year-old *Homo habilis*, among the first of our ancestors to make stone tools; *Homo erectus*, the first to leave Africa 1.8 million years ago; *Homo neanderthalensis* (the Neanderthals), who survived in Europe until less than 30,000 years ago; and finally our own species, *Homo sapiens sapiens*, appearing 100,000 years ago. Such ancestors are known only through their fossil remains and the material residues of their behaviour – those stone tools, broken bones and carved figurines.

The most ambitious attempt so far to reconstruct the minds of these ancestors has been by the psychologist Merlin Donald. In his book *The Origins of the Modern Mind* (1991), he drew substantially on archaeological data to propose a scenario for the evolution of the mind. I want to follow in Donald's footsteps, although I believe he made some fundamental errors in his work – otherwise there would be no need for this book.[4] But I want to turn the tables on Donald's approach. Rather than being a psychologist drawing on archaeological data, I am writing as an archaeologist who wishes to draw on ideas from psychology. Rather than having archaeology play the supporting role, I want it to set the agenda for understanding the modern mind. So here I provide *The Prehistory of the Mind.*

The last two decades have seen a remarkable advance in our understanding of the behaviour and evolutionary relationships of our ancestors. Indeed many archaeologists now feel confident that the time is ripe to move beyond asking questions about how these ancestors looked and behaved, to asking what was going on within their minds. It is time for a 'cognitive archaeology'.[5]

The need for this is particularly evident from the pattern of brain expansion during the course of human evolution and its relationship – or the lack of one – to changes in past behaviour. It becomes clear that there is no simple relationship between brain size, 'intelligence' and behaviour. In Figure 1 I depict the increase in brain size during the last 4 million years of evolution across a succession of human ancestors and relatives whom I will introduce more fully in the next chapter. But here just consider the manner in which brain size increased. We can see that there were two major spurts of brain enlargement, one between 2.0 and 1.5 million years ago, which seems to be related to the appearance of *Homo habilis*, and a less pronounced one between 500,000 and 200,000 years ago. Archaeologists tentatively link the first spurt to the development of toolmaking, but can find no major change in the nature of the archaeological record correlating with the second period of rapid brain expansion. Our ancestors continued the same basic hunting and gathering lifestyle, with the same limited range of stone and wooden tools.

The two really dramatic transformations in human behaviour occurred long after the modern size of the brain had evolved. They are both associated exclusively with *Homo sapiens sapiens*. The first was a cultural explosion between 60,000 and 30,000 years ago, when the first art, complex technology and religion appeared. The second was the rise of farming 10,000 years ago, when people for the first time began to plant crops and domesticate animals. Although the Neanderthals (200,000–30,000 years ago) had brains as large as ours today, their culture remained extremely limited – no art, no complex technology and most probably no religious behaviour. Now big brains are expensive organs, requiring a lot of energy to maintain – 22 times as much as an equivalent amount of muscle requires when at rest.[6] So here we find a dilemma – what was all the new brain processing power before the 'cultural explosion' being used for? What was happening to the mind as brain size

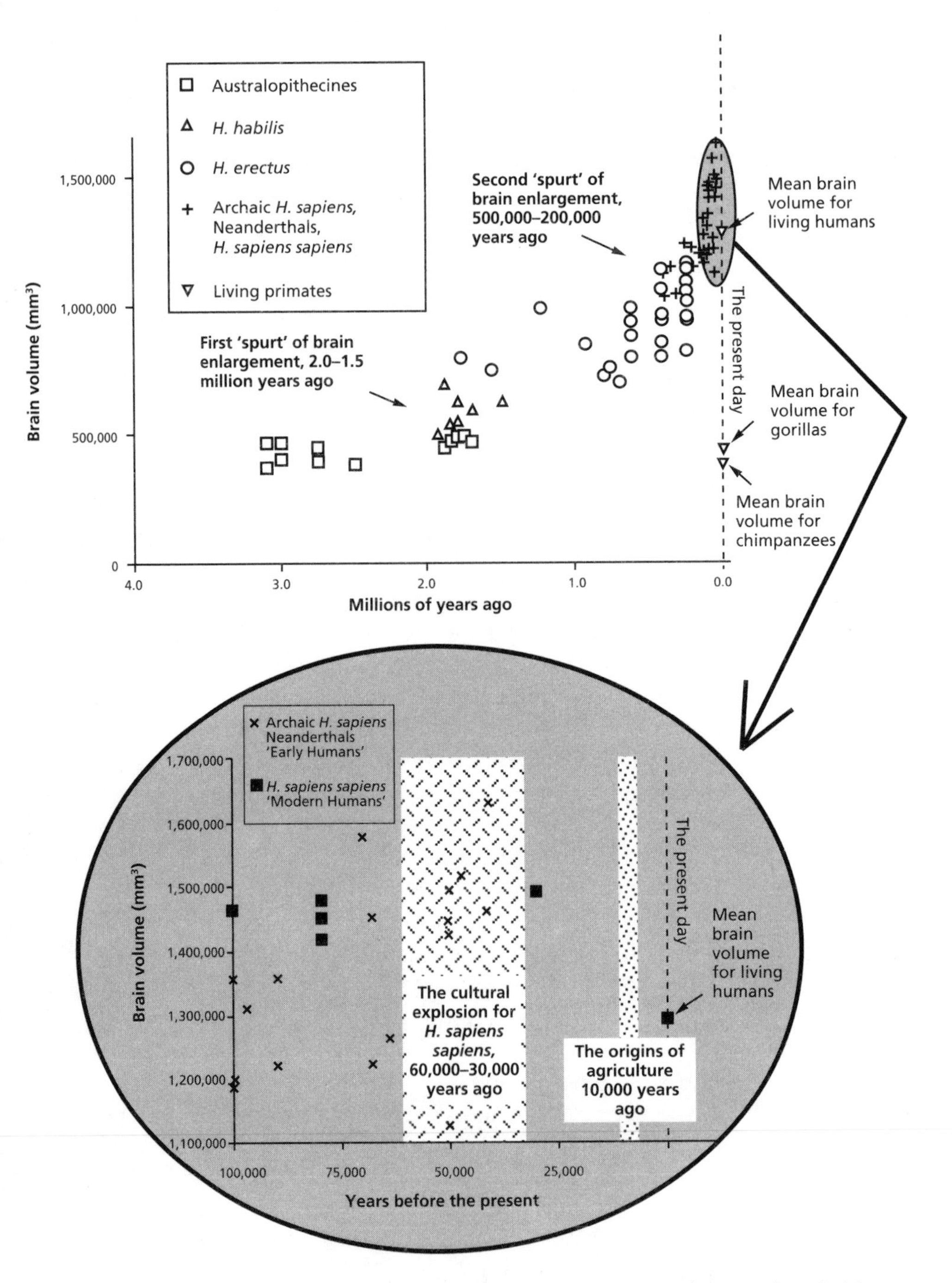

1 The increase in brain volume during the last 4 million years of human evolution. Each symbol denotes a specific skull from which brain volume has been estimated by Aiello & Dunbar (1993). Upper graph based on figure in Aiello (1996a) who discusses the evidence for the two bursts of brain enlargement separated by over a million years of stasis.

expanded in the two major spurts during human evolution? And what happened to it between these spurts, and to the mind of *Homo sapiens sapiens* to cause the cultural explosion of 60,000–30,000 years ago? When did language and consciousness first arise? When did a modern form of intelligence arise – what indeed *is* this intelligence and the nature of the intelligence that preceded it? What are the relationships of these, if any, to the size of the brain? To answer such questions we must reconstruct prehistoric minds from the evidence I introduce in Chapter 2.

We will only be able to make sense of the evidence, however, if we have some expectations about the types of minds that our ancestors may have possessed. Otherwise we will simply be faced with a bewildering mass of data, not knowing which aspects of it may be significant for our study. It is the task of Chapter 3 to begin to set up these expectations. I am able to do so because psychologists have realized that we can understand the modern mind only by understanding the process of evolution. Consequently while archaeologists have been developing a 'cognitive archaeology', psychologists have been developing an 'evolutionary psychology'. These two new sub-disciplines are in great need of each other. Cognitive archaeology cannot develop unless archaeologists take note of current thinking within psychology; evolutionary psychologists will not succeed unless they pay attention to the behaviour of our human ancestors as reconstructed by archaeologists. It is my task within this book to perform a union, the offspring of which will be a more profound understanding of the mind than either archaeology or psychology alone can achieve.

Chapter 3 will be concerned with outlining the developments in psychology that need to be brought into contact with the knowledge we have of past behaviour. One of the fundamental arguments of the new evolutionary psychology is that it is wrong to view the mind as a general-purpose learning mechanism, like some sort of powerful computer. This idea is dominant within the social sciences, and is indeed a 'common-sense' view of the mind. The evolutionary psychologists argue that we should replace it with a view of the mind as a series of specialized 'modules', or 'cognitive domains' or 'intelligences', each of which is dedicated to some specific type of behaviour[7] (see Box p. 14) – such as modules for acquiring language, or tool-using abilities, or engaging in social interaction. As I will explain in the following chapters, this new view of the mind does indeed hold a key to unlocking the nature of both the prehistoric and modern mind – although in a very different way from that in which the evolutionary psychologists currently believe. The contrast between a 'generalized' and 'specialized' mentality will emerge as a critical theme throughout this book.

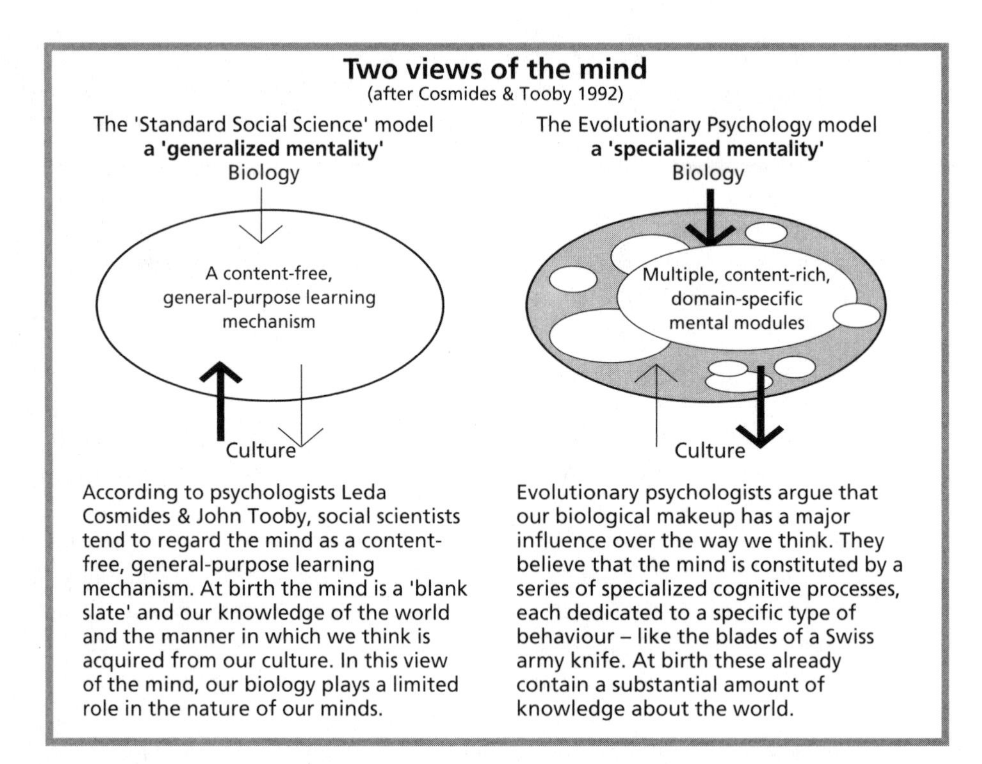

As we look at the new ideas of evolutionary psychology, we will find another dilemma that requires resolution. If the mind is indeed constituted by numerous specialized processes each dedicated to a specific type of behaviour, how can we possibly account for one of the most remarkable features of the modern mind: a capacity for an almost unlimited imagination? How can this arise from a series of isolated cognitive processes each dedicated to a specific type of behaviour? The answer to this dilemma can only be found by exposing the prehistory of the mind.

In Chapter 4 I will draw upon the ideas of evolutionary psychology, supplemented by ideas from other fields, such as child development and social anthropology, to suggest an evolutionary scenario for the mind. This will provide the template for the reconstruction of prehistoric minds in the following chapters. In Chapter 5 we will begin that task by tackling the mind of the common ancestor to apes and humans who lived 6 million years ago. We have no fossil traces or archaeological remains of that ancestor and will consequently make an assumption that the mind of this ancestor was not fundamentally different from that of the chimpanzee today. We will ask questions such as what do the tool-using and foraging abilities of chimpanzees tell us about the chimpanzee mind – and hopefully that of the 6-million-year-old common ancestor?

In the next two chapters we will reconstruct the minds of our human ancestors prior to the appearance of *Homo sapiens sapiens* – our own species – in the fossil record 100,000 years ago. In Chapter 6 we will focus on the first member of the *Homo* lineage, *Homo habilis*. As well as being the first identifiable ancestor to make stone tools, *Homo habilis* was also the first to have a diet with a relatively large quantity of meat. What do these new types of behaviour tell us about the *Homo habilis* mind? Did *Homo habilis* have a capacity for language? Did this species possess a conscious awareness about the world similar to ours today?

In Chapter 7 we will look at a group of human ancestors and relatives whom I will refer to as the 'Early Humans'. The best known of these are *Homo erectus* and the Neanderthals. The Early Humans existed between 1.8 million years ago and a mere 30,000 years ago. It will be when reconstructing the Early Human mind that we face the problem of explaining what the new brain processing power that appeared after 500,000 years ago was doing, given that we see limited change in Early Human behaviour during this period – which is why we can group all these ancestors together as Early Humans.

The Neanderthals provide us with our greatest challenge, a challenge I take up when I ask in Chapter 8 what it may have been like to have the mind of a Neanderthal. Popularly thought to be rather lacking in intelligence, we will see how in many ways Neanderthals were very similar to us, such as in terms of their brain size and their level of technical skill as evident from their stone tools. Yet in other ways they were very different, such as in their lack of art, ritual and tools made from anything but stone and wood. This apparent contradiction in Neanderthal behaviour – so modern in some ways, so primitive in others – provides vital evidence for reconstructing the nature of the Neanderthal mind. By doing so we will gain a clue as to the fundamental feature of the modern mind – a clue that remains hidden from psychologists, philosophers and indeed any scientist who ignores the evidence from prehistory.

The climax of our enquiry then comes with Chapter 9, 'The big bang of human culture'. We will see that when the first modern humans, *Homo sapiens sapiens*, appeared 100,000 years ago they seem to have behaved in essentially the same manner as Early Humans, such as Neanderthals. And then, between 60,000 and 30,000 years ago – with no apparent change in brain size, shape or anatomy in general – the cultural explosion occurred. This resulted in such a fundamental change in lifestyles that there can be little doubt that it derived from a major change in the nature of the mind. I will argue that this change was nothing less than the emergence of the modern mind – the same mentality that you and I possess today. Chapter 9 will be concerned with describing the new mentality, while Chapter 10 will then suggest how it arose.

In Chapter 11, my final chapter, I will move from considering the prehistory of the mind, to the evolution of the mind. Whereas the course of the book tracks how the mind has changed during the last 6 million years, in that final chapter I will adopt a truly long-term perspective by beginning 65 million years ago with the very first primates. By doing so we will be able to appreciate how the modern mind is the product of a long, slow evolutionary process – although a process that has a remarkable and hitherto unrecognized pattern.

I complete my book with an epilogue which addresses the origins of agriculture 10,000 years ago. This event transformed human lifestyles and created new developmental contexts for young minds – contexts within sedentary farming societies rather than a mobile hunting and gathering existence. Yet I will show in the course of this book that the most fundamental events which defined the nature of the modern mind occurred much earlier in prehistory. The origins of agriculture are indeed no more than an epilogue to the prehistory of the mind.

In this book I intend to specify the 'whats', 'whens' and 'whys' for the evolution of the mind. While following its course I will be searching for – and will find – the cognitive foundations of art, religion and science. By exposing these foundations it will become clear how we share common roots with other species – even though the mind of our closest living relative, the chimpanzee, is indeed so fundamentally different from our own. I will thus provide the hard evidence to reject the creationist claim that the mind is a product of supernatural intervention. At the end of this prehistory I hope I will have furthered an understanding of how the mind works. And I also hope to have demonstrated why one should ask an archaeologist about the human mind.

2 The drama of our past

TO FIND THE ORIGINS of the modern mind we must look into the darkness of prehistory. We must go back to a time before the first civilizations, which began a mere 5,000 years ago. We must go back further than the first domestication of plants and animals 10,000 years ago. We must flash past the first appearance of art 30,000 years ago and even that of our own species, *Homo sapiens sapiens*, in the fossil record 100,000 years ago. Not even 2.5 million years ago, the time when the very first stone tools appear, is adequate. Our starting point for the prehistory of the mind can be no less than 6 million years ago. For at that time there lived an ape whose descendants evolved in two separate directions. One path led to the modern apes, the chimpanzees and gorillas, and the other to modern humans. And consequently, this ancient ape is referred to as the common ancestor.

Not only the common ancestor but also the missing link. It is this species that links us to the living apes, and it remains missing from the fossil record. We have not a single fossil fragment. But we cannot doubt that the 'missing link' existed. Scientists are hard on its heels. By measuring the differences in the genetic makeup of modern apes and humans, and by estimating the rate at which genetic mutations arise, they have tracked it down to living about 6 million years ago. And we can be confident that it lived in Africa, for – just as Darwin declared – Africa does indeed seem to have been the cradle of humankind. No other continent has yielded the requisite ancestral human fossils.

Six million years is a vast span of time. In order to begin to comprehend it, to grasp its salient pattern of events, it helps to think of those events as constituting a play, the drama of our past. A very special play, for no one wrote the script: 6 million years of improvisation. Our ancestors are the actors, their tools are the props and the incessant changes of environment through which they lived the changes of scenery. But as a play do not think of it as a 'whodunit', in which action and ending are all. For we already know the ending – we are living it. The Neanderthals and the other Stone Age actors all died out leaving just one single survivor, *Homo sapiens sapiens*.

Think of our past not as a novel by Agatha Christie or Jeffrey Archer but as a Shakespearean drama. Think of it as a story in which prior knowledge of the dénouement enriches enjoyment and understanding. For we need not worry about *what* is going to happen. Instead we can be concerned with *why* things happen – the mental states of the actors. We don't watch Macbeth to find out whether or not he will murder Duncan, nor do we have a sweepstake on whether Hamlet will live or die. Similarly, in this book our interest is not so much with what our Stone Age ancestors did or did not do, as with what their actions tell us about their mentality.

So look upon this short chapter as the play's programme notes. Different producers – the writers of archaeological textbooks – stress different versions even of the main events, which is why a few comments on the alternative versions have been added. I have divided the drama into four acts, and provide below a brief summary of the action, as well as 'biographical details' for the actors, and notes about the props and scene changes. These may be read either now or used as a source of reference later in the book. The changes of lighting I refer to reflect the variable quality and quantity of our knowledge about each of these acts of prehistory. And when I refer to 'he' or 'his', and 'she' or 'her' I am adopting these on an arbitrary basis simply to avoid the inelegant he/she and his/her. There is no implication that either of the sexes was necessarily more important than the other at any time in our past.

Act 1

6–4.5 million years ago

A long scene of little action.

To be watched virtually in total darkness.

Our play opens somewhere in Africa around 6 million years ago and has a single actor, the ancestral ape. This actor has not one but two stage names, common ancestor and missing link. Until some fossil traces are found, its true identity – a scientific name – must remain a blank. As we know nothing about the environment in which this ancestral ape lived, and as it appears to have left no stone tools, the stage for this whole act remains bare and silent. Some producers would be inclined to add trees and provide a set of simple tools, much like the termite sticks used by chimpanzees today. But this risks over-interpretation. We must leave the stage bare and have no action throughout this act. We are indeed virtually in total darkness.

Act 2

4.5–1.8 million years ago

This has two scenes which together last just over 2.5 million years.

They should be lit only by a flickering candle.

Act 2 takes place in Africa, initially just in regions such as Chad, Kenya, Ethiopia and Tanzania, and then the stage enlarges to encompass South Africa for the second scene. The act begins 4.5 million years ago with the appearance of *Australopithecus ramidus*, an actor only made known to the world in 1994. He is the first of the so-called australopithecines (literally 'southern apes'). After about 300,000 years a second player appears, *A. anamensis* – an even more recent arrival, having been found in 1995. Both of these actors are living in wooded environments and are principally vegetarian. By 3.5 million years they have both departed stage left and been replaced by a performer so famous that she has been given a stage name, Lucy (because her discoverer happened to be listening at the time to the Beatles' song, 'Lucy in the Sky with Diamonds'). Her true identity is *Australopithecus afarensis*. It seems most likely that she is descended from *A. ramidus*, but she may well have evolved from *A. anamensis*, or someone else altogether. Lucy is such an impressive character, adept at both walking upright on two legs and climbing trees, that the lack of props – tools – is hardly noticeable. She leaves the stage after just 0.5 million years and the play enters another period of silence until the second scene begins at 2.5 million years ago. But right at the very end of the first scene, we see some pieces of stone scattered on the stage. These seem little different from naturally cracked pieces of rock, but in fact they are the first props of the play. Unfortunately we cannot see the actor who made them.

Scene 2 opens at 2.5 million years ago with a rush of actors on to the stage. Most of these look similar to those of Scene 1, although they come in a variety of shapes and sizes. These are more australopithecines: they are Lucy's children. In fact one of these, which has a noticeably light build and is referred to as a gracile australopithecine, is very similar to Lucy, although we see him in South rather than East Africa. This is *A. africanus*, who behaves rather like a modern baboon, although he spends more time on two legs. The other australopithecines are physically much more robust, with representatives in both East and South Africa. These remind us of gorillas rather than baboons.

By 2 million years ago, after *A. africanus* has disappeared, a new group of actors appear who are big headed and seem rather precocious. Indeed they are the first members of the *Homo* lineage, and have brains 1.5 times larger than the australopithecines. But, as with the australopithecines, they show considerable variability in size and shape. Some commentators discern just a single actor, *Homo habilis*, but it is likely that three are present – *Homo habilis*, *Homo rudolfensis* and *Homo ergaster.* Nevertheless, because they are so difficult to differentiate, we will simply refer to them collectively as *Homo habilis*.

Homo habilis is definitely carrying tools, stone artifacts described as the Oldowan industry. Perhaps the robust australopithecines are as well, it is hard to tell. The anatomy of their hands would certainly allow them to do so. We can see *Homo habilis* butchering animals with his tools, but we cannot be confident as to whether the carcasses had been hunted or just scavenged from the kills of lions and leopards. As the scene comes to an end, the behaviour of *Homo habilis* and his robust australopithecine cousins appears to be diverging markedly, with the first becoming more proficient in making tools and including more meat in his diet, while the australopithecines seem to be chewing their way to an even more robust morphology.

Act 3

1.8 million–100,000 years ago

Two scenes, which have an exciting start at around 1.8–1.5 million years ago, but which lapse into utter tedium. The lighting is still poor, although it improves slightly for the second scene.

Act 3 opens with a grand announcement: 'The Pleistocene begins'. The ice sheets start to form in high latitudes. On to our stage at 1.8 million years ago strides a new figure, *Homo erectus*. She is descended from *Homo habilis* (or maybe one of the other types of *Homo*), who now leaves the action, and is taller and larger-brained. The robust australopithecines hang around in the shadows until 1 million years ago, but take no part in the events of this act. The astonishing thing about the appearance of *Homo erectus* is that her arrival seems to be practically simultaneous in three parts of the world, East Africa, China and Java – and consequently the stage has now had to expand to include the Near East, Eastern and Southeast Asia. Gradually we see *Homo erectus*, or her discarded tools, in all these areas. But it is difficult to tell exactly when she arrived in particular places and quite what she is doing.

After more than a million years of *Homo erectus* – during which there appears to have been no further expansion of the brain – we begin to see some new performers on the stage. As with the earliest *Homo*, it is unclear how many species we actually have. *Homo erectus* continues living in East Asia until a mere 300,000 years ago, but elsewhere in Asia and in Africa we see actors with more rounded skulls who are rather awkwardly referred to as archaic *Homo sapiens*. These are likely to be descended from *Homo erectus* in their respective continents and mark a return to a period of increasing brain size. By 500,000 years ago, the stage has become further enlarged to include Europe. The actor here is called *Homo heidelbergensis*, another descendent of *Homo erectus* who seems to have a particularly large physique.

While the props of Act 2 continue to be used throughout this act, some rather more impressive ones appear. Most notable are symmetrical pear-shaped stone tools called handaxes. Soon after these have first appeared in East Africa, at around 1.4 million years ago, they become pervasive in almost all parts of the world except for Southeast Asia, where no tools are discernible at all – some commentators think that they are made here from perishable bamboo.

The second scene of this act, beginning around 200,000 years ago, is traditionally referred to by archaeologists as the 'Middle Palaeolithic', distinguishing it from the 'Lower Palaeolithic' of the preceding scene. But the boundary between these is so blurred that this distinction is gradually being phased out. Yet it is clear that by this date there have been some significant changes in the props being used by the actors. These have become rather more diverse, and handaxes have become less prominent. New tools include those made with a new technique called the Levallois method which produces carefully shaped flakes and points of stone. Indeed, for the first time it looks as though performers in different parts of the stage are each carrying a different range of tools. In Africa alone we see a predominance of Levallois flakes in the north, heavy-duty stone 'picks' in sub-Saharan regions, and long thin flakes of stone in the south.

By 150,000 years ago a new actor has appeared in Europe and the Near East, *Homo neanderthalensis*, popularly known as Neanderthal man. He has a propensity to use tools made from the Levallois technique and can be seen to hunt large game. Like the other characters of this act, the Neanderthals are having to cope with frequent and dramatic changes of scenery: this is the period of the ice ages, and we watch ice sheets repeatedly advance and then retreat across Europe, and with them a change in vegetation from tundra to forest. Yet even with such changes, the action seems rather monotonous. Indeed one distinguished commentator on Acts 2 and 3, the archaeologist Glynn Isaac, described how 'for almost a million years, toolkits tended to involve the same essential ingredients seemingly being shuffled in restless, minor, directionless changes'. While some of these tools seem to be very finely crafted, they are all made of either stone or wood. Although unmodified pieces of bone and antler are used, no carving of these materials takes place.

The curtain falls on another long act. It has lasted more than 1.5 million years, and although much of the Old World has now become the stage, the props have become more diverse, brain size has reached its modern dimensions and a range of new actors have appeared, one has nevertheless to describe it as tedious stuff. We have now been watching this play for a fraction under 6 million years, but there is still nothing that we can call art, religion or science.

Act 4

100,000 years ago–present day

A much shorter act, into which are squeezed three scenes packed with more dramatic action than in all the rest of the play.

Scene 1 of Act 4 covers the period from 100,000 to around 60,000 years ago, although as we will see the boundary between Scenes 1 and 2 is rather blurred. But the start is clear cut: a new figure enters – our own species, *Homo sapiens sapiens*. He is first seen in South Africa and the Near East and joins a cast that continues to include the Neanderthals and archaic *Homo sapiens*. Perhaps surprisingly there is no major change in the props as a whole at this time: our new actor continues making the same range of stone tools as his forebears of the final scene of Act 3. Indeed in practically all respects his behaviour is no different from theirs. But there are hints of something new. In the Near East we see *Homo sapiens sapiens* not only burying their dead within pits – as indeed are the Neanderthals – but they are placing parts of animal carcasses on to the bodies seemingly as grave goods. In South Africa they are using lumps of red ochre, although it is unclear what they are doing with these, and are grinding pieces of bone to make harpoons. These are the very first tools made from materials other than wood or stone.

Scene 2 of this final act begins at around 60,000 years ago with a remarkable event: in Southeast Asia *Homo sapiens sapiens* builds boats and then makes the very first crossing to Australia. Quite soon we see new things happening in the Near East. Instead of flakes being produced using the Levallois method, long thin slivers of flint are removed that look like, and indeed are called, blades. And then quite suddenly – at around 40,000 years ago – the play becomes transformed in Europe, and in Africa. The props have come to dominate the action. To mark such dramatic behavioural change archaeologists use these props to define the start of a new period of our past, known as the Upper Palaeolithic in Europe and Late Stone Age in Africa. A similar transformation also occurs in Asia, but as we can only dimly make out that region, it is unclear whether this occurs at the same time as in Europe and Africa, or later, perhaps around 20,000 years ago.

In place of the small range of stone tools, the props are now diverse and made from a whole host of new materials, including bone and ivory. The actors are building the scenery themselves – constructing dwellings and painting the walls. Some sit carving animal and human figures from stone and ivory, others are sewing clothes with bone needles. And on their bodies they wear beads and pendants – whether those bodies are living or deceased. Who are the actors? Well, *Homo sapiens sapiens* is clearly setting the pace. We saw how she makes the sea crossing to Australia in the very first few moments of this scene, and then enters Europe 40,000 years ago. For about 10,000 years after that the Neanderthals of Europe may be trying to mimic the new types of blade tools that *Homo sapiens sapiens* is making and the necklaces of beads she is wearing. But the Neanderthals soon fade away, as have done all the other actors in the play. *Homo sapiens sapiens* is now left alone on the world stage.

The pace of the action slowly accelerates. Europe is ablaze with the colour of cave art between 30,000 and 12,000 years ago, even though the landscapes have become deeply frozen in the midst of the last ice age. As the ice sheets begin to retreat the stage becomes yet larger, with the addition of North and South America. The scenery shows dramatic fluctuations from periods of warm/wet climate to cold/dry climate as the ice age comes to an end, signing off with a period of rapid global warming at 10,000 years ago. This marks the end of the Pleistocene, when the actor is ushered into the warm world of the Holocene and the final scene of the play.

As soon as the third scene of Act 4 begins, we see people in the Near East planting crops, and then domesticating animals. Events now flash past at bewildering speed. People create towns, and then cities. A succession of empires rise and fall and the props become ever more dominant, diverse and complex: in no more than an instant carts have become cars and writing tablets word processors. After almost 6 million years of relative inaction, we find it difficult to make sense of this final, hectic scene.

The actors...

A. ramidus and **A. anamensis**

A. ramidus is the oldest known human ancestor, dating to 4.5 million years ago. It is defined by 17 fossil specimens found in the Middle Awash area of Ethiopia in 1994, which display more ape-like features than any other human ancestor. The body of *A. ramidus* may have been similar to that of a chimpanzee. It has been suggested that these fossils should in fact be placed within a new genus, *Ardipithecus*. The abundance of fossil wood, seeds and monkeys from the sediments in which the fossils were found suggests that *A. ramidus* lived in a forested environment.

A. anamensis is defined by nine fossil specimens from Kanapoi, Kenya, which were discovered in 1995. This species appears to have lived between 4.2 and 3.9 million years ago and is also thought to have occupied wooded or bushland habitats. It appears to have been rather larger than *A. ramidus*, but the absence of postcranial skeletal fragments makes a comparison between the two species difficult. They are likely to have overlapped in date and their relationship with *A. afarensis* remains unclear.

ACT 2

Gracile australopithecines
A. afarensis and **A. africanus**

These two species are jointly referred to as the 'gracile australopithecines' and lived between 4 and 2.5 million years ago. *A. afarensis* is best known from the nearly half complete fossil skeleton nicknamed 'Lucy'. This was found in the Hadar area of Ethiopia, where numerous other specimens of *A. afarensis* have also been recovered. *A. afarensis* is likely to have been 1–1.5 m (3ft 3 in–5 ft) tall and weighed 30–75 kg (66–165 lb), with a brain size of 400–500 cc. It had a light build with long arms relative to its legs and curved fingers and toes. These features suggest that *A. afarensis* may have been neither fully bipedal, nor fully arboreal. A trail of footprints dating to 3.5 million years ago found at Laetoli, Tanzania, are likely to have been made by *A. afarensis*.

The fossils of *A. africanus* are found in southern Africa. This species was about the same size as *A. afarensis* and had the same brain capacity. It appears to have been adapted for bipedal locomotion. Contrasts are found in the shape of the skull, with that of *A. africanus* having a higher forehead and less prominent brow ridges. With regard to dentition, *A. africanus* had smaller incisor-like canines and larger molars than *A. afarensis*.

ACT 2

Robust australopithecines
P. boisei and **P. robustus**

The australopithecines which evolved particularly robust features have been placed into a separate genus named *Paranthropus*. In southern Africa these are referred to as *P. robustus* and weighed between 40 and 80 kg (90 and 175 lb). This suggests that like modern gorillas the males were considerably larger than the females. The East African form, *P. boisei,* had an even greater range of size, and may have been a little taller at 1.4 m (4 ft 6 in).

The anatomical features of the robust australopithecines indicate a diet involving the processing of much plant food and the generation of considerable force between the teeth. The most notable features are the thick lower jaws, the very large molars and the sagittal crest of bone on the cranium which provided the attachment for powerful chewing muscles. After having appeared in the fossil record 2.5 million years ago, *Paranthropus* species survived until 1 million years ago.

ACT 2

The earliest *Homo*
H. habilis, H. rudolfensis and **H. ergaster**

At around 2 million years ago, new types of fossils appear which have been assigned to the genus *Homo*. These show considerable variation in size and form and consequently are likely to represent several species. They are all characterized by a larger brain size than the australopithecines, reaching between 500 and 800 cc. The most important localities for these finds are Olduvai Gorge, Tanzania, and Koobi Fora, Kenya, where the best-preserved specimen of *H. habilis*, KNM-ER 1470, was recovered. *H. habilis* appears to have had a body that was more australopithecine in character but a human-like face and dentition, while *H. rudolfensis* had a human-like body but retained facial and dental features of the australopithecines. By 1.6 million years ago the fossils of these early *Homo* species are no longer found, appearing to have been replaced by *H. erectus,* which probably evolved from a further type of early *Homo*, *H. ergaster.*

ACT 2

H. erectus

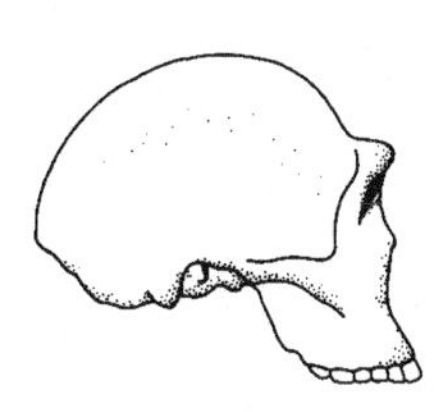

The first fossils of *H. erectus* are found in the Koobi Fora region of Africa and in Java at 1.8 million years ago. *H. erectus* is thought to have evolved from early *Homo* in Africa and to have then rapidly dispersed into Asia. A mandible of *H. erectus* has also been recovered from Dmanisi in Georgia, where it is thought to date to *c.* 1.4 million years old. *H. erectus* had a larger brain size than the earliest *Homo,* 750–1250 cc, with prominent brow ridges and a robust skeleton. The skulls of Asian *H. erectus,* such as those from the cave of Zhoukoudian which were once known as 'Peking man', are more heavily buttressed with ridges of bone than those of Africa. The most spectacular *H. erectus* fossil is that of an almost complete skeleton of a 12-year-old boy dated to 1.6 million years old from Nariokotome, Kenya, which provides evidence for a rapid rate of child development. This appears characteristic of early humans. He has the physique characteristic of humans living in tropical environments. *H. erectus* survived until around 300,000 years ago.

ACT 3

Archaic ***H. sapiens/ H. heidelbergensis***

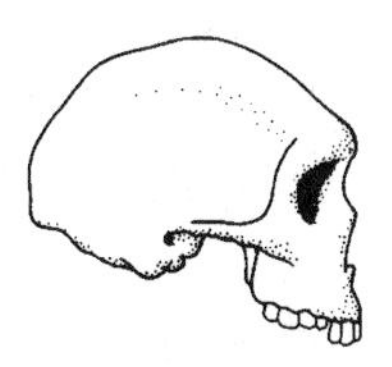

Specimens of archaic *H. sapiens* are found in Africa and Asia from between *c.* 400,000 and 100,000 years ago. Important specimens come from the sites of Broken Hill, Florisbad and Omo in Africa, and Dali and Maba in East Asia. This is an ill-defined species but is distinguished from *H. erectus* by a larger brain size, 1100–1400 cc, and a cranium which is higher and more rounded. Little is known about the rest of the skeleton, but it is thought to have been as robust and muscular as that of *H. erectus.*

H. heidelbergensis is the name used for the first humans in Europe and is a descendant of *H. erectus.* Very few remains are known, just a jawbone from Mauer in Germany and part of a leg bone from Boxgrove in England, both dating to around 500,000 years ago. Both of these specimens suggest that *H. heidelbergensis* was a large and robust species. Human fossils from Atapuerca in Spain, recently dated to at least 780,000 years old, may also belong to *H. heidelbergensis.*

ACT 3

ACT 4

The Neanderthals
H. neanderthalensis

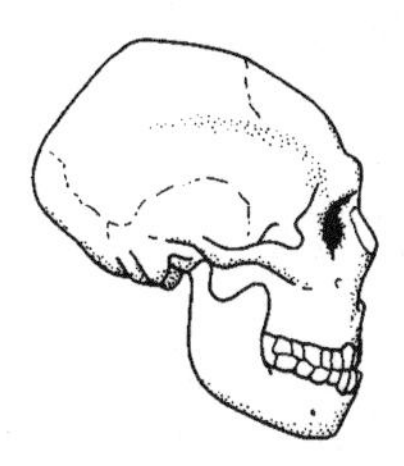

H. neanderthalensis is believed to have evolved from *H. heidelbergensis* by 150,000 years ago. Well-defined Neanderthal features are present on specimens from Pontnewydd Cave, North Wales, dating to 220,000 years ago. The 'classic' Neanderthals are found at sites in Europe and the Near East between 115,000 and 30,000 years ago, notably Saint Césaire in France (33,000), and Tabūn (110,000) and Kebara (63,000) in the Near East. *H. neanderthalensis* is distinguished from *H. erectus* by a larger brain size of 1200–1750 cc, larger noses and reduced brow ridges. Their bodies were very strongly built, being stout and muscular with short legs and large barrel-like chests. Many of their anatomical features are adaptations to living in glacial environments. Neanderthal bodies seem to have suffered a high degree of physical injuries and degenerative diseases that are likely to reflect a physically demanding lifestyle.

ACT 3

ACT 4

Anatomically modern humans
H. sapiens sapiens

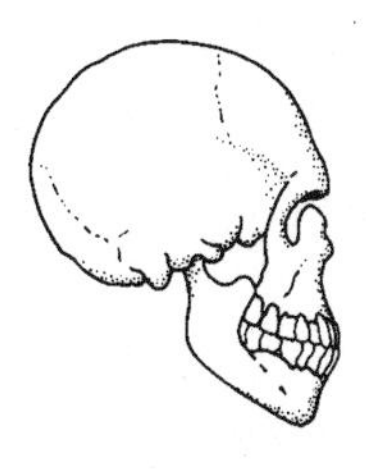

The earliest anatomically modern humans (AMHs) are found in the Near East, in the caves of Qafzeh and Skhūl, and in South Africa at Border Cave and Klasies River Mouth at about 100,000 years ago. Fossil specimens from Jebel Irhoud in North Africa are also likely to be *H. sapiens sapiens.* AMHs are believed to be descended from archaic *H. sapiens* in Africa. The fragmentary specimens from Klasies River Mouth show some archaic features and may represent a transitional form. AMHs are distinguished from both archaic *H. sapiens* and *H. neanderthalensis* by a less robust physique, the reduction and often absence of brow ridges, a more rounded skull, and smaller teeth. The brain size at between 1200 and 1700 cc is the same as, or slightly smaller, than that of *H. neanderthalensis.*

Soon after, 100,000 years ago AMHs are likely to have dispersed throughout Africa and into East Asia. They colonized Australia soon after 60,000 years ago, and first entered Europe 40,000 years ago. After 30,000 *H. sapiens sapiens* is the only surviving member of the *Homo* lineage.

ACT 4

The props...

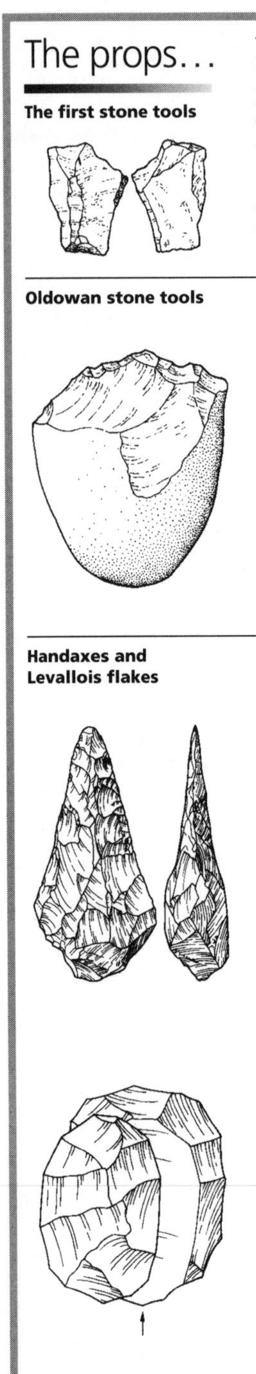

The first stone tools

The very first stone tools date to between 3 and 2 million years ago and are often difficult to distinguish from naturally occurring rocks. These artifacts have been grouped together and termed the Omo industrial complex, after the Omo area of Ethiopia. The artifacts from this area come from the Shungura formation which has sediments spanning the period between 3 and 1 million years ago. The earliest of these consist of flaked and smashed up quartz pebbles. Similar artifacts thought to date to 2.7 million years ago have been found at Kada Gona, Ethiopia. A further early site is that of Lokalalei (GaJh 5) found near the base of the Kalochoro member of the Nachukui formation of West Turkana, Kenya, where the artifacts are dated to 2.36 million years ago.

ACT 2

Oldowan stone tools

Between 2 and 1.5 million years ago, the stone tools found in East and South Africa consist of flakes removed from pebbles, and the remaining 'core'. These are referred to as the Oldowan industry, named after the artifacts from Bed I at Olduvai Gorge. These artifacts come in various shapes and sizes and are characterized as heavy duty tools, light duty tools, utilized pieces and débitage.

Olduvai Gorge remains the most important site for Oldowan stone tools. This is a 100-m-deep (330-ft) gash stretching for 50 km (30 miles) in the Serengeti Plain, Tanzania, created by a river cutting through sediments laid down during the last 1.8 million years. It has an extensive series of archaeological sites found in four main beds containing artifacts and fossils, numerous of which were excavated by Mary Leakey. There are several other locations in East Africa of similar importance to Olduvai Gorge. Most notable is the area of Koobi Fora, Kenya, where extensive fieldwork by Glynn Isaac yielded many early sites.

ACT 2

Handaxes and Levallois flakes

Handaxes are a type of artifact made by the bifacial flaking of a stone nodule or a large flake. This means that flakes are alternately removed from either side of the artifact. Handaxes are typically pear shaped, while similar tools with a straight edge, rather than a pointed or curved tip, are called cleavers. When handaxes/cleavers are found at relatively high frequencies within stone artifact assemblages, those assemblages are referred to as Acheulian. The bifacial technique is first found in Bed II at Olduvai Gorge, and when present the stone industry is referred to as the Developed Oldowan. The earliest true handaxes are known from Konso-Gardula in Ethiopia where they date to 1.4 million years ago. They also abruptly appear in the archaeological record at *c.* 1.4 million years ago at the sites of Olorgesailie and Kesem-Kebana. Handaxes are found at sites throughout Europe, West and South Asia during Act 3; often they are found in very large numbers. For instance at Olorgesailie in Tanzania, many thousands of handaxes have been found in 16 artifact assemblages around the edge of an ancient lake basin. A notable site in Europe is Boxgrove in southern England, dated to 500,000 years ago, where perfectly preserved scatters of knapping debris from the manufacture of handaxes have been excavated. The only part of the Old World where early humans do not appear to have made handaxes is Southeast Asia. They are also very rare in China. In the regions that they are found, they are not ubiquitous and are absent from many sites at which tools remain similar to Oldowan or Developed Oldowan technology. Such sites include Verteszöllös in Hungary, Bilzingsleben in Germany and the lowest levels at the stratified sites of Ùbeidiya, Israel, and Swanscombe, England.

The Levallois method is a technique for removing flakes and stone points of predetermined size by careful preparation of the core. It first appears in the archaeological record 250,000 years ago and is widely found in Africa, the Near East and in Europe. Many of the assemblages from North Africa, such as in the cave of Haua Fteah, and the Near East, such as in the caves of Tabūn and Kebara, are dominated by this method. In some assemblages, such as at Pontnewydd in North Wales, the Levallois technique is found together with handaxes.

ACT 3

1 2 3 4

Wooden artifacts

Artifacts made from wood are extremely rare in the archaeological record, but the few which survive indicate that they were being made by Early Humans. Pointed sticks, which were probably spears, have been recovered from the sites of Clacton-on-Sea and Lehringen and a polished wooden plank has been found at Gesher Benot Ya'aqov in Israel. It is most likely that the working of wood to make artifacts stretches back to the common ancestor, 6 million years ago.

ACT 3 ACT 4

Blade technology

Long thin slivers of flint are referred to as blades rather than flakes, and are usually removed from cores which have been carefully prepared, often into a prismatic shape. The earliest blades are found in the industries termed the Pre-Aurignacian from the cave of Haua Fteah, North Africa, and the Amudian from the Near East, both dating to before 100,000 years ago. But it is not until 40,000 years ago that blade production begins on a systematic scale, after which it becomes the dominant stone working technique throughout the Old World. Blade cores come in various sizes, with the smaller ones referred to as bladelet or micro-blade cores. Blades themselves are often chipped into specific shapes, such as projectile points, endscrapers and burins (chisel-like engraving tools).

ACT 4

Bone artifacts

Although there is evidence of bones being used as tools as much as 500,000 years ago, the first worked artifacts – harpoons made by grinding bones – are only found 90,000 years ago at Katanda in Zaire. These harpoons remain as unique finds for it is not until after 40,000 years ago that another artifact of worked bone is known. After this date bone artifacts are found in all regions of the Old World. For instance, 39,000 years ago arrowheads were made from grinding bone at Border Cave, while in the Near East and Europe bone was carved to make tools such as points and awls. From around 20,000 years ago bone was used to make harpoons, particularly in the societies living in Europe towards the end of the last ice age. Bone needles are first found at 18,000 years ago. The first architecture used the bones of mammoths for dwellings in Russia and Siberia over 20,000 years ago.

ACT 4

Objects of art and personal adornment

Although fragments of red ochre have been found at sites which date to 250,000 years ago, the first objects of art appear 40,000 years ago. The most impressive and abundant of these are in Europe, where beads, necklaces and pendants were made from ivory, animal and human figures were carved and a wide array of abstract and naturalistic images were painted and engraved on cave walls. In Africa slabs of stone painted with animal figures are found dating to 27,500 years ago, while ostrich egg shell beads date back to 39,000 years ago. In East Asia the first beads are dated to 18,000–13,000 years ago from the cave of Zhoukoudian, while a decorated piece of red deer antler dated to 13,000 years ago has come from Longgupo Cave in China. Engravings made into soft mud on cave walls in Australia have been dated to 23,000–15,000 years ago, while it is likely that some of the rock art stretches back to a date of 40,000 years ago. At Mandu Mandu rockshelter a collection of 20 shell beads has been found dated to 34,000–30,000 years ago.

ACT 4

Computers and other modern props

The first computer, Charles Babbage's analytical engine, was designed in 1834. Less than 160 years later the global computer network called the Internet had been established. These developments took place no more than 90,000 years after the first piece of bone was carved. This contrasts with the more than 2 million years that it took to get from the production of the first stone tool to the carving of that piece of bone. This difference reflects the remarkably rapid rate of technological innovation and change that was hinted at 90,000 years ago, began in earnest 40,000 years ago and continues apace today. Notable landmarks during that 40,000 years were the first use of ceramic technology 26,000 years ago for making clay figurines, which had become widespread for making pots by 8,000 years ago. The first plants and animals were domesticated 10,000 years ago. The first writing began 5,000 years ago, and metal smelting 4,000 years ago. It took only 20,000 years to get from the bow and arrow to the atomic bomb, and 6,000 years from the first wheeled vehicles to spacecraft.

ACT 4

Acts 1 and 2: African origins

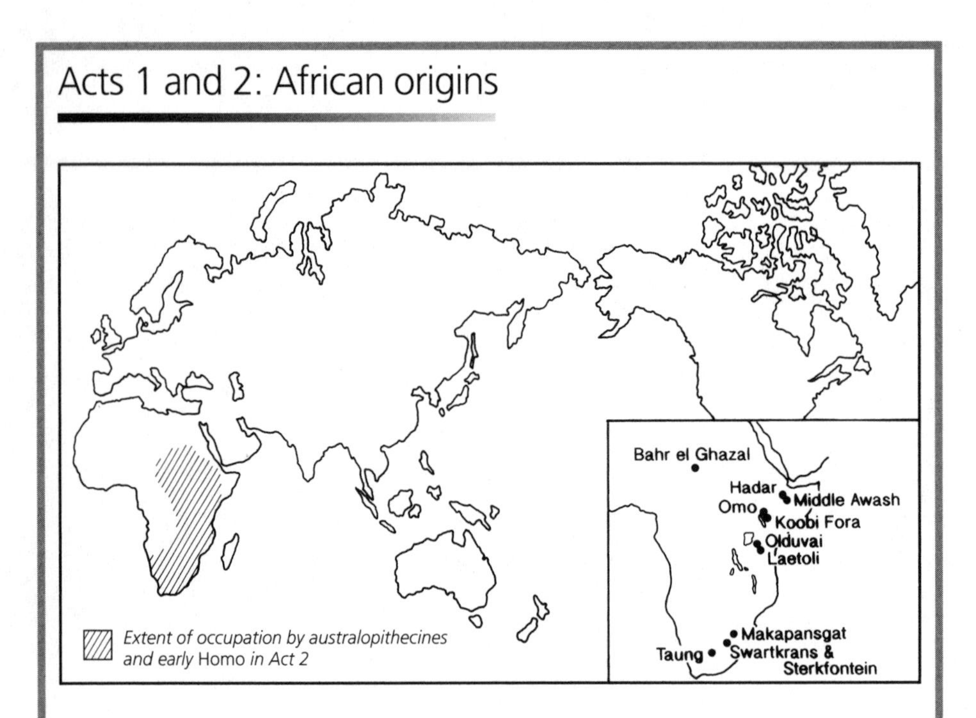

Fossil apes from the period 10–5 million years ago are known from Africa, Europe and Asia and it remains unclear where the common ancestor of 6 million years ago actually lived. But it is most likely to have been East Africa, in light of the diversity of australopithecine fossils from that region and the ape-like features of the earliest of these. Fossils of australopithecines and earliest *Homo* are found from cave deposits in South Africa and from open sites in East Africa. The most important sites in South Africa are Makapansgat, Sterkfontein and Swartkrans, all of which provide a diverse array of animal fossils. It is unlikely that these human ancestors actually occupied the caves and their remains were either washed in, or taken in by carnivores. Of these caves Sterkfontein has *H. habilis* fossils and a stratified sequence of early stone tools. The fossils and early stone tools from East Africa are found eroding from exposed sediments, notably at Hadar, Middle Awash, Olduvai Gorge, Koobi Fora and Omo. Their discovery and dating have been possible due to the faulting and erosion that has occurred in the African Rift Valley which has exposed ancient sediments, and the lenses of volcanic tuffs between these, which can be dated by a variety of radiometric methods.

Act 3: The colonization of Europe and Asia

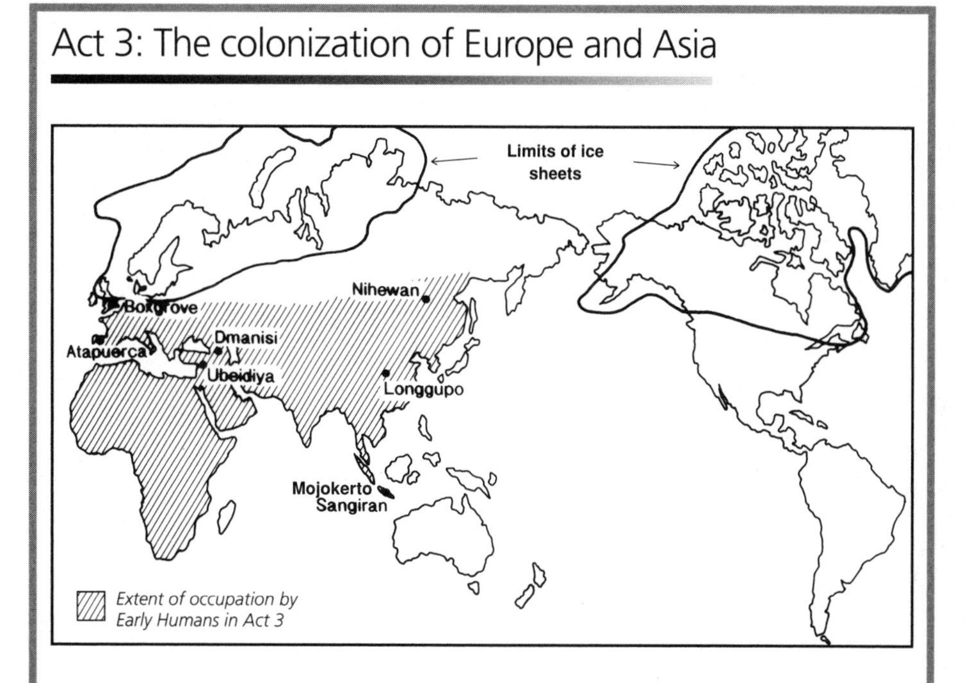

H. erectus fossils from Mojokerto and Sangiran on Java have been controversially dated to 1.6–1.8 million years ago, making them almost 1 million years older than previously thought. A tooth possibly dating to 1.9 million years ago and claimed to be early *Homo* has been found at Longgupo Cave in central China. If these new dates are correct, they imply that *H. erectus* dispersed from Africa very rapidly, or that an earlier species of *Homo* had left Africa, and the origins of *H. erectus* may in fact be in Asia itself. There have been claims for Oldowan-like stone tools from the Riwat area of Pakistan dating to 2 million years old, but it remains unclear whether or not these are true artifacts. A human jawbone attributed to *H. erectus* has been recovered from Dmanisi in Georgia. This was found above sediments which have been dated to 1.8 million years ago. It was associated with Oldowan-like stone tools, and most likely dates to between 1.5 and 1 million years ago. As such it may be similar in date to the earliest occupations at Ùbeidiya in western Asia. The earliest archaeological sites from East Asia come from the Nihewan basin in China, which are likely to date to between 0.75 and 1 million years ago. With these early fossils and sites in Asia, the absence of well-dated sites in Europe earlier than 500,000 years ago remains a puzzle. Sites such as Vallonet in France are claimed to date earlier than 1 million year ago, but, as at Riwat, it is unclear that the stone 'tools' are not simply naturally fractured pieces of rock. The earliest dates for human fossils come from Gran Dolina, Atapuerca in Spain where they are dated to 780,000 years ago, although some confirmation for these dates is required. At and soon after 500,000 years ago there are several archaeological sites in Europe. Most notable is Boxgrove in southern England, where handaxes and a part of an early human leg bone have been found.

Act 4: The colonization of Australasia and the Americas

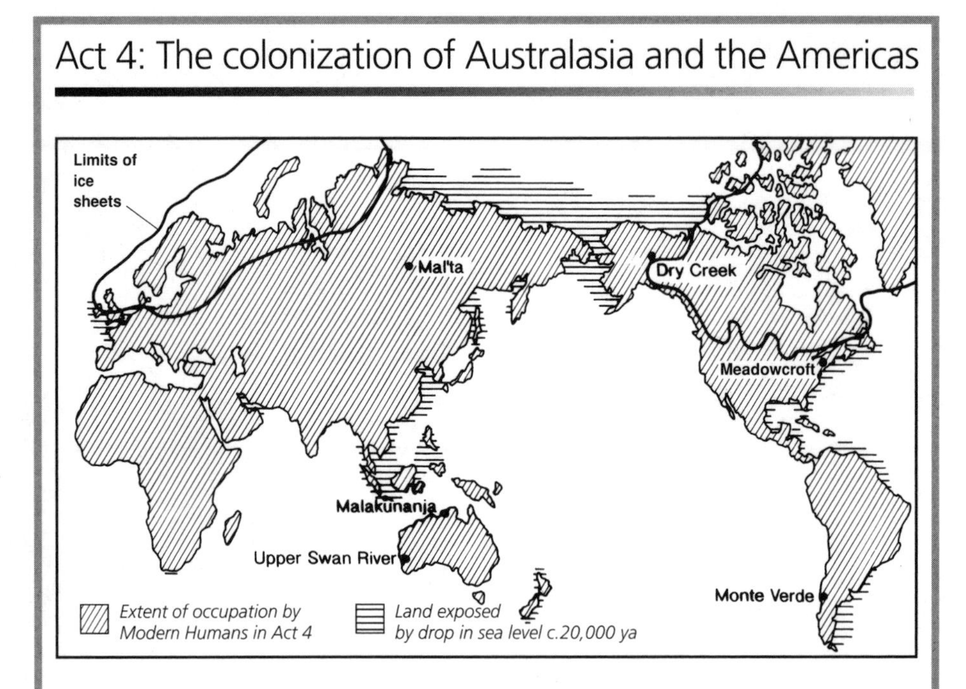

Australia is most likely to have been colonized 50,000–60,000 years ago in view of luminescence dates for occupation in Malakunanja II and Nauwalabila rockshelters in the Northern Territory. Other than these sites, the earliest dates are less than 40,000 years old, but this may reflect the 'time barrier' for radiocarbon dating. The site of Upper Swan on the outskirts of Perth is dated to 39,500±2300 years ago, and there are a significant number of sites dated to 35,000–30,000 years ago. Australia was colonized by *H. sapiens sapiens*, but there is some controversy as to whether these represent a dispersing population from Africa, or had evolved locally from *H. erectus* ancestry in Southeast Asia. Human fossils in Australia dating to 30,000–20,000 years ago show considerable variability, ranging from very gracile to very robust anatomy. The Americas were colonized by a route that led through northern Siberia, where the earliest well-dated sites are 35,000 years old. The richest of these is the 25,000-year-old site of Mal'ta which has large quantities of art objects. Entry into the Americas was across the now submerged landmass of Beringia, but the date of this colonization remains unclear. Claims have been made for sites in South America dating to 40,000 years ago, but these are unlikely to be accurate. The earliest well-verified dates come from sites such as Dry Creek in Alaska and Meadowcroft Rockshelter in Pennsylvania at around 12,000 years ago. There are numerous sites dating to between 11,500 and 11,000 years ago, when people appear to have been hunting megafauna such as mammoths. By 11,000 years ago there are many sites in South America, notably Monte Verde. As with Australia, it is likely that colonization was not a single event, but involved numerous influxes of people over a wide time range.

Evolutionary relationships between human ancestors

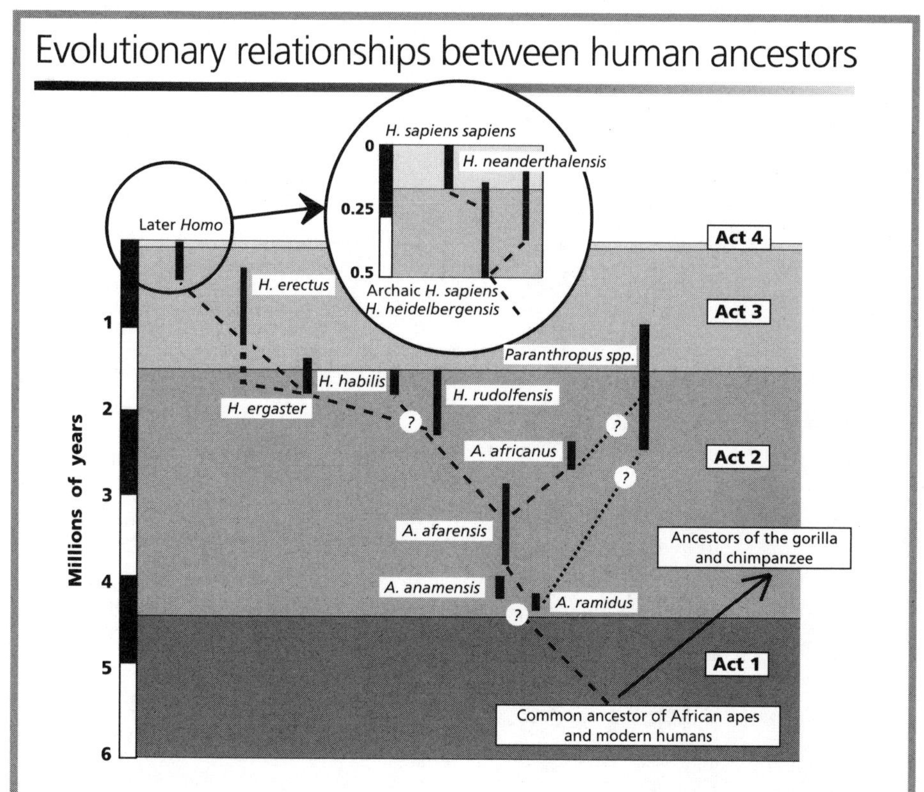

Reconstructing the evolutionary relationships between human ancestors is a task fraught with difficulties due to the paucity of the fossil evidence. This diagram is based on that provided by Bernard Wood (1993), in which the black bars denote the timing of the first and last appearance of a species. Relationships between the australopithecines are particularly hard to establish due to the scarcity of their fossils and their morphological variability: it is often unclear whether one is dealing with the male and female of the same species, or two separate species. Perhaps the most contentious part of the evolutionary tree is the most recent part concerning the origins of *H. sapiens sapiens.* Views about this fall into two broad camps. Some believe that there was a single origin in Africa, and that all existing populations such as Neanderthals in Europe and archaic *H. sapiens* in Asia, were replaced by this new species and made no contribution to the modern gene pool. Others dispute this, arguing for multiple origins of *H. sapiens sapiens* in different parts of the world, evolving from the resident early human populations. Between these two extremes are various other positions, such as those arguing for a dispersing population of modern humans from Africa around 100,000 years ago, but with a degree of interbreeding with the archaic *H. sapiens* populations. The study of human genetics can also provide a means for reconstructing evolutionary history. The limited amount of genetic variability between modern humans suggests that we have had a very recent origin, while measuring the difference between humans and chimpanzees has established the date of the common ancestor at 6 million years ago. Attempts are being made to use the variation in the DNA of human populations in different parts of the world to distinguish between a single or multiple origin for modern humans, and if the former, identify when and where this happened. This book adopts the position of a single African origin followed by a replacement of all archaic *Homo sapiens,* but is sympathetic to the idea of limited hybridization between populations dispersing from Africa and resident early humans.

Changes of scenery during Acts 3 and 4

The Pleistocene climate as recorded in deep sea core V28-238 taken in the Pacific Ocean

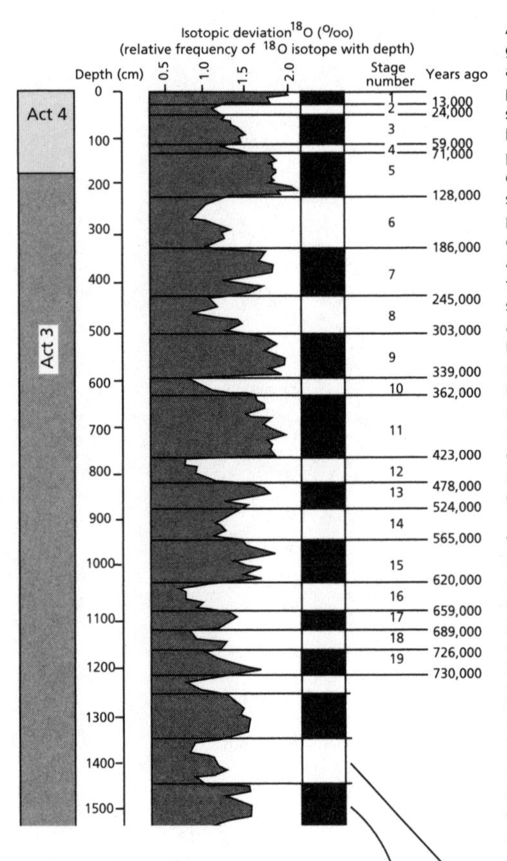

Acts 3 and 4 of prehistory cover the geological periods known as the Middle and Upper Pleistocene. During these the planet experienced a long and complex sequence of climatic changes, dominated by swings from glacial to interglacial phases. We see this alternation most clearly in cores taken from marine sediments. These can be analyzed to provide a record of changes in the ratio of two isotopes of oxygen, which in turn are directly related to climatic fluctuations from glacial to interglacial stages. These cores, which first became available in the 1970s, show that there have been eight cycles from glacial to interglacial during the Middle and Upper Pleistocene. Moreover, there have been numerous smaller oscillations, with marked periods of cold, called stadials, during interglacial periods and conversely periods of warmth, called interstadials, during cold glacial periods.

These climatic oscillations provide us with a chronological structure for the Pleistocene as each climatic stage has a number with glacial periods denoted by even, and warm periods by odd, numbers. Moreover, the fluctuations within a climatic phase are denoted by subscripts of letters. For instance, stage 5 is the whole period of the last interglacial (128,000–71,000 years ago), which is divided up into 5 substages referred to as 5a–5e, with the latter marking the highest sea level. Other particularly important oxygen isotope stages are stage 12 (which is thought to be the Anglian glaciation which covered northern Europe 478,000–423,000 years ago), and stage 2 (which denotes the last glaciation, 24,000–13,000 years ago).

Warm phases

During the warm phases of the Pleistocene the ice sheets melted, resulting in a rise in sea level, cutting areas such as Britain off from continental Europe. As the climate warmed the landscapes were colonized by plants and trees and animal communities were transformed. The marine sediment and ice cores show that the transition to warm phases often involved very rapid periods of global warming.

Cold phases

As global temperatures fell more water became locked up in ice sheets which expanded across high latitudes. In the low latitudes climates became drier. The falling sea levels exposed large areas of landmass which are now flooded. In Europe tundras developed which were exploited by large migratory herds of reindeer. Areas such as the Near East suffered drought conditions.

3 The architecture of the modern mind

WHAT CAN BE LEARNT from the modern mind today that will help us in our quest for the minds of our earliest ancestors?

It helps to start our enquiry briefly not with minds, but with bodies.[1] If we want to find out how people looked or behaved in the past we may go to a museum and look at exhibits of human fossils or stone tools. If it is a good museum there may be a reconstruction, perhaps a hairy Neanderthal crouching at the entrance to a cave cooking food or sharpening a spear. But there is a much easier way to start learning about the past, even about the most ancient of human ancestors. And that is to sit in the bath. As the water cools, you get goose bumps. Your skin reacts in this fashion because our Stone Age ancestors were much hairier than we are today. When they got cold they also got goose bumps, which made their hair stand on end and trap a layer of warm air against their skin. We have (largely) lost the hairy bodies today, but the goose bumps remain. They provide a clue to the way we used to look many millennia ago.

In fact our bodies are a Stone Age detective's paradise. Watching how a gymnast can swing like a gibbon provides a clue that this is what our arms and shoulders were once designed to do. The extent of heart disease in modern Western populations provides a clue that our high fat diet is not what our bodies were designed to consume.[2] Is it the same with our minds? Can the nature of the modern mind betray the nature of the Stone Age mind? Can we find clues in the way we think today to the way that our ancestors thought thousands, even millions, of years ago? We can indeed – although the clues are perhaps not as readily apparent as those concerning our anatomy. In fact we can find more than just clues, for the modern mind has an architecture built up by millions of years of evolution. We can start to reconstruct the prehistory of the mind by exposing that architecture, and then taking it apart.

The mind as a sponge, the mind as a computer

Exposing the architecture of the modern mind is the task of psychologists. But we have all engaged in this activity from time to time: we are all expert mind users. We constantly and compulsively peer into our own minds and wonder what is going on in the minds of others. Sometimes we think we know. Now this is a risky business because we may begin to delude ourselves. Look at the world and it seems to be flat. Look at the mind and it seems to be ... well let us start by looking at what the mind does seem to be. And let us start by looking at some of the most fertile and extraordinary minds in existence: those of young children.

Watching my own children develop has in many ways been as helpful to my search for the prehistory of the mind as the academic papers and books that I have read during the last decade. When Nicholas, my son, was almost three years old we were playing with his toy zoo and I asked if he wanted to put the seal into the lake. His eyes glanced at the animal and then he looked at me in silence for a moment. 'Yes', he said, 'but actually it's a walrus'. He was right. I may have got them confused, but my son had meticulous knowledge of his animals. He needed telling just once and the differences between armadillos, aardvarks and anteaters would become embedded in his mind. As with the minds of all children, his seemed to be like a sponge soaking up knowledge. New facts and ideas were sucked into an endless array of empty pores. Moreover, young minds in different parts of the world will soak up different things; they will acquire different cultures. And cultures, so anthropologists tell us, are not just lists of facts about the world, but specific ways of thinking and understanding: the sponge-mind is one that soaks up the processes of thought itself.[3]

The idea that the mind is an empty sponge waiting to be filled is one that pervades both our everyday thinking, and much of academia. The process of acquiring knowledge is about filling up the pores and remembering is about squeezing the sponge. The idea of an IQ test is based on the notion that some sponges are better than others with regard to mopping up and wringing out. The evolution of the human mind appears to be no more than the gradual enlargement of the sponge within our heads.

But this analogy doesn't help us think about how minds solve problems, how they learn. This is more than simply amassing and then regurgitating facts; it is about comparing and combining bits of information. Sponges cannot do this, but computers can. The mind as a *computer* is perhaps an even more persuasive idea than the mind as a *sponge*. We can think of the mind as taking in data, processing it, solving the problem, and making our bodies perform the output. The brain is the hardware, the mind is the software.[4] But what programs are running?

Usually we think of the mind as running a single, powerful general-purpose program. We normally give this program the simple name of 'learning', and say no more. So as the child begins to soak up knowledge it will also start running the general-purpose learning program. One day the child will start entering data about the sounds it hears coming from people's mouths and their actions which follow – the program runs and the child will learn the meaning of words. Another day the input data will be the shape of marks it sees on paper and the adjacent pictures of objects – the child learns to read. Another day the input data may be about numbers on a page, or about balancing on a two-wheeled object and this remarkably flexible computer program we call 'learning' enables the child to understand mathematics or ride a bicycle. The same program just keeps on running, even into adulthood.

If the mind is a computer, how should we think of the minds of our prehistoric ancestors? Easy. Different types of minds are like computers with different memory capacities and processing chips. During the last decade we have seen a dramatic increase in the power and speed of computers and this almost begs to be used as an analogy for the prehistory of the mind. Not long ago I took my children to the Science Museum in London and we looked at the reconstruction of Charles Babbage's analytical engine, the first computer. It is many, many times larger and slower than the tiny laptop computer on which I am writing this book. I wondered whether Babbage's analytical engine and my laptop are analogous to the Neanderthal and the modern mind. Or is a better analogy simply that of having a different amount of memory in your PC?

The mind as a sponge and the mind as a computer. Both ideas are very appealing. Both seem to describe a little of how the mind works. How can the mind seem to be such different types of things at once? It seems so easy to say what the mind is like, and so hard to say what the mind actually is.

But are sponges and computers really good analogies for the mind? The mind doesn't just accumulate information and then regurgitate it. And nor is it indiscriminate in the knowledge it soaks up. My children – like all children – have soaked up thousands of words effortlessly, but their suction seems to lose its power when it comes to multiplication tables. Nor does the mind simply solve problems in the way a computer does. The mind does something else: it creates. It thinks of things which are not 'out there', in the world. Things which *could not* be out there in the world. The mind thinks, it creates, it imagines. This cannot happen within a computer. Computers just do what programs tell them to do; they cannot be truly creative in the way that appears compulsive for a four-year-old child.[5] Maybe when we think of the mind as either a sponge or a computer program we are joining the psychological equivalent of the flat earth society.

In reality what I found provocative when my son declared that 'actually it was a walrus' was not that he was right, but that in a fundamental way he was wrong. How could he possibly have thought that it was a walrus? It was no more than a little piece of moulded orange plastic. A walrus is blubbery and wet, fat and smelly. That little piece of plastic was all these things – but only in his mind.

The ideas of Thomas Wynn and Jean Piaget

My own interest in the origins of the human mind was first sparked not by my children, but by a remarkable paper I read as an undergraduate. In 1979 an American archaeologist by the name of Thomas Wynn had published an article which claimed that by 300,000 years ago the modern mind was already in place.[6] Recall that this is within Act 3 of the play that is our past, before Neanderthals, let alone anatomically modern humans, had appeared on the stage. The evidence that Thomas Wynn used for his claim were the fine symmetrical handaxes made by *Homo erectus* and archaic *Homo sapiens* during the first scene of Act 3.

How did he reach this conclusion? He began by using an idea that has been hotly debated by academics for many years: that the phases of mental development in the child reflect the phases of cognitive evolution of our human ancestors. In jargon, this is referred to as the idea that 'ontogeny recapitulates phylogeny'.[7] This is a 'big idea', and one to which I will return later in this chapter and the next. Think of it as implying that the mind of, say, *Homo erectus* or perhaps a chimpanzee today may have structural similarities to that of a young child, although obviously they will possess a vastly different content. To use this idea, Tom Wynn needed to know what the minds of young children were like; he needed to know the phases of mental development. Not surprisingly he looked to the work of the child psychologist Jean Piaget, by far the most influential figure at that time.

Piaget was a psychologist who firmly believed that the mind is like a computer. According to his theories, the mind runs a small set of general-purpose programs which control the entry of new information into the mind, and which serve to restructure the mind so that it passes through a series of developmental phases.[8] He called the last of these phases, reached when the child is about 12 years old, formal operational intelligence. In this phase the mind can think about hypothetical objects and events. This type of thinking is absolutely essential for the manufacture of a stone tool like a handaxe. One must form a mental image of what the finished tool is to look like before starting to remove flakes from the stone nodule. Each strike follows from a hypothesis as to its effect on the shape of the tool. As a consequence, Tom Wynn felt confident in attributing formal operational intelligence, and hence a fundamentally modern mind, to the makers of handaxes.

To a student of archaeology, this was an absolutely stunning conclusion. Here was someone who could actually read the mind of an extinct human ancestor from the stone tools discarded and lost in prehistory. But could the prehistory of the mind really have been over so soon in the course of human evolution? Did the appearance of art, bone tools and global colonization, the events of Act 4, require no new cognitive underpinnings? This seemed implausible to say the least.

A scrutiny of Tom Wynn's work showed that he had been faultless in using Piaget's ideas. To make a handaxe which was simultaneously symmetrical in three dimensions certainly seemed to involve the types of mental processes that Piaget argued were characteristic of formal operational intelligence. So maybe it was Piaget's ideas that were wrong. This has indeed been the message from many psychologists during the last decade: the mind does *not* run general-purpose programs, and nor is it like a sponge, indiscriminately soaking up whatever information is around. Psychologists have introduced a new type of analogy for the mind: it is like a Swiss army knife. A Swiss army knife? One of those chunky knives with lots of specialized devices, like little scissors and saws and tweezers. Each of these is designed for coping with a very specific type of problem. When the knife is closed up, one wouldn't dream that such a multitude of specialized devices exist. Perhaps our minds are closed to us. But if the mind is a Swiss army knife, how many devices are there? What problems are these designed to solve? How did they get there? And is this analogy any better at helping us understand imagination and creative thought?

Many psychologists since 1980 have addressed such questions. They have adopted terms such as 'modules', 'cognitive domains' and 'intelligences' to describe each of the specialized devices. There are lots of disagreements about the number and nature of the specialized devices, but by scrutinizing their work we will be more successful at exposing the architecture of the mind than when we idly ponder the mind as we play with children. And that architecture looks fundamentally different from the one suggested by Piaget. So now we must follow how this Swiss-army-knife view of the mind has arisen and how it has developed during the last few years.[9]

Fodor's two-tier architecture for the mind

Our starting point is with two big books published in 1983. In fact the first of these books is a small slim volume, but it has some big ideas about the architecture of the mind, and gives some major clues to its past: *The Modularity of Mind*, by Jerry Fodor.[10]

Jerry Fodor is a psycho-linguist with very clear ideas about the architecture of the mind. He proposes that it should be split into two parts which he calls perception, or input systems, and cognition, or the central systems. Their respective architectures are very different; input systems are like the blades on a Swiss army knife and he describes these as a series of discrete and independent 'modules', such as sight, hearing and touch. He includes language as one of these input systems. In contrast the central systems have no architecture at all, or at least their architecture will always remain hidden from us. This is where those mysterious processes happen, known as 'thought', 'problem solving' and 'imagination'. It is where 'intelligence' resides.

Fodor argues that each input system is based on independent brain processes. For instance, those we use for hearing are utterly different from those we use for sight, or for language: they are like different blades within the Swiss army knife that just happen to be contained within the same case. This modularity of input systems is attested by numerous lines of evidence which include their apparent association with specific parts of the brain, the characteristic patterns of development in the child, and their propensity to exhibit specific patterns of breakdown. Fodor also stresses how the input systems operate very quickly and are mandatory: one cannot help to hear, or to see, when given the appropriate stimuli.

While few would contest these features of the input systems, further features proposed by Fodor are more open to controversy. First is the notion that input systems do not have direct access to the information being acquired by other input systems. Hence what I am seeing at this moment is not influenced by what I am hearing. Fodor uses the term 'encapsulated' to describe this feature of the input systems. A second feature is that the input systems have only limited information from the central systems. This, for Fodor, is a crucial architectural feature, for it means that the knowledge possessed by any individual has a limited, perhaps even marginal, influence on the way they perceive the world. A neat example he uses to illustrate this is optical illusions: these persist even when we know that what we are seeing is untrue.

The idea that cognition only marginally influences perception runs counter to the relativist ideas of the social sciences. Recall that when we were thinking about the mind as a sponge, young children were supposed to soak up the knowledge of their culture. Well to the majority of social scientists that knowledge also includes how to perceive the world. Fodor is saying that this is wrong: the nature of perception is already *hard-wired into the mind* at birth. Fodor hates relativism almost as much as he hates fibreglass powerboats, which I assume means he hates it quite a lot.[11]

According to Fodor, input systems are encapsulated, mandatory, fast operating and hard wired. He calls them stupid. As such they contrast with cognition, the 'smart' central system. Fodor argues that we know almost nothing about how the central systems work, other than that they have a series of features which are the opposite of the input systems: they operate slowly, are unencapsulated and domain neutral; in other words, the processes of thought and problem solving turn on the integration of information from all input systems, in addition to that which is being internally generated. Unlike the input systems, the processes of the central systems cannot be related to specific parts of the brain.

The fundamental character of cognition is that it is holistic, the exact opposite of the input systems which are all dedicated to dealing with one specific type of information alone. And this is what Fodor sees as the most puzzling feature of cognition: 'its non encapsulation, its creativity, its holism and its passion for the analogical'.[12] Fodor feels defeated by the central systems, declaring they are impossible to study. For him, 'thought', 'problem solving', 'imagination' and 'intelligence' are unresolvable.

In summary, Fodor believes the mind has a two-tier architecture, the lower one is like a Swiss army knife, the upper one is like ... well we can't say for we have nothing else like it in the world.

At first sight the combination of input and central systems appears to provide a rather odd architecture for the mind, a dramatic and unsightly clash of styles. But Fodor argues that the architect of the modern mind – the processes of human evolution – has in fact come up with a most ingenious design. It is well-nigh perfect for allowing us to adapt to the world around us. Perception has been built to detect what is right in the world: in situations of danger or opportunity a person needs to react quickly and without thinking. According to Fodor 'it is, no doubt, important to attend to the eternally beautiful and true. But it is more important not to be eaten.'[13] At other times, however, one survives by contemplating the nature of the world in a slow, reflective manner, integrating many different types and sources of information. Only by this can one come to recognize the regularities and structure of the world. 'Nature has contrived to have it both ways', Fodor argues, 'to get the best out of fast dumb systems and slow contemplative ones, by simply refusing to choose between them.'[14]

Gardner's theory of multiple intelligences

In the same year that Fodor's book was published, another one appeared: *Frames of Mind: The Theory of Multiple Intelligences*, by Howard Gardner.[15] In some ways this contrasts dramatically with Fodor's work. Gardner is as much concerned with practical matters in terms of devising education policies for schools, as with purely philosophical issues concerning the mind. He also draws on information from more than just psychology and linguistics to bear on the mind, bringing in data from disciplines such as social anthropology and educational studies.

Gardner proposes a very different type of architecture for the mind; he does away with the distinction between input and central systems and instead focuses on the notion of intelligence – which to Fodor is unresolvable. He questions whether there is a single, generalized intellectual capacity – the size of one's sponge, or speed of one's computer – and replaces it with no less than seven different types of intelligence. He claims that these are based in different parts of the brain, having their own dedicated and independent neurological processes. So here too we have a Swiss-army-knife architecture for the mind, with each blade now described as an intelligence.

To identify the multiple intelligences of the mind Gardner uses a stringent set of criteria. For instance, he feels that there should be evidence that the core capacity may become isolated by brain damage, either in terms of losing the capacity (while all others remain unimpaired), or losing all other capacities yet remaining competent in the proposed intelligence. He also feels that one should be able to see a distinct developmental history in the child for the intelligence, and that it ought to be developed to different degrees in different individuals. By using such criteria, Gardner arrives at his set of seven intelligences: his blades for the Swiss army knife of the modern mind.

Gardner's seven intelligences are: linguistic, musical, logical-mathematical, spatial, bodily-kinesthetic and two forms of personal intelligence, one for looking in at one's own mind, and one for looking outward towards others. The function of each intelligence is largely defined by its name. Logical-mathematical is perhaps the closest to what we generally mean when we invoke the word intelligence, as it is ultimately about logical and scientific thought. The awkwardly named bodily-kinesthetic intelligence is about the co-ordination of one's body movements, as exemplified by sportsmen and dancers. Now each of these intelligences meets the criteria that Gardner puts forward. For instance, language certainly seems to rely on its own unique brain processes; and we all probably know children that seem to have particularly advanced levels of musical or logical-mathematical intelligence.

So Gardner suggests that the architecture of the mind is constituted by a series of relatively autonomous intelligences. Not only does he suggest this, but the case is very powerfully made. In doing so, he seems to depart quite radically from the type of architecture proposed by Fodor. Gardner's intelligences are very different from Fodor's modules. The former have a developmental history – their character is heavily influenced by the cultural context of the individual. The blades of Gardner's Swiss army knife are concerned with thinking and problem solving, not just with the acquisition of information as undertaken by a Fodorian module. There is one more fundamental difference. But, ironically, this brings the ideas of Fodor and Gardner much closer together than they initially appear.

While Fodor's modules are absolutely independent from each other, Gardner continuously stresses how interaction between the multiple intelligences is fundamental to the workings of the mind. Gardner emphasizes that 'in the normal course of events, the intelligences actually interact with, and build upon, one another.'[16] It is a characteristic feature of human development, he argues, that young infants have a capacity to build connections between domains. And his book is full of examples of the intelligences working together to create the patterns of behaviour and the cultural achievements of humankind. Indeed it is difficult to conceive of musical intelligence, for instance, not being intimately linked with intricate body movements deriving from bodily-kinesthetic intelligence, or linguistic intelligence being used independently from personal intelligence. So Gardner's position is that, in spite of the independent core processes of each intelligence, 'in normal human intercourse one typically encounters complexes of intelligences functioning together smoothly, even seamlessly, in order to execute intricate human activities.'[17] And the wisest individuals, he suggests, are those who are most able at building connections across domains, as exemplified in the use of metaphors and analogies.

The word 'analogy' immediately takes us back to think of how Fodor described the central systems: they have 'a passion for analogical thought'. Could it be that Fodor could see no modularity in the central systems simply because the intelligences or modules within it function so smoothly together that one is unaware that any modularity exists?[18]

Interlude: Fodor versus Gardner

Let us pause for a moment in this spin through recent thought in psychology to assess how far we have come in exposing the architecture of the mind. Fodor has given us a two-tier architecture, and the role of each tier appears to be of evolutionary interest: one can imagine a mind working with just the input systems, but not with just a central system. Insects and amoebas need input systems, but they don't require the processes of the central systems. So perhaps the latter have been added on sometime during evolution. Gardner has given us a Swiss-army-knife model for the processes of thought which, if the multiple intelligences can truly function together sufficiently smoothly and seamlessly, appears not substantially different from the manner in which Fodor characterized the central systems. So, perhaps the mind is not just a single Swiss army knife, but in fact two knives: one for input systems in which the blades remain truly independent, and one for thought in which the blades are somehow working together for most of the time. But if that is true, why are there separate blades for thought in the first place? Why not have a general-purpose learning/thinking/problem-solving program? Or in other words, a general intelligence? And what confidence can we have that Gardner has identified the correct number and types of blades on the knife? Gardner himself admits that someone else looking at the mind might find a different range of intelligences. To answer these questions we had better think about who put this Swiss army knife/knives of the mind together – that is, about the architect of the mind: the processes of evolution. To do this we must return to our study of recent thought in psychology and meet a gang of psychologists who have been shouting the loudest during the 1990s: the evolutionary psychologists.

Enter the evolutionary psychologists

The leaders of the gang of evolutionary psychologists are Leda Cosmides and John Tooby, two charming people with razor-sharp minds.[19] During the late 1980s and early 1990s they published a succession of papers culminating in a long essay, entitled 'The psychological foundations of culture', published in *The Adapted Mind*, a 1992 book they edited with Jerome Barkow.[20] By adopting an explicitly evolutionary approach their work has challenged many of the conventional notions about the mind – the mind as a sponge, the mind as a general-purpose computer program. In fact it was Leda Cosmides who I saw a few months ago starting a lecture by holding up a Swiss army knife and declaring it to be the mind.[21] I'll refer to Cosmides and Tooby as C&T.

The reason that they parade under the banner of evolutionary psychology is that the gang argue that we can only understand the nature of the modern mind by viewing it as a product of biological evolution. The starting point for this argument is that the mind is a complex, functional structure that could not have arisen by chance. If we are willing to ignore the possibility of divine intervention, the only known process by which such complexity can have arisen is evolution by natural selection.[22] In this regard C&T treat the mind as one treats any other organ of the body – it is an evolved mechanism which has been constructed and adjusted in response to the selective pressures faced by our species during its evolutionary history. More specifically, they argue that the human mind evolved under the selective pressures faced by our human ancestors as they lived by hunting and gathering in Pleistocene environments – the central Acts and Scenes of our prehistory. As that lifestyle ended no more than a fraction of time ago in evolutionary terms, our minds remain adapted to that way of life.

As a consequence of this, C&T argue that the mind consists of a Swiss army knife with a great many, highly specialized blades; in other terms, it is composed of multiple mental modules. Each of these blades/modules has been designed by natural selection to cope with one specific adaptive problem faced by hunter-gatherers during our past. Just as Gardner argued, the mind has more than a capacity for 'general intelligence' – there are multiple specialized types of intelligence, or ways of thinking. As with Gardner's intelligences, it is likely that each module has its own specific form of memory and reasoning process.[23] But the modules of C&T's mind are very different from the intelligences of Gardner. In fact they are far more like Fodor's input processes: they are hard-wired into the mind at birth and universal among all people. Whereas the character of Gardner's multiple intelligences were open to influence by the cultural context in which young minds developed, this is not the case with C&T's modules.

These modules have a critically important feature that we have not come across yet: they are 'content rich'. In other words, the modules not only provide sets of rules for solving problems, but they provide much of the information that one needs to do so. This knowledge reflects the structure of the real world – or at least that of the Pleistocene in which the mind evolved. This information about real-world structure, together with a multitude of rules for solving problems, each contained in its own mental module, is already in a child's mind at birth. Some modules are sparked into action immediately – modules for eye contact with the mother – others need a little time before they get busy, such as the modules for language acquisition.

Now before we look at the types of modules that C&T believe to be within their mind, it is important to understand why they believe the mind is like a Swiss army knife, rather than like a sponge, or a general-purpose computer, or something else. They have three major arguments.

First they suggest that because each type of problem faced by our hunter-gatherer ancestors had a unique form, trying to solve all of them using a single reasoning device would have led to many errors. Consequently, any human who had specialized mental modules dedicated to specific types of problems would have avoided errors and solved them more successfully. That person would have had a selective advantage and his/her genes would have spread in the population, encoding the construction of Swiss army knives in the minds of his/her offspring.

The criteria for choosing sexual partners can illustrate the value of mental modules. If a man is choosing who to have sex with he should avoid someone who is biologically related. But if he is choosing someone to share food with, then he should not avoid kin. Someone using a simple reasoning rule that stated, 'always be friendly to kin', or 'always ignore kin' would not have as much reproductive success as someone with a set of mental rules, each dedicated to a particular problem.

The second argument used by C&T to support the notion of content-rich mental modules is that young children rapidly learn so much about so many complex subjects that it is simply unbelievable that this could happen unless their minds were pre-programmed to do so. This argument was originally known as the 'poverty of the stimulus' and was used by Noam Chomsky with regard to language. How is it possible, he asked, for children to acquire the many and complex rules of grammar from the limited series of utterances they hear from their parents' lips? How could a generalized learning program in the mind possibly deduce these rules, memorize them and then allow a four-year-old child to use them to near perfection? Well, quite simply it couldn't. Chomsky argued that the mind contains a genetically fixed 'language acquisition device' dedicated to learning language, that comes already geared up with a blueprint for grammatical rules. Fodor and Gardner concurred with this viewpoint, which is why both had language as a specialized feature of the mind.

C&T generalize the 'poverty of the stimulus' argument to all domains of life. How can a child learn the meaning of facial expressions, or the behaviour of physical objects, or how to attribute beliefs and intentions to other people, unless that child was helped by content-rich mental modules dedicated to these tasks.

Their third argument is known as the frame problem and is about the difficulty of making decisions. It is the same argument that Fodor used when explaining why stupid input systems exist. Imagine that a prehistoric hunter turned a corner and was suddenly faced with a lion. What should he do? If he had no more than a general-purpose learning program, the time taken to evaluate the intentions of the lion and weigh up the pros and cons of running or staying put might well be too great. He would, as Fodor noted, very probably have been eaten.

The problem with general-purpose learning rules, according to C&T, is that there are no bounds as to what information should be excluded from making a decision, and as to which alternative courses of action should be ignored. Every single possibility should be examined. Our prehistoric ancestors would have quietly starved as they tried to decide where and what to hunt. But if one of the hunters had a specialized mental module for making hunting decisions, which prescribed the types of information to consider and how to process them, he would have prospered. This would, no doubt, have increased his reproductive success, and soon the community would be populated with his offspring, each with this specialized mental module for making hunting decisions.[24]

Now these are powerful arguments. If it is legitimate to think of the mind as a product of natural selection, the case for a Swiss-army-knife design seems overwhelming. So what sort of blades should we find on the knife? This takes us to perhaps the most significant aspect of C&T's arguments: they suggest that we can actually predict what devices should exist within the knife. We do not need to be like Gardner and rely on hunches and guesses. At least, we can predict the blades if we know the types of problems that our prehistoric hunter-gatherers had regularly to face and solve. C&T think that they do and suggest that the mind is teeming with a multitude of modules. These include:

> A face recognition module, a spatial relations module, a rigid objects mechanics module, a tool-use module, a fear module, a social-exchange module, an emotion-perception module, a kin oriented motivation module, an effort allocation and recalibration module, a child care module, a social inference module, a friendship module, a semantic-inference module, a friendship module, a grammar acquisition module, a communication-pragmatics module, a theory of mind module, and so on![25]

This extensive and incomplete list of possible modules is perhaps not that different from what Gardner was suggesting. For from such lists one can readily group modules together, such as those about social interaction, or those about physical objects. C&T have called these groupings 'faculties'. As such, these faculties seem similar to Gardner's notion of an intelligence. But the fundamental difference from Gardner's ideas is that his intelligences are arbitrary – no more than his hunches as to what goes on in the mind. C&T, on the other hand, predict what modules should be present by drawing on the fact that the mind is a product of evolution during the Pleistocene in which natural selection can be assumed to have played a dominant role. Moreover, Gardner's intelligences are moulded by the cultural context of development. C&T's are immune to the outside world. But so many modules? Can we really have so many independent psychological processes in our minds? I wonder if such ideas are what Fodor feared when he warned of 'modularity theory gone mad'.[26]

Interlude: Hunter-gatherers and Cambridge dons versus the evolutionary psychologists

Let us break from the psychologists and see how the idea of the modern human mind as the Swiss army knife of a prehistoric hunter-gatherer fares with our experience of the world. Pretty poorly is the answer.

To begin with, consider the idea that the modern mind evolved as a means of solving the problems faced by Stone Age hunter-gatherers in Pleistocene environments. The logical arguments for this are overwhelming: how could it be otherwise? But how then can we account for those things that the modern mind is very good at doing, but which we can be confident that Stone Age hunter-gatherers never attempted: such as reading books and developing cures for cancer. For some of these we may use modules which originally evolved for different, but related, tasks. So modules intended for the acquisition of spoken language might well be co-opted when we learn to read and write. And perhaps we can learn to do geometry because we can use C&T's 'spatial relations module', not now for finding our way around a landscape, but for finding our way around the sides of a triangle.

Other types of non-hunter-gatherer-like thoughts and behaviour may well use some general-purpose learning rules such as associative learning and trial-and-error learning. I group all these together under the title of general intelligence. Even C&T admit that some general-purpose learning rules must exist within the mind. But, if their arguments are correct, these could only solve simple problems. Anything more difficult requires some dedicated, or co-opted, specialized mental processes.

Consider mathematics. Children certainly have a far more difficult time learning the rules of algebra than they do the rules of language. This certainly suggests that the mind is preadapted for learning language but not for mathematics. So perhaps we learn mathematics by using the rules within general intelligence. But could this account for those adults, and indeed children, who are outstanding at mathematics?

Consider the case of a mathematician by the name of Andrew Wiles. In June 1993 he announced that he had a proof for what is known as Fermat's last theorem.[27] Fermat was a 17th-century mathematician who jotted in the margin of a notebook that he had proved that the equation $x^n+y^n=z^n$ has no integer solution when n is greater than 2 and x, y and z are not zero. But he forgot to leave us the proof itself, which ever since has been one of the Holy Grails of mathematics. Wiles claimed he had it: more than a thousand pages of equations utterly unintelligible to the vast majority of people in the world. But someone understood them, and told poor Andrew Wiles that he had got it wrong! One year later a revised proof was submitted, which has been acclaimed as one of the greatest achievements in 20th-century mathematics. Now, if minds are just adapted for solving the problems of hunting and gathering how could this proof have been devised? How indeed could Fermat have thought of a last theorem, or even a first theorem? Could Fermat and Wiles have been using no more than a second-hand cognitive process which had been evolved for another task? Or maybe a general-purpose learning ability? Both of these seem implausible.

Of course it is not just the ability of modern humans to do pure mathematics that poses this problem to Cosmides and Tooby's ideas about the mind. When I first read their work I was a very junior Research Fellow at a Cambridge college, Trinity Hall. Once a week all the Fellows would gather for dinner at High Table. And there I would sit, fresh out of my Ph.D., surrounded by some of the great intellects in the country. People like Sir Roy Calne, the transplant surgeon (and talented artist); Professor John Polkinghorne, who had not only been a professor of mathematical physics but had also been ordained as an Anglican priest; and the distinguished linguist, Sir John Lyons, the Master of the college. On special occasions the honorary Fellows of the college would dine, including the famous physicist Professor Stephen Hawking. Could these surgeons, linguists and theoretical physicists be expanding the boundaries of human knowledge in such diverse and complex fields by using minds which were adapted for no more than a hunter-gatherer existence?

Perhaps we should look at modern hunter-gatherers for a moment and consider how their minds seem to work. The Inuit, Kalahari Bushmen and Australian Aborigines are not relics of the Stone Age. They are just as modern as you and me. They simply have a lifestyle that happens to be the closest analogy for that of the Pleistocene. Indeed by having to hunt and gather for their food, these modern people share many of the adaptive problems faced by Pleistocene hunter-gatherers. Yet there is a vast gulf between the manner in which they appear to think about their activities, and how they should do so according to C& T.

One of C&T's fundamental arguments is that specific types of problems need specific ways to solve them. A girl choosing fruit using the same reasoning devices she uses for choosing a mate is likely to end up with severe stomach ache because she will choose unripe fruit – fruit which seems to have good muscle tone. Yet as soon as we look at modern hunter-gatherers this seems to be precisely what they do; not get stomach ache from eating unripe fruit, but reason about the natural world as if it were a social being.

Nurit Bird-David has lived with people following a traditional hunting and gathering lifestyle in tropical forests, such as the Mbuti of Zaire. She found that all these groups share a common view of their environment: they conceive of the 'forest as parent', it is a 'giving environment, in the same way as one's close kin are giving'.[28] Similarly the Inuit of the Canadian Arctic 'typically view their world as imbued with human qualities of will and purpose'.[29] Modern hunter-gatherers do not live in landscapes composed merely of animals, plants, rocks and caves. Their landscapes are socially constructed. Among the Aborigines of Australia the wells in the landscape are where their ancestors had dug in the ground, the trees are where digging sticks had been placed, and deposits of red ochre where they had shed blood.[30]

2 *During the mythological creation period of the Inuit, animals and humans lived together and easily metamorphosed into each other. This picture is from a drawing by Davidialuk Alasuaq and shows a polar bear dressed Inuit-style cordially greeting a male hunter.*

This propensity to think of the natural world in social terms is perhaps most evident in the ubiquitous use of anthropomorphic thinking – attributing animals with humanlike minds. Consider the Inuit and the polar bear. This animal is highly sought after and is 'killed with passion, butchered with care and eaten with delight'.[31] But it is also treated in some respects as if it is another male hunter. When a bear is killed the same restrictions apply to activities that can be undertaken as when someone dies in the camp. The polar bear is thought of as a human ancestor, a kinsman, a feared and respected adversary (see Figure 2). In the mythology of the Inuit there was a time when humans and polar bears could easily change from one kind to another. This idea – that in the past humans and non-human animals could be transformed into each other – is indeed a pervasive feature of the minds of hunter-gatherers. It is the basis of totemic thought, the study of which is a foundation stone of social anthropology.[32]

In general all modern hunter-gatherers appear to do precisely what C&T say they should not do: they think of their natural world as if it were a social being. They do not use a different 'blade' for thinking about such different entities. This has been nicely summed up by the anthropologist Tim Ingold. He writes: 'For them [modern hunter-gatherers] there are not two worlds of persons (society) and things (nature), but just one world – one environment – saturated with personal powers and embracing both human beings, the animals and plants on which they depend, and the landscape in which they live and move.'[33] The social anthropologist/philosopher Ernest Gellner goes even further. Writing about non-Western, 'traditional' societies he concludes that 'the conflation and confusion of functions, aims and criteria, is the normal, original condition of mankind.'[34]

The overwhelming impression from the descriptions of modern hunter-gatherers is that all domains of their lives are so intimately connected that the notion that they think about these with separate reasoning devices seems implausible. Killing and eating animals appears to be as much about constructing and mediating social relationships as it is about getting food.[35] Hunter-gatherers have to build huts within their settlements for shelter, but the act of placing a hut at one location rather than another makes an important social statement.[36] Similarly everything that is worn on the body acts both to keep the person warm but also to send social messages about identity and how that person wants to be treated.[37] When designing the shape of an arrowhead hunters take into account the physical properties of the raw material, the functional requirements of the arrowhead, such as whether it should pierce vital organs or slash arteries, and also how the shape can send social messages about either personal identity or group affiliation.[38] In a nutshell, any one action of a modern hunter-gatherer does not address one single adaptive problem. It simultaneously and intentionally impinges on a whole host of problems. If – and it is a very big if – these modern hunter-gatherers are indeed a good analogy for those of the Pleistocene, how could selective pressures have existed to produce a Swiss army knife for the mind?

I have not been lucky enough to sit with Inuit or Kalahari Bushmen at their meal times. But I have sat with Cambridge dons at a High Table and there seems to be little difference in their behaviour. For while the food provided nutrition, it was also used for sending social messages. It was expensive, excessive and exotic, especially when guests were invited to the college: conspicuous consumption acting to bond the group of Fellows together and to establish their prestige. The seating arrangements in the dining hall were as much socially inspired as those of hunter-gatherers when they seat themselves around a fire: the Fellows' High Table literally on a podium, looking down to where the undergraduates would sit. The Master seated in the centre. I remember the many frowns I received from Senior Fellows when I accidentally sat in a place that did not befit my rank. And also the scowls when I forgot to pass the port – similar (but less serious) to those received by a young hunter if he forgets to divide his kill. The gowns that Fellows wear are of course their tribal dress, the different colours and designs used to establish social rank. Cambridge dons and

Kalahari Bushmen, they are all the same. They all have the architecture of the modern mind – which seems to be something fundamentally different from a collection of specialized devices each for solving a unique adaptive problem.

Now one doesn't need to look at exotic human cultures to recognize that what C&T are telling us about the mind runs counter to how people actually seem to think. Let us return to children. Give a child a kitten and she will believe it has a mind like her own: anthropomorphizing appears to be compulsive. Give a child a doll and she will start talking to it, feeding it and changing its nappy. That inert lump of moulded plastic never smiles at her, but she seems to use the same mental process for interacting with it as she uses for interacting with real people.

Now sit with children and watch cartoons on the television. Immediately one enters a world in which every single rule which could have been imposed on their minds by evolution appears to be violated. You will see talking animals, objects that can change shape and come to life, people that can fly. This surreal world is understood effortlessly by young minds. How could this be if the evolutionary psychologists are correct and the child's mind is composed of content-rich mental modules reflecting the structure of the real world? Surely, if that is the case, they should be confused, bewildered, terrified by their cartoons?

So we are left with a paradox. The evolutionary psychologists make a very powerful argument that the mind should be like a Swiss army knife. It should be constituted by multiple, content-rich mental modules, each adapted to solve a specific problem faced by Pleistocene hunter-gatherers. One cannot fault the logic of their argument. I find it compelling. But as soon as we think about Cambridge dons, Australian Aborigines, or young children this idea seems almost absurd. For me it is the human passion for analogy and metaphor which provides the greatest challenge to Cosmides and Tooby's view of the mind. Simply by being able to invoke the analogy that the mind is like a Swiss army knife, Leda Cosmides appears to be falsifying the claim that is being made.

How can we resolve this paradox? I think we should start by looking once again at children's minds, but this time with a little help from another group of experts: the developmental (rather than evolutionary) psychologists.

Child development and the four domains of intuitive knowledge

Are children really born with content-rich mental modules that reflect the structure of the real (Pleistocene) world, as C&T would have us believe? The answer from developmental psychology is overwhelmingly in their favour. Young children seem to have intuitive knowledge about the world in at least four domains of behaviour: about language, psychology, physics and biology. And their intuitive knowledge within each of these appears to be directly related to a hunting and gathering lifestyle long, long ago in prehistory. We have already considered language, so now let us turn to the evidence for these other types of intuitive knowledge, starting with that of psychology.

INTUITIVE PSYCHOLOGY

By the time children reach the age of three years old they attribute mental states to other people when attempting to explain their actions. In particular, they understand that other people have beliefs and desires and that these play a causal role in behaviour. As Andrew Whiten mentions in the introduction to his edited book, *Natural Theories of Mind* (1991), this has been variously described as an 'intuitive psychology', a 'belief-desire psychology', a 'folk psychology' and a 'theory of mind'.[39] The basic concepts of belief and desire that children use, whatever their cultural background, could not be constructed from the evidence available to them during the earliest stages of their development. Consequently these concepts appear to derive from an innate psychological structure – a content-rich mental module which creates mandatory interpretations of human behaviour in mentalistic terms.

The study of this intuitive psychology has been one of the most dynamic fields of enquiry in child development during the last decade. Most interest has focused on what is known as the 'theory of mind' module: an ability to 'read' other people's minds, described for example in the work of Alan Leslie. One of the most interesting proposals is that the condition of autism, in which children have severe difficulties engaging in social interaction, appears to arise from an impairment of this one module. Autistic children seem to be unaware of what other people are thinking, indeed they seem to be unaware that other people may have thoughts in their minds at all. Simon Baron-Cohen has described their condition as 'mindblindness'. Yet autistic children appear to be quite normal in other aspects of thought. It is as if one blade of their mental Swiss army knife has broken off, or got stuck and won't open. All the other blades carry on as normal – or maybe are enhanced as in the cases of people with severe impairments in some areas of mental activity who display prodigious talents in others, the *idiots savants*.[40]

An evolutionary rationale for a theory of mind module was proposed 20 years ago by Nicholas Humphrey.[41] In fact it was Humphrey who delivered evolutionary psychology into the academic world; the current gang have simply picked up as nurse maids during its kindergarten years. In a seminal academic paper entitled 'The social function of intellect',

Nicholas Humphrey argued that when individuals are living within a group, and entering into a diverse set of co-operative, competitive and mutualistic relationships, individuals with an ability to predict the behaviour of others will achieve the greatest reproductive success. Moreover powers of social forethought and understanding – what he termed a social intelligence – are essential for maintaining social cohesion so that practical knowledge, such as about toolmaking and foraging, can be passed around. In other words, there will be selective pressures for abilities to read the contents of other people's minds. We use a clever trick for this: it is called consciousness. We are going to look at Humphrey's ideas in more detail in Chapter 5, when we will also start to come to grips with the idea of consciousness. Here we should simply note that we can both identify selective pressures for a theory of mind module and find evidence in developmental psychology for its existence. C&T seem to be bang on the mark.

INTUITIVE BIOLOGY

Similar evidence exists for an intuitive understanding of biology. Research in child development has shown that children appear to be born with an understanding that living things and inanimate objects are fundamentally different. Children as young as three seem to have a compulsion to attribute an 'essence' to different types of living things and to recognize that a change in manifest appearance does not reflect a change in kind.[42] For instance, Frank Keil has shown that children can understand that if a horse is put into striped pyjamas, this does not turn it into a zebra. Similarly if a dog is born mute and with only three legs, it is nevertheless a dog, which is a barking quadruped.[43] Just as the experience of young children appears inadequate to account for how they acquire language, so too does their experience of the world seem inadequate to account for their understanding of living things.

We are all familiar with this notion of species essence. It is because of this notion that we demand that a severely brain-damaged person should have the same rights as a university professor, or a physically disabled person the same rights as an Olympic sportsman. They are all 'human', whatever their intellectual and physical abilities. Similarly many people feel uncomfortable about the idea of genetic engineering because it often seems to be about combining the essences of two different species.

Another reason for believing in an intuitive biological knowledge is that all cultures share the same set of notions concerning the classification of the natural world, just as all languages share the same grammatical structure. This has been documented by Scott Atran in his book on the *Cognitive Foundations of Natural History* (1990).[44] He describes how all known cultures appear to entertain notions of (1) biological species of vertebrates and flowering plants; (2) sequential patterns of naming , e.g. 'oak', 'shingle oak', 'spotted shingle oak'; (3) taxa constructed by an appreciation of overall patterns of morphological regularity; (4) over-arching animal 'life-form' groupings that closely match those of modern zoological classes such as fish and bird; and (5) overarching plant 'life-form' groupings that have ecological significance, such as 'tree', and 'grass', although these have no place in modern botanical taxonomy.

The universality and complexity of the hierarchical classifications of the natural world that people adopt are most parsimoniously (and perhaps only) explained by a shared, content-rich mental module for 'intuitive biology'. It is simply impossible that people could generalize from the limited evidence available to them during development to the complex taxonomies universally adopted, unless they possessed a 'blue-print' for the structures of the living world hard-wired into their minds.

There are further similarities between biological knowledge and that of psychology and language. For instance, just as people seem to be unable to restrain themselves from thinking about other people's actions in terms of a 'belief-desire' psychology, so too do people seem unable to prevent themselves imposing a complex taxonomic classification on the world, even when it is of little utilitarian value. The anthropologist Brent Berlin has shown, for example, that among the Tzeltal Maya of Mexico and the Aguarana Jivar of Peru more than a third of named plants have no social or economic uses, nor are they poisonous or pests.[45] But they are nevertheless named and grouped according to perceived similarities.

Another similarity with notions of beliefs and desires is the ease with which biological information is transmitted. Scott Atran has described how the structure, scope and depth of taxonomic knowledge are comparable in different societies, regardless of the effort put into transmitting that knowledge. The Hanunóo of the Philippines, for example, have detailed botanical knowledge, which they frequently discuss and pontificate about. The Zafimaniry of Madagascar, living in a similar environment and with a similar subsistence organization, have an equally detailed botanical knowledge. But they pass this information on quite informally, with neither instruction nor commentary.

A critical component of this information refers not to the taxonomy of animals and plants, but to their behaviour. There are several cases of cognitive pathologies in which people either lose an intuitive understanding of animal behaviour, or appear to have one enhanced as they lose other types of knowledge. One of the best examples is provided by the clinical neurologist Oliver Sacks, who has described the case of Temple Grandin. She is autistic and cannot decipher even the simplest social exchange between humans. Yet her intuitive understanding of animal behaviour is daunting. Sacks describes his impression of her after spending some time with Temple on her farm:

I was struck by the enormous difference, the gulf, between Temple's immediate, intuitive recognition of animal moods and signs and her extraordinary difficulties understanding human beings, their codes and signals, the way they conduct themselves. One cannot say that she is devoid of feeling or has a fundamental lack of sympathy. On the contrary, her sense of animals' moods and feelings is so strong that these almost take possession of her, overwhelm her at times.[46]

So we have good evidence that the mind has a specialized device for learning about the natural world. I become particularly convinced about this when I see children showing such effortless ease and enjoyment when learning about animals in their games – this reflects their intuitive biology at work. Could such intuitive biology be accounted for by selective pressures on prehistoric hunter-gatherers, as C&T would have us believe? Quite clearly it could. Of all lifestyles, that of hunting and gathering requires the most detailed knowledge of the natural world. This is quite clear when looking at modern hunter-gatherers: they are compulsive and expert naturalists, able to interpret the tiniest clues in their environments as to their implications for the location and behaviour of animals.[47] Their success as hunter-gatherers, often in marginal environments, depends far more on their understanding of natural history than on their technology, or the amount of labour they put into their lives. We can well imagine that in the evolutionary environment of modern humans, those individuals born with content-rich mental modules to facilitate the acquisition of this knowledge would have had a substantial selective advantage.

INTUITIVE PHYSICS

The evidence from developmental psychology appears conclusive: the ease with which children learn about language, other minds and biology appears to derive from a cognitive foundation of innate content-rich mental modules. Such modules appear to be universally shared by all humans. This finding also applies to a fourth cognitive domain: intuitive physics. From a very early age children understand that physical objects are subject to a different set of rules from those which govern mental concepts and living things. It appears impossible for them to have acquired such knowledge from their limited experience of the world.

This has been demonstrated by the psychologist Elizabeth Spelke.[48] She has undertaken sets of experiments with young children to demonstrate that they have an intuitive knowledge about the properties of physical objects. Concepts of solidity, gravity and inertia appear to be hard-wired into the child's mind. While the life experiences of a young child are dominated by that of people, they nevertheless understand that objects have fundamentally different properties. They cannot, for instance, cause 'action at a distance', as a stranger can do when he or she enters a room.

Children understand that the appropriate way to classify physical objects is very different from that needed for living things. The notion of essence is entirely absent from their thought about artifacts. Whereas a dog is a dog is a dog, even if it has three legs, they appreciate that a crate can be something to store things in, or to sit on, or to use as a table or a bed. Unlike living things, the identity of an object depends upon context. It has no essence. It is subject neither to hierarchical classifications nor to ideas about growth and movement.[49]

From an evolutionary point of view the benefit of possessing content-rich mental modules for understanding physical objects is readily apparent. If one risked using ideas appropriate to living things to think about inert objects, life would be full of mistakes. By having an intuitive knowledge of physics one can rapidly draw on culturally transmitted knowledge about those particular objects required for one's lifestyle – perhaps the stone tools needed by prehistoric hunter-gatherers – without having first to learn about how physical objects differ from living things and mental concepts.

Developing minds: the rise and fall of a Swiss-army-knife mentality

In this tussle between our everyday experience of the world and the academic ideas of evolutionary psychologists, the latter seem to have won this second round hands down. There is a mass of ever-accumulating data from developmental psychology that children are indeed born with a great deal of information about the world hard-wired into their minds. This knowledge appears to fall into four cognitive domains: language, psychology, biology and physics. For each of these one can imagine strong selective pressures for the evolution of content-rich mental modules – for the specialized blades on the Swiss army knife which appears to be the mind.

Nevertheless this cannot be a complete account of the mind. Recall for a moment the way in which a child will play with an inert doll, investing it with the attributes of a living being. A critical feature of that child's mind is not simply that she is able to apply the evolutionarily inappropriate rules of psychology, biology and language to play with her inert physical object, but that she is utterly compelled to do so. This compulsion, and the effortless ease with which it is achieved, appears to be just as strong as that to acquire language or a belief-desire psychology.[50] It too must reflect a fundamental feature of the evolved architecture of her mind.

So now let us now climb back into the ring for round three with C&T. And my boxing gloves are going to be a pair of developmental psychologists who have looked at how children's minds change during their first few years of life. As we look at their ideas we must remember that compelling idea introduced earlier in this chapter, that the stages in the development of a child's mind reflect the stages of cognitive evolution in our ancestors: the idea that 'ontogeny recapitulates phylogeny'.

The very young infant: from a generalized to a domain-specific mentality

The conclusive evidence we have seen for content-rich mental modules has predominantly come from children aged two and three. What about their minds before and after this period?

The developmental psychologist Patricia Greenfield has suggested that up until the age of two, the child's mind is not like a Swiss army knife at all; in fact it is like that general-purpose learning program that we met earlier in this chapter.[51] She argues that the capacities for language and object manipulation displayed by the young infant rely on the same cognitive processes: it is only afterwards that modularization occurs.

To make this argument, Greenfield stresses the similarity between the hierarchical organization of object combination and of speech by very young children. With regard to objects, elements are combined to make constructions, while in language, phonemes are constructed to make words. It is only after the age of two that the language explosion occurs; prior to that the child seems to acquire rudiments of language by using learning rules which are not restricted to language alone. The mind is running a simple, general-purpose computer program – it has a general intelligence. Greenfield argues that in this respect the mind of a two-year-old child is similar to that of a chimpanzee, which she also sees as using general-purpose learning processes for manipulating physical objects and symbols – an idea we will explore in Chapter 5. Among humans, it is only after the age of two that the content-rich mental modules containing knowledge about language, physics, psychology and biology overwhelm the general-purpose learning rules.

So we seem to have a strange metamorphosis of the mind from a computer program to a Swiss army knife. Is this metamorphosis like that of a tadpole to a frog, the end of the affair, or is it like that of a caterpillar to a chrysalis – implying that the final, and most startling, change is yet to happen? Annette Karmiloff-Smith believes it is the latter and that the final stage of mental development is like the emergence of a butterfly.[52]

The child: from a domain-specific to a cognitively fluid mentality

In her book *Beyond Modularity* (1992) Karmiloff-Smith concurs with Greenfield that modularization is a product of development. Now for Karmiloff-Smith, the modules which develop are to some extent variable in different cultural contexts – an idea that is anathema to the evolutionary psychologists, but which aligns her work with the ideas of Howard Gardner. She fully accepts the role of intuitive knowledge about language, psychology, biology and physics, which has indeed been conclusively demonstrated by the work of people such as Noam Chomsky, Alan Leslie, Scott Atran and Elizabeth Spelke as we saw above. But for Karmiloff-Smith, these simply provide the kick-start for the development of cognitive domains. Some of the domains/faculties/intelligences that she believes develop in the mind are the same as those which the evolutionary psychologists would accept, such as language and physics. And they are constituted in the same manner: whereas C&T group mental modules into faculties, Karmiloff-Smith divides domains into micro-domains. So within the faculty/domain of language, pronoun acquisition would be described as either a module or a micro-domain, depending on whose book one is reading.

But fundamental to the ideas of Karmiloff-Smith is that the cultural context in which a child develops also plays a role in determining the type of domains that arise. This is due to the plasticity of early brain development. She suggests that 'with time brain circuits are progressively selected for different domain-specific computations'.[53] And consequently, although Pleistocene hunter-gatherers may not have been great mathematicians – their lives did not require it – children today may nevertheless develop a specialized cognitive domain of mathematics. The kick-start to this may lie in one of the modules of intuitive physics or some other aspect of intuitive knowledge that children are born with. In the appropriate cultural conditions this may become elaborated into a fully developed domain of mathematical knowledge, as indeed has been explored by the psychologist David Geary.[54] The mind is still a Swiss army knife; but the types of blades present may vary from person to person. A man who uses a Swiss army knife to go fishing needs a different assortment of blades from one who goes camping.

So Karmiloff-Smith agrees with C&T that the mind of a young child is a Swiss army knife. But for Karmiloff-Smith, this is just a stage prior to the emergence of the butterfly. For she argues that soon after modularization has occurred, the modules begin working together. She uses a very awkward term for this: 'representational redescription' (RR). But what she means is quite simple. The consequence of RR is that in the mind there arise 'multiple representations of similar knowledge' and consequently 'knowledge becomes applicable beyond the special purpose goals for which it is normally used and perceptual links across domains can be forged'.[55] In other words, thoughts can arise which combine knowledge which had previously been 'trapped' within a specific domain.

A very similar idea has been independently proposed by the developmental psychologists Susan Carey and Elizabeth Spelke. They have argued that the emergence of 'mapping across domains' is a fundamental feature of cognitive development, and one which accounts for cultural diversity: 'Although infants the world over share a set of initial systems of knowledge, these systems are spontaneously overturned over the course of development and learning, as children and adults construct, explore and adopt mappings across knowledge systems.'[56]

Accounting for creativity

With these ideas of Karmiloff-Smith, Carey and Spelke we are immediately drawn back to those attributes of the mind that Jerry Fodor and Howard Gardner had found most impressive, and believed to be a fundamental part of its architecture. Recall how Fodor characterized the most puzzling features of the mind as 'its non-encapsulation, its holism, and its passion for the analogical'. Recall how Gardner had described how 'one typically encounters complexes of intelligences functioning together smoothly, even seamlessly, in order to execute intricate human activities.' Gardner had suggested that the wisest of human beings are those who are most able at building connections across domains – or mappings – as exemplified in the use of analogy and metaphor.

Indeed this seems to be the essence of human creativity. In her book *The Creative Mind* (1990), Margaret Boden explores how we can account for creative thought and concludes that this arises from what she describes as the transformation of conceptual spaces.[57] Now for Boden, a conceptual space is much like a cognitive domain, intelligence or faculty that we have been discussing. Transformation of one of these involves the introduction of new knowledge, or new ways of processing the knowledge that is already contained within the domains. In her book she describes how Arthur Koestler had accounted for human creativity, way back in 1964. He had argued that this arises from 'the sudden, interlocking of two previously unrelated skills or matrices of thought'.[58] A matrix of thought sounds suspiciously like one of Gardner's intelligences or C&T's faculties.

The evidence for thought which requires knowledge from multiple cognitive domains is so overwhelming, and this is clearly such a critical feature of mental architecture, that even some evolutionary psychologists have explored how it can be accounted for. There have been two proposals. The first was in fact made 20 years ago by Paul Rozin, who joins Nicholas Humphrey as one of the midwives of evolutionary psychology. Rozin developed ideas very similar to those of C&T.[59] He argued that the processes of evolution should result in a host of modules within the mind, which he described as 'adaptive specializations' (C&T's technical term, coined 20 years later, was 'Darwinian Algorithms'). But the critical question that he asked is how can behavioural flexibility evolve? C&T suggest that this comes from simply adding more and more specialized devices to the Swiss army knife. Rozin, on the other hand, argued that some form of accessibility between mental modules/domains is the critical feature in both child development and evolution: the 'hall mark for the evolution of intelligence ... is that a capacity first appears in a narrow context and later becomes extended into other domains'.[60] That statement could easily switch places with that by Karmiloff-Smith written almost two decades later: 'knowledge becomes applicable beyond the special purpose goals for which it is normally used'.

All of these arguments by Fodor, Gardner, Karmiloff-Smith, Carey, Spelke and Rozin appear to do away with a strictly modular architecture for the fully developed modern mind. This lack of modularity appears essential to creative thought. But the cognitive scientist Dan Sperber has argued that we can have it both ways – a strictly modular but also a highly creative modern mind.[61] He has argued that during the course of evolution the mind has simply evolved another, and rather special, module. This he calls the 'module of metarepresentation' (MMR). This name is almost as awkward as Karmiloff-Smith's term representational redescription and indeed there is a fundamental similarity in their ideas: the multiple representations of knowledge within the human mind. Whereas the other modules of the mind contain concepts and representations of things, such as those about dogs and what dogs do, Sperber suggests that this new module only holds 'concepts of concepts' and 'representations of representations'.

Sperber explains himself by using an example not about dogs but about cats. Now somewhere deep within our minds, we have a concept of 'cat' which is linked to our intuitive knowledge about living things. This conceptual cat cannot bark, because that is not in the cat essence. As we are told something new about cats it initially enters our minds into the MMR. From there, anything about cats that is compatible with our existing concept of cats is combined with, and may slightly change, that concept. So the MMR is like a clearing house, through which new ideas must pass before they can find a home. But even when they have found their home, they are free to come back and visit the clearing house whenever they like. Some new ideas, such as that cats might bark, do not have a proper home to go to. And consequently they just stay in the clearing house. Now in this clearing house all sorts of mischief can occur. Ideas from different modules, and those which have no home to go to, can get together in some peculiar ways. For instance, knowledge about dogs can get mixed up with knowledge about physical objects and with knowledge about beliefs and desires, so that when a child is given a toy dog – an inert lump of stuffed material – he or she makes it behave like a dog, while also giving it human-like beliefs, desires and intentions.

How could this clearing house have evolved? Or if this clearing house is not really present, how could evolution have drilled holes between the walls of our cognitive domains to let knowledge flow between them or to get replicated in different parts of the mind, as Gardner, Karmiloff-Smith and Rozin suggest? To find some kind of an answer we need to know the Prehistory of the Mind. For this crossing over between domains is after all exactly what C&T argued should not happen in evolution, since it can lead to all sorts of behavioural mistakes. I might go for lunch and see a bowl of plastic bananas. Rather than checking whether or not these yellow objects conform to what I know about edible things (i.e. that they are not made of plastic) I might just bite into them. And all because of some mischief in my mental clearing house that led knowledge of inert physical objects and of (once) living things to get mixed up.

I'm back from lunch and there was not a plastic banana in sight. Actually there was never a risk of eating one as the mind doesn't seem to make mistakes like that. We can create wild and wacky concepts, but often (not always) we seem very able at separating these from the real world. Yet the ability to think of such concepts has certainly evolved, and psychologists can offer no answers as to why this is the case. The only psychologists to have thought seriously about evolutionary issues, C&T, have no explanation as to how or why the multitude of mental modules they believe exist in the mind can lead to such ideas. For they are committed to the idea of the mind as a Swiss army knife.

In this chapter we have seen that the mind is more than simply a Swiss army knife. It may not be an indiscriminate sponge or a computer with a single all-purpose program, as earlier theorists would have it, but nor is it solely a Swiss army knife. It is too creative and unpredictable for that. So perhaps the ideas of Karmiloff-Smith, Carey, Spelke and Sperber about a kind of clearing house can be reconciled with those of Cosmides and Tooby, if seen in an evolutionary context. It is the task of the next chapter to propose just such a framework.

4 A new proposal for the mind's evolution

THE 'GUIDES' who took us around the modern mind in the previous chapter were interested in how the mind works today, and how it develops during childhood. But my interest is with evolutionary history. Since I am trained as an archaeologist I can hardly help trying to identify evolutionary phases whenever faced with a complex structure – whether that structure is a building of stone or the modern mind. Let me give you a taste of how we need to approach the mind by briefly recounting my own experience of an archaeological excavation.

During my summer vacations when a student I worked on the excavation of the medieval Benedictine Abbey of San Vincenzo in Molise, Italy.[1] I supervised the investigation of a particularly complex building, known as the 'South Church'. This involved exposing, recording and interpreting a large series of walls, floors and tombs: the remnants from a remarkable palimpsest of buildings. How could the walls and other remains be made to yield up the secrets of the building's history – its architectural phases and their dates? Much of archaeology entails the painstaking scraping away of the past, layer by layer. It also requires the study of complex intercuttings of certain walls by others, to deduce which are earlier, which later. Those walls must then be dated by reference perhaps to the different types of pottery found in the floor deposits that abut them. All these techniques of archaeological detection are then brought together to recreate as best one can the architectural phases of the building. In the case of the South Church, we deduced that there had been five phases in all, spanning the first 1,000 years AD and culminating in an elaborate multi-storey building housing many of the precious relics of the Abbey. The transitions between each phase had involved the demolishing and constructing of walls, the laying of new floors, the addition of new storeys, and the blocking of doors.

When I look at the evidence about the modern mind provided by the psychologists in the previous chapter, I am reminded of our work at the South Church at San Vincenzo – or indeed any modern church or cathedral. The task of this chapter is the task that we faced after having amassed the information from the South Church excavations: identifying a series of architectural phases.

In this short chapter I will propose an evolutionary history for the mind in terms of three architectural phases. This will provide the framework for the rest of my study – the archaeological data we are going to explore in later chapters will be used to evaluate, refine, develop and date this framework. Without a provisional framework we would be simply swamped with data, knowing neither what we should be looking for nor what it might mean. In order to propose these phases I will draw on the theories outlined in the previous chapter. I will also draw on one of the biggest ideas in biology, one that has been significant in studies of evolution since the time of Aristotle, although the last two decades has seen it lose its once preeminent position: recapitulation, or 'ontogeny follows phylogeny'.

I briefly introduced this idea in the previous chapter. In essence recapitulation proposes that the sequence of developmental stages that a juvenile of a species goes through, its ontogeny, reflects the sequence of adult forms of its ancestors, its phylogeny. Ernest Haeckel stated this idea in his biogenetic law of 1866: 'ontogeny is the short and rapid recapitulation of phylogeny'.[2] Haeckel had thought that during the course of evolution the rate of development had accelerated, and consequently ancestral adult forms had been pushed back, or 'telescoped into', the juvenile stages of descendants.

The origin and history of this idea have been traced in the seminal book by Stephen Jay Gould entitled *Ontogeny and Phylogeny* (1977). He explains that parallels between development and evolution pervade the biological world and that for many scientists of the 19th and early 20th centuries recapitulation appeared to be the key for understanding the past. Gould quotes the biologist E. Conklin writing in 1928: 'recapitulation promised to reveal not only the animal ancestry of man and the line of his descent but also the method of origin of his mental, social and ethical faculties.'[3] Jean Piaget, the most influential developmental psychologist of the 1960s and 1970s, was sympathetic to the idea of parallels between ontogeny and phylogeny, although he did not adopt an explicit position regarding recapitulation. But as I noted in the previous chapter, the archaeologist Thomas Wynn was drawn to the notion of recapitulation as a means to infer the intelligence of our ancestors by relying on the developmental phases for the mind as proposed by Piaget. Indeed the psychologist Kathleen Gibson has recently written that 'ontogenetic perspectives have become the rule, rather than the exception, among serious scholars of cognitive and linguistic evolution.'[4]

Today biologists take a rather more liberal view of the relationship between ontogeny and phylogeny than that adopted by Haeckel. As

Stephen Jay Gould explains, while there is evidence for the accelerated development of some traits, just as Haeckel proposed, and hence the pushing of ancestral adult forms into the juvenile stages of descendants, there is also evidence for the converse: the slowing up of the development of other traits so that certain juvenile features of ancestors appear in the adult descendants. This is referred to as neoteny, and is thought to be as common as recapitulation. It is most dramatically illustrated by the manner in which juvenile chimpanzees have a striking resemblance to adult humans – a similarity that is lost as chimpanzees mature. Consequently if there is any value in the notion of recapitulation, it will be found in the study of individual organs, rather than organisms as a whole.

Gould devotes much of his book to neoteny, demonstrating that this is of critical importance for understanding human evolution. But as both Kathleen Gibson and the psycho-linguist Andrew Lock have argued, while neoteny may help explain the morphological development of modern humans, this cannot account for the development of intelligence and knowledge.[5] These do not remain infantile during development, as does the shape of the skull, for instance. And so, if there are parallels between the development and the evolution of the mind, recapitulation rather than neoteny is a more likely scenario.[6]

I am going hesitantly to adopt the notion of recapitulation and propose a series of architectural phases for the evolution of the mind. My hesitation is for two reasons. First, as Gould describes in *The Mismeasure of Man* (1981), the idea of recapitulation 'provided an irresistible criterion'[7] for late-19th-century and 20th-century scientists to rank human groups as higher or lower. It provided pseudo-scientific support for racist and sexist ideas. So, although these ideas reflect a misunderstanding and misuse of recapitulation, one must always use it with great caution. The second reason for my hesitation is that I have no theoretical conviction that recapitulation of the evolution of the mind during development necessarily occurs. If it does, I am sure that it is likely to be manifest in some broad parallels rather than any strict correspondence of phylogenetic and ontogenetic stages.

Whether or not recapitulation of the mind is correct, it provides a means to establish the framework of hypothetical architectural phases which is needed to continue with my study.[8] Indeed it would seem a missed opportunity verging on academic negligence if I were to ignore the idea of recapitulation. After all, I am already in possession of information about the development of the mind in the child, as described in the previous chapter, and by the end of my study I also intend to have information about the evolution of the mind acquired from the materials of the archaeological and fossil records. So by adopting the notion of recapitulation an intriguing prospect looms: will we see the developmental stages of the minds of children today paralleled in the evolution of human ancestral minds?

In the previous chapter we looked at the work of several developmental psychologists, notably Patricia Greenfield, Annette Karmiloff-Smith, Susan Carey and Elizabeth Spelke. It will be largely by drawing on their work that I will suggest the architectural phases for the evolution of the mind. I say largely because I believe that there were also clues provided by all the psychologists whose work we considered in that chapter, clues which in fact support the proposed phases as drawn from studies of child development.

Three phases for the evolution of the mind

Let me now simply state the three broad architectural phases for the evolution of the mind that will serve as the framework for interpreting the archaeological and fossil data in later chapters, prior to elaborating on these in the rest of this chapter.

Phase 1. Minds dominated by a domain of general intelligence – a suite of general-purpose learning and decision-making rules.

Phase 2. Minds in which general intelligence has been supplemented by multiple specialized intelligences, each devoted to a specific domain of behaviour, and each working in isolation from the others.

Phase 3. Minds in which the multiple specialized intelligences appear to be working together, with a flow of knowledge and ideas between behavioural domains.

The correspondence between these and the development processes described in the previous chapter should be clear. The first is paralleled by the domain-general learning processes identified as critical to the very young infant; the second parallels the modularization of the mind with the development of domain-specific thought and knowledge; and the third parallels what Karmiloff-Smith describes as 'representational redescription' and Carey and Spelke describe as 'mapping across domains' – when knowledge becomes available for use in multiple domains of activity.[9]

These three broad phases are suggested as no more than a hypothetical framework for guiding the rest of my study. I want to spend the remainder of this chapter elaborating on this framework. There are further clues yet to be extracted from the observations about the modern mind made by the psychologists we considered in the previous chapter.

It is also important to clarify the relationship between development and evolution. As Stephen Jay Gould stressed in *Ontogeny and Phylogeny*, when we talk about evolution, we are normally just talking about the evolution of the adult forms of past species. But just as with any individual today, an australopithecine or member of an early *Homo* species went through a period of development, possibly with his/her mind going through a series of substantial changes. There is, therefore, considerable potential for confusion between the development and evolution of the mind. Let me try to clarify the relationship by pursuing an analogy of the mind as a cathedral.

The mind as a cathedral

We can think of the mind of each individual as a new cathedral being built as he or she develops from an infant to a mature adult. It is built according to an architectural plan encoded in the genetic constitution of that individual, as inherited from his/her parents, and under the influence of the particular environment in which he/she develops. As we all vary in our genetic constitution and/or developmental environment, we all have a unique mind. But as members of the same species, we share substantial similarities in the architectural plans that we inherit and the minds we develop.

This situation has been the same for all our ancestors. But the architectural plans have been constantly tinkered with by evolution. Random changes were brought about by genetic mutations. Most of these changes had no effect on the mind. A few had negative effects: these 'damaged' plans did not survive for long in the gene pool because the individuals with such minds were out-competed by other individuals for resources and for mates. Some other mutations resulted in beneficial effects, enabling individuals to compete more successfully and pass on to the next generation these 'improved' architectural plans. Of course, while these mutations were happening, the environment was also changing. Our ancestors constantly faced new types of problems, requiring new types of thought processes for their solution – different types of buildings are appropriate in different types of environment.

With the joint effects of variation caused by random genetic mutations, inheritance, differential reproductive success, and constant environmental change, the suite of architectural plans evolved. In other words, it was shaped by natural selection.[10] The architectural plans may have been continually tinkered with, but no plan was ever started again from scratch. Evolution does not have the option of returning to the drawing board and beginning anew; it can only ever modify what has gone before. This is, of course, why we can only understand the modern mind by understanding the prehistory of the mind. It is why ontogeny may contain clues to phylogeny. It is why we can look at the cathedral of the modern mind and find clues to the architecture of past minds.

We also know that even though two cathedrals may have shared the same architectural plan, they will not have looked exactly the same due to the unique environments in which they were built. Different types of stone, topographic settings and workforces would have been available. It is impossible to separate the influence of the building environment and the architectural plan on the finished cathedral, claiming for instance that a particular feature is due to one or the other. Similarly when trying to understand the character of a modern mind, it is impossible to separate the effects of genes and the developmental environment.

In the last chapter we looked at several different modern cathedrals – the minds of young children and mature adults, the minds of Cambridge dons and Kalahari Bushmen, the minds of brilliant mathematicians and those who suffer from cognitive pathologies such as autism. We were guided by various psychologists, each trying to identify the common and significant features of modern minds, but each stressing different features. To my mind they all rather neglected the importance of architectural joints and how buildings change in design and function throughout their long histories. This, of course, was not their concern: their interest was in how the modern mind works today. But my concern is with architectural history, so let me now return to those three phases I stated above and elaborate these by pursuing my analogy of the mind as a cathedral (see Box p. 67).

Phase 1

Minds dominated by a central nave of generalized intelligence.

The minds of the first proposed phase have no more than a single nave in which all the services take place; these are the processes of thought. Information is delivered to this nave via a series of input modules – earlier versions of those that Jerry Fodor described when looking at the modern mind. The nave does not contain the complex central systems that Fodor saw within the mind. It is a nave of general intelligence, which has few traces surviving in the modern mind. Two of our guides – Patricia Greenfield and Annette Karmiloff-Smith – found traces of this type of intelligence in the minds of young children. Two other guides, John Tooby and Leda Cosmides, acknowledged that traces of this nave might be somewhere in the modern mind, but were not interested in searching for them, believing that general intelligence plays a limited role in the modern mind. Of course, if I had chosen another guide – Jean Piaget – he would have seen little else but this nave in all

The mind as a cathedral

N.B. These are schematic, metaphorical illustrations. They carry no implications for the spatial location of cognitive processes within the brain.

Phase 3: Two possible architectural plans for Phase 3 minds.
These represent minds of people living by hunting and gathering. For those with other lifestyles, it is likely that other types of specialized intelligences will develop, although social and linguistic intelligence are likely to be universal.

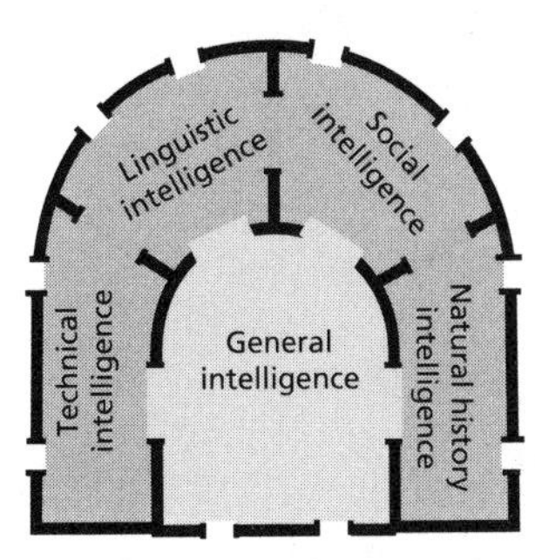

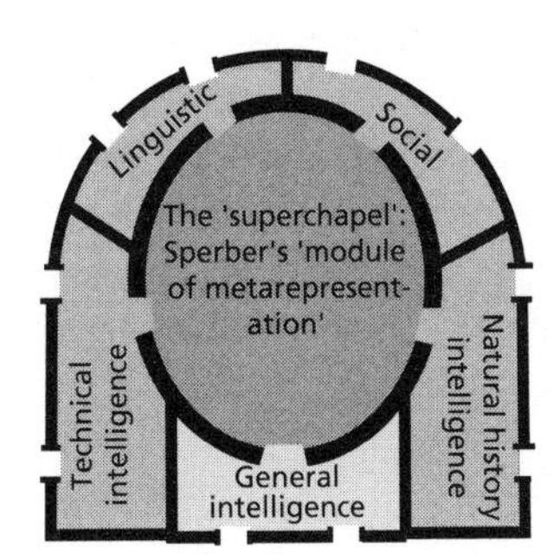

Phase 2
Minds with a 'nave' of general intelligence and multiple 'chapels' of specialized intelligences. It remains unclear how that of language is related to the other cognitive domains. As we can assume that all minds of this phase were of people living by hunting and gathering, the three 'chapels' are social, technical and natural history intelligence.

Linguistic intelligence
?
Social intelligence
?
?
Technical intelligence
General intelligence
Natural history intelligence

Phase 1
Minds with a 'nave' of general intelligence. The 'doors' represent the passage of information from modules concerned with perception.

General intelligence

Evolutionary time

the minds we visited. This general intelligence would have been constituted by a suite of general-purpose learning and decision-making rules. Their essential features are that they can be used to modify behaviour in the light of experience in any behavioural domain. But they can only produce relatively simple behaviour – the rate of learning would be slow, errors would be frequent and complex behaviour patterns could not be acquired.

Phase 2

Minds in which isolated chapels of specialized intelligences are built.

Minds of this second proposed phase are distinguished by the construction of a series of 'chapels' of specialized intelligences, as Howard Gardner called them, alternatively known as cognitive domains or faculties, as described by Leda Cosmides and John Tooby. Just as the greater number of side chapels in Romanesque cathedrals of the 12th century reflect the increasing complexity of church ritual at that time, so too do these chapels reflect the increasing complexity of mental activity.

The nave of general intelligence remains as an essential feature of the architectural design. But the services of thought within the nave are now overshadowed by those of greater complexity being undertaken in each of the chapels. Bundles of closely related mental modules relating to one specific domain of behaviour are found within each specialized intelligence. Some of the modules may in fact have been present in Phase 1, where they would have been scattered around the nave rather than being grouped together in the appropriate isolated specialized intelligence.

Each specialized intelligence looks after a specific domain of behaviour and is essential to the functioning of the mind as a whole. All knowledge about the domain is contained within that chapel and cannot be found anywhere else within the mind. Learning within these behavioural domains is now rapid and with a minimum of errors. Complex behavioural patterns can be acquired, and these can be easily modified due to new experience relating to that specific behavioural domain. So in Phase 2 we have minds with multiple specialized intelligences, or chapels of the mind. How many chapels were there, and what domains of behaviour were they dedicated to?

We know that the architectural plans for these minds evolved, and the minds themselves developed, while people were living as hunter-gatherers. And we saw in the last chapter that the modern mind still has modules that provide us with an intuitive knowledge of biology, physics and psychology. These modules are likely to be the surviving foundations of the chapels/intelligences which were once built in the minds of this second phase. Consequently there are likely to have been at least three dominant chapels/intelligences in the second phase:

1. The traces of an intuitive psychology imply a chapel of **social intelligence,** used for interacting with other human individuals, and including modules for 'mind reading'.
2. Similarly the traces of an intuitive biology within the modern mind suggest that there was once a chapel of **natural history intelligence** – a bundle of modules concerned with understanding the natural world, an understanding essential to life as a hunter-gatherer.
3. Intuitive physics may be the surviving foundations of a chapel of **technical intelligence** that once existed in the minds of some of our early ancestors, housing the mental modules for the manufacture and manipulation of stone and wooden artifacts, including those for throwing such artifacts.[11]

A critical design feature of these chapels is that their walls are thick and almost impenetrable to sound from elsewhere in the cathedral. There is no access between the chapels. In other words, knowledge about different behavioural domains cannot be combined together. Moreover the modules used for thinking within each intelligence are largely restricted to that intelligence alone. There may be some exceptions: on some occasions modules may indeed be used in an inappropriate domain of behaviour – a module evolved for social interaction being used for interacting with animals – but when this happens the module cannot work effectively. We may think of this as the sounds emanating from one chapel being heard in a heavily muffled and indistinct form elsewhere in the cathedral.

Minds in this second proposed phase of cognitive evolution use the chapels for thinking complex thoughts about toolmaking, natural history and social interaction. But when a single thought is required which could benefit from knowledge or modules from more than one chapel – such as thoughts about designing a tool for hunting a specific animal – the mind must rely on general intelligence. Consequently, thought and behaviour at 'domain-interfaces' would appear far simpler than that within a single domain. Nevertheless, the nave remains an essential part of the building, for without it the structure would simply collapse.

There may be a fourth chapel within the cathedrals of this phase: that of **linguistic intelligence**. As we saw in the previous chapter, this is also constituted by a bundle of mental modules. But could linguistic intelligence ever have been isolated from the other intelligences of the mind? Unlike them it serves no function in itself – people do not talk about grammar for its own sake. And we saw in the previous chapter how Jerry Fodor characterized language as one of the 'input' processes rather than as a feature of the central systems. So at present, while we recognize that a chapel of linguistic intelligence may have existed, we cannot specify its architectural relationship to general intelligence and the other specialized intelligences. This will have to wait until we have acquired further evidence later in this book.

The previous chapter gave us a large number clues to the existence of this evolutionary phase of the modern mind, which partly reflects my choice of guides. One of the biggest clues came from the study of child development. Annette Karmiloff-Smith describes how, after having passed through a phase in which thought is dominated by general intelligence, children develop 'domain-specific' thought processes. Because of the highly variable environments in which children develop today, the numbers and types of domains are quite variable – they are not those which are necessarily appropriate to a hunter-gatherer way of life. They are, however, built upon, or in Karmiloff-Smith's term 'kick started' by, the surviving foundations of the Phase 2 specialized intelligences.

Phase 3

Minds in which the chapels have been connected, resulting in a 'cognitive fluidity'.

The minds of the third phase share a new architectural feature: direct access between the chapels. With this feature, knowledge once trapped within different chapels can now be integrated together. It is not quite clear how this direct access was achieved. Some of our guides described how they could see knowledge crossing between domains/intelligences, as if passing through doors and windows which had been inserted in the chapel walls. But one of our guides, Dan Sperber, thought he could see a 'superchapel' – his module of metarepresentation. In this superchapel, knowledge from specialized intelligences is replicated in much the same way that Karmiloff-Smith argued that knowledge becomes replicated in different parts of the mind during development. Clearly we need more evidence before the specific architectural design of Phase 3 minds can be described; all we know at present is that the combining of thoughts and knowledge of the different specialized intelligences is possible and that this has significant consequences for the nature of the mind.

As occurred in Phase 1, a 'single service' of thought can be conducted. But these single services of Phase 3 draw upon and harmonize the previously isolated services practised perhaps for millennia within each of the chapels of Phase 2. For instance, Howard Gardner stresses how in the modern mind complexes of intelligences function smoothly and seamlessly together; Paul Rozin, Annette Karmiloff-Smith, Susan Carey and Elizabeth Spelke have written about the importance of knowledge being used in multiple domains of thought. Moreover, the single service now has a complexity that was previously absent: for this single service is what Jerry Fodor described as the central system of the mind.

Experience gained in one behavioural domain can now influence that in another. Indeed distinct behavioural domains no longer exist. And brand new ways of thinking, subjects to think about and ways to behave arise. The mind acquires not only the ability but a positive passion for metaphor or analogy.

The differences between the Phase 2 and Phase 3 minds are analogous to those between Romanesque and the succeeding Gothic cathedrals of stone. In Gothic architecture sound and light emanating from different parts of the cathedral can flow freely around the building unimpeded by the thick heavy walls and low vaults one finds in Romanesque architecture. In a Gothic design, sound, space and light interact to produce a sense of almost limitless space. Similarly, in the Phase 3 mental architecture, thoughts and knowledge generated by specialized intelligences can now flow freely around the mind – or perhaps just around the superchapel. As both Arthur Koestler and Margaret Boden recognized, when thoughts originating in different domains can engage together, the result is an almost limitless capacity for imagination. So we should refer to these Phase 3 minds as having a 'cognitive fluidity'.

Why the tinkering of evolution led to the ability to combine thoughts and knowledge from specialized intelligences, and indeed why the specialized intelligences were constructed in the first place, remains unclear. But this is not important at this stage in our enquiry. All we need at present is a basic architectural history.

How should we date the different phases of our architectural history? When in the course of human evolution did the architectural plans encode information for the construction of no more than a central nave? When were chapels first built? Were they built simultaneously, or introduced piecemeal so that there was a gradual change from Phase 1 to Phase 2 buildings? How did the chapel of linguistic intelligence fit in? When was the direct access between chapels first created? How was this direct access achieved, by the construction of a superchapel, or simply a series of doors and windows?

These questions are similar to those a medieval archaeologist might ask when devising a programme of excavations to refine an architectural history. They are the questions we need to answer when we turn to examine the archaeological and fossil evidence for the evolution of the mind in later chapters. But a good archaeologist never rushes to dig holes. First he or she searches for further clues in the modern world. He or she looks around the landscape to find a building dating to an early period and not subjected to later construction work which might have destroyed the original design. Indeed a few years after digging at San Vincenzo I was able to accompany the director of those excavations to southern Albania where we saw intact 9th-century monastic buildings. These had been constructed with architectural plans similar to those used for the buildings at San Vincenzo, but which we had struggled to reconstruct from no more than wall fragments and foundations.

So for one more chapter we must remain in the modern world. But the landscape we must now explore is not occupied by churches and abbeys; it is one populated by chimpanzees. We must try to expose the architecture of the chimpanzee mind, because this is likely to share features with that of the common ancestor of 6 million years ago. In this sense we can now raise the curtain on Act 1 of our prehistory.

5 Apes, monkeys and the mind of the missing link

ACT I OF OUR PREHISTORY begins 6 million years ago. But, as we saw in Chapter 2, the stage is bare and our actor, the missing link, is absent. There are no bones or artifacts to inspect which might give clues to past behaviour and past mental activity. How then can we reconstruct the mind of this distant ancestor? To what architectural phase should we assign her mind? Phase 1, with no more than a general intelligence? Or perhaps Phase 2, with one or more specialized cognitive domains working alongside, but blocked off from each other and a general intelligence? How can we use the mind of the missing link to help in understanding the prehistory of the mind? These are all challenging questions to answer.

Our only hope is to take a look at that great ape from whom our forebears diverged on the ancestral family tree 6 million years ago: the chimpanzee.

There is a long history in science of using the chimpanzee as an analogy for our earliest human ancestor.[1] This assumes that there has been minimal cognitive evolution during the last 6 million years along the ape line. We can indeed be confident that there has not been significant evolution in terms of brain processing power, for the brain size of the chimpanzee at about 450 cc is not significantly less than that of the australopithecines and a figure that seems reasonable for the missing link. Similarly, as we go back in time from *H. erectus*, to *H. habilis*, to *A. afarensis* and *A. ramidus*, anatomy becomes increasingly ape-like in character – more and more like that of living chimpanzees. And if we look at the archaeological record that chimpanzees leave behind them, it is practically indistinguishable from that of our earliest ancestors because it hardly exists at all. There are no more than a few stone flakes (unintentionally created when hammering nuts) which can barely be distinguished from flakes created by natural processes. Such flakes are likely to have been lost within the litter of nature.

So we will follow convention and assume that the mind of the chimpanzee is a good approximation for the mind of the missing link. What does the behaviour of chimpanzees tell us about the architecture of their minds? Let us start with a type of behaviour which was once thought to be uniquely human – the manufacture and use of tools – and ask whether chimpanzees have a chapel of technical intelligence.

Technical intelligence: Chimp the toolmaker?

Fifty years ago it was generally believed that humans were the only species to make and use tools, summed up in the epithet 'Man the toolmaker'. Then in the late 1950s Jane Goodall began to study wild chimpanzees at Gombe in Tanzania and soon described how the chimpanzees stripped leaves off sticks to use as probes for ants and to make fishing sticks for termites.[2] Since that time many other observations of chimpanzee tool manufacture and use have been made by researchers such as by Bill McGrew and Christophe and Hedwige Boesch. We now know that a wide range of tools are made, and used for a variety of tasks, by chimpanzees.[3] In addition to catching insects, small sticks are used for acquiring honey, removing nuts from their shells, picking bits of brain from skulls and cleaning eye orbits. Leaves are crushed together to form a sponge to gather up ants or water. Leaves are also used by chimpanzees to clean the cranial cavities of prey, and to clean themselves. They even use leaves as a plate – a plate to catch their own faeces which are then inspected for undigested food items. In the forests of West Africa chimpanzees use hammers and anvils to crack open nuts (see Figure 3). In sum, chimpanzees appear adept at manufacturing and manipulating physical objects. Does this imply that they have specialized cognitive processes dedicated to such tasks – does their mental architecture have a chapel of technical intelligence? Or do chimpanzees simply rely on the processes of general intelligence, such as trial-and-error learning, for making and using tools?

As a first stab at answering this question we might consider how complex chimpanzee tool behaviour appears to be: the more complex it

3 A chimpanzee using a stone hammer and anvil to crack open nuts.

is, the more likely it is to arise from specialized cognitive processes. Bill McGrew, author of the most comprehensive study of chimpanzee material culture,[4] firmly believes that chimpanzee tool use is of considerable complexity. Indeed, in an (in)famous article written in 1987, he directly compared the toolkits of chimpanzees to those of Tasmanian Aborigines and concluded that they were at an equivalent level of complexity. For this comparison McGrew chose to measure complexity by counting 'technounits', which is simply an individual component of a tool, whatever material that component is made from and however it is used. So a hoe used by, say, a peasant farmer, comprising a shaft, a blade and a binding, has three technounits, while the suite of computerized robots operated by a modern car worker has perhaps three million technounits.

When McGrew measured the technounits in the tools of the Tasmanian Aborigines and those of the Tanzanian chimpanzees he found that the mean number of technounits per tool was not substantially different. All chimpanzee tools and most of the Aboriginal tools were made from a single component. The most complex Aboriginal tool, a baited hide, had only four technounits. All other tools, such as spears, stone missiles, ropes, hides and baskets, appeared to be directly comparable in their technounit complexity to the termite sticks and leaf sponges of the chimpanzees. Consequently if the modern mind, as possessed by Tasmanian Aborigines, has an intuitive physics then we should also attribute this to the chimpanzee mind.

McGrew's conclusion, however, is unhelpful. The tools of the peasant farmer may have several million fewer components than those of the factory worker, but they may require far greater skill and knowledge to use effectively. Once the computers and robots are in place, pressing a button can build a car, but to till the ground a hoe needs to be manipulated with care.

Counting technounits as a measure of tool complexity can also be seen to be of limited value when we consider how the tools are made. One requires a tool to make a sharpened stick. This may simply be a flake of stone, but nevertheless that flake must be found or, more likely, struck from a nodule. A termite probe can be made by simply tearing off the leaves and biting the stick to an appropriate length. When Aborigines make tools their physical actions are unique to toolmaking: there is nothing comparable in other domains of human behaviour to the chipping of stone or the whittling of a stick. When chimpanzees make tools they simply use the same set of actions which are employed in feeding: removing twigs from bushes, stripping leaves, biting them into shorter pieces.[5]

McGrew did in fact address manufacturing complexity in his comparison of Aboriginal and chimpanzee tools, and again argued that the similarities outweigh the differences. But I find some of his examples unconvincing. For instance, Aborigines regularly use a production principle of 'replication' when making their tools. This is the combining of several identical elements, as in a bunch of tied-up grass. McGrew argued that chimpanzees also use this principle – but the only example he could find was that of a leaf sponge, a crushed mass of essentially identical leaves.

Aborigines also regularly use 'conjunction', which is the joining of two or more technounits together. But only one single example of conjunction by a chimpanzee has ever been witnessed. This was on 16 January 1991, when Testuro Matsuzawa observed Kai, an old female chimpanzee, take two stones for nutcracking, one for the hammer and one for the anvil.[6] To steady the anvil she placed another stone below it to act as a wedge. Until there are other examples, I'm not convinced that this is sufficient evidence that chimpanzees employ conjunction in their toolmaking – something that is present in practically every single tool made by humans.

The gist of my argument should now have become clear: we cannot attribute chimpanzees with specialized cognitive processes dedicated to the manipulation and transformation of physical objects i.e. a technical intelligence. Further confirmation of this can be found when we look at the distribution of tool use among different chimpanzee groups – although this evidence is normally used to argue the exact converse. Chimpanzees appear to have cultural traditions regarding tool use.[7] Only the chimpanzees of the Tai forest in West Africa extract bone marrow with sticks; the chimpanzees of Mahale in Tanzania do not use tools to probe for ants, although they feed upon these insects. Similarly those of the Tai forest do not go ant fishing, although they do go ant eating. Unlike chimpanzees of Gombe, the Mahale and Tai chimpanzees do not use tools for personal hygiene.

These differences cannot be explained on genetic or ecological grounds alone: chimpanzee tool use appears to be largely based on tradition. This finding has been like a blast of trumpets for those who have wanted to minimize the differences between chimpanzee and human behaviour. For it seems to say that chimpanzees are like humans: animals with culture. But I interpret this finding rather differently. Human cultural traditions rarely impinge on the use of simple tools for simple tasks, especially when they dramatically increase the efficiency with which that task is completed (as is the case with using sticks for termite fishing). All human groups use knives, for instance. Human cultural traditions are usually about different ways of doing the same task, rather than whether that task is undertaken or not. To take a trivial example, Frenchmen used to wear berets and Englishmen bowlers, but they both wore hats. Chimpanzee tool-use traditions appear fundamentally different from human cultural traditions. The failure of Tai chimpanzees to use termite sticks is most likely to arise simply from the fact that no individual within that group has ever thought of doing such a thing, or discovered it accidentally, or managed to learn it from another chimp before that chimp forgot how to do it, or passed away with his great tool-use secret. This is not cultural behaviour; it is simply not being very good at thinking about making and using physical objects. It is the absence of a technical intelligence.

This conclusion can be strengthened when we actually look at the pattern of learning about tool use. Recall that the intuitive physics and technical intelligence within the human mind facilitate rapid and efficient learning about the world of objects. Now if we see chimpanzees struggling to learn about the simplest object manipulation tasks, this may indicate that their minds lack such intuitive knowledge. And this is precisely what we do see.

We commonly think of chimpanzees as very rapid learners – a species that has mastered the art of imitation. Indeed we commonly use the verb 'to ape' as another way of saying 'to imitate'. But this is far from the truth: chimpanzees do not seem to be very good at imitating behaviour at all. In fact, some primatologists argue that chimpanzees cannot imitate – all that happens is that their attention is drawn to certain objects and then learning takes place on a trial-and-error basis.[8] So if one chimpanzee sees another poking sticks in a hole and licking the termites off, and then starts to do something similar, this is unlikely to be imitation in terms of understanding both the goal of the action and the means to achieve it. It is more likely that his attention was simply drawn to sticks and holes. This is perhaps why in more than 30 years of observation of chimpanzee tool use there have been no technological advances: each generation of chimpanzees appears to struggle to attain the technical level attained by the previous generation.

Unfortunately we lack systematic studies of how techniques such as termite fishing and ant dipping are acquired by chimpanzees, although there are various reports of juveniles watching their mothers at work and 'playing' with sticks.[9] Christophe and Hedwige Boesch, however, have made a detailed study of the acquisition of the nutcracking technique as used by the chimpanzees in the Tai forest of West Africa.[10] For you, me or most young children this technique is easy. A nut is placed on an anvil and struck with a hammer. Yet juvenile chimpanzees appear to have great difficulty in learning to do this. They do not fully acquire the skill before adulthood and require four years of practice before any net benefits are achieved. Juveniles seem to spend a lot of time hitting hammers directly against anvils without putting a nut between them, or bringing nuts to anvils without hammers.

Here is a summary of the evidence about toolmaking and using by chimpanzees. Their tools are very simple. They are made by using physical actions common to other domains of behaviour. They are used for a limited range of tasks, and chimpanzees appear to be rather poor at thinking about new ways to use tools. They are slow at adopting the tool-use methods currently practised within their group. Now these attributes do not constitute the type of behavioural repertoire that we would expect if the chimpanzee mind had a technical intelligence devoted to manipulating and transforming physical objects. They are much more like those we would expect from the use of a general intelligence – processes such as trial and error and associative learning – which are not specifically designed for making and using tools.

Natural history intelligence: mental maps and hunting behaviour

Chimpanzee tool use is predominantly about getting food. So we must now turn to foraging and ask whether the chimpanzee mind has a natural history intelligence in terms of a suite of cognitive processes dedicated to acquiring and processing information about resources, such as plants, animals and raw materials.

Chimpanzees certainly appear to be very adept at making foraging decisions, for they display goal-directed movements towards particular food patches. Such behaviour is likely to derive from a detailed knowledge about the spatial distribution of resources – a continually updated mental map – and knowledge of the ripening cycles of many plants. Some of the most detailed observations of chimpanzee foraging behaviour have been made by Richard Wrangham.[11] He studied the Gombe chimpanzees of Tanzania and concluded that they have an intimate knowledge of their environment, being excellent botanists and able to discriminate between subtle visual clues of species type or plant condition. By using such botanical knowledge and a mental map chimpanzees were able to move directly to patches with ripe plant material.

Wrangham could find no evidence, however, that chimpanzees could find food patches about which they had no prior knowledge. To do so would have necessitated the development of hypotheses for food distribution – an insightful and complex use of knowledge to create a new idea about the world, which is one of the hallmarks of a specialized intelligence. Chimpanzees appear to rely on noticing and remembering sufficient information about the environment on their daily travels.

The possession of mental maps in chimpanzees has been demonstrated by formally testing their ability to find and remember the location of objects hidden in enclosures.[12] But the most interesting study has been undertaken by Christophe and Hedwige Boesch regarding the transport of hammers and nuts to anvils in the West African Tai forest.[13] By monitoring the movement of hammerstones, weighing them and measuring the distance between trees, the Boeschs inferred that the chimpanzees have a spontaneous means of measuring the distance between two locations in the forest – a means as accurate as the Boeschs' own measuring ropes, even when there are intervening obstacles such as fallen trees and rivers. They claim that chimpanzees are able to abstract and compare distances between sets of paired locations, identify the shortest of these, and include the influence of the weight of the hammer to be transported when deciding where to aim for. This mental feat is all the more impressive when one recognizes that mental maps need continual updating to account not only for the movement of hammers, but also the activity of other nutcracking chimps. Indeed one of the reasons for the few sub-optimal decisions appears to be that a hammerstone had been expected in one location, but had already been moved by other individuals.

It is most likely that this well-developed mental mapping exhibited by Tai chimpanzees derives from the need to exploit patchy resources under conditions of poor visibility. This has indeed been proposed as a general explanation for the evolution of intelligence among primates[14] – before intelligence was thought of as a Swiss army knife of specialized devices.

These observations by Wrangham and the Boeschs leave us in a rather equivocal position regarding the possibility of a specialized domain of natural history intelligence. Certain elements of this appear to be present: the interest and ability to build up a large database of natural history knowledge and the processing of this to make efficient foraging decisions. Yet this is effectively no more than rote memory – there does not seem to be a creative or insightful use of that knowledge. And we must remember that many animals, particularly birds, construct very elaborate mental maps for the distribution of resources.[15] We need to look for further evidence regarding chimpanzee interaction with the natural world, which we can find by considering a rather more challenging type of foraging behaviour – hunting.

In 1989 the Boeschs published a detailed study of the hunting behaviour of the Tai chimpanzees in which they undertook a comparison with hunting by the chimpanzees of Gombe and Mahale.[16] The Tai chimpanzees appear to be very proficient hunters; on over 50 per cent of their hunting events clear hunting intentions were apparent within the group before any prey had been seen or heard. In contrast, all the hunts by the Gombe and Mahale chimpanzees appear to be opportunistic.

The Tai chimpanzees concentrate on one type of prey, colobus monkeys, while those of Gombe and Mahale regularly hunt bushpigs, bushbuck and blue duiker. This difference can be explained on ecological grounds alone, as young duiker are rare in the Tai forest and bushpigs live in relatively large groups and are difficult to hunt.

With regard to hunting success, this is considerably higher among the Tai chimpanzees. It appears to reflect the fact that they hunt in larger groups within which there is a relatively high degree of cooperation. When the Gombe chimpanzees hunt in groups they tend to chase the prey in different directions, which serves to confuse it. In contrast the Tai chimpanzees disperse under the prey, often out of sight of each other, but all remain focussed on the same victim. As the hunt progresses they reunite when cornering their victim.

Why do the Tai chimpanzees show this greater degree of intentionality and cooperation in their hunting activity? The Boeschs argue that it reflects the challenge of hunting in a thickly forested environment in which visibility is limited to about 20 metres (65 feet). There is, however, an alternative to this argument. In the Tai forest the chimpanzee hunters rely on acoustic clues to locate their prey. The Boeschs give several examples of this, such as how a hunting group will alter their direction when they hear the grunting of forest hogs. In more open environments, such as in Gombe and Mahale, a chimpanzee will need to have as much, if not greater, reliance on visual clues, such as the sight of the animal and its tracks left on the ground. Now visual clues may be inherently more difficult for a chimpanzee to use. This is certainly the case with vervet monkeys, who seem unable to understand the danger implied when they see the signs that their predators are nearby, such as the trail left by a python or the carcass from a recent leopard kill.[17] If chimpanzees are also relatively poor at drawing inferences from visual clues – as appears to be the case[18] – then hunting in relatively open environments may be more difficult than in those environments in which acoustic clues are dominant.

My suspicion that hunting by Tai chimpanzees may appear more complex than it really is finds a little support in a curious anecdote provided by the Boeschs. They describe an incident in which a group of infants and juveniles had caught a very young blue duiker and were playing with it. An adult female joined the play session, during which the animal was killed by their rough behaviour. Yet throughout, the adult males showed no interest and the carcass of the animal was abandoned without being eaten. This appears rather bizarre in view of the excitement shown by the males whenever a small colobus monkey was killed. It would be very difficult to imagine a human hunter ignoring such an opportunistic kill; it is not the sort of behaviour one expects if a specialized domain of natural history intelligence is present.

To summarize, the cognitive basis for the chimpanzee's interaction with the natural world is difficult to assess. On the one hand there is the acquisition of large amounts of information, and the processing of it to make efficient foraging decisions. On the other hand there appears to be a marked absence of a creative use of such knowledge; foraging behaviour appears to be characterized by a significant degree of inflexibility. And there is severe doubt that chimpanzees are proficient at reading the mass of visual clues available in the environment. The most reasonable conclusion is to attribute the chimpanzee mind with some microdomains enabling the construction of mental maps, but not a fully developed natural history intelligence.

Social intelligence: Machiavellian behaviour and the role of consciousness

Now let us turn to the cognitive basis of social interaction. In 1988 a remarkable collection of papers was published in a book entitled *Machiavellian Intelligence: Social Expertise and the Evolution of Intellect in Monkeys, Apes and Humans.*[19] Edited by Dick Byrne and Andrew Whiten, some of the papers had been originally published more than 30 years ago. They all contributed to making one major argument: that there is something very special about the cognitive processes used for social interaction. These processes lead to social behaviour which is fundamentally more complex than that found in any other domain of activity. In effect they argued that monkeys and apes have a discrete domain of social intelligence, constituted by a whole bundle of mental modules. The term Machiavellian seemed particularly apposite since cunning, deception and the construction of alliances and friendships are pervasive in the social life of many primates.

One of the key papers re-published in that volume was 'The social function of intellect' by Nicholas Humphrey that I briefly referred to in Chapter 3. That had set out the problems that group living poses to primates and the need for specialized cognitive processes to compete successfully within the social milieu. Picking up on this argument, Byrne and Whiten described the tangled social web in which chimpanzees, and many other primates, live. Such animals need to:

balance a diverse range of competitive and co-operative options. Individuals may compete not only over mates, but (for example) over feeding resources, sleeping sites, location in the group (which may affect not only feeding, but predator avoidance), allies, grooming partners, playmates and access to infants, and they may cooperate with each other not only in mating, but in (for example) grooming and support in agnostic encounters.[20]

It sounds a lot harder than pulling a few leaves off a twig to make a termite stick or building up a mental map of plant distribution.

One of the best accounts of this tangled social web within which chimpanzees live is Franz de Waal's marvellous description of the chimpanzee politics he witnessed during his observations of a colony at the Burgers' zoo, Arnhem.[21] He provides a story of ambition, social manipulation, sexual privileges and power takeovers that would put any aspiring politician to shame – and it was all done by (Machiavellian-minded) chimpanzees. For instance, de Waal describes a two-month-long power struggle between the two eldest males, Yeroen and Luit. This began with Yeroen as the dominant male and proceeded through a series of aggressive encounters, bluff displays and reconciliation gestures to the social isolation and eventual dethronement of Yeroen. To achieve this, Luit carefully nurtured the support of the females within the group, who began as Yeroen's supporters. When Yeroen was present, Luit ignored the females; but when Yeroen was out of sight he paid them attention and played with their children. And before an intimidation display against Yeroen, Luit systematically groomed each female in turn as if to arouse their support. Luit's eventual success depended upon a coalition he developed with another male, Nikkie. During conflicts with Yeroen, Luit relied upon Nikkie to fight off Yeroen's supporters, the females. Nikkie had much to gain by this. He began with very low status in the group, being ignored by the females, yet he became second-in-command in the hierarchy above the females and Yeroen once Luit became leader. As soon as this happened, Luit's social attitudes changed. Rather than being the source of conflict he became the champion of peace and stability. When females were fighting he broke up the contests without taking sides and hit anyone who continued fighting. In other situations Luit prevented the escalation of conflict within the group by supporting the weaker participant in a conflict. He would chase away Nikkie, for instance, when Nikkie attacked Amber, one of the females. After a few months as the dominant male, Luit was himself toppled from power by Nikkie. And this was only achieved by Nikkie developing a powerful coalition with none other than Yeroen.

The two centrepieces of social intelligence are the possession of extensive social knowledge about other individuals, in terms of knowing who allies and friends are, and the ability to infer the mental states of those individuals. When we watch chimpanzees engage in deception of others, we can be confident that both are working together smoothly. Dick Byrne and Andrew Whiten have given many examples of deception used by apes.[22] Here are three of them. Female gorillas have been seen to engineer situations carefully in which they and a young male become separate from the bulk of the group, especially the dominant male. They then copulate, suppressing the cries that normally go with this act. Male chimpanzees are just as cunning. When courting females in the presence of a higher-ranking competitor, they have been seen to place a hand over their erect penis so that it remains visible to the female but hidden from the viewpoint of the other male. Deception is as useful for stealing food as it is for stealing sex. Another incident Byrne and Whiten relate is one in which a high-ranking individual left an area in which another individual had been concealing food items. He left as if suspecting nothing, but then peeped from behind a tree until the food was exposed. And then he stole it.

David Premack has explored the character of the 'theory of mind' that chimpanzees possess by laboratory experiments.[23] In one experiment a chimpanzee called Sarah was instrumental in allowing one of her carers to acquire food items because she had control of the button which opened the door to the cabinet in which the food was placed. Behind this door the cabinet was divided into two halves, one stocked with good food items such as cakes, and the other with bad food items such as rubber snakes and even a cup of faeces about which the carer had gestured to Sarah her utter disgust. In the experiment the carer entered the room and Sarah pressed the button which opened the cabinet door so that the carer reached in and took something from the side with the good food items. This was repeated many times. Then Sarah was allowed to watch an 'intruder', a human unknown to Sarah, prise open the cabinet and switch the locations of the good and bad food items. The next time the carer entered Sarah knew about the switch and she should also have known that the carer did not know. If the door was opened the carer would place her hand in a very inappropriate place. Yet Sarah pressed the button as usual.

Premack uses this experiment to argue that the chimpanzee's theory of mind is rather less sophisticated than that of humans. For Sarah appeared unable to hold within her mind a representation of her own knowledge, as well as that of the carer's which was different from her own. Premack argues that attributing knowledge which is different from one's own to another individual is beyond the mind capabilities of a chimpanzee. Yet isn't this precisely what chimpanzees are doing in the cases of deception? The naughty chimp with the erect penis is surely holding representations of his own, the dominant male's and the female's knowledge of his sexually excited state in his mind all at the same moment. I suspect that the reason that Sarah seemed unable to do this was because her carer was not another chimpanzee. Reading the minds of other chimpanzees may be difficult but attainable; crossing the species boundary and reading the mental state of a human may simply be impossible for chimpanzees.

This returns us to the notion – discussed in Chapter 3 – that the theory of mind module within the domain of social intelligence is likely to have evolved to facilitate interaction with other members of one's social group. The essence of a theory of mind is that it allows an individual to predict the behaviour of another. Social life is about building and testing hypotheses – unlike decision making in chimpanzee foraging activity, which is simply rote memory. Nicholas Humphrey argues that this is the biological function of consciousness.[24] In effect we explore our own mind and use it as the best model we have for the mind of another individual. We reflect on how we would feel and behave in a particular context and assume that another individual will do likewise. This is a very powerful argument for the evolution of reflexive consciousness: it is elegant, makes common sense and conforms to all we understand about evolution. It persuades me that chimpanzees have a conscious awareness of their own minds. But if Humphrey is correct, this conscious awareness should extend only to their thoughts about social interaction. If consciousness is a trick to predict the behaviour of others, there is no evolutionary reason why chimpanzees should have a conscious awareness about their (limited) thoughts about toolmaking or foraging. Yet our own conscious awareness seems to cover our thoughts about all domains of activity. We will see as this prehistory of the mind unfolds that the broadening of conscious awareness has a very critical role to play in creating the modern mind.

Our next task is to look at the would-be Dr Doolittles, those who have tried to talk with the animals.

A linguistic capacity? Chatting with chimps

Chimpanzees cannot talk to us because they do not have the vocal apparatus to do so. But do they have the cognitive basis for language? If we could plug a chimpanzee into a pair of vocal cords, would the chimpanzee have much to say? Well we cannot do this, but the next best thing has been to teach chimpanzees the use of sign language.

In the 1960s Beatrice Gardner and her husband and research colleague Allen Gardner trained a chimpanzee called Washoe to use sign language.[25] Washoe lived in a caravan next to their house and whenever in his presence they signed to him and to each other. Washoe learnt to sign back. Within three years he had acquired at least 85 signs and could hold a 'conversation' with humans and make requests. 'Gimme tickle, gimme, gimme tickle' is not the most profound and articulate request ever made, although it may have been one of the most sincere. Washoe's most acclaimed statement during his time as the star performer of the chimpanzee world occurred when he saw a swan and signed water and then bird in quick succession. A swan is indeed a water-bird.

During the same decade David Premack embarked on a series of language experiments with Sarah, whom we met just a moment ago.[26] Premack used plastic chips of different colours and shapes, each of which was represented by a different object. Using these he argued that Sarah could be seen to understand abstract concepts such as 'same', 'different', 'colour of' and 'name of'.

In the early 1970s a long-term research programme was begun at the Yerkes Language Research Centre in the U.S. by Duane Rumbaugh and Sue Savage-Rumbaugh.[27] They used symbols on a computer keyboard to represent words. They claimed to demonstrate that chimpanzees were able to classify objects by semantic class, such as 'fruit' or 'tool'. More importantly, they argued that their experiments demonstrated a correspondence between what chimpanzees intend to say and what they actually do say. The use of symbols by chimpanzees, they argued, is not simply a series of tricks or conditioned routines, but involves an understanding of the significance of utterances in much the same way as humans.

The validity of these experiments and results did not go unchallenged. At Columbia University a study was made of the 'linguistic' capacity of a chimpanzee called Nim Chimpsky by Herbert Terrace.[28] He concluded that the claims made by the Gardners, by Premack and by Rumbaugh's group were false. They had, he argued, all inadvertently exaggerated the linguistic abilities of their chimpanzee students by adopting a poor methodology that did not preclude simple associative learning or even random signing. In the academics' desire to see evidence for a linguistic ability they over-interpreted their data; any movement that could conceivably be a sign was recorded as one. So was Washoe's 'water-bird' just a chance association of two words that happened to make a meaningful combination in the context of when they were uttered?

In 1979 Terrace and his colleagues published an academic paper which posed a question: can an ape create a sentence? They gave a simple answer. No. In a series of academic papers during the early 1990s Sue Savage-Rumbaugh and her colleagues have been giving the opposite answer. Yes, they have argued, chimpanzees can create a sentence. Or at least the new star performer of the chimpanzee world can. This is a pygmy chimpanzee or bonobo who goes by the name of Kanzi.[29]

Kanzi was not formally taught to use symbols in the manner of previous apes. He was simply encouraged to use them by being placed in a learning environment that had as many similarities with a natural situation as was possible. Consequently Kanzi and his siblings were reared in a 55-acre forest and much of their communication was related to normal chimpanzee-type activities, such as looking for food.

Kanzi's learning process involved understanding a spoken word and its referent, and then learning the symbol for it on a computer keyboard. By the age of six Kanzi could identify 150 different symbols upon hearing the spoken word. He could also understand the meanings of sentences when different words were strung together to make novel requests not previously encountered. When he was eight, Kanzi's linguistic abilities were formally compared with those of a two-year-old girl called Alia. She was the daughter of one of Kanzi's carers and had developed in a similar environment. Their linguistic abilities appeared to be markedly similar.

Sue Savage-Rumbaugh and her colleagues have laid great stress on what appears to be Kanzi's ability to use rules of grammar. He appeared to adopt some of the grammatical rules used by his carers. For instance, there seemed to be a progressive ordering of words in two-word phrases away from a random combination towards the order used in English, in which an action word precedes an object word. So Kanzi became more prone to say 'bite ball' and 'hide peanut' and rather less prone to say 'ball bite' and 'peanut hide'.

They also claim that Kanzi has 'invented' his own rules of grammar. For example, Kanzi frequently makes two-word combinations of action words. A statistical analysis of these utterances demonstrated that certain words, such as 'chase', 'tickle' and 'hide', were more likely to be in the first position, while other words were more likely to come second, such as 'slap' and 'bite'. Savage-Rumbaugh and her colleagues argued that this ordering reflects the sequence in which events occur: the first word tends to be an invitation to play, while the second describes the content of the play that follows. In such cases, Kanzi combines words with grammatical rules. He creates sentences.

But they are not very good sentences. In fact they are awful, whether compared with those of William Shakespeare or any three-year-old child. Savage-Rumbaugh and her colleagues acknowledge that Kanzi's range of vocabulary and use of grammatical rules is not as advanced as that of a three-year-old. But they do not recognize the yawning gulf that in fact exists. The gulf has been stressed by the linguist Steven Pinker.[30]

By the age of three a child frequently strings ten words together by the use of complex grammatical rules. By the age of six a child will have a vocabulary of about 13,000 words. Young children are constant commentators on the world around them and on what others say. Almost the entire sample of Kanzi's utterances are demands for things; his comments on the world are extremely rare.

Indeed the whole pattern of acquiring language is so radically different between apes and humans that it is difficult to imagine how ape language could ever have been thought of as anything other than a very weak analogy for that of humans. A much stronger analogy appears to be bird song. As the biologist Peter Marler once described, there are several important points of similarity between the way that children acquire language and young birds acquire their song.[31] Both learn the correct pattern of vocalization from adults. Both have a critical period during which the learning of language/song is at a premium. The 'subsong' of young birds appears to be analogous to the babbling of young children. There is also a similarity in terms of the brain structures which enable language/song to be learnt. In both birds and humans these are found in the cerebral cortex, while in primates vocalizations are controlled by other parts of the brain, such as the brain stem.[32]

The similarities between acquisition of language by children and that of song by young birds are as striking as the differences from 'language' acquisition by chimpanzees. Song plays a much more important role in the life of birds than does vocalization in the life of non-human primates; it is possibly as important as the role of language among humans. We should therefore perhaps expect that both birds and humans will have specialized cognitive processes designed for the rapid acquisition of complex song/language, traits that may be less developed, perhaps even absent among non-human primates. Convergent evolution has meant that these bird-song and human-language modules are strongly analogous. It is perhaps not surprising that the most impressive non-human linguist is not an ape, but an African Grey parrot called Alex.[33]

Steven Pinker's description of chimpanzee linguists as 'highly trained animal acts' may be a bit harsh. But we do not appear to be witnessing in these language acquisition experiments the release of some latent linguistic ability, trapped in the animals' minds by the absence of vocal cords. We simply see clever chimps at work, using aspects of general intelligence such as associative learning to understand the links between a set of signs and their referents, and how to combine those signs to gain rewards. Using a general-purpose learning rule for language acquisition can take a chimpanzee only so far when learning vocabulary and grammar: that distance appears to be similar to the 'language' of a two-year-old human child. And recall, as we saw in the previous chapter, that up to the age of two human children may also be using generalized learning rules for language – the language explosion only occurs after that age, with specialized language modules coming into operation. But no such thing happens in the chimpanzee mind. There is no linguistic intelligence.

Brick walls or open windows? Thought at domain interfaces in the chimpanzee mind

We have tried to established the cognitive processes that lie behind tool use, foraging, social behaviour and 'language' acquisition by chimpanzees. How is the architectural plan of the chimpanzee mind shaping up?

There appear to be three main features (see Figure 4). The first is a general intelligence, which includes modules for trial and error learning, and associative learning. These are used for a wide range of tasks: making foraging decisions, learning about tool use, acquiring an understanding of symbolic meanings. We should not minimize the importance of this general intelligence: chimpanzees are without doubt clever chimps. Secondly, there is a specialized domain of social intelligence. This enables a chimpanzee's interaction with the social world to be an order of magnitude greater in complexity than its interaction with the non-social world, involving aspects such as hypothesis formation which are evidently lacking from foraging behaviour and tool use. Thirdly, there is a small set of mental modules concerned with building up large mental databases about resource distribution, an incipient natural history intelligence.

This proposed suite of features for the mental architecture of the chimpanzee has been identified by looking at toolmaking, foraging, linguistic and social behaviour in isolation from each other. It can be strengthened when we look at the interfaces between them.

Consider that between toolmaking and foraging. This seems to be so fluid that differentiating between them is impossible. The Tai chimpanzees seem very proficient at choosing hammerstones of the appropriate weight for cracking the specific type of nuts they have acquired.[34] Similarly they manufacture sticks of appropriate size for the job in hand: small sticks for extracting bone marrow and nuts, longer and thinner sticks for ant dipping and getting honey.[35] The Gombe chimpanzees select stems and grass blades of an appropriate size for termite fishing and bite them to optimize their length or rejuvenate the stiffness of the ends. Bill McGrew has described how Kate, a rehabilitated chimpanzee

4 The chimpanzee mind.

in the Gambia, used four tools in succession to acquire honey from a bees nest in a hollow tree.[36] Each tool appeared to be very well chosen for the particular stage that she had reached in this delicate task.

In general, chimpanzees appear very good at making and choosing tools which are just right for the job in hand. This is indeed what we should expect if both toolmaking and foraging are using the same mental processes, general intelligence.

Now consider the interface between social behaviour and toolmaking. This seems quite the opposite, characterized by an awkwardness and what appears to be many missed opportunities. Consider the social interactions between mothers and their infants in the context of using hammers and anvils to open nuts in the Tai forest.[37] It is not surprising, in view of the nutritional value of nuts but the difficulty of nutcracking, that mothers help their infants acquire the skill. They may leave a hammer on an anvil, or nuts close by an anvil. Moreover, active teaching appears to have been observed. The Boeschs report two instances in which mothers saw their infants having difficulty in cracking nuts and provided demonstrations of how to solve the problem. In one case the correct positioning of a nut on an anvil prior to striking was demonstrated, while in the other the proper way to grip a hammerstone was shown to an infant who immediately seemed to adopt the grip with some success.

What is remarkable, however, is that such active teaching, or even passive encouragement, should be so rare. The two instances that the Boeschs describe constitute less that 0.2 per cent of almost 1,000 maternal interventions in nutcracking seen during 4,137 minutes of observation. Why don't they do more of it? The time and effort juveniles invest in cracking nuts is substantial, as is the nutritional benefit once the skill is attained. We have seen evidence that chimpanzees are able to imagine what is going on inside the mind of another chimpanzee, so should not a mother be able to appreciate the problems her offspring is facing when trying to use tools? It would seem to make very great evolutionary sense for mothers to provide their offspring with more instruction. But they don't. It seems a missed opportunity. It appears that this capacity for imagining the thoughts of another individual does not extend to thoughts about toolmaking but is restricted to those of the social domain alone.

Nor do chimpanzees use material culture in their social strategies. We have seen these to be Machiavellian in character: deception, cunning, ambition are rife. Chimpanzees *seem* to use any means possible to gain social advantage – but in fact they don't. For they do not employ material culture to this end. No chimpanzee has ever been seen wearing or using material items to send social messages about status and aspiration. Imagine if our politicians acted with the same self-restraint in their competitive posturing: no pin-striped suits and no old school ties. Material culture is critical to the Machiavellian social antics of modern humans, but is strangely absent from those of chimpanzees. If social status is so important to them, why not use tools to maintain it? Why not display the head of a little monkey that one had killed, or use leaves to exaggerate the size of one's chest? The failure of chimpanzees to act in this way seems another missed opportunity at this awkward cognitive interface between social behaviour and tool use.

There seems to be a brick wall between social and tool behaviour – the relationship between these lacks the fluidity that exists between foraging and tool use. We can explain this brick wall by the very different types of cognitive processes used by chimpanzees to interact with physical objects (general intelligence) and those used for social interaction (social intelligence). In short they seem unable to integrate their thoughts about toolmaking with their thoughts about social interaction. They may be able to read each other's minds, but not when a mind is 'thinking' about tool use. I suspect that this is because they have no mental awareness of their own knowledge and cognition concerning making and using tools. These are not part of their conscious awareness.

The existence of this brick wall between general and social intelligence is not to say that there is no relationship between social and toolmaking behaviour at all. Clearly there is, because the patterns of social behaviour provide the means by which knowledge about tool use is maintained within a group. As the Boeschs have noted, it is probably no coincidence that the Tai chimpanzees have both the most complex patterns of tool use and the greatest degree of social complexity among chimpanzee groups.[38] The food sharing that occurs from mothers to juveniles is probably essential in order to allow the juveniles time and energy to invest in learning the nutcracking technique. The intensity of social life in chimpanzee groups is also essential for maintaining the tool-use traditions, which require constant watching of other individuals and hence unsolicited opportunities for being stimulated to use tools. The critical point is that the relatively higher frequency of tool use among chimpanzees living in socially complex groups is simply a *passive* reflection of that social complexity; the tools are not playing an active role within social strategies.

I suspect that the same relationship holds between social and foraging behaviour, especially hunting patterns. There are indeed 'traditions' regarding animal exploitation that do not appear to have an ecological explanation. There are some striking culinary preferences: 'Tai chimpanzees keep the rump or the ribcage for last, consistently share the brain, and always swallow their leaf wadges. By contrast, Gombe chimpanzees keep the brain, which they rarely share, for last, spit out their leaf wadges, suck the blood of their prey, and eat with delight the fecal content of the large intestine.'[39] Butchery differences are interesting: Tai chimpanzees tend to kill their prey by disembowelling them, while Gombe chimpanzees smash the heads of their prey against tree trunks or rocks, or tear them apart by their limbs. Like tool traditions, these appear to play a passive role in social interaction; they are nothing like the culinary and butchery traditions between human groups, which have an active role in defining social identity.

More generally, the exploitation of resources appears to have no direct social implications. Food sharing among chimpanzees is tolerated theft rather than the provisioning of individuals to build up social obligations, as among humans. Even among the Tai chimpanzees, food sharing is essentially a passive reflection of social structure, rather than an active means to manipulate social relationships. The apparent effectiveness of Tai chimpanzees at hunting is a consequence of large group size, a high degree of mother-juvenile sharing, and an abundance of acoustic clues, rather than evidence for a natural history intelligence.

Further evidence to support the proposed mental architecture for the chimpanzee is what happens to chimpanzees when they are taken into captivity and come under the influence of socially complex, tool proficient, linguistically talented humans. We do not see any fundamental change in the complexity of chimpanzee social behaviour. The social strategies they adopt in captivity are essentially the ones they adopt in the wild. But just look at what happens to their toolmaking and using capacities. These become highly elaborated, with chimpanzees even learning to flake stone nodules. Indeed many primates suddenly become proficient tool users in captivity when provided with appropriate stimulus. And the same happens with chimpanzees' 'linguistic abilities' – a capacity for using symbols suddenly emerges. Now recall from the previous two chapters that one of the fundamental attributes of a specialized intelligence built upon intuitive knowledge is that the behavioural skills need only minimal stimulus from the social and natural environment to develop. If chimpanzees had a 'technical intelligence' we would expect to see them performing very little better with tools in the laboratory than in the wild; on the other hand, if they are simply clever chimps in terms of having general intelligence, the more stimulus and encouragement they receive, the better tool and language users they are likely to become. This seems to be precisely what we observe. Social behaviour, on the other hand, is already built upon a base of specialized cognitive processes and is not significantly influenced by an increased intensity of social interaction when in captivity.

The origins of social intelligence

Let me summarize the arguments of this chapter. We wanted to interpret the action of Act 1 of our prehistory in this chapter, but the theatre was in darkness and our actor was missing. To compensate for this we have considered the behaviour of the chimpanzee, assuming that the chimpanzee mind has a similar architecture to that of the common ancestor of 6 million years ago.

We watched the chimpanzee make and use tools, learn to use symbols in the laboratory, go foraging and hunting and engage in complex social strategies. Our interpretation of this behaviour is that the chimpanzee mind has a powerful general intelligence, a specialized domain of social intelligence, and a number of mental modules which are used for building up a large database about resource distributions. If we return to the analogy of the mind as a cathedral and our proposed architectural history for the mind, it can be suggested that the mind of the 6-million-year-old ancestor is at the interface between Phase 1 and Phase 2. We now know that the chapels were not built simultaneously; the first erected was the chapel of social intelligence.

When did a specialized domain of social intelligence first appear in the primate mind? To answer this we must first look to another common ancestor, ancestral to ourselves, chimpanzees and monkeys. This common ancestor appears to have lived about 35 million years ago and is likely to have possessed a mind similar to that of the monkeys which live today.[40]

Robert Seyfarth and Dorothy Cheney drew on years of field observations and experiments to 'look inside' the monkey mind in their 1990 book *How Monkeys See the World.* They found a rather less powerful general intelligence than the one we found inside the chimpanzee mind; one that did not lead monkeys to use tools in the wild, although it enabled them to learn tool use when given sufficient stimulus in laboratory contexts. Cheney and Seyfarth also found evidence for a specialized domain of social intelligence in the monkey mind which, as in that of chimpanzees, was closed off from general intelligence. Monkeys seem able to solve problems in the social world far more effectively than problems in the non-social world, even when those problems appear essentially the same. They can, for instance, rank the social status of their conspecifics, but cannot rank the amount of water in a series of containers. And they have a thirst for social knowledge, but an indifference to that about the non-social world.[41] But the social intelligence of monkeys appears less complex and powerful than that of chimpanzees. Monkeys appear unable to work out what other monkeys are thinking, or indeed that they may be thinking at all: they have no theory of mind module. And place a monkey in front of a mirror and he gets upset at the other monkey who has suddenly entered the room: unlike chimpanzees and gorillas, they cannot recognize themselves and have no concept of self.[42]

Now let us look at yet another common ancestor. We will venture even further back in time to look at the common ancestor to humans, apes, monkeys and lemurs. This common ancestor lived as much as 55 million years ago, and probably had a mind much like that of modern lemurs. Dick Byrne and Andrew Whiten have suggested that this mind has a general intelligence, but lacks any cognitive processes specialized for social behaviour.[43] The interaction that lemurs have with their social worlds appears to be no more complex than that with the non-social world.

To summarize, a specialized domain of social intelligence first appeared in the course of human evolution after 55 million years ago. This gradually increased in complexity with the addition of further mental modules, such as that for a theory of mind between 35 and 6 million years ago. As this domain of social intelligence increased in complexity, so too did the capacity for general intelligence. And mental modules first appeared relating to foraging activity, enabling the mind to construct large databases of resource distribution.

Act 2 of our prehistory is now almost upon us. The programme notes have told us that actors will now appear, and a candle will be lit to watch them by. Time has flown. It is now 4.5 million years ago. Has there been any new building work in the cathedral of the mind?

6 The mind of the first stone toolmaker

THE FIRST SCENE of the second act begins 4.5 million years ago and has three actors, *A. ramidus*, *A. anamensis* and *A. afarensis*. As I noted in Chapter 2, we can learn a certain amount about their behaviour from the few fossil fragments of these species that survive, but we have no direct evidence of their toolmaking – if indeed they made tools at all – and foraging activities. With the start of scene two at 2.5 million years ago there is a rush of actors on to the stage: first the later australopithecines and then by 2 million years ago the earliest members of the *Homo* lineage. The fossil fragments of these show significant anatomical and thus behavioural developments, such as the appearance of more effective bipedalism – habitual walking on two legs – a behavioural event to which I will return later in this book. Moreover we can see our ancestors setting off in two different evolutionary directions. The australopithecines went down a route of ever-increasing robusticity as specialized plant-grinding machines, while early *Homo* took a more cerebral route of increasing brain size. It is the mind of the earliest *Homo* which is the subject of this chapter.

There are likely to have been several species of early *Homo* at this time, but I will use the shorthand in this chapter of referring to one single species, *H. habilis*. Although the fossil remains of *H. habilis* are sparse, they are more substantial than those of the gracile australopithecines living prior to 2 million years ago, and we thus have more opportunities to make inferences about behaviour and mental activity. Moreover we now have direct evidence for foraging and toolmaking in the form of scatters of stone tools and the debris from their manufacture, as well as scatters of bone fragments of the animals that were exploited. It is only in a very few cases, however, that we can confidently attribute these archaeological remains to *H. habilis*. Many of the stone tools may have been made by the australopithecines, who may also have been responsible for some of the scatters of animal bone fragments. But I will follow convention in this chapter by assuming that the majority of the archaeological remains do indeed derive from the activity of *H. habilis*. My aim is to reconstruct the architecture of the mind of *H. habilis*. I must start with the hardest evidence available, Oldowan stone tools, and ask whether there was a specialized domain of technical intelligence.

Technical intelligence: do the first stone tools mark a cognitive breakthrough?

Oldowan artifacts are named after the site of Olduvai Gorge in East Africa, where they have been found eroding from sediments. Numerous other locations in East and South Africa have yielded similar artifacts. They are principally made from basalt and quartzite[1] and come in a range of shapes and sizes. Some are flakes removed from nodules, others are the remnant nodules themselves, referred to as cores. A few of the flakes have had smaller flakes removed from them. Are these artifacts indicative of specialized cognitive processes of a kind that seem absent from the mind of the common ancestor 6 million years ago? In the 4 million years that have elapsed since that ancestor, has evolution created a technical intelligence?

We need to start by asking how different these stone artifacts are from the tools made from plant material used by chimpanzees. By definition they are different: they are made from stone. Some archaeologists have felt that that is the end of the matter and that in all other respects the Oldowan and chimpanzee technologies are essentially the same.[2] But this misses two important differences, which have considerable implications for the mental processes underlying tool manufacture. First, although the function of Oldowan artifacts remains unclear, there is little doubt that some were made to make other tools – such as the production of a stone flake to sharpen a stick.[3] The making of a tool to make another tool is unknown among chimpanzees. It involves holding in one's mind the qualities of two contrasting types of raw material, such as stone and wood, and an understanding of how one can impinge on the other.

A second point is that when a chimpanzee makes a termite stick, the bits that must be removed from the twig are strongly dictated by the nature of the material and the future task themselves – you cannot poke a stick down a hole when it has got leaves on, and it is clear where these should be detached. But *H. habilis* had a more difficult task when removing bits from stone nodules. Just hitting a nodule in a random fashion is either unlikely to make any impact at all, or it will shatter the rock into many tiny pieces. To detach the type of flakes one finds in the sites of Olduvai Gorge, one needs to recognize acute angles on the nodules, to select so-called striking platforms and to employ good hand-eye co-ordination to strike the nodule in the correct place, in the right direction and with the appropriate amount of force[4] (see Figure 5). Members of *H. habilis* were working stone nodules in a fundamentally different manner from the way chimpanzees work their raw materials. They could indeed locate appropriate angles and adjust the force and direction of their striking actions.

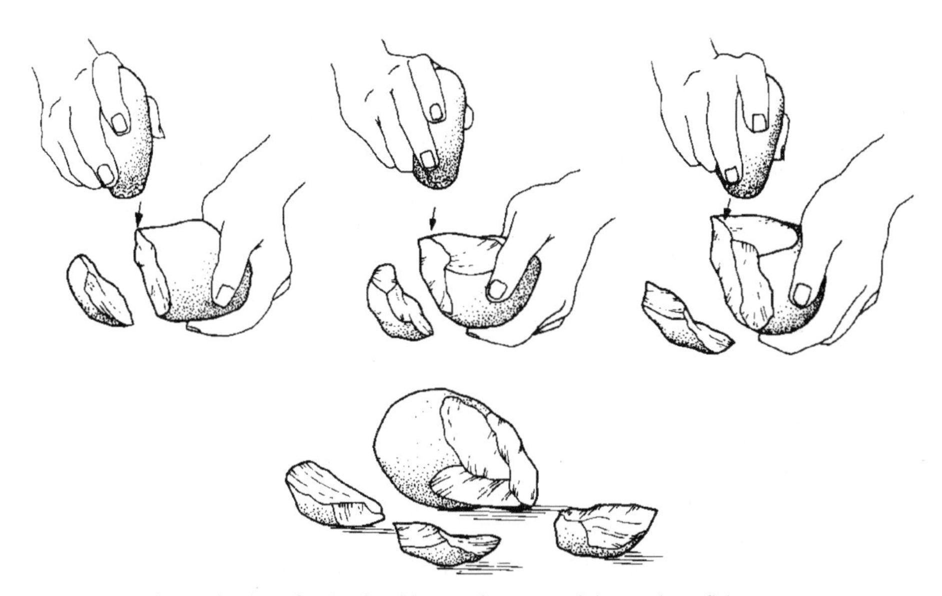

5 *The production of a simple Oldowan chopper and the resultant flakes.*

In 1989 Tom Wynn and Bill McGrew, both of whom we have already met in this prehistory, suggested that a chimpanzee could make Oldowan-like stone tools. This has now been tested. And they can't. Or at least that linguistic star of the chimpanzee world, Kanzi, is unable to do so. And if he can't it seems unlikely that other chimpanzees can. Nicholas Toth, the foremost expert on Oldowan technology, and his colleagues motivated Kanzi to want sharp-edged cutting tools, tempting him with treats locked in a box tied with string. Kanzi was shown the principles of producing stone flakes and provided with rocks. He did indeed learn to produce stone flakes, cut the string and win his reward. But he didn't win Nicholas Toth's vote as a modern Oldowan toolmaker. For Kanzi has never developed the concept of searching for acute angles, using flake scars as striking platforms or controlling the amount of force in percussion. His failure to do this does not reflect a lack of adequate manual dexterity, for Kanzi has learnt to do things like tie shoelaces and undo buttons. And it seems implausible, although a possibility, that he may learn the Oldowan-type flaking strategies with more practice.[5]

Now if Kanzi cannot produce Oldowan-like artifacts, what implications does this have for the minds of those who did 2 million years ago? There are two possibilities. The first is that a more powerful general intelligence had evolved so that the techniques of Oldowan technology could gradually be learnt, with presumably many trials and a lot of error. Alternatively, specialized cognitive processes dedicated to the manipulation and transformation of stone nodules had appeared – an intuitive physics in the mind of *H. habilis*. Perhaps even a technical intelligence.

If this is the case then our best bet for when it appeared is in the short interval between Scenes 1 and 2 of this second act of prehistory. Recall that just at the end of the first scene, between 3 and 2 million years ago, there were props scattered on the stage although we could see no actors to use them. Well these props are the tools of the Omo industrial tradition, which precedes the Oldowan. They are only found in a few places in East Africa, notably at Omo itself and at the site of Lokalalei in West Turkana.[6] These 'tools' are little more than smashed nodules, requiring less technical skill to make than those of the Oldowan. Indeed, they look like the sort of stone flakes that Kanzi can produce. So perhaps we are witnessing a greater need for stone flakes within the behavioural repertoire of the forebears of *H. habilis* prior to 2 million years ago, which then provided the selective pressures for the specialized cognitive mechanisms we see expressed in the Oldowan technology.

We should tread very carefully here, however, for while Oldowan stone tools appear beyond the cognitive capacities of chimpanzees, they are nevertheless extremely simple artifacts by human standards. As Nicholas Toth has shown, the aim of Oldowan artifact makers appears to have been simply to produce flakes with sharp edges, and nodules which could be held in the hand while having sufficient mass for tasks such as breaking open bones for marrow. In the 1970s archaeologists spent much time dividing Oldowan artifacts into different 'types', like polyhedrons, spheroids and choppers. These are easily thought of as equivalent to our 'types' of tools today, such as hammers, saws and screwdrivers. But we now know that this was too complex a classification. Oldowan artifacts in fact show a continuous pattern of variability. The form of the artifact can be explained simply by the character of the original nodule, the number of flakes removed and the sequence in which they were detached. We can see no evidence for an intentional imposition of form.[7] We should also note that although working stone is technically more demanding than stripping leaves off twigs, the Oldowan toolmakers, mainly using stone such as basalt and quartzite, appear to have been unable to work more intractable rocks such as cherts.[8] For this we must wait until the next act of our prehistory.

We must conclude, therefore, on a rather equivocal note. On the one hand the making of Oldowan stone tools requires an understanding of fracture dynamics that appears beyond the capacity of the chimpanzee mind. On the other hand the stasis in Oldowan technology, the absence of imposed form and the preference for the easier raw materials prevent us attributing *H. habilis* with a technical intelligence beyond that of a few micro-domains.

Natural history intelligence: the rise of the meat eaters?

While Oldowan stone tools are likely to have been used for a variety of purposes, their main function was probably the processing of animal carcasses. The sharp flakes were most likely used to cut hide and tendons, and to remove pieces of meat. The heavy nodules were probably employed to smash apart joints, or to break open bones to remove marrow.[9] This takes us, therefore, to a second aspect of *H. habilis* lifestyles for which we might expect specialized cognitive processes to have evolved: interaction with the natural world. In the previous chapters we saw that chimpanzees are capable of building up substantial mental databases of resource distribution. I attributed this to the presence of dedicated mental modules for this task. But the lack of hypothesis building and the creative use of knowledge about resource distribution suggested that attributing chimpanzees with a domain of natural history intelligence was unwarranted. Is there any evidence that it had evolved by the time of *H. habilis*?

To answer this we must focus on the one major difference from the behaviour of the chimpanzee/common ancestor that we can be confident about – members of *H. habilis* were consuming larger quantities of meat. We know this because many archaeological sites dating between 2 and 1.5 million years ago have large numbers of fragments of animal bones intermingled with stone artifacts. These dense accumulations are normally assumed to have derived from meal times – Mary Leakey described these sites as 'living floors'.

During the 1980s a vast amount of attention was paid to these bone fragments, engendering a vociferous and acrimonious debate as to how they should be interpreted. The fragments are those found at sites such as HAS at Koobi Fora, a 1.6-million-year-old scatter of stone artifacts and animal bones, dominated by those of a hippopotamus.[10] Or those at FLK 22, Olduvai Gorge where 40,172 bone fragments and 2,647 stone artifacts were found and have been studied in immense detail – this is one of the most intensively studied sites from any period or region in the whole world.[11] The problem with these bone fragments is that they are usually extremely small, and it is often not clear from what type of bone they derived, let alone the types of animal to which they belonged. When these animals can be identified, it is clear that *H. habilis* exploited a wide range of species, including zebras, antelopes and wildebeest.

The debates about *H. habilis* lifestyles were initiated by the publications of the late Glynn Isaac.[12] He proposed that these dense artifact and bone scatters represented 'home bases' – places where *H. habilis* shared food and the care of infants. Food sharing was the critical feature. Isaac suggested that the wide range of species typically represented on these

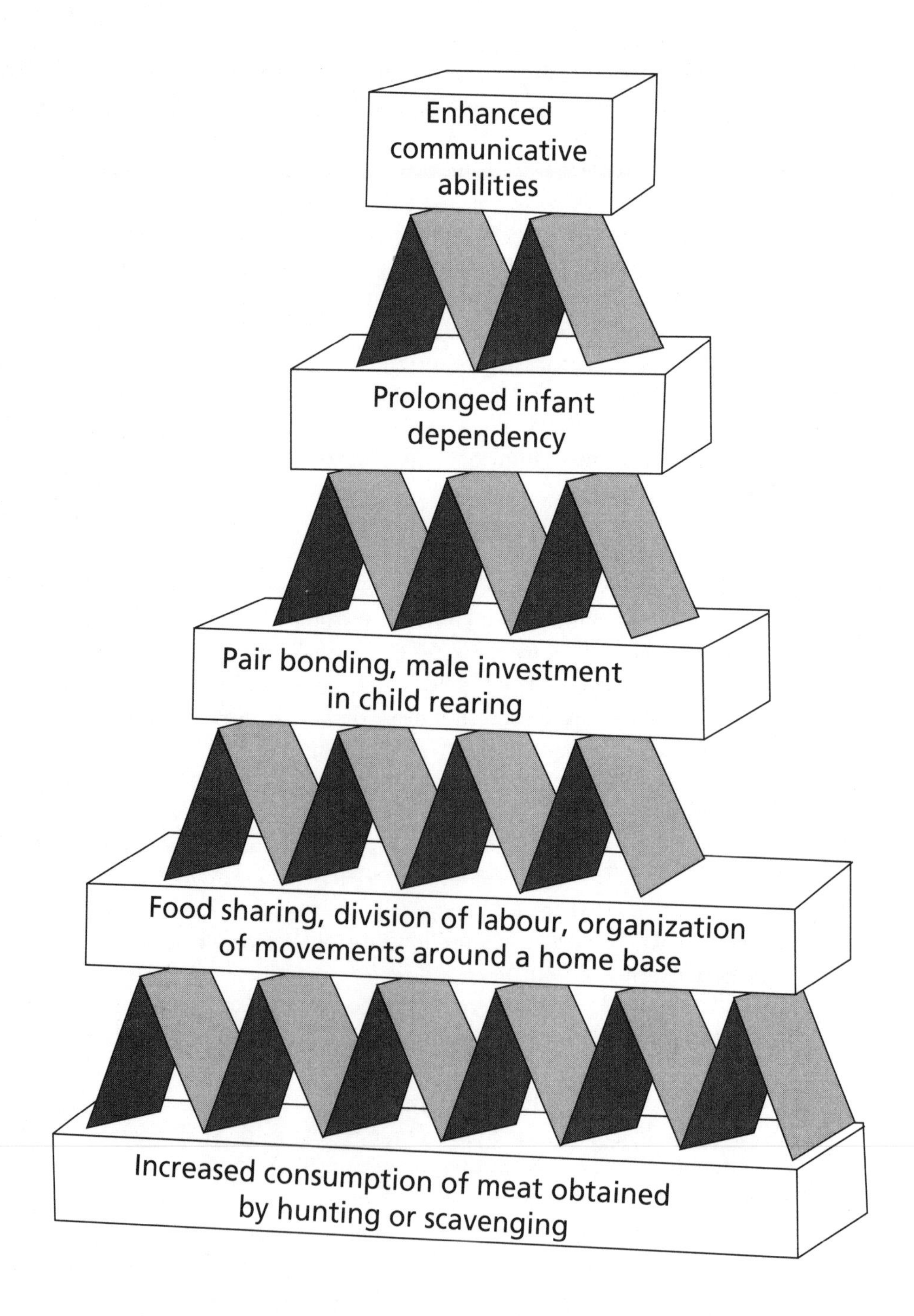

***6** Glynn Isaac's home base and food sharing hypothesis as a stack of cards. If Isaac's conclusion that early* Homo *was consuming a large quantity of meat is wrong, then all his other ideas concerning social behaviour and cognition come tumbling down.*

sites implied that members of *H. habilis* were transporting foodstuffs from different types of ecological zones in the landscape to a central place. Food sharing was the basis for a pyramid of inferences – some would say a house of cards – culminating in the presence of prolonged infant dependency and linguistic communication (see Figure 6). The home base model was published in the late 1970s and transformed the field of Palaeolithic archaeology, shifting it away from mere descriptions of stone artifacts and subjective guesses as to what they might mean.[13] For a few years it became widely accepted. And then in 1981 Lewis Binford published one of the truly significant archaeological books of the last 30 years, *Bones: Ancient Men and Modern Myths*,[14] which further transformed the study of the earliest archaeological sites.

During the 1980s Lewis Binford was the big-punching heavyweight of Palaeolithic archaeology. He took on all comers about how the stone tools and bone fragments of the archaeological record should be interpreted. His strength in debate came from a knowledge about how the archaeological record is formed – the processes of decay and change that affect the items that hunter-gatherers leave behind them in the millennia until they are found by archaeologists. He had acquired this knowledge in the Arctic and the Australian desert where he lived with modern hunter-gatherers, making meticulous records of their activities, what is thrown away and how this would look to an archaeologist.

Binford argued that there was no evidence for the transport and consumption of large quantities of meat. Instead, he suggested that members of *H. habilis* acquired just tiny morsels of meat, if indeed any at all. They were not merely scavengers, but 'marginal scavengers'. They did no more than take the tit-bit leftovers at the bottom of the hierarchy of meat eaters on the African savannah, trailing in after the lions, the hyenas and the vultures had had their fill (see Figures 7 and 8). Take away the large meat packages, and Isaac's home bases and his pyramid of inferences come tumbling down.

Following Binford's first onslaught against Isaac's model in 1981 a lengthy debate ensued, often with Isaac's students rather than himself arguing the case for hunting or scavenging from freshly killed carcasses by *H. habilis* and hence the maintenance of large meat parcels in the diet.[15] New models were proposed, supplementing the home base and marginal scavenging hypotheses. Binford himself developed the theme of marginal scavenging into a 'routed' foraging model in which the movements of foragers were constrained around a series of fixed points in the landscape, such as trees used for shade.[16] Richard Potts suggested that members of *H. habilis* were creating caches of unworked stone nodules or artifacts at strategic points in the landscape to minimize search

7, 8 *Glynn Isaac's and Lewis Binford's contrasting models for early* Homo *lifestyles. In the upper figure we see early* Homo *living in large social groups and using specific nodes in the landscape as home bases for the sharing of food. At these home bases co-operative behaviour involving the division of labour is planned. In the lower figure we see Lewis Binford's interpretation of the same evidence in which individuals, or at most small groups, scavenge morsels of meat and marrow from carcasses, trailing in after other predators and scavengers.*

time for stone when a carcass had been located.[17] Robert Blumenschine suggested that members of *H. habilis* concentrated their activities in woodland near water sources, since this provided a scavenging niche not being exploited by other species.[18]

Yet in spite of the intensity of research, our understanding of *H. habilis* subsistence patterns remains limited, with no consensus about the extent of hunting and scavenging, the use of central places or of routed foraging. Two factors explain this lack of consensus. First, the archaeological record is probably just too poorly preserved to make inferences about *H. habilis* lifestyles with regard to day-to-day activities.[19] Second – and rather more optimistically – the true answer to the *H. habilis* lifestyle is probably that it was marked by diversity; a flexibility between hunting and scavenging, and between food sharing and feed-as-you-go, to suit the particular ecological circumstances of the moment. *H. habilis* is likely to have been behaviourally flexible, a non-specialized forager. The only type of animal exploitation that appears absent from the Olduvai assemblages is the marginal, scrounging type of scavenging.[20]

It is indeed most likely that meat eating was a regular part of the diet of *H. habilis*.[21] In addition to the animal bones, sometimes showing butchery cutmarks from the stone tools found at archaeological sites, the relatively large brain of *H. habilis* implies the consumption of a high-quality diet, measured in terms of calorific intake per unit of food. The brain is a highly expensive organ in terms of the quantity of energy it consumes. As the anthropologists Leslie Aiello and Peter Wheeler have argued, to compensate for the amount of energy used by an enlarged brain, the requirements of another part of the body must be reduced to maintain a stable basal metabolic rate.[22] They argue that this has to be the gut; as the brain gets bigger, the gut has to get smaller. And the only way for the gut to get smaller is by increasing the quality of the diet, such as by the consumption of greater quantities of meat as opposed to plant foods. So the fact that *H. habilis* has a brain size significantly larger than the australopithecines suggests that meat had become a larger part of the diet – whether or not the intellectual challenge of finding animal carcasses provided a selective pressure for brain enlargement. Indeed, as will be argued below, the need to live within larger groups was probably a far more important selective pressure in this regard.

Behavioural flexibility involving meat eating implies cognitive complexity. Does this in its turn imply the existence of a specialized natural history intelligence? What new cognitive capacities would regular meat eating have required from the mind of *H. habilis*?

In view of the prevalence of tooth and gnaw marks on the bones from early archaeological sites, animal carcasses appear to have been competed for by several carnivores and scavengers, and many of these competitors would have been a threat to the members of *H. habilis.* Knowledge of carnivore behaviour and distribution would therefore appear to have been critical to early *Homo*: competing carnivores may have provided both a threat and an indication of a possible scavenging opportunity. In this light it would seem improbable that *H. habilis* could have exploited the carcass niche if it had not mastered the art of using inanimate visual clues, such as animal footprints and tracks. In contrast to monkeys, chimpanzees and the 6-million-year-old common ancestor, members of *H. habilis* are likely to have been able to read the visual clues indicating that a carnivore was in the vicinity.

On a more general level, the switch to a higher meat diet may have required a more sophisticated ability to predict resource locations than that needed by the predominantly vegetarian australopithecine forebears. Random searching for animals or carcasses, or even for the visual clues which indicate carcass location, is unlikely to have been feasible within such predator-rich environments. Unlike plant foods, animals are mobile and carcasses can disappear within a relatively short space of time, eaten by carnivores ranging from hyenas to vultures.[23] Simply building up an information store and mental map of their distribution – as we saw chimpanzees can do for plant and hammerstone distributions – would be inadequate. Members of *H. habilis* are likely to have needed one further cognitive trick – the ability to use their natural history knowledge to develop hypotheses about carcass/animal location.

The evidence that members of *H. habilis* were engaging in prediction about resource distribution comes from the recovery of stone nodules away from their raw material source and incomplete sets of knapping debris at archaeological sites. These reflect the transport of unworked nodules and stone artifacts across the landscape. Such artifacts were not carried for great distances – 10 km appears to be the very maximum and transport distances are usually much shorter.[24] Indeed the predominant pattern remains one of extremely local use of raw materials. Yet the fact that some items were transported, possibly to create caches, indicates that *H. habilis* had mental maps of raw material distribution, and could anticipate the future use of artifacts for subsistence activities.[25] There appear to be three important differences between *H. habilis* artifact transport, and that of hammerstones by Tai forest chimpanzees. First, *H. habilis* artifact transport occurs over a larger spatial scale than the transport of hammerstones by chimpanzees. Second, chimpanzees transport stone to fixed locations (nut trees), whereas the carcass destinations for *H. habilis* artifacts were continually changing. Third, it is as likely that members of

H. habilis transported the foodstuffs that needed processing to the tools (rather than just the other way around), and very often both tools and foodstuffs were transported from separate sources to a third location.

So far in this section the evidence from the archaeological record has been in favour of a considerable development of mental modules for interaction with the natural world. But there is some conflicting evidence, guarding against the inference of an evolved natural history intelligence. For one thing, much of *H. habilis* activity appears to be constrained to a narrow range of environments in comparison to the humans who appear in the fossil record after 1.8 million years ago. At a coarse spatial scale, it appears unlikely that any *Homo* prior to *H. erectus* moved out of their African evolutionary environment.[26] Even within the region of East Africa the activity of *H. habilis* was focused in a narrow range of microenvironments, as compared with the wide range of environments exploited by *H. erectus*, let alone modern humans. Much of the activity of *H. habilis* appears to have been 'tied' to the edges of permanent water sources.[27]

This tethering to natural features for the foci of activities appears to be reflected in the 'stacking' of archaeological sites in Olduvai Gorge. Sites such as FLK North I and MNK Main-II consist of vertical distributions of artifacts through several stratigraphic layers.[28] Hominids appear to have repeatedly returned to such locations in spite of fairly substantial changes in fauna, climate and landscape. The diversity of the faunal remains on the sites, with regard to body size and habitat preference, suggests that members of *H. habilis* did range quite widely into a variety of microenvironments when procuring animal parts. The fact that these were repeatedly transported to the same type of environmental context implies the absence of the behavioural flexibility indicative of a full natural history intelligence.[29]

Let me summarize the evidence we have for the mind of *H. habilis* regarding interaction with the natural world. We can start from the basis of an ability to construct large mental databases and maps for resource characteristics and distributions, as this was found in the mind of the common ancestor in the previous chapter. This now appears to be supplemented with abilities to develop hypotheses concerning resource location and to use inanimate visual clues. On the other hand members of *H. habilis* remained within a rather narrow environmental setting, and within that appear to be tethered to natural features for much of their activity. We seem to have reached a similar conclusion to that concerning technical intelligence: evolution has been at work laying further foundations for a chapel of natural history intelligence, but the walls are yet to be completed and general intelligence continued to play a dominant role in thought about the natural world.

A burgeoning social intelligence: safety in numbers

In the last chapter we saw that the common ancestor to modern humans and the chimpanzee at 6 million years ago already had a discrete domain of social intelligence. How, if at all, had the nature of social intelligence changed by the time of *H. habilis*?

To address this question we must begin with a short digression and think about the problems of group living, soap operas and brain size. As a general rule the more people that one chooses to live with, the more complex life becomes: there is a wider choice of possible partners with whom to share food or sex, and each of those partners will have a greater number and more diverse relationships with other members of the group. It is a considerable challenge to keep track of who is friends with whom, who are enemies, and who bear grudges or desires, and then to try to decide with whom to make friends without upsetting your other friends. We have all had some experience of this. In fact we seem to quite enjoy the social manoeuvrings that become paramount as groups enlarge, especially if we are bystanders. Why else are soap operas so popular? As a new character enters the script we watch the havoc caused to existing social relationships. Somebody often gets heartache, while someone else gets a headache.

It is therefore not surprising to find that among living primate species there is a strong positive relationship between group size and brain size – species which tend to have a terrestrial lifestyle in large groups also tend to have bigger brains. They need the brain processing power to keep track of the increased number of social relationships that arise as groups increase in size. This was discovered by the anthropologist Robin Dunbar who consequently argued that among living primates brain size is a direct measure of social intelligence.[30] Dick Byrne concurs with this result by finding a strong positive relationship between brain size and the frequency of deception in social strategies – the more complex the social scene, the more devious you are going to need to be to win more friends without winning more enemies.[31]

Now a critical question for reconstructing the prehistory of the mind is whether these relationships hold for extinct primates, like the australopithecines and *H. habilis*. The reason that they may not is that, as we have seen, the mind of *H. habilis* had a greater number of mental modules for making tools and interacting with the natural world than in any living primate and these must take up some brain processing power. Nevertheless, those domains seem only to have just got off the ground by 2 million years ago and so the relationship that exists for living primates between brain size and group size may also be applicable for *H. habilis*.

Robin Dunbar used the cranial volume of the fossil skulls of *H.*

habilis to estimate brain size. He then plugged these figures into an equation he had derived from living primates relating brain size to group size, to predict that australopithecines would have been living in groups with a mean size of 67 individuals, and a member of *H. habilis* with its larger brain size would usually have had about 82 other members of *H. habilis* for company. These compare with a predicted group size for chimpanzees of 60 individuals. The group sizes are for something that Dunbar refers to as the 'cognitive group', that is the number of individuals of whom one has social knowledge, as opposed to with whom one might live on a daily basis.

There is good circumstantial evidence that *H. habilis* would have been living in larger groups than his ancestors. If we again look at modern primates, there appear to be two ecological situations in which primates choose to live in larger groups, and suffer the accompanying social challenges.[32] One of these is when they face a high risk from predators. In that case it is better to be with some friends because then you can work together to fend off an attack, or failing that you might hope that the attacker will eat one of your friends rather than yourself. Now we know that our earliest ancestors did become the prey of carnivores – we have skulls pierced with the teeth marks of leopards to prove it.[33] And we know that their predilection for morsels of meat from carcasses may have been pitting them against hyenas. At just 1.5 m (under 5 ft) tall and 50 kg (110 lbs) in weight at most,[34] and with no more than a few lumps of stone to throw, they were not particularly well equipped for hand-to-hyena combat. So group living seems a necessity for *H. habilis*.

The other ecological condition which favours group living is when food comes in large parcels that are irregularly distributed around the landscape. Finding these may not be easy, but once found there is plenty of food to be had. So it is often beneficial to live within a relatively large group, search for food packages individually or in pairs, but then share food with other group members. On the next day it may be someone else who is the lucky one and finds the food. This scenario is likely to apply to *H. habilis* searching for carcasses on the savannahs of East Africa 2 million years ago. Indeed the archaeologist Mark Lake has demonstrated the plausibility of such an idea by building a computer simulation model of *H. habilis* searching for carcasses and seeing how well different individuals get on when they are lonely introverts or social extroverts.[35] The gregarious loudmouths consistently win the prize of the smelly rotting carcass.

We have therefore good ecological criteria for believing that *H. habilis* would be choosing to live in relatively large groups, and their large brain size implies that they had the social intelligence to do so. In other words the enlarged brain of the *H. habilis* suggests that the domain of social intelligence has become yet more powerful and complex. What might the new elements have been? We can only speculate, but one possibility is that they could cope with more 'orders of intentionality' than could their chimpanzee-like ancestors.

'Orders of intentionality' is a term that the philosopher Daniel Dennett introduced to help us think about how social intelligence works.[36] If I believe you to know something, then I can cope with one 'order of intentionality'. If I believe that you believe that I know something, then I can cope with two orders of intentionality. If I believe that you believe that my wife believes that I know something, then I can cope with three orders of intentionality. We modern humans regularly encounter three orders of intentionality – or at least we do if we believe soap operas, which often revolve around beliefs of what others believe a third party believes, and which often turn out to be false beliefs. Five orders of intentionality seem to be our limit. Daniel Dennett demonstrated this quite effectively when he asked if 'you wonder whether I realize how hard it is for you to be sure that you understand whether I mean to be saying that you recognize that I can believe you to want me to explain that most of us can keep track of only about five or six orders of intentionality under the best of conditions'.[37] Under the best of conditions chimpanzees are likely to manage just two orders of intentionality. Perhaps the new architectural features in the chapel of social intelligence had increased this to three or four in early *Homo*.

Incipient language? Investigating brain casts and social grooming

In the preceding passage I suggested that members of *H. habilis* had probably been 'gregarious loudmouths'. All sorts of animals can become loudmouths in a metaphorical sense when they want to threaten another animal or show off to the opposite sex. Peacocks are loudmouths with their tails, so too are gorillas when they beat their chest and sticklebacks when their stomachs go red. Members of *H. habilis* were surely loudmouths in this sense – displaying to impress the opposite sex, or to assert their authority with the group. But were they literally loudmouths, with plenty of words to speak? Did they have a capacity for language?

In the last chapter we could try and chat to chimps, whether by gestures or with computer keyboards. But now we have no more than *H. habilis* fossil bones and stone tools to interrogate. Looking more closely at stone tools is not going to be of any help. Language is a modularized cognitive capacity, reliant on its own unique neural processes. In contrast, as we saw in Chapter 3, the object manipulation and vocalizations of very

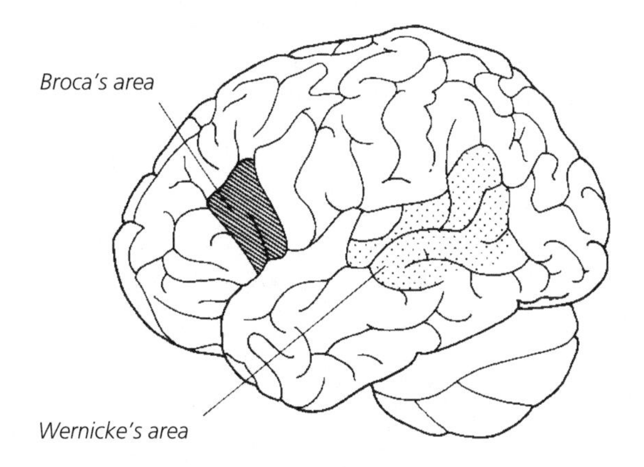

9 *A side view of the brain showing the locations of Broca's area and Wernicke's area. These are thought to be associated with the production and the comprehension of language.*

young children prior to their development of language, as well as those of chimpanzees, derive from 'general intelligence' rather than language modules. When we see a child making a hierarchically structured object we can infer that this child also makes hierarchically structured vocalizations, even if we can only see those objects. But fully developed language relies on mental modules specialized for language alone; we cannot infer the existence of these in the mind of *H. habilis* from the character of the physical objects being made.[38]

Can we infer a linguistic capacity from the shape of the brain itself? The neural processes which provide the capacity for language appear to be concentrated in specific areas of the brain, principally in the left hemisphere. Within this area, two regions appear to be particularly important: Broca's area and Wernicke's area[39] (see Figure 9). People who have suffered damage to either of these lose some of their linguistic capacity. Damage to Broca's area appears mainly to affect the use of grammar, while that to Wernicke's area affects comprehension. Damage to the connecting tissue between these areas, or to the tissue that connects these areas to the rest of the brain, can also result in severe language defects. But the relationships between specific parts of the brain and specific features of language are complex and little understood; all that we can be truly confident about is that certain areas of the brain are important for language.

So what do the brains of *H. habilis* look like? Can we see a development of Broca's and Wernicke's areas? The closest we can get to looking at their brains is to look at casts of the insides of their fossilized skulls.[40] We must hope that the humps and bumps on these casts reflect the humps and bumps of the brain of *H. habilis*. A risky business to say the least. Remember that these fossils have remained within the ground for as much as 2 million years, often becoming fossilized under the massive weight of overlying sediments. Humps and bumps on these casts are perhaps as likely to reflect the squashes and strains of the fossilization processes as much as the structure of the brain.

The fossil skull of a 2-million-year-old *H. habilis* specimen from Koobi Fora, referred to as KNM-ER 1470, is particularly well preserved. This has been examined by Phillip Tobias, one of the foremost authorities on the evolution of the brain. He is confident that a significant development of Broca's area can be seen, which has been confirmed by the work of another leading specialist, Dean Falk. In contrast, no such development of Broca's area can be seen in the brains of the australopithecines.[41]

Another clue to the presence of a linguistic intelligence may come not from the shape of the brain, but simply from its size. The two people who have thought about this in most detail have reached rather opposing conclusions.

The neuroscientist Terrence Deacon has argued that the enlargement of the brain that occurs with the first members of the *Homo* lineage involved a disproportionate increase of the part of the brain known as the pre-frontal cortex.[42] By drawing on extensive studies of the neural circuits involved in primate vocalizations and human language, Deacon argued that this relative enlargement of the pre-frontal cortex would have led to a re-organization of connections within the brain which would have favoured the development of a linguistic capacity – although whether that was sufficiently developed 2 million years ago to be termed language remains unclear.

The anthropologist Robin Dunbar looked at the size of the brain of *H. habilis* from a very different perspective.[43] Recall that we have already referred to his work regarding the relationship between brain size and group size – living within a larger group requires more brain-processing power to keep up with the ever-changing sets of social relationships. When living in groups, primates have to transfer information between each other and the principal way they do this is by grooming each others' bodies – picking out all the fleas and the lice. Who one chooses to groom, how long one grooms, and who you let watch while you do it, function as much to send social messages as to get rid of parasites. In the Burgers' zoo chimpanzee group that we looked at in the previous chapter grooming between males reached a peak when their relationships were unstable. Grooming sessions among the males lasted nine times as long in periods when there was an oestrus female in the group; de Waal suggests that the grooming may amount to 'sexual bargaining'.

Dunbar found that as group size increases, so too does the amount of time that primates spend grooming. This is not because there are more lice about but because one has to invest more and more time in social communication. But grooming is time consuming, and there are other things to do such as finding food to eat. Dunbar reckons that the longest any primate can afford to groom others is about 30 per cent of its time budget. Once above that limit, the individual may be a mastermind at social relationships, but be very hungry and lack the energy to exploit this knowledge to his or her social advantage.

So what can be done when group size is so large that even spending 30 per cent of one's time grooming leaves one ignorant of many important social relationships within the group? Well, maybe another means for transferring social information could be used – or in evolutionary terms would be selected for. Dunbar suggests that that other means is language. He argues that language evolved to provide a means for exchanging social information within large and socially complex groups, initially as a supplement to grooming, and then as a replacement for it. Language can do this because it is a much more efficient way of transferring information. An ambidextrous chimp may be able to groom two of his mates at once, but an articulate human can chat away to whoever is listening.

We will explore this social origin theory of language more thoroughly in the next chapter, but here we must ask whether *H. habilis* could have achieved the transfer of sufficient social information by grooming alone. Dunbar fed his estimates for the group size of *H. habilis* into his equation relating group size to grooming time, derived from his study of living primates. He found that early *H. habilis* just manages to dip under the 30 per cent threshold, with a social grooming time requirement of 23 per cent. With such a high percentage of time required for grooming it is likely that those individuals who could reduce their grooming time by inferring social information from the vocalizations of others, or who could begin to embed social information into their own vocalizations, may have gained some selective advantage.

The anthropologist Leslie Aiello suggests that these vocalizations may have been analogous to the chattering observed in Gelada baboons today and functioned to spread feelings of mutual content and well-being.[44] Perhaps they may also have been analogous to the purring of a cat when it is stroked. Or perhaps it is the sighs of pleasure when we stroke each other. These oohs, aahs, and ouches are social communication: do some more of this please, a little less of that. Dunbar has in fact argued that in our more intimate moments we return to our ancient means of social communication – physical grooming – although we now lack the body hair and (hopefully) the lice and the fleas.

Opening a crack in the cathedral door

Some cathedrals and churches are easier to get into than others. One of the churches I recently visited was in the small town of Angles in France. The main doors were locked and we had to search for a small side entrance. When inside it was initially so dark that we could hardly see our way around. Visiting that church was like trying to visit the mind of *Homo habilis*. With such a poorly preserved archaeological record, and no living species to provide an adequate analogy, finding a way into this prehistoric mind has been very difficult. The Oldowan stone tools have perhaps been able to prise apart a crack in the cathedral door. But peeping through this has been like the first few moments in the church at Angles, it all looks very dark and gloomy: it is hard to see what the basic architectural design actually is, let alone appreciate any of the details.

When my eyes grew accustomed to the lack of light in the church at Angles I was startled by the simplicity of the building; there was just a simple nave with bare stone walls and plain wooden pews. A few candles were burning in a small chapel. For some reason I had expected it to be more elaborate – architecturally more complex with ornate decorations. I feel the same about what I have managed to see of the mind of *H. habilis*. The first appearance of stone tools sounds such a grand event in human prehistory – indeed it is the starting point for the discipline of archaeology – that we expect it to be marked by some major cognitive event. But the mind of *H. habilis* at 2 million years ago seems to have been little more than an elaborate version of the mind of the common ancestor of 6 million years ago, with no fundamental changes in design (see Figure 10). Let me quickly summarize what we have seen in the mind of *H. habilis*.

OUR SOCIALLY PRECOCIOUS ANCESTOR

The toolmaking and foraging behaviour of *H. habilis* is certainly more complex than that of chimpanzees and what we expect of the common ancestor. Both the production of stone tools and the regular exploitation of animal carcasses are likely to have required specialized cognitive processes of a type absent from the chimpanzee mind. *H. habilis* appears to have been able to understand the fracture dynamics of stone and to have constructed hypotheses about resource distributions, both of which are likely to be beyond the capacity of general intelligence that dominates the toolmaking and foraging behaviour of the chimpanzee. Yet these specialized cognitive processes in the mind of *H. habilis* do not appear to be embedded within a matrix of other specialized processes relating to the same domain of activity. General intelligence appears to have continued to play an important role in conditioning toolmaking and foraging behaviour of *H. habilis*. And as a consequence, the making of stone arti-

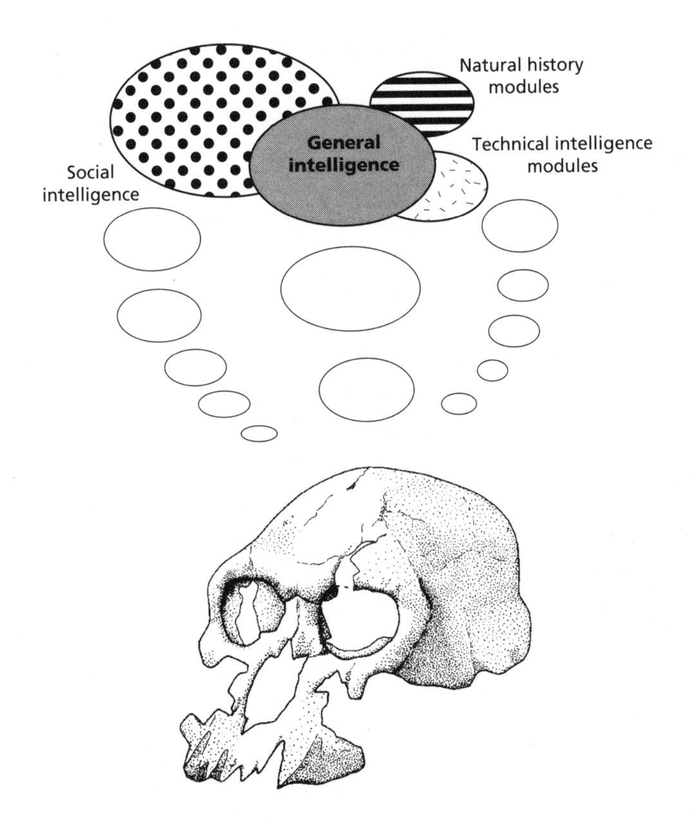

***10** The mind of early* Homo. *The drawing depicts the* H. habilis *skull known as KNM-ER 1470. This was discovered in 1972 at Koobi Fora, Kenya, and dates to 1.9 million years ago.*

facts and the exploitation of animal carcasses appear to be thoroughly integrated. They seem to be part of a single stream of activity, just as we recognized for the tool-using and foraging behaviour of the chimpanzee.

Social intelligence has become more complex and powerful than that within the mind of the chimpanzee. But it remains just as isolated from the thoughts about toolmaking and foraging as in the chimpanzee mind. There is no evidence that *H. habilis* used tools in social strategies. As noted above, the form of Oldowan artifacts appears to reflect no more than the character of the original nodule and the number of flakes removed. There is no imposition of social information on to the tools, as is pervasive among modern humans. Similarly, there are no examples in the archaeological record of spatial structure on archaeological sites which might reflect a social use of space. Material culture was not used in social strategies, even though we must conclude that those social strategies were even more complex and Machiavellian than we see among chimpanzees today.

Yet this increased social complexity is likely to have had a passive influence over the foraging and technical behaviour of *H. habilis*. As we saw in the previous chapter, the complexity of the tool-using and hunting behaviour of the Tai chimpanzees, as compared with those of Gombe, can partly be attributed to their larger group size and more intense social relationships. These provide greater opportunities for social learning and the cultural transmission of behavioural patterns. From this perspective, much of the increase in behavioural complexity of *H. habilis* over that of the common ancestor, in terms of the manufacture of stone tools and the exploitation of animal carcasses, might simply be accounted for as a spin-off from increased social complexity. The frequent use of the term 'food sharing' when discussing the behaviour of early *Homo* is probably misleading. It is more appropriate to view this as 'tolerated theft'. In terms of the play that is our past, the extra power and complexity of social intelligence appears to be the most important feature to explain the action of the second scene of Act 2.

In summary, the architectural plans inherited by members of *H. habilis* encoded the construction of a mental cathedral that appears to have had the same basic design as that encoded in the mind of the common ancestor 6 million years ago. The nave was larger, the chapel of social intelligence more elaborate, the walls of the chapels of technical and natural history intelligence a little higher and incorporating more modules. But those chapels remained incomplete.

7 The multiple intelligences of the Early Human mind

Act 3 of prehistory, from 1.8 million to 100,000 years ago, is the most puzzling period of our past. The quality of the archaeological record is substantially improved over that of Act 2, often enabling detailed and accurate reconstructions of past behaviour to be made. But when we study that behaviour, it frequently seems almost bizarre in its nature. It appears fundamentally different from what went before and from what comes afterwards in that rush towards the present day in Act 4.

While we still have much to learn about our ancestors of Act 2, discussed in the previous chapter, we can nevertheless accept that their ways of life were fine-tuned adaptations to the African woodland and savannahs between 4.5 and 1.8 million years ago. Because their lifestyles are so alien to us, it seems clear how they should be studied: once we have reconstructed the behaviour of the earliest *Homo*, for instance, we try to understand it as if we were an ecologist trying to understand the behaviour of any other primate species. We can also feel confident about how we should approach the performance of Act 4, especially in the second and third scenes after 60,000 years ago. During that period the pace of cultural change is so fast that it feels familiar, because this is precisely what we are accustomed to in our own short lives. And for the majority of these scenes we have a single type of human improvising the script – ourselves, *H. sapiens sapiens*. So we try to be more like an anthropologist than an ecologist when explaining human behaviour in Act 4.

Between these two periods we find the no-man's land of Act 3, where neither ecologist nor anthropologist can tread with confidence. Indeed this also applies to much of the first scene of Act 4, particularly when we are looking at the behaviour of the final Neanderthals. During these periods some features of the actors' behaviour seem so familiar to us that we could readily believe that they have the modern mind; but in other ways their behaviour appears as alien as that of the earliest *Homo* on the African savannah. Act 3 is indeed a period full of puzzles – we will come across eight of them within this chapter. Each actor seems to be like the man that Charles Colton was thinking about when he wrote early in the last century that 'Man is an embodied paradox, a bundle of contradictions'.[1] The task of the next two chapters is to unravel this bundle to see what type of mind is hidden inside.

Let us begin by reminding ourselves of the salient points of the third act.

Act 3 has an exciting start: the appearance of *H. erectus* 1.8 million years ago, followed by new types of stone tools, handaxes, 1.4 million years ago. Through the course of this act we watch how *H. erectus* diversifies and evolves into a range of new human ancestors. While the size of the brain appears to have remained stable between 1.8 and 0.5 million years ago – as *H. erectus* and her immediate descendants colonized much of the Old World – this period is brought to a close by a return to a period of rapidly expanding brain size, similar to that which had happened 2 million years ago, and which ends at around 200,000 years ago with the brain at an equivalent size to that of Modern Humans today. The new larger-brained actors after 500,000 years ago are classified as types of archaic *H. sapiens* in Africa and China, while in Europe the scant fossil remains are referred to as *H. heidelbergensis*. This last species then seems to give rise to *H. neanderthalensis* – the Neanderthals – found in Europe and the Near East after about 150,000 years ago and which survives in Europe until as late as 30,000 years ago. For this chapter I am going to group all of these actors together and refer to them as 'Early Humans' to distinguish them from *H. sapiens sapiens* appearing at the start of Act 4, whom I will refer to as 'Modern Humans'.

While these evolutionary events were occurring, the scenery was going through a hectic series of changes. This period of our past is dominated by a succession of global environmental changes as the planet went through at least eight major glacial-interglacial cycles. If we look at Europe, we can see the landscapes repeatedly changing from ice-covered tundras, to thick forests and back again, with accompanying changes in animal fauna. And even within one climatic phase, there were a host of shorter-term climatic fluctuations – successions of years, or even individual years, when the climate was abnormally cold or warm, wet or dry.

So with regard to the evolution of human anatomy and climatic change, Act 3 is teeming with action. But the props that the actors are using do not seem to match this tempo of change. After the initial appearance of the handaxe at 1.4 million years ago, we have a single major technical innovation at around 250,000 years ago with the appearance of a new production technique called the Levallois method. But other than this there seem to be hardly any changes in material culture. Indeed many of the props seem little different from those used by *H. habilis* on the African savannah in Act 2. As a whole, the archaeological record between 1.4 million and 100,000 years ago seems to revolve around an almost limitless number of minor variations on a small set of technical and economic themes.

By the start of Act 3, over 4 million years have passed since the time of the common ancestor. This has taken us to a mind with two dominant features: a bundle of mental modules dedicated to social interaction alone, which can be characterized as a discrete social intelligence, and a suite of generalized learning and problem-solving rules which are used irrespective of the behavioural domain and are referred to as general intelligence. Supplementing these are a number of specialized mental modules which relate to understanding physical objects and the natural world, although these appear to be relatively few in number. We must now see what happens to this mind during the next act of prehistory.

As I have just indicated, there are several different types of human ancestors during this act, each of whom is likely to have had a slightly different type of mental architecture. I say 'slightly' because I am going to start with the premise that the similarities between their mental architectures are more significant than the differences. My aim in this chapter is to try to reconstruct the architecture for a generic Early Human mind, drawing freely on data from the different types of Early Humans of this act. Indeed I will also step into the start of Act 4, when looking at the behaviour of the last of the Neanderthals – behaviour that appears to be no different from that of Act 3, but which can be reconstructed in rather more detail. Only at the end of this chapter will I try to draw some distinctions between the mental architectures of *H. erectus* and *H. neanderthalensis*, thereby exploring the evolution of the mind during the course of Act 3.

This act is full of behavioural paradoxes, if not plain contradictions. A theme running through this chapter will be how Early Humans appear to be so much like Modern Humans in some respects, yet so remarkably different in others. I believe that these puzzles and paradoxes are in fact the key to reconstructing the architecture of the Early Human mind. In order to proceed, we must consider the evidence for each of the four cognitive domains I defined in Chapter 4 – technical, natural history, social and linguistic intelligence – as well considering how these interacted, if at all. So let us start once again with technical intelligence and the evidence from stone tools.

Technical intelligence: imposing symmetry and form

We must begin by recognizing a quite dramatic increase in technical skill over that possessed by *H. habilis* in Act 2. The most characteristic artifact produced by Early Humans was the handaxe. Even a brief look at handaxes indicates a number of significant differences from those artifacts produced within the Oldowan tradition. They often display high degrees of symmetry, sometimes simultaneously in three dimensions, and indi-

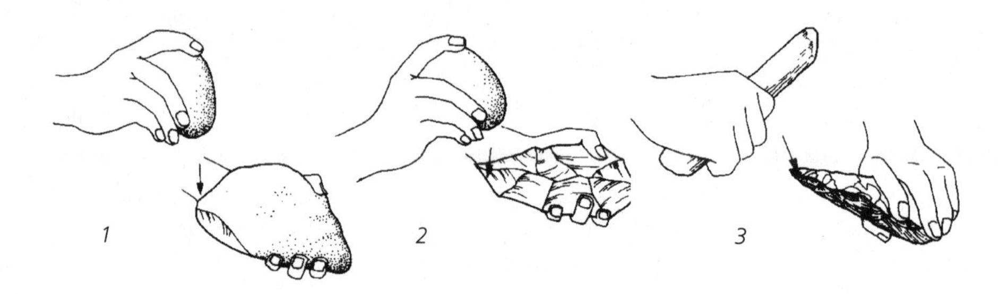

11 The production of a symmetrical handaxe involves three major stages. Beginning with either a large flake or a nodule (1), a hard hammer of stone is used to achieve the basic shape by detaching flakes from alternate sides of the artifact (2). The handaxe is finished by using a 'soft' hammer, of either bone, antler or wood, to remove 'thinning' flakes (3) and to achieve the final form of the artifact.

cate that the knapper was imposing form on to the artifact, rather than just creating sharp edges as with an Oldowan chopper.

To achieve such symmetry and form, longer knapping sequences were required. These can be appreciated from the refitting of knapping debris from sites such as Boxgrove in southern England, where handaxes were made 500,000 years ago.[2] To make a handaxe, great care must be paid to the initial selection of the stone nodule with regard to its shape, quality and likely fracture dynamics. Manufacture involves roughing out the handaxe using a stone hammer followed by final shaping, often with a 'soft' hammer made of bone or wood (see Figure 11). Flakes are removed from alternate sides of the artifact in turn, which is why the technique is often described as bifacial knapping, and the artifacts as bifaces. A soft hammer can detach flakes with shallow scars to create an artifact that is relatively thin. Prior to the removal of each thinning flake, the edge of the artifact may be ground for a few moments or have small flakes removed, in preparation for a strike.

The difficulty in achieving a symmetrical handaxe of a specified form has been stressed by Jacques Pelegrin, who has many years' experience at replicating handaxes. He has explained how the goal of the knapper is not simply to obtain a sharp cutting edge but to extricate an artifact of a specific form independent from the starting shape of that nodule. Planning ahead is essential if symmetry is to be achieved, and maintained as the piece is developed. The knapper needs to assess both what is desirable and what is possible, and achieve such ends by blows of a specific force and direction at specific points on the artifact. Each nodule worked by a knapper will have its own unique characteristics and challenges. Consequently to produce standardized forms, the knapper needs to exploit and adapt his or her toolmaking knowledge, rather than just follow a fixed set of rules in a rote fashion.[3] This final point is particularly important since many collections of handaxes from single sites are of very similar shape and size. If we assume that the original nodules are unlikely to have been exactly the same shape, then we have a fine example of the imposition of a specified form.[4]

Many of the above comments regarding the technical difficulty in producing handaxes also apply to the use of the Levallois method – the archetypal knapping technique used by the Neanderthals. Indeed, the Levallois method may involve even greater technical skill that that required to make handaxes.[5] The essence of the method is the removal of a flake, the size and shape of which is predetermined by the preparation of the core. The core is created with two distinct surfaces. One of these is domed, with flake scars to guide the removal of a flake. The other surface is the striking platform. If flake removal is to be successful, the angle between these two surfaces, the angle at which the core is struck and the force used must all be precisely right. Otherwise the detached flake may plunge over the side of the core, or deviate to one side or the other.

A modern-day flintknapper and archaeologist has recently remarked that 'even today, there are few students of lithic technology that ever achieve a Neanderthal's level of expertise in producing good Levallois cores or flakes, while the number of contemporary flint knappers that have successfully mastered the technique for producing good Levallois points probably number less than a score'.[6] He goes on to argue that the production of a blade from a prismatic core – as is characteristic of the Upper Palaeolithic period beginning 40,000 years ago in Act 4 – is 'incomparably easier' than the manufacture of a Levallois point (see Figure 12).

The Neanderthal stone technology from the Near East illustrates the technical sophistication of the Levallois technique. Consider, for instance, the demanding process by which Levallois points were produced at Kebara Cave between 64,000 and 48,000 years ago.[7] After the cortex of the core had been removed, flakes were struck from the core to create a convex profile in both the longitudinal and transverse directions. Following this, a special type of striking platform was created, referred to as a *chapeau de gendarme*. This has a central protrusion which aligns with the axis of the 'Y' form on the main ridge on the dorsal side of the core created by the initial preparation. This combination then acts to guide the removal of a flake so that the desired symmetrical point is obtained. The Kebara Neanderthals removed several Levallois flakes from each core before restoring its convexity to enable a further sequence of Levallois points to be removed. These points were most frequently used just as they came off the core; no further shaping was required.

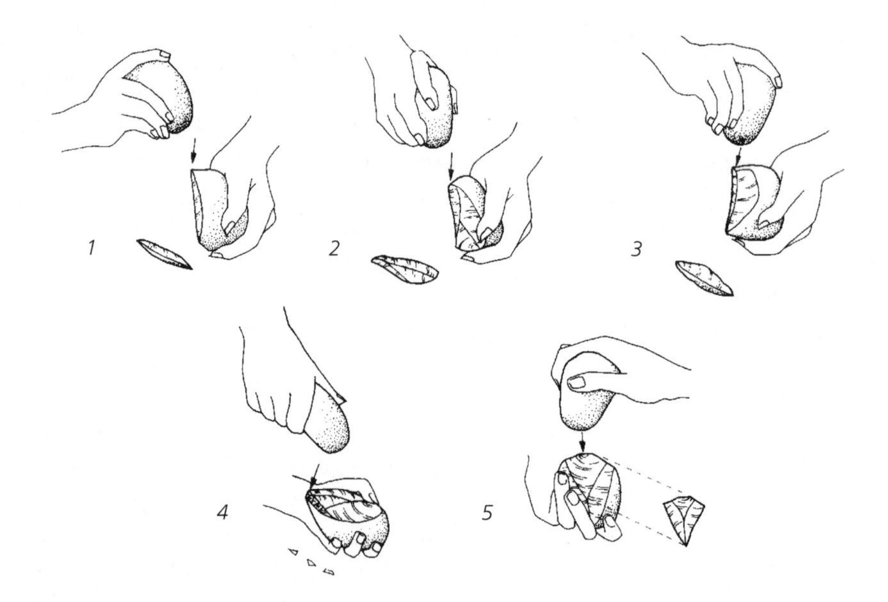

__12__ To make a Levallois point one must remove flakes from the surface of a core to leave a series of ridges on a domed surface (1–3) which will then guide the removal of the final pointed flake. A striking platform is prepared perpendicular to the domed surface of the core (4) and the Levallois point removed by a single blow (5).

As with the making of handaxes, it is critical to appreciate that Levallois flakes cannot be successfully removed by a mechanical adherence to a set of rules. Each nodule of stone has unique properties and a unique 'pathway' through the nodule must be found. Nathan Schlanger has described this when exploring the knapping actions undertaken 250,000 years ago by the Early Human who made 'Marjories core', a Levallois core from the site of Maastricht-Belvédère in the Netherlands that has had many of the waste flakes refitted.[8] Schlanger stresses how the knapper needed to have used both visual and tactile clues from the core, to have constantly monitored its changing shape, and to have continually adjusted his or her plans for how the core should develop.[9]

The technical intelligence of Early Humans is also apparent from the range of raw materials that they worked. Some of the earliest handaxes indicate an ability to work raw materials with less predictable patterns of fracture than those of the Oldowan. Consider, for instance, the collection of artifacts containing handaxes stratified immediately above the Oldowan at Sterkfontein in South Africa.[10] In this we see the introduction of a new raw material, diabase, and much better use of the difficult rock types, such as quartzite and chert. Indeed, throughout the Old World we find bifacial and Levallois flaking methods being applied successfully to relatively intractable materials.[11]

Moreover we can see a clear preference in some sites for making particular types of artifacts from particular types of raw materials. For instance, at Gesher Benot in Israel, a site more than 500,000 years old, basalt was preferentially used for handaxes, while limestone was used for choppers. Similarly at the site of Terra Amata in southern France, one of the earliest occupations in Europe, limestone was used for choppers and bifaces, while flint and quartz were used for the small tools.[12]

Puzzling over technical conservatism

We have seen evidence for an advanced technical intelligence among Early Humans. There can be little doubt that in terms of understanding the fracture dynamics of stone, and putting that understanding into practice to make stone artifacts conforming to a series of preconceived mental templates, Early Humans possessed equivalent abilities to the Modern Humans of Act 4. But, when we consider other features of Early Human technology, we see types of behaviour that are in dramatic contrast to those of Modern Humans. There are indeed four puzzles about Early Human technology:

Puzzle 1. Why did Early Humans ignore bone, antler and ivory as raw materials? Although there is evidence that Early Humans used pieces of unworked bone, such as for hammers when making handaxes, there are no carved artifacts made from bone, antler or ivory. A few pieces have scratches on the surfaces, or even chips removed from their edges – although it is often difficult to distinguish these from carnivore gnawing. But there is nothing remotely requiring the type of technical skill that is so readily apparent from stone tools. If Early Humans had been working materials such as ivory and bone, we would surely have some of the results in the enormous collections of bones which are found intermingled with the stone artifacts made by Neanderthals from sites such as Combe Grenal in France and Tabūn in the Near East. Both of these have long sequences of occupation horizons with many thousands of stone tools and animal bones. Consequently we cannot invoke poor preservation to explain the absence of carved bone artifacts. Nor can we explain it by invoking anatomical constraints in terms of Early Humans' lack of manual dexterity. Even though the anatomy of the Neanderthal hand differed slightly from that of *H. sapiens sapiens*,[13] Neanderthals seem to display equivalent sophistication to Modern Humans in their manipulation of stone artifacts during manufacture. Moreover, Early Humans made simple wooden artifacts, such as the sharpened sticks from Clacton in Britain and Lehringen in Germany, and a 'polished plank' from Gesher Benot in Israel, which required similar motor movements to working bone. And finally we cannot explain the absence of bone, antler and ivory artifacts by suggesting that they would have been of little value to Early Humans. These raw materials have physical properties, such as an ability to sustain impacts without fracturing, which give them advantages over stone when making projectiles for hunting large ungulates,[14] an activity which we will see was a central element of Early Human lifestyles. So why did they ignore such raw materials?

Puzzle 2. Why did Early Humans not make tools designed for specific purposes? Microscopic analysis of the edges of stone tools has shown that the stone artifacts of Early Humans were typically used for a wide range of tasks. Moreover there appears to be no relationship between the form of a tool and its likely function.[15] Handaxes, or simple flakes, appear to have been used as general-purpose tools, such as for woodworking, chopping plant material, cutting animal hides and removing meat. The generalized nature of Early Human tools is particularly noticeable for spear points. These show hardly any variability in size and shape across the Old World, although many different types of animals were hunted. As we will see in Chapter 9, Modern Humans of the Upper Palaeolithic – 40,000–10,000 years ago – made an immense diversity of spear and projectile points indicating that specific types of weapons were made to hunt specific types of game.[16] Early Humans do not appear to have done this. In fact nor did the earliest Modern Humans in the first scene of Act 4.

Puzzle 3. Why did Early Humans not make multi-component tools? There is nothing to suggest that *H. erectus* hafted any stone artifacts. Neanderthals appear to have been the first to do this with the stone points they made using the Levallois method. Those points found in the caves of the Near East have breakage and wear patterns consistent with hafting and their use as spear points.[17] Hafting involves making a shaft, ensuring the end is the appropriate size and shape, acquiring the binding and resin and then using these to achieve a secure attachment. It is a time-consuming business, but transforms the effectiveness of hunting weapons. From the evidence of the fracture patterns of the Levallois points from the Near East, it is clear that Early Humans had mastered the technique. The odd thing, however, is that these hafted tools remained so few in number and with so few components. If one stone flake can be attached, why not create artifacts with multiple components which, in view of their dominance among later hunter-gatherers, appear to have been considerably more efficient? So if Early Humans had mastered the art of combining different types of raw materials to make composite artifacts, why did they stop at making such simple tools? The most complex tool that Neanderthals made is unlikely to have had more than two or three parts.

Puzzle 4. Why did Early Human stone tools show such limited degrees of variation across time and space? Perhaps the most startling feature of the stone technology of Early Humans is its limited degree of variability. In Chapter 2 I quoted the archaeologist Glynn Isaac who remarked on the 'shuffling of the same essential ingredients' of Early Human technology for more than a million years of 'minor, directionless change'. Other prominent archaeologists have also stressed this puzzling aspect of Early Human technology. For instance, Lewis Binford has written how we have collections of handaxes 'from many different environments in Africa, western Europe, the Near East and India, and, except for possible minor variations that can be understood in terms of the types of raw materials available for those artifacts' production and distribution ... no patterned differentiations convincingly covary with grossly different environments.'[18] Large-scale statistical analyses of handaxe shape have supported such views.[19] Similarly with regard to the period after 200,000 years ago, Richard Klein, one of the authorities on the behaviour of archaic *H. sapiens* in South Africa, has described how their toolkits have little to distinguish them from those of the Neanderthals living in the Near East and Europe.[20] Why was there no degree of variability in technology to match that of environment? Why was there such limited innovation?

One possible solution to these puzzles is simply that Early Humans had no need for tools made from organic materials other than wood, or with specialized functions, or of many component parts. But this solution can easily be seen to be inadequate: when we consider the interaction between Early Humans and their natural environment, we see that many Early Humans appear to have been under considerable adaptive stress that could have been alleviated by such tools. So before finding the solution to these puzzles we must consider the nature of this interaction with the environment, and in so doing examine a second cognitive domain of the Early Human mind: natural history intelligence.

Natural history intelligence: expanding minds, expanding territories

Natural history intelligence is an amalgam of at least three sub-domains of thought: that about animals, that about plants and that about the geography of the landscape, such as the distribution of water sources and caves. As a whole it is about understanding the geography of the landscape, the rhythms of the seasons, and the habits of potential game. It is about using current observations of the natural world to predict the future: the meaning of cloud formations, of animal footprints, of the arrival and departure of birds in the spring and autumn.

Were Early Humans natural historians *par excellence* like modern hunter-gatherers? In the previous chapter we arrived at a rather equivocal situation for the earliest members of the *Homo* lineage. We concluded that their success as hunters, gatherers and scavengers on the savannah of East Africa implied an ability to use natural history clues, such as footprints, and the ability to develop hypotheses about resource distribution. These abilities are likely to have gone far beyond those of the 6-million-year-old common ancestor we considered in Chapter 5. But we nevertheless characterized these abilities as a small cluster of micro-domains, too limited in number and scope to deserve the title of a natural history intelligence.

The most obvious indication that we should now be prepared to use this title for a component of the Early Human mind is the colonization of landscapes outside Africa. Recall from Chapter 2 that *H. erectus* or his descendants had begun living in Southeast Asia and perhaps China by 1.8 million years ago, western Asia by 1.0 m.y.a., and Europe perhaps by 0.78 m.y.a. and certainly by 0.5 m.y.a.

While these new environments varied greatly from one another, they were all substantially more seasonal than the low latitudes of Africa. If the earliest *Homo* had mastered low-latitude savannah environments, Early Humans had the capacity to learn about a much wider range of new environments, most notably those of the high latitudes with their very different landscapes, resources and climates. The increased technical intelligence discussed above, and the developments in social organization and language that we will consider below, may well have facilitated the exploitation of new environments. But ultimately the Early Humans would have needed to understand the habits of new types of game, the distribution of new plants and a new set of environmental clues. Consequently the presence of Early Humans from Pontnewydd Cave, North Wales, in the far northwest corner of the Old World to the Cape of South Africa implies a sophisticated natural history intelligence.

Yet Early Humans remained absent from several regions of the Old World, and made no entry into Australasia or the Americas. Clive Gamble, one of the foremost authorities on Early Human behaviour, has recently reviewed the evidence for global colonization and concluded that Early Humans were unable to cope with very dry and very cold environments.[21] These appear to have been too challenging, even if Early

Humans had a well-developed natural history intelligence and were able to make artifacts such as handaxes.

The manner in which Early Humans exploited these diverse environments, particularly in the first scene of Act 3, remains unclear. We only rarely find the animal bones which derived from Early Human hunting and scavenging activity, and those we have are often very poorly preserved.[22] But the evidence we do have suggests that Early Humans had been eclectic and flexible foragers, using a mixture of plant gathering, scavenging and hunting. In the second scene of Act 3 and the first scene of Act 4, the period between 200,000 and *c.* 60,000 years ago, the interaction between Early Humans and the natural world becomes a little clearer. So let us now explore the natural history intelligence of Early Humans by considering one specific actor in one specific part of the Old World: the Neanderthals of western Europe.

THE NEANDERTHALS: SURVIVING AGAINST THE ODDS

If the stone tools of the Neanderthals are impressive, then so too is the fact that these Early Humans lived successfully in the particularly challenging glaciated landscapes of Europe. The demands of living in such high latitudes, predominantly open tundra, cannot be underestimated.

The faunal remains from caves and open sites indicate very diverse animal communities. Among the herbivores were mammoth and woolly rhino, bison, deer and horse, reindeer, ibex and chamois. The carnivore element included species that today are only found in very different environments, such as cave bear, hyena, lion and wolf.[23] In general the animal communities appear to have been substantially more diverse than any in the modern world.

With this diversity of game, it might initially appear that Neanderthals were living in a Garden of Eden; but far from it. Acquiring the necessities of life – food, shelter, warmth – would have been immensely challenging. The animal and plant resources may have been diverse, but they are not likely to have been abundant. Each animal would have been linked into a complex foodweb resulting in frequent and unpredictable fluctuations in their numbers. And with the frequent environmental changes, whether these were from an advance or a retreat of the ice sheets, or even a few years of relative warmth or cold, the composition and links of these foodwebs would have been constantly changing. Even within a single year, the availability of plants and game would have shown dramatic variations over the seasons, with a marked deterioration during the winter months.[24]

The problems that Neanderthals faced in such environments were further exacerbated by their technology, or rather their lack of it. As I have discussed, Neanderthals appear to have mastered very complex sequences of stone tool production. Yet in spite of this technical proficiency, the range of tools appears remarkably narrow, and to have made a limited contribution to coping with the glaciated landscapes.

It is important here to appreciate the type of technology that modern hunter-gatherers such as the Inuit (Eskimo) use to survive in glaciated landscapes. These modern hunter-gatherers are as reliant upon a highly complex technology as they are upon their detailed knowledge of the natural world and an extensive series of social alliances between groups.[25] They have tools with multiple components and various complex facilities, including those for storing foodstuffs to cope with seasonal shortages.[26] To make their tools they use a wide array of raw materials, notably bone and ivory. Many of their tools are 'dedicated' to very specific tasks (see Box p. 127). As I noted above, there is no evidence that Neanderthals, or indeed any Early Humans, had such technologies. This reliance of Modern Humans on a complex and diverse technology to exploit glaciated landscapes makes the technologically-simple Neanderthal achievement particularly impressive – an achievement that lasted over 200,000 years.

That life was never easy for the Neanderthals is demonstrated by the fact that they died so young: 70–80 per cent of individuals were dead by the age of 40. Not only were Neanderthals living on the edge of the Old World, they were quite literally living on the edge of life itself. A very high proportion of Neanderthals suffered from stress fractures, and degenerative diseases. In fact they show a very similar pattern of physical injuries to rodeo riders today.[27] It would indeed be difficult to think of any group of people more in need of a wide variety of tools, or ones dedicated to specific tasks.

So how did they survive? As the environmental conditions would not have favoured substantial plant gathering, Neanderthals must have been reliant upon exploiting game, particularly during the harsh winter months. The collections of animal bones from Neanderthal occupations in the caves of western Europe typically represent many different species, but are dominated by large herbivores such as red deer, reindeer, horse and bison. These bones have been subject to intense debate concerning whether they reflect opportunistic scavenging by Neanderthals or well-planned game hunting.[28]

The most important bone collections are those from the cave site of Combe Grenal in southwest France. These have been studied by Phillip Chase who looked at the types of bones present, examining whether they would once have provided large quantities of meat or just tit-bit morsels from scavenged carcasses. He also examined the location of cutmarks

Tool complexity of Inuit hunter-gatherers

The most complex tool Early Humans appear to have made was a short thrusting spear created from a stone point hafted on to a wooden shaft. In contrast modern Inuit hunter-gatherers routinely make and use tools with many components, and which are 'dedicated' to killing specific types of animals in specific circumstances. The anthropologist Wendell Oswalt has made a study of Inuit technology and shown that tools for killing terrestrial mammals, such as caribou, similar to the reindeer hunted by the Neanderthals, typically have several components and are made from several raw materials such as stone points, antler foreshafts and wooden shafts. It is likely that the bone artifacts from the earliest Upper Palaeolithic sites after 40,000 years ago came from tools of equivalent complexity. The most complex tools used by the Inuit were for marine hunting, such as this harpoon for sealing employed by the Angmagsalik hunters of Greenland. This was carried on the side of a kayak and launched when a seal came into sight. Wendell Oswalt (973, 137–8) describes its component parts:

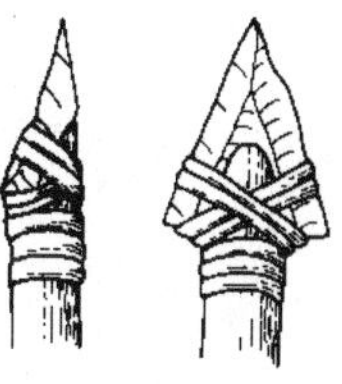

Reconstruction of a hafted Levallois point as made by Neanderthals.

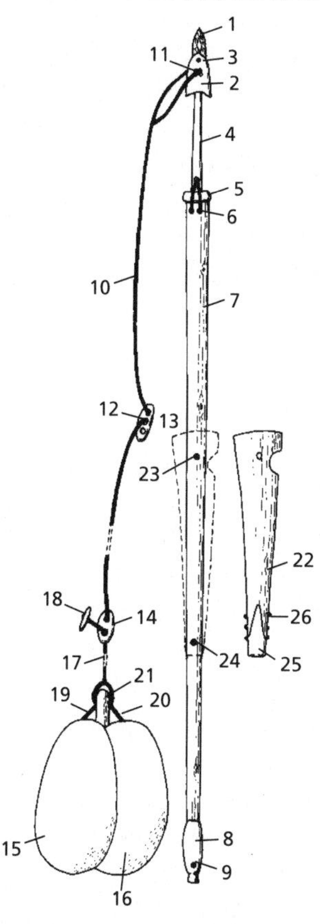

The stone point (1) was attached to the toggle head of bone (2) with a peg (3), and the distal end of the ivory foreshaft (4) fitted into a hole at the base of the harpoon head. The proximal end of the foreshaft fitted into a hole in the top of the bone socketpiece (5) and was held in place by thongs (6) which passed through a hole in the foreshaft and through two holes in the wooden shaft (7). At the base of the shaft was a bone counterweight (8) held with pegs (9). The harpoon line (10) was attached to the harpoon head through two holes (11), and it extended through two holes in a bone clasp (12). A third hole in the clasp was fitted over a bone peg (13) wedged into the shaft. The line continued on to another bone clasp (14) to which the end was tied. The floats (15, 16) were held by a single line (17) which ended in a toggle bar (18) where it was attached to a line leading from the harpoon head. The double floats consisted of two blown-up sealskins which were bound together at the middle, presumably with a thong, and had thongs which closed the opening at the head end of each (19, 20). A section of wood (21) which served to join the floats at the front was forked at the ventral surface in order to fit over a strap across the rear decking of the kayak.... The harpoon was launched with a throwing-board (22) and was readied for throwing by fitting the two bone pegs (23, 24) in the shaft through matching holes in the throwing-board. The throwing-board consisted of a strip of wood with a bone inset at the distal end (25) held in place with a series of bone pegs (26).

from stone tools on the bones, which can indicate how the animals were butchered and thus how they were acquired. Chase concluded that the Neanderthals at Combe Grenal were proficient hunters of reindeer and red deer. The method by which bovids and horse were exploited is more equivocal and is likely to have been a mix of hunting and scavenging.[29] Other cave sites, such as Grotta di Sant'Agostino in western Italy, have also yielded conclusive evidence that Neanderthals were hunters, in that case of red and fallow deer.[30] This hunting activity is likely to have been undertaken with short thrusting spears, requiring that the hunters got close to their prey, perhaps by stranding the animals in marshes or rivers.[31]

Neanderthals also scavenged animals which had either been killed by other predators, or died natural deaths, as demonstrated at the site of Guattari in western Italy.[32] Clive Gamble has stressed the likely importance of scavenging during the winter months when game would have been scarce and Neanderthals may have been dependent upon locating and then thawing frozen carcasses, a food niche not open to other predators.[33] Indeed, it is most likely that hunting and scavenging were alternative tactics open to Neanderthals which they chose to employ in the appropriate circumstances.

We have seen, therefore, that Neanderthals survived in Europe by employing a mixture of scavenging and hunting. The Early Humans in the Levant (Neanderthals) and those in South Africa (archaic *H. Sapiens*) employed a similar mix of subsistence tactics, adapted to their particular resource characteristics.[34] How could Early Humans have achieved such effective patterns of subsistence, particularly in the harsh glaciated landscapes of Europe, in view of their limited technological repertoire?

There appear to be three answers. The first is that they lived in large groups which mitigated the dangers of a failure in the food supply for any single individual or subgroup of foragers. We will consider the evidence for this below. A second reason is that they worked very hard. The Neanderthal short lifespan partly reflects physically demanding lives.[35] Their lower limbs were particularly robust in character, which, together with other postcranial anatomical features and a high frequency of stress fractures, indicates that Neanderthals were habitually engaged in prolonged periods of locomotion involving strength and endurance.[36] Their large nasal apertures and projecting noses are likely to have been partly to get rid of excess body heat during prolonged bouts of activity.

But simply having lots of friends and working hard would not have been enough. The third, and most important, answer to their technologically-challenged survival must be within their minds. The circumstantial evidence is conclusive: Neanderthals (and other Early Humans) must have possessed a sophisticated understanding of their environment and the animals within it; they had an advanced natural history intelligence.

Natural history intelligence would have been essential for building mental maps of their environment – maps at a vastly greater geographical scale than those used by chimpanzees that we considered in Chapter 5. One of the critical features of these mental maps would have been the location of rockshelters and caves. These were needed for shelter and warmth. Neanderthal clothing is likely to have been rather unsophisticated, as they lacked the technology to make sewn garments – bone needles are first found at 18,000 years ago, well into Act 4.[37] The evidence for Neanderthal occupation in caves is often marked by extensive layers of ash and evidence of burning. These have traditionally been interpreted as 'home bases', but a novel idea is that they may have principally served as 'defrosting chambers' for carcasses.[38] Whatever the role of caves, Neanderthals' mental maps of the location of caves and rockshelters, and an ability to infer the presence of resident carnivores, would have been essential for survival.

A natural history intelligence would also have been essential for hunting. Neanderthals would have needed to get close to game for an effective use of their short thrusting spears. For this they had to understand animal behaviour and how to entice prey into disadvantaged situations: planning is essential to effective hunting, and knowledge of animal behaviour is essential to effective planning. Neanderthals could only have been successful at hunting large game if they had mastered the use of visual clues such as hoofprints and faeces, and possessed an intimate knowledge of the habits of their game. Successful scavenging behaviour would also have relied on a natural history intelligence, perhaps even more so than for the earliest *Homo* on the African savannah. The prediction of carcass location, rather than random searching, would have been a necessity. This would require not only a knowledge of animal behaviour, including the hunting patterns of predators whose prey might be scavenged, but also of the physical processes that lead to the movement, burial and exposure of carcasses.

In summary, a well-developed natural history intelligence appears to have been essential for Early Human lifestyles as inferred from the archaeological record. And surely it must have been a natural history intelligence as sophisticated as that of modern hunter-gatherers, who have the advantage of highly complex, multi-component tools. Indeed, without the use of complex tools, Early Humans are likely to have relied even more heavily on a natural history intelligence than do Modern Humans. They literally must have thought their way through the hazards of living by hunting and gathering in glaciated landscapes.

Yet even this well-developed natural history intelligence may have been inadequate when the environments in northern Europe became very harsh during the height of one of the later ice ages of the Pleistocene period. At those times Neanderthals employed a further strategy for survival: they left. Similarly Neanderthals seem to have been unable to cope with the thickly forested woodland of northwest Europe at 125,000 years ago, a period of climatic warmth squeezed in between two periods of cold tundra environments and expanded ice sheets.[39] We should also note that while Early Humans were effective big-game hunters, they do not appear to have systematically exploited small game, birds and fish. Even their big-game hunting appears to have been restricted to the killing of individuals or at least small groups of animals. It is only with behaviourally modern hunter-gatherers beginning in Act 4 that we find systematic mass slaughters. So as with their manufacture of tools, in some ways Early Humans appear to be very modern, and in others they seem to be very distant human ancestors.

Solving the puzzle of Early Human technology

Having established that Neanderthals – as our representatives of Early Humans – possessed both a technical intelligence, as manifest in their stone tools, and a natural history intelligence, as manifest in their hunting activities and indeed their mere survival in ice age Europe, we must return to our four puzzles about Early Human technology. As will become apparent, there is I think a simple solution to these enigmas: a barrier between the technical and natural history intelligences within the Early Human mind – a barrier like that of a thick wall dividing two chapels in a medieval cathedral. Let us consider each of the puzzles in turn.

The first was the absence of artifacts made from bone, antler or ivory. This can only be explained by recognizing that Early Humans could not think of using such materials for tools: these materials were once parts of animals and animals were thought about in the domain of natural history intelligence. The conceptual leap required to think about parts of animals using cognitive processes which had evolved in the domain of inert, physical objects appears to have been too great for Early Humans.

Do the few examples of minimally scratched and chipped bone by Early Humans indicate that this cognitive barrier was occasionally overcome? Perhaps they do, for the fact that they were chipped suggests that they may have been thought of as stone. For instance, Paola Villa has described a piece of elephant bone from the site of Castel di Guido in Italy, at least 130,000 years old, which has a series of scars from where it had been struck as if it were a nodule of stone. She interprets the piece as an attempt to make a handaxe out of bone.[40] Alternatively the scratching and chipping of bone may simply reflect the use of general intelligence – which could never achieve artifacts of any complexity, or develop working methods appropriate to these raw materials. Indeed, general intelligence is likely to have supplied the cognitive processes for the working of wood as a raw material.

A cognitive barrier preventing the integration of knowledge about animal behaviour and toolmaking also appears to explain the second puzzle, the absence of artifacts dedicated to specific activities. As we saw above, Early Humans relied on general-purpose tools – they did not design specific tools for specific tasks. To do so would have required an integration of technical and natural history intelligence. For instance, if one wishes to design a projectile to kill one type of animal, say a red deer, in a particular situation then one must think about the animal's anatomy, pattern of movement and hide thickness, while also thinking about the raw material and how to work it. We have seen that Early Humans could think in complex ways about these things, but they do not seem to have been able to think about them in this manner at the same time. When activity at the domain interface of toolmaking and hunting was required, this was undertaken by general intelligence and resulted in behavioural simplicity.

This also explains the third puzzle: the absence of tools with multiple components. Among modern hunter-gatherers these are principally produced with specific types of prey in mind. The most complex tools, for example, are found among groups such as the Inuit and are used for hunting marine mammals (see above).[41] Each of the components is designed for solving a specific problem concerned with locating, killing and retrieving an animal. If animals and tools cannot be thought about in such an integrated fashion, it seems unlikely that tools with more than a few components would ever be produced.

This same cognitive constraint might be invoked to explain the fourth puzzling feature about Early Human technology: its remarkable conservatism across time and space. There can be little doubt that the behaviour of Early Humans varied across the inhabited part of the Old World as they encountered different types of resources, competed with different type of carnivores and coped with different climatic regimes. They had an advanced natural history intelligence which enabled them to adapt to new resources. If the chimpanzees of Gombe and the Tai forest can have such different feeding patterns as we saw in Chapter 5, we should expect no less of Early Humans. Yet, when viewed at this scale, technology shows minimal variation. The making of stone tools simply does not appear to be fully integrated with subsistence behaviour and the reason must be that thought about stone tools was inaccessible to thought about natural history. As archaeologists we are left with a million years of technical monotony that *mask* a million years of socially and economically flexible behaviour.

This is not to argue that there was no relationship between the types of environments exploited by Early Humans and the types of tools they made. Different environments provided different types of raw materials. If only small nodules were available, or the stone was of poor quality, Early Humans were restricted in the types of stone artifacts they could make. Moreover, access to raw material sources was influenced by the manner in which people moved around the landscape, and the extent of vegetation and snow cover. When access appears to have been restricted, such as in France when snow cover was particularly thick or in west-central Italy when wide-ranging scavenging behaviour resulted in infrequent visits to raw material sources, we see Early Humans using their raw materials more conservatively. For instance, we see repeated re-sharpening of artifacts, or the adoption of knapping methods which could remove a relatively large number of flakes from a single nodule of stone.[42] But this variability in technology is no more than a *passive reflection* of past environments and the manner in which they were exploited, requiring only general intelligence to make simple cost/benefit decisions about raw material use.[43]

Now let us consider social intelligence.

Social intelligence: expanding minds, expanding social networks

The social intelligence of Early Humans is both the easiest and the most difficult of our cognitive domains to assess. The easy part is that we can simply assert that *H. erectus*, Neanderthals and other Early Humans are likely to have possessed a complex social intelligence given its existence in non-human primates and the earliest *Homo*, as we have seen in Chapters 5 and 6. If chimpanzees have a theory of mind and engage in cunning Machiavellian social tactics, there can be little doubt that Early Humans were at least as socially intelligent. We can indeed find substantial evidence for the existence of a domain of social intelligence – perhaps one as complex as that of Modern Humans – within the Early Human mind. This evidence comes not from the tools and animal bones they left behind, but from their anatomy and from the environments within which they lived.

The most significant piece of evidence is the size of the Early Human brain, and the implications this has for the average size of social groups – which, as I discussed in the previous chapter, is a proxy measure for the degree of social intelligence. Recall how the biological anthropologist

Robin Dunbar demonstrated a strong correlation between brain size and the average group size for living non-human primates.[44] Using estimates for the brain size of Early Humans, and extrapolating from this relationship, Leslie Aiello and Robin Dunbar predict that *H. erectus* would have lived in groups with a mean size of 111, archaic *H. sapiens* in groups of 131, and Neanderthals in groups of 144, not significantly different from the group size for Modern Humans of about 150.[45] These are not predictions for the day-to-day groups within which Early Humans lived, but for the number of individuals about whom any one person had social knowledge. There are many problems with this study which make me cautious about the specific figures. Aiello and Dunbar, for example, ignore the complex technical and foraging behaviour of Early Humans, which must have used some brain-processing power and contributed to brain expansion. Yet Dunbar provides some supporting evidence for these predictions in terms of the group sizes of Modern Humans in recently documented hunter-gatherer societies.[46] In view of such inferences we have good reason to expect that Early Humans, especially those after 200,000 years ago, were as socially intelligent as Modern Humans.

Living in large groups – though probably not as large as Dunbar suggests – would appear to make ecological sense for Early Humans. In many regions of the world they are likely to have been at risk from carnivores, a danger alleviated, as we saw in the last chapter, by group living. Even so, we know of several cases in which Early Humans seem to have fallen victim to carnivores.[47] The character of the food supply would also have encouraged the formation of large groups. Food is likely to have come predominantly in 'large packages' in the shape of animal carcasses, either hunted or scavenged. This would have been especially true in the glaciated tundra-like environments of Europe. One 'large package' could have fed many mouths, thus encouraging Early Humans to live within large groups.[48] Moreover the chances of finding and killing an animal on one's own or in a small group would have been minimal.[49]

While in most circumstances the appropriate social strategy would have been to live in large social groups, in some environments Early Humans would have found it more advantageous to live in relatively small groups. There are many disincentives to group living, such as competition for resources and aggressive encounters between group members, the frequency of which are likely to have increased with the size of the group.[50] It is most likely that when Early Humans in Europe were living in relatively wooded environments, such as during warmer interludes between the advances of the ice sheets, they would have formed much smaller groups. Thick vegetation provides a means to evade and escape potential predators, and plant resources are more evenly distributed and provide food in smaller packages than animal carcasses. Consequently we should expect Early Humans to have constantly altered their group size in accordance with environmental conditions. This would require an adjustment of social relationships between individuals. The capacity for such social flexibility is at the heart of social intelligence.

Early Human skeletal remains may provide one further glimpse of complex social relations. Neanderthals clearly took care of their sick and elderly – those who could only make a limited contribution, if any, to the welfare of the group. A classic example of this is the Neanderthal from Shanidar Cave in Iraq who appears to have lived for several years in spite of having suffered head injuries and a crushing of the right side of his body, possibly from a cave rock fall, and blindness in his left eye. It is unlikely that he could have moved very far at all and yet he lived for several years with these severe injuries, no doubt being cared for by other members of his social group.[51]

Social intelligence: the contradictory evidence from archaeology

The anatomical and environmental evidence I have so far considered supports the idea that Early Humans frequently lived in large groups and had an advanced level of social intelligence. Yet as soon as we turn to the archaeological evidence we find some more puzzles. If we accept – as we must – that the brain size of Early Humans implies a high degree of social intelligence, resulting in Machiavellian social tactics adopted by individuals often living in large groups, then four more aspects of the archaeological record are very odd indeed:

Puzzle 5. Why do the settlements of Early Humans imply universally small groups? Archaeologists attempt to make inferences concerning past group size and social organization from the spatial extent of archaeological sites and the distribution of artifacts and features within the sites.[52] This is not an easy task when dealing with the sites of Act 3: poor preservation and the limited extent of many excavations make it very difficult to assess the original area of an occupation. Nevertheless, the leading authorities on the archaeological record of Early Humans have all agreed that such data indicate that they were living in very small groups as compared with Modern Humans. For example, Lewis Binford describes groups of Neanderthals as 'uniformly small',[53] while Paul Mellars suggests that 'communities ... were generally small ... and largely lacking in any clear social structure or definition of individual social or economic roles'.[54] Randall White has described Neanderthal social organization as 'internally un- or weakly differentiated'.[55] Similarly Olga Soffer, the leading authority on the archaeology of the Central Russian Plain, argues that Neanderthals lived in 'small sized groups' and that there was an 'absence of social differentiation'.[56] As is evident, there is a dramatic contrast between these views about group size among Early Humans gained from the archaeological record, and those of the biological anthropologists such as Robin Dunbar gained by looking at Early Human brain size.

Puzzle 6. Why do distributions of artifacts on sites suggest limited social interaction? It is not only the size of Early Human occupation sites that is very different from those of Modern Humans. They also show very different distributions of artifacts and bone fragments. Rather than being found in patterned arrangements, such as around hearths or huts, artifacts and bones are found in seemingly randomly distributed piles of knapping and butchery debris.[57] It is as if each individual or small group were operating with no desire to observe and interact with other group members – quite the opposite of what is expected from high social intelligence. Indeed, Clive Gamble interprets the lack of spatial structure as reflecting an episodic behavioural pattern – a 15-minute culture.[58] But an essential feature of the advanced social intelligence implied by Early Human brain size is a long time depth to social relationships.

Puzzle 7. Why is there an absence of items of personal decoration? A characteristic feature of all Modern Humans, whether they are prehistoric hunter-gatherers or 20th-century business people, is that they use material culture to transmit social information. As I have noted already, this is an essential part of our complex social behaviour – it is unimaginable how sufficient social information could be passed between people living in large social groups without the help of material culture. Yet we have no evidence that Early Humans were doing this: no beads, pendants or necklaces, or paintings on cave walls. There are a few pieces of bone that are claimed to have been pierced by Neanderthals, but it is likely that the piercing was done by the canines of carnivores. And a few pieces of red ochre found in Early Human sites in South Africa may imply body painting.[59] Yet if they do, then the absence of any actual artifact for body decoration in more than 1.5 million years of prehistory becomes even more bizarre.

Puzzle 8. Why is there no evidence for ritualized burial among Early Humans? This is a puzzle because while there is clear evidence that Neanderthals were burying some individuals in pits, there is no evidence of graveside ritual accompanying such acts, nor of the placing of artifacts within the pits/graves along with the dead, as is characteristic of Modern Humans. Isolated burials of Neanderthals have been found in several caves, such as Teshik Tash, La Ferrassie and Kebara. It was once believed that a 'flower burial' had occurred in Shanidar Cave, high pollen frequencies in the soil seeming to indicate that the body of a deceased Neanderthal had been covered with a wreath of flowers. But this pollen is now believed to have been blown into the cave, or even brought in on workmen's boots.[60]

The significance of these Neanderthal burials remains unclear. They may simply represent an hygienic disposal of corpses so as not to attract scavenging carnivores. Alternatively the act of burial, and the resulting existence of a grave within an occupied cave, may reflect the importance of ancestors in on-going social relations. And it is this which makes the absence of any ritual and grave-goods so puzzling.

Solving the enigma of social intelligence

In summary, the evidence for the social intelligence of Early Humans leaves us with a paradox. The brain size of Early Humans and the environmental evidence appear conclusively to show an advanced level of social intelligence; the archaeology shows the exact converse – it implies that Early Humans lived in small groups apparently with little or no social structure. A resolution to this paradox is quite simple: archaeologists are making a major mistake in their interpretation of the data. They are assuming that the Early Human mind was just like the modern mind – that there was a cognitive fluidity between social, technical and natural history intelligences. We can only make sense of the archaeological record, and solve the puzzles we have found, by recognizing that these were isolated from each other. Just as there was a cognitive barrier between technical and natural history intelligence, so too were there barriers between these and social intelligence.

This provides a ready solution to why the character of Early Human sites appears to suggest a simple social behaviour, while brain size implies a sophisticated social intelligence. If technical intelligence was not integrated with social intelligence, there is no reason to expect that social activity and technical activity took place at the same place in the landscape. We know that it did for Modern Humans, epitomized by the manufacture or repair of tools while people were seated around a hearth and engaged in conversation. Because of this intimacy between technical and social activities, the artifact distributions of Modern Humans may well reflect the size of social groups and their social structure. But the artifact scatters left by Early Humans have no such implications. They show no more than where tools were made and used: the complex social behaviour and large social aggregations of Early Humans took place elsewhere in the landscape, perhaps no more than a few metres away – and are archaeologically invisible to us today (see Figures 13 and 14). Similarly, the butchering and sharing of food is as much a social as an economic activity among modern hunter-gatherers today, and consequently the distribution of butchery remains provides information about social behaviour. But if social and natural history intelligence were not linked, the animal bones from the sites of Early Humans will provide no information about past social behaviour.

Food sharing is nonetheless likely to have been prevalent in Early Human society because food sources would often have come in large packages – animal carcasses. Moreover, the relatively large brain size of Early Humans, particularly Neanderthals and archaic *H. sapiens*, suggests that nursing mothers would have required a high-quality diet to meet the feeding demands of the infant. The provisioning of females with meat appears a very likely scenario – it is difficult to imagine how a nine-months pregnant Neanderthal, or one with a young infant, could have survived without some provisioning of food by either other females or perhaps her sexual partner. Yet the articulation of food within a social relationship could have been handled by general intelligence.

As we will see in the next chapter, the provisioning of pregnant or nursing mothers with food may be the behavioural context for a selective pressure for an integration of social and natural history intelligence. But this comes later in human evolution. The provisioning and sharing of food among Early Humans appear to have been handled by general intelligence in view of the absence of spatial patterning in artifact and bone distributions on sites. I therefore suspect that the formalized rules for food sharing found in many modern hunter-gatherer groups were lacking among Early Humans. These often involve very strict rules which define which part of a carcass should go to which relative.[61] The carcass is itself interpreted as a map of social relations within the group – the distribution of meat provides a means to reinforce those social relationships. Food sharing among Early Humans was probably a rather simpler affair. Similarly I doubt if feasting took place of the kind seen in the Potlatches of the Northwest Coast Indians of America or the pig feasts among New Guinea Highlanders. In these ritualized feasts, food is used as a medium for social interaction rather than to appease hunger.

General intelligence is also likely to have been adequate to build the links between interaction with the social and natural environments required for coordinating group hunting. It seems improbable that either hunting or scavenging could have been successful without some degree

13, 14 *Modern and Early Human spatial behaviour compared. In the upper figure we see how Early Humans undertook activities such as social interaction, making stone tools and butchering carcasses in spatially discrete locations. Among Modern Humans of the Upper Palaeolithic, for whom the boundaries between different types of activities were much more blurred, each activity was undertaken within the same spatial area. The result for archaeologists are two very different types of archaeological record.*

of social cooperation, either in these activities themselves, or in terms of sharing information. But we must be careful not to exaggerate the extent of social cooperation required here: we can see cooperative hunting and information-sharing in many different types of animals, including lions and chimpanzees, as I described in Chapter 5.

The most persuasive piece of evidence for a cognitive barrier between social and technical intelligence is the absence of any artifacts used for body decoration, such as beads and pendants. The manufacture of these objects involves a type of thinking equivalent to that for making specialized hunting weapons, as I described above. One needs to keep in mind the social purposes of these artifacts – such as to communicate social status or group affiliation – while performing the technical acts themselves. If social and technical intelligence are closed to each other, the opportunities for making such artifacts is lost. Due to this cognitive barrier, any body decoration by Early Humans would need to have been undertaken by using general intelligence alone. This in its turn would have meant that such body decoration sent only very simple social messages, or perhaps merely drew attention to parts of the body. Indeed it is this sort of behaviour that probably explains the pieces of red ochre found at an extremely small number of Early Human archaeological sites.

In summary, the relationship between the technical and social intelligence of Early Humans appears to mirror that between technical and natural history intelligence. Just as tools were not made for specific forms of interaction with the natural world, nor were they made for specific patterns of social interaction. Just as the limited variation in technology provides a very poor reflection of the diversity of hunting and gathering behaviour, so too does the limited variability in settlement size provide a poor reflection of social variability and complexity.

A further similarity, however, is that past patterns of social behaviour may be *passively reflected* in Early Human technology. For instance, it is apparent that those European Early Humans before 100,000 years ago who were living in small social groups in wooded environments did not make complex artifacts such as handaxes and lacked strong toolmaking traditions. A good example of these are the Early Humans who made the tools classified as the Clactonian industry in southern England, dating to before 250,000 years ago and lacking any handaxes. In contrast those who probably lived on tundra-like environments in large groups had very strong traditions, such as in the shapes of handaxes which seem to have been copied from generation to generation. Those who lived in southern England both before and after those who made Clactonian tools used the same raw materials to produce very fine handaxes. The Clactonian toolmakers simply had fewer other toolmakers to observe, and did so less frequently. Consequently there was little stimulus to enable the intuitive physics within their minds to mature into a technical intelligence, as happened when Early Humans lived in large social groups on open tundras.[62]

We must now turn to language.

A social language

There are three features of the fossil crania of Early Humans which can be used to draw inferences concerning linguistic capacities: brain size, neural structure as inferred from the shape of the brain, and the character of the vocal tract.

With regard to brain size, the most important point is also the simplest: the brain sizes of the majority of *H. erectus*, and all archaic *H. sapiens* and Neanderthals, fall within the range of that of Modern Humans. Indeed the mean brain size of Neanderthals is rather larger than that of anatomically Modern Humans.[63] Now recall that in the previous chapter I introduced the ideas of Robin Dunbar that related brain size to group size, and group size to the amount of social grooming required to maintain social cohesion. He suggested that the maximum percentage of time a primate can devote to grooming without interfering with other activities (such as foraging) is about 30 per cent. By the time of archaic *H. sapiens*, *c.* 250,000 years ago, the predicted grooming time had risen to almost 40 per cent. Leslie Aiello and Robin Dunbar have argued that to alleviate this, the use of language with a significant social content would have been essential.[64]

On such evidence Aiello and Dunbar concluded that the basis of the language capacity appeared early in the evolution of the genus *Homo*, at least by 250,000 years ago. A critical feature of their argument is that the subject matter of the earliest language was social interaction; it was in effect a 'social language'. There was thus a co-evolution of increasing group size/social intelligence and a capacity for language. Evidence for this may indeed be found in the structure of the brain. The prefrontal cortex is not only the area of the brain responsible for many aspects of language, but also that where the ability to reflect on one's own and other people's mental states, which I have argued is a central fact of social intelligence, are found.[65] The general-purpose character of language as we know it today, and its symbolic features evolved, Aiello and Dunbar argued, at a later date – although how much later is left unclear in their work. On a far more intuitive basis, it is indeed difficult to imagine how an Early Human could have had a brain size equivalent to that of ourselves today, but lacked a linguistic capacity.

Further support for a linguistic capacity can be found by looking at the shape of the Early Human brain, as reconstructed from the bumps on the insides of their crania. We saw in Chapter 6 that *H. habilis* appears to have had a well-developed Broca's area, which is conventionally associated with speech. Broca's area also appears well formed on the *H. erectus* cranium of KNM-WT 15000,[66] a particularly well-preserved 12-year-old boy dating to 1.6 million years ago and found at East Turkana in Kenya. With regard to more recent Early Humans, palaeoneurologists have argued that the brain shape is practically identical to that of Modern Humans. Ralph Holloway, in particular, has argued that both Broca's and Wernicke's areas can be identified on Neanderthal brain casts and that they show no difference from their appearance on the brains of Modern Humans.[67]

A third source of evidence for a linguistic capacity is the nature of the vocal tract of Early Humans. There has been a long history of efforts at reconstructing the vocal tract, particularly for the Neanderthals.[68] Since it is principally composed of soft tissue – the larynx and pharynx – one must rely on consistent relationships between the organization of soft tissue and those parts of the cranium that can survive in an archaeological context. The most recent reconstructions imply that the Neanderthal vocal tract would not have differed significantly from that of Modern Humans: Neanderthals would have had essentially modern powers of vocalization and speech.

This has received support from the discovery of a hyoid bone, surviving in a Neanderthal skeleton buried in Kebara Cave in Israel and dated to 63,000 years ago.[69] The hyoid is a bone that can provide detailed information about the structure of the vocal tract. Its movement affects the position and movement of the larynx to which it is attached. That found at Kebara, lying in an undisturbed position with the mandible and cervical vertebra, is virtually identical to that of a Modern Human with regard to its shape, muscular attachments and apparent positioning. This implies that the morphology of the vocal tract of this Neanderthal was not significantly different from that of Modern Humans. If the cognitive capacity for language was present, there appears no reason why the full range of human sounds could not have been produced.

Of course the 'if' in the last statement is a rather big 'if'. On purely logical grounds, however, it would be a little odd if Neanderthals had the vocal structures but not the cognitive capacity for speech. The structure of the human vocal tract differs markedly from other animals in having a single rather than a two-tube system. As a result adult humans carry with them the possibility of fatal choking by food becoming lodged in the pharynx. The selective disadvantage of this is over-ridden by the selective benefits of the wide range of vocalizations – and thus articulate speech – that can be made with this particular structure.[70] It would be evolutionarily bizarre indeed if Neanderthals were exposed to the possibility of choking, without being able to complain about their food.

All the fossil evidence I have briefly reviewed is ambiguous and open to different interpretations. Yet during the last few years the argument that both archaic *H. sapiens* and Neanderthals had the brain capacity, neural structure and vocal apparatus for an advanced form of vocalization, that should be called language, is compelling.

If humans began using language to talk about their social relationships, did they also start to use it to talk about toolmaking, plant gathering and hunting before the end of Act 3? In other words, had language become transformed to have the general-purpose functions which are familiar to us today – a means to communicate information irrespective of the behavioural domain? It might indeed be argued that it would have been too difficult to have acquired, say, the Levallois method for flake production without verbal instruction. Or that the cooperation implied by hunting and scavenging could not have been achieved without talking about game movements. Countering such arguments, one might point out that *H. erectus*, the earliest of Early Humans, appears to have been a very proficient toolmaker and forager even though his/her linguistic capacity is likely to have been rather limited. Moreover, if language was used within the technical and natural history domains of behaviour as frequently and effectively as in the social domain, we would expect a greater integration between behaviour in these domains. Communication by spoken language is, after all, the means by which Dan Sperber proposed that the metarepresentational module would evolve, as was described in Chapter 3.

Consequently, I am in sympathy with the suggestion from Robin Dunbar that language first evolved to handle social information, and I believe that it remained exclusively a 'social language' for the whole of Act 3.

The Early Human mind

We have now looked at all four specialized cognitive domains of the Early Human mind, and the nature of the connections between these domains. The Early Human mind we have found is illustrated in Figure 15. This is what may be described as a generic Early Human mind, because I have constructed it by freely drawing on evidence from different types of Early Humans, although the quality of the evidence has led me to focus on the Neanderthal mind which this diagram fits most closely. The archaeological data have been too sparse or ambiguous to deal with each

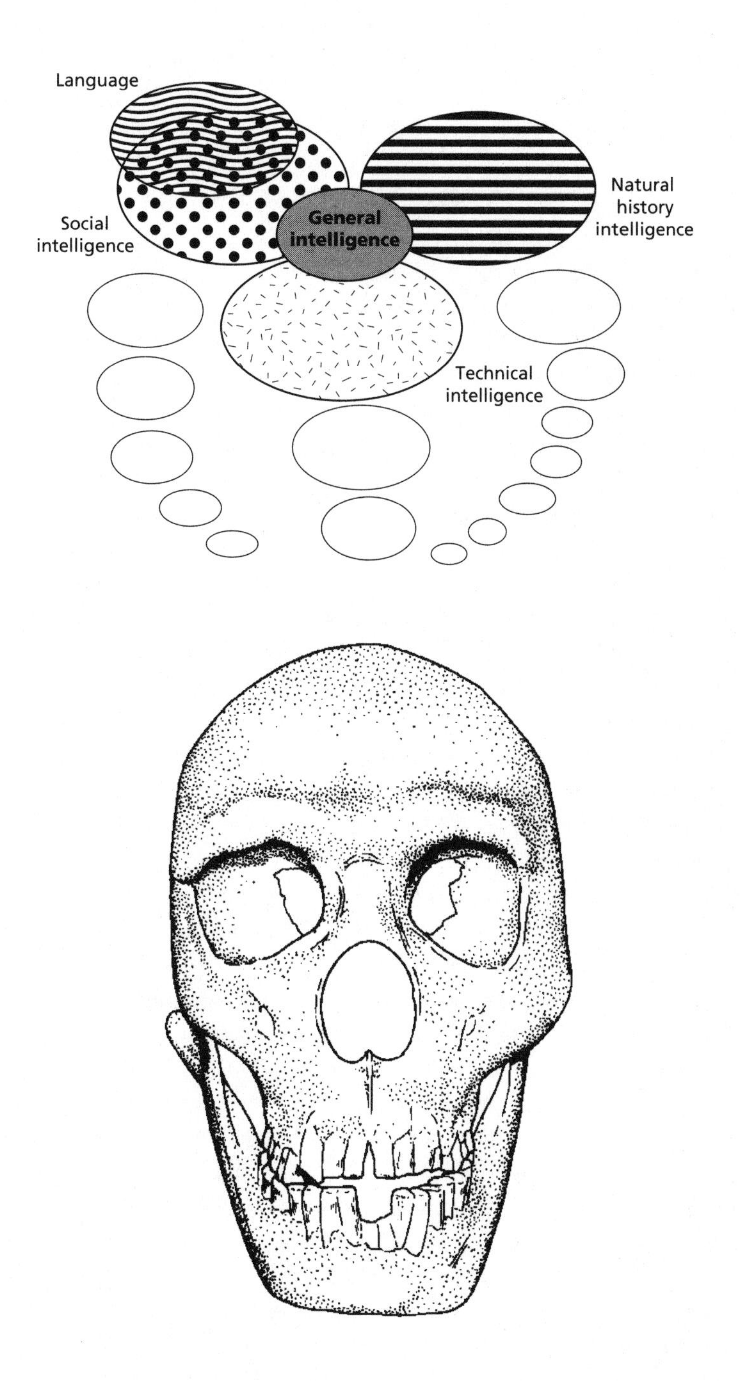

***15** The Neanderthal mind. The drawing depicts the Neanderthal skull known as Shanidar I, a man who had suffered substantial injuries and was probably blind in his left eye. This model for the mind is also applicable to archaic* H. sapiens *after* c. *200,000 years ago.*

type of Early Human in turn and to identify the cognitive variability that no doubt existed between them. There are nevertheless some pointers as to what those differences may have been.

There was a very significant enlargement of brain size during the course of Act 3, from the value of 750–1250 cc for earliest *H. erectus* to 1200–1750 cc for Neanderthals. This was not a gradual increase: brain size appears to have been at a plateau between 1.8 million and 500,000 years ago, and then to have rapidly increased in association with the appearance of archaic *H. sapiens* and then the Neanderthals. In view of the arguments I have made and reviewed in this chapter, we should expect such an expansion to reflect a growth in both social intelligence and linguistic capacity. Indeed my hunch is that this expansion in brain size reflects the change to a form of language with an extensive lexicon and a complex series of grammatical rules, although remaining a 'social language'.

Thus while *H. erectus*'s vocalizing capacity may have been considerably enhanced over that of any living primate, it remained too simple to be called language. As Leslie Aiello has noted, the anatomy of the most complete *H. erectus* skeleton, KNM-WT 15000, suggests that the muscle control essential for the fine regulation of respiration in human speech was absent.[71] We should perhaps think of *H. erectus* as having been able to produce a wide range of sounds in the context of social interaction which related to feelings of contentment, anger or desire and which mediated social relationships. But compared with Modern Humans, the range of sounds and their meanings would have been limited, with none of the grammatical rules that allow an infinite number of utterances to be made from the finite number of sounds available. Perhaps very elaborate versions of cat purring is an appropriate analogy.

A case can also be made that the Levallois method, appearing roughly at the end of the period of brain expansion (250,000 years ago), is more technically and cognitively demanding than bifacial knapping used to make handaxes. And consequently the appearance of the new method may reflect an increase in technical intelligence. I rather doubt this, however, and suspect that it is a reflection of more intense social interactions which enabled greater amounts of technical knowledge to be passively and unintentionally transmitted. Similarly, it is clear that the high latitudes of Europe were occupied rather later than those of Asia, perhaps as much as a million years after *H. erectus* had first moved out of Africa. This late entry into Europe is surprising and one may wonder whether there was some feature of Pleistocene environments in Europe which were beyond the cognitive capacities of the earliest Early Humans to cope with – perhaps the degree of seasonal variation. A case can be

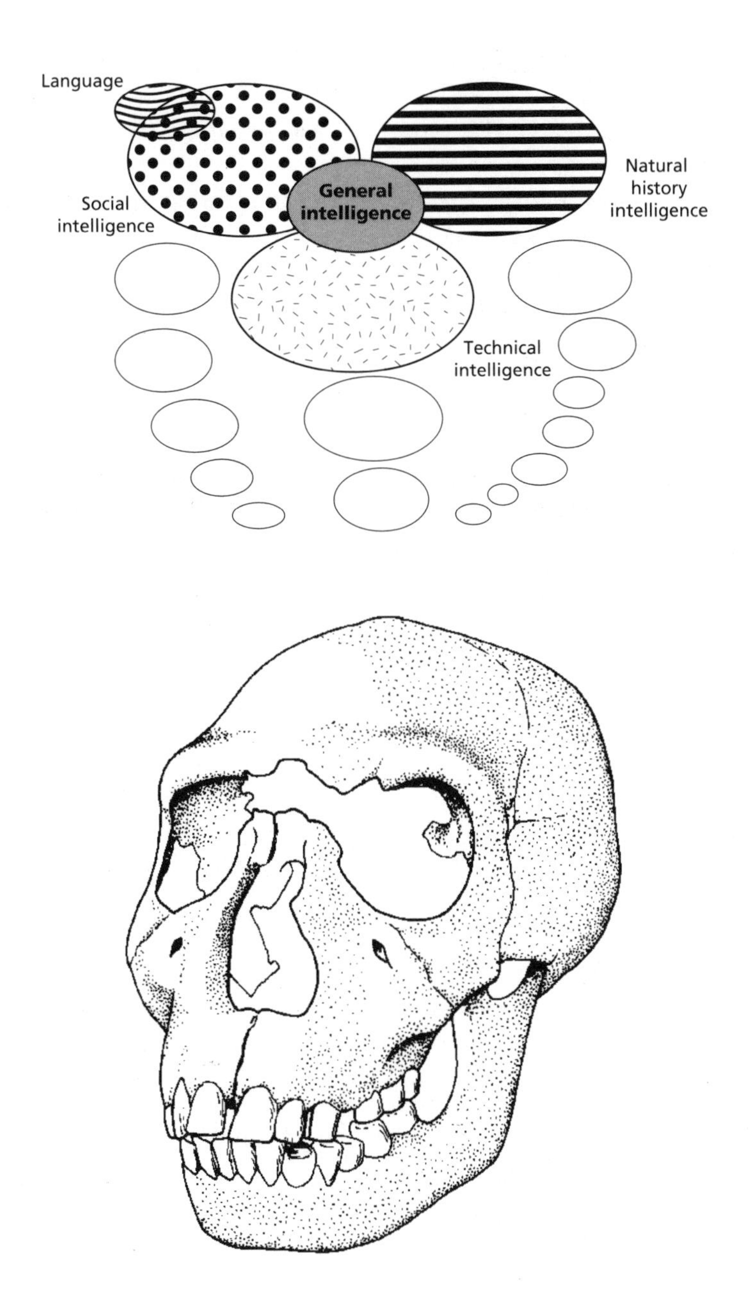

***16** The mind of* H. erectus. *The drawing depicts the skull denoted by KNM-WT 15000, otherwise known as the Nariokotome boy. This was discovered in Kenya in 1984 and dates to around 1.6 million years ago.*

made therefore, although a weak one, for some increase in natural history intelligence during the course of Act 3. But the fundamental difference between the mind of *H. erectus* and *H. neanderthalensis* lies in the extent of linguistic intelligence (see Figure 16).

In conclusion, we can safely state that in spite of linguistic differences, all Early Humans shared the same basic type of mind: a Swiss-army-knife mentality. They had multiple intelligences, each dedicated to a specific domain of behaviour, with very little interaction between them. We can indeed think of the Early Human mind as a cathedral with several isolated chapels within which unique services of thought were undertaken, each barely audible elsewhere in the cathedral. We have reached Phase 2 in the architectural history proposed in Chapter 4. Early Humans seem to have been so much like us in some respects, because they had these specialized cognitive domains; but they seem so different because they lacked a vital ingredient of the modern mind: cognitive fluidity.

8 Trying to think like a Neanderthal

Before we look at what happened to the mind at the start of Act 4 with the appearance of the first Modern Humans, we must ask an important question: what would it have been like to have had the mind of an Early Human such as a Neanderthal?

To address this question we must return to the issue of consciousness. In this book I am following Nicholas Humphrey's argument that consciousness evolved as a cognitive trick to allow an individual to predict the social behaviour of other members of his or her group. Humphrey suggested that it evolved to enable us to use our minds as models for those of other people. At some stage in our evolutionary past we became able to interrogate our own thoughts and feelings, asking ourselves how we would behave in some imagined situation. In other words, consciousness evolved as part of social intelligence.

This has significant consequences for how the stream of subjective states of awareness and sentience which would have been experienced by Neanderthals contrasts with that inside our minds today. In the Neanderthal mind social intelligence was isolated from that concerning toolmaking and interaction with the natural world. With regard to our cathedral of the mind analogy, consciousness was firmly trapped within the thick and heavy chapel walls of social intelligence – it could not be 'heard' in the rest of the cathedral except in a heavily muffled form. As a consequence, we must conclude that Neanderthals had no conscious awareness of the cognitive processes they used in the domains of technical and natural history intelligence.

Now before pursuing this proposal I must enter the caveat that consciousness is a multifaceted phenomenon that no one really understands. Whether Daniel Dennett did indeed explain consciousness in his 1991 book *Consciousness Explained* is a moot point. Some suggest that he merely explained it away. There appear to be at least two different types of consciousness.[1] There is the type that we refer to as 'sensation', such as our awareness of itches on our body, colour and sounds. Nicholas Humphrey calls this a 'lower order' of consciousness than that which relates to reasoning and reflection about one's own mental states. It is this higher order of 'reflexive consciousness' which I suspect was lacking from the Neanderthal mind in connection with toolmaking and interaction with the natural world, although it was present with regard to their thoughts about the social world.

I believe that Early Humans experienced the type of consciousness when making their stone tools that we experience when driving a car while engaged in conversation with a passenger. We finish the journey with no memory of the roundabouts, traffic lights and other hazards we negotiated and appear to have passed safely through these without thinking about driving at all. As Daniel Dennett has remarked, while this type of driving is often described as a classic case of 'unconscious perception and intelligent action', it is in fact a case of 'rolling consciousness with swift memory loss'.[2]

When Early Humans engaged in their toolmaking and foraging they may well have experienced this type of 'rolling consciousness'. It resulted from the heavy 'muffling' of consciousness when it is 'heard' from outside the chapel of social intelligence. In other words, when the mental modules that create consciousness were applied in domains different from those they had evolved to serve, they could not work effectively. This left Neanderthals with a rolling, fleeting, ephemeral consciousness about their own knowledge and thoughts concerning toolmaking and foraging. There was no introspection.

This argument is perhaps easier to accept when dealing with the 6-million-year-old common ancestor and the 2-million-year-old *H. habilis* than it is with the Neanderthals. Neither of the former had particularly advanced thought processes for toolmaking and natural history and consequently consciousness about these does not appear as a major issue. But with the Neanderthals, or indeed any type of Early Human, it is a struggle to imagine what it could possibly have been like to be such a skilled toolmaker or natural historian, but not be aware of the depth of one's knowledge or the cognitive processes that one uses. We find it extremely difficult to imagine making a tool without at the same time thinking in detail what the tool will be used for and then utilizing those thoughts in designing the artifact. Similarly when choosing what clothes (i.e. material artifacts) to wear in the morning, we automatically think about the social contexts within which we will find ourselves that day.

We have to struggle so hard to imagine what it may have been like to have had a Swiss-army-knife-type mentality that the plausibility of such a mentality is called into question. How could a Swiss-army-knife-like mind possibly have existed? But in moments of such doubt we can remind ourselves that we have many complex cognitive processes going on inside our minds about which we have no awareness. Indeed, we are probably aware of only a tiny fraction of what goes on inside our minds. For example, we have no conscious awareness of those processes we use to comprehend and generate linguistic utterances. We are not aware of the great number of linguistic rules we use in our everyday speech, or of the many thousands of words that we know the meaning of. Generating grammatically correct, meaningful utterances is perhaps the most complex thing we do – the number of cognitive processes we use is likely to be far in excess of those needed by Neanderthals to make their stone tools – and we do it with no conscious awareness of what is going on inside our minds.

Daniel Dennett has stressed the importance of other types of unconscious thought. To prove their existence he gives the example of knocking your coffee cup over your desk: 'In a flash, you jump up from the chair, narrowly avoiding the coffee that drips over the edge. You were not conscious of thinking that the desk top would not absorb the coffee, or that coffee, a liquid obeying the law of gravity, would spill over the edge, but such unconscious thoughts must have occurred – for had the cup contained table salt, or the desk been covered with a towel, you would not have leaped up'.[3]

A different example of unconscious thought is perhaps the most persuasive argument that Early Humans could have made their stone tools and gone foraging with limited, if any, conscious awareness of the thought processes and knowledge that they were using. Some unfortunate people suffer sudden loss of functions in their higher brain stem which results in 'petit mal' seizures. These involve a loss of conscious experience. Yet the sufferers are still able to continue with their activities, whether they be simply walking, or even driving cars or playing pianos. They continue with these goal-directed activities, which involve selective responses to environmental stimuli, with no conscious awareness of their thought processes. When acting in this way their behaviour takes on a rather mechanical nature – something to which we will return in a later chapter – but they nevertheless continue to perform their complex activities.[4]

I am not suggesting that the Early Human mind was equivalent to someone today suffering a petit mal seizure. I simply use this example as a further demonstration that the absence of conscious awareness about one's thought processes would not mean that those thought processes were not occurring and could not lead to complex forms of behaviour. If people can drive cars and play pianos without conscious awareness, then the possibility of Neanderthals making stone tools and foraging without conscious awareness becomes more plausible.

Plausible, perhaps, but still practically impossible to imagine. Yet this difficulty in imagining what it may have been like to have thought as a Neanderthal may simply reflect a constraint on our own type of thinking put in place by evolution. At the heart of Nicholas Humphrey's ideas about the evolution of consciousness is the notion that it enables us to use our own minds as a model for the minds of other people. Thinking that other people think in the same way as us appears to have been of immense evolutionary value. But the corollary of this is that we find it inherently difficult to think that another human (of whatever species) thinks in a manner that is fundamentally different from our own.

We are perhaps not in quite as bad a position as was the philosopher Thomas Nagel when he famously asked, writing in 1974, 'what is it like to be a bat?'. We are, after all, much closer in evolutionary terms to Neanderthals than to bats. Nagel didn't want to know what it would be like for him to be a bat, but what it is like for a *bat* to be a bat. 'If I try to imagine this', he wrote, 'I am restricted to the resources of my own mind, and those resources are inadequate to the task. I cannot perform it either by imagining additions to my present experience, or by imagining segments gradually subtracted from it, or by imagining some combination of additions, subtractions, and modifications'.[5]

All we can ever achieve then is perhaps a fleeting experience of how a Neanderthal may once have thought as we for example concentrate on some task and block out the rest of the world from our minds. But this experience lasts no more than an instant. As with Nagel and his bats, we are unable to know what it was like for a *Neanderthal* to have been a Neanderthal. Evolution has guarded against this possibility and we are left struggling with the idea of a Swiss-army-knife mentality for Early Humans.

But to help us with this struggle we have the archaeological record, the empirical evidence, perhaps worth more than all the theorizing by philosophers and psychologists. It is indeed the often bizarre nature of this record that is the most compelling argument for a fundamentally different type of human mind. So much of Early Human behaviour looks modern, epitomized by the technical skill apparent from stone tools. But so much else looks positively weird: the monotony of industrial traditions, the absence of tools made from bone and ivory, the absence of art. All of this is epitomized by the 'type' artifact of Early Humans, the handaxe. As the archaeologist Thomas Wynn has recently stated, 'it would be difficult to over-emphasize just how strange the handaxe is when compared to the products of modern culture'.[6] It seems to me that the only way to explain the archaeological record of Early Humans is by invoking a fundamentally different type of mind from that which Modern Humans possess.

9 The big bang of human culture: the origins of art and religion

THERE WAS a cultural explosion in the fourth and final act of our past. This happened in the time period 60,000–30,000 years ago, which marks the blurred start of the second scene of Act 4. The start of the act itself is marked by the entry of the final, and sole surviving, actor, *H. sapiens sapiens* at 100,000 years ago. This new actor appears immediately to have adopted certain forms of behaviour never previously seen in the play. Most notable are the making of bone artifacts in southern Africa, and the placing of parts of animals into human burials in the Near East – the only two areas of the world where 100,000-year-old *H. sapiens sapiens* fossils are known. But other than these glimpses of something new, the props of *H. sapiens sapiens* in the first scene of Act 4 are almost identical to those of the Early Humans. I will therefore refer to these first *H. sapiens sapiens* as Early Modern Humans. The cultural explosion only occurs after they have been on the stage for at least 40,000 years. And consequently it is the start of Scene 2, and not the first appearance of *H. sapiens sapiens*, which archaeologists denote as one of the major turning points in prehistory, referring to it in an ungainly phrase as the 'Middle/Upper Palaeolithic transition'.

In this chapter I want to look at the behaviour of *H. sapiens sapiens* in the first two scenes of Act 4 – immediately before and after this transition – and ask how their minds were different from those of Early Humans. But I want to take the two scenes in reverse order, beginning with the dramatic cultural changes which happened after 60,000 years ago, notably the origin of art.

Now recall that by the start of Act 4 the cathedral of the modern mind is almost complete. The four chapels of technical, natural history, social and linguistic intelligence, the traces of which we saw when we looked at the modern mind in Chapter 3, are in place. But the walls of these chapels are solid; the chapels are closed to each other, trapping within them the thoughts and knowledge of each specialized intelligence – except for the flows between the chapels of linguistic and social intelligence. To constitute the modern mind, the thoughts and knowledge located in all these chapels must be allowed to flow freely around the cathedral – or perhaps within one 'superchapel' – harmonizing with each other to create ways of thought that could never have existed within one chapel alone.

Archaeologists have often described the Middle/Upper Palaeolithic transition as a cultural explosion. Recall from Chapter 2 that it is at, or soon after, this transition that Australia was colonized, that bone tools became widespread (after having made their very first appearance in Act 4 Scene 1), and wall paintings were created. Scene 2 of Act 4 is a frenzy of activity, with more innovation than in the previous 6 million years of human evolution. As the start of this scene is so often described as a cultural explosion, it seems obvious to ask whether this noise is an explosion at all; perhaps it is the sound of doors and windows being inserted into the chapel walls, or even the noise of a 'superchapel' being constructed. In other words, the start of the final phase of our architectural history of the mind.

It is quite easy to think of the Middle/Upper Palaeolithic transition as a cultural explosion, or a big bang – the origins of the universe of human culture. Indeed a 'big bang' is the shorthand description I will use in this chapter. Yet if we look a little more closely at the boundary between Scenes 1 and 2 we see that there is not so much a single big bang as a whole series of cultural sparks that occur at slightly different times in different parts of the world between 60,000 and 30,000 years ago. The colonization of Australia, for instance, seems to reflect a cultural spark which happened between 60,000 and 50,000 years ago, yet at this time all remained relatively quiet elsewhere in the world. In the Near East a cultural spark happened between 50,000 and 45,000 years ago when the Levallois technology was replaced by that of blade cores. The cultural spark in Europe seems not to have been until 40,000 years ago with the appearance of the first objects of art. Indeed, it is perhaps only after 30,000 years ago that we can be confident that the hectic pace of cultural change had begun in earnest throughout the globe. Some archaeologists go so far as to deny that there is such a thing as a major transition at all, and view the cultural changes as no more than the result of a long process of gradual change. They suggest that the new types of artifacts that appear in the archaeological record during Act 4 reflect better preservation and recovery rather than new forms of behaviour.[1] But I disagree.

As with the majority of archaeologists I believe something fundamental occurs at the Middle/Upper Palaeolithic transition, even if at slightly different times in different parts of the world. There have been several ideas previously put forward as to what this fundamental thing might be. These include notions about the 're-structuring of social relations',[2] the appearance of economic specialization,[3] a technological 'invention' similar to that which caused the transition to agriculture 30,000 years later,[4] and the origin of language.[5] I think that these are all

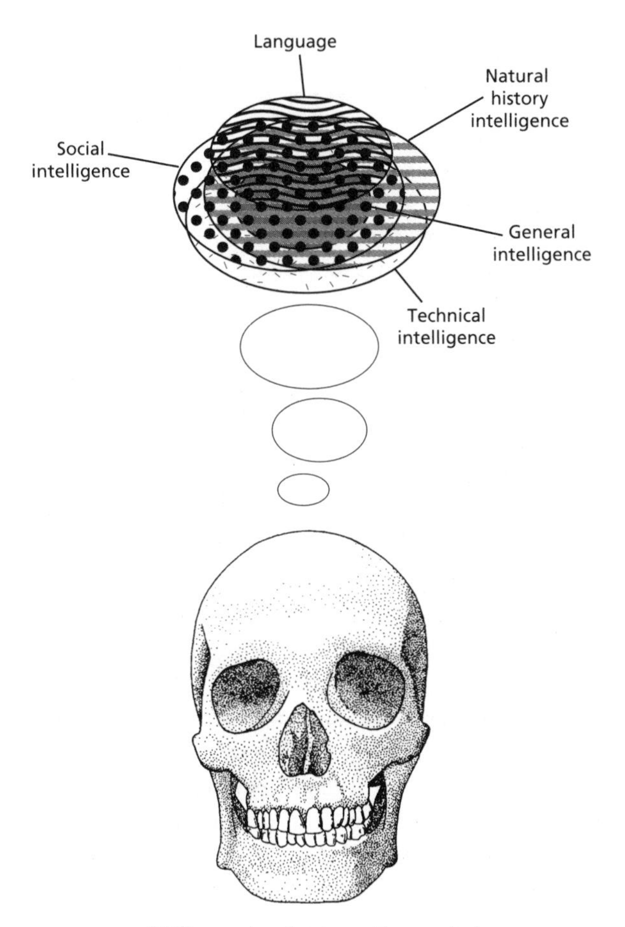

17 The modern hunter-gatherer mind.

wrong: either they are merely consequences rather than causes of the transition, or they fail to recognize the complexity of social and economic life of the Early Humans.

My explanation of the big bang of human culture is that this is when the final major re-design of the mind took place. It is when the doors and windows were inserted in the chapel walls, or perhaps when a new 'super-chapel' was constructed. The modern mind might thus be represented as in Figure 17. With these new design features the specialized intelligences of the Early Human mind no longer had to work in isolation. Indeed I believe that during the last two decades of research the explanation for the Middle/Upper Palaeolithic transition has been found – not by archaeologists but by the cognitive scientists whose work we examined in Chapter 3.

Recall how Jerry Fodor finds the 'passion for the analogical' to be a central feature of the distinctly non-modular central processes of the mind and how Howard Gardner believes that in the modern mind multiple intelligences function 'together smoothly, even seamlessly in order to execute complex human activities'. We saw how Paul Rozin concluded that the 'hall mark for the evolution of intelligence ... is that a capacity first appears in a narrow context and later becomes extended into other domains' and Dan Sperber had reached a similar idea with his notion of a metarepresentational module, the evolution of which would create no less than a 'cultural explosion'. Also recall the ideas of Annette Karmiloff-Smith regarding how the human mind 're-represents knowledge', so that 'knowledge thereby becomes applicable beyond the special-purpose goals for which it is normally used and representational links across different domains can be forged', which is so similar to the notion of 'mapping across knowledge systems' as proposed by Susan Carey and Elizabeth Spelke, and the ideas of Margaret Boden regarding how creativity arises from the 'transformation of conceptual spaces'.[6]

None of these cognitive scientists was writing about the Middle/Upper Palaeolithic transition. Nor were they necessarily writing about the same aspects of the modern mind: some were addressing child development while others were discussing cognitive evolution, or simply how we think as we go about our daily lives. But their ideas share a common theme: that in both development and evolution the human mind undergoes (or has undergone) a transformation from being constituted by a series of relatively independent cognitive domains to one in which ideas, ways of thinking and knowledge flow freely between such domains. Although they did not know it, Gardner, Rozin, Boden and the others were providing the answer to the Middle/Upper Palaeolithic transition.

At least I think they were. It is the purpose of this chapter and the next to evaluate this proposition. I will begin by asking whether such developments can explain the new types of behaviour we see early on in Act 4, when people continued to live by hunting and gathering during the period we call the Upper Palaeolithic. In the Epilogue I will take us a little bit closer to the present day and lifestyles that are familiar to us by considering the origin of agriculture.

We must start with the event of Act 4 that at last brings some colour to the play: the appearance of art.

What is art?

We cannot discuss the origin of art unless we agree what we are talking about. Art is another of those words pervading this book which defy easy definition, words like mind, language and intelligence. As with those words, the definition of art is culturally specific. Indeed many societies who create splendid rock paintings do not have a word for art in their language.[7] The communities of the Upper Palaeolithic are likely to have had a very different concept of art (if one at all) from that which is the most popular today: non-utilitarian objects to be placed on pedestals in galleries. Yet these prehistoric hunter-gatherers were producing artifacts which we regard as priceless today, and which are very readily placed on pedestals in our own galleries and museums. Let us for a moment consider the earliest pieces of art known to us, before generalizing about their essential qualities.

In the debris left from Act 3 a few pieces of scratched stone and bone have been found which some have claimed to be of symbolic significance, such as a bone from Bilzingsleben in Germany with incised parallel lines.[8] I doubt if there is any justification for such claims, and these objects should be excluded from our admittedly ill-defined category of art. The majority can be explained as by-products of other activities, such as cutting plant material on a bone support – but there may be some exceptions to which I will return below.

Membership of the elite group of artifacts that we call 'art' must go to those which are either representational or provide evidence for being part of a symbolic code, such as by the repetition of the same motifs. The earliest phase of the Upper Palaeolithic provides us with examples of both.

In terms of representational art we can do no better than start with the ivory statuette from Hohlenstein-Stadel in southern Germany, some 30,000–33,000 years old (see Figure 18). This is a figure of a man with a lion's head carved from the tusk of a mammoth, a remarkable combination of technical expertise and powerful imagery. It was found shattered in tiny pieces and meticulously restored to provide us with the earliest work of art known.[9] Also from southern Germany at this time we have a series of animal figures carved in ivory including felines and herbivores such as mammoth, horse and bison. Some of these have incised markings on their bodies.[10]

Contemporary with this representational art, we find images which appear to be part of a symbolic code being created in southwest France (see Figure 19). These are predominantly 'V'-shaped signs engraved on to limestone blocks in the caves of the Dordogne. Although they have been traditionally described as images of vulvas, archaeologists now discount the idea that they have any simple representational status. The critical feature is that the motifs which have the same form are repeatedly engraved.[11]

***18** The lion/man ivory statuette from Hohlenstein-Stadel, southern Germany, c. 30,000–33,000 years old. Height 28 cm.*

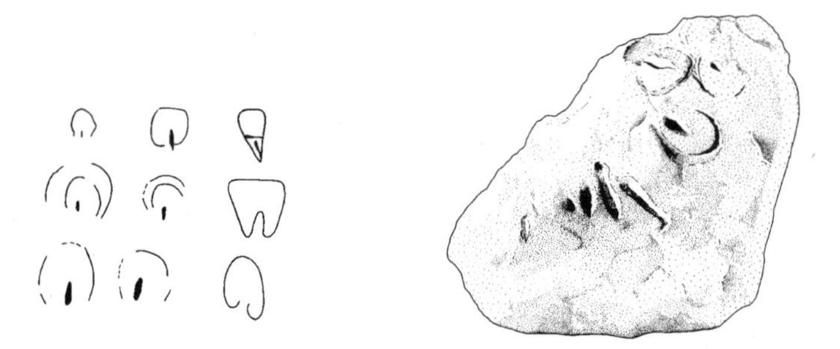

19 (Right) Engraved symbols on a small boulder, 60 cm wide, from Abri Cellier, Dordogne, France, c. 30,000–25,000 years old. Images such as these are repeated in other sites in southwest France during this period, including Abri Blanchard, Abri de Castanet and La Ferrassie, as illustrated on the left.

Along with these pieces of art, the period between 40,000 and 30,000 years ago saw the first production of items for personal decoration such as beads, pendants and perforated animal teeth. At the site of La Souquette in southwest France ivory beads were carved to mimic sea shells.[12] At the same time as, or soon after, these items were being produced the first caves in southwest Europe were being painted with images of animals, signs and anthropomorphic figures, a tradition which would culminate in the paintings of Lascaux at around 17,000 years ago.[13] Indeed some of the paintings in Chauvet Cave in the Ardèche region of France, a cave discovered as recently as 18 December 1994, have been dated as being 30,000 years old. The 300 or more paintings of animals in this cave – including rhinoceroses, lions, reindeer, horses and an owl – are quite remarkable. Many of them are highly naturalistic and demonstrate an impressive knowledge of animal anatomy and outstanding artistic skill. The cave is perhaps on a par with Lascaux, and certainly with Altamira in Spain, with regard to the spectacular nature of its art.[14] Although this is the very first art known to humankind, there is nothing primitive about it.

While the production of art was most prolific in Europe, it was a worldwide phenomenon by, or soon after, 30,000 years ago. In southern Africa the painted slabs from Apollo Cave are well dated to 27,500 years ago while wall engravings in Australia date back beyond 15,000 and perhaps to 40,000 years ago.[15] Art remains rare, or even absent in several regions of the world until 20,000 years ago. But that is just 20,000 years after its first appearance in Europe – an almost insignificant amount of time when set against the more than 1.5 million years that Early Humans lived without art.

The variability in the intensity with which art was produced can be attributed to variation in economic and social organization, which in turn can be largely attributed to environmental conditions. The archaeological record shows us that Stone Age art is not a product of comfortable circumstances – when people have time on their hands; it was most often created when people were living in conditions of severe stress. The florescence of Palaeolithic art in Europe occurred at a time when environmental conditions were extremely harsh around the height of the last ice age.[16] Yet there is unlikely to have been a human population living under more adaptive stress than the Neanderthals of western Europe. But they produced no art. They lacked the capacity to do so.

There can be little doubt that by 30,000 years ago this capacity was a universal attribute of the modern human mind. What does it entail? While the definition of a visual symbol is notoriously difficult, at least five properties are critical:

1. The form of the symbol may be arbitrary to its referent. This is one of the fundamental features of language, but also applies to visual symbols. For instance, the symbol '2' does not look like two of anything.[17]
2. A symbol is created with the intention of communication.[18]
3. There may be considerable space/time displacement between the symbol and its referent. So, for example, I might draw a picture about something that happened long in the past, or what I imagine may happen some time in the future.
4. The specific meaning of a symbol may vary between individuals and indeed cultures. This often depends upon their knowledge and experience. A Nazi swastika has a different meaning to a young child, than to a Jew whose family was lost in the Holocaust. The swastika is in fact an ancient symbol, found in cultures as far apart as Mexico and Tibet.
5. The same symbol may tolerate some degree of variability, either deliberately or unintentionally imposed. For instance, we are able to read different people's handwriting although the specific forms of the letters are variable.

These properties of visual symbols become particularly apparent when we consider the art created by recent hunter-gatherers, such as the Aboriginal communities of Australia. The last decade has seen a tremendous development in our understanding of this art.[19] We now know that even the simplest of images, such as a circle, can have many different referents. Among the Walpiri of the Central Australian Desert, for example, a circle can represent an almost unlimited number of referents: campsites, fires, mountains, waterholes, women's breasts, eggs, fruit and other items. The intended meaning of the circle in any one composition can only be identified by the associated motifs. Such simple geometric motifs may have a wider range of possible meanings than complex naturalistic images[20] (see Box p. 158).

Naturalistic images, perhaps of animals or ancestral beings, can also

Complex meanings in simple designs of hunter-gatherer art

The complex and multiple meanings that may be found in the simplest geometric designs found in Palaeolithic art can be illustrated with an example from the art of the Australian Aborigines. The social anthropologist Howard Morphy has described how many of their paintings have a basic geometric template underlying the design. Each part of the template may encode a series of meanings. For instance, consider the image below which has two 'loci', (a) and (b).

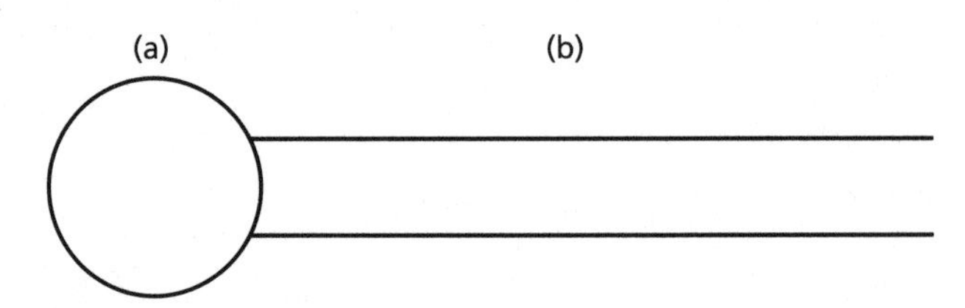

At locus (a), the following meanings are encoded: 'well', 'lake', 'vagina'. At locus (b) the meanings 'digging stick', 'river' and 'penis' are encoded. Consequently three different interpretations of this image would be a river flowing into a lake, a digging stick being used to dig a well, and a penis going into a vagina. All three of these are 'correct' interpretations, but each is appropriate in a different social context. Moreover, the interpretations may be connected within a single mythic sequence:

> A kangaroo ancestor was digging a well with a digging stick. When he finished, a female wallaby bent down to drink the fresh water, and the kangaroo seized his opportunity to have sexual intercourse with her. The semen flowed out of her body and into the waterhole. Today a river flows into the lake at that place and the kangaroo's penis was transformed into a digging stick which can be seen as a great log beside the lake.

If such simple geometric designs can 'encode' such complex meanings, and by doing so express the transformational aspects of Ancestral Beings, one can only wonder at the types of meanings encoded in the geometric designs from the Palaeolithic period.

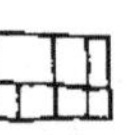

have complex and multiple meanings. An Aboriginal child, lacking in knowledge about the Dreamtime (the mythical past/present), may initially interpret images in a literal fashion. To a child, images of fish, for instance, are about fishing which is an economically important activity for many Aboriginal groups. Such literal interpretations can be described as the 'outside' meanings of the art – they are learned in the context of daily life and are in the public domain. As the child matures and acquires knowledge about the ancestral world, the same image will be interpreted in a more metaphorical sense, often relating to the actions of the Ancestral Beings. There may be various levels of these, each requiring additional knowledge about the ancestral past, which may be restricted to certain classes of individuals. Consequently these are described as 'inside' meanings. For example, the child may gradually learn how fish are a potent symbol of spiritual transformation of both birth and death. They are good to paint not just because they are good to eat, but also because they are good to think. The metaphorical meanings of fish images, concerning birth and death, do not replace the literal interpretation concerning the practice of fishing, they are complementary. As a result, many images have different meanings to different people depending on their access to knowledge about the ancestral past.[21]

Whatever meaning is attributed to an image, that image is most likely to be displaced in time and space from the inspiration for the image. The waterhole referred to by a circle may be far away, while the Ancestral Being has no clear location in either time or space.

We can find many of these features in the rock art tradition of other modern hunter-gatherers, such as the San of southern Africa.[22] Indeed, we cannot doubt that the images created in the Upper Palaeolithic also had complex symbolic and multiple meanings involving those five properties listed above. Archaeologists are more likely to have success at reconstructing the 'outside' meanings of this art, rather than the 'inside' meanings which require access to the lost mythological world of the prehistoric mind – a world to which I will return at the end of this chapter when I consider the origins of religious ideas.

Cognitive fluidity and the origins of art

Having considered some of the properties of visual symbols, let us consider what mental attributes are involved in creating and reading them. There are at least three:

1. The making of a visual image involves the planning and execution of a preconceived mental template.

2. Intentional communication with reference to some displaced event or object.

3. The attribution of meaning to a visual image not associated with its referent.

From what we established in the previous chapter – and as I will explain below – it is likely that Early Humans were competent in each of these cognitive processes. They are likely to have existed in as complex and as advanced a state as in the Modern Human mind. So why no art? The answer would appear to be that although they possessed these processes, they were found in different cognitive domains. They were inaccessible to each other and the origin of art only occurred following a marked increase in the connections between cognitive domains. So where in the Early Human mind were these processes located?

The making of marks on objects is something that happens unintentionally in the course of activities by many animals – marks such as hoof-prints, scratches on trees and gnawmarks on bones. Some non-human animals also create marks intentionally: chimpanzees have created striking paintings in laboratories, although these do not appear to have symbolic meanings and are not created in the wild.[23] I would interpret such 'artistic achievements' in the same manner as the 'linguistic' achievements of chimpanzees – as the product of a generalized learning capacity. The earliest members of the *Homo* lineage we encountered in Chapter 6 were making marks with stone tools on bones in the process of butchery. We also have the series of artifacts made by Early Humans which have incised lines on them, such as a fossil nummulite from Tata in Hungary, which appears to have a line intentionally engraved perpendicular to a natural crack to make a cross and is thought to be 100,000 years old, and the marked bone from Bilzingsleben[24] in Germany (see Figure 20). Although it has yet to be demonstrated, I am sympathetic to the idea that some of these lines may have been intentionally created, and I will return to how they should be interpreted shortly. Similarly, the few pieces of red ochre from Early Human sites in southern Africa – no more than a dozen from the period prior to 100,000 years ago[25] – may suggest that archaic *H. sapiens* were marking their bodies. But there is no reason to believe that this is equivalent to the symbolic behaviour involved in producing objects of art. What we need to find in the mind of Early Humans is a capacity to intentionally create marks or objects of a preconceived form.

This can indeed be found – in the domain of technical intelligence. We have seen that Early Humans were regularly imposing form on to their stone artifacts. Handaxes and Levallois flakes required the extraction of objects of a preconceived form from nodules of stone. In view of such technical intelligence, the failure to make three-dimensional objects of art cannot reflect difficulties in conceiving of objects 'within' a block of

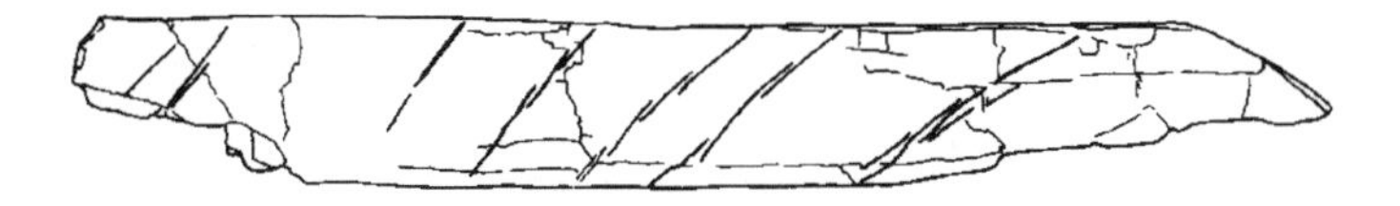

20 *Fragment of a rib of a large mammal from Bilzingsleben, Germany. On its surface there is a series of parallel lines, each engraved by the repeated application of a stone tool probably by a Neanderthal. Length 28.6 cm, width 3.6 cm.*

stone or ivory, or the mental planning and manual dexterity to 'extract' them. The cognitive processes located in the domain of technical intelligence used for making stone artifacts appear to have been sufficient to produce a figurine from an ivory tusk. But they were not used for such ends.

With regard to the second of the three critical cognitive capacities for art, intentional communication, this was established in the previous chapter as a critical feature of Early Human social intelligence. Indeed Early Humans were probably as dependent on intentional communication as are modern humans today. Among the last of the Early Humans this capacity became manifest in spoken language; in the earlier ones it was probably restricted to vocalizations too simple to be described as language, as well as gesture. In Chapter 5 we saw that both monkeys and apes also engage in intentional communication, suggesting that this capacity has had a long evolutionary history: there can be little doubt that not only Early Humans, but also the common ancestor and the earliest *Homo* were engaging in frequent, intentional communication.

The third element of a capacity for art is an ability to attribute meaning to inanimate objects or marks displaced from their referents.[26] Can this ability be found within one of the cognitive domains of Early Humans? It certainly can: the capacity to attribute meaning to the unintentionally made tracks and trails of potential prey is a critical component of natural history intelligence. As I have argued in previous chapters, the ability to draw inferences from marks such as footprints most likely reaches back to when earliest *Homo*, or indeed australopithecines, began hunting and scavenging on the African savannah. These inferences often include the type, age, sex, state of health and current behaviour of the animal which made them.

The unintentionally made marks left by animals share a number of properties with the intentionally made 'marks' or symbols of Modern Humans, such as paintings on rock faces or drawings in the sand.[27] They are inanimate. They are both spatially and temporally displaced from the event which created them and that which they signify. Footprints, just like symbols, must be placed into an appropriate category if correct meaning is to be attributed. For instance, the hoofprint of a deer will vary depending upon whether it is made in mud, snow or grass, just as the drawing of a symbol will vary according to rock surface and the individual style of the artist. The marks left by animals will often be non-representational. While the hoofprint of a deer may look like the base of the hoof, it does not look like the event that is inferred from it, such as the passing of a male stag. Many marks have no visual resemblance to the animal which created them, such as the parallel lines left by the wriggling of a snake. And finally, the meaning of marks will vary according to the knowledge of the person viewing the mark, in a similar way that the meaning of symbols vary. For example a child may identify a hoofprint as coming from a deer, whereas a mature and skilled hunter may be able to infer that the deer is a pregnant female which passed two hours ago.

These points of similarity suggest that the same cognitive processes which are used to attribute meaning to marks unintentionally made by animals would be equally effective at attributing meaning to marks intentionally created by humans. But we have no evidence that they were used for such purposes before the arrival of Modern Humans.

The three cognitive processes critical to making art – mental conception of an image, intentional communication and the attribution of meaning – were all present in the Early Human mind. They were found in the domains of technical, social and natural history intelligence respectively. But the creation and use of visual symbols requires that they function 'seamlessly and smoothly together' (to quote Gardner). This would require 'links across domains' (to quote Karmiloff-Smith). And the result would be a 'cultural explosion' (to quote Sperber).

We do see a cultural explosion beginning 40,000 years ago in Europe as the first works of art were produced and I would suggest that this can be explained by new connections between the domains of technical, social and natural history intelligence. The three previously isolated cognitive processes were now functioning together, creating the new cognitive process which we call visual symbolism, or simply art (see Box p. 163).

If I had to choose just one feature of the earliest art to support this argument it would be that the very first images are of such technical skill and emotive power. No analogy can be drawn between the origins of art in evolutionary time and the development of artistic skills by a child. The latter consists of a gradual change from scribbles to representational images, and then a gradual improvement in the quality of those images. For some young artists one can then see a gradual understanding of how to use line and colour to convey not just a record of what is seen but one's feelings for it. There is nothing gradual about the evolution of the capacity for art: the very first pieces that we find can be compared in quality

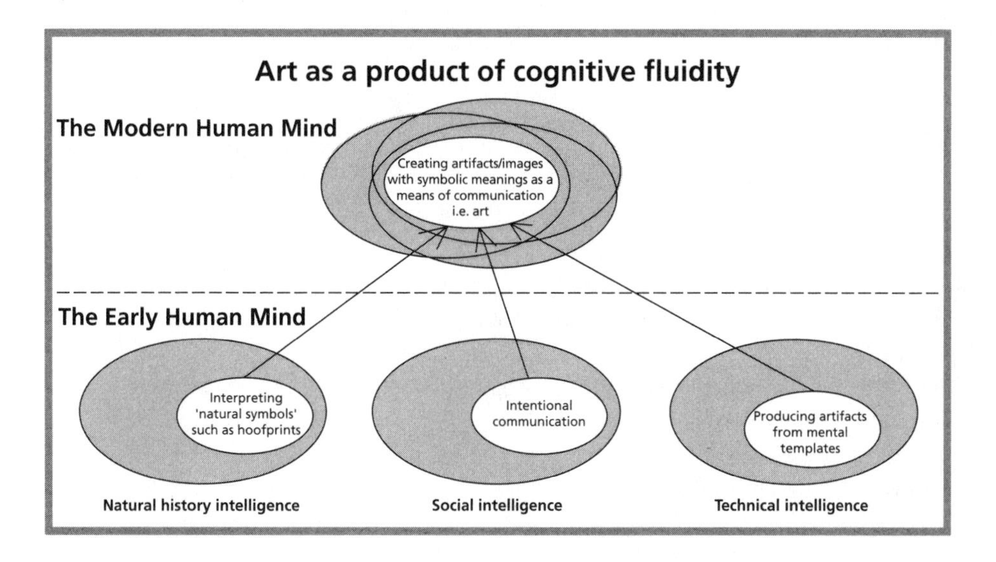

with those produced by the great artists of the Renaissance. This is not to argue that the ice age artists themselves did not go through a process of learning; we can indeed find many images which appear to be those drawn by children or apprentice artists.[28] But the abilities to impose form, to communicate and to infer meaning from images, must have already been present in the Early Human mind – although there was no art. All that was needed was a connection between these cognitive processes which had evolved for other tasks to create the wonderful paintings in Chauvet Cave.

But before we leave the origins of art we must return to those scratched pieces of bone and ivory made by Early Humans, such as from Bilzingsleben and Tata. If – and it is a big if – these lines were intentionally made, how can they be accounted for? I suggest that they reflect the maximum amount of symbolic communication that can be achieved by relying on general intelligence alone. Early Humans may have been able to associate marks with meanings by using their capacities for associative learning alone. But relying on this would have severely constrained the complexity of the marks and meanings. There is a similarity between the simplicity of the toolmaking capacities of chimpanzees as compared with those of Early Humans, and the simplicity of Early Human intentional markings as compared with those of Modern Humans. Chimpanzees rely on general intelligence for toolmaking, just as Early Humans relied on general intelligence for 'symbolic' communication. As a result, chimpanzees and Early Humans appear to 'underachieve' in these activities in light of their accomplishments in behavioural domains for which they have specialized intelligences.

Humans as animals, animals as humans: anthropomorphism and totemism

The new flow of knowledge and thought processes between cognitive domains of the modern mind can be readily seen not only in the existence of art, but also in its contents. Consider once again the image in Figure 18. This figure has a lion's head and human body. We cannot prove, but equally cannot doubt, that it represents a being in the mythology of the Upper Palaeolithic groups of southern Germany. Whether it is an image of an animal that has taken on certain human attributes – reflecting anthropomorphic thinking – or a human who is descended from a lion – reflecting totemic thought – we do not know. But, whichever of these is correct (and the answer is probably both), the ability to conceive of such a being requires a fluidity between social and natural history intelligences.

Images like this pervade not only the art of Upper Palaeolithic groups, but that of almost all hunter-gatherer societies, and indeed those living by agriculture, trade and industry.[29] We have many spectacular examples from prehistory. In the art of the Upper Palaeolithic they include the 'sorcerer' from Trois-Frères – a painted figure that has an upright posture, legs and hands that look human, but the back and ears of a herbivore, the antlers of a reindeer, the tail of a horse, and a phallus positioned like that of a feline (see Figure 21) – as well as a bird-headed man from Lascaux and a female figurine from Grimaldi Cave paired back to back with a carnivore.[30] Indeed one of the paintings in the newly discovered Chauvet Cave, some of which are dated to 30,000 years old, is a

21 The sorcerer from Trois-Frères, Ariège, France, as drawn by Henri Breuil. Height 75 cm.

figure with the head and torso of a bison and the legs of a human. Similarly the prehistoric hunter-gatherers who lived 7000 years ago in the forests of Europe after the ice had retreated made monumental carvings of fish/humans at the site of Lepenski Vir on the Danube.[31] As I noted in Chapter 3, among the modern hunter-gatherers described by anthropologists, animals are frequently attributed with human-type minds.

Anthropomorphic thinking is something that pervades our own everyday lives. We indulge in anthropomorphic thinking in our relations with pets by attributing to them feelings, purposes and intentions. This may indeed be reasonable with regard to dogs and cats, but with a moment's reflection it seems far-fetched with regard to pets such as goldfish. We seem unable to help anthropomorphizing animals – some claim that it is built into us by both nature and nurture – and while this gives us considerable pleasure, it is a problem that plagues the study of animal behaviour, for it is unlikely that animals really do have human-like minds.[32] Anthropomorphism is a seamless integration between social and natural history intelligence (see Box p. 166). The very first pieces of Palaeolithic art indicate that it stretches back to the cultural explosion of 40,000 years ago. But I doubt if it goes back any further.

Totemism is the other side of the human/animal coin. Rather than attributing animals with human characteristics, it involves embedding human individuals and groups within the natural world, epitomized by tracing descent from a non-human species. The study of totemism – and attempts to define it – formed the core of social anthropology as it developed during the 19th century. Between 1910 and 1950 major works on totemism were produced by the pioneers of social anthropology including Frazer, Durkheim, Pitt-Rivers, Radcliffe-Brown and Malinowski. Such works provided the foundations for Levi-Strauss' *The Savage Mind.* This in turn has been followed as from the 1970s by a renewed surge of interest in totemism.[33]

In the light of this long history of study, it is not surprising that totemism has been defined and interpreted in a variety of ways. Lévi-Strauss' position is perhaps the most widely known: animals are not just good to eat but also 'good to think'. He viewed totemism as the practice of humanity brooding on itself and its place in nature. To his mind, the 'study of natural species, provided nonliterate and prescientific groups with a ready-to-hand means of conceptualizing relations between human groups'.[34]

Whether or not this is a correct interpretation, we may simply note three features of totemism that are particularly relevant for an understanding of the evolution of the modern mind. First, when broadly defined, totemism is universal among human groups who live by a

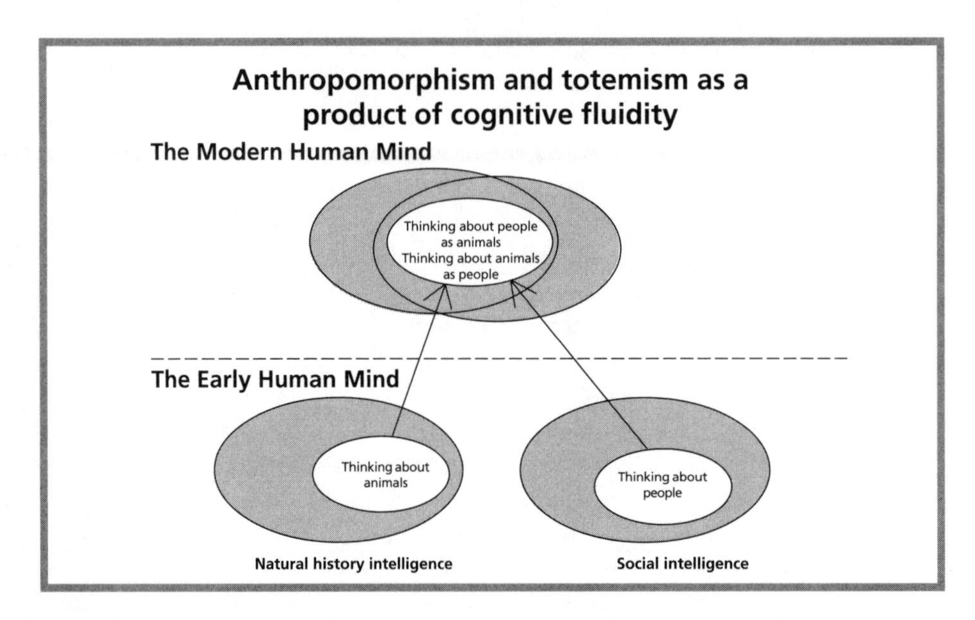

hunting-gathering lifestyle; second, it requires a cognitive fluidity between thinking about animals and people; and third, on the basis of archaeological evidence it is likely to have been pervasive in human society since the start of the Upper Palaeolithic. The evidence we can invoke here includes that of imagery in Palaeolithic art and that from burials, such as at the 7800-year-old cemetery at Oleneostrovski Mogilnik in Karelia where we find two clusters of graves, one associated with effigies of a snake, and the other with effigies of an elk.[35] In contrast, we have no reason to believe that Early Human society was structured on a totemic basis.

We must also note here that it is not just other living things which are thought of as possessing human qualities. Hunter-gatherers do not just live in a landscape of animals and plants, rocks, hills and caves. Their landscapes are socially constructed and full of meaning. Once again the Aboriginal communities of Australia provide a good example. The wells in their landscape are where ancestral beings dug in the ground, the trees where they had placed their digging sticks and the deposits of red ochre where they had bled.[36] John Pfeiffer has argued that the encompassing of the features of the landscape in a web of myths and stories is of great utility to the Aborigines, for it helps them to remember enormous quantities of geographic information.

Whether or not this is the case, when we look at a region such as that of southwest France in which we find both a range of topographic features universally attributed with social and symbolic meanings by modern hunter-gatherers,[37] and caves and rockshelters covered with paintings, we can be in no doubt that the Upper Palaeolithic hunters were also living in a landscape full of symbolic meanings.

It is useful to recall here the words of Tim Ingold that I quoted in Chapter 3: 'For them [modern hunter-gatherers] there are not two worlds of persons (society) and things (nature), but just one world – one environment – saturated with personal powers and embracing both human beings, the animals and plants on which they depend, and the landscape in which they live and move.'[38] The anthropomorphic images and painting of caves and rockshelters that begin after 40,000 years ago suggests that the earliest Upper Palaeolithic hunter-gatherers had a similar attitude to the social and natural worlds: they were one and the same. One consequence, of benefit to us today, is that they expressed this view within their art, creating some of the most powerful and beautiful images ever made. But this collapse of the cognitive barrier between the social and natural worlds also had significant consequences for their own behaviour, for it fundamentally changed their interaction with the natural world. It is to this that we must now turn.

A new proficiency at hunting: special strategies, special tools

The hunter-gatherers of the Upper Palaeolithic were hunting the same types of animals as the Early Humans. In Europe, for instance, reindeer, red deer, bison and horse continued as the mainstay of their economies, while in southern Africa animals such as eland, cape buffalo and seals remained the most important prey. What differed, however, is the manner in which these animals were hunted. Modern Humans appear to have been considerably more proficient at predicting game movements and planning complex hunting strategies.

This is readily apparent from Europe. Almost all the sites of Early Humans have a mix of animal species, suggesting that these were hunted as individuals on an opportunistic basis. The site of Combe Grenal in southwest France is typical in this regard. Each occupation level usually contains a few individuals of each of the types of large game being hunted. As the climate grew colder, animals such as reindeer become more prevalent in the occupation deposits, while red deer increase during periods of relative warmth. The Neanderthals were simply hunting whatever animals were available – although as I indicated in the last chapter, we should certainly not minimize their achievement at exploiting such game.

The first Modern Humans in Europe hunted in a very different fashion. Although they continued to kill individual animals, or at most small groups, they began to specialize on specific animals at specific sites.[39] Consequently many sites are dominated by one species alone, very often reindeer. Indeed certain sites seem to have been selected for ambush hunting, indicating that Modern Humans were much better at predicting the movements of animals than Early Humans. This becomes very apparent when we look at hunting methods in the period *c.* 18,000 years ago, when the last ice age was at its peak. At about this time, Modern Humans shifted from hunting individual and small groups of animals to slaughtering mass herds of reindeer and red deer. These are likely to have been attacked at critical points on their annual migration routes when the animals were constrained in narrow valleys, or when crossing rivers.[40]

The same contrast between Early and Modern Humans can be seen in other parts of the Old World. In northern Spain, for example, animals such as ibex began to be hunted for the first time. This is significant because, as the archaeologist Lawrence Straus has written, ibex hunting required 'elaborate strategies, tactics, weapons and ... logistical camps'. By 'logistical camps' he refers to sites specifically located for ibex hunting.[41] Similarly on the Russian Plain, Olga Soffer has described how the first Upper Palaeolithic hunters were locating sites for exploiting specific animals at specific times of the year. She suggests that they were taking greater account of the seasonal and long-term fluctuations in animal numbers and behaviour patterns.[42] The same can be seen in southern Africa. For instance, Richard Klein has suggested that a new awareness of the seasonal variation in seal numbers had arisen, and was being used to plan hunting trips to the coast. This replaced a more opportunistic pattern of hunting and scavenging.[43]

In general, the Modern Humans of the Upper Palaeolithic appear to have had a significantly greater ability both to predict the movements of animals and to use that knowledge in their hunting strategies. How were they managing to do this? The answer lies in what has already been a major theme of this chapter: anthropomorphic thinking. This is universal among all modern hunters and its significance is that it can substantially improve prediction of an animal's behaviour. Even though a deer or a horse may not think about its foraging and mobility patterns in the same way as Modern Humans, imagining that it does can act as an excellent predictor for where the animal will feed and the direction in which it may move.

This has been recognized in several studies of living hunter-gatherers, such as among the G/Wi and the !Kung of the Kalahari, the Valley Bisa of Zambia and the Nunamiut of the Canadian Arctic. Anthropomorphizing animals by attributing to them human personalities and characters provides as effective a predictor for their behaviour as viewing them with all the understanding of ecological knowledge possessed by Western scientists.[44] The anthropologist Mary Douglas sees the similarity in the categories used for understanding the natural and social worlds as primarily being of practical value in terms of understanding and predicting the ways of animals. She suggests that this is of far more importance than using the natural world for addressing profound metaphysical problems about the human condition, as proposed by Lévi-Strauss.[45]

Anthropomorphic thinking, therefore, has clear utilitarian benefits. Yet the new powers of prediction would have been of limited value had Modern Humans not also been able to develop new types of hunting weapons. And we do indeed see a striking elaboration of technology at the start of the Upper Palaeolithic. In Europe, Modern Humans could make all those types of tools which Neanderthals, with their Swiss-army-knife mentality, could not even think about: tools which required an integration of technical and natural history intelligences.

For example, we see many new types of weapons made from bone and antler, notably harpoons and spearthrowers. Experimental studies using replica artifacts have shown that these were very effective at piercing animal hides and organs.[46] We see many new types of stone projectile points, and find associations between specific types of points and specific types of animals.[47] We can see evidence for complex, multi-component tools being made, such as in the presence of microliths – small blades of flint used as points and barbs. Lying at the heart of these new technological innovations was the switch to 'blade technology', which provided standardized 'blanks', each of which could be turned into part of a highly specialized tool (see Figure 22).

It is not simply the introduction of new tools at the start of the Upper Palaeolithic which is important. It is how these were then constantly modified and changed. Throughout the Upper Palaeolithic we can see the processes of innovation and experimentation at work, resulting in a constant stream of new hunting weapons appropriate to the prevailing environmental conditions and building on the knowledge of previous generations. As the environments became very harsh at the height of the last ice age 18,000 years ago, large points were manufactured, specialized for ensuring that large game would be despatched on the tundra. As the climate began to ameliorate, and a wider range of game became available, hunting technology became more diverse, with an emphasis on multi-component tools.[48] Lawrence Straus has appositely described this as a Palaeolithic arms race.[49] Such behaviour, geared to maintaining if not maximizing hunting efficiency, is markedly different from the monotony of the hunting tools of Early Humans during the equally variable environments that they exploited. It could only have arisen owing to a new connection between natural history and technical intelligence.

The design of hunting weapons is perhaps the best example of this new type of thinking, but it also resulted in a wide range of other technological developments. For instance, by 18,000 years ago people in North Africa were using grinding stones for preparing plant material. Such artifacts required integrated thought about the characteristics of both stone and plant material.[50] The elaboration in the range of scraping and engraving tools used for such tasks as cleaning hides and carving bone required thought about the nature of animal products during the process of tool manufacture. And perhaps most impressive of all is the development of facilities for trapping animals, such as small game or fish, and the technology for storing food, whether it be reindeer meat during the Upper Palaeolithic or hazelnuts once forests had spread across Europe after the end of the last ice age 10,000 years ago.[51] The design and use of all these involve an integration of natural history and technical knowledge, resulting in a constant innovation of new technology.

Art as stored information

Many of the new bone and antler tools of the Upper Palaeolithic carried elaborate designs engraved on to their surfaces, or were even carved into animal figures themselves, such as the spearthrower from Mas d'Azil (see Figure 23). Indeed it is very difficult to draw any division between what is a piece of 'art' and what is a 'tool', and such artifacts epitomize the absence of any boundaries between different domains of activity. Many of the art objects can indeed be thought of as a brand new type of tool: a tool for storing information and for helping to retrieve information stored in the mind.

The simplest tools of this new type are pieces of bone with incised parallel lines. The most complex have many hundreds of marks made by a number of different tools, creating a complex pattern on the face of the artifact, such as on the Taï plaque from eastern France (see Figure 24).[52] The interpretation of these has always been controversial. When first discovered they were described as '*tailles de chasse*' – hunting tallies recording the number of animals killed. A range of other interpretations have since been made, for example that they record the number of people attending social gatherings and lunar calendars.[53]

Detailed microscopic study of such artifacts by Alexander Marshack and Francesco D'Errico has confirmed that on several of them the marks come in such regular patterns that they appear to be a system of notation.[54] These artifacts are likely to have acted as a form of visual recording device, most probably about environmental events. They look very similar to notched and engraved artifacts made by modern hunter-gatherers which are known to have been mnemonic aids and recording

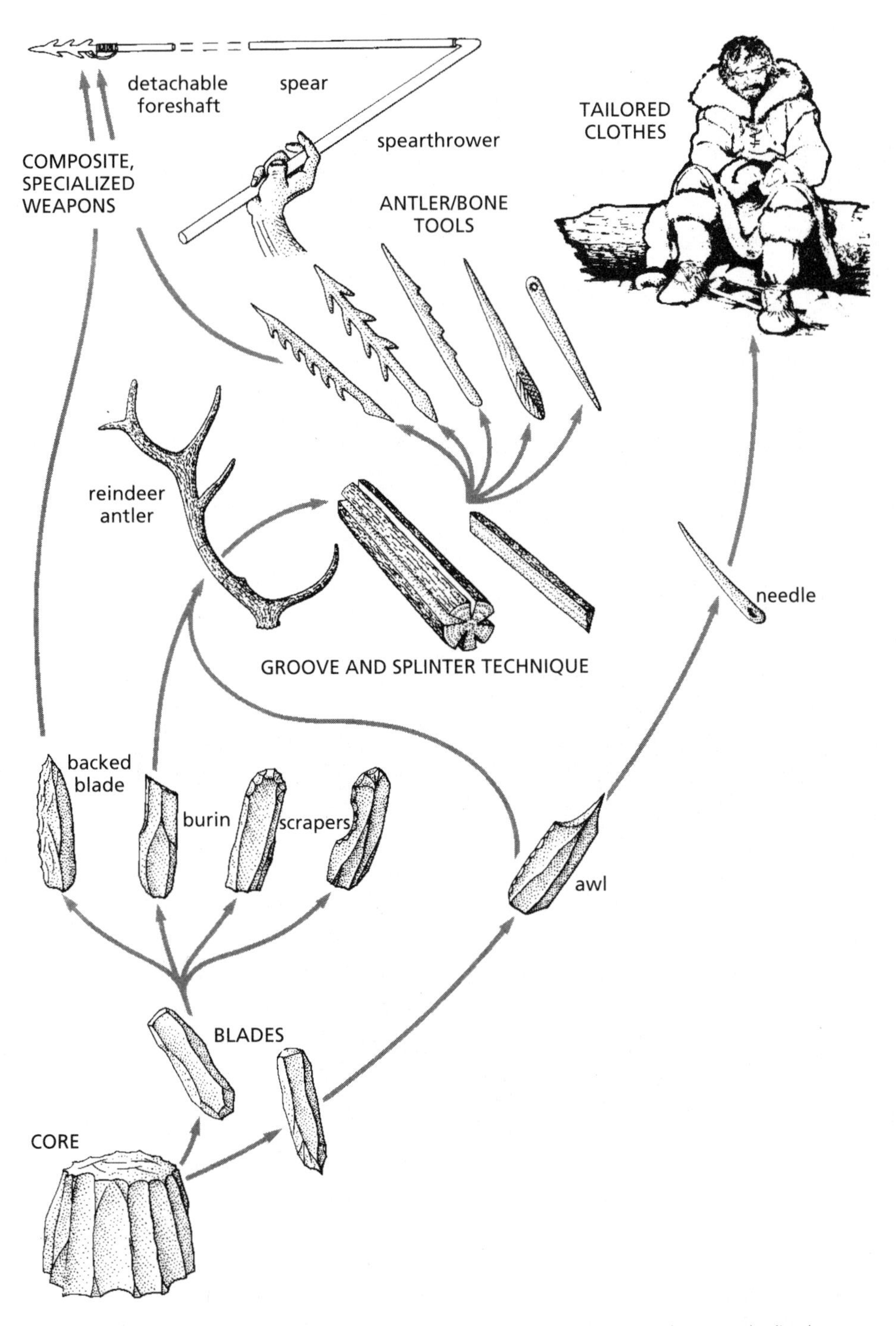

22 *Systematic blade production in the Upper Palaeolithic was a means to produce standardized 'blanks' that could be easily modified for use in a wide range of multi-component tools.*

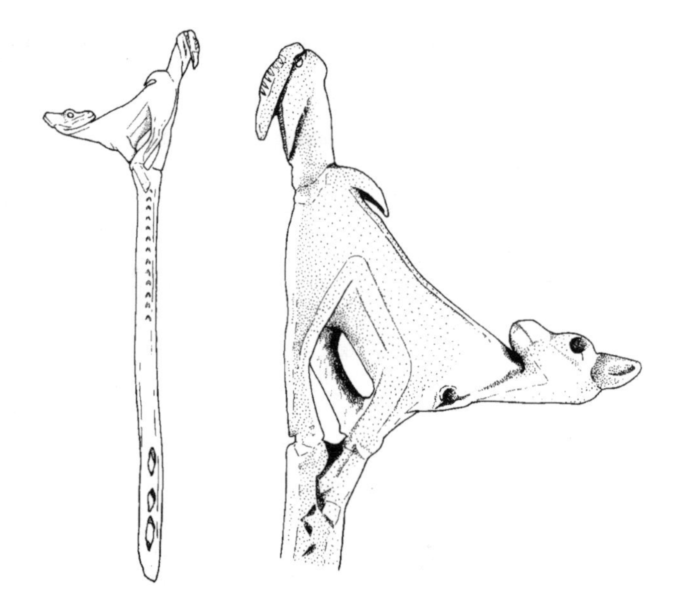

23 Antler spearthrower from Mas d'Azil, Ariège, France. This depicts an ibex that is either giving birth, or excreting a large turd on which two birds are perched. Total length 29.6 cm.

devices, such as the calendar sticks made from ivory by the Yakut people of Siberia.[55]

Like the engraved pieces of bone, cave paintings also appear to have been used to store information about the natural world, or at least facilitate its recall by acting as a mnemonic device. Indeed, these paintings have been described as the 'tribal encyclopedia' by John Pfeiffer.[56] I myself have suggested that much of the animal imagery within this art served to help recall information about the natural world stored within the mind.[57] For instance, I have argued that the manner in which many of the animals were painted makes direct reference to the ways in which information was acquired about their movements and behaviour. In some images, while the animals were painted in profile, their hooves were painted in plan, as if hoofprints were being depicted to facilitate the memorizing and recall of tracks seen while in the environment, or even the teaching of children. Similarly the choice of imagery itself was selective towards those animals which provide knowledge about forthcoming environmental events. The bird imagery is particularly telling, dominated as it is by ducks and geese, which are likely to have been migratory. Modern hunters in glaciated environments keep a very close lookout for the annual arrival and departure of such birds, since such information gives a clue as to when the big freeze of the winter, or the spring thaw, will happen. Some of the most evocative images of this type are ivory carvings of geese in flight found at the Siberian site of Mal'ta, where the hunters had relied on mammoths for food but no doubt eagerly watched for the passing of migrating birds indicating the arrival of spring.[58]

The way in which Upper Palaeolithic cave paintings may have functioned to help store information about the natural world is perhaps analogous to the way in which Wopkaimin hunter-horticulturalists of New Guinea use the bones from the animals they hunt. These bones are placed on the rear walls of their houses where they are described as 'trophy arrays'. But they are carefully arranged to act as a mental map for the surrounding environment to facilitate the recall of information about that environment and animal behaviour. They thus play an important role in decision-making about use of resources and improving the predictions about animal location and behaviour.[59] There is clear patterning in the arrangement of animal figures in the cave paintings of the Upper Palaeolithic.[60] Michael and Anne Eastham have suggested that the paintings and engravings in the caves of the Ardèche region of France served as a model or a map for the specific terrain around the caves.[61]

In summary, although the specific roles that prehistoric artifacts may have played in the management of information about the natural world remain unclear, there can be little doubt that many of them served to store, transmit and retrieve information. Major benefits of this will have been enhanced abilities to track long-term change, to monitor seasonal fluctuations and to devise hunting plans. Many of the paintings, carvings and engravings of Modern Humans were tools with which to think about the natural world.

Sending social messages: objects of personal adornment

Beads, pendants and other items of personal decoration first appear at the start of the Upper Palaeolithic. They too arise from the new cognitive fluidity of the mind – an integration between technical and social intelli-

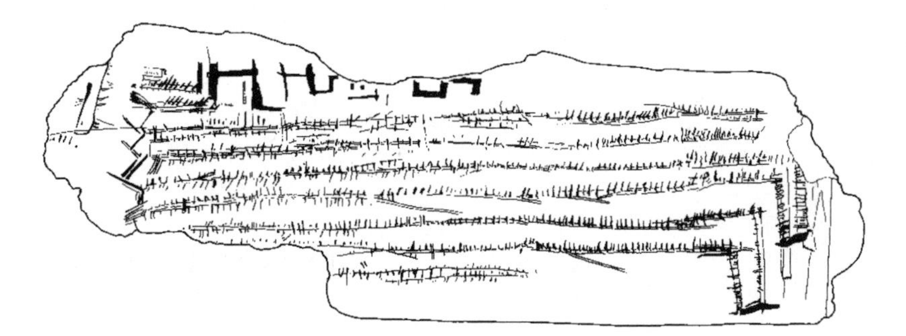

24 Engraved bone plaque from Grotte du Taï, Drôme, France. Length, 8.8 cm.

gence. Such artifacts are initially found in abundance in occupation deposits of caves in southwest France, and are particularly important during the very harsh climatic conditions at around 18,000 years ago.[62] They are often found in burials, most dramatically on the 28,000-year-old burials at Sungir in Russia (see Box p. 175). Describing beads and pendants as 'decoration' risks belittling their importance. They would have functioned to send social messages, such as about one's status, group affiliation and relationships with other individuals, just as they do in our own society today. And of course these messages need not have been 'true'; beads and pendants provide new opportunities for deception in the kind of social tactics that we saw are prevalent even among chimpanzees. To have produced such artifacts required not only specialized social and technical intelligences – as possessed by Early Humans – but also an ability to integrate these.

It is likely that all types of artifacts, including those that might appear to be mundane tools for hunting or even processing animal hides, became imbued with social information at the start of the Upper Palaeolithic.[63] In effect the 'goal posts' of social behaviour were moved; whereas for Early Humans the domains of hunting, toolmaking and socializing were quite separate, these were now so integrated that it is impossible to characterize any single aspect of Modern Human behaviour as being located in just one of these domains. Indeed as Ernest Gellner stated: 'the conflation and confusion of aims and criteria, is the normal and original condition of mankind'.[64]

The rise of religion

Many of the new behaviours I have been describing, such as the anthropomorphic images in the cave paintings and the burial of people with grave goods, suggest that these Upper Palaeolithic people were the first to have beliefs in supernatural beings and possibly an afterlife. We are indeed seeing here the first appearance of religious ideologies. This can be explained by the collapse of the barriers that had existed between the multiple intelligences of the Early Human mind.

Just as we did with art, we must first reach some agreement on quite what we mean by the notion of religion. While it is difficult to identify features universal to all religions, there are nevertheless a series of recurrent ideas. The importance of these has been stressed by the social anthropologist Pascal Boyer in his 1994 book *The Naturalness of Religious Ideas*. Boyer explains that a belief in non-physical beings is the most common feature of religions; it may indeed be universal. In fact, ever since the classic work of E.B. Tylor in 1871 on *Primitive Cultures*, the idea of non-physical beings has been taken for the very definition of

Sending social information by material culture: the Sungir burials

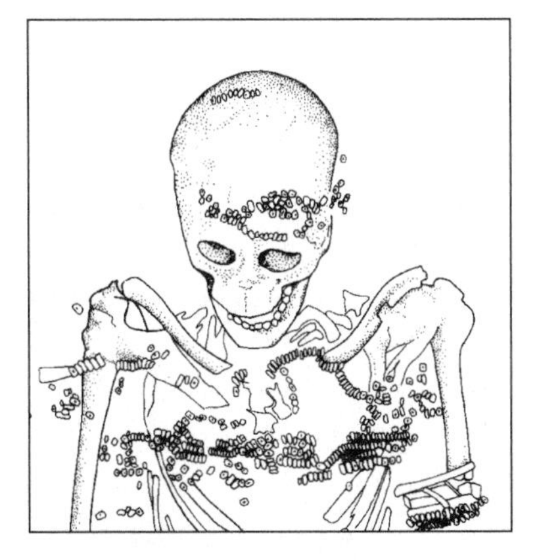

The burials at Sungir, Russia, have been dated to 28,000 years old. They consist of the graves of a 60-year-old man, and a joint burial of a male and a female adolescent. Each of these individuals were decorated with thousands of ivory beads, which had probably been attached to clothing. The archaeologist Randall White has studied these graves and provides the following descriptions:

The man was adorned with 2936 beads and fragments arranged in strands found on all parts of his body including his head, which was apparently covered with a beaded cap that also bore several fox teeth. His forearms and biceps were each decorated with a series of polished mammoth-ivory bracelets (25 in all), some showing traces of black paint.... Around the man's neck he wore a small flat schist pendant, painted red, but with a small black dot on one side....

The supposed small boy was covered with strands of beads – 4903 of them – that were roughly 2/3 the size of the man's beads, although of exactly the same form. Unlike the man, however, he had around his waist – apparently the remains of a decorated belt – more than 250 canine teeth of the polar fox. On his chest was a carved ivory pendant in the form of an animal. At his throat was an ivory pin, apparently the closure of a cloak of some sort. Under his left shoulder was a large ivory sculpture of a mammoth. At his left side lay a medial segment of a highly polished, very robust human femur, the medullary cavity of which was packed with red ochre. At his right side ... was a massive ivory lance, made from a straightened woolly mammoth tusk.... Near it is a carved ivory disc which sits upright in the soil.

The supposed girl had 5274 beads and fragments (also roughly 2/3 the size of the man's beads) covering her body. She also wore a beaded cap and had an ivory pin at her throat, but her burial contains no fox teeth whatsoever. Nor does she have a pendant on her chest. However, placed at each of her sides there was a number of small ivory 'lances', more appropriate to her body size than that accompanying the boy. Also at her side are two pierced antler batons, one of them decorated with rows of drilled dots. Finally, she was accompanied by a series of three ivory disks with a central hole and lattice work, like that adjacent to the supposed boy's burial.

(White 1993, 289–292)

religion itself. Boyer notes three other recurrent features of religious ideologies. The first is that in many societies it is assumed that a non-physical component of a person can survive after death and remain as a being with beliefs and desires. Second, it is very frequently assumed that certain people within a society are especially likely to receive direct inspiration or messages from supernatural agencies, such as gods or spirits. And third, it is also very widely assumed that performing certain rituals in an exact way can bring about change in the natural world.

If we look at the archaeological evidence from the start of the Upper Palaeolithic, we get hints that each of these features was present. Few can doubt that the painted caves, some of which were located deep underground, were the locus for ritual activities. Indeed the anthropomorphic images within this art, such as the sorcerer from the cave of Les Trois-Frères, are most easily interpreted as being either supernatural beings or shamans who communicated with them. As was most forcefully argued by the French prehistorian André Leroi-Gourhan, these painted caves are likely to reflect a mythological world with concepts as complex as those of the Dreamtime held by the Australian Aborigines.

In addition to the art we have the evidence from the burials. It is difficult to believe that such investment would have been made in burial ritual, as at Sungir, had there been no concept of death as a transition to a non-physical form. Indeed, since only a tiny fraction of the Upper Palaeolithic population seems to have been buried, it is likely that these people played a special religious role within their society.

Pascal Boyer has explored how the characteristics of supernatural beings as found in religious ideologies relate to the intuitive knowledge about the world genetically encoded in the human mind. In Chapter 3 I described three types of intuitive knowledge, that regarding psychology, biology and physics, and argued that these 'kickstarted' the formation of cognitive domains or multiple intelligences during child development. Boyer argues that a typical feature of supernatural beings is that they have characteristics which violate this intuitive knowledge.

For example, Boyer explains that the supernatural beings of religious ideologies commonly violate intuitive biological knowledge. While they may have bodies, they do not undergo the normal cycle of birth, maturation, reproduction, death and decay. Similarly, they may violate intuitive physics by being able to pass through solid objects (as with ghosts) or simply be invisible. Nevertheless, supernatural beings also have a tendency to conform to some intuitive knowledge; for instance, they are very frequently intentional beings who have beliefs and desires like normal human beings. The Ancestral Beings of the Australian Aborigines provide an excellent example of such entities which both violate and conform to intuitive knowledge of the world. On the one hand, they have very weird characteristics, such as existing in both the past and the present. On the other hand, in many of the stories they play tricks and engage in deception in a manner which is very human.[65] A more familiar example to many people will be the gods of Greek legends who have supernatural powers but also suffer jealousies and petty rivalries much like those of normal people.

Boyer argues that it is this combination of violation of, and conformity to, intuitive knowledge that characterizes supernatural beings in religious ideologies. The violations make them something different, but by conforming to some aspects of intuitive knowledge people are able to learn about them; if there was nothing about supernatural beings which conformed to intuitive knowledge of the world, the concept of them would simply be too difficult for the human mind to grasp.

An alternative way of viewing this feature of supernatural beings is as a mixing up of knowledge about different types of entities in the real world – knowledge which would have been 'trapped' in separate cognitive domains within the Early Human mind. For example, Early Humans would have known that rocks are not born and do not die like living things. And Early Humans would also have known that people have intentions and desires, while inert nodules of stone do not. Because they had isolated cognitive domains, there was no risk of the Early Human mind getting these entities mixed up, and arriving at a concept of an inert object that is neither born nor dies, but which nevertheless has intentions and desires. Such concepts, which Boyer argues are the essence of a supernatural being, could only arise in a cognitively fluid mind.

Boyer himself suggests that a combination of knowledge about different types of entities explains another recurrent feature of religious ideologies – the fact that some individuals are believed to have special powers of communication with supernatural beings. At the heart of this notion, Boyer argues, is the belief that some people have a different 'essence' from others in the group. I discussed the notion of essence in Chapter 3, where it was explained to be a critical feature of intuitive biology, a means by which even young children are able to classify animals into different species. Boyer explains the differentiation of people into different social roles, exemplified by that of shaman, as an introduction of the notion of essence into thought about the social world. In other words, it is a consequence of cognitive fluidity.

We cannot, of course, reconstruct the religious ideologies of the earliest Upper Palaeolithic societies. But we can be confident that religious ideologies as complex as those of modern hunter-gatherers came into existence at the time of the Middle/Upper Palaeolithic transition and have remained with us ever since. This appears to be another consequence of the cognitive fluidity that arose in the human mind, which resulted in art, new technology, and a transformation in the exploitation of the natural world and the means of social interaction.

Towards cognitive fluidity: the mind of Early Modern Humans

The new cognitive fluidity transformed the human mind and all aspects of human behaviour (see Figure 25). It is not surprising that with new abilities to use materials such as bone and ivory for tools, and to use artifacts to store and transmit information, humans were able to colonize new areas of the world. At around 60,000 years ago a second major pulse of movement across the globe began, following that of the first Early Humans to leave Africa more than 1.5 million years ago. As Clive Gamble has described in his recent study of global colonization,[66] Australasia was colonized by extensive sea voyages, and then the North European Plain, the arid regions of Africa and the coniferous forests and tundra of the far north were colonized soon after 40,000 years ago. Early Humans may have temporarily entered these environments, but they did not remain on a long-term basis. Modern Humans not only colonized them but used them as stepping stones to the Americas and the Pacific islands.

The emergence of a cognitively fluid mentality provides the answer to the Middle/Upper Palaeolithic transition. But remember that this transition does not happen until half-way through Act 4. The start of that act is defined by the appearance of *H. sapiens sapiens* in the fossil record at 100,000 years ago. We must complete this chapter by asking how the minds of these Early Modern Humans – those who lived before the Middle/Upper Palaeolithic transition – were different from those of the Early Humans of Act 3 (who also continued into the first scene of Act 4), and the Modern Humans who lived after the Middle/Upper Palaeolithic transition, among whom we must include ourselves.

There is, I believe, a simple answer to this question. The Early Modern Humans seem to have been achieving some degree of integration between their specialized intelligences, but not gaining the full cognitive fluidity that arose after 60,000 years ago. Their minds were a half-way house between a Swiss-army-knife and a cognitively fluid mentality.

We can see this most clearly in the Near East, where we find the remains of Early Modern Humans in the caves of Skhūl and Qafzeh dating to between 100,000 and 80,000 years ago. While their stone tools are practically indistinguishable from those of the Neanderthals who used the cave of Tabūn before the Early Modern Humans arrived (*c.* 180,000–90,000 years ago), and Kebara after they left (63,000–48,000

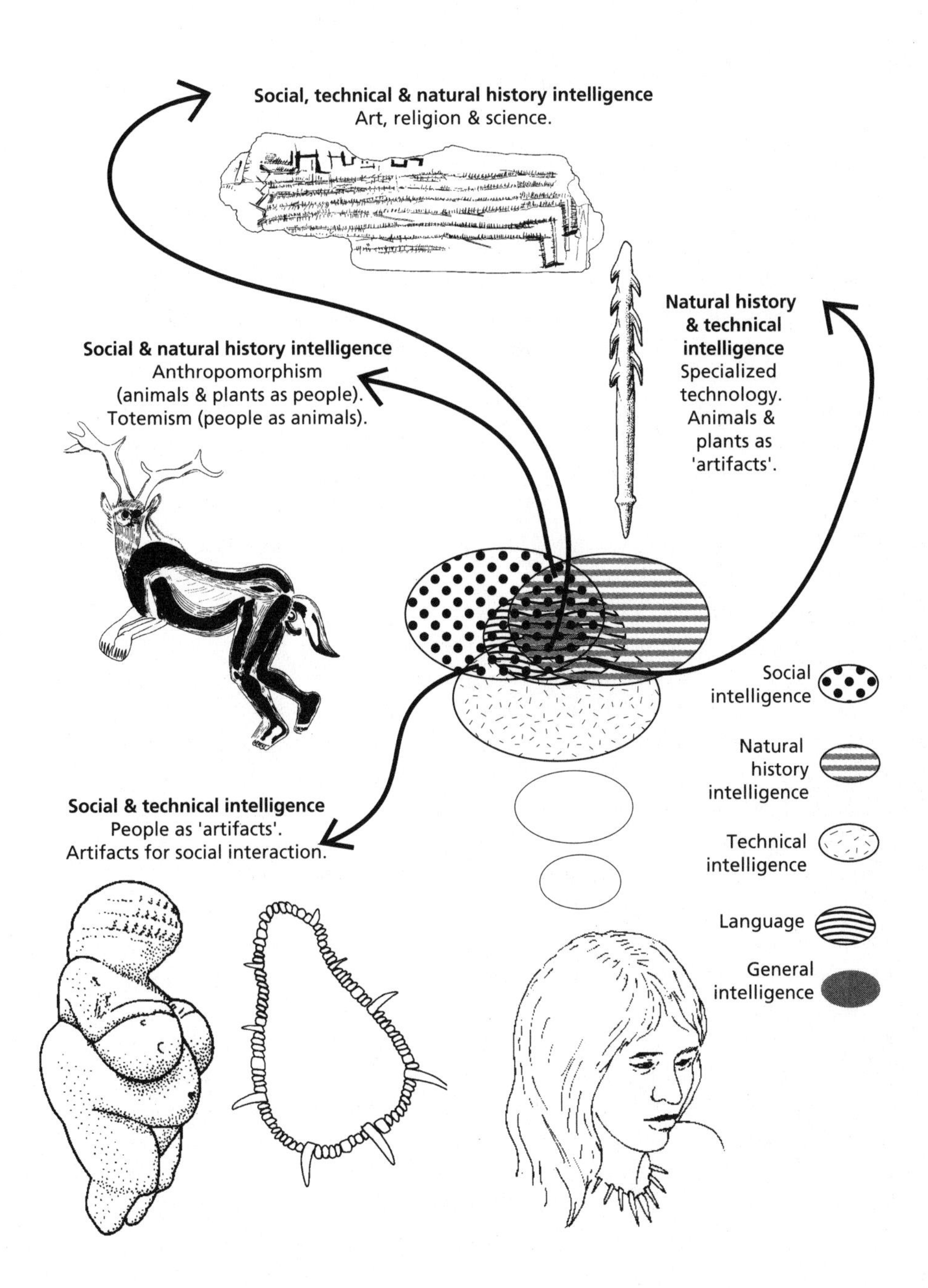

***25** The cultural explosion as a consequence of cognitive fluidity.*

years ago), the Early Modern Humans seem to have had two unique features to their behaviour.

The first is that they placed parts of animal carcasses within human graves. For instance, in the cave of Qafzeh a child was found buried with the skull and antlers of a deer. At Skhūl one of the burials contained a body which had been laid on its back, with the jaws of a wild boar placed within its hands.[67] These seem to imply ritualized burial activity, and a belief in religious ideologies. Recall that while Neanderthals did bury some individuals, there is no evidence for the intentional placing of items within the graves, or for any ritual activity associated with the act of burial.

The second contrast concerns the hunting of gazelle. This was the most important animal hunted by both Neanderthals and Modern Humans, and both appear to have used short thrusting spears with stone points. But their hunting patterns were quite different. The Early Modern Humans used their caves on a seasonal basis, and probably expended less physical energy in their hunting behaviour. In addition, they appear to have needed to repair their spears less frequently.[68] In other words, they were hunting with greater degrees of planning and more efficiently than the Neanderthals. This, in turn, is likely to reflect an enhanced ability at predicting the location and behaviour of their prey.

At first glance these two differences between the Early Modern Humans and the Neanderthals of the Near East appear unrelated. But there is in fact a very significant relationship: both derive from an integration of natural history and social intelligence in the minds of Early Modern Humans. As I argued earlier in this chapter, improvements in the ability to predict animal behaviour over what can be achieved with a natural history intelligence alone probably derive from anthropomorphic thinking, as is universal among living hunter-gatherers. I also discussed how concepts of religious belief arise from cognitive fluidity, particularly the integration of natural history and social intelligence. The placing of animal parts within the burials of Early Modern Humans implies that some associations were being made between people and animals, probably reflecting some form of totemic thought. It is significant, I think, that artifacts were not placed within the burials, which is common practice during the Upper Palaeolithic. This suggests that technical intelligence remained isolated within the Early Modern Human mind. This is indeed confirmed by the fact that in spite of their abilities at predicting the behaviour of gazelle, Modern Humans continued to use the same types of hunting weapons as the Neanderthals. They do not appear to have been designing more effective hunting weapons, which would have arisen if technical and natural history intelligence had been integrated,

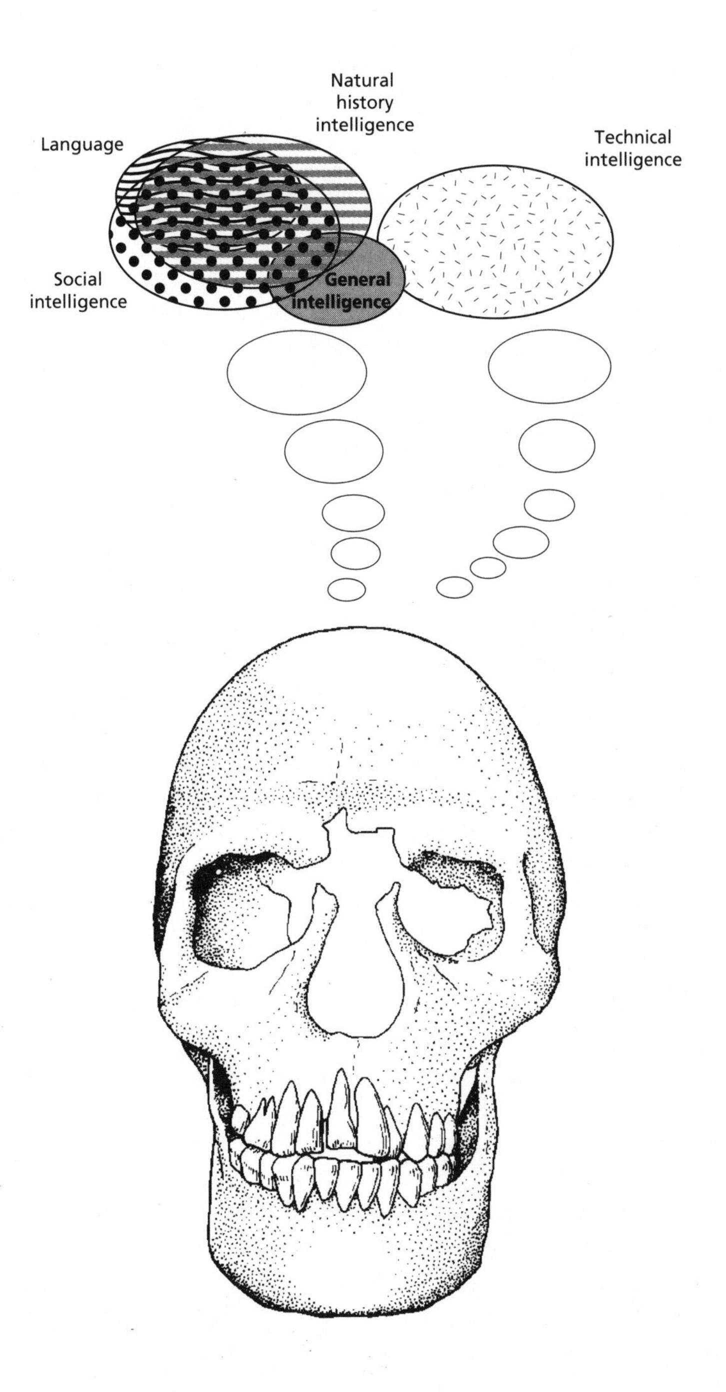

***26** The Early Modern Human mind. The drawing depicts the skull known as Qafzeh 9 dating to c. 100,000 years ago. This is from a young adult who appears to have been buried with a child at its feet.*

nor were they investing their stone tools with social information, as would have arisen if technical and social intelligence were integrated.

In summary, the minds of the Early Modern Humans of the Near East seem to be a half-way house between the Swiss-army-knife mentality of Early Humans and the cognitively fluid mentality of Modern Humans (see Figure 26).

We reach a similar conclusion when we consider the Early Modern Humans of South Africa. Their fossils, found in the caves of Klasies River Mouth and Border Cave, are less well preserved than those of the Near East, but date to the same time period of around 100,000 years ago. The South African specimens contain some archaic features and this region is likely to have been the original source of *H. sapiens sapiens*.[69]

The long stratified sequence of archaeological deposits in Klasies River Mouth is of most interest.[70] It covers the period between around 140,000 years ago and 20,000 years ago. Towards the end of this sequence, at around 40,000 years ago, we see a change in stone technology from a predominantly flake to a blade production method, which denotes the Middle/Upper Palaeolithic transition – although in Africa this is referred to by archaeologists as the change from the Middle to Later Stone Age. Prior to this event, the stone tools in almost the whole of this sequence are very similar to those made by Early Humans elsewhere in the African continent during Act 3, even though those after 100,000 years ago appear to have been made by Early Modern Humans, the first *H. sapiens sapiens*.

However, the levels likely to correlate with the first appearance of Early Modern Humans are notable for a significant increase in the quantity of red ochre.[71] Some of these pieces seem to have been used as crayons. The pieces of red ochre remain quite rare, less than 0.6 per cent of the artifacts from any one layer, but are nevertheless at much higher frequencies than in sites associated with Early Humans. Indeed there are no pieces of red ochre known prior to 250,000 years ago, and only a dozen pieces before 100,000 years ago. Red ochre is also found at other sites in southern Africa after this date, and there have even been claims that it was mined at Lion Cavern in Swaziland. It remains unclear what the Early Modern Humans were doing with the ochre. As the anthropologists Chris Knight and Camilla Powers have argued, body painting is the most likely explanation, since there are no objects of art known in South Africa prior to 30,000 years ago, nor are there any beads or pendants.[72]

A few other traces can be found of new types of behaviour by the Early Modern Humans in southern Africa. In Border Cave there appears to have been a burial of an infant within a grave dating to between 70,000 and 80,000 years ago. This is the only burial known from the Middle Stone Age of the region and it is notable for not only being that of an Early Modern Human, but for also containing a perforated *Conus* shell that had originated more than 80 kilometres away.[73] Another innovation – alongside the more widespread stone flake technology – was the introduction of small blades, made from higher quality stone and chipped into forms which would not be out of place in the Upper Palaeolithic of Europe. These blades look as if they were designed for multi-component tools.[74] A final type of novel behaviour is the working of bone. The most dramatic evidence comes from the sites at Katanda in Zaire, where bone harpoons with multiple barbs have been found. These are as complex as any bone artifact from the Upper Palaeolithic of Europe. They were made by grinding and are at least 90,000 years old – making them 60,000 years earlier than any other known examples. They are associated with typical Middle Stone Age stone artifacts.[75]

If we are indeed dealing with a single type of human in southern Africa after 100,000 years ago, then the mentality of the Early Modern Humans appears to drift in and out of cognitive fluidity. It is as if the benefits of partial cognitive fluidity were not sufficient for this mental transformation to have been 'fixed' within the population. The minds of these Early Modern Humans seem like those of the Early Modern Humans of the Near East in showing some degree of cognitive fluidity, but one that did not match what arose after the start of the Upper Palaeolithic.

Nevertheless, this partial cognitive fluidity was to prove absolutely critical in giving Early Modern Humans the competitive edge as they spread from Africa and the Near East throughout the world between 100,000 and 30,000 years ago. The Early Modern Humans of the Near East are likely to be representatives of – or at least closely related to – the source population of *H. sapiens sapiens* that left Africa, spread into Asia and Europe and replaced all existing Early Humans.[76]

The strongest evidence for this replacement scenario is the limited amount of genetic diversity among living humans today. Although there is considerable controversy as to how modern genetic variability should be interpreted, there is strong evidence that there has been a recent and severe 'bottleneck' in human evolution. In general, living Africans have a higher degree of genetic variability than people elsewhere in the world, suggesting that as the first *H. sapiens sapiens* left Africa there was a considerable loss of genetic variation. This implies that for a short period of time there was a very small breeding population. One recent estimate has suggested no more than six breeding individuals for 70 years, which would reflect an actual population size of around 50 individuals, or 500 individuals if this bottleneck lasted for 200 years.[77]

If the Early Modern Humans of the Near East are indeed part of this source population, or closely related to them, then as they spread throughout the world, they took with them their partially cognitively fluid minds. This feature of their mentality was presumably encoded within their genes. It was their integration of natural history and social intelligence which enabled them to compete successfully with resident Early Human populations, pushing the latter into extinction – although the possibility of some hybridization remains. And consequently we find *H. sapiens sapiens* in China at 67,000 years ago, represented by the fossil skull from Liujang.[78]

At slightly different times in different parts of the world the final step to a cognitively fluid mind was taken. This was the integration of technical intelligence with the already combined social and natural history intelligences. That all *H. sapiens sapiens* populations dispersed throughout the world took this final step – a case of parallel evolution – was perhaps inevitable. There was an evolutionary momentum to cognitive fluidity; once the process had begun it could not be halted. It appears that as soon as a set of adaptive pressures arose in each area, technical intelligence became part of the cognitively fluid mind, the final step on the path to modernity.

In this chapter I have argued that the events of Act 4 can be explained by the emergence of cognitive fluidity in the human mind. This process began with the very first appearance of *H. sapiens sapiens* and its culmination caused the cultural explosion that archaeologists call the Middle/Upper Palaeolithic transition. But, as in so much of science, answering one question merely raises another. How did it happen? How did the thoughts and knowledge escape from their respective chapels of the Early Human mind?

10 So how did it happen?

IN AN EARLIER chapter I suggested that we should view the past as if it were a drama. The interest in such a play is not so much the action, but what is going on in the minds of the actors when various events occur and actions are undertaken. I have concluded that the diverse range of new behaviours that appear in Act 4 of the play derive from a fundamental change in mental architecture. Thoughts and knowledge which had been previously trapped within chapels of specialized intelligence could now flow freely around the cathedral of the mind – or at least a part of it – harmonizing with each other to create new types of thoughts as part of an almost limitless imagination: a cognitively fluid mentality.

Explaining the rise of the flexible mind

My argument remains incomplete, because I have yet to explain how the new cognitive fluidity arose. I believe the explanation relates to changes in the nature of language and consciousness within the mind. Let me start my explanation with a simple proposition: once Early Humans started talking, they just couldn't stop.

To understand how this led to cognitive fluidity we must first recall that in previous chapters I have followed the proposals of Robin Dunbar that the language of Early Humans was a 'social language' – they used language as a means to send and receive social information. This contrasts with our language today which is a general-purpose language, playing a critical role in the transmission of information about the non-social world, although a social bias remains. Now although the language of Early Humans can be characterized as a social language – and for the Early Humans after 250,000 years ago, as a language with an extensive lexicon and grammatical complexity – I believe there would nevertheless have been 'snippets' of language about the non-social world, such as about animal behaviour and toolmaking.

These would have arisen from two sources. The first is general intelligence. As I argued in Chapter 7, general intelligence was extremely important in the Early Human mind as it conditioned behaviour at the domain interfaces, such as the use of tools for hunting and use of food for establishing social relationships. As a result, behaviour at these domain interfaces remained extremely simple, because general intelligence could not access the cognitive processes located within each of the specialized intelligences. General intelligence is also likely to have enabled Early Humans to associate particular vocalizations with non-social entities and consequently produced 'snippets of conversation' about the non-social world – which would have been few in number and lacking in grammatical complexity. Indeed these snippets are likely to have been similar in complexity to the use of symbols by chimpanzees when trained in laboratories which, as I argued in Chapter 5, arises simply from possessing a general intelligence, rather than any linguistic capacity. The non-social 'language' of Early Humans may thus have amounted to a small range of 'words', used predominantly as demands, and with no more than two or three being strung together in a single utterance. They would have contrasted with the grammatically complex and diverse flow of utterances relating to the social world produced by Early Humans arising from their specialized social and linguistic intelligences. Yet the non-social vocalizations may have been embedded within this social language.

A second way for snippets of non-social conversation to arise may have been that the specialized intelligences were never totally isolated from each other, although the degree of isolation was sufficient to prevent them working together. I gave an example of this in Chapter 8 when I suggested that although Neanderthals may have lacked reflexive consciousness about their toolmaking and foraging activities, they may have had a fleeting, ephemeral, rolling consciousness about these – a 'snippet of consciousness', insufficient to have provided any introspection about their thoughts and knowledge in these domains. I explained why this may have been the case by using my analogy of the mind as a cathedral. The 'sounds' of reflexive consciousness at work may have seeped through the chapel walls of social intelligence, and then seeped into the chapels of technical and natural history intelligence, arriving in a heavily muffled or watered down form. I gave another example in Chapter 7 when I noted that in those very rare instances when Early Humans did work bone, they chipped it as if it were stone. This implies that if technical intelligence was indeed being used, it was not working effectively, since chipping is an inappropriate method for working bone. So we may also imagine that seeping in through the walls of social and linguistic intelligence were the muffled thoughts and knowledge coming from the chapels of technical and natural history intelligence. Consequently these were also available for use by linguistic intelligence when generating utterances.

What would have happened to these snippets of language about the non-social world? They must have entered the minds of other individuals as part of the flow of social language and have been decoded by linguistic intelligence and interpreted by social intelligence. In other words, the chapel of social intelligence began to be invaded by non-social information. Those individuals who could exploit these invasions to increase their own knowledge about the non-social world would have been at a selective advantage. They would have been able to make more informed decisions about hunting and toolmaking, enabling them to compete more successfully for mates and provide better care for offspring.

Further selective advantage would have been attained by those individuals who could add more non-social linguistic snippets into conversation, such as by introducing questions about animal behaviour or toolmaking methods. Perhaps these were individuals who, due to random changes made in the architectural plans they inherited, had particularly permeable walls between their specialized intelligences. These talkative individuals were gaining their selective advantage by exploiting the non-social knowledge of other individuals by using language, as opposed to relying on behavioural observations alone. As a consequence, social language would very rapidly (in evolutionary time) have moved to a general-purpose language; my guess would be in the time period between 150,000 and 50,000 years ago. Natural selection, the most important architect of the mind, simply would not have allowed this opportunity to improve the exchange of non-social information, and hence increase reproductive success, to pass by.[1]

There is evidence of this switch from a social to a general-purpose language surviving in our conversation today. As Robin Dunbar described, we still predominantly talk about social issues – we have a love of gossip. Moreover, when we talk about physical objects we often appear to ascribe to them an intrinsic tendency towards motion and imply that they possess 'minds' as if they are living, social beings. This has been explained by the linguist Leonard Talmy.[2] He argues that sentences such as 'the book toppled off the shelf' and 'the ball sailed through the window' imply that these objects move under their own power, since they are equivalent in their structure to sentences such as 'a man entered the room'. More generally, utterances appear to use the same range of concepts and structures whether they are referring to mental states, social beings or inert objects – which linguists refer to as the 'thematic relations hypothesis'.[3] They assume that the original use of language was for the last of these, and those concepts became transferred into utterances about the social/mental world by 'metaphorical extension'. Yet it makes more sense to see it the other way round: the structure of language arose when talking about the social world and was metaphorically extended for talking about physical objects.

The superchapel of the mind

Returning to our evolutionary scenario of a switch from social to general-purpose language, we must ask what happened to the chapel of social intelligence as it began to be invaded by non-social ideas and information? The cognitive scientist Dan Sperber has provided the answer: it became a type of superchapel in the cathedral of the mind. As we saw in Chapter 3, he described this superchapel as the 'module of metarepresentation' (MMR). He suggested that the MMR is an expanded version of the theory of mind module, although my position conceives of it as an expanded – perhaps even exploded – version of a more general domain of social intelligence. Sperber states: 'As a result of the development of communication, and particularly of linguistic communication, the actual domain of the meta-representational module is teeming with representations made manifest by communicative behaviours.... An organism endowed with ... a meta-representational module ... may form representations of concepts and beliefs pertaining to all conceptual domains, of a kind that the modules in those domains might be unable to form on their own.'[4] (see Figure 27)

The critically important point that Sperber is trying to express is that knowledge about the world comes to be represented in two different locations within the mind – within the specialized cognitive domain where it 'belongs', and within what had been the domain of social intelligence but which now contains knowledge about both the social and the non-social world. Indeed, the multiple representations of knowledge within the mind is a critical feature of Annette Karmiloff-Smith's idea for how cognitive fluidity arises during development.

This idea helps us understand what often appear to us to be contradictory views held by living hunter-gatherers, and indeed any Modern Human, about their world. Recall, for instance, the attitude to the polar bear held by the Inuit that I described in Chapter 3. This animal is thought of as a fellow kinsman, but it is also killed and eaten with delight. This combination of a deep respect for the animals they hunt, often expressed in terms of social relationships, and the lack of any qualms about actually killing them appears to be universal among hunter-gatherers. Such a combination of attitudes appears contradictory to us, until we appreciate that knowledge about these animals may be contained in two different cognitive domains – one where it relates to natural history and the problems of securing food, and one where it is mixed up with social intelligence. Another example is the attitude of the Australian Aborigines to their landscapes. To exploit these they rely upon a profound understanding of ecology. They are expert natural historians with detailed knowledge about the cycles of life and death. Yet they also

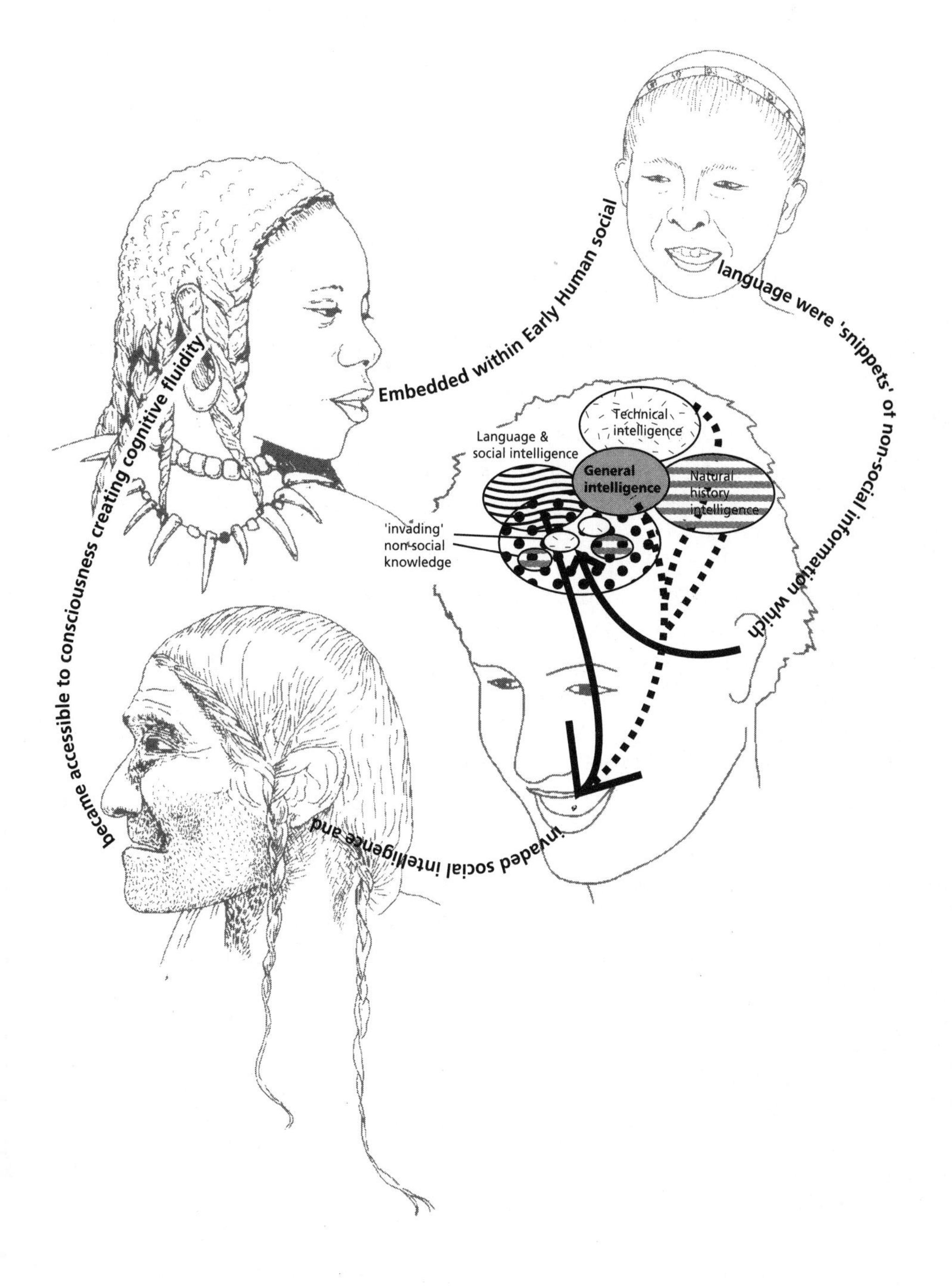

27 *The role of language in creating cognitive fluidity.*

understand their landscape as continuously created by Ancestral Beings, who have no respect for any laws of ecology. There is no contradiction or confusion in the Aboriginal mind: they simply have two mental representations of their environment, located in different cognitive domains.

Sperber suggested that the invasion of social intelligence by non-social information would trigger a 'cultural explosion'.[5] We do, of course, see precisely that cultural explosion at the start of the Upper Palaeolithic, and indeed see a rumbling anticipation of it after the first Modern Humans enter the play of our past 100,000 years ago. And as part of that cultural explosion we see the appearance of concepts and beliefs which no single domain could create by itself, concepts such as art and religion.

A new role for consciousness

A critical feature of the change to a cognitively fluid mind was a change in the nature of consciousness. Throughout this book I have followed Nicholas Humphrey's arguments that (reflexive) consciousness evolved as a critical feature of social intelligence: it enabled our ancestors to predict the behaviour of other individuals. But just like any other micro-domain of social intelligence, consciousness was not accessible to thought in other cognitive domains – there is no reason to expect Early Humans to have had an awareness about their own knowledge and thought processes concerning the non-social world (other than the ephemeral rolling consciousness I described in Chapter 8). But if, via the mechanism of language, social intelligence starts being invaded by non-social information, the non-social world becomes available for reflexive consciousness to explore. This is, in essence, the argument that Paul Rozin made in 1976 regarding the evolution of advanced intelligence. The critical feature of his notion of accessibility was the 'bringing to consciousness' of the knowledge which was already in the human mind but located within the 'cognitive unconsciousness'.[6]

Quite how much knowledge was brought to a level of conscious awareness is unclear. As I discussed in Chapter 8, a large proportion of our mental activity is likely to remain closed to us in our unconscious mind. Craftspeople, for instance, often appear unaware of the technical knowledge and skills they are using. When asked how they undertake tasks such as throwing a pot they often have difficulty explaining what they do unless they can provide a demonstration. Actions do indeed speak louder than words when technical knowledge is trapped within a specialized cognitive domain. This emphasizes the importance of verbal teaching of technical skills, which only began at the start of the Upper Palaeolithic as is implied by the spatial proximity of knapping debris produced by skilled and unskilled knappers at sites such as Etiolles in France and Trollesgave in Denmark.[7] When knowledge is acquired by verbal instruction it is by definition passed into what had once been the chapels of social and linguistic intelligences, where it becomes available for reflexive consciousness.[8]

The new role for consciousness in the human mind is likely to have been the one identified by the psychologist Daniel Schacter. In an article written in 1989 he argued that, in addition to creating the subjective feelings of 'knowing', 'remembering' and 'perceiving', consciousness should be viewed as 'a global database that integrates the output of modular processes.' He goes on to argue that such an 'integrative mechanism is crucial in any modular system in which processing and representations of different types of information are handled in parallel by separate modules.'[9] In the Early Human mind, general intelligence was the only device available to play this integrating role, and it hardly played it at all. But because language acted as the vehicle for delivering non-social thoughts and knowledge into the chapel of social intelligence, consciousness could start to play this new integrating role within the cathedral of the mind.

We have seen the consequence of integrating knowledge from separate domains in the previous chapter – a vast increase in human creativity. A final argument that consciousness is playing a fundamental role in achieving this integration and resulting creativity comes from the philosopher John Searle. In his 1992 book *The Rediscovery of the Mind*, he considered those sufferers of petit mal seizures that I referred to in Chapter 8. Recall that during their seizures they were able to continue with their goal-directed behaviour but without any consciousness. Referring to the change in the manner in which they undertook their activities, such as piano playing, Searle writes: 'the patients were performing types of actions that were habitual, routine and memorized ... normal human conscious behaviour has a degree of flexibility and creativity that is absent from ... [these] ... cases of unconscious drivers and unconscious pianists.... One of the evolutionary advantages conferred on us by consciousness is the much greater flexibility, sensitivity and creativity we derive from being conscious.'[10]

Early Humans did not lack consciousness altogether; it was simply restricted within their domain of social intelligence. And consequently their social interactions showed considerable flexibility, sensitivity and creativity. But this was markedly absent from their non-social activity – as anyone who has had the task of describing handaxe, after handaxe, after handaxe will know. But as soon as language started acting as the vehicle for delivering non-social information and ideas into the domain of social intelligence, reflexive consciousness could also get to grips with the non-social world. Individuals could now become introspective about their non-social thought processes and knowledge. As a result, the whole of human behaviour was pervaded with the flexibility and creativity that is characteristic of Modern Humans.

Nursing females, cognitive fluidity and extended childhood

The scenario I have offered for the evolution of cognitive fluidity suggests that by 150,000 years ago the Swiss-army-knife mentality was beginning to break down. Those individuals who were able to exploit snippets of non-social conversation were at a selective advantage as they could integrate knowledge which had been 'trapped' within specialized intelligences. We can, I think, identify one particular class of individual within these societies who would have been under particular selective pressure to achieve cognitive fluidity: sexually mature females.

Females at any time during human evolution were only able to give birth to relatively small-brained infants. This is due to the anatomy of the pelvis which needs to be narrow to allow efficient walking on two legs.[11] Consequently the offspring of Modern Humans have a brain size no larger than that of a newborn chimpanzee – about 350 cc. Yet unlike the chimpanzee, in the immediate period after birth the human brain continues to grow at the same rate as that of a foetus. By the age of four a human brain has tripled in size, and when maturity is reached it is around 1400 cc, four times the size at birth. In contrast the chimpanzee brain has only a small postnatal increase in size to around 450 cc.[12] During the period of brain growth after birth, human infants have a very high degree of dependency on adults. There are substantial demands on the mothers to supply the energy to fuel the growth of the infant brain, and indeed anatomy in general. These demands would have become particularly strong during the second period of rapid brain expansion that began after 500,000 years ago.

The social anthropologist Chris Knight and his colleagues have argued that the Early Modern Human females solved the problem of how to 'fuel' the production of increasingly large-brained infants by extracting 'unprecedented levels of male energetic investment'.[13] They suggest that coordinated behaviour by females forced males to provide them with high-quality food from hunting. An important element of the female action was a 'sex strike' and the use of red ochre as 'sham menstruation'. They describe this as the first use of symbolism and find evidence for it in the increase of red ochre after 100,000 years ago associated with the Early Modern Humans of southern Africa.

While I am sceptical about their ideas of coordinated female action, they have identified a social context in which food becomes critical in negotiating social relationships between the sexes. In this context 'snippets' of language about food and hunting may have been especially valuable in the social language between males and females. Females, in particular, may have needed to exploit this information when developing their social relationships with males. This may indeed explain why the first step towards cognitive fluidity, as seen in the behaviour of the Early Modern Humans of the Near East, was an integration of social and natural history intelligence.

The increase in the time between birth and maturity that arose as brain size enlarged during the course of human evolution[14] has another consequence for the switch from a Swiss-army-knife to a cognitively fluid mentality. This is simply that it provides the time for connections between specialized intelligences to be formed within the mind. As I described in Chapter 3, the developmental psychologist Annette Karmiloff-Smith has argued that the mind of a modern child passes through a phase during which cognition is essentially domain-specific, after which knowledge becomes applicable beyond the special-purpose goals for which it is normally used. In Chapter 7 I argued that the cognitive development for young Early Humans effectively ceased after the specialized domains of thought had arisen and before any connections had been built. Consequently, with regard to development, the source of cognitive fluidity must lie in a further extension of the period of cognitive development.

There is indeed evidence in the fossil record that child development of Modern Humans is considerably longer than that of Early Humans. This comes in the form of the skeletal remains of the few Neanderthal children that exist. These show that Neanderthal children grew up rather quickly, developing robust limbs and a large brain at an early age compared with Modern Humans. A particularly important specimen comes from the site of Devil's Tower on Gibraltar and dates to around 50,000 years ago. This consisted of no more than five fragments, but reconstructions have shown it to be of a three- or four-year-old child. The teeth of this child demonstrate that dental eruption occurred earlier than in Modern Humans. Of more interest, however, is that at this young age the brain size of this Neanderthal, at 1400 cc, was approaching that of a mature adult. Such a rapid rate of brain expansion appears to be a general feature of Neanderthal children, being found in several other specimens.[15] The most recently discovered and best-preserved Neanderthal child is a two-year-old from Dederiyeh Cave in Syria. This appears to have possessed a brain size equivalent to that of a six-year-old Modern Human.[16]

In essence, there was no time for cognitive fluidity to arise before the development of the Neanderthal mind – and I assume the Early Human mind in general – had ceased. Unfortunately we lack any child skulls of the 100,000-year-old Early Modern Humans from the Near East, or those of the first Upper Palaeolithic hunter-gatherers. But my guess would be for a gradual extension of the period of development between 100,000 and 50,000 years ago.

The rise of the modern mind: an overview

Let me conclude this chapter by summarizing my explanation for the evolution of cognitive fluidity. The seeds were sown with the increase of brain size that began 500,000 years ago. This was related to the evolution of a grammatically complex social language. The utterances of this language, however, carried snippets of non-social information as well. Those individuals who were able to exploit such non-social information gained a reproductive advantage. In particular, females who were nursing infants for prolonged periods – and therefore unable to feed themselves adequately – would have come under selective pressure to adapt in this way, because their patterns of social interaction with males had become bound up with a need for food. As social language switched to a general-purpose language, individuals acquired an increasing awareness about their own knowledge of the non-social world. Consciousness adopted the role of an integrating mechanism for knowledge that had previously been 'trapped' in separate specialized intelligences.

The first step towards cognitive fluidity appears to have been an integration between social and natural history intelligence that is apparent from the Early Modern Humans of the Near East, 100,000 years ago. This is before Modern Humans dispersed into Asia and Europe where they either replaced or interbred with existing Early Human populations. The final step to a full cognitive fluidity occurred at slightly different times in different populations between 60,000 and 30,000 years ago. This involved an integration of technical intelligence, and led to the changes in behaviour that we refer to as the Middle/Upper Palaeolithic transition. In other words, it created a cultural explosion: the appearance of the modern mind.

11 The evolution of the mind

THE CRITICAL STEP in the evolution of the modern mind was the switch from a mind designed like a Swiss army knife to one with cognitive fluidity, from a specialized to a generalized type of mentality. This enabled people to design complex tools, to create art and believe in religious ideologies. Moreover, as I argue in the Boxes on pp. 196–97 and 198, the potential for other types of thought which are critical to the modern world can be laid at the door of cognitive fluidity. So too can the rise of agriculture as I will explain in the Epilogue to this book – for agriculture and its consequences do indeed constitute the cultural epilogue to the evolution of the mind.

The switch from a specialized to a generalized type of mentality between 100,000 and 30,000 years ago was a remarkable 'about turn' for evolution to have taken. The previous 6 million years of evolution had seen an ever-increasing specialization of the mind. Natural history, technical and then linguistic intelligence had been added to the social intelligence that was already present in the mind of the common ancestor to living apes and humans. But what is even more remarkable is that this recent switch from specialized to generalized ways of thinking was not the only 'about turn' that occurred during the evolution of the modern mind. If we chart the evolution of the mind not just over the mere 6 million years of this prehistory, but over the 65 million years of primate evolution, we can see that there has been an oscillation between specialized and generalized ways of thinking.

In this final chapter I want to put the modern mind in its truly long-term context by charting and explaining this long-term oscillation in the nature of the mind. Only by doing so can we appreciate how we are products of a long, slow gradual process of evolution and how we differ so much from our closest living relative, the chimpanzee. And in doing so I want firmly to embed the evolution of the mind into that of the brain, and indeed the body in general. I must begin by introducing some rather shadowy new actors who now appear in a long prologue to the play that is our past (see Figure 28).[1]

Sixty-five million years of the mind

We must start 65 million years ago with a creature known as *Purgatorius*, represented by sparse cranial and dental fragments coming from eastern

Racist attitudes as a product of cognitive fluidity

In Chapter 9 I argued that cognitive fluidity led to anthropomorphic and totemic thinking, since the accessibility between the domains of natural history and social intelligence meant that people could be thought of as animals, and animals could be thought of as people. The consequences of an integration of technical and social intelligence are more serious. Technical intelligence had been devoted to thought about physical objects, which have no emotions or rights because they have no minds. Physical objects can be manipulated at will for whatever purpose one desires. Cognitive fluidity creates the possibility that people will be thought of in the same manner.

We are all aware of such racist attitudes in the modern world, typified in the treatment of racial minorities. The roots of denying people their humanity would appear to stretch back to the dawn of the Upper Palaeolithic. Perhaps this is indeed what we see with the burial of part of a polished human femur with one of the children at Sungir 28,000 years ago and the defleshing of human corpses at Gough's Cave in Somerset, England, 12,500 years ago, which were discarded in the same manner as animal carcasses. Early Humans, with their Swiss-army-knife-like mentality, could not think of other humans as either animals or artifacts. Their societies would not have suffered from racist attitudes. For Neanderthals, people were people, were people. Of course those early societies could not have been peaceful Gardens of Eden with no conflict between individuals and groups. The idea that our ancestors may have lived in an idyllic state of cooperation and harmony was shown to be nonsense as soon as Jane Goodall, in her 1990 book *Through a Window* about the chimpanzees of Gombe, described how she saw bloodthirsty brutal murder and cannibalism of one chimpanzee by another. There can be little doubt that Early Humans engaged in similar conflicts as they attempted to secure and maintain power within their groups, and access to resources. But what Early Humans may have lacked were beliefs that other individuals or groups had different types of mind from their own – the idea that other people are 'less than human' which lies at the heart of racism.

The social anthropologists Scott Atran and Pascal Boyer have both independently suggested that the idea that there are

Montana, USA. This animal was a member of a group known as the plesiadapiforms. *Purgatorius* appears to have been a mouse-sized creature which lived on insects. The best preserved of its group was known as *Plesiadapis*: about the size of a squirrel, it fed on leaves and fruit (see Figure 29).

It is unclear whether or not the plesiadapiforms should be classified as primates. They lack characteristic primate features in certain regions of their skulls and in their mode of locomotion, as far as these can be reconstructed from fragmentary fossil remains. It is in fact possible that rather than being primates, the plesiadapiforms shared a common ancestor with the earliest true primates which appeared after 55 million years ago. In view of this uncertain evolutionary status, plesiadapiforms are best described as 'archaic primates'.

different human races comes from a transfer into the social sphere of the concept of 'essences' for living things that, as we saw in Chapter 3, is a critical part of intuitive biology. This transfer appears to happen spontaneously in the minds of young children. As another social anthropologist, Ruth Benedict, made clear in her classic 1942 study entitled *Race and Racism*, believing that differences exist between human groups is very different from believing that some groups are inherently inferior to others. For this view, which we can call racism, we seem to be looking at the transfer into the social sphere of concepts about manipulating objects, which indeed do not mind how they are treated because they have no minds at all. My argument here is that the cognitive fluidity of the Modern Human mind provides a potential not only to believe that different races of humans exist, but that some of these may be inferior to others due to the mixing up of thoughts about humans, animals and objects. There is no compulsion to do this, simply the potential for it to happen. And unfortunately that potential has been repeatedly realized throughout the course of human history.

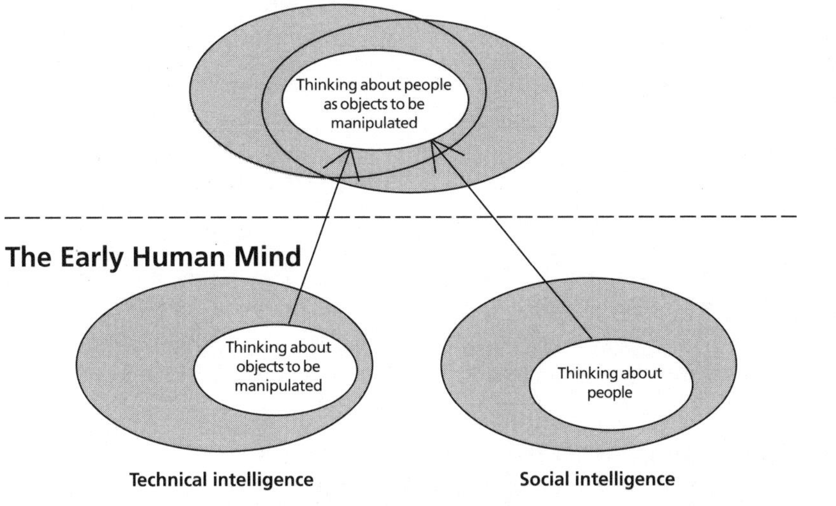

Our concern is with the type of mind that should be attributed to these creatures. It would seem appropriate to characterize their pattern of behaviour as more directly under the control of genetic mechanisms than of learning. A strict division between these – between 'nature' and 'nurture' – has long been rejected by scientists. Any behaviour must be partly influenced by the genetic make-up of the animal and partly by the environment of development. Nevertheless, the relative weighting of these varies markedly between species, and indeed between different aspects of behaviour within a single species.

It is useful here briefly to consider some findings from laboratory studies on the learning capacities of different types of animals. These studies require animals to solve problems, such as about getting food by pressing the correct levers, and have shown that primates as a whole have

Humour as a product of cognitive fluidity

Here is a joke:

> A kangaroo walked into a bar and asked for a scotch and soda. The barman looked at him a bit curiously and then fixed the drink. 'That will be two pounds fifty' said the barman. The kangaroo pulled out a purse from his pouch, took out the money and paid. The barman went about his business for a while, glancing from time to time at the kangaroo, who stood sipping his drink. After about five minutes the barman went over to the kangaroo and said, 'You know, we don't get many kangaroos in here.' The kangaroo replied, 'At two pounds fifty a drink, it's no wonder.'

This joke was quoted by Elliot Oring in his 1992 book *Jokes and their Relations* to illustrate what he believes to be a fundamental feature of successful humour: 'appropriate incongruities'. In this joke there are lots of incongruities: kangaroos walking into bars, speaking English and drinking scotch. But the response of the kangaroo to the barman's remark is an 'appropriate incongruity' due to the way the barman framed his remark. This implied that there were scotch-drinking, English-speaking kangaroos around, but that they simply were not visiting his particular bar.

It is readily evident that the potential to entertain ideas that bring together elements from normally incongruous domains arises only with a cognitively fluid mind. Had Neanderthals known about kangaroos, scotch and bars, they could not have thought of the incongruous situation of kangaroos buying a drink because their knowledge about social transactions would have been in one cognitive domain and that about kangaroos in another. And consequently their Swiss-army-knife mentality may have denied them what seems to be an essential element of a sense of humour.

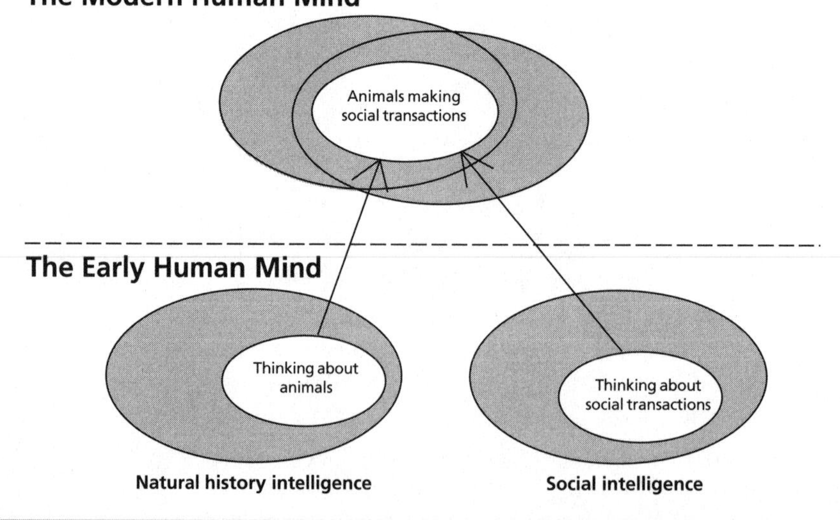

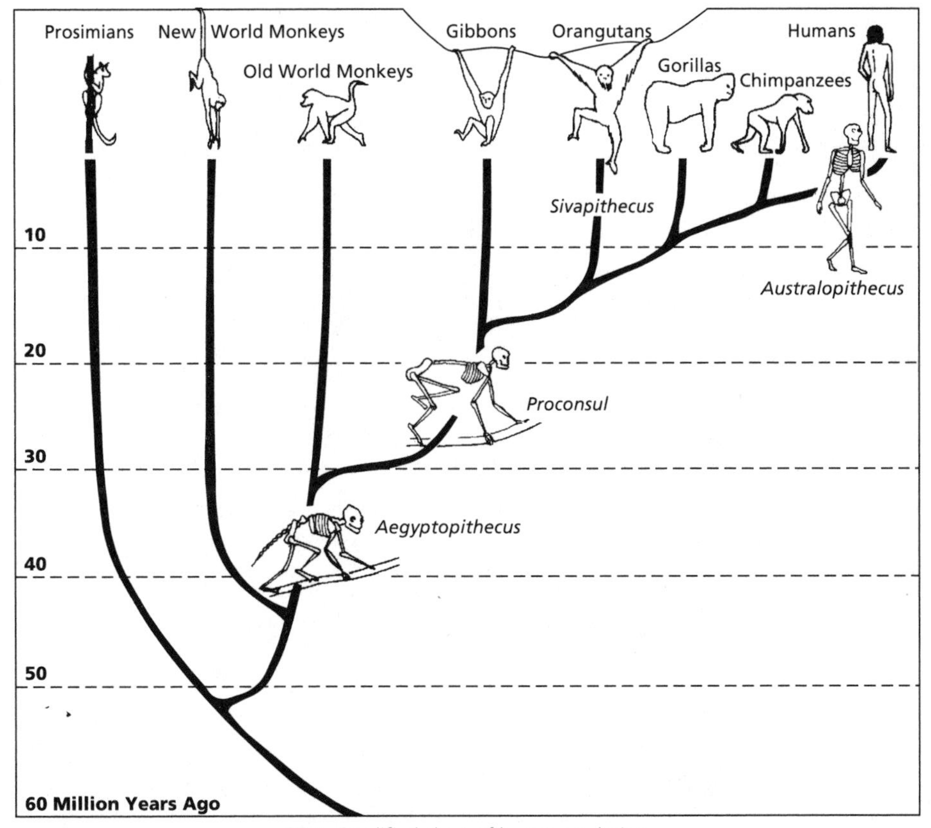

28 *A simplified chart of human evolution.*

29 Plesiadapis.

a greater capacity for learning than other animals, such as rats, cats and pigeons. By 'learning', I am referring here to what I have called throughout this book 'general intelligence' – a suite of general-purpose learning rules, such as those for learning associations between events. Only primates appear able to identify general rules that apply in a set of experiments, and to use the general rule when faced with a new problem to solve. While rats and cats can solve simple problems, they do not show any improvement over a series of learning tasks.[2]

Returning to the plesiadapiforms, and remembering that they may not be primates at all, it would seem likely that they would fall in with the rats and the cats on such tasks, rather than with the primates. In other words, we should attribute them with a minimal general intelligence, if one at all. The lives of the plesiadapiforms were probably dominated by relatively innately specified behaviour patterns, that arose as a response to specific stimuli and which were hardly modified at all by experience. We could indeed think of the plesiadapiform mind/brain as being constituted by a series of modules, encoding highly specialized knowledge about patterns of behaviour. To put it in other words, they possessed a type of Swiss-army-knife mentality.

The plesiadapiforms declined in abundance around 50 million years ago. This coincided with a proliferation of rodents, which probably outcompeted the plesiadapiforms for leaves and fruit. However, by around 56 million years ago two new primate groups had appeared, referred to as the omomyids and the adapids. These are the first 'modern primates' and looked similar to the lemurs, lorises and the tarsier of today. These first modern primates were agile tree dwellers, specialized for eating fruit and leaves. The best preserved is *Notharctus*, whose fossil remains come from North America (see Figure 30).

The most notable feature of these early primates is that they were the first to possess a relatively large brain. By this I mean that they had a brain size larger than what one would expect on the basis of their body size alone when compared with other mammals of their time period.[3] In general, larger animals need larger brains, simply because they have more muscles to move and coordinate. Primates as a group, however, have brains larger than would be predicted by their body size alone. The evolution of this particularly large brain size is described as the process of encephalization – and we can see that it began with these early primates of 56 million years ago.

I referred to this group at the end of Chapter 5 when we were considering the evolution of social intelligence. As I noted, if their minds were similar to those of lemurs today, it is unlikely that they possessed a specialized social intelligence. It is probable, however, that they pos-

30 Notharctus.

sessed a 'general intelligence', supplementing the modules for relatively innately specified behaviour patterns. The biological anthropologist Katherine Milton has argued that the selective pressure for this general intelligence was the spatial and temporal 'patchiness' of the arboreal plant resources they were exploiting. Simple learning rules allowed primates to lower the food acquisition costs and improve foraging returns.[4] Yet general intelligence may also have had benefits in other domains of behaviour, such as by facilitating the recognition of kin.

It is at this date, therefore, of about 56 million years ago, that we have the first 'about turn' in the evolution of the mind. We can see a switch from a specialized type of mentality possessed by archaic primates, with behavioural responses to stimuli largely hard-wired into the brain, to a generalized type of mentality in which cognitive mechanisms allow learning from experience. Evolution appears to have exhausted the possibilities for increasing hard-wired behavioural routines: an alternative evolutionary path was begun of generalized intelligence.

General intelligence required a larger brain to allow the information processing required to make simple cost/benefit calculations when choosing between behavioural strategies, and to enable knowledge to be acquired by associative learning. For a larger brain to have evolved, these early modern primates would have needed to exploit high-quality plant foods such as new leaves, ripe fruits and flowers – as is confirmed by their dental features. Such dietary preferences were essential in order to permit a reduction in gut size and consequently the release of sufficient metabolic energy to fuel the enlarged brain while maintaining a constant metabolic rate.[5]

The next important group of primates come from Africa, notably the sedimentary deposits of the Fayum depression in Egypt. The most important of these is *Aegyptopithecus*, which lived around 35 million years ago. This was a fruit-eating primate, living in the tall trees of monsoonal rainforests. Its body appears to have been adapted for both climbing and leaping. Like all the previous primates, it was a quadruped committed to moving on all four limbs. The most important primate fossils from the period 23–15 million years ago are likely to represent several species, but are referred to as *Proconsul*. These fossils are found in Kenya and Uganda, and show both monkey-like and ape-like features (see Figure 31).

The mind of *Aegyptopithecus* probably differed from that of *Notharctus* and the other early modern primates in two major respects. First the domain of general intelligence became more powerful – giving greater information processing power. The second change is of more significance: the evolution of a specialized domain of social intelligence.

If we follow the scenario put forward by Dick Byrne and Andrew Whiten, by 35 million years ago there was a form of social intelligence which resulted in significantly more complex behaviour in the social domain than in the interaction with the non-social world – as I discussed

31 Proconsul.

in Chapter 5. This domain of social intelligence evolved thanks to the reproductive advantage it gave individuals in terms of being able to predict and manipulate the behaviour of other members of the group. As argued by Leda Cosmides and John Tooby, those individuals with a suite of specialized mental modules for social intelligence are likely to have had more success at solving the problems of the social world. In other words, by 35 million years ago evolution seems to have exhausted the possibilities of improving reproductive success by enhancing general intelligence alone: an evolutionary turn around was made which began an ever-increasing specialization of mental faculties that continued until almost the present day.

It is during this period that Andrew Whiten's characterization of brain evolution as deriving from a 'spiralling pressure as clever individuals relentlessly selected for yet more cleverness in their companions' is appropriate.[6] As Nicholas Humphrey has described, when intellectual prowess is correlated with social success, and if social success means high biological fitness, then any heritable trait which increases the ability of an individual to outwit his fellows will soon spread through the gene pool.[7]

This 'spiralling pressure' probably continued in the period between 15 and 4.5 million years ago, during which the fossil record is particularly sparse.[8] It was in this time period, at around 6 million years ago, that the common ancestor of modern apes and humans lived, and it was with this missing actor that I began the play of our past. Byrne and Whiten suggest that by the time of the common ancestor, social intelligence had become sufficiently elaborated to involve abilities at attributing intentions to other individuals and to imagining other possible social worlds.

When the fossil record improves after 4.5 million years ago, the australopithecines are established in East Africa and possibly elsewhere in that continent. As we saw in Chapter 2, the best preserved of these, *A. afarensis*, displays adaptations for a joint arboreal and terrestrial lifestyle. As can be seen in Figure 1, the fossils between 3.5 and 2.5 million years ago suggest that this was a period of stability with regard to brain size. Why should the 'spiralling pressure' for ever greater social intelligence, and consequently brain expansion, have come to an end – or at least a hiatus? The probable answer is that evolution now confronted two severe constraints: bigger brains need more fuel, and bigger brains need to be kept cool. With regard to fuel, brains are very greedy, requiring over 22 times more energy than muscle tissue while at rest. With regard to temperature, an increase of only 2°C (3.6°F) can lead to impaired functioning of the brain.[9]

The australopithecines are likely to have been mainly vegetarian and lived in the equatorial, wooded savannahs. This lifestyle constrained the amount of energy that could be supplied to the brain, and exposed them to constant risk of overheating. Brain expansion could therefore not have occurred, even if the selective pressures for it had been present.

Had it not been for a remarkable conjunction of circumstances, it is likely that australopithecines would still be foraging in Africa and that the *Homo* lineage would not have evolved. But as we saw in Figure 1, at around 2 million years ago there started a very rapid period of brain expansion, marking the appearance of the *Homo* lineage. This could only have arisen if the constraints on brain expansion had been relaxed – and of course if selective pressures were present. When trying to explain how this happened, the interrelationships between the evolution of the mind, the brain and the body become of paramount importance. There are two behavioural developments in this period which are of critical importance: bipedalism – habitual walking on two legs – and increased meat eating.

The evolution of bipedalism had begun by 3.5 million years ago. Evidence for this is found in the anatomy of *A. afarensis* (see Figure 32), and, more dramatically, by the line of australopithecine footprints preserved at Laetoli in Tanzania. The most likely selective pressure causing the evolution of bipedalism was the thermal stress suffered by the australopithecines when foraging in the wooded savannahs of East Africa. With their tree-climbing and tree-swinging ancestry, the australopithecines had a body already conditioned for an upright posture. The anthropologist Peter Wheeler has shown that by adopting bipedalism australopithecines could achieve a 60 per cent reduction in the amount of solar radiation they experienced when the sun was overhead. Moreover, the energetic costs of locomotion would have been reduced. Bipedalism enabled australopithecines to forage for longer periods without the need for food and water, to forage in environments which had less natural shade, and thus to exploit foraging niches not open to other predators who were more heavily tied to sources of shade and water.[10] The shift to increasingly efficient bipedalism may have been partly related to the environmental change to more arid and open environments that occurred in Africa at around 2.8 million years ago,[11] increasing the value of reducing exposure to solar radiation by adopting an upright posture.

Bipedalism required a larger brain for the muscle control needed for balance and locomotion. But bipedalism and a terrestrial lifestyle had several other consequences for brain enlargement. Some of these have been discussed by the anthropologist Dean Falk.[12] She explains how a new network of veins covering the brain must have been jointly selected for with bipedalism to provide a cooling system for the brain – or a 'radiator' as she describes it. Once in place, the constraint of overheating on

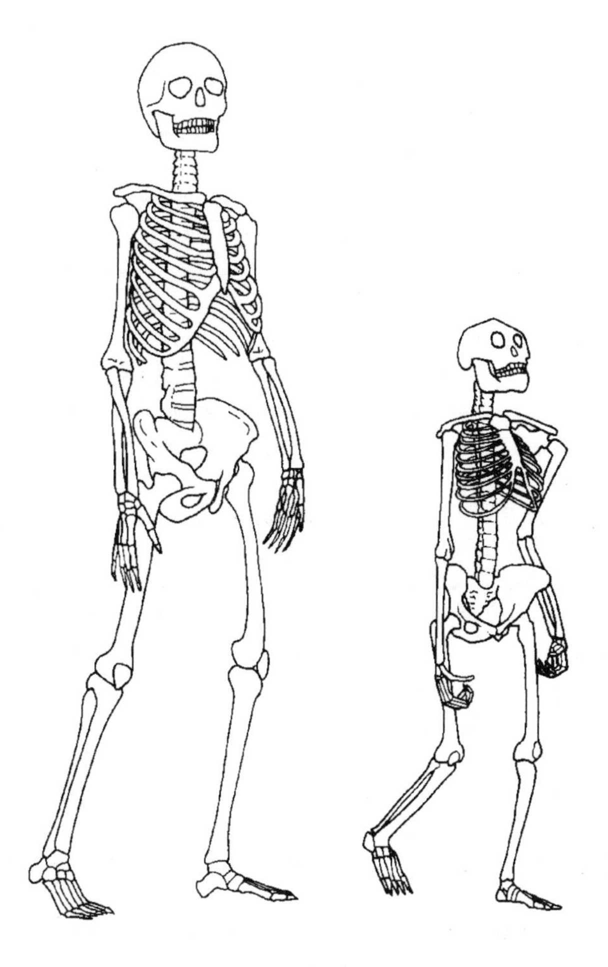

32 *A comparison of the size and posture of 'Lucy' (right) –* A. afarensis *– and a Modern Human female (left). Lucy was about 105 cm (3 ft 5 in) tall, with notably long arms.*

further expansion of the brain was relaxed as this radiator could easily be modified. Consequently the possibility (not necessity) arose of further brain enlargement.

Dean Falk also suggests that bipedalism would have led to a reorganization of the neurological connections within the brain: 'once feet had become weight bearers (for walking) instead of graspers (a second pair of hands) areas of cortex previously used for foot control were reduced thus freeing up cortex for other functions'.[13] This of course went with the 'freeing' of the hands, providing opportunities for enhanced manual dexterity for carrying and toolmaking. There may also have been significant changes in the perception of the natural environment due to an increase in the distances and directions regularly scanned; and a change in the social environment by an increase in face-to-face contact, enhancing the possibilities for communication by facial expression.

Perhaps the most significant consequence of bipedalism, however, is that it facilitated the exploitation of a scavenging niche. A 'window of opportunity' was opened to exploit carcasses during periods of the day when carnivores needed to find shade. As Leslie Aiello and Peter Wheeler have discussed, with an increasing amount of meat in the diet, the size of the gut could be further reduced, releasing more metabolic energy to the brain while maintaining a constant basal metabolic rate.[14] And in this way a further constraint on the enlargement of the brain was relaxed.

The main selective pressures for brain enlargement no doubt continued to come from the social environment: the spiralling pressures caused by socially clever individuals creating the selective pressure for even more social intelligence in their companions. And this pressure itself was present due to the need for large social groups that a terrestrial lifestyle in open habitats required, partly as a defence against predators.

Confirmation of the importance of the social environment for the expansion of brain size was found in Chapter 6. As we saw in that chapter, it is clear that the Oldowan stone tools of early *Homo* demanded more knowledge to make than those which chimpanzees use today, and therefore those likely to have been used by the australopithecines. But this knowledge probably arose from the enhanced opportunities for social learning in larger groups rather than as a consequence of selection for a domain of technical intelligence. Similarly, the narrow range of environments exploited by early *Homo* suggests that a discrete domain of natural history intelligence had not yet evolved and that the information requirements for scavenging were also being met as a by-product of living in larger social groups.

In my reconstruction of the evolution of the mind I only found the first evidence for distinct domains of natural history and technical intelligence at 1.8–1.4 million years ago with the appearance of *H. erectus*, and the technically demanding handaxes. What were the causes, conditions and consequences for these new domains of intelligence?

The ultimate cause for these new specialized intelligences was the continuing competition between individuals – the cognitive arms race that had been unleashed when the constraints on brain enlargement had been relaxed. But the evolution of these specific intellectual domains may well reflect the appearance of a constraint on any further enhancement of social intelligence itself. As Nicholas Humphrey noted, 'there must surely come a point when the time required to solve a social argument becomes insupportable'.[15] So, just as the possibilities of increasing reproductive success by enhancing general intelligence alone by natural selection had been exhausted by 35 million years ago, we might also conclude that the 'path of least resistance' for a further evolution of the mind in the conditions existing at 2 million years ago lay not in enhanced social intelligence but in the evolution of new cognitive domains: natural history and technical intelligence.

In other words, those individuals gaining most reproductive success were the ones who were most efficient at finding carcasses (and other food resources) and most able to butcher them. These individuals gained a better quality of diet, and spent less time exposed to predators on the savannah. As a result, they enjoyed a better state of health, could compete more successfully for mates, and produced stronger offspring. With regard to toolmaking, behavioural advantage was gained by those individuals who were able to have ready access to suitable raw materials for removing meat and breaking open bones of a carcass. The advantages of artifacts such as handaxes may well have been that they could be carried as raw material for flakes, as well as used as a butchering tool themselves. Experimental studies have repeatedly shown that they are very effective general-purpose tools.

Bipedalism, the scavenging niche, the existence of raw materials, the competition from other carnivores – these were all conditions that enabled the enhanced intellectual abilities at toolmaking and natural history to be selected for. Had one of these conditions been missing, we might still be living on the savannah.

The most significant behavioural consequence of these new cognitive domains was the colonization of large parts of the Old World. The evolution of a natural history and technical intelligence thus opened up a further window of opportunity for human behaviour. Within less than 1.5 million years, our recent relatives were living as far apart as Pontnewydd Cave in north Wales, the Cape of South Africa and the tip of Southeast Asia. There could be no more effective demonstration that the Swiss-army-knife mentality of Early Humans provided a remarkably effective adaptation to the Pleistocene world. Indeed, there appears to have been no further brain enlargement and no significant changes in the nature of the mind between 1.8 and 500,000 years ago.

This is not to argue that all minds were exactly the same; the *H. erectus* and *H. heidelbergensis* populations that dispersed throughout much of the Old World were living in diverse environments, resulting in subtle differences in the nature of their multiple intelligences. An example I gave in Chapter 7 referred to juveniles living in relatively small social groups in wooded environments during interglacial periods who will have had less opportunity to observe toolmaking, and whose minds consequently will not have developed the technical skills found in other Early Human populations.

The fourth cognitive domain to have evolved in the Early Human mind was that of language. It is likely that as far back as 2 million years ago, selective pressures existed for enhanced vocalizations. In this book I have followed Robin Dunbar's and Leslie Aiello's arguments that language initially evolved as a means of communicating social information alone rather than information about subjects such as tools or hunting. As group sizes enlarged, mainly due to the pressures of a terrestrial lifestyle, those individuals who could reduce the time they needed to spend in building social ties by grooming – or who acquired greater amounts of social knowledge with the same time investment – were reproductively more successful.

Just as the tree-living ancestry of the australopithecines enabled bipedalism to evolve, so too did bipedalism itself make possible the evolution of an enhanced vocalization capacity among early *Homo*, and particularly *H. erectus*. This has been made clear by Leslie Aiello.[16] She has explained how the upright posture of bipedalism resulted in the descent of the larynx, which lies much lower in the throat than in the apes. A spin off, not a cause, of the new position of the larynx was a greater capacity to form the sounds of vowels and consonants. In addition, changes in the pattern of breathing associated with bipedalism will have improved the quality of sound. Increased meat eating also had an important linguistic spin off, since the size of teeth could be reduced thanks to the greater ease of chewing meat and fat, rather than large quantities of dry plant material. This reduction changed the geometry of the jaw, enabling muscles to develop which could make the fine movements of the tongue within the oral cavity necessary for the diverse and high-quality range of sounds required by language.

The linguistic capacity was intimately connected with the domain of social intelligence within the Early Human mind. But technical and natural history intelligence remained isolated from these, and from each other. As I discussed in Chapter 7, this created the distinctive characteristics of the Early Human archaeological record, appearing very modern in some respects, but very archaic in others.

As I explained at the end of Chapter 7, while *H. erectus* probably possessed a capacity for vocalizing substantially more complex than what we see in apes today, it is likely to have remained relatively simple compared with human language. The evolution of the two principal defining features of language, a vast lexicon and a set of grammatical rules, seems to be related to the second spurt of brain enlargement that happened between 500,000 and 200,000 years ago. Yet even with these elements present, it remained in essence a social language. Explanations for this second period of brain enlargement are less easy to propose than for the initial spurt, which is clearly related to the origin of bipedalism and a terrestrial lifestyle.

One possibility is that the renewed brain enlargement relates to a further expansion of the size of social groups, resulting in those individuals with enhanced linguistic capacities being at a selective advantage. But the need for large group size is unclear – even remembering that this refers to the wider 'cognitive group', not necessarily the narrower group within which one lives on a day-to-day basis. Aiello and Dunbar suggest that it may simply reflect the increase in global human population and the need for defence not against carnivores, but other human groups.[17]

Yet here again another new window of opportunity arose for evolution. As soon as language acted as a vehicle for delivering information into the mind (whether one's own or that of another person), carrying with it snippets of non-social information, a transformation in the nature of the mind began. As I suggested in Chapter 10, language switched from a social to a general-purpose function, consciousness from a means to predict other individuals' behaviour to managing a mental database of information relating to all domains of behaviour. A cognitive fluidity arose within the mind, reflecting new connections rather than new processing power. And consequently this mental transformation occurred with no increase in brain size. It was, in essence, the origins of the symbolic capacity that is unique to the human mind with the manifold consequences for hunter-gatherer behaviour that I described in Chapter 9. And, as we can now see, this switch from a specialized to a generalized type of mentality was the last in a set of oscillations that stretches back to the very first primates.

As I discussed in Chapter 10, one of the strongest selective pressures for this cognitive fluidity is likely to have been the provisioning of females with food. The expansion of the brain had resulted in an extension of infant dependency which increased the expenditure of energy by females and made it difficult for them to supply themselves with food. Consequently male provisioning is likely to have been essential, resulting in a need for connections between natural history and social intelligence. It is perhaps not surprising, therefore, that these cognitive domains appear to have been the first two to have become integrated – as is apparent from the behaviour of the Early Modern Humans of the Near East – to be followed somewhat later by technical intelligence. Moreover, the prolonged period of infancy provided the time for cognitive fluidity to develop.

This transition to a cognitively fluid mind was neither inevitable nor pre-planned. Evolution simply capitalized on a window of opportunity that it had blindly created by producing a mind with multiple specialized intelligences. It may be the case that by 100,000 years ago the mind had reached a limit in terms of specialization. It might be asked why cognitive fluidity did not evolve in the other types of Early Humans, the Neanderthals, or the archaic *H. sapiens* of Asia. Well, there may indeed be a trace of cognitive fluidity between social and technical intelligence in the very latest Neanderthals in Europe, as they seem to start making artifacts whose form is restricted in time and space, and consequently may be carrying social information.[18] Yet before this could develop fully, they were pushed into extinction by the incoming Modern Humans, who had already achieved full cognitive fluidity.

Cognitive fluidity enabled people to engage in new types of activities, such as art and religion. As soon as these arose the developmental contexts for young minds began to change. Children were born into a world where art and religious ideology already existed; in which tools were designed for specific tasks, and where all items of material culture were imbued with social information. At 10,000 years ago the developmental contexts began to change even more fundamentally with the origins of an agricultural way of life, which, as I will explain in my Epilogue, is a further product of cognitive fluidity. As I described in Chapter 3, with these new cultural contexts, the hard-wired intuitive knowledge within the minds of growing infants may have 'kick-started' new types of specialized cognitive domains. For instance, a young child growing up in an industrial setting may no longer have developed a 'natural history intelligence'. Instead, in some contexts, a specialized domain for mathematics may have developed, kick-started by certain features of 'intuitive physics', even though no prehistoric hunter-gatherer had ever developed such a domain.

The hectic and ongoing pace of cultural evolution unleashed by the appearance of cognitive fluidity continues to change the developmental contexts of young minds, resulting in new types of domain-specific knowledge. But all minds develop a cognitive fluidity. This is the defining property of the modern mind.

Oscillations in the evolution of the mind

If we stand back from this 65 million years, we can see how the selective advantages during the evolution of the mind have oscillated from those individuals with specialized intelligence, in terms of hard-wired modules, up to 56 million years ago, to those with general intelligence up to 35 million years ago, and then back again to those with specialized intelligence in the form of cognitive domains up until 100,000 years ago.

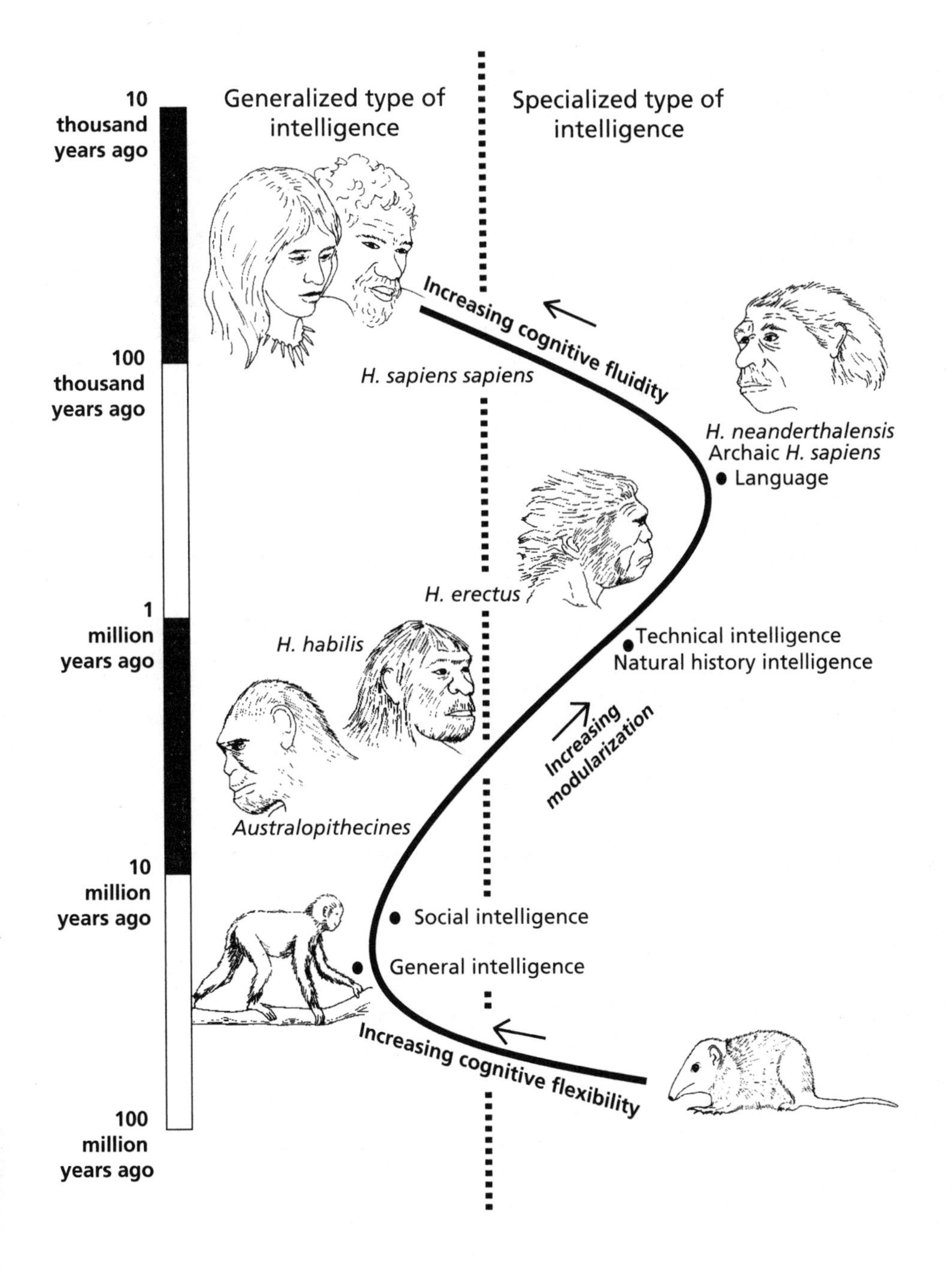

33 *The evolution of human intelligence.*

The final phase of cognitive evolution involved a further switch back to a generalized type of cognition represented by cognitive fluidity.

In the light of this evolutionary trajectory, as illustrated in Figure 33, it is not surprising that the modern mind is so frequently compared with that of a chimpanzee. Both have a predominantly generalized type of mentality (although chimpanzees have a specialized, isolated social intelligence), and therefore both look superficially similar. When we look at chimpanzees and modern hunter-gatherers we see a very smooth fit in each case between their technology and subsistence tasks. Both are very adept at making 'tools for the job'. Chimpanzees often behave in a similar way to humans, especially when they are taught and encouraged by humans to make tools, or paint pictures or use symbols. We are led to believe that the chimpanzee and the human mind are essentially the same: that of Modern Humans simply being more powerful because the brain is larger, resulting in a more complex use of tools and symbols. The evolution of the mind, as I have documented in the preceding pages, shows this to be a fallacy: the cognitive architecture of the chimpanzee mind and the modern mind is fundamentally different.

Yet this poses an important question. If the end point of cognitive evolution has been to produce a mind with a generalized type of mentality, superficially similar to the generalized type of mentality of the chimpanzee (excepting social intelligence) and the one we attribute to our early primate ancestors, then why did it bother to go through a phase of multiple, specialized intelligences which had limited integration? Why did natural selection not simply build on general intelligence, gradually making it more complex and powerful?

The answer is that a switch between specialized and generalized systems is the only way for a complex phenomenon to arise, whether it is a jet engine, a computer program or the human mind. Indeed my colleague Mark Lake believes that repeated switching from general-purpose to specialized designs is likely to be a feature of evolutionary processes in general.[19] To explain it let me return to one of the first analogies for the mind that I used in this book: the mind as a computer. Actually, let me be more specific and characterize the mind as a piece of software, and natural selection as the computer programmer – the designer. Both are common analogies, but no more. The mind/brain is as much a chemical soup as a series of electronic circuits, and natural selection has no goal; it is in Richard Dawkins memorable phrase the 'Blind Watchmaker'.[20] Let us briefly consider how natural selection blindly wrote the computer programs of the mind.

How is a complex piece of software produced? There are three stages. First one must write an overall plan for the program, often in the form of a series of separate routines that are linked together. The aim of this stage is simply to get the program to 'run', for all the routines to work together. This is analogous to natural selection building the general intelligence of our early primate ancestors: no complexity but a smoothly functioning system. The next stage is to add the complexity to the program *in a piecemeal fashion.* A good programmer does not try to add the required complexity to a program as a whole and all at once: if this is attempted, de-bugging becomes impossible and the program repeatedly crashes. The faults cannot be located and they pervade the system.

The only way to move from a simple to a complex program is to take each routine in turn, and develop it on an independent basis to perform its own specialized and complex function, ensuring that it remains compatible with the initial program design. This is what natural selection undertook with the mind; specialized intelligences were developed and tested separately, using general intelligence to keep the whole system running. Only when each routine has been developed on an independent basis does a programmer glue them back together in order simultaneously to perform their complex functions as an advanced computer program. This integration is the third and final stage of writing a complex program. Natural selection did it for the mind by using general-purpose language and consciousness as the glue. The result was the cultural explosion I described in Chapter 9.

In this regard, natural selection was simply being a very good (though blind) programmer when building the complex modern mind. If it had tried to evolve the complex, generalized type of modern mind directly from the simple, generalized type of mind of our early ancestors, without developing each cognitive domain in an independent fashion, it would simply have failed. Moreover, it is perhaps not surprising that we have found in this book a similar sequence of changes in the cognitive development of the child as in the cognitive evolution of the species.

The cognitive origins of science

Knowing the prehistory of the mind provides us with a more profound understanding of what it means to be human. I have used it to understand the origins of art and religion. And I must draw this book to a close by considering the third of the unique achievements of the modern mind, science, which I referred to in my introductory chapter, since this will lead us to identify the most important feature of our cognitively fluid minds.

Science is perhaps as hard to define as art or religion.[21] But I believe there are three critical properties. The first is the ability to generate and test hypotheses. This is something which, as I argued in previous chapters, is fundamental to any specialized intelligence: chimpanzees are evidently generating and testing hypotheses about the behaviour of other individuals when they engage in deceptive behaviour by using their social intelligence. I argued that early *Homo* and Early Humans were needing to generate and test hypotheses about the distribution of resources, especially carcasses for scavenging, by using their natural history intelligence.

A second property of science is the development and use of tools to solve specific problems, such as a telescope to look at the moon, a microscope to look at a flea, or even a pencil and paper to record ideas and results. Now although the hunter-gatherers of the Upper Palaeolithic did not make telescopes and microscopes, they were nevertheless able to develop certain dedicated tools by being able to integrate their knowledge of natural history and toolmaking. Moreover, they were using material culture to record information in what the archaeologist Francesco D'Errico has described as 'artificial memory systems':[22] the cave paintings and engraved ivory plaques of the Upper Palaeolithic are the precursors of our CD-Roms and computers. The potential to develop a scientific technology emerged with cognitive fluidity.

So too did the third feature of science. This is the use of metaphor and analogy, which are no less than the 'tools of thought'.[23] Some metaphors and analogies can be developed by drawing on knowledge within a single domain, but the most powerful ones are those which cross domain boundaries, such as by associating a living entity with something that is inert, or an idea with something that is tangible. By definition these can only arise within a cognitively fluid mind.

The use of metaphor pervades science.[24] Many examples are widely known, such as the heart as a mechanical pump and atoms as miniature solar systems, while others are tucked away in scientific theories, such as the notion of 'wormholes' in relativity theory and 'clouds' of electrons in particle physics. Charles Darwin conceived of the world in metaphor 'as a log with ten thousand wedges, representing species, tightly hammered in along its length. A new species can enter this crowded world only by insinuating itself into a crack and popping another wedge out.'[25] The biologist Richard Dawkins is a master at choosing appropriate metaphors to explain evolutionary ideas, such as 'selfish' DNA, 'natural selection as a blind watchmaker' and 'evolution as a flowing river'. Mathematicians are prone to talk about their equations and theorems using terms such as 'well behaved' and 'beautiful', as if they were living things rather than inert marks on pieces of paper.

The significance of metaphors for science has been discussed at length by philosophers, who recognize that they play a critical role not only in the transmission of ideas but in the practice of science itself. In his 1979 essay entitled 'Metaphor in Science', Thomas Kuhn explained that the role of metaphor in science goes far beyond that of a device for teaching and lies at the heart of how theories about the world are formulated.[26] Much of science is perhaps similar to Daniel Dennett's description of the study of human consciousness – a war of competing metaphors.[27] Such a battle has indeed been fought in this book. If we could not think of the mind as a sponge, or a computer, or a Swiss army knife, or a cathedral, would we be able to think about and study the mind at all?

In summary, science like art and religion, is a product of cognitive fluidity. It relies on psychological processes which had originally evolved in specialized cognitive domains and only emerged when these processes could work together. Cognitive fluidity enabled technology to be developed which could solve problems and store information. Of perhaps even greater significance, it allowed the possibility for the use of powerful metaphors and analogy, without which science could not exist.

Indeed, if one should want to specify those attributes of the modern mind that distinguish it not only from the minds of our closest living relatives, the apes, but also our much closer, but extinct, ancestors, it would be the use of metaphor and what Jerry Fodor described as our passion for analogy. Chimpanzees cannot use metaphor and analogy, because with one single type of specialized intelligence, they lack the mental resources for metaphor, not to mention the language with which to express it. Early Humans could not use metaphor because they lacked cognitive fluidity. But for Modern Humans, analogy and metaphor pervade every aspect of our thought and lie at the heart of art, religion and science.

The human mind is a product of evolution, not supernatural creation. I have laid bare the evidence. I have specified the 'whats', the 'whens' and the 'whys' for the evolution of the mind. I have explained how the potential arose in the mind to undertake science, create art and believe in religious ideologies, even though there were no specific selection pressures for such abstract abilities at any point during our past. I have demonstrated that we can only understand the nature of language and consciousness by understanding the prehistory of the mind – by getting to grips with the details of the fossil and archaeological records. And I have found the use of metaphor and analogy in various guises to be the most significant feature of the human mind. I have myself only been able to think and write about prehistory and the mind by using two metaphors within this book: our past as a play and the mind as a cathedral.

It is perhaps fitting, therefore, that this last chapter has been largely written while staying in the Spanish city of Santiago de Compostela.

This was one of the great centres of pilgrimage in the medieval world. The town has a remarkable collection of religious buildings which were built, and constantly modified, during the Middle Ages. These range from the simplicity of small churches with no more than a single nave to the complexity of the cathedral. Built on the site of a small ninth-century church, the cathedral is one of the masterpieces of Romanesque architecture. It has a three-aisled nave and no fewer than 20 chapels, each of which is dedicated to a different saint. The original Romanesque design has been modified by Gothic and later additions. My guide book to this cathedral and the other churches of Santiago tells me that walking within and between them will be like walking through history. But for me, it has been like walking through the Prehistory of the Mind.

Epilogue: the origins of agriculture

AROUND 10,000 years ago, people changed from being hunter-gatherers to farmers in many different regions of the world. This transformation took place quite independently in parts of Southwest Asia, Equatorial Africa, the Southeast Asian mainland, Central America and in lowland and highland South America. The onset of farming is frequently invoked as *the* turning point of prehistory. Without agriculture we would not have had towns, cities and state society. It is these that have so fundamentally changed the contexts in which the minds of individuals develop today from those of our hunter-gatherer ancestors. So how did this change come about? In my Epilogue I will argue that the rise of agriculture was a direct consequence of the type of thinking that evolved with the emergence of cognitive fluidity. More specifically, I will propose that there were four aspects of the change in the nature of the mind which resulted in a reliance on domesticated plants and animals when environmental conditions abruptly altered 10,000 years ago. Before looking, however, at just what these changes in the mind might have been, we need to consider briefly some of the broader issues involved in the origins of agriculture.

The introduction of farming is viewed as one of the great mysteries of our past. Why did it happen? Certainly not because of the crossing of a threshold in accumulated knowledge about plants and animals, enabling people to domesticate them.[1] As I have argued in this book, hunter-gatherers – whether Early or Modern Humans – are and were expert natural historians. We can be confident that knowledge about how animals and plants reproduce, and the conditions they need for growth, had been acquired by human minds as soon as a fully developed natural history intelligence had evolved, at least 1.8 million years ago.

The knowledge prehistoric hunter-gatherers possessed about animals is readily apparent from the diversity of species we know they hunted, to judge by the bones found at their settlements. It is only quite recently, however, that archaeologists have been able to document a similar level of exploitation of plant foods by prehistoric hunter-gatherers. Consider, for instance, the 18,000-year-old sites in the Wadi Kubbaniya, which lies to the west of the Nile Valley. The charred plant remains discovered here indicate that a finely ground plant 'mush' had been used, probably to wean infants. A diverse array of roots and tubers had been exploited, possibly all the year round, from permanent settlements.[2] Similarly, at Tell Abu Hureyra in Syria, occupied by hunter-gatherers between 20,000 and 10,000 years ago, no fewer than 150 species of edible plants have been identified, even though roots, tubers and leafy plants were not preserved.[3] At both these locations we see the technology for pounding and grinding plant material – the same as that used by the first farmers (see Figure 34). In summary, these sites demonstrate that the origins of agriculture 10,000 years ago are not to be sought in a sudden breakthrough in technology, or the crossing of a threshold in botanical knowledge.

So why did people take up farming? An element of compulsion must have been involved. Despite what we might intuitively imagine, farming did not automatically liberate our Stone Age ancestors from a hand-to-mouth, catch-as-catch-can existence. Indeed quite the opposite. Living by agriculture comes a very poor second when compared with living by hunting and gathering. The need to look after a field of crops ties down some members of a community to a particular spot, creating problems of sanitation, social tensions and the depletion of resources such as firewood. Hunter-gatherers easily solve these problems by being mobile. As soon as their waste accumulates, or firewood is depleted, they move on to another campsite. If individuals or families have disagreements, they can move away to different camps. But as soon as crops need regular weeding, and labour has been invested in building storage facilities or irrigation canals which need maintaining, the option to move on is lost. It is no coincidence that the earliest agricultural communities of the Near East show substantially poorer states of health than their hunter-gatherer forebears, as we know from studies of their bones and teeth.[4]

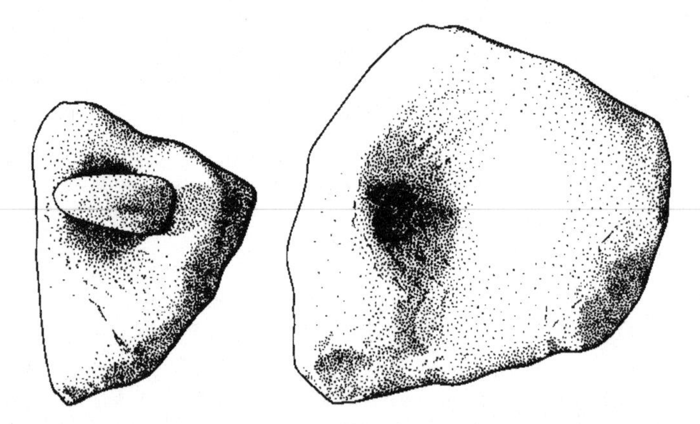

34 *Mortar and pestle for processing plants from site E-78-4, Wadi Kubbaniya, c. 18,000 years old.*

People therefore must have had some *incentive* to switch to farming. Moreover that incentive must have been on a worldwide scale 10,000 years ago, if we are to account for the fact that diverse methods of food production started independently in such a relatively short time period around the globe.[5] The crops being cultivated varied markedly, from wheat and barley in Southwest Asia, to yams in West Africa, to taro and coconuts in Southeast Asia.

Conventionally, two explanations are put forward for this near-simultaneous adoption of agriculture. The first is that at around 10,000 years ago population levels had gone beyond those that could be supported on wild food alone. The world had effectively become full up with hunter-gatherers and there were no new lands to colonize. As a result, new methods of subsistence were required to provide more food, even if they were labour intensive and came with an assortment of health and social problems.[6]

This idea of a global food crisis in prehistory is both implausible and not supported by the evidence. We know from studies of modern hunter-gatherers that they have many means available for controlling their population levels, such as infanticide. Mobility itself constrains the size of population due to the difficulties of carrying more than one child. Furthermore, we know that in some instances at least the health of the last hunter-gatherers in a region where agriculture was adopted appears to have been significantly better than that of the first farmers. This is evident from the study of pathologies on the bones of the last hunter-gatherers and the first farmers. Such evidence shows that the onset of agriculture brought with it a surge of infections, a decline in the overall quality of nutrition and a reduction in the average length of life.[7] The rise of farming was certainly not a solution to health and nutritional problems faced by prehistoric populations; in many cases it appears to have caused them. Nevertheless, although a global population crisis is implausible, the possibility remains that production of foodstuffs became necessary to feed relatively high local populations.

A second and partially more convincing explanation for the introduction of farming 10,000 years ago is that the whole world at that time was experiencing dramatic climatic changes associated with the end of the last ice age. There was a period of very rapid global warming – recent research indicating perhaps as much as an astonishing 7°C (over 12°F) in a few decades – that marked the end of the last glacial period.[8] This was preceded by a series of fluctuations 15,000–10,000 years ago, switching the globe from periods of warm/wet to cold/dry climate and back again. These climatic fluctuations were truly global affairs. The near-simultaneous adoption of farming in different parts of the world therefore appears to represent local responses, to the local environmental developments, caused by the global climatic changes immediately before and at 10,000 years ago as the last ice age came to an end. As we shall see, this cannot entirely account for the rise of farming, since Early Humans experienced similar climatic fluctuations without abandoning their hunting and gathering way of life. But first let us pause in our argument to consider one particular region, so as to understand better what really happened as farming took hold.

We can see the close relationship between changing methods of food procurement and late ice age climatic instabilities in Southwest Asia, where the origins of agriculture have been studied in most detail. Here we see the first farming communities of domesticated cereals (barley and wheat) and animals (sheep and goat) at sites such as Jericho and Gilgad at around 10,000 years ago. These settlements are found in precisely the area where the wild ancestors of these domesticated cereals had grown and had been exploited by the hunter-gatherers, such as those from Abu Hureyra.

Indeed the stratified sequence of plant remains at Abu Hureyra, as studied by the archaeobotanist Gordon Hillman and briefly referred to above, is very informative about the switch from a hunting and gathering to a farming lifestyle.[9] Between 19,000 and 11,000 years ago the environmental conditions in Southwest Asia improved, as the ice sheets of Europe retreated, leading to warmer and moister conditions, particularly during the growing season. This is likely to have been a period during which hunter-gatherer populations increased, since they were able to exploit ever more productive food plants, and gazelle herds moving along predictable routes.[10] At Abu Hureyra we find evidence in fact that a wide range of plants was being gathered. Between 11,000 and 10,000 years ago, however, there was a marked return to much drier environmental conditions, even drought.[11]

This drought had severe consequences for the hunter-gatherers of Abu Hureyra. In successive archaeological layers at the site we see the loss of tree fruits as a source of food – reflecting the loss of trees because of the drought – and then the loss of wild cereals, which were unable to survive the cold dry environments. To compensate we see a marked increase in small seeded legumes, plants which were more drought resistant but which also required careful detoxification to make them edible. At around 10,500 years ago Abu Hureyra was abandoned; when people returned there 500 years later, they came to live as farmers.

The significance of this drought, and possibly earlier climatic fluctuations, for the change in hunter-gatherer lifestyles is seen throughout Southwest Asia. In the region of the Levant, to the south and west of

Abu Hureyra, we can see that around 13,000–12,000 years ago hunter-gatherers changed from a mobile to a sedentary lifestyle probably in response to a short, abrupt climatic crisis of increased aridity which resulted in dwindling and less predictable food supplies.[12] Although people continued to live by hunting and gathering, the first permanent settlements with architecture and storage facilities were constructed.[13] This period of settlement is known as the 'Natufian', and lasted until 10,500 years ago when the first true farming settlements appear.

The Natufian culture marked a dramatic break with what went before.[14] Some of the new settlements were extensive. That at Mallaha involved digging underground storage pits and levelling slopes to create terraces for huts. The range of bone tools, art objects, jewellery and ground stone tools expanded markedly. Some of the Natufian flint blades have what is known as a 'sickle gloss', which suggests that stands of wild barley were being intensively exploited. But the people living in these settlements still supported themselves by wild resources alone. The critical importance of the Natufian for the origins of agriculture is that it constituted what has been described by the archaeologists Ofer Bar-Yosef and Anna Belfer-Cohen as 'a point of no return'.[15] Once that sedentary lifestyle had been put in place it was inevitable that the level of food production would need to increase, because the constraint on population growth imposed by a mobile lifestyle had been relaxed. Although it remains unclear quite why the sedentary lifestyle was chosen, it seems to have arisen out of decisions made by hunter-gatherers when faced with the short, abrupt climatic fluctuations at the very end of the last ice age.

It is likely that elsewhere in the world hunter-gatherers also reacted to the climatic fluctuations of the late Pleistocene in ways that involved either the direct cultivation of plants, or the adoption of a sedentary lifestyle which eventually committed them to a dependence on domesticated crops. But this cannot be the whole story of the origins of agriculture. As I have stressed at several places in this book, the Early Humans of Act 3 lived through successive ice ages. They too had been faced with marked climatic fluctuations, and experienced a dwindling of plant foods and the need for change in their hunting and gathering practices. But at no time did they develop sedentary lifestyles or begin to cultivate crops or domesticate animals. So why did so many groups of Modern Humans, when faced with similar environmental changes, independently develop an agricultural way of life?

The answer lies in the differences between the Early Human and the Modern Human mind. If my proposals for the evolution of the mind are correct, then Early Humans simply could not have entertained the idea of domesticating plants and animals, even when suffering severe economic stress, hypothetically surrounded by wild barley and wheat, and magically provided with pestles, mortars and grinding stones. The origins of agriculture lie as much in the new way in which the natural world was thought about by the modern mind, as in the particular sequence of environmental and economic developments at the end of the Pleistocene. There are four aspects of the change in the nature of the mind which were critical to the origins of agriculture.

1. **The ability to develop tools which could be used intensively to harvest and process plant resources. This arose from an integration of technical and natural history intelligence.** Little more needs to be said about this ability, for such technological developments were discussed in Chapter 9. We see the appropriate technology for the cultivation of plants in use at Wadi Kubbaniya and Abu Hureyra by 20,000 years ago.

2. **The propensity to use animals and plants as the medium for acquiring social prestige and power. This arose from an integration of social and natural history intelligence.** We can see several examples of this in the behaviour of hunter-gatherers after 40,000 years ago in Europe. Consider, for instance, the way in which the storage of meat and bone was used on the Central Russian Plain between 20,000 and 12,000 years ago, a period during which people constructed dwellings from mammoth bones and tusks (see Figure 35). The stored resources came from animals such as bison, reindeer and horse which were hunted on the tundra-like environments of the last ice age. Olga Soffer has described how during the course of this period access to stored resources came increasingly under the control of particular dwellings.[16] Individuals appear to have been using stored meat, bone and ivory not just as a source of raw material and food, but as a source of power.

We can see something similar in the hunter-gatherer communities of southern Scandinavia between 7,500 and 5,000 years ago. These people exploited game such as red deer, wild pig and roe deer in thick mixed-oak forests. By looking at the frequencies with which different species were hunted, and by studying the hunting patterns with computer simulation, we can deduce that they were focussing on red deer – even though this often left the hunters returning to their settlements empty-handed, because red deer were much scarcer and more difficult to kill than, say, the smaller and more abundant roe deer.[17] Why were they doing this? It is most likely that the preference for red deer arose from the larger size of the animal. More meat could be given away from a red deer carcass, pro-

***35** Mammoth-bone dwellings and storage pits on the Central Russian Plain, c. 12,000 years ago.*

viding greater social prestige and power. Day-to-day fluctuations in meat from hunting could be coped with by exploiting the rich plant, coastal and aquatic foods in the region, especially by using facilities such as fish traps that could be left unattended, some of which have been found almost perfectly preserved in waterlogged conditions. This idea is confirmed when we look at the burials of the hunter-gatherers. Antlers of red deer and necklaces made from their teeth are prominent in the grave goods.[18]

This use of animals, and no doubt plants, as the means for gaining social control and power within a society was absent from Early Humans. Their thought about social interaction and the natural world was undertaken within isolated cognitive domains and could not be brought together in the required fashion. This difference is critical to the origins of agriculture. While sedentary farming may represent a poorer quality of life for a community as a whole, when compared with a mobile hunting-gathering lifestyle, it provides particular individuals with opportunities to secure social control and power. And consequently, if we follow the proper Darwinian line of focussing on individuals rather than groups, we can indeed see agriculture as just another strategy whereby some individuals gain and maintain power.[19]

The archaeologist Brian Hayden favours this explanation for the origins of agriculture. In a 1990 article he argued that 'the advent of competition between individuals using food resources to wage their competitive battles provides the motives and the means for the development of food production'.[20] He used examples from various modern hunter-gatherer societies to show that when technological and environmental conditions allow it, individuals try to maximize their power and influence by accumulating desirable foods and goods, and by claiming ownership of land and resources.

When Hayden looked at the Natufian culture, he felt that the evidence for the long-distance trade of prestige items, and the abundance of jewellery, stone figurines and architecture were all clear signs of social inequality, reflecting the emergence of powerful individuals. Once that social structure had arisen, there was a need for the powerful individuals continually to introduce new types of prestige items and to generate economic surpluses to maintain their power base. Food production is an inevitable consequence – as long as there are suitable plants and animals in the environment for domestication. As Hayden notes, many of the first domesticates appear to be prestige items – such as dogs, gourds, chilli peppers and avocados – rather than resources which could feed a population grown too large to be supported by wild resources alone.

3. The propensity to develop 'social relationships' with plants and animals, structurally similar to those developed with people. This is a further consequence of an integration of social and natural history intelligence. In order to domesticate animals and plants, it was necessary for prehistoric minds to be able to think of them as beings with whom 'social' relationships could be established. As I have argued, Early Humans with their Swiss-army-knife mentality could not have entertained such ideas.

We can see evidence for the emergence of 'social relationships' between people and wild animals and plants among the prehistoric hunter-gatherers of Europe. For instance, in the Upper Palaeolithic cave sites of Trois-Frères and Isturitz in France reindeer bones have been found with fractures and injuries that would have seriously inhibited the animals' ability to move and feed. Nevertheless these reindeer survived for sufficient time to allow the fractures to start healing and it has been proposed that they were cared for by humans[21] – in much the same way as the crippled Neanderthal from Shanidar Cave referred to in Chapter 7 had been looked after.

There are also a few intriguing examples of horse depictions from Palaeolithic art which seem to show the animals wearing bridles – although it is difficult to tell, and the marks may simply identify changes in colour or bone structure (see Figure 36).[22] We know for sure, however, that dogs were domesticated shortly after the end of the ice age. Indeed in the hunter-gatherer cemeteries of southern Scandinavia dating to around 7,000 years ago, we find dogs which had received burial ritual and grave goods identical to those of humans. There is also a grave from the Natufian settlement of Mallaha which has a joint burial of a boy with a dog.[23]

The ability to enter into social relationships with animals and plants is indeed critical to the origins of agriculture. The psychologist Nicholas Humphrey drew attention to the fact that the relationships people have

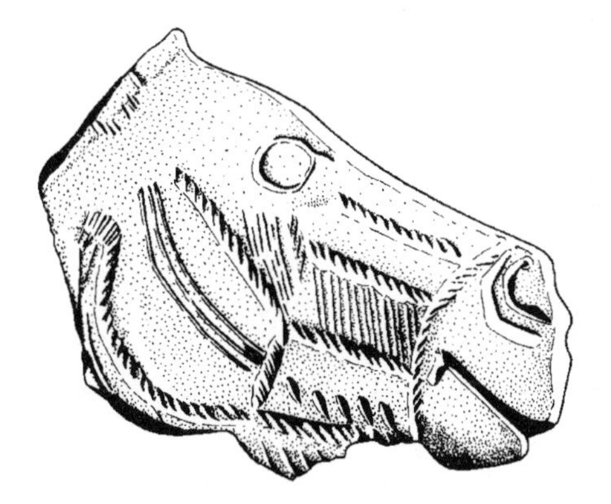

36 *Horse's head from St-Michael d'Arudy, Pyrénées-Atlantiques, France. Length 4.5 cm.*

with plants bear close structural similarities to those with other people. Let me quote him:

the care which a gardener gives to his plants (watering, fertilising, hoeing, pruning etc.) is attuned to the plants' emerging properties.... True, plants will not respond to ordinary social pressures (though men *do* talk to them), but the way in which they give to and receive from a gardener bears, I suggest, a close structural similarity to a simple social relationship. If ... [we] ... can speak of 'conversation' between a mother and her two month old baby, so too might we speak of a conversation between a gardener and his roses or a farmer and his corn.

As Humphrey goes on to note, 'many of mankind's most prized technological discoveries, from agriculture to chemistry, may have had their origin ... in the fortunate misapplication of social intelligence.'[24]

4. The propensity to manipulate plant and animals, arising from an integration of technical and natural history intelligence. We can think of this as the misapplication of technical intelligence, for just as Modern Humans appear to have begun treating animals and plants as if they were social beings, so too did they treat them as artifacts to be manipulated. Perhaps the best example of this is from the hunter-gatherers of Europe, who lived in the mixed-oak forests after the end of the last ice age. They were deliberately burning parts of the forest.[25] This is a form of environmental management/manipulation that acts to encourage new plant growth and attract game. It is a practice that has been well documented among the Aboriginal communities of Australia who undertook it perfectly aware that by doing so they were removing exhausted plant growth and returning nutrients to the soil to facilitate new growth. Indeed, by looking at the accounts of how the indigenous Australians exploited their environments we find evidence for many practices which are neither simple hunting and gathering, nor farming. For instance, in southwestern Australia, when yams were intensively collected, a piece of the root was always left in the ground to ensure future supplies.[26]

Modern Humans living as hunter-gatherers during prehistory probably developed relationships with plants and animals of a similar nature to those observed among recent hunter-gatherers. They are unlikely to have been simple predators, but engaged in the manipulation and management of their environments – although this fell short of domesticating resources. This was indeed recognized a quarter of a century ago by the Cambridge archaeologist Eric Higgs.[27] He encouraged a generation of research students to challenge the simple dualism between hunting-gathering and farming. We now know that these are just two poles on a continuum of relationships developed by prehistoric hunter-gatherers. But these relationships were only developed after 40,000 years ago, when ideas about animals and plants as beings to be manipulated at will or with whom 'social relationships' could be developed arose.

The four abilities and propensities I have outlined fundamentally altered the nature of human interaction with animals and plants. When people were faced with immense environmental changes at the end of the last ice age it was the cognitively fluid mind that made it possible for them to find a solution: the development of an agricultural lifestyle. In any one region there was a unique historical pathway to agriculture, in which some of these mental abilities and propensities may have been more important than others. But while the seeds for agriculture may have been first planted 10,000 years ago, they were first laid in the mind at the time of the Middle/Upper Palaeolithic transition. It is this key epoch and not the period of the birth of agriculture that lies at the root of the modern world. I have therefore treated the origins of agriculture as no more than an epilogue to my book. Nevertheless agriculture fundamentally changed the developmental contexts for young minds: for the vast majority of people alive today, the world of hunting and gathering, with its specialized cognitive domains of technical and natural history intelligence, have been left behind as no more than prehistory.

I have tried to demonstrate in this book the value of reconstructing that prehistory. For our minds today are as much a product of our evolutionary history as they are of the contexts in which we as individuals develop. Those stone tools, broken bones and carved figurines that archaeologists meticulously excavate and describe can tell us about the prehistory of the mind. And so, if you wish to know about the mind, do not ask only psychologists and philosophers: make sure you also ask an archaeologist.

Notes and further reading

Ch. 1. Why ask an archaeologist about the human mind? (pp. 9–16)

1 The evolution of the human mind's capacities for art and science is perhaps the key problem concerning the mind. The evolutionary linguist Steven Pinker describes this as a 'fundamental problem'. How could it have been possible, he asks, for evolution to 'have produced a brain capable of intricate specialized achievements like mathematics, science, and art, given the total absence of selective pressures for such abstract abilities at any point in history' (1989, 371).

2 Creationists in this context are not necessarily those who are anti-science or anti-evolution with regard to human anatomy. For instance Alfred Wallace Russell, the co-discoverer of the theory of natural selection, believed that human intelligence can only be explained by divine creation (Gould 1981, 39). In his 1989 book *The Evolution of the Brain*, the Nobel-prize-winning neurologist Sir John Eccles concludes that human consciousness derives from 'supernatural spiritual creation' (1989, 287).

3 I use the term 'ancestors' in a rather loose sense here as the evolutionary relationships between members of the australopithecines and *Homo* are highly contentious. Whether a species was a direct ancestor, or merely a relative, remains unclear in many cases, especially with *H. neanderthalensis* as will be discussed later in this book.

4 Merlin Donald's 1991 book *The Origins of the Modern Mind* was an excellent and very important attempt to integrate data and ideas from psychology, evolutionary biology and archaeology. He proposes that the mind has passed through three major stages: an 'episodic culture' associated with australopithecines, earliest *Homo* and living apes; a 'mimetic culture' associated with *H. erectus* and a 'mythic' culture associated with *H. sapiens*. The last of these involved the ability to construct conceptual models and was closely related to the evolution of language. He believes that with this third stage the 'mind' became extended in the sense of beginning to use external storage devices i.e. material symbols. Any readers of my book are highly recommended to read *The Origins of the Modern Mind* as an alternative interpretation of how data and ideas from psychology and archaeology can be integrated. The principal weakness in Donald's work is his use of archaeological data: the complexity and variability of this is often not appreciated, and certainly not exploited to its full extent. Lake (1992) makes numerous perceptive criticisms in this regard. Donald also appears to underestimate the cognitive capacities of living apes, as the type of intelligence he attributes to *H. erectus* is similar to that found in chimpanzees today (Byrne, personal communication). Donald (1994) provides a précis which is followed by a critical discussion of his book.

The psychologist Michael Corballis (1992) has also drawn on archaeological data, especially when exploring the evolution of language. He argues that the origin of language was gesture – speech only became the principal medium for language relatively late in human evolution, at the time of the Middle/Upper Palaeolithic transition (*c.* 40,000 years ago). He supports this idea by referring to the expansion in the range of technical behaviour at the time of the transition, in the sense of bone, antler and ivory working, the production of art and the use of prismatic blade cores for stone tools. These arose, he suggests, because the hands had become freed from being used as the medium of communication due to the evolution of speech. The major problem with this is that the lithic technology of the Middle Palaeolithic involved as much manual dexterity as the techniques of the Upper Palaeolithic, as explained in my Chapter 6. Nevertheless, as with Donald's (1991) work, this is a valuable attempt to integrate ideas and data from psychology and archaeology.

5 The most explicit call for a 'cognitive archaeology' came from Colin Renfrew (1983). Prior to that, however, Thomas Wynn (1979, 1981) and Alexander Marshack (1972a,b) had attempted to draw inferences about past cognition from specific types of artifacts. More recently, archaeologists have shifted their attention to the evolution of language (e.g. Davidson & Noble 1989; Whallon 1989; Mellars 1989a) but with little concern as to the relationship between language and other aspects of cognition. As far

as I know, no archaeologist has attempted to track the evolution of the mind throughout the course of prehistory.

6 Aiello (1996a).

7 As we will see in Chapter 3, this is in fact not a particularly new idea and one that does not necessarily require an explicit evolutionary argument for support.

Ch. 2. The drama of our past (pp. 17–32) Further reading

Human evolution

Jones *et al* (1992) contains a series of excellent chapters covering all aspects of human evolution, with descriptions of fossils and what can be learnt from living primates and human genetics. For a discussion of the methods of molecular taxonomy for reconstructing human and primate evolutionary relationships see Byrne (1995, Chapter 1). The most recent australopithecine discoveries are described by White *et al* (1994), WoldeGabriel *et al* (1994), Leakey *et al* (1995) and Brunet *et al* (1995), while Wood (1994) and Andrews (1995) discuss their significance. Susman (1991) discusses the anatomy of the australopithecine hand, with regard to their potential for making stone tools. Johanson & Eddy (1980) provide an account of the discovery of 'Lucy' and a discussion of her significance. A review of the earliest fossils of *Homo* is provided by Wood (1992), while Tobias (1991) is a comprehensive study of the hominid fossils from Olduvai Gorge.

The evolution of *H. erectus* is discussed by Rightmire (1990), while dates for the *H. erectus* fossils in Java are provided by Swisher *et al* (1994); and in China by Wanpo *et al* (1995). The significance of the new finds in China and the problems of their taxonomic identification are discussed by Wood & Turner (1995) and Culotta (1995). A detailed study of the *H. erectus* specimen known as KNM-WT 15000 is provided by Walker & Leakey (1993). The evolution of modern humans has been a matter of intense debate during the last decade, between those supporting multi-regional and those supporting out of Africa scenarios. Important papers regarding the contribution of molecular genetics include Cann *et al* (1987) and Templeton (1993), while summaries of the debating points regarding hominid fossils are found in Hublin (1992), Frayer *et al* (1993, 1994), Aiello (1993), Stringer & Bräuer (1994) and Wolpoff (1989; Wolpoff *et al* 1984). The earliest fossils in Europe are described by Arsuaga *et al* (1993), Carbonell *et al* (1995) and Roberts *et al* (1994). Stringer (1993) provides a summary of differing interpretations. The evolution and nature of the Neanderthals are described in Stringer & Gamble (1993) and Trinkaus & Shipman (1993). A summary of the dating evidence for the earliest anatomically modern humans is given by Grün & Stringer (1991).

There are numerous edited volumes dealing with the origins of modern humans. The most notable are by Akazawa *et al* (1992), Mellars & Stringer (1989), Bräuer & Smith (1992) and Nitecki & Nitecki (1994).

Stone tool technology

General introductions to stone tool technology describing the different techniques and the periods in which they are found are provided by Bordes (1961a, 1968) and Inizan *et al* (1992).

The archaeology of Act 2

The earliest stone tools are described by Merrick & Merrick (1976), Chavaillon (1976), Roche (1989), Roche & Tiercelin (1977) and Kibunjia (1994; Kibunjia *et al* 1992). Harris & Capaldo (1993) provide a review of the earliest archaeological sites and their interpretation. The archaeology of Olduvai Gorge is described by Leakey (1971), while Hay (1976) provides the critical geological background. Good accounts of the Oldowan industry are provided by Toth (1985) and Schick & Toth (1993), while Potts (1988) summarizes the archaeology of Bed I. Isaac (1984) provides a summary of other site complexes in East Africa, such as Koobi Fora. With regards to the interpretation of animal bones associated with these stone tools see Binford (1981, 1985, 1986), Bunn (1981, 1983a, 1983b), Bunn & Kroll (1986), Potts (1988) and Potts & Shipman (1981). The collected papers of Glynn Isaac (B. Isaac 1989) are essential reading for an understanding of the archaeology of Act 2. Useful papers concerning the environmental context of early hominids are those by Cerling (1992) and Sikes (1994). Claims for 2-million-year-old stone tools in Pakistan have been made by Dennell *et al* (1988a,b).

The archaeology of Act 3

The earliest use of bifacial technology is described by Leakey (1971) while Asfaw *et al*

(1992) provide dates for the first handaxes. For a general review of the dispersal of early humans into Asia and Europe see Gamble (1993, 1994). Bar-Yosef (1994a) describes the site of Dmanisi, while the earliest sites in West Asia are described by Bar-Yosef (1980, 1989, 1994a), Bar-Yosef & Goren-Inbar (1993) and Goren-Inbar (1992). For the earliest sites in East Asia see Schick & Zhuan (1993), while Zhoukoudian is summarized by Wu & Lin (1983). The debate about the first colonization of Europe is discussed by Roebroeks & van Kolfschoten (1994), while the early dated artifacts from Atapuerca are briefly described by Parés & Pérez-González (1995). Claims for occupation prior to 1 million years ago are made by Bonifay & Vandermeersch (1991). The site of Boxgrove is described by Roberts (1986), and questions about its date are raised by Bowen & Sykes (1994).

The archaeology of Africa between 1.5 million and 200,000 years ago, the Lower Palaeolithic, is summarized by Isaac (1982) and Phillipson (1985). Particularly important sites are Olorgesailie in Kenya (Isaac 1977; Potts 1989, 1994); Isimila in Tanzania (Howell 1961); Gadeb in Ethiopia (Clark & Kurashina 1979a, 1979b) and Sterkfontein in South Africa (Kuman 1994). For sites in West Asia for this period see Bar-Yosef (1980, 1994a), in East Asia see Schick & Zhuan (1993), and in Southeast Asia see Ayers & Rhee (1984), Bartstra (1982), Sémah *et al* (1992), Pope (1985, 1989) and Yi & Clark (1985). Early sites in Europe are discussed by Roebroeks *et al* (1992) and Gamble (1986). Roe (1981) summarizes the sites in Britain while Villa (1983) does likewise for France, focusing on the site of Terra Amata. Other important sites are Pontnewydd Cave in Wales (Green 1984); High Lodge in England (Ashton *et al* 1992) and La Cotte on Jersey (Callow & Cornford 1986). Sites lacking handaxes are described by Svoboda (1987) and Vértes (1975).

For the period between 200,000 and 50,000 years ago, Clark (1982) outlines the archaeology of Africa, while Allsworth-Jones (1993) provides a useful review of the associations between human species and stone tool industries. Particularly important sites with stratified sequences of material are the Haua Fteah in North Africa (McBurney 1967), Muguruk in Kenya (McBrearty 1988), Kalambo Falls in Zaire (Clark 1969, 1974), Klasies River Mouth in South Africa (Singer & Wymer 1982; Thackeray 1989) and Border Cave, also in South Africa (Beaumont *et al* 1978). Reviews for sites of this period in West Asia are provided by Bar-Yosef (1988, 1994b) and Jelenik (1982). Recent work in the important cave site of Kebara is described by Bar-Yosef *et al* (1992). For Europe, Gamble (1986) and Roebroeks *et al* (1992) provide a general review, while important studies are those of Laville *et al* (1980) of the rockshelters from Southwest France, Tuffreau (1992) for sites in North France, Kuhn (1995) for sites in Western Italy and Conrad (1990) for sites in the central Rhine Valley. The archaeology of East Asia for this time period is very poorly known. Schick & Zhuan (1993) and Zhonglong (1992) review the currently known, but often very poorly dated, sites.

The use of marine sediment cores to reconstruct the changing environments of this period is described by Dawson (1992), while important papers are those of Shackleton & Opdyke (1973) and Shackleton (1987). Initial results from the study of ice cores are described by Alley *et al* (1993), Johnsen *et al* (1992) and Taylor *et al* (1993).

The archaeology of Act 4

For the earliest use of red ochre in South Africa see Knight *et al* (1995), and for bone harpoons dating to earlier than 90,000 years ago see Yellen *et al* (1995). Roberts *et al* (1990, 1993, 1994) and Allen (1994) describe the earliest dated sites in Australia, while discussions of the colonization process are provided by Gamble (1993) and Bowdler (1992). Davidson & Noble (1992) discuss the implications of the colonization for cultural capacities, while Bahn (1994) provides dates for the earliest art in Australia. Bowdler (1992) and Brown (1981) examine the varying morphology of the modern humans in Australia while Flood (1983) describes the archaeology of the first Australians. For the colonization of North America see Hoffecker *et al* (1993), C. Haynes (1980), G. Haynes (1991), Gamble (1993) and Greenberg *et al* (1986). Larichev *et al* (1988, 1990, 1992) summarizes the evidence for occupation in northern Siberia. Important sites in the Americas regarding the earliest occupation include Meadowcroft Rockshelter (Adovasio *et al* 1990), Monte Verde in Chile (Dillehay 1989; Dillehay & Collins 1988) and Pedra Furada in Brazil (Guidon *et al* 1994; Meltzer *et al* 1994). Dillehay *et al* (1992) review the earliest archaeology of South America.

The changes in technology and behaviour at 40,000 years ago in Africa are discussed by Smith (1982), Parkington (1986) and Wadley (1993). The new technology in the Haua Fteah is summarized by Close (1986) while important cultural developments in the Wadi Kubbaniya, such as grinding stones, are described by Wendorf *et al* (1980). The first technological changes happening in West Asia are described by Bar-Yosef (1988, 1994b), Gilead (1991), Gilead & Bar-Yosef (1993) and Olszewski & Dibble (1994). With regard to East Asia, Bednarik & Yuzhu (1991) and Aikens & Higuchi (1982) describe the earliest pieces of art while Zhonglong (1992) and Reynolds & Barnes (1984) describe changes in stone tools. Anderson (1990) and Groube *et al* (1986) describe the first known archaeological sites in Southeast Asia.

Important summaries for the cultural changes in Europe after 40,000 years ago are provided by Mellars (1973, 1989a, 1989b, 1992), White (1982), Gamble (1986) and Allsworth-Jones (1986). Crucial dating evidence for the spread of modern humans is provided by Hedges *et al* (1994), Bischoff *et al* (1989) and Cabrera & Bischoff (1989). The earliest bone technology is considered by Knecht (1993a, 1993b) and bead technology by White (1989a, 1993a, 1993b). The earliest art is described by Delluc & Delluc (1978) and Hahn (1993), while claims for art in Act 3 are made by Bednarik (1992, 1995) and Marshack (1990). Interpretations of the relationship between Neanderthals and modern humans are considered by Harold (1989) and Mellars (1989a). The art of the last ice age from Europe is described by Bahn & Vertut (1988), while technological developments and adaptations to the last glacial maximum are described by Straus (1991), Jochim (1983) and Gamble & Soffer (1990). For later European prehistory see Barton *et al* (1992) and Cunliffe (1994).

Ch. 3. The architecture of the modern mind (pp. 33–60)

1 Whether or not there is a valid distinction to make here has troubled philosophers for many years; the mind-body problem being one of the major issues of philosophy. Dennett (1991) gives an entertaining introduction to this problem while MacDonald (1992) provides a review of mind-body identity theories. For body-mind concepts in the ancient world see Hankoff (1980).

2 Our bodies are physiologically adapted to the diet of Pleistocene hunter-gatherers: wild game, nuts, fruit and fresh vegetables. The fact that our diet today (and for much of later prehistory) contrasts with this in terms of the consumption of dairy products, cereals, fatty meat, sugars, oils and alcohol has profound consequences for our health today: heart attacks, strokes, cancers and diabetes are all nutritionally related.

3 Tooby & Cosmides (1992) have reviewed the manner in which most social scientists (they claim) see the mind as a 'tabula rasa', a blank slate, waiting to be filled by the cultural context of development. For instance Clifford Geertz, perhaps the most influential social anthropologist of the 20th century, has written about how the mind is 'desperately dependent upon such extragenetic, outside-the-skin control mechanisms ... for the governing of behaviour' (Geertz 1973, 44). Closely allied with this is what might be interpreted as a denial of human nature: 'humanity is as various in its essence as in its expression' (ibid, 37).

4 The view of the brain as hardware and the mind as software has been expressed by the archaeologist, Colin Renfrew: 'The hardware (directly dependent upon the genetic base) may have changed little over the time-span [of the past 40,000 years] but it is in the software ("culture") that the radical transformations from the hunter-gatherer to the space age have to be understood' (Renfrew 1993, 249).

5 Whether or not computers can be truly creative has been discussed by the cognitive scientist Margaret Boden (1990), who is more sympathetic to the cause of creative computers than I am myself. As with making computers intelligent, it hinges on how the term 'creativity' is defined.

6 The need to reconstruct the cognition of our earliest ancestors was always implicit in Glynn Isaac's work (e.g. 1978, 1981) and was addressed directly in Isaac (1986). Other Palaeolithic archaeologists were more disparaging about both the need and our ability to make cognitive interpretations. For instance, Lewis Binford, perhaps the most influential Palaeolithic archaeologist of the 20th century, condemns attempts at 'palaeopsychology'. Similarly, but much more recently, another highly influential Palaeolithic archaeologist, Clive Gamble, has written that 'stone tools can tell us ... precious little about intelligence or its potential' (1993, 170). Wynn (1979, 1981, 1989) thought precisely the opposite. In his early work Thomas Wynn clung onto the idea that intelligence is a single, generalized capacity. In his later work (e.g. Wynn 1991, 1993) he has become less ambitious with regard to inferring the mental capacities of early hominids by recognizing that intelligence may be a modular phenomenon. And consequently he now uses the morphological attributes of early stone tools to infer levels of spatial competence rather than overall intelligence.

7 The notion that 'ontogeny recapitulates phylogeny' was originally proposed by Haeckel in the 19th century, although the roots of this idea can be traced back to Aristotle. Gould (1977) is a seminal volume discussing the relationship between phylogeny and ontogeny, while Gould (1981) explains how the notion of recapitulation was used in the 19th and 20th centuries to justify racist and sexist attitudes. With regard to recent work, several psychologists have suggested that the ontogeny of language recapitulates its phylogeny, notably Parker & Gibson (1979). Although there continue to be major disagreements about recapitulation, ontogenetic perspectives are now commonplace in discussions of cognitive evolution. This is amply illustrated by papers in Gibson & Ingold (1993). I will return to the notion of recapitulation in Chapter 4.

8 Piaget published his ideas in a whole stream of books, and they showed a certain degree of development throughout his lifetime. A good starting place is his 1971 book *Biology and Knowledge*. He argued that there were just three 'programs' running in the mind which he referred to as 'assimilation', 'accommodation' and 'equilibration'. The first of these is the manner in which new knowledge becomes integrated with that already in the mind, while the second refers to how existing knowledge is changed to accommodate new knowledge. These are therefore reciprocal processes working in tandem. Equilibration was proposed as a term to describe the mental restructuring that occurs during development. Piaget proposed a stage model of development with mental restructuring marking the start of each new stage. In its simplest form Piaget proposed four stages: sensorimotor intelligence (birth–2 yrs), preoperational intelligence (2–6/7 yrs), concrete operational intelligence (6/7–11 yrs) and formal operational intelligence after the age of about 12 yrs. During the sensorimotor stage there is an absence of internalized, representational thought which only emerges with preoperational intelligence and allows the development of language. The two forms of operational intelligence involve a series of mental operations that allow, among other things, long-term planning of actions. Formal operational intelligence is particularly concerned with thinking about hypothetical objects and events.

9 Many more psychologists have adopted this Swiss-army-knife view of the mind than I am willing to discuss in my main text. For instance while Gardner (1983) has 'cut the cake' of intelligence into seven pieces, Robert Sternberg (1988) cut it into just three, which he named analytical, creative and practical intelligence. The neurophysiologist Michael Gazzaniga (1985; Gazzaniga & Lerdoux 1978) has argued that the mind is a coalition of bundles of semi-independent agencies, and Khalfa (1994) has written in the introduction to a book entitled *What is Intelligence?* that there are 'many types of intelligence and they cannot be easily compared, let alone rated on a common scale.' The cake of memory has also been sliced up in various ways during the last two decades. One slicing has created working, short-term and long-term memory. Endel Tulving (1983) has cut this cognitive cake into procedural and propositional memories, which approximates to a distinction between knowing about skills and knowing about knowledge. Propositional memory has then been cut again into episodic and semantic memories. The first is involved in the recording and subsequent retrieval of memories of personal happenings and doings, the second is concerned with knowledge of the world that is independent of a person's identity and past.

10 Fodor (1983). A summary and critical discussion of Fodor's book is provided in Fodor (1985).

11 This quote by Fodor is so good it is worth repeating: ' "But look," you might ask, "why do you care about modules so much? You've got tenure; why don't you take off and go sailing?" This is a perfectly reasonable question and one that I often ask myself.... But ... the idea that cognition saturates perception belongs with (and is, indeed, historically connected with) the idea in the philosophy of science that one's observations are comprehensively determined by one's theories; with the idea in anthropology that one's values are comprehensively determined by one's culture; with the idea in sociology that one's epistemic commitments, including especially one's science, are comprehensively determined by one's class affiliations; and with the idea in linguistics that one's metaphysics is comprehensively determined by one's syntax. All these ideas imply a kind of relativistic holism: because perception is saturated with cognition, observation by theory, values by culture, science by class, and metaphysics by language, rational criticism of scientific theories, ethical values, metaphysical worldviews, or whatever can take place only *within* the framework of assumptions that – as a matter of geographical, historical or sociological accident – the interlocutors happen to share. What you can't do is rationally criticize the framework.

The thing is: I hate relativism. I hate relativism more than I hate anything else, excepting, maybe, fibreglass powerboats. More to the point I think that relativism is very probably false. What it overlooks, to put it briefly and crudely, is the fixed structure of human nature.... Well, in cognitive psychology the claim that there is a fixed structure of human nature traditionally takes the form of an insistence on the heterogeneity of cognitive mechanisms and the rigidity of the cognitive architecture that effects their encapsulation. If there are faculties and modules, then not everything affects everything else; not everything is plastic. Whatever the All is, at least there is more than One of it.' (Fodor 1985, 5).

12 Fodor (1985, 4).

13 Fodor (1985, 4).

14 Fodor (1985, 4).

15 Gardner (1983). *Frames of Mind* was also published as a 10th-anniversary edition in 1993 and accompanied by a sequel *Multiple Intelligences: The Theory in Practice* (Gardner 1993).

16 Gardner (1983, 279).

17 Gardner (1983, 279).

18 This was suggested by Gallistel & Cheng (1985) when commenting on Fodor's ideas.

19 In addition to Cosmides and Tooby, other prominent evolutionary psychologists are Steven Pinker (1994) who focuses on the evolution of language and the psychologist David Buss (1994) who researches human mate selection using cross-cultural data.

20 My discussion of Cosmides and Tooby's work draws on Cosmides (1989), Cosmides & Tooby (1987, 1992, 1994) and Tooby & Cosmides (1989, 1992).

21 At the joint meeting of the Royal Society/British Academy entitled 'The evolution of social behaviour patterns in primates and man', London, 4–6 April 1995.

22 The notion of divine intervention is perhaps harder to resist when dealing with the mind than with other parts of the body and person. For instance when describing the evolution of the brain, the Nobel-prize-winning scientist Sir John Eccles decided that it was necessary to invoke supernatural spiritual creation for the qualities of the human mind (Eccles 1989).

23 At the meeting of the 'Human Behavior and Evolution Society', Santa Barbara, 28 June–1 July 1995, John Tooby argued that episodic memory, as defined by Tulving (1983), is fundamentally related to the 'theory of mind' module. Tooby wishes to cut the cake of memory into many thin slices, with each cognitive module having its own independent memory system.

24 Kaplan & Hill (1985) provide evidence for a relationship between hunting ability and reproductive success among modern hunter-gatherers.

25 Tooby & Cosmides (1992, 113).

26 Fodor (1987, 27).

27 For an account of Andrew Wiles' announcement of a proof see *New Scientist* 3 July 1993 and 5 November 1994.

28 Bird-David (1990).

29 Riddington (1982, 471). Also quoted in Ingold (1993, 440).

30 Morphy (1989b) provides a succinct discussion of how the landscape was created by the Ancestral Beings during the Dreamtime. As he describes, the Ancestral past is more appropriately thought of as a dimension of the present and consequently the landscape is not simply a record of past mythological events but plays an active role in creating those events.

31 Saladin D'Anglure (1990, 187). This work discusses the complex and often ambiguous conception of the polar bear by the Inuit. The Inuit draw parallels between humans and the polar bear due to similarities in behaviour: the bear stands on two legs, constructs winter shelters, travels across land and sea, and hunts seals using similar tactics to those of the hunters. The bear plays a central role in many of the rituals during the growing up of an Inuit boy and is associated with masculine sexual powers. For instance killing one's first bear is a sign of adult virility and sterile women eat polar bear penises.

32 Willis (1990) provides a review of changing definitions and interpretations of totemism in the introduction to his edited volume about human meaning in the natural world. As he describes, Lévi-Strauss raised the whole level of the totemic debate to a level of generality about universal human thought processes by the publication in 1962 of his two major works, *Le Totémisme Aujourd'hui* and *La Pensée Sauvage* (The Savage Mind). Douglas (1990, 35) characterizes Lévi-Strauss' views as the practice of humanity brooding on itself and place in nature.

33 Ingold (1992, 42).

34 Gellner (1988, 45) emphasizes that the seemingly absurd associations that are made in the thought and language of non-Western traditional societies, reflect a complex and sophisticated cognition which serves to accomplish many ends at once. It is the 'single strandedness, the neat and logical division of labour, the separation of functions' that is characteristic of modern Western society which is the anomaly and which needs explaining. Ingold (1993) makes a very similar argument to Gellner, by suggesting that the cognitive separation between 'nature', 'society' and 'technology' is a product of Western thought. Modern hunter-gatherers make no such distinctions and exhibit unrestrained cognitive fluidity. The issue that neither Ingold nor Gellner addresses and which is central to this book is that this may not have been the case for pre-modern hunter-gatherers.

35 For instance, in the case of the polar bear and the Inuit referred to above, the bear is strongly associated with male strength. By associating themselves with the polar bear, the Inuit males use the bear as a potent ideological tool to consolidate their domination of women. Saladin D'Anglure (1990).

36 Whitelaw (1991) has made a detailed cross-cultural study of the use of space in hunter-gatherer camps, demonstrating how community layout maps kinship relations, and how space is an active medium for social interaction. To quote him: 'spatial organization is used by different individuals and in different cultures to generate, amplify, facilitate, manipulate and control social interaction and organization' (1991, 181).

37 To quote the social anthropologist Andrew Strathern: 'what people wear, and what they do to and with their bodies in general, forms an important part of the flow of information – establishing, modifying and commenting on major social categories, such as age, sex and status' (quoted in White 1992, 539–40). Similarly, Turner stated that 'the surface of the body ... becomes the symbolic stage upon which the drama of socialization is enacted, and bodily adornment ... becomes the language through which it is expressed' (quoted in White 1992, 539).

38 The tools of modern humans display very effective designs for their functional tasks (e.g. Oswalt 1976; Torrence 1983; Bleed 1986; Churchill 1993). But at the same time these tools are used in conducting social relationships. Polly Wiessner (1983) has documented this for the arrows of the Kalahari San. While these are very effective hunting weapons, the shapes of the arrow heads carry information about group affiliation. Their use in hunting the eland, an animal central to San mythology, results in the arrows also having considerable symbolic significance.

39 Whiten & Perner (1991). See also Gopnik & Wellman (1994), Whiten (1991) and Wellman (1991).

40 For the relationship between autism and the impairment of the theory of mind module see Leslie (1991, 1994), Frith (1989) and Baron-Cohen (1995). These works describe how other aspects of cognition may be left unaffected. Some autistic children appear to have prodigious talents in the fields of art, music or mathematics. For an account of these see Sacks (1995), particularly the essay within that volume entitled 'Prodigies'. A remarkable case of an *idiot savant* is described by Smith & Tsimpli (1995). This is a man known as Christopher who at the age of 35 has an IQ of between 40 and 70 (human average is 100) and who fails tests set for five year olds. He has to live in sheltered accommodation because he cannot look after himself. Yet Christopher can speak more than 15 languages in addition to his native English.

41 Humphrey (1976). His ideas have also been elaborated in Humphrey (1984, 1993).

42 Atran (1990, 1994).

43 Keil (1994) and Atran (1994).

44 Atran (1990).

45 Berlin (1992; Berlin *et al* 1973) and Atran (1994).

46 Sacks (1995, 269). Other examples are described in Atran (1990).

47 Mithen (1990, 52–88) reviews the methods by which modern hunter-gatherers gath-

er information from their environments, and how this information is used in decision making. Particularly useful ethnographic accounts, which include examples of the extensive and detailed natural history knowledge that hunter-gatherers rely upon, are as follows: !Kung (Lee 1976, 1979; Lee & DeVore 1976; Marshall 1976; Blurton-Jones & Konner 1976), G/Wi (Silberbauer 1981), Valley Bisa (Marks 1976), Ache (Hill & Hawkes 1983), Mistassini Cree (Tanner 1979; Winterhalder 1981), Koyukon (Nelson 1983), Kutchin (Nelson 1973), Ten'a (Sullivan 1942), Nunamiut (Gubser 1965; Binford 1978), Groote Eylandt Islanders (Levitt 1981), Gidjingali (Meehan 1982), Tiwi (Goodale 1971) and Canadian Indians (Jennes 1977).
48 Spelke (1991; Spelke *et al* 1992). See also Pinker (1994, 423–24).
49 Atran (1990, 57).
50 Kennedy (1992) argues that people are prone to a compulsive anthropomorphizing. The idea that animals are conscious and have purpose appears to be built into us by nature. He does not discuss what appears to be a similar compulsiveness for children to attribute minds to inert physical objects.
51 Greenfield (1991). See also Lock (1993). There is, however, considerable disagreement on this issue and intuitive knowledge systems may be present and working in the mind from birth.
52 Karmiloff-Smith (1992). A summary of her book and a critical discussion of the ideas are found in Karmiloff-Smith (1994).
53 Karmiloff-Smith (1994, 695).
54 Geary (1995) uses the term 'primary biological abilities', rather than intuitive knowledge, to refer to those abilities which are hard-wired into the brain as a consequence of our evolutionary history. He argues that the kick start to the development of mathematical knowledge is a pan-human capacity for counting. This provides a set of 'skeletal principles' that guide counting behaviour before children have acquired the use of number words.
55 Karmiloff-Smith (1994, 701, 706). It is important to note that Karmiloff-Smith's model for mental development is not a simple stage model. She believes that there are two distinct parallel processes happening at the same time: 'one of progressive modularization, the other of progressive explicitness of knowledge representations' (1994, 733).
56 Carey & Spelke (1994, 184). The precise similarities and differences between the ideas of Carey and Spelke and Karmiloff-Smith have yet to be explored. Carey and Spelke draw interesting comparisons between conceptual change in the history of science and during child development arguing for similarities in how children and scientists construct mappings across different knowledge domains.
57 Boden (1990). A summary and critical discussion of Boden's ideas are found in Boden (1994).
58 Koestler, quoted in Boden (1990).
59 Rozin (1976); Rozin & Schull (1988).
60 Rozin (1976, 262).
61 Sperber (1994).

Ch. 4. A new proposal for the mind's evolution (pp. 61–72)

1 The excavation and phasing of the South Church are described in Hodges & Mithen (1993).
2 Quoted in Gould (1977, 76).
3 Gould (1977, 116).
4 Gibson (editorial, p. 276 in Gibson & Ingold 1993).
5 Lock (1993).
6 As the psychologist Daniel Povinelli stated in 1993 regarding the evolution of a theory of mind, 'comparing the ontogeny of psychological capacities should allow evolutionary psychologists to reconstruct the order in which particular features of mental state attribution evolved' (Povinelli 1993, 506). This is precisely my aim in this chapter – although my intention is to do this with regard to the mind in general.
7 Gould (1981, 115).
8 Lock (1993) argues that the use of ontogenetic information for developing hypothetical scenarios for evolution to be tested by other data is an appropriate method of research.
9 I must stress here that Karmiloff-Smith does not separate progressive modularization of the mind and 'representational redescription' into two consecutive processes; she argues that these happen in parallel with each other. However, a time lag is implied between them as knowledge has to become part of a specialized module, before becoming explicitly represented and applicable between domains.
10 Natural selection is unlikely to have done all the shaping by itself. There were other evolutionary processes at work, such as genetic drift and founder effects, which may

have also played a significant role in the continual tinkering. The relative importance of natural selection is a matter of considerable debate among evolutionary biologists.
11 The significance of throwing for the evolution of the mind has been explored by Calvin (1983, 1993).

Ch. 5. Apes, monkeys and the mind of the missing link (pp. 73–94)

1 Examples of the use of the chimpanzee as an analogy for early human ancestors are McGrew (1992) and Falk (1992). Byrne (1995, 27–30) explains how a better approach is to reconstruct the behaviour and cognition of our ancestors by using the methods of cladistics.
2 Goodall's work is summarized in her two books (Goodall 1986, 1990).
3 Twenty years after Goodall first recognized tool use by chimpanzees Christophe and Hedwige Boesch in West Africa have been extending the observed repertoire of chimpanzee tool use by describing the use of anvils and hammerstone to crack nuts in the Tai forest (e.g. 1983, 1984a, 1984b, 1990, 1993). There have also been a large number of studies of chimpanzee technology undertaken by Bill McGrew and his colleagues, culminating in his book entitled *Chimpanzee Material Culture* published in 1992. Together with studies by other primatologists such as Sugiyama (1993) and Matsuzawa (1991) a very substantial database concerning chimpanzee tool use has been created, which, as McGrew argues, has considerable implications for human evolution – although quite what those implications are remains contentious.
4 McGrew (1992).
5 Boesch & Boesch (1993) explain that just seven types of actions are used for making the whole repertoire of chimpanzee tools: (1) detaching a leafy twig or branch from a plant to use as a stick; (2) cutting a stick to a specific length with teeth or hands; (3) removing the bark or leaves from a stick with teeth or hands; (4) sharpening the end of a stick using teeth; (5) modifying the length of a stick (after initial use) with teeth or hands; (6) breaking a branch or stone in two by hitting it on a hard surface to make a hammer; (7) breaking a branch in two by pulling while standing on it to make a hammer. There have been no observations of intentional flaking of stone. Among the Tai chimpanzees the first four actions are often used in succession while 83% of the observed modifications to sticks involved the first three.
6 Matsuzawa (1991).
7 Nishida (1987), Boesch & Boesch (1990) and McGrew (1992).
8 The processes of social learning have been the subject of much discussion in recent literature about primates, e.g. Clayton (1978), Galef (1988, 1990), Whiten (1989), Visalberghi & Fragaszy (1990), Tomasello *et al* (1987, 1993), Tomasello (1990) and Byrne (1995). In addition to imitation, social learning might involve the processes of stimulus enhancement and response facilitation. Stimulus enhancement is the process in which an animal's interest in objects may be stimulated simply by the activities of another. The actual process of learning to use the objects as tools may follow on a trial-and-error basis. Another social learning process is response facilitation in which the presence of a conspecific performing an action increases the likelihood that another animal seeing it will do the same. A critical difference between this and imitation is that for the latter it is normally supposed that the action must be new to the animal, whereas response facilitation evokes actions that already existed in the animal's behavioural repertoire. Many primatologists now believe that monkeys never imitate, and some extend this to chimpanzees especially when they are in wild situations. Even if imitation is present among chimpanzees it seems to be at a markedly lower intensity than in modern humans. Yet these types of social learning are likely to be the primary processes by which tool use diffuses within chimpanzee populations.
9 For example, McGrew (1992, 186-7), Byrne (1995, 86–8).
10 Boesch (1991, 1993).
11 Wrangham (1977).
12 Menzel (1973, 1978).
13 Boesch & Boesch (1984a)
14 Katherine Milton has proposed that the greatest environmental challenges are faced by those primates which rely on fruit because this resource is the most widely dispersed in space and time (Milton 1988). Primates must solve the problem of remembering the location of fruit trees, and exploiting the fruit at the appropriate time in its ripening cycle. This, she argued, would have created a selective pressure for greater intelligence and she suggested that there is indeed a correlation between brain size and diet among the primates. Similarly Kathleen Gibson has

stressed the selective pressures on cognition that 'omnivorous extractive foraging' would create (Gibson 1986, 1990). By this she refers to the practice of removing food from various types of matrices – kernels from nut shells, ants from mounds, eggs from shells. These foodstuffs, which come encased in an inedible layer, are typically high in energy and protein. They are often available during the dry season, when other resources may be scarce. They are, however, difficult to exploit, requiring either very specialized anatomical adaptations or the use of tools and an intelligence that can conceive of 'hidden' food sources.

Robin Dunbar has since shown that the correlations between brain size and foraging patterns are likely to be spurious (Dunbar 1992), while McGrew has dismissed the idea that there is a clear relationship between the use of tools and brain size (McGrew 1992). Moreover, Cheney and Seyfarth have pointed out that when we look at animals in general, rather than just primates, diet, foraging behaviour and brain size vary widely with no clear correlations (Cheney & Seyfarth 1990). In addition, they point to the difficulty in making a distinction between ecological and social pressures. Primates use social strategies to cope with environmental complexity. Patchy and irregular food supplies provide selective pressures for greater cooperation in foraging, abilities to detect cheaters in food sharing and for communication about resource distribution. Group size among primates, for instance, which is Dunbar's measure of social complexity, is strongly related to predator risk and food availability (Dunbar 1988).

15 Consider, for instance, the little bird known as Clark's nutcracker. This small bird has a brain weighing less than 10g, but each winter hides more than 30,000 seeds for winter stores. Not only does it hide them, but it regularly finds at least half of the hidden nuts. Laboratory studies have shown that this bird has a prodigious spatial memory, far greater than that of humans (Mackintosh 1994).

16 Boesch & Boesch (1989).

17 Cheney & Seyfarth (1990) undertook an extensive series of experiments to explore the types of clues from which vervet monkeys could infer information, focusing on clues which one would expect to be of significance for the monkeys. For instance one of the species feared by vervet monkeys are humans, in the form of the local Maasai people who herd cattle and goats. The monkeys tend to give a human alarm call and then flee whenever Maasai appear. Can the monkeys use the approach of cows to infer the approach of the Maasai? Cheney and Seyfarth used hidden loud speakers to play the lowing of cows. They found a positive reaction. Although cows offer no threat to the monkeys, they reacted to the lowing as if they were hearing the Maasai themselves, indicating that they have a mental association between these two species. The monkeys' reacted in a similar fashion when the ringing of bells was played, another sound associated with approaching Maasai. Consequently the monkeys appeared adept at using such secondary auditory clues and mental associations to infer approaching danger.

Conversely however, when the secondary clues are visual rather than auditory the monkeys appear to be much less 'intelligent'. For instance they do not react to the distinctive dust clouds created by the approach of Maasai with their cows, and only flee when the cows and people emerge. The monkeys difficulty with visual clues was explored in a series of experiments using a stuffed gazelle carcass placed in a tree to mimic a leopard kill. Leopards are one of the major predators of the monkeys and normally remain in the close vicinity of their recent kills. The carcass was placed in a tree during the night so that it would be readily visible to the monkeys the next morning. Yet they ignored it and undertook their normal activities as if the carcass was simply not there.

Similarly the monkeys appear not to understand the implications of fresh python tracks. Pythons are another major predator of monkeys and they leave distinctive trails in the sand. Cheney and Seyfarth observed that when monkeys approach such tracks they show no increase in vigilance or any change of behaviour. Indeed, they watched monkeys follow such tracks to bushes and then become shocked when they stumbled upon a python!

18 It is likely that humans are the only primate able to draw inferences from visual clues which are displaced from their referent e.g. footprints (Davidson & Noble 1989; Hewes 1986, 1989).

19 Byrne & Whiten (1988).

20 Byrne & Whiten (1988, editorial p. 4).

21 de Waal (1982).

22 Byrne & Whiten (1991, 1992), Byrne

(1995, 124–40). Heyes (1993) provides an important critical review of studies such as those drawing on anecdotal data by Byrne and Whiten which purport to demonstrate a 'theory of mind' in non-human primates.
23 Premack & Woodruff (1978), Premack (1988).
24 Humphrey describes his ideas in two very readable short books (Humphrey 1984, 1993 (originally published 1986)). In his more recent work (Humphrey 1992) he deals with consciousness as raw sensation rather than what he describes as the second order mental faculties 'thoughts about feelings' and 'thoughts about thoughts'. It is this type of consciousness, however, that remains my interest when dealing with the evolution of the human mind.
25 Gardner *et al* (1989).
26 Premack & Premack (1972).
27 Savage-Rumbaugh & Rumbaugh (1993).
28 Terrace (1979), Terrace *et al* (1979).
29 Greenfield & Savage-Rumbaugh (1990), Savage-Rumbaugh & Rumbaugh (1993). Sue Savage Rumbaugh argues that the small size and other morphological traits of the bonobo make it a better model for the common pongid/hominid ancestor than the common chimpanzee. Kanzi was born in captivity in 1980 to Matata, who had been caught in the wild. Matata never performed well on language tasks, although her social skills were excellent.
30 Pinker (1994, 151).
31 Marler (1970).
32 The cerebral cortex is the outer layer of the cerebral hemispheres referred to as 'grey matter', comprising layers of nerve cells and their interconnections which are thrown into a series of folds and troughs. In contrast, the vocal calls of primates are controlled by neural processes in the brain stem (the part of the brain connecting the cerebral hemispheres to the spinal cord) and limbic systems (the nerve pathways and networks within the temporal lobes of the cerebral hemispheres) (Marler 1970).
33 Alex is an African Grey parrot who exhibits cognitive capacities that appear to be analogous (though not homologous) to those of primates and humans. Alex has been a good subject to explore inter-species cognitive similarities since he has learnt to speak and hence one of the major constraints on exploring primate minds can partly be overcome. Pepperberg (1990) provides a review of her studies of Alex and their implications.
34 Boesch & Boesch (1983).
35 Boesch & Boesch (1989).
36 This episode of Kate's tool use was described by Brewer & McGrew (1990). She first used a stout chisel and then a finer chisel to make an indentation in the nest. A sharp pointed stick was then used to puncture the nest wall and finally a longer, flexible stick was used to dip for honey. Overall, Kate appears to have sequentially used a set of tools each appropriate for a specific task. McGrew feels justified in describing these as a toolkit.
37 Boesch (1991, 1993).
38 Boesch & Boesch (1989).
39 Boesch & Boesch (1989, 569).
40 Byrne (1995).
41 Cheney & Seyfarth (1988, 1990).
42 While monkeys appear unable to recognize themselves in mirrors, they are able to learn to use mirrors, such as to see if another monkey is around the corner (Byrne 1995).
43 Byrne & Whiten (1992).

Ch. 6. The mind of the first stone toolmaker (pp. 95–114)

1 When discussing Oldowan technology, it is more appropriate to use the term 'artifact' than 'tool'. When archaeologists find these Oldowan flakes and cores it is not clear whether they are the pieces thrown away during manufacture (like the leaves from a twig when stripping it for a termite stick) or those pieces kept for some task or other. It is not even clear that the actors themselves had any idea of this division between 'waste' and 'tools'. So archaeologists, being cautious creatures, use a neutral term, artifacts. Potts (1988, table 8.6) provides data on frequency of raw material use by weight and number of artifacts at four sites from Bed I, Olduvai: DK, FLKNN-3, FLK 'Zinj' and FLK North-6. At FLK 'Zinj' 90.2% of artifacts are made from quartzite, although as these are small they constitute only 27.6% of the total weight of the assemblage. Artifacts made from vesicular basalt, on the other hand, compose only 4.7% of the total number of artifacts, but 44.7% of the total weight. DK is notable for having a relatively high frequency of nephelinite (a type of lava) in terms of artifact numbers (22.7%) and weight (12.6%). Chert, gneiss and feldspar never reach more than 0.2% of an assemblage by number or weight, except at FLK North-6 where 1.6% of the artifacts are made from chert.

2 Wynn & McGrew (1989).
3 Traces of 'polish' from woodworking have been found on the edges of 1.5-million-year-old artifacts from Koobi Fora (Keeley & Toth 1981). The possible functions of Oldowan artifacts have been discussed by Schick & Toth (1993, 150–86).
4 Schick & Toth (1993, 118–22) summarize the manufacturing techniques of Oldowan stone tools.
5 Toth *et al* (1993). The basic format of the experiment involved placing a desired object within a box with a transparent lid which could only be opened by cutting a cord. Kanzi was shown how stone flakes could be produced from nodules and used for this purpose. At first he was simply provided with flakes to cut the cord, but then he was given nodules and had to produce the flakes himself. During these experiments Kanzi employed two basic techniques for producing flakes: hard hammer percussion involving striking two rocks against each other; and throwing rocks so that they shattered. In both of these some degree of improvement could be observed, but the resulting artifacts consistently remained very different from those of the Oldowan. Toth & Schick (1993, 351) note that the argument that chimpanzees may be constrained from modifying stones in an Oldowan manner due to a lack of motor skills seems implausible, since they have shown abilities to tie shoelaces and unbutton shirts. Westergaard (1995) describes the stone-flaking abilities of capuchin monkeys. These appear similar to Kanzi's and significantly different to those of Oldowan hominids.
6 Lokalalei (GaJh 5) has an age slightly younger than 2.36 ± 0.04 million years ago and was excavated in 1991. The artifacts are in a fresh condition and made from a medium-grained lava which has good conchoidal fracture. These, together with the geological context of the site and faunal assemblage, are described by Kibunjia (1994).
7 Toth (1985) undertook thousands of replication experiments to explore this. He demonstrates how in the Koobi Fora region the variation in artifact form across the landscape can be explained by the variation in raw material characteristics and availability. See also Potts (1988, 235–37).
8 This can be seen at Sterkfontein where an introduction of new types of raw materials occurs with the Acheulian in a stratified sequence of assemblages (Kuman 1994).
9 Direct evidence for the use of stone tools in processing carcasses comes from cutmarks on animal bones (Bunn 1981; Potts & Shipman 1981) and wear patterns on stone tools (Keeley & Toth 1981). Indirect evidence comes from the regular association of stone artifacts and animal bones on archaeological sites, and the effectiveness of stone artifacts at processing carcasses in experimental work (Schick & Toth 1993).
10 The HAS site is found in 1.6-million-year-old sediments in the Koobi Fora region. Amongst the hippopotamus bones were 119 chipped stones and a pebble which had been used as a hammerstone (Isaac 1978).
11 Potts (1988) summarizes the archaeology at FLK 22, together with the other sites from Bed I at Olduvai Gorge.
12 Isaac was one of the most significant Palaeolithic archaeologists of the 20th century on the basis of his contributions to the discovery and excavation of new sites, analytical methods and theory. He tragically died in 1983 at the pinnacle of his career as a professor at Harvard. His contribution to the discipline can be appreciated from his collected papers, edited by his wife (B. Isaac 1989).
13 Isaac's home base model was most clearly set out in his 1978 paper in *Scientific American* entitled 'The food sharing behaviour of proto-human hominids'. Potts (1988) provides an excellent summary and critique of the model.
14 Binford (1981)
15 The debate concerning the prevalence of hunting, primary scavenging (i.e. scavenging from a recently killed carcass which provides an equivalent amount of meat to that of an animal which had been hunted) and marginal scavenging partly arose out of, and partly stimulated, a remarkable advance in the methods archaeologists use to interpret their materials, especially animal bones. These included microscopic analysis of gnawing, tooth and cutmarks on bones, the analysis of body part representation and inferences about the extent of bone weathering. All these advances were reliant upon programmes of ethnoarchaeological and actualistic studies concerning the processes of site formation. These debates were marred, however, by the failure of the participants even to agree on the contents of the archaeological record, let alone its interpretation. One theme was the implications of stone tool cutmarks on bones in terms of their temporal

relationships to carnivore gnawmarks, their frequency and the type of butchery they implied. Body part representation was also intensely debated since this may provide a means to differentiate between marginal scavenging and hunting. Only with the latter would one expect to find the major meat-bearing bones on a site, although primary scavenging in which a hominid has access to a freshly killed carcass is likely to result in a similar body-part signature. Major papers in this dispute include: Binford (1984b, 1985, 1986, 1988), Binford *et al* (1988), Bunn (1981, 1983a, 1983b, 1994), Bunn & Kroll (1986), Isaac (1983a, 1983b), Kroll (1994), Kroll & Isaac (1984), Oliver (1994), Potts & Shipman (1981) and Shipman (1983, 1986).

16 This is most extensively described in Binford (1984a).

17 The 'stone cache' hypothesis is described in Potts (1988). Minimization of search time for sharp flakes to be used for entering/butchering the carcass would have been essential due to the high level of predator risk faced by the hominids. (See note 25.)

18 This was largely based on actualistic studies identifying the most feasible scavenging niche for early hominids (Blumenschine 1986, 1987; Blumenschine *et al* 1994).

19 Stern (1993, 1994) has stressed the difficulties of landscape archaeology in East Africa. She describes the inverse relationship between the area of an ancient landscape being sampled, the quantity of archaeological data available for study and the amount of time represented by that debris and the encasing sediments (1994, 89). As an example she uses the archaeological sites of the lower Okote member of Koobi Fora for which the finest time resolution is 65 ± 5 k.y.a. Consequently ethnographic scale observations of the interactions between individuals and their environment across the landscape can only be made by ignoring this time dimension of the data.

20 Potts (1988, 308). The likely diversity of hominid lifestyles has been noted by Potts (1994) and Blumenschine *et al* (1994). The latter suggest that variability in hominid ecology would have been largely due to variability in competition from carnivores for animal tissues.

21 A major difficulty with the interpretation of this material is that the exploitation of carcasses is practically the only evidence we have for hominid subsistence. We have little idea of the relative importance of meat in the hominid diet in relation to plant foods. Research on the likely contribution of plant foods to the hominid diet takes the form of actualistic studies in modern African environments which consider the availability of possible plant foods, and the costs and benefits of exploiting them (e.g. Hatley & Kappelman 1980; Sept 1994).

22 Aiello & Wheeler (1995). They find a correlation between gut size and brain size among primates in general. Organs such as the heart and liver cannot be reduced in size to compensate for the metabolic requirements, as they are physiologically constrained. The relatively large brains of australopithecines as compared to those of non-human primates suggest that they were consuming a range of high-quality plant foods, such as underground tubers.

23 See Blumenschine (1986). This has been explored using sophisticated computer simulation modelling by Lake (1995).

24 Several archaeologists have stressed the importance of stone transport. The identification of this at Olduvai was made possible by the geological studies of Hay (1976) which located the raw material sources. For Isaac (1978), stone transport was a further reason for building his home base hypothesis. Binford (1989) has argued that it was predominantly the core tools which were transported across the landscape, as these are not normally found with their manufacturing debris. Toth (1985) has devised a methodology for inferring artifact transport which relies on replicated assemblages and the frequencies of different artifact types in complete assemblages, as employed at FxJj50. The small spatial scale of such transport activity is indicated by the sites of FxJj and FeJj in East Turkana. These were occupied at *c.* 1.8 m.y.a. and are only 25 km apart. The lithic remains at each site are made only from the locally available raw material, lava at FxJj and quartz at FeJj (Rogers *et al* 1994, 151).

25 Richard Potts suggested that one reason for transporting stone nodules and artifacts was to create caches. Such caches would have allowed rapid access to stone artifacts/raw materials when they were needed to exploit a carcass. Using time efficiently may have been essential for survival in a predator-rich environment. This remains one of the most plausible explanations for the accumulations of artifacts, especially manuports (unmodified nodules) and faunal remains as specific points in the landscape. It remains unclear, however, whether hominids were intentionally creating such caches, or simply using those unintentionally created during previous carcass butchery. If they were being created, then this would provide further evidence for predicting and planning for future resource distributions. The stone cache hypothesis has been described in most detail in Potts (1988) where he demonstrates the functional benefit of creating caches with simple computer models. (See note 17.)

26 There are two examples of possible evidence for movement out of Africa by a hominid prior to *Homo erectus*. First, claimed artifacts from Riwat in Pakistan dating to 2 m.y.a. (Dennell *et al* 1988a, 1988b). I suspect these are natural 'artifacts', although Dennell provides a challenging defence that they were produced by early *Homo*. Second, hominid dental fragments from Longgupo Cave, China (Wanpo *et al* 1995). These have been dated to 1.9 m.y.a. and possibly belong to early *H. erectus*. However, they appear to possess some primitive features and the possibility remains that they are *H. ergaster* (a species I am including within the broad category of *H. habilis* and which is most likely directly ancestral to *H. erectus*). If so, this implies that *H. ergaster* may have dispersed out of Africa, and *H. erectus* evolved within Asia, to then return to Europe and Africa. But there is no consensus on the taxonomic identification of these hominid remains; indeed some even doubt that they are hominid at all. The range of different interpretations are discussed in Wood & Turner (1995) and Culotta (1995).

27 An attempt systematically to compare landuse before and after 1.6 m.y.a. has been made by Jack Harris and colleagues for the East Lake Turkana region (Rogers, Harris & Feibel 1994). They compared the distribution of settlement at three successive time intervals, 2.3 m.y.a., 1.9–1.8 m.y.a. and 1.7–1.5 m.y.a. and attribute the more diverse location of archaeological sites in the third of these to the wider ranging behaviour of *H. erectus*. They concluded that only after this date were more diverse types of environmental settings used and activities detached for the first time from landscape features, such as raw material sources and shade trees. In the period before 1.6 m.y.a. archaeological sites were 'tied' to the edges of permanent water sources where cobbles were available in gravels. After this date, sites were found in floodplain locations, some distance from both permanent water and raw materials. The early hominids appear to have been more constrained than the early humans by the distribution of natural resources. A similar conclusion was reached by Richard Potts (1994) when he compared the archaeology of Bed I at Olduvai (1.8–1.7 m.y.a.) and Member I at Olorgesailie dating to 0.9 m.y.a.

28 See Leakey (1971) and Potts (1988, 1994). For instance the MNK main occupation in Bed II at Olduvai has six main archaeological layers in 1.5 m (5 ft) of sediment. Binford (1987a) has argued that sites such as these are in fact no different in terms of past behaviour than the dense concentration of artifacts and bone fragments found at discrete vertical levels, such as FLK 'Zinj'. The contrast simply reflects the rate at which sediments are accumulating, and consequently whether one ends up with a palimpsest or a vertically diffuse artifact distribution. Even when we do not have this stacking of sites through deep sedimentary layers, the evidence from bone weathering indicates that the 'living floor' assemblages accumulated over several years (Potts 1986; Behrensmeyer 1978).

29 This was the basic feature of the faunal assemblages that led Isaac to develop his home base hypothesis, for it implies the transport of animal body parts between micro-environments. Plummer & Bishop (1994) have suggested that the morphological variability in bovid metapoidals from Olduvai Bed I sites indicates that the Olduvai hominids were utilizing habitats ranging from open to closed, perhaps the full range in the lake margin zone. Blumenschine (1986, 1987) suggested that river-side woodland provided the optimal scavenging region. Sikes (1994) has used the stable isotope composition of paleosols from early hominid sites to estimate the original proportion of grasses (C4) to woody (C3) vegetation, finding the latter to be dominant. She concluded that Plio-Pleistocene hominids in East Africa may have preferred relatively closed, woodland habitats that may have offered shade, food and predator refuge. More generally Cerling (1992) has argued that open grasslands with >90% C4 biomass did not become established in East Africa until around 1.0 m.y.a. Nevertheless, the diversity of animal species in faunal assemblages indicates that early *Homo* was foraging in a variety of environments, including open savannah conditions.

30 Testing for a relationship between brain size and measures of social complexity is by no means easy. The difficulty is that brain size is itself extremely difficult to measure in a meaningful fashion for inter-species comparison (e.g. see Jerison 1973; Clutton-Brock & Harvey 1980; Deacon 1990; Dunbar 1992). While larger animals have larger brains to cope with increased sensory and motor demands, brain size does not increase in a simple linear fashion with body size. One must also take into account differences in diet. A primate that is dependent upon eating leaves requires a larger gut and consequently has a larger body size, although no expansion in brain capacity is needed. In contrast primates who live on fruit tend to have a smaller body size as only a short gut is required. These complexities have led to various different measures of brain size being used in comparative studies. These rely on measures of allometric scaling which take into account body size effects and produce linear correlations between brain and body size. When such correlations are produced for either primates or mammals in general, one can inspect the residuals from the regression line for each species. Large positive residuals mark species out as having a relatively larger brain than one would expect for an animal of that size. For primates, the strepsirhines (lemurs) have the sort of brain sizes one would expect for their body size, while monkeys and apes have brain sizes almost twice as large as expected. The brain size of humans is very substantially larger than expected.

Of the brain size measures that have been used, that of the ratio of neocortex volume to the rest of the brain has been one of the most robust in face of the critical discussion surrounding this area. Robin Dunbar explored the correlation between neocortex ratio and factors that relate to the foraging and mobility behaviour of non-human primates, notably range area, day journey length and the amount of fruit in the diet (Dunbar 1992). A correlation here would suggest that the selective pressure for brain enlargement (used as a proxy measure for intelligence) was environmental complexity. Yet no correlations were found. In contrast, the neocortex ratio was correlated with mean group size of primates. Group size may be a reflection of social complexity as it reflects the number of animals an individual needs to monitor and take account of when making behaviour decisions. This has been, therefore, an explicit test of the Machiavellian hypothesis, with a positive result.

31 As his measure of social complexity Byrne used the extent of tactical deception. By drawing on the reports of tactical deception in a range of primate species, he also found a strong positive correlation between its frequency and neocortex ratio. This supports the idea that the selective pressure for brain enlargement during hominoid evolution has been the social environment (Byrne 1995; see also Byrne & Whiten 1985, 1991, 1992).

32 For studies of group size see Clutton-Brock & Harvey (1977), van Schaik (1983), Foley (1987), Wrangham (1987), Dunbar (1988), Chapman (1990) and Isbell *et al* (1991). There have been very few explicit tests of the relative importance of predator risk and resource patchiness to group size because of the inherent problems of measuring such variables (Wrangham 1987). Any particular group size is likely to derive from a range of ecological, evolutionary and historical factors (Wrangham 1987; Dunbar 1988). Moreover, the idea that 'group size' is a useful social variable can be questioned. More profitable research is likely to derive from considering specific types of groups, such as feeding or reproductive groups, and taking account of the different social strategies employed by each sex (Cheney *et al* 1987). Yet due to the resolution of the archaeological record, prehistorians appear to be forced to consider group size as a coarse-grained social variable.

33 For instance, the cranium from Swartkrans known as SK54 of an australopithecine child has two holes which were probably caused by the lower canines of a leopard as it grasped the child within its jaws (Brain 1981). Brain suggests that early hominids would have been preyed on by a range of large carnivores. It has also been suggested that the juvenile australopithecine represented by the skull from Taung had once been the prey of an eagle which had swooped down to steal it from its mother, as they are observed to do today with monkeys (*New Scientist* 9 September 1995, p. 7).

34 Jones *et al* (1992).

35 Lake (1995).

36 Dennett (1988).

37 Dennett (1988, 185–86).

38 Dibble (1989) reviews the various attempts to make inferences about linguistic capacities from stone artifacts.

39 The significance of Broca's and Wernicke's area for language have been discussed in several recent publications concerned with the evolution of the brain and language (e.g. Corballis 1991, 1992; Donald 1991; Falk 1983, 1990, 1992; Pinker 1994), but there remains some confusion about their function. After a lengthy description of the possible roles of Broca's and Wernicke's area for language, Steven Pinker recently concluded that 'to be honest no one really knows what either Broca's or Wernicke's area is for' (1994, 311).

40 These are referred to as endocasts. Some are created naturally as brain cases become filled with fine-grained sediment that turns to stone as the brain case decays, leaving a copy of the contours of the inside of the brain case. Others are made artificially by using a latex mould.

41 Tobias (1987, 741), Falk (1983).

42 Deacon's (1992) work was based on trying to understand how evolution could move from the vocal communications of apes to the language of modern humans when these appear to be produced by different parts of the brain. Primate calls have their source in subcortical areas, whereas human language depends on activity within the neocortex (see Chapter 5, note 32). Deacon argues that rather than language requiring completely new circuits, it may be accounted for by shifts in the relative proportions of circuits in different parts of the brain as these enlarge by different amounts during encephalization.

43 Aiello & Dunbar (1993), Dunbar (1991, 1992, 1993).

44 Aiello (1996a).

Ch. 7. The multiple intelligences of the Early Human mind (pp. 115–146)

1 Charles Caleb Colton, *Lacon* (1820), vol i, No. 408.

2 Gowlett (1984). At Boxgrove the debris from making ovate handaxes has been excavated in undisturbed contexts and refitted so that each strike of the knapper's hammer can be reconstructed. Here the fine, shallow finishing flakes across the artifacts indicate that the knappers used at least two different types of hammers – hard hammers of stone and soft hammers of bone. Indeed these bone hammers have recently been found at Boxgrove with minute flint flakes still embedded in the striking ends (Bergman & Roberts 1988; Roberts 1994).

3 Pelegrin (1993). Following rules in a rote fashion enable many non-human animals, particularly social insects, to create 'artifacts' of considerable complexity and symmetry, epitomized by a honeycomb. Such 'artifacts' have been compared with handaxes to suggest that Early Humans were not so clever after all. But this comparison is flawed since knapping is a process of reduction, rather than construction, and one must continually modify one's plans due to the unpredictability of fracture.

4 There are many groups of handaxes which contain artifacts of great similarity. One of the most impressive collections in this regard is that from the Wolvercote Channel near Oxford (Tyldesley 1986). These show near perfect symmetry, partly accomplished by the removal of tiny finishing flakes which would appear to have limited, if any, functional value. Many of these artifacts are almost exact replicas of each other in both size and shape.

5 Our understanding of the Levallois method has advanced considerably during the last few years by extensive refitting of Levallois debitage and replication experiments (e.g. Boëda 1988, 1990; Roebroeks 1988). Inizan *et al* (1992) suggest that it may be the most technically demanding knapping method.

6 Hayden (1993, 118).

7 The definition of a Levallois point is an artifact produced by the Levallois method which has a 'symmetrical morphology, a clearly pointed distal end with the overturned "Y" dorsal scar pattern obtained by three or at most four removals regardless of their direction' (Bar-Yosef & Meignen 1992, 175).

8 Schlanger (1996). Maastricht-Belvédère has several discrete clusters of knapping debris. 'Marjories core' consists of 41 refitted flakes out of 145 which are thought to have derived from the same core. None of the refitted flakes have been retouched or used, and nine of them have been classified as Levallois flakes. The core appears to have been brought to the site in a partially worked condition since there are no flakes from the outside part of the flint nodule.

9 The technical intelligence of Early Humans can also be appreciated from artifact types and production methods which are not widespread throughout the Old World. For instance, archaic *H. sapiens* in sub-Saharan Africa made long bifacial implements, which are described as Lumpeban bifaces. These are often impressive due to their size, symmetry and the fact that some specimens are made from very intractable rocks. One specimen from Muguruk in western Kenya is 267mm (10 1/2 inches) long, with a maximum thickness of only 35mm(1 2/5 inches). Such artifacts were made by bifacial knapping, with the use of both hard and soft hammers (McBrearty 1988). We should also note here that in a few rare instances Early Humans engaged in a blade technology of a type very similar to that of the Upper Palaeolithic, at the start of Act 4. Assemblages made by Early Humans which include blades are described by Ronen (1992) who characterizes them as 'PUP' for Pre-Upper Palaeolithic. Conrad (1990) discusses blade assemblages made by Neanderthals during the last interglacial of North West Europe. In the latter case at least, however, there is a marked difference between the type of blades being produced in these assemblages, and those of the Upper Palaeolithic. For instance, the Early Humans were not making prismatic blade cores but removing blades from a variety of directions on a core.

In one industry, the Howieson's Poort of South Africa dating to after 75,000 years ago, blades were turned into small crescent-shaped artifacts, described as microliths. Parkington (1990) reviews the dating of the Howieson's Poort. He draws together evidence from numerous sites in South Africa to argue that some Howieson's Poort assemblages could by as young as 40,000 years old. This view has been supported by electron spin resonance (ESR) dates which suggest that the Howieson's Poort artifacts from Klasies River Mouth are between 40,000 and 60,000 years old and those from Border Cave between 45,000 and 75,000 years old. One of the problems is that the Howieson's Poort industry may not be a unitary phenomenon, and it may have appeared at different times in different sites between 100,000 and 40,000 years ago. Parkington notes that only at three sites in South Africa are Howieson's Poort artifacts overlain by Middle Stone Age (MSA) flake/blade assemblages. In others, it is overlain by assemblages which are transitional to the Late Stone Age (LSA) with increasing numbers of bladelet cores. Other than in this industry – which may in fact belong to Act 4 – microliths are confined to the toolkits of Modern Humans which begin to appear towards the end of the last ice age, many thousands of years after the start of Act 4.

10 Kuman (1994). See also Clarke (1988).

11 For instance, during the Middle Stone Age in Africa a range of relatively intractable materials were worked, contrasting substantially to earlier periods (Clark 1982).

12 Goren-Inbar (1992), Belfer-Cohen & Goren-Inbar (1994) and Villa (1983).

13 The handbones of Neanderthals imply a somewhat less precise grip than that of Modern Humans between the thumb and forefinger (Jones *et al* 1992). Dennell (1983, 81–3) suggests that Early Humans lacked the motor abilities to work bone, antler and ivory. This seems unlikely in light of the need for these actions to make the few wooden artifacts of the archaeological record, and the diversity of motor actions used in tasks such as animal butchery and plant processing.

14 Knecht (1993a) has demonstrated the effectiveness of organic materials as projectiles in a series of experimental studies, while Straus (1990a) compares the suitability of lithic and organic materials used for projectiles in the context of the Later Upper Palaeolithic. Wooden artifacts made by Early Humans are described by Oakley *et al* (1977) and Belitzky *et al* (1991).

15 Unfortunately there are rather few microwear studies of early prehistoric artifacts, largely due to the unsuitability of their raw material for such studies. Microwear studies on African handaxes, demonstrating that they were general-purpose tools, have been undertaken by Keeley & Toth (1981), and studies of Acheulian and Clactonian artifacts from England gave similar results (Keeley 1980). Experimental use of replicated artifacts (e.g. Jones 1980, 1981) also supports the notion that early artifacts were general-purpose rather than dedicated tools. Anderson-Gerfund (1990) and Béyries (1988) have found similar results with Mousterian artifacts.

16 Kuhn (1993) discusses the narrow range of variability in Mousterian points, while relationships between Upper Palaeolithic weapons and specific types of game are demonstrated by Peterkin (1993) and Clark *et al* (1986). Straus (1990a, 1993) examines weapon specialization during the Upper Palaeolithic, which is considered in Chapter 9.

17 Shea (1988, 1989; Lieberman & Shea 1994) has demonstrated breakage patterns, microfracturing debitage and abrasive wear on pointed artifacts. Wear analysis has also been undertaken on Mousterian artifacts from western Europe, but with no clear evidence for their use as spear points (Anderson-Gerfund 1990; Béyries 1988).

18 Binford (1989, 28).

19 One study has shown that when more than 1000 handaxes from 17 sites in Europe, Africa, India and the Near East were statistically compared, only those from one of these regions appeared to show any distinctive shape (Wynn & Tierson 1990). As this sample includes sites from high to low latitudes, in which different types of animals were exploited, and plant foods probably had different degrees of importance in the Early Human diet, the only conclusion is that handaxe morphology bears very little relation to variability in the natural environment and subsistence behaviour.

20 Klein (1989).

21 Gamble (1993).

22 Many of the faunal assemblages from the Middle Pleistocene, such as the elephant dominated assemblage from Torralba in Spain, the assemblages from Zhoukoudian in China and those from Olorgesailie in Africa, were originally interpreted as reflecting big-game hunting (e.g. Howell 1965; Isaac 1978; Shipman *et al* 1981). Binford reinterpreted many of these during the 1980s as the product of hominid scavenging (Binford 1985, 1987b; Binford & Ho 1985; Binford & Stone 1986; Binford & Todd 1982). However, many of these faunal assemblages may be simply too disturbed and poorly preserved to extract any inferences about past behaviour (Villa 1983, 1990, 1991; Stopp 1988).

23 See summaries in Gamble (1986) and Stringer & Gamble (1993). For more detailed studies of Pleistocene fauna see Stuart (1982). High degrees of species diversity are generally thought to reflect a true difference between the animal communities of the Pleistocene and the modern world. But we must remember that Pleistocene faunal assemblages often have a very poor chronological resolution and are invariably palimpsests. The recent data from ice cores tell us that there were many short-lived, but quite marked, environmental fluctuations, during which certain species may temporarily have extended their range. Consequently the idea that such diverse communities (as opposed to assemblages) were a typical feature of the Pleistocene may be unfounded.

24 A further environmental feature which may have challenged the Neanderthals was that Pleistocene vegetation showed a markedly lower degree of zonation than is found today, with plant communities having a patchwork or plaid distribution. Today we find distinctive types of vegetation, such as woodland, grassland and tundra, coming in broad bands, within which a typical range of animal species will be found. But prior to the end of the last ice age at 10,000 years ago vegetation types appear to have been much more inter-mingled with each other (Guthrie 1984, 1990). Evidence for this comes both from pollen and, more importantly, the remarkable diversity of game found in Pleistocene landscapes. Guthrie explains this contrast in vegetation pattern by the richer soils, longer growing season and the greater degree of variability between growing seasons. This would have reduced the predictability of game species making their exploitation even more difficult than that in high latitude environments today.

Adding to the Neanderthal difficulties was the fact that in these fluctuating and unpredictable environments they would have been competing with carnivores for both food and shelter. This competition is apparent from the mixture of human and carnivore activity often represented within the same faunal assemblages (Straus 1982). Gamble (1986, 1989) attempts to monitor the variation in competitive pressure between carnivores and humans across Pleistocene Europe, and suggests that this may partly account for the variation in the extent to which Neanderthal skeletons and burials survive.

25 For information concerning Inuit technology see Oswalt (1973) and for modern hunter-gatherers in general see Oswalt (1976). Torrence (1983) has demonstrated that technological complexity is related to latitude and she interprets this as reflecting time stress. Hence groups such as the Inuit have to ensure that attempted kills are successful due to the limited opportunities of a second chance. In addition, it is likely that the exploitation of aquatic mammals requires particularly complex technology since the animal must be retrieved as well as killed. A very useful discussion of weapon technology and hunting methods among modern hunter-gatherers is provided by Churchill (1993).

26 Soffer (1989b) reviews the different storage technologies available to hunter-gatherers. For permanent storage these include the use of various types of pits, storehouses and other devices, while for portable storage the drying of meat is useful, but labour intensive. Social storage is also possible in terms of building up reciprocal obligations and is likely to include the use of artifacts to symbolize debts. Finally, one form of storage Neanderthals are likely to have used was storage in the self by building up fat reserves.

27 Trinkaus (1995) provides a comprehensive study of Neanderthal mortality patterns. Two factors may question the apparent high levels of mortality. First, the sample is drawn from across the Old World and combines Neanderthals from many tens of thousands of years. Consequently it may not reflect any true population. Secondly, the sample is inevitably composed of individuals from cave situations. If individuals of different ages died in different parts of the landscape, sampling just one type of context may lead to very biased conclusions. A comparison between the injuries of Neanderthals and rodeo riders is made by Berger (*National Geographic* 1996, 189, p. 27).

28 A review of Middle Palaeolithic faunal assemblages is provided by Chase (1986). Part of the problem with the interpretation of these cave faunas is that the products of human activity are often mixed together with that of hyenas, bears and other carnivores. It is often difficult to distinguish between the two. Most of the debate about their interpretation has been stimulated by Binford (1985) who suggested that Neanderthals were essentially scavengers. Mellars (1989a) and Stringer & Gamble (1993) review interpretations of the relevant faunal assemblages.

29 Chase (1986, 1989). The patterns of body part representation at the site (predominantly meat-bearing bones) and the presence of cutmarks at those locations on the skeleton where fillets would be removed, are the exact opposite of what would be expected from opportunistic scavenging near the bottom of the predator hierarchy. Bovid and horse remains have relatively high frequencies of less utilitarian carcass parts (as might be left at kill sites by carnivores), although butchery marks on limb bones are still present (Chase 1986). Levine (1983) has shown that horse remains have a catastrophic mortality profile (i.e. animals of different ages are represented in the same proportions as in a living herd) which is more likely a product of hunting rather than scavenging.

30 The fauna from Grotta di Sant'Agostino has been analyzed by Mary Stiner (Stiner & Kuhn 1992).

31 Evidence for Neanderthal hunting has also come from open sites, as opposed to cave occupations. At both Mauran in the Pyrenees and La Borde in the Lot valley the substantial faunal assemblages are dominated by bovids. At Mauran there are the remains of at least 108 bovids, constituting over 90% of the assemblage. The site is at the base of a steep riverside escarpment and may reflect 'cliff-fall' hunting (Girard & David 1982; Mellars 1989a). There are no absolute dates for the site and Straus (1990b) has questioned the dating of the site to the Middle Palaeolithic, noting that this is essentially done by circular reasoning and that the lithic assemblage does not preclude an early Upper Palaeolithic date. He also notes that the faunal assemblage is likely to have formed over a long period of time and consequently there may not have been the mass slaughter of bovids that cliff-fall hunting implies. La Borde is apparently well dated at 120,000 BP (Stringer & Gamble 1993, 163). Had Neanderthals been opportunistic scavengers we would expect such sites to have a more even distribution of game species. Another possible case of cliff-fall hunting is La Cotte on Jersey, a cave site at the base of a cliff dated to 180,000 years ago (Scott 1980; Callow & Cornford 1986). Mellars (1989a) argues that sites such as La Cotte imply that Neanderthals were practising cliff-fall hunting of an equivalent nature to the massive bison-jump kill sites created by Palaeo-Indians of North America. Gamble (Stringer & Gamble 1993, 162) also interprets La Cotte as reflecting specialist hunting but has suggested that it might reflect 'dangerous driving by desperate people' rather than carefully controlled and planned hunting. Piles of mammoth and rhino bones within this cave have been interpreted as parts of carcasses dragged into the cave after animals were forced off the cliff above to fall to their death.

32 Stiner (1991).

33 Gamble (1987).

34 As we move into lower latitudes the environmental challenges faced by Early Humans may have been reduced, but nevertheless remained substantial. The faunal assemblages from the caves of the Levant indicate that diverse animal faunas were a common feature of the Pleistocene, as was the competition for prey and shelters between humans and carnivores. The Neanderthals using Kebara Cave appear to have had the upper hand in this competition as the gnawmarks on the fauna generally postdate the human cutmarks (Bar-Yosef *et al* 1992).

Both the Neanderthals and anatomically Modern Humans in the Near East made Mousterian industries, and both appear to have been competent hunters. The Levallois points from both Kebara and Qafzeh caves, associated with Neanderthals and Modern Humans respectively, have wear traces and fracture patterns that indicate they had been hafted and used as spear tips (Shea 1988, 1989).

These spear tips were used for hunting a range of game species including gazelle, fallow deer and roe deer. The first of these appears to have been the major prey item, constituting over 75% of the faunal remains from Kebara. While both Neanderthals and anatomically Modern Humans were hunting such animals, the precise patterns of their hunting behaviour appear to have differed (Lieberman & Shea 1994), with Neanderthals practising a less mobile strategy that nevertheless required a higher daily expenditure of effort than the anatomically Modern Humans. This agrees with the skeletal evidence indicating high degrees of physical activity by the muscular anatomy and high frequencies of stress fractures (Trinkaus 1995). As in Europe, the long-term success and effective hunting strategies of these Early Humans in the Levant imply a sophisticated natural history intelligence. An understanding of animal behaviour and the ability to 'read' visual cues are both implied by the long-term success of Early Humans in the Levant. The knowledge bases of Early Humans in Europe and western Asia are bound to have been different, however, not only because of the different range of game, but also because of the greater availability of plant foods in lower latitudes. We have archaeological evidence for their exploitation, such as the fruits of *Celtis* sp. from Doura Cave and wild peas in the hearths at Kebara (Bar-Yosef 1994b; Bar-Yosef *et al* 1992). But such evidence still remains sparse.

The subsistence behaviour of the Early Humans of the Middle Stone Age (MSA) in South Africa shares many similarities to that in the Levant and Europe. There are also similar disputes concerning interpretation of the faunal remains following Binford's (1984a) controversial volume on Klasies River Mouth. Klein (1989) provides the most reasonable interpretation of MSA subsistence patterns and how they differ to those of the Late Stone Age (LSA). The faunal remains from Klasies River Mouth indicate that eland were hunted, while the larger bovids such as cape buffalo were likely to have been scavenged. The MSA Early Humans also exploited seals and gathered shellfish, demonstrating the application of an advanced natural history intelligence to the exploitation of coastal resources. As with the Neanderthals of Europe, the Early Humans of South Africa do not appear to have actively gone fishing and fowling.

35 Trinkaus (1987, 1995). Neanderthals have a high frequency of traumatic injuries and developmental stress indicators. Their low survival rate may also reflect frequent population crashes, perhaps from seasonal shortages of food which may have been induced by environmental fluctuations or hunting failure.

36 This is a feature they share with other Early Humans except for the early anatomically Modern Humans (Trinkaus 1987).

37 Some very fine bone needles come from the site of Combe Saunière in southwest France dated to 18,000 years ago (Geneste & Plisson 1993).

38 Gamble (1994).

39 The evidence for the ability of Early Humans to exploit interglacial environments has been discussed by Gamble (1986, 1992) and Roebroeks *et al* (1992). The absence of any archaeological traces from the Ipswichian of Britain (i.e. the last interglacial, *c.* 125, 000 BP – stage 5e, see Box p. 32) when there was abundant game but relatively thick forest cover may well indicate that the technologically-challenged Neanderthals could not exploit such environments. Alternatively, if the Neanderthals were living in small groups, their archaeological record may simply be extremely sparse, or their absence due to their failure to colonize Britain before it was cut off by rising sea levels after the preceding glacial maximum.

40 Villa (1983), see also Stepanchuk (1993).

41 Oswalt (1973, 1976).

42 The manner in which climate influenced the toolmaking of Neanderthals in France has been discussed by Nicholas Rolland and Harold Dibble (1990; Dibble & Rolland

1992). (See also Turq (1992) for an explanation of how the Quina Mousterian variant is a reflection of time-stressed activities during harsh climatic conditions.) They have shown that when the climate was relatively mild, artifacts were produced which had a relatively low degree of reduction – i.e. they were relatively large and were infrequently resharpened. In contrast, when climatic conditions were severely cold, artifacts were more frequently resharpened and toolmakers were more conservative with their raw material. To explain this, they argue that the long winters of these cold phases would have forced groups to minimize journeys and reduced access to raw materials. During milder conditions Neanderthals would have changed their habitation sites more often. This would have allowed more frequent replenishment of raw materials, resulting in less intensively reduced assemblages.

Mary Stiner and Steven Kuhn have explored the connection between variability in stone tool technology and collections of animal bones from four cave sites in west-central Italy, each of which had been occupied by Neanderthals (Grotta Breuil, Grotta Guattari, Grotta dei Moscerini and Grotta di Sant'Agostino). The character of the animal bones prior to *c.* 55,000 years ago suggested that animal carcasses were acquired by scavenging. The tools and flakes associated with these bones are relatively large and exhibit evidence of prolonged use and relatively high frequencies of transport between sites. After 55,000 years ago Neanderthals appear primarily to have been hunting animals such as deer and horse. And their stone artifacts had changed. They were now dominated by production techniques that yielded relatively large numbers of small flakes, and the artifacts were neither worked intensively nor transported over long distances.

While there is a clear association between the variation in stone tool technology and the manner in which meat was acquired, there is no direct or obvious functional link between them. The stone tools from either pre- or post-55,000 years ago are mainly sidescrapers. Stone points remain at about the same low frequency in both collections. Stiner & Kuhn (1992) argue that differences in the Neanderthals' patterns of movements across the landscape, as they engaged in either carcass scavenging or hunting, provided different opportunities to replenish their raw materials for toolmaking. Scavenging and gathering imply relatively wide-ranging search patterns, and the production of large flakes by centripetal core reduction techniques would be advantageous because such blanks would be suitable when gathering/scavenging in areas where raw materials were scarce. Similarly, the persistent resharpening made possible by such blanks is a way of coping with the uncertainty about when and where raw materials for manufacturing new tools will be available. After 55,000 years ago, hunting is likely to have involved targeting concentrated food patches, reducing the ranging area of the hominids, increasing the duration of occupations within caves and reducing uncertainties about raw material availability. As a consequence, greater numbers of light tools were made using a platform core reduction technique producing blanks which could be used unmodified, or after light retouching, for processing animal tissue. This case study illustrates once again how the variation in Early Human toolmaking at a regional level is essentially a passive reflection of mobility and the distribution of raw materials. It did not structure mobility and hunting patterns in the way that toolmaking does among modern hunter-gatherers. Additional studies of artifact transport and mobility by Early Humans are provided by Roebroeks *et al* (1988) and Féblot-Augustins (1993). For earlier interpretations of Middle Palaeolithic technology see Binford & Binford (1969), Binford (1973) and Bordes (1961b, 1972).

43 Similar passive reflections of environmental variability and the making of simple cost/benefit decisions are apparent in several other regions. In the Aquitaine area, Geneste (1985) has recognized that the 'utilization' index (UI) of raw materials progressively increases with the distance from the sources at which they were procured – the UI is a measure of the intensity of use of a raw material once it has been procured. In a 5-km radius, the UI is only 5%; for sources between 5–20 km from the sites the UI was 10–20%; while for exotic materials from 50–80 km away the UI was 75–100%. Moreover the form in which the raw material entered the sites systematically varied, with prepared blocks only for the 5–20-km distant sources, and pieces at the final stage of the reduction sequence for those materials from exotic sources.

Otte (1992) has explained how at the site of Sclayn, where occupation is dated to

130,000 BP, Early Humans made simple denticulates from local chert, the quartz from a slightly more distant origin was used to make becs and perforators, flint from about 30 km away was used to make heavily retouched sidescrapers, while Levallois flakes made of a fine sandstone had been transported into the site from a distant source.

Callow (Callow & Cornford 1986) attributes a substantial amount of the technological variability at La Cotte to changes in raw material availability. When the sea levels were high and raw material access difficult, artifacts were small and made of thick flakes with an inverse or bifacial retouch. When the sea level was lower, and raw materials more readily available, these traits diminished.

44 Dunbar (1992) explores this using various different measures of brain size, all of which shows some degree of correlation with mean group size. The strongest correlation is when brain size is estimated by the ratio of the neocortex to the rest of the brain.

45 Aiello & Dunbar (1993). These are mean figures taken from data provided in their table 1.

46 Dunbar (1993). A figure of 147.8 is given for Modern Humans. All these estimates have wide 95% confidence limits, that for Modern Humans ranging between 100.2 and 231.1. The extrapolation beyond the range of X-variable values is rather poorly justified on the basis that the study is exploratory rather than explanatory. A range of methodological issues are discussed in the commentary following Dunbar's article. He suggests that the predicted group size for Modern Humans fits well with the size of intermediate-level grouping among hunter-gatherers, lying between the group that lives together on a day-to-day basis (30–50 individuals) and the population unit (500–2000 individuals). The intermediate-level groups range in size between 100 and 200, with a mean not significantly different to that of his predicted figure of 147.8. Dunbar also suggests that there are many groupings within prehistoric farming and modern societies (such as in armies) of around 150 individuals and these support the idea that Modern Humans are cognitively constrained to maintaining personal contact with this size of group; a rather tenuous argument, to say the least.

47 Neanderthal remains from Grotta Guattari and Krapina have been substantially chewed by carnivores (Trinkaus 1985, White & Toth 1991). It is not clear whether the Neanderthals were already dead before the carnivores chewed them. This is perhaps the most likely story, although there is clear evidence that early hominids were hunted and killed by carnivores (e.g. Brain 1981).

48 A nice example of this from Africa is the elephant butchery site of Mwanganda's Village (Clark & Haynes 1970). Dennell (1983) notes the consequences of megafaunal food packages for group size.

49 Even among modern hunter-gatherers with firearms the rate of hunting success is often very low. For instance Marks (1976) describes the rarity of the Valley Bisa actually succeeding in killing an animal, even though they used shotguns.

50 Wrangham (1987) discusses the competition for food as a disincentive to group living. The frequency of aggressive encounters in groups of non-human primates appears to be directly correlated to group size and the degree to which food is clumped (Dunbar 1988, 113–15). This is likely to be a major cause of the fusion-fission pattern frequently noted among large primate groups (Beauchamp & Cabana 1990).

51 Stringer & Gamble (1993), Trinkaus (1983).

52 For example, see Naroll (1962), Yellen (1977). O'Connell (1987) provides one of the most useful studies demonstrating how the spatial area of artifact distributions is influenced by both the number of people occupying a site, and the duration of occupation.

53 Binford (1989, 33).

54 Mellars (1989a, 358).

55 White (1993a, 352).

56 Soffer (1994, 113).

57 This is a widely held view (see Mellars 1989a and for a specific example of apparent lack of spatial structure in butchery sites, Farizy & David 1992). This is not a function of preservation, for, as Clive Gamble (1994; Stringer & Gamble 1993) stresses, we have several well-preserved and extensive undisturbed occupation areas from the Early Human sites of Hoxne and Boxgrove in England, Biache-St-Vaast in Northern France and Maastricht-Belvédère in the Netherlands. None of these have pits, postholes, hearths or stone structures of the type that are used to structure social interaction among Modern Humans. Precisely the same phenomenon has been found in the 0.99-million-year-old sediments at Olorgesailie. As Richard Potts has described, even though the archaeological sediments of these sites have preserved footprint trails and animal burrows, there are no signs of hearths, shelters or 'traces of distinctive social units' (Potts 1994, 18). Hayden (1993) has challenged this view, suggesting that there are numerous Middle Palaeolithic sites with spatial structure in artifact distributions and indeed features such as post-holes and wall constructions indicating a social use of space. Few, if any, of his examples, however, stand up to scrutiny and cannot be explained in more parsimonious terms.

58 Stringer & Gamble (1993, 154–58), Gamble (1994, 24–6).

59 A recent review of this data by Knight *et al* (1995) concludes that there are no more than 12 such pieces from the whole of the period prior to the start of the Upper Palaeolithic, all of which date to after 250,000 years ago. Nevertheless, they believe that these lumps of red ochre indicate that Early Humans were engaging in body painting. They argue that ochre was used as a symbol of menstrual blood and construct an intriguing, but unconvincing, argument for the origins of ritual and symbolic behaviour, building on the previous work of Knight (1991).

60 Gargett (1989) reviews the evidence for Neanderthal burial (for Kebara, see Bar-Yosef *et al* 1992). With regard to Shanidar (Solecki 1971), he suggests that it is more likely that the pollen was deposited in the cave by wind, while Gamble (1989) notes the possibility that flower pollen had been introduced into the cave by workmen during the excavation. Gamble (1989) highlights that the distribution of Neanderthal burials appears to be inversely correlated with the intensity of carnivore activity. Akazawa *et al* (1995) have described what they claim is a burial of a Neanderthal child from Dederiyeh Cave in Syria. From the brief report they provide there seems to be no evidence for a pit, but the excellent preservation may well indicate a burial. They claim that a piece of flint was intentionally placed over the heart of the child, but they provide insufficient data to support such an assertion.

61 These are described for Inuit groups by Birket-Smith (1936) and Weyer (1932) while Knight (1991) draws numerous accounts together from all over the world.

62 Mithen (1994) discusses this in detail with regard to the Acheulian and Clactonian from southeast England (Wymer 1974, Ashton *et al* 1994), drawing on Wymer's (1988) tentative correlation of assemblages with past environments. Gamble (1992, table 2) correlates Early Palaeolithic sites lacking handaxes from northwest Europe with interglacial stages, while Valoch (1984) and Svoboda (1992) have also argued that pebble/flake industries come from wooded environments. See also McNabb & Ashton (1995) and Mithen (1995).

The chain of consequences from wooded environments, to small group size, to a predominance of trial-and-error individual learning over social learning, resulting in a stone technology displaying a low level of technical skill (see Mithen 1996, figure 7.2), may also explain the stone tools from the site of Gran Dolina, one of many caverns in the limestone hill of Atapuerca in Spain. These stone tools may well be the earliest artifacts found in Europe, as they come from a deposit which has been dated to at least 780,000 years ago. This deposit also contains many fossil remains of animals and those of at least four Early Humans, which have been tentatively assigned to *H. heidelbergensis.* The tools exhibit a very low level of technical skill and are comparable to those of the Oldowan. What is significant is that the types of animals that are represented by the fossils are those of wooded environments, such as beaver, wild boar, red deer and fallow deer. These Early Humans appear to have been living in wooded environments and hence would have lacked the social structure to maintain a high level of technical skill within the group. The date for the deposits at Gran Dolina must remain provisional until it is confirmed by additional methods of dating. The hominids and stone tools from this site are described in Carbonell *et al* (1995) and the dating method in Parés & Pérez-González (1995).

John Shea (personal communication 20 June 1994) suggests that a relationship between industry and environment may also be seen at `Ubeidiya in Israel. This site had a long (but probably intermittant) occupation between *c.* 1.4 and 0.85 m.y.a. Many of the artifacts in the lower levels of this site are similar to those of the Oldowan industry and reflect limited technical skill. The environment in which they were made, as reconstructed from pollen in associated sediments, appears to have been thick woodland. This would suggest small social groups, which in turn imply low degrees of social learning.

Higher up in the Ubeidiya formation, handaxes were being made. These appear to be associated with steppe/savannah environments, in which larger group sizes, and therefore more social learning, are expected. The result would be an increase in technical skill and cultural tradition – as are indeed reflected in the production of the technically more demanding handaxes.

63 Holloway (1985) attributes the degree of Neanderthal brain enlargement over that of Modern Humans as due to a metabolic adaptation to cold environments.

64 Aiello & Dunbar (1993), Dunbar (1993). Dunbar suggests that language is a considerably more efficient means of transmitting social information than grooming for two reasons: first it can be undertaken at the same time as other activities; and secondly one can speak to many people at once, whereas grooming is restricted to one person alone.

65 Aiello (1996a).

66 Begun & Walker (1993).

67 Holloway (1981a, 1981b, 1985), Holloway & de la Coste-Lareymondie (1982). Similarly, LeMay (1975, 1976) has argued that Neanderthal endocasts imply an essentially modern neural structure.

68 A very influential reconstruction of a Neanderthal vocal tract was presented by Phillip Lieberman and Ed Crelin in 1971. They suggested that Neanderthal crania show significant similarities to the morphology of a new born rather than an adult Modern Human, and on that basis reconstructed the vocal tract. The size and shape of this was found to be only capable of producing a limited range of vowel sounds, when compared with Modern Humans. As a result, while they claimed that Neanderthals had language and speech, this was very restricted in its vocal range. Fremlen (1975) showed that this restricted range of vowels would have had little consequence for the nature of language in the following manner: '... et seems emprebeble thet ther speech wes enedeqwete bekes ef the leck ef the three vewels seggested. the kemplexete ef speech depends en the kensenents, net en the vewels, es ken be seen frem the generel kemprehensebelete ef thes letter.' Perhaps rather surprisingly, by using the same method as before Lieberman and Crelin found that archaic *H. sapiens*, in contrast to Neanderthals, were capable of fully modern speech. A similar conclusion was reached by Jeffrey Laitman and his colleagues who reconstructed the vocal tract by using the shape of the base of the cranium, which they argued was correlated with the positioning of soft tissues (Laitman *et al* 1979, 1991, 1993). By measuring this on a range of Neanderthal and archaic *H. sapiens* fossils they reached the same conclusion as Lieberman and Crelin: Neanderthals, unlike archaic *H. sapiens*, were unlikely to have had the full range of modern vocalizations. Both of these studies have received severe criticisms, summarized in Schepartz (1993). See also Frayer (1992) and Houghton (1993). One of the most important of the criticisms is that the reconstructions of the Neanderthal skulls used by Lieberman and others, notably that from the site of Chapelle-aux-Saints, are inaccurate.

69 Arensburg *et al* (1989). There has been marked disagreements over the implications of this tiny ancient bone (Arensburg *et al* 1990; Laitman *et al* 1990; Lieberman 1993).

70 Lieberman (1984).

71 Aiello (1996b).

Ch. 8. Trying to think like a Neanderthal (pp. 147–150)

1 Block (1995) discusses different types of consciousness.

2 Dennett (1991, 137).

3 Dennett (1991, 308).

4 The consequences of 'petit mal' seizures are described in Penfield (1975) and summarized in Block (1995).

5 Nagel (1974).

6 Wynn (1995, 21).

Ch. 9. The big bang of human culture: the origins of art and religion (pp. 151–184)

1 The idea that the Middle/Upper Palaeolithic transition marks a dramatic break in human behaviour is the most widely accepted position and is particularly favoured by Mellars (e.g. 1973, 1989a,b) and White (e.g. 1982, 1993a,b). Marshack (1990) however argues that the capacity for visual symbolism evolved gradually during the Pleistocene, while Lindly and Clark (1990) suggest that the changes in behaviour at *c.* 20,000 BP are of much greater significance than those at 40,000–35,000 BP. They seem to forget about the sudden appearance and abundance of items of personal ornamentation at *c.* 40,000 BP when coming to this conclusion. Bednarik (1994) has suggested that the current chronological and spatial patterning in 'art objects' is purely a reflection of preservation and discovery and has no bearing on patterns of past behaviour. This extremely bleak view is also extremely wrong. For instance the taphonomic contrasts between later Middle Palaeolithic and early Upper Palaeolithic assemblages in southwest Europe cannot account for the different quantities of art. There are a vast number of organic objects surviving from many thousands of years of Neanderthal activity in the form of the bones of the animals they were hunting. But not one of these has evidence for the carving or engraving of images with symbolic meanings. Also, while the Early Palaeolithic record as a whole may be relatively poorly preserved, we nevertheless do have some almost perfectly preserved sites, such as Boxgrove, and, as discussed in Chapter 7, these give no indication of activities with symbolic meaning.

2 White (1982, 176) has written of the 'total restructuring of social relations across the Middle/Upper Palaeolithic boundary' and of the 'transformation from internally un- or weakly-differentiated social systems' (1993a, 352). Soffer (1994) provides a social scenario for the transition in which the sexual division of labour and biparental provisioning of young were absent in the Middle Palaeolithic. In this regard she sees the origin of the home base/food sharing model, that Isaac (1978) had proposed, occurring at 2 million years ago, at the start of the Upper Palaeolithic. Her evidence for this is slim, to say the least, and the social intelligence and likely social complexity of Early Humans, as discussed in Chapter 6, suggest the proposals of Soffer and White regarding a simple form of social organization in the Middle Palaeolithic are wide of the mark.

3 Orquera (1984) suggests that the transition can be accounted for by an increase in specialized hunting technology. Hayden (1993) believes that the contrast between Middle and Upper Palaeolithic communities in Europe is equivalent to that between generalized and complex hunter-gatherers, as documented in the ethnographic record. The latter are characterized by food storage, private ownership and social differentiation, while generalized hunter-gatherer communities are small in size and highly mobile. The problem with this idea is that the Middle Palaeolithic populations in Europe were living in precisely those environments and under the type of adaptive stress in which we would expect the attributes of complex hunter-gatherer societies to develop. But they didn't. This implies that there were cognitive constraints preventing Neanderthals from making technical and economic innovations. Hayden perhaps acknowledges this when he suggests there may 'have been some changes in mental capacity and composition from Neanderthal to fully modern human forms' (1993, 137), although he goes on to suggest these would not appear to have been significant changes.

4 Bar-Yosef (1994b) has made an explicit comparison between the origin of the Upper Palaeolithic and that of agriculture. He suggests that archaeologists should adopt a similar research strategy to the Middle/Upper Palaeolithic transition, as has been undertaken for the origins of agriculture. This would include trying to identify the 'core area' where critical technical developments occurred and then the process by which these spread, either by migration or technological diffusion. A problem with this comparison is that the changes at the Middle/Upper Palaeolithic transition appear to be much more diverse and profound than those at 10,000 years ago without just one 'big idea' (such as domesticating plants), and appear to have occurred in many regions of the world in a very short space of time.

5 The language interpretation varies, some arguing that the transition marked the switch from gestural to spoken language (e.g. Corballis 1992), others that this switch was from a proto-language lacking a full range of tenses to fully modern language (Whallon 1989). Mellars suggests that the 'emergence of complex, highly structured language' could 'potentially, have revolutionized the whole spectrum of human culture' (Mellars 1989a, 364), without specifying quite what is meant by 'complex' and 'highly structured', nor how the revolution would have taken place. Gamble and Stringer (1993) refer to the lack of symbolic capacities in the Middle Palaeolithic, but it is not clear whether they are including linguistic and visual symbolism in the same capacity.

6 Fodor (1985, 4), Gardner (1983, 279), Rozin (1976, 262), Sperber (1994, 61), Karmiloff-Smith (1994, 706), Carey & Spelke (1994, 184) and Boden (1994, 522).

7 White (1992) suggests that the difficulty in defining art has been a serious hindrance to explaining the origin of 'art'. Conkey (1983,

1987) has discussed how the adoption by archaeologists of the modern concept of art as a universal category is a handicap to explaining the cultural developments at the start of the Upper Palaeolithic.

8 Bednarik (1995) makes extravagant claims about such artifacts. He describes pieces of bone with simple scratches on as having 'concept mediated' markings, with no explanation of what he means by this term. Simple sets of juxtaposed lines are claimed to be 'structured sets', 'identically angled', having an 'extraordinary straightness' and being 'intentional', with no attempt to justify such claims. His discussion of these illustrates the type of uncritical, subjective interpretation of archaeological data that severely constrains our progress towards understanding the pattern of cognitive evolution.

9 Marshack (1990, 457–98).

10 Aurignacian figurative art in Central Europe is restricted to four sites: Vogelherd, Hohlenstein-Stadel, Geißenklösterle, all in Germany, and Stratzing/Krems-Rehberg in Austria. The largest single collection of ten statuettes comes from Vogelherd Cave, consisting of 2 mammoths, 1 horse, 2–3 felids or other indeterminable animals, a half relief mammoth head on a retoucher, a half relief lion, a fully sculptured bison, a lion's head and an anthropomorph (Hahn 1972, 1984, 1993). Marshack (1990) describes how his microscopic examination of the Vogelherd figurines revealed that the animal figures were often marked and over marked, as if in periodic ritual.

11 Delluc & Delluc (1978).

12 White (1989, 1992, 1993a,b) has made a detailed study of the production and distribution of these items throughout Europe, indicating their considerable complexity and their abundance in southwest Europe. Of the many important aspects of his studies, we might note that the beads form a distinct time horizon at *c.* 40,000 BP and that in southwest Europe they are not from burial contexts but occupation layers. White stresses that we should view these beads as objects of art, rather than trivializing them by simply calling them decorative items.

13 Bahn & Vertut (1989) and Clottes (1990) review the problems of dating rock art. Our knowledge of the chronology of Palaeolithic art is being dramatically changed by the use of AMS radiocarbon dating (e.g. Valladas *et al* 1992), which hopefully will become widely used.

14 The art in Chauvet Cave is described in Chauvet, Deschamps & Hillaire (1996). In addition to its early date, 10,000 years earlier than many experts were expecting, the cave is also notable for the dominance of rhinoceroses and carnivores in the art. In other caves these tend to be rather infrequent, outnumbered by paintings of horses and bison. In addition, all the other 'classic' painted caves have been found in the Perigord/Quercy and Pyrenees regions of France or in Cantabria, Spain. The discovery of Chauvet Cave has fundamentally changed our knowledge of Palaeolithic cave painting.

15 Bahn (1991, 1994) reviews Pleistocene art outside Europe. There are numerous Australian sites with Pleistocene dates. At Sandy Creek in Queensland, engravings have been dated to 32,000 BP by the sediments which cover them, and red paint has been directly dated to 26,000 BP. AMS dating of organic material in varnish covering petroglyphs in south Australia has provided dates of 42,700 BP for an oval figure at Wharton Hill and 43,140 ± 3000 BP for a curved line at Panaramitec North. These very early dates are controversial and should not be accepted without confirmation. Items of art of Pleistocene age are now also claimed to come from China and South America.

16 Mithen (1989, 1990) argues that the combination of severe climatic conditions and the intensification of hunting led to fluctuations in the principal prey items, which in turn created the conditions in which Palaeolithic art flourished. More generally Jochim (1983) has emphasized the role of southwest Europe as a population refugia during the time of the last glacial maximum, resulting in the cave art and associated rituals which served to mark territories and cope with the resulting social stress of high population densities. See also Soffer (1987).

17 Chase (1991) provides a useful discussion of the complex terminology surrounding symbol and style in archaeology, and different ways in which the word 'arbitrary' is used. He distinguishes between 'icons', which point to something by resembling it (such as a portrait), 'indexes', which point to something by being associated with it (such as smoke from a fire) and 'symbols', which have an entirely arbitrary relationship with their referent that has to be learnt.

18 This is perhaps the critical difference

between an artifact that has symbolic as opposed to stylistic attributes (Chase 1991). Sackett (1982) distinguishes between 'active style', in which there is an intention to communicate, and 'passive style', in which an artifact adopts certain attributes distinctive to an individual or group, although there was no intention to communicate such identity by the artisan. Something with active style will act as a symbol (Wobst 1977). Halverson (1987) suggests that Palaeolithic cave art may have no meaning (and consequently was created with no intention of communication) – 'no religious, mythic or metaphysical reference' (1987, 63). This seems extremely unlikely in light of the very narrow range of subject matter that Palaeolithic artists chose to depict.

19 Layton (1994) provides an excellent synthesis of our current understanding of Aboriginal art.

20 Faulstich (1992) discusses the use of abstraction and naturalism in Walpiri art. He describes how abstractions usually have various levels of meaning, while a naturalistic image will have a single referent, although that referent in itself may have multiple meanings.

21 Tacon (1989) provides an account of the representation of fish in the art of western Arnhem Land, explaining their economic and symbolic importance. With regard to the latter he describes how among the Kunwinjku of central Arnhem Land fish are such a potent symbol of fertility, sexual relations and rebirth that coitus is often described as a 'women netting a fish' in everyday speech. This refers to a similarity between the role of nets to catch fish and legs to catch a penis, and points to a symbolic link between fish and penises as the sources of human life. Fish are also good to paint and to think about due to their anatomy. In paintings, their bones – symbols of the transformation from life to death – can be well displayed. They are also good to paint and think about due to their colour because, more than any other animal, they exhibit the quality of 'rainbowness', which is associated with the essence of Ancestral Beings. Fascinating discussions of the multivalency of images in Aboriginal art are given by Taylor (1989) for the Kunwinjku of western Arnhem Land, and by Morphy (1989b) for the Yolngu of eastern Arnhem Land.

22 Lewis-Williams (1982, 1983, 1987, 1995) has made particularly detailed studies of the rock art of South Africa exposing its complex symbolic meanings. He has stressed the presence of 'entoptic' phenomena in this art's images generated by the nervous system when under states of altered consciousness (Lewis-Williams & Dowson 1988; Lewis-Williams 1991). Similar images, he argues, are found in many rock art traditions including Palaeolithic art. A good example of multivalency from San rock art is the image of a nested series of U-shaped curves from Natal Drakensberg which are surrounded by tiny flying insects (Lewis-Williams 1995). In one respect this is a painting of a beehive, probably reflecting the great love of honey found among all hunter-gatherers. But Lewis-Williams also explains how this image is likely to have entoptic significance and also reflect the work of shamans.

23 Morris (1962) contains many splendid paintings by chimpanzees.

24 There are numerous artifacts from the Early Palaeolithic which have been claimed to be 'art' or have symbolic meanings due to the presence of engraved lines (see note 8). These have been reviewed in a favourable light by Marshack (1990) and Bednarik (1992, 1995). However, the majority of these can be explained as artifacts which have become unintentionally marked, whether by human activities (such as cutting grass on a bone support), by carnivores or during the physical processes of site formation (Chase & Dibble 1987, 1992; Davidson 1990, 1991, 1992; Pelcin 1994). The few remaining artifacts exist in isolation from each other in terms of space or time and there is no reason to believe that the marks upon them constituted part of a symbolic code.

25 Knight *et al* (1995).

26 This is very different to the attribution of meaning to the behaviour of another individual by inferring the contents of his/her mind, at which Early Humans are likely to have excelled. In this type of meaning attribution, the signified (the cognitive state) is spatially and temporally close to the signifier (observed behaviour). This is a central feature of social intelligence and one that non-human primates show varying degrees of competence in. As we saw in Chapter 4, non-human primates appear unable to attribute meaning to inanimate marks or objects displaced from their referents.

27 This has also been independently noted by White (1992, 558) and Hewes (1989, 145). Hewes states that 'I see no perceptual difference between the decoding of animal tracks, not produced deliberately, and the decoding of man-made "depictions", although the effective reading of hoofprints may demand greater cognitive ability'.

28 Bégouen & Clottes (1991) suggest that some of the engravings on bone from the cave of Enlène in the Pyrenees may have been the work of novice artists, as they show considerably less skill than the engravings on the walls of the adjacent caves of Tuc d'Audoubert and Trois-Frères. However, they are reluctant to return to the rather simplistic idea of Capitan and Bouyssonie, put forward in 1924, that Enlène represents a workshop where apprentices worked under the supervision of master artists. More generally, while the technically accomplished and realistic animal images are most frequently depicted in books, Palaeolithic art contains numerous images of disproportioned animals which may have been made by an untrained hand (Bahn & Vertut 1989).

29 Morphy (1989a) provides a collection of papers illustrating the diverse and complex ways in which animals are used in art. Particularly good examples of anthropomorphism can be seen in the ceramic art of the Ilama potters, an Amerindian group flourishing during the first millennium BC in Colombia (pp. 87–97), and the art of the Solomon Islands (pp. 318–42). Anthropomorphic images are also described within the rock art of Kenya, the Aboriginal art of Australia, and the art of the Hopi and Zuni Pueblo groups of Arizona and New Mexico.

30 Anthropomorphic imagery in Palaeolithic art is reviewed by Bahn & Vertut (1989, p. 144 for the description of the Trois-Frères sorcerer), while Lorblanchet (1989) discusses the continuity between images of humans and animals. The splendid figure from Grimaldi is 47.2 mm (1 9/10 inches) high and made from green serpentine. The female and animal are connected at the back of the heads, the shoulders and the feet. This is one of a group of figurines from Grimaldi which were 'rediscovered' in Montreal in 1991, after having been dug up in Grimaldi some time between 1883 and 1895 (Bisson & Bolduc 1994). Human figurines from the Palaeolithic are described by Delporte (1979, 1993) and Gvozdover (1989) and interpreted by Gamble (1982, 1993), Duhard (1993) and Rice (1981).

31 Srejovic (1972).

32 Kennedy (1992) provides an overview of anthropomorphic thinking, particularly its pervasiveness in ethology, which he suggests has resulted in many mistaken interpretations of animal behaviour. He describes how even those scientists who attempt to avoid anthropomorphizing animals unwittingly slip into it from time to time. He suggests that people are prone to compulsive anthropomorphizing because the idea that animals are conscious and have purpose appears to be built into us by nature and nurture.

33 Willis (1990) provides a review of changing definitions and interpretations of totemism in the introduction to his edited volume about human meaning in the natural world.

34 Willis (1990, 4).

35 In the cemetery of Oleneostrovski Mogilnik in Karelia, dating to *c.* 7800 BP, the graves are distributed into a northern and southern cluster. In the northern one effigies of elk were present in the graves, while in the southern one effigies of snakes and humans were present. This has been interpreted as reflecting two groups divided on a totemic basis (O'Shea & Zvelebil 1984).

36 Morphy (1989b, 145). As the Ancestral Beings are continually being created anew through the performance of ceremonies, the Ancestral past is more appropriately conceived of as a dimension of the present, and consequently the landscape is not simply a record of past mythological events but plays an active role in creating those events.

37 Carmichael *et al* (1994) contains a set of papers which suggests that humans universally assign symbolic meanings to topographic features such as caves, odd-shaped rocks and rivers.

38 Ingold (1992, 42).

39 The hunting tactics of the early Upper Palaeolithic appear to have been based on the stalking and killing of individual animals rather than the mass slaughter of herds, and in this regard they are more typical of the Middle Palaeolithic. Enloe (1993), for instance, has demonstrated this for Level V at Abri du Flageolet (25,700 ± 700 BP) and it conforms to the Aurignacian reindeer-hunting pattern that Spiess (1979) inferred at Abri Pataud, and those of red deer that Pike-Tay (1991, 1993) has reconstructed for Roc de Combe and La Ferrassie. Pike-Tay argues that during the Upper Perigordian hunting was not organized in such a logistic manner as during the later Upper Palaeolithic.

Mellars (1989a, 357–38) however refers to the reindeer-dominated assemblages of Abri Pataud, Roc de Combe, La Gravette and Le Piage, all of which date to between 32,000 and 34,000 BP, in which 95–99% of the faunal remains are reindeer. The dominance of these early Upper Palaeolithic assemblages by a single species remains a significant contrast to the Middle Palaeolithic assemblages from the same region. Only the Middle Palaeolithic site of Mauran appears to have an equivalent level of dominance by a single species, in that case bovids. Specialized reindeer hunting during the later Upper Palaeolithic is described by Audouze (1987), Audouze & Enloe (1992), Bokelmann (1992), Bratlund (1992) and Grønnow (1987).

40 White (1989); Mithen (1990).

41 Straus (1992, 84). Specialized ibex hunting is a feature of late Upper Palaeolithic subsistence throughout mountainous regions of southern Europe (Straus 1987b). Sites such as Bolinkoba and Rascaño in Cantabrian Spain, however, in steep cliff side locations, also have early Upper Palaeolithic levels.

42 Soffer (1989a, 714–42).

43 Klein (1989, 540–41).

44 Silberbauer (1981) provides a particularly detailed description of the anthropomorphic models used by the G/Wi. In this case human attributes are imposed on mammals in particular, and to a lesser extent on birds, reptiles and amphibians. Silberbauer explains how attributing such animals with human personalities and characteristics serves to predict their behaviour both before and after they are shot (and while being tracked when wounded). Marks (1976) highlights a similar point regarding the Valley Bisa, as does Gubser (1965) for the Nunamiut. Blurton-Jones & Konner (1976) have recognized how the !Kung knowledge of animal behaviour, based on anthropomorphic models, is as good as that of Western scientists.

45 Douglas (1990, 33). Her argument was developed with specific regard to the Lele people of Zaire. These have numerous prohibitions about eating spotted animals, which appear to relate to their interest in skin diseases including smallpox. She suggests that they 'are not using animals for drawing elaborate pictures of themselves, nor are they necessarily using them for posing and answering profound metaphysical problems. The argument is that they have practical reasons for trying to understand and predict the animals' ways, reasons to do with health, hygiene and sickness. The principles of seniority, marriage exchange, territory and political hegemony they use for explaining their own behaviour they also use for prediction about animal behaviour'.

46 Knecht (1993a,b, 1994) has made extensive experimental studies in the manufacture and use of early Upper Palaeolithic organic hunting weapons. She has also explicitly compared the utility of stone and antler as raw materials for hunting weapons, noting that while the former may have greater penetrating and cutting ability and are quicker to work, tools made from organic material are more durable and easier to repair. Pike-Tay (1993) discusses how her faunal studies and Knecht's technological studies imply that Upper Perigordian foragers were skilled hunters. She interprets the organic weapons from the early Upper Palaeolithic as being made to hunt a variety of game, rather than being dedicated to specific types.

47 For instance, Clark *et al* (1986) have undertaken a multivariate statistical analysis of the lithic and faunal assemblages from La Riera and showed a persistent association between Solutrean points and ibex. Using similar methods, Peterkin (1993) demonstrates a positive association between the haft length of lithic artifacts and the proportion of bovines within assemblages from the Upper Palaeolithic in southwest France, indicating the use of durable hafting technology for the procurement of bovines. See Bergman (1993) for development of bow technology.

48 This can be recognized by using the criteria that Bleed (1986) put forward regarding the optimal design of hunting weapons (see also Torrence 1983). He contrasted two different design alternatives: reliable and maintainable tools, each appropriate for different circumstances. When food resources are predictable, but available in very short time periods (a situation that Torrence (1983) would describe as 'time-stressed') one would expect tools to be reliable. As such they would be 'over-designed', having redundant parts, and be dedicated to specific resources and produced by specialists. When food resources are more evenly distributed in time and relatively unpredictable, the optimal tools would have a maintainable design. These are tools which can be repaired and maintained during use, often having multiple standardized components. At a very broad scale of analysis we do indeed find reliable tools being manufactured in the time-stressed environments of the last glacial maximum, as we should expect, and a switch to a maintainable technology in the forested environments of the Holocene in which game was more dispersed and less predictable. Straus (1991) and Geneste & Plisson (1993) describe the specialized hunting technology in southwest Europe at the height of the last glacial maximum, while Zvelebil (1984) contrasts this with the microlithic and maintainable technology of the Mesolithic. He provides an excellent description of how Mesolithic technology was very well suited to hunting in forested environments (Zvelebil 1986). The contrast between reliable and maintainable tools can also be seen at a finer scale of analysis. For instance, Pike-Tay & Bricker (1993) note that while Gravettian artifact assemblages in southwest France are dominated by lithic artifacts from tools they believe to be easily maintainable hunting weapons for red deer and reindeer exploitation, the Gravettian assemblage from Abri Pataud Layer 4 is dominated by organic weapons. This layer is also characterized by a tight seasonal period of hunting, the spring and fall only, which appears to have resulted in the production of reliable organic tools, just as Bleed's theory would suggest.

49 Straus (1990a) uses this phrase to characterize the interplay between microlithic technology, organic harpoons and large projectile points during the Solutrean and Magdalenian. But it is probably also appropriate as a general description of technological developments among Modern Humans.

50 Wendorf *et al* (1980).

51 The most impressive evidence for storage from the Upper Palaeolithic comes from the Russian Plain, where Soffer (1985) has described storage pits on many sites which had been used to cache frozen meat supplies. In the Late Pleistocene/Early Holocene, the communities in Japan (Jomon) and the Near East (Natufian) were building storage facilities for plant material (Soffer 1989b). It is widely accepted that Mesolithic groups were routinely storing foods, although the archaeological evidence remains rare.

52 This is a piece of bone from the Grotte de Taï (Drôme, France), dating to the Magdalenian, which has 1020 incisions on one side and 90 on the other, all of which are arranged in parallel lines following the axis of the bone. Marshack (1991) provides a very detailed description, and interprets the piece as representing a system of notation, and more specifically a lunar calendar.

53 The interpretations of these artifacts have included the following: hunting tallies, lunar calendars, a 'mathematical conception of the cosmos', the 'knowledge of a numbering or calculating system', and 'a rhythmical support for traditional recitation ... or musical instruments' (D'Errico & Cacho 1994, 185).

54 Both Marshack (1972a, 1972b, 1991) and D'Errico (1991; D'Errico & Cacho 1994) have used microscopic examination of the marks to try and ascertain the manner and order in which they have been made. While Marshack innovated this research, D'Errico has introduced a much higher degree of objective evaluation of the marks, partly by using experimentally produced artifacts to establish the criteria to be used in drawing inferences concerning the direction, type and changes of tool. Perhaps not surprisingly, there has been some disagreement between them, with D'Errico sceptical of many of Marshack's methods and interpretations (D'Errico 1989a, 1989b, 1991, 1992; Marshack 1989). The most robust cases for inferring systems of notation from these artifacts are D'Errico & Cacho's (1994) study of the Upper Palaeolithic engraved artifact from Tossal de la Roca, Spain, and D'Errico's (1995) study of the engraved antler from La Marche, France. Robinson (1992) provides a perceptive critique of Marshack's work.

55 Good ethnographic examples are the calendar stick from North America described by Marshack (1985) and the Siberian Yakut calenders made from fossil ivory strips (Marshack 1991).

56 Pfeiffer (1982).

57 Mithen (1988, 1990).

58 These carvings from Mal'ta, and many other pieces of Palaeolithic art, are beautifully illustrated in the *National Geographic*, Vol 174, no. 4 (October 1988).

59 The trophy arrays of the Wopkaimin of central New Guinea are described and interpreted as mental maps by Hyndman (1990). He emphasizes their role as a trigger in recalling the characteristics of specific places and areas of their environment. The arrangement of bones in the trophy array of the Bakonabip men's house is as follows: 'Ancestral relics (*menamen*) are stored in string bags centrally at eye level on the trophy level. These belong to the *ahip* [inner circle of hamlets] realm in the relatively long-term hamlet sites ... placed centrally in the homeland. Domestic pigs are fostered to select families residing a short distance from the hamlets, and mandibles from these animals are displayed below the ancestral relics.... Wild pig bones are placed lower than domestic ones; they come from *gipsak*, the lowest zone of rainforest encircling the inner garden and hamlet zones.... Marsupial mandibles are displayed highest off the floor, they primarily come from the mid to highest rainforests. Cassoway pelvis and thigh bones are placed in association with the wild pigs and the marsupials representing the coexistence of these animals in the outer rainforests' (Hyndman 1990, 72).

60 Leroi-Gourhan (1968) suggests that there is deliberate patterning in the layout of figures within painted caves, with animals such as carnivores being found in deep recesses, and bison being found in central areas. This proposal has never been formally tested, partly due to the difficulty of identifying original entrances, and where entrance, central and rear parts of the caves begin and end. Sieveking (1984) believes that the patterning Leroi-Gourhan claims to identify could be related to the ecological characteristics of the animals which were regularly associated together, in much the same manner as these are encoded in the trophy arrays of the Wopkaimin.

61 Eastham & Eastham (1991).

62 See White (1989b, 1992, 1993a, 1993b) for the early Upper Palaeolithic items of personal adornment, and Soffer (1985) for those manufactured on the Russian Plain during the later Upper Palaeolithic.

63 This is likely to explain the discrete spatial and temporal distributions of points which have very specific forms and have been given their own special name by archaeologists such as the 'Font Robert points' from western Europe and 'Emireh points' from the Near East. These artifacts, so useful to archaeologists as they can be used as chronological markers when other dating information is absent, were probably carrying social information about group membership, intentionally invested on the tool at the time of manufacture. Other aspects of variability between tools, such as markings on harpoons, may have been used to communicate individual ownership. The belief that these typologically distinct artifacts of the Upper Palaeolithic were carrying social information is widely held by archaeologists (e.g. Mellars 1989b). An excellent ethnographic study which illustrates how artifacts are invested with social information is by Wiessner (1983). She explores which items of material culture among the Kalahari San carry social information, and finds that projectile points are very well suited for carrying information about groups and boundaries because of their widespread social, economic, political and symbolic importance. She refers to this type of information as 'emblemic' style and contrasts it with 'assertive' style, which is information about individual ownership. With regard to the Palaeolithic we should perhaps expect assertive style to be present on organic artifacts, such as harpoons and arrow shafts, which may involve greater investment of time to produce than chipped stone points. In addition, the very process of manufacture had acquired new significance. Sinclair (1995, 50) argues that 'the symbolic aspects of [Upper Palaeolithic] technology is not restricted to the external form of tools.... Symbolism pervades the entire process of manufacture, through the use of a salient set of skills and desires which are common to both technology and other practices within societies'.

64 Gellner (1988, 45).

65 Morphy (1989b) provides a summary of the characteristics of the Ancestral Beings.

66 Gamble (1993).

67 The Skhūl burial was described by McCown (1937) and that at Qafzeh by Vandermeersch (1970). Lindly & Clark (1990) have questioned whether the animal parts were deliberately included with the anatomically Modern Humans at the time of burial. But due to the very close association between animal and human bones, there appears little doubt that parts of animal carcasses were intentionally placed in graves.

68 Lieberman & Shea (1994). The inferences regarding seasonality are made by using the cementum layers on gazelle teeth, while those concerning the intensity of hunting are made by the frequency of points within the artifact assemblages and the character of impact fractures. Evidence for a greater expenditure of energy by the Neanderthals comes from the character of their post-cranial skeleton (Trinkaus 1992).

69 Grün *et al* (1990), Grün & Stringer (1991), Stringer & Bräuer (1994).

70 Singer & Wymer (1982). A summary of the archaeological sequence at Klasies River

Mouth is provided by Thackeray (1989).
71 The evidence for the use of red ochre in the Middle Stone Age has been summarized by Knight *et al* (1995).
72 Knight *et al* (1995), Knight (1991).
73 This site was excavated in 1941 and the true date of the grave, if indeed it is a grave, remains unclear. Unfortunately the bone material itself cannot be dated (Grün & Stringer 1991).
74 Parkington (1990) draws together the dating evidence for the Howieson's Poort industry, and shows that some of these assemblages could be as young as 40,000 years old. He suggests that this industry is unlikely to be a unitary phenomenon, and that it appeared at various times between 100,000 and 40,000 years ago.
75 Yellen *et al* (1995).
76 I am here choosing just one of the possible scenarios for the origin and distribution of Modern Humans throughout the world. The major opposing view is that of multiregional evolution (see Mellars & Stringer 1989, Nitecki & Nitecki 1994 for debates about the origins of Modern Humans). The strongest argument supporting the multiregional hypothesis of evolution is the continuity in morphological features of fossils in different parts of the world, especially Southeast Asia/Australasia and China. I suspect that this continuity can be explained by the emergence of a similar set of adaptive features and by some degree of hybridization between incoming and resident populations.
77 Jones & Rouhani (1986), Jones *et al* (1992).
78 We should expect to find in the period between 100,000 and 60,000–30,000 years ago archaeological sites created by Early Modern Humans that do indeed look a bit like those of Early Humans, and a bit like those of fully Modern Humans. One such site is likely to be Prolom II in the Crimea which has stone tools typical of those made by Neanderthals, but also a large number of bones, some of which are pierced, engraved or chipped (Stepanchuk 1993). The site is as yet undated and there are no human skeletal remains associated with it. My guess is that it will prove to be an archaeological site of Early Modern Humans who had a glimmer of cognitive fluidity.

Ch. 10. So how did it happen? (pp. 185–194)

1 Dunbar makes this point in the following terms: 'ecologically related information exchange might be a subsequent development that capitalized on a window of opportunity created by the availability of a computer with a substantial information-processing capacity' (1993, 689).
2 Talmy (1988).
3 Pinker (1989).
4 Sperber (1994, 61).
5 Intriguingly, the philosopher Daniel Dennett suggests a similar scenario to that provided by Sperber for the evolution of the mind when playing one of his 'thought experiments' in his 1991 book *Consciousness Explained*. In his case, however, he emphasizes the importance not of talking to other people but of talking to oneself. He describes this as 'autostimulation' and the consequences he proposes are what I have been describing as 'cognitive fluidity'. Let me quote Dennett (1991, 195–96): 'the practice of asking oneself questions could arise as a natural side-effect of asking questions of others, and its utility would be similar: it would be a behaviour that could be recognized to enhance one's prospects by better informed action-guidance.... Suppose ... that although the right information is already in the brain, it is in the hands of the wrong specialist; the subsystem in the brain that needs the information cannot obtain it directly from the specialist – because evolution simply has not got around to providing such a "wire". Provoking the specialist to "broadcast" the information into the environment, however, and then relying on an existing pair of ears (and an auditory system) to pick it up, would be a way of building a "virtual wire" between the relevant subsystems. Such an act of autostimulation could blaze a valuable new trail between one's internal components.' Replace Dennett's terms of 'specialist' with 'specialized intelligence', and 'virtual wire' with 'cognitive fluidity' and his argument conforms to the one I have proposed, except that he suggests that any 'specialist' could 'broadcast' information, whereas I argue that this is likely to have been restricted to social intelligence.
6 Rozin (1976, 246).
7 Pigeot (1990), Fischer (1990).
8 It is significant to note here that although Modern Humans do have a capacity for verbal instruction, specialized craftspeople often acquire their technical skills not by explicit

teaching but by observation and trial-and-error learning: Wynn (1991) describes this for several modern groups, acquiring skills ranging from those of trawler fishing to those of toolmaking in traditional societies. Such a learning method may ensure that technical knowledge is built up within a specialized intelligence, as opposed to simply becoming part of what Sperber (1994) calls the meta-representational module, where knowledge acquired by language is placed. Psychologists refer to the type of knowledge that can only be expressed by demonstration as 'procedural' memory. They contrast this with 'propositional memory' which is divided into two types: episodic and semantic. This distinction has been proposed and explored in detail by the psychologist Endel Tulving (1983). While these types of memory share many features, they differ in that episodic memory refers to memories of personal happenings and doings, while semantic memory refers to knowledge of the world that is independent of a person's identity and past. With regard to the evolutionary scenario I have proposed, episodic memory is likely to be the original form of memory within social intelligence, and would have been possessed by Early Humans – just as they would have possessed forms of procedural memory within natural history and technical intelligences. Semantic memory, however, might be a unique possession of the Modern Human mind. If the principal difference between this and episodic memory is the type of information they deal with – and Tulving emphasizes that the critical differences between these two types of memory remain unclear – then semantic memory may have arisen from the invasion of social intelligence by non-social information. This information became available to those mental modules which had previously been dedicated to creating memories concerning only personal events within social intelligence, just as it became available for reflexive consciousness.

9 Schacter (1989, 360).
10 Searle (1992, 108–9).
11 Aiello (1996a), Wills (1994).
12 Wills (1994).
13 Knight *et al* (1995).
14 Smith *et al* (1995).
15 Stringer & Gamble (1993), Dean *et al* (1986), Zollikofer *et al* (1995). See also Smith *et al* 1993.
16 Akazawa *et al* (1995).

Ch. 11. The evolution of the mind (pp. 195–216)

1 The following brief summary of primate evolution draws on Martin (1990) and Simons (1992).
2 McFarland (1987).
3 Simons (1992).
4 Milton (1988).
5 Aiello & Wheeler (1995).
6 Whiten (1990, 367).
7 Humphrey (1984, 22).
8 The phylogenetic relationships between Eurasian fossil primates found between 15 and 4.5 m.y.a. and hominids remains unclear. The best represented of these fossils is *Dryopithecus*, with remains found in Hungary, southern France and Spain. A particularly well-preserved specimen of *D. laietanus* was recently found in the Valle Penedes region of Spain. This shows the dryopithecines swung from branches and moved on four legs, in a similar manner to orang-utans today (Moyà-Solà & Köhler 1996). Andrews & Pilbeam (1996) comment on the phylogenetic reconstruction of this period.
9 Aiello (1996a).
10 Wheeler (1984, 1988, 1991, 1994).
11 deMenocal (1995).
12 Falk (1990).
13 Falk (1990, 334).
14 Aiello & Wheeler (1995).
15 Humphrey (1984, 23).
16 Aiello (1996a, 1996b).
17 Aiello & Dunbar (1993). Aiello (1996b) draws on recent work by Robert Foley to suggest that a very gradual increase at an exponential rate in human population, beginning with *H. erectus* 1.8 million years ago, might lead to a seeming population explosion, forcing people to live within large groups.
18 The most notable of these are bifacially worked artifacts similar to handaxes which are found in the very final Mousterian assemblages from sites such as Combe Grenal. Clive Gamble (1993, 1994; Stringer & Gamble 1993) has suggested that one can see further features in Neanderthal behaviour after 60,000 years ago which foreshadow the behavioural developments of the Upper Palaeolithic, such as a greater amount of spatial structure on archaeological sites. He refers to this period as a 'pioneer phase'. But the evidence for any cognitive fluidity remains very slight, and there is nothing that approaches a capacity for symbolism.

19 Lake suggests: 'It seems plausible that evolution by natural selection typically occurs by repeatedly isolating, honing and then re-integrating parts. Natural selection is most efficacious when genotypic variability and fitness are closely correlated; it is impossible when they are completely uncorrelated. The degree of correlation is likely to be weakest in generalized systems since fitness will be subject to a larger number of selective pressures which require conflicting adaptive responses. For this reason natural selection might be expected to operate most successfully on specialized systems. However, such systems are often brittle in the sense that there is simply no way of adapting them to cope with a radical change in selective conditions. Thus it would appear that the long-term persistence of a type of system (or lineage) requires that it possess the contradictory properties of predictability and flexibility. I suggest that natural selection has frequently solved this conundrum by decomposing systems into weakly coupled parts. In this way it can respond to small changes in selective conditions by adapting the relevant subsystem without radically affecting the rest of the system. Equally, however, the possibility of rearranging the links between the subsystems provides the flexibility required to cope with radically altered selective conditions' (personal communication 16 November 1995).

20 Dawkins (1986).

21 The problem of trying to define quite what science is can be seen by contrasting two very different viewpoints. The first view is that held by the philosophers and historians of science. They have discussed the nature of science ever since Francis Bacon published his works at the start of the 17th century arguing that science must involve empirical observation of the world and experiment. Following Bacon's work, various other definitions of science have been proposed. Karl Popper challenged the view that science is the process of generalization from a mass of observations, by arguing that the essence of science is the ability to falsify one's hypotheses. Thomas Kuhn introduced the notion that science is deeply embedded in a social matrix and proceeds in sudden jumps ('paradigm changes') rather than a gradual accumulation of knowledge. More recently the whole notion that there is such as thing as a scientific method at all has been challenged by philosophers such as Paul Feyerbend.

There are many books that provide reviews of these changing ideas of science (e.g. Gillies 1993) and others that describe the development of scientific thought, perhaps most notably the seminal 1957 work of Herbert Butterworth, *The Origins of Modern Science 1300–1800*. As can be seen from that title, such histories of science almost invariably begin at the end of the Medieval period and focus on the work of figures such as Galileo, Copernicus, Newton and Einstein. Indeed, in such works there is an assumption that although the intellectual foundations for these scientists may be found in the work of Classical and Islamic scholars, science is a product of Western civilization. One recent review article in the *British Journal for the History of Science*, concluded that science is no more than 250 years old and confined to western Europe and America (Cunningham & Williams 1993).

Now let us look at a radically different view of science, one that has come from a scientist himself. In his 1995 book, *The Trouble with Science,* Robin Dunbar – whose views about the evolution of language we have considered – argues that science is 'a method for finding out about the world based on the generation of hypotheses and the testing of predictions derived from those hypotheses.' As such this is a fairly conventional position. But Dunbar takes a radical stance by questioning the assumption that this is unique to modern Western culture.

In his book, Dunbar argues that not only can the technological inventions of the Chinese during the 1st millennium BC, such as printing, silk and gunpowder, be described as arising from science, but so too can the knowledge that Aristotle acquired about the natural world in the 4th century BC and the developments in mathematics and physics made by Islamic scholars during the 9th to 12th centuries AD. This much is no doubt acceptable to the majority of his readers. But he goes on to argue that science is rife in traditional non-Western societies. According to Dunbar, 'science' is the method used to acquire the prodigious and accurate knowledge about the natural world possessed by hunter-gatherers, pastoralists and farmers. As if this was not enough, Dunbar proceeds to argue that many non-human animals also engage in science, because hypothesis testing appears to be one of the means by which they acquire their knowledge of the world. He concludes that 'science is a genuine universal, characteristic of all advanced life forms' (p. 75).

22 D'Errico (1995). Donald (1991) similarly emphasizes the importance of these which he describes as 'external storage devices'.

23 Dennett (1991).

24 In his book *The Trouble with Science* (1995) Robin Dunbar argues that the use of metaphors appears most commonly in physics and evolutionary biology, as these subjects involve ideas which are alien to our everyday experience. To understand these, scientists are prone not only to use metaphors, but to choose those which draw on the social world of humans. For instance the geneticist Steve Jones (1993) uses the metaphor of the genetic code as possessing a language; as Pinker (1994) describes, the use of a linguistic metaphor in genetics has been widely adopted. Dunbar provides examples of many other metaphors used in biological thought, such as the intriguing 'Kamikaze Sperm' hypothesis.

25 Gould (1990, 229).

26 Kuhn (1979).

27 Dennett (1991, 455).

Epilogue. The origins of agriculture (pp. 217–226)

1 Hole (1992) provides a brief overview of ideas concerning the origins of agriculture.

2 Wendorf *et al* (1990) describe the archaeology of Wadi Kubbaniya, while Hillman (1989) summarizes the Late Palaeolithic food remains.

3 Hillman *et al* (1989).

4 Cohen & Armelagos (1984).

5 Hole (1992).

6 This argument was forwarded in most detail by Nathan Cohen in a 1977 book entitled *The Food Crisis in Prehistory*.

7 Cohen & Armelagos (1984).

8 Dansgaard, White & Johnsen (1989).

9 The following summary follows Moore & Hillman (1992).

10 Legge & Rowley-Conwy (1987).

11 This is the period of the Younger Dryas, a global environmental event which saw the re-advance of the ice sheets in Europe. It was a short, sharp cold interval that was followed by the very rapid global warming which marked the true end of the last ice age.

12 Bar-Yosef & Belfer-Cohen (1989).

13 The architecture itself is not necessarily indicative of sedentism; mobile hunter-gatherers do in some circumstances build substantial dwellings and facilities which are returned to on a regular basis. Bar-Yosef & Belfer-Cohen (1989) suggest that the best evidence for sedentism comes from the appearance of house sparrows, mice and rats in the fauna from these sites.

14 For a summary of Natufian settlement and economy see Byrd (1989) and Bar-Yosef & Belfer-Cohen (1989).

15 Bar-Yosef & Belfer-Cohen (1989, 490).

16 This is evident from the spatial relationships between storage pits and dwellings. At Radomyshl' we see several dwellings surrounding a central storage pit, implying 'open, visible and equal access to stored resources for all inhabitants of the site'. At the slightly later site of Dobranichevka we see similar numbers of similar-sized storage pits distributed around each dwelling, implying that the residents of each dwelling now owned their own stored resources, although the distribution of resources remained equitable. At later sites, such as Mezin, Gontsy and Eliseevichi, the storage pits are preferentially distributed around one single dwelling. For instance at Mezin there appears to have been 5 dwellings, but 6 out of the 7 (or 8) storage pits there were located adjacent to just one of these dwellings. The residents of this dwelling, therefore, appear to have controlled access to stored resources (Soffer 1985, 459–63).

17 Mithen (1990).

18 See Albrethsen & Petersen (1976), Larsson (1983) and Clark & Neeley (1987).

19 For differing views on how a Darwinian perspective should be used when looking at prehistoric behaviour see Clark (1992) and Mithen (1993).

20 Hayden (1990, 35).

21 Bahn (1978). This evidence has been critically assessed by White (1989b).

22 Bahn (1978).

23 For burial of dogs in southern Scandinavia see Larsson (1983); for the Natufian see Byrd (1989).

24 Humphrey (1984, 26–7)

25 Evidence for the management and manipulation of plants resources in the European Mesolithic has been summarized by Zvelebil (1994).

26 Yen (1989) and Hallam (1989) summarize evidence for the 'domestication' of the environment by indigenous Australians. See also Chase (1989) and Jones & Meehan (1989).

27 See Higgs & Jarman (1969), Higgs (1972).

Bibliography

Adovasio, J.M., Donahue, J. & Stuckenrath, R. 1990. The Meadowcroft Rockshelter radiocarbon chronology. *American Antiquity* 55, 348–54.

Aiello, L. 1993. The fossil evidence for modern human origins in Africa: a revised view. *American Anthropologist* 95, 73–96.

Aiello, L. 1996a. Terrestriality, bipedalism and the origin of language. In *The Evolution of Social Behaviour Patterns in Primates and Man*, ed., J. Maynard-Smith. London: Proceedings of the British Academy (in press).

Aiello, L. 1996b. Hominine preadaptations for language and cognition. In *Modelling the Early Human Mind*, eds., P. Mellars & K. Gibson. Cambridge: McDonald Institute Monograph Series.

Aiello, L. & Dunbar, R.I.M. 1993. Neocortex size, group size and the evolution of language. *Current Anthropology* 34, 184–93.

Aiello, L. & Wheeler, P. 1995. The expensive-tissue hypothesis. *Current Anthropology* 36, 199–221.

Aikens, C.M. & Higuchi, T. 1982. *Prehistory of Japan*. New York: Academic Press.

Akazawa, T., Aoki, K. & Kimura,T. 1992. *The Evolution and Dispersal of Modern Humans in Asia*. Tokyo: Hokusen-Sha.

Akazawa, T., Muhesen, M., Dodo, Y., Kondo, O. & Mizoguchi, Y. 1995. Neanderthal infant burial. *Nature* 377, 585–86.

Albrethsen, S.E. & Petersen, E.B. 1976. Excavation of a Mesolithic cemetery at Vedbaek, Denmark. *Acta Archaeologica* 47, 1–28.

Allen, J. 1994. Radiocarbon determinations, luminescence dates and Australian archaeology. *Antiquity* 68, 339–43.

Alley, R.B., Meese, D.A., Shuman, C.A., Gow, A.J., Taylor, K.C., Gorrtes, P.M., Whitell, J.W.C., Ram, M., Waddington, E.D., Mayewski, P.A. & Zielinski, G.A. 1993. Abrupt increase in Greenland snow accumulation at the end of the Younger Dryas event. *Nature* 362, 527–29.

Allsworth-Jones, P. 1986. *The Szeletian and the Transition from the Middle to Upper Palaeolithic in Central Europe*. Oxford: Clarendon Press.

Allsworth-Jones, P. 1993. The archaeology of archaic and early modern *Homo sapiens*: an African perspective. *Cambridge Archaeological Journal* 3, 21–39.

Anderson, D.D. 1990. *Lang Rongrien Rockshelter: A Pleistocene-Early Holocene Archaeological Site from Krabi, Southwestern Thailand*. Philadelphia: The University Museum, University of Pennsylvania.

Anderson. J. R. 1980. *Cognitive Psychology and its Implications* (2nd edition). New York: W.H. Freeman.

Anderson-Gerfund, P. 1990. Aspects of behaviour in the Middle Palaeolithic: functional analysis of stone tools from southwest France. In *The Emergence of Modern Humans*, ed., P. Mellars, pp. 389–418. Edinburgh: Edinburgh University Press.

Andrews, P. 1995. Ecological apes and ancestors. *Nature* 376, 555–56.

Andrews, P. & Pilbeam, D. 1996. The nature of the evidence. *Nature* 379, 123–24.

Arensburg, B., Tillier, A-M., Vandermeersch, B., Duday, H., Schepartz, L.A. & Rak, Y. 1989. A Middle Palaeolithic hyoid bone. *Nature* 338, 758–60.

Arensburg, B., Schepartz, L.A., Tillier, A-M., Vandermeersch, B. & Rak, Y. 1990. A reappraisal of the anatomical basis for speech in Middle Palaeolithic hominids. *American Journal of Physical Anthropology* 83, 137–46.

Arsuaga, J-L., Martinez, I., Gracia, A., Carretero, J-M. & Carbonell, E. 1993. Three new human skulls from the Sima de los Huesos Middle Pleistocene site in Sierra de Atapuerca, Spain. *Nature* 362, 534–37.

Ashton, N.M., Cook, J., Lewis, S.G. & Rose, J. (eds.) 1992. *High Lodge: Excavations by G. de G. Sieveking 1962–68 & J. Cook 1988*. London: British Museum Press.

Ashton, N.M. & McNabb, J. 1992. The interpretation and context of the High Lodge flint industries. In *High Lodge: Excavations by G. de G. Sieveking 1962–68 & J. Cook 1988*, eds., N.M. Ashton, J. Cook, S.G. Lewis & J. Rose, pp. 164–68. London: British Museum Press.

Ashton, N.M., McNabb, J., Irving, B., Lewes, S. & Parfitt, S. 1994. Contemporaneity of Clactonian and Acheulian flint industries at Barnham, Suffolk. *Antiquity* 68, 585–89.

Asfaw, B., Beyene, Y., Suwa, G., Walter, R.C., White, T., WoldeGabriel, G. & Yemane, T. 1992. The earliest Acheulean from Konso-Gardula. *Nature* 360, 732–35.

Atran, S. 1990. *Cognitive Foundations of Natural History: Towards an Anthropology of Science*. Cambridge: Cambridge University Press.

Atran, S. 1994. Core domains versus scientific theories: evidence from systematics and Itza-Maya folkbiology. In *Mapping the Mind: Domain Specificity in Cognition and Culture*, eds., L.A. Hirschfeld & S.A. Gelman, pp. 316–40. Cambridge: Cambridge University Press.

Audouze, F. 1987. The Paris Basin in Magdalenian times. In *The Pleistocene Old World*, ed., O. Soffer, pp. 183–200. New York: Plenum Press.

Audouze, F. & Enloe, J. 1992. Subsistence strategies and economy in the Magdalenian of

the Paris Basin. In *The Late Glacial in North-West Europe: Human Adaptation and Environmental Change at the End of the Pleistocene*, eds., N. Barton, A.J. Roberts & D.A. Roe, pp. 63–71. London: Council for British Archaeology Research Report No. 17.
Ayers, W.S. & Rhee, S.N. 1984. The Acheulian in Asia? A review of research on the Korean Palaeolithic culture. *Proceedings of the Prehistoric Society* 50, 35–48.
Bahn, P.G. 1978. On the unacceptable face of the West European Upper Palaeolithic. *Antiquity* 52, 183–92.
Bahn, P.G. 1991. Pleistocene images outside of Europe. *Proceedings of the Prehistoric Society* 57 (i), 99–102.
Bahn, P.G. 1994. New advances in the field of Ice Age art. In *Origins of Anatomically Modern Humans*, eds., M.H. Nitecki & D.V. Nitecki, pp. 121–32. New York: Plenum Press.
Bahn, P.G. & Vertut, J. 1988. *Images of the Ice Age*. London: Windward.
Bar-Yosef, O. 1980. Prehistory of the Levant. *Annual Review of Anthropology* 9, 101–33.
Bar-Yosef, O. 1989. Geochronology of the Levantine Middle Palaeolithic. In *The Human Revolution*, eds., P. Mellars & C. Stringer, pp. 589–610. Edinburgh: Edinburgh University Press.
Bar-Yosef, O. 1994a. The Lower Palaeolithic of the Near East. *Journal of World Prehistory* 8, 211–65.
Bar-Yosef, O. 1994b. The contributions of southwest Asia to the study of the origin of modern humans. In *Origins of Anatomically Modern Humans*, eds., M.H. Nitecki & D.V. Nitecki, pp. 23–66. New York: Plenum Press.
Bar-Yosef, O. & Belfer-Cohen, A. 1989. The origins of sedentism and farming communities in the Levant. *Journal of World Prehistory* 3, 447–97.
Bar-Yosef, O. & Goren-Inbar, N. 1993. *The Lithic Assemblages of the Site of Ubeidiya, Jordan Valley*. Jerusalem: Qedem 34.
Bar-Yosef, O. & Meignen, L. 1992. Insights into Levantine Middle Palaeolithic cultural variability. In *The Middle Palaeolithic: Adaptation, Behaviour and Variability*, eds., H.L. Dibble & P. Mellars, pp. 163–82. Philadelphia: The University Museum, University of Pennsylvania.
Bar-Yosef, O., Vandermeersch, B., Arensburg, B., Belfer-Cohen, A., Goldberg, P., Laville, H., Meignen, L., Rak, Y., Speth, J.D., Tchernov, E., Tillier, A-M. & Weiner, S. 1992. The excavations in Kebara Cave, Mt. Carmel. *Current Anthropology* 33, 497–551.
Baron-Cohen, S. 1995. *Mindblindness*. Cambridge MA: MIT Press.
Barkow, J.H., Cosmides, L. & Tooby, J. 1992. *The Adapted Mind: Evolutionary Psychology and the Generation of Culture*. Oxford: Oxford University Press.
Barton, N., Roberts, A.J. & Roe, D.A. (eds.) 1992. *The Late Glacial in North-West Europe: Human Adaptation and Environmental Change at the End of the Pleistocene*. London: Council for British Archaeology Research Report No. 77.
Bartstra, G. 1982. *Homo erectus erectus:* the search for his artifacts. *Current Anthropology* 23, 318–20.
Beauchamp, G. & Cabana, G. 1990. Group size and variability in primates. *Primates* 31, 171–82.
Beaumont, P.B., Villers, D. & Vogel, J.C. 1978. Modern man in sub-Saharan Africa prior to 49,000 BP: a review and evaluation with particular reference to Border Cave. *South African Journal of Science* 74, 409–19.
Bednarik, R.G. 1992. Palaeoart and archaeological myths. *Cambridge Archaeological Journal* 2, 27–57.
Bednarik, R.G. 1994. A taphonomy of palaeoart. *Antiquity* 68, 68–74.
Bednarik, R.G. 1995. Concept-mediated marking in the Lower Palaeolithic. *Current Anthropology* 36, 605–34.
Bednarik, R.G. & Yuzhu, Y. 1991. Palaeolithic art in China. *Rock Art Research* 8, 119–23.
Bégouen, R. & Clottes, J. 1991. Portable and wall art in the Volp caves, Montesquieu-Avantès (Ariège). *Proceedings of the Prehistoric Society* 57 (i), 65–80.
Begun, D. & Walker, D. 1993. The endocast. In *The Nariokotome Homo erectus Skeleton*, eds., D. Walker & R. Leakey, pp. 26–358. Berlin: Springer Verlag.
Behrensmeyer, A.K. 1978. Taphonomic and ecologic information from bone weathering. *Palaeobiology* 2, 150–62.
Belfer-Cohen, A. & Goren-Inbar, N. 1994. Cognition and communication in the Levantine Lower Palaeolithic. *World Archaeology* 26, 144–57.
Belitzky, S., Goren-Inbar, N. & Werker, E. 1991. A Middle Pleistocene wooden plank with man-made polish. *Journal of Human Evolution* 20, 349–53.
Bergman, C.A. 1993. The development of the bow in western Europe: a technological and functional perspective. In *Hunting and Animal Exploitation in the Later Palaeolithic and Mesolithic of Eurasia*, eds., G.L. Peterkin, H.M. Bricker & P. Mellars, pp. 95–105. Archaeological Papers of the American Anthropological Association, No. 4.
Bergman, C.A. & Roberts, M.B. 1988. Flaking technology at the Acheulian site of Boxgrove, West Sussex (England). *Revue Archéologique de Picardie* 1–2, 105–13.
Berlin, B. 1992. *Ethnobiological Classification: Principles of Categorization of Plants and Animals in Traditional Societies.* Princeton: Princeton University Press.
Berlin, B., Breedlove, D. & Raven, P. 1973. General principles of classification and nomenclature in folk biology. *American Anthropologist* 87, 298–315.
Béyries, S. 1988. Functional variability of lithic

sets in the Middle Paleolithic. In *Upper Pleistocene Prehistory of Western Eurasia*, eds., H.L. Dibble & A. Montet-White, pp. 213–23. Philadelphia: The University Museum, University of Pennsylvania.

Binford, L.R. 1973. Interassemblage variability – the Mousterian and the functional argument. In *The Explanation of Culture Change*, ed., C. Renfrew, pp. 227–54. London: Duckworth.

Binford, L.R. 1978. *Nunamiut Ethnoarchaeology*. New York: Academic Press.

Binford, L.R. 1981. *Bones: Ancient Men and Modern Myths*. New York: Academic Press.

Binford, L.R. 1984a. *Faunal Remains from Klasies River Mouth*. Orlando: Academic Press.

Binford, L.R. 1984b. Butchering, sharing and the archaeological record. *Journal of Anthropological Archaeology* 3, 235–57.

Binford, L.R. 1985. Human ancestors: changing views of their behavior. *Journal of Anthropological Archaeology* 4, 292–327.

Binford, L.R. 1986. Comment on 'Systematic butchery by Plio/Pleistocene hominids at Olduvai Gorge' by H.T. Bunn & E.M. Kroll. *Current Anthropology* 27, 444–46.

Binford, L.R. 1987a. Searching for camps and missing the evidence? Another look at the Lower Palaeolithic. In *The Pleistocene Old World: Regional Perspectives*, ed., O. Soffer, pp. 17–31. New York: Plenum Press.

Binford, L.R. 1987b. Were there elephant hunters at Torralba? In *The Evolution of Human Hunting*, eds., M.H. Nitecki & D.V. Nitecki, pp. 47–105. New York: Plenum Press.

Binford, L.R. 1988. Fact and fiction about the Zinjanthropus floor: data, arguments and interpretations. *Current Anthropology* 29, 123–35.

Binford, L.R. 1989. Isolating the transition to cultural adaptations: an organizational approach. In *The Emergence of Modern Humans: Biocultural Adaptations in the Later Pleistocene*, ed., E. Trinkaus, pp. 18–41. Cambridge: Cambridge University Press.

Binford, L.R. & Binford S.R. 1969. Stone tools and human behavior. *Scientific American* 220, 70–84.

Binford, L.R. & Chuan Kun Ho 1985. Taphonomy at a distance: Zhoukoudian, 'the cave home of Beijing Man'. *Current Anthropology* 26, 413–42.

Binford, L.R. & Stone, N.M. 1986. Zhoukoudian: a closer look. *Current Anthropology* 27, 453–75.

Binford, L.R., Mills, M.G.L. & Stone, N.M. 1988. Hyena scavenging behavior and its implications for the interpretation of faunal assemblages from FLK 22 (the Zinj floor) at Olduvai Gorge. *Journal of Anthropological Archaeology* 7, 99–135.

Binford, L.R. & Todd, L. 1982. On arguments for the 'butchering' of giant geladas. *Current Anthropology* 23, 108–10.

Birket-Smith, K. 1936. *The Eskimos*. London: Methuen.

Bird-David, N. 1990. The 'giving environment': another perspective on the economic system of gatherer-hunters. *Current Anthropology* 31, 189–96.

Bischoff, J.L., Soler, N., Maroto, J. & Julia, R. 1989. Abrupt Mousterian/Aurignacian boundary at *c.* 40 ka bp: accelerator 14C dates from L'Arbreda cave. *Journal of Archaeological Science* 16, 563–76.

Bisson, M.S. & Bolduc. P. 1994. Previously undescribed figurines from the Grimaldi Caves. *Current Anthropology* 35, 458–68.

Bleed, P. 1986. The optimal design of hunting weapons. *American Antiquity* 51, 737–47.

Block, N. 1995. On a confusion about the function of consciousness. *Behavioral and Brain Sciences* 18, 227–87.

Blurton-Jones, H. & Konner, M.J. 1976. !Kung knowledge of animal behavior. In *Kalahari Hunter-Gatherers*, eds., R. Lee & I. DeVore. Cambridge MA: Harvard University Press.

Blumenschine, R.J. 1986. *Early Hominid Scavenging Opportunities*. Oxford: British Archaeological Reports, International Series 283.

Blumenschine, R.J. 1987. Characteristics of an early hominid scavenging niche. *Current Anthropology* 28, 383–407.

Blumenschine, R.J., Cavallo, J.A. & Capaldo, S.D. 1994. Competition for carcasses and early hominid behavioural ecology: a case study and conceptual framework. *Journal of Human Evolution* 27, 17–213.

Boden, M. 1990. *The Creative Mind: Myths and Mechanisms*. London: Weidenfeld and Nicolson.

Boden, M. 1994. Précis of 'The Creative Mind: Myths and Mechanisms'. *Behavioral and Brain Sciences* 17, 519–70.

Boëda, E. 1988. Le concept laminaire: rupture et filiation avec le concept Levallois. In *L'Homme Neanderthal, Vol. 8, La Mutation*, ed., J. Kozlowski, pp. 41–60. Liège, Belgium: ERAUL.

Boëda, E. 1990. De la surface au volume, analyse des conceptions des débitages Levallois et laminaires. *Mémoires du Musée de Préhistoire*. 3, 63–8.

Boesch, C. 1991. Teaching among wild chimpanzees. *Animal Behavior* 41, 530–32.

Boesch, C. 1993. Aspects of transmission of tool-use in wild chimpanzees. In *Tools, Language and Cognition in Human Evolution*, eds., K.G. Gibson & T. Ingold, pp. 171–83. Cambridge: Cambridge University Press.

Boesch, C. & Boesch, H. 1983. Optimization of nut-cracking with natural hammers by wild chimpanzees. *Behaviour* 83, 265–86.

Boesch, C. & Boesch, H. 1984a. Mental maps in wild chimpanzees: an analysis of hammer transports for nut cracking. *Primates* 25, 160–70.

Boesch, C. & Boesch, H. 1984b. Possible causes of sex differences in the use of natural hammers by wild chimpanzees. *Journal of Human Evolution* 13, 415–40.

Boesch, C. & Boesch, H. 1989. Hunting behavior of wild chimpanzees in the Taï National Park.

American Journal of Physical Anthropology 78, 547–73.

Boesch, C. & Boesch, H. 1990. Tool-use and tool-making in wild chimpanzees. *Folia Primatologica* 54, 86–99.

Boesch, C. & Boesch, H. 1993. Diversity of tool-use and tool-making in wild chimpanzees. In *The Use of Tools by Human and Non-human Primates*, eds., A. Berthelet & J. Chavaillon, pp. 158–74. Oxford: Clarendon Press.

Bokelmann, K. 1992. Some new thoughts on old data on humans and reindeer in the Arhensburgian tunnel valley in Schleswig-Holstein, Germany. In *The Late Glacial in North-West Europe: Human Adaptation and Environmental Change at the End of the Pleistocene*, eds., N. Barton, A.J. Roberts & D.A. Roe, pp. 72–81. London: Council for British Archaeology Research Report No. 17.

Bonifay, E. & Vandermeersch, B. (eds.) 1991. *Les Premiers Européens*. Paris: Editions du C.T.H.S.

Bordes, F. 1961a. *Typologie du Paléolithique Ancien et Moyen*. Publications de l'Institut de Préhistoire de l'Université de Bordeaux, Memoiré No 1, 2 Vols.

Bordes, F. 1961b. Mousterian cultures in France. *Science* 134, 803–10.

Bordes, F. 1968. *Tools of the Old Stone Age*. London: Weidenfeld & Nicolson.

Bordes, F. 1972. *A Tale of Two Caves*. New York: Harper and Row.

Bowdler, S. 1992. *Homo sapiens* in Southeast Asia and the Antipodes: archaeological versus biological interpretations. In *The Evolution and Dispersal of Modern Humans in Asia*, eds., T. Akazawa, K. Aoki & T. Kimura, pp. 559–89. Tokyo: Hokusen-Sha.

Bowen, D.Q. & Sykes, G.A. 1994. How old is Boxgrove Man? *Nature* 371, 751.

Boyer, P. 1990. *Tradition as Truth and Communication*. New York: Cambridge University Press.

Boyer, P. 1994a. *The Naturalness of Religious Ideas. A Cognitive Theory of Religion*. Berkeley: University of California Press.

Boyer, P. 1994b. Cognitive constraints on cultural representations: natural ontologies and religious ideas. In *Mapping the Mind: Domain Specificity in Cognition and Culture*, eds. L.A. Hirschfeld & S.A. Gelman, pp. 391–411. Cambridge: Cambridge University Press.

Brain, C.K. 1981. *The Hunters or the Hunted?* Chicago: University of Chicago Press.

Bräuer, G. & Smith, F.H. (eds.) 1992. *Continuity or Replacement? Controversies in Homo sapiens Evolution*. Rotterdam: Balkema.

Bratlund, B. 1992. A study of hunting lesions containing flint fragments on reindeer bones at Stellmoor, Schleswig-Holstein, Germany. In *The Late Glacial in North-West Europe: Human Adaptation and Environmental Change at the End of the Pleistocene*, eds., N. Barton, A.J. Roberts & D.A. Roe, pp. 193–207. London: Council for British Archaeology Research Report No. 17.

Breuil, H. 1952. *Four Hundred Centuries of Cave Art*. Montignac: Centre d'Etudes et de Documentation Préhistoriques.

Brewer, S.M. & McGrew, W.C. 1990. Chimpanzee use of a tool-set to get honey. *Folia Primatologica* 54, 100–04.

Brothwell, D. 1986. *The Bogman and the Archaeology of People*. London: British Museum Press.

Brown, P. 1981. Artificial cranial deformations as a component in the variation in Pleistocene Australian crania. *Archaeology in Oceania* 16, 156–67.

Brunet, M., Beauvilain, A., Coppens, Y., Heintz, E., Moutaye, A.H.E. & Pilbeam, D. 1995. The first australopithecine 2,500 kilometres west of the Rift Valley (Chad). *Nature* 378, 273–74.

Bunn, H.T. 1981. Archaeological evidence for meat eating by Plio-Pleistocene hominids from Koobi Fora and Olduvai Gorge. *Nature* 291, 574–77.

Bunn, H.T. 1983a. Evidence on the diet and subsistence patterns of Plio-Pleistocene hominids at Koobi Fora, Kenya and Olduvai Gorge, Tanzania. In *Animals and Archaeology: 1. Hunters and their Prey*, eds., J. Clutton-Brock and C. Grigson, pp. 21–30. Oxford: British Archaeological Reports, International Series 163.

Bunn, H.T. 1983b. Comparative analysis of modern bone assemblages from a San hunter-gatherer camp in the Kalahari Desert, Botswana, and from a spotted hyena den near Nairobi, Kenya. In *Animals and Archaeology: 1. Hunters and their Prey*, eds., J. Clutton-Brock and C. Grigson, pp. 143–48. Oxford: British Archaeological Reports, International Series 163.

Bunn, H.T. 1994. Early Pleistocene hominid foraging strategies along the ancestral Omo River at Koobi Fora, Kenya. *Journal of Human Evolution* 27, 247–66.

Bunn, H.T. & Kroll, E.M. 1986. Systematic butchery by Plio-Pleistocene hominids at Olduvai Gorge, Tanzania. *Current Anthropology* 27, 431–52.

Buss, D. 1994. *The Evolution of Desire: Strategies of Human Mating*. New York: Basic Books.

Byrd, B.F. 1989. The Natufian: settlement, variability and economic adaptations in the Levant at the end of the Pleistocene. *Journal of World Prehistory* 3, 159–97.

Byrne, R.W. 1995. *The Thinking Ape: Evolutionary Origins of Intelligence*. Oxford: Oxford University Press.

Byrne, R.W. & Whiten, A. 1985. Tactical deception of familiar individuals in baboons (*Papio ursinus*). *Animal Behavior* 33, 669–73.

Byrne R.W. & Whiten, A. (eds.) 1988. *Machiavellian Intelligence: Social Expertise and the Evolution of Intellect in Monkeys, Apes and Humans*. Oxford: Clarendon Press.

Byrne, R.W. & Whiten, A. 1991. Computation and mindreading in primate tactical deception. In *Natural Theories of Mind*, ed., A. Whiten, pp. 127–41. Oxford: Blackwell.

Byrne, R.W. & Whiten, A. 1992. Cognitive evolution in primates: evidence from tactical deception. *Man (N.S.)* 27, 609–27.

Cabrera, V. & Bischoff, J. 1989. Accelerator 14C dates for Early Upper Palaeolithic at El Castillo Cave. *Journal of Archaeological Science* 16, 577–84.

Callow, P. & Cornford, J.M. (eds.) 1986. *La Cotte de St Brelade 1961–1978: Excavations by C.B.M. McBurney*. Norwich: GeoBooks.

Calvin, W.H. 1983. A stone's throw and its launch window: timing, precision and its implications for language and hominid brains. *Journal of Theoretical Biology* 104, 121–35.

Calvin, W.H. 1993. The unitary hypothesis: a common neural circuitry for novel manipulations, language, plan-ahead and throwing. In *Tools, Language and Cognition in Human Evolution*, eds., K.R. Gibson & T. Ingold, pp. 230–250. Cambridge: Cambridge University Press.

Cann, R.L., Stoneking, M. & Wilson, A. 1987. Mitochondrial DNA and human evolution. *Nature* 325, 32–6.

Carbonell, E., Bermúdez de Castro, J.M., Arsuaga, J.C., Diez, J.C., Rosas, A., Cuenca-Bercós, G., Sala, R., Mosquera, M. & Rodriguez, X.P. 1995. Lower Pleistocene hominids and artifacts from Atapuerca-TD6 (Spain). *Science* 269, 826–30.

Carey, S. & Spelke, E. 1994. Domain-specific knowledge and conceptual change. In *Mapping the Mind: Domain Specificity in Cognition and Culture*, eds., L.A. Hirschfeld and S.A. Gelman pp. 169–200. Cambridge: Cambridge University Press.

Carmichael, D.L., Hubert, J., Reeves, B. & Schanche, A. 1994. *Sacred Sites, Sacred Places.* London: Routledge.

Cerling, T.E. 1992. The development of grasslands and savanna in East Africa during the Neogene. *Palaeogeography, Palaeoclimateology and Palaeoecology* 97, 241–47.

Chapman, C. 1990. Ecological constraints on group size in three species of neotropical primates. *Folia Primatologica* 55, 1–9.

Chase, A.K. 1989. Domestication and domiculture in northern Australia: a social perspective. In *Foraging and Farming: The Evolution of Plant Exploitation*, eds., D.R. Harris & G.C. Hillman, pp. 42–78. London: Unwin Hyman.

Chase, P. 1986. *The Hunters of Combe Grenal: Approaches to Middle Palaeolithic Subsistence in Europe*. Oxford: British Archaeological Reports, International Series, S286.

Chase, P. 1989. How different was Middle Palaeolithic subsistence? A zooarchaeological perspective on the Middle to Upper Palaeolithic transition. In *The Human Revolution*, eds., P. Mellars & C. Stringer, pp. 321–37. Edinburgh: Edinburgh University Press.

Chase, P. 1991. Symbols and palaeolithic artifacts: style, standardization and the imposition of arbitrary form. *Journal of Anthropological Archaeology* 10, 193–214.

Chase, P. & Dibble, H. 1987. Middle Palaeolithic symbolism: a review of current evidence and interpretations. *Journal of Anthropological Archaeology*, 6, 263–93.

Chase, P. & Dibble, H. 1992. Scientific archaeology and the origins of symbolism: a reply to Bednarik. *Cambridge Archaeological Journal* 2, 43–51.

Chauvet, J-M., Deschamps, E.B. & Hillaire, C. 1996. *Chauvet Cave: The Discovery of the World's Oldest Paintings.* London: Thames and Hudson; New York: Abrams.

Chavaillon, J. 1976. Evidence for the technical practices of early Pleistocene hominids. In *Earliest Man and Environments in the Lake Rudolf Basin: Stratigraphy, Paleoecology and Evolution*, eds., Y. Coppens, F.C. Howell, G. Isaac & R.E.F. Leakey, pp. 565–73. Chicago: Chicago University Press.

Cheney, D.L. & Seyfarth, R.S. 1988. Social and non-social knowledge in vervet monkeys. In *Machiavellian Intelligence: Social Expertise and the Evolution of Intellect in Monkeys, Apes and Humans*, eds., R.W. Byrne & A. Whiten, pp. 255–70. Oxford: Clarendon Press.

Cheney, D.L. & Seyfarth, R.S. 1990. *How Monkeys See the World.* Chicago: Chicago University Press.

Cheney, D.L., Seyfarth, R.S., Smuts, B.B. & Wrangham, R.W. 1987. The future of primate research. In *Primate Societies*, eds., B.B. Smuts, D.L. Cheney, R.M. Seyfarth, R.W. Wrangham & T.T. Struhsaker, pp. 491–96. Chicago: Chicago University Press.

Churchill, S. 1993. Weapon technology, prey size selection and hunting methods in modern hunter-gatherers: implications for hunting in the Palaeolithic and Mesolithic. In *Hunting and Animal Exploitation in the Later Palaeolithic and Mesolithic of Eurasia*, eds., G.L. Peterkin, H.M. Bricker & P. Mellars, pp. 11–24. Archaeological Papers of the American Anthropological Association, No. 4.

Clark, G.A. 1992. A comment on Mithen's ecological interpretation of Palaeolithic art. *Proceedings of the Prehistoric Society* 58, 107–09.

Clark, G.A. & Neeley, M. 1987. Social differentiation in European Mesolithic burial data. In *Mesolithic Northwest Europe: Recent Trends*, eds., P.A. Rowley-Conwy, M. Zvelebil & H.P. Blankholm, pp. 121–27. Sheffield: Department of Archaeology and Prehistory.

Clark, G.A., Young, D., Straus, L.G. & Jewett, R. 1986. Multivariate analysis of La Riera industries and fauna. In *La Riera Cave*, eds., L.G. Straus & G.A. Clark, pp. 325–50. Anthropological Research Papers 36, Tempe: Arizona State University.

Clark, J.D. 1969. *The Kalambo Falls Prehistoric Site, Vol I.* Cambridge: Cambridge University Press.

Clark, J.D. 1974. *The Kalambo Falls Prehistoric*

Site, Vol II. Cambridge: Cambridge University Press.
Clark, J.D. 1982. The cultures of the Middle Palaeolithic/Middle Stone Age. In *The Cambridge History of Africa, Volume 1, From the Earliest Times to c. 500 BC*, ed., J.D. Clark, pp. 248–341. Cambridge: Cambridge University Press.
Clark, J.D. & Haynes, C.V. 1970. An elephant butchery site at Mwanganda's Village, Karonga, Malawi. *World Archaeology* 1, 390–411.
Clark, J.D. & Kurashina, H. 1979a. An analysis of earlier stone age bifaces from Gadeb (Locality 8E), Northern Bale Highlands, Ethiopia. *South African Archaeological Bulletin* 34, 93–109.
Clark, J.D. & Kurashina, H. 1979b. Hominid occupation of the east-central highlands of Ethiopia in the Plio-Pleistocene. *Nature* 282, 33–9.
Clarke, R.J. 1988. Habiline handaxes and Paranthropine pedigree at Sterkfontein. *World Archaeology* 20, 1–12.
Clayton, D. 1978. Socially facilitated behaviour. *Quarterly Review of Biology* 53, 373–91.
Close, A. 1986. The place of the Haua Fteah in the late Palaeolithic of North Africa. In *Stone Age Prehistory*, eds., G.N. Bailey & P. Callow, pp. 169–80. Cambridge: Cambridge University Press.
Clottes, J. 1990. The parietal art of the Late Magdalenian. *Antiquity* 64, 527–48.
Clutton-Brock, T.H. & Harvey, P. 1977. Primate ecology and social organisation. *Journal of the Zoological Society of London* 183, 1–39.
Clutton-Brock, T.H. & Harvey, P. 1980. Primates, brains and ecology. *Journal of the Zoological Society of London* 190, 309–23.
Cohen, M.N. 1977. *The Food Crisis in Prehistory*. New Haven CT: Yale University Press.
Cohen, M.N. & Armelagos, G.J. 1984. *Paleopathology at the Origins of Agriculture*. New York: Academic Press.
Conkey, M. 1980. The identification of prehistoric hunter-gatherer aggregation: the case of Altamira. *Current Anthropology* 21, 609–30.
Conkey, M. 1983. On the origins of Palaeolithic art: a review and some critical thoughts. In *The Mousterian Legacy: Human Biocultural Change in the Upper Pleistocene*, ed., E. Trinkaus, pp. 201–27. Oxford: British Archaeological Reports 164.
Conkey, M. 1987. New approaches in the search for meaning? A review of research in 'Palaeolithic art'. *Journal of Field Archaeology* 14, 413–30.
Conrad, N. 1990. Laminar lithic assemblages from the last interglacial complex in Northwest Europe. *Journal of Anthropological Research* 46, 243–62.
Cook, J. 1992. Preliminary report on marked human bones from the 1986–1987 excavations at Gough's Cave, Somerset, England. In *The Late Glacial in North-West Europe: Human Adaptation and Environmental Change at the End of the Pleistocene*, eds., N. Barton, A.J. Roberts & D.A. Roe, pp. 160–78. London: Council for British Archaeology Research Report No. 17.
Cook, J. & Welté, A.C. 1992. A newly discovered female engraving from Courbet (Penne-Tarn), France. *Proceedings of the Prehistoric Society* 58, 29–35.
Corballis, M.C. 1991. *The Lopsided Ape*. Oxford: Oxford University Press.
Corballis, M.C. 1992. On the evolution of language and generativity. *Cognition* 44, 197–226.
Cosmides, L. 1989. The logic of social exchange: has natural selection shaped how humans reason? Studies with the Wason selection task. *Cognition* 31, 187–276.
Cosmides, L. & Tooby, J. 1987. From evolution to behaviour: evolutionary psychology as the missing link. In *The Latest on the Best: Essays on Evolution and Optimality*, ed., J. Dupré, pp. 277–306. Cambridge: Cambridge University Press.
Cosmides, L. & Tooby, J. 1992. Cognitive adaptations for social exchange. In *The Adapted Mind*, eds., J.H. Barkow, L. Cosmides & J. Tooby, pp. 163–228. New York: Oxford University Press.
Cosmides, L. & Tooby, J. 1994. Origins of domain specificity: the evolution of functional organization, In *Mapping the Mind: Domain Specificity in Cognition and Culture*, eds., L.A. Hirschfeld & S.A. Gelman, pp. 85–116. Cambridge: Cambridge University Press.
Culotta, E. 1995. Asian hominids grow older. *Science* 270, 1116–17.
Cunliffe, B. (ed.) 1994. *The Oxford Illustrated Prehistory of Europe*. Oxford: Oxford University Press.
Cunningham, A. & Williams, P. 1993. De-centering the 'big' picture: the origins of modern science and the modern origins of science. *British Journal of the History of Science* 26, 407–32.
Currant, A.P., Jacobi, R.M. & Stringer, C.B. 1989. Excavations at Gough's Cave, Somerset 1986–7. *Antiquity* 63, 131–36.
Dansgaard, W., White, J.W.C. & Johnsen, S.J. 1989. The abrupt termination of the Younger Dryas climate event. *Nature* 339, 532–34.
Darwin, C. 1859. *The Origin of Species*. London: John Murray.
Darwin, C. 1913 [1871]. *The Descent of Man*. London: John Murray.
Davidson, I. 1990. Bilzingsleben and early marking. *Rock Art Research* 7, 52–6.
Davidson, I. 1991. The archaeology of language origins: a review. *Antiquity* 65, 39–48.
Davidson, I. 1992. There's no art – To find the mind's construction – In offence (reply to R. Bednarik). *Cambridge Archaeological Journal* 2, 52–7.
Davidson, I. & Noble, W. 1989. The archaeology of perception: traces of depiction and language. *Current Anthropology* 30, 125–55.
Davidson, I. & Noble, W. 1992. Why the first

colonisation of the Australian region is the earliest evidence of modern human behaviour. *Archaeology in Oceania* 27, 113–19.

Dawkins, R. 1976. *The Selfish Gene*. Oxford: Oxford University Press.

Dawkins, R. 1986. *The Blind Watchmaker.* Harmondsworth: Penguin Books.

Dawkins, R. 1995. *River Out of Eden*. London & New York: Weidenfeld & Nicolson.

Dawson, A.G. 1992. *Ice Age Earth: Late Quaternary Geology and Climate*. London: Routledge.

Deacon, T.W. 1990. Fallacies of progression in theories of brain-size evolution. *International Journal of Primatology* 11, 193–236.

Deacon, T.W. 1992. The neural circuitry underlying primate calls and human language. In *Language Origin: A Multidisciplinary Approach*, eds., J. Wind, B. Chiarelli, B. Bichakhian & A. Nocentini, pp. 121–62. Dordrecht: Kluwer Academic Publishing.

Dean, M.C., Stringer, C.B. & Bromgate, T.G. 1986. Age at death of the Neanderthal child from Devil's Tower Gibraltar and the implications for studies of general growth and development in Neanderthals. *American Journal of Physical Anthropology* 70, 301–09.

Delluc, B. & Delluc, G. 1978. Les manifestations graphiques aurignaciennes sur support rocheux des environs des Eyzies (Dordogne). *Gallia Préhistoire* 21, 213–438.

Delporte, H. 1979. *L'Image de la Femme dans l'Art Prehistorique*. Paris: Picard.

Delporte, H. 1993. Gravettian female figurines: a regional survey. In *Before Lascaux: The Complex Record of the Early Upper Palaeolithic*, eds., H. Knecht, A. Pike-Tay & R. White, pp. 243–57. Boca Raton: CRC Press.

deMenocal, P.B. 1995. Plio-Pleistocene African Climate. *Science* 270, 53–9.

Dennell, R. W. 1983. *European Economic Prehistory*. London: Academic Press.

Dennell, R.W. & Rendell, H. 1991. De Terra and Paterson and the Soan flake industry: a new perspective from the Soan valley, North Pakistan. *Man and Environment* XV 1, 91–9.

Dennell, R.W., Rendell, H. & Hailwood, E. 1988a. Early tool making in Asia: two million year old artifacts in Pakistan. *Antiquity* 62, 98–106.

Dennell, R.W., Rendell, H. & Hailwood, E. 1988b. Late Pliocene artifacts from North Pakistan. *Current Anthropology*, 29, 495–98.

Dennett, D. 1988 The intentional stance in theory and practice. In *Machiavellian Intelligence: Social Expertise and the Evolution of Intellect in Monkeys, Apes and Humans*, eds., R.W. Byrne & A. Whiten, pp. 180–202. Oxford: Clarendon Press.

Dennett, D. 1991. *Consciousness Explained*. New York: Little, Brown & Company.

Dibble, H.L. 1987. The interpretation of Middle Palaeolithic scraper morphology. *American Antiquity* 52, 109–17.

Dibble, H.L. 1989. The implications of stone tool types for the presence of language during the Lower and Middle Palaeolithic. In *The Human Revolution*, eds., P. Mellars & C. Stringer, pp. 415–32 Edinburgh: Edinburgh University Press.

Dibble, H.L. & Rolland, N. 1992. On assemblage variability in the Middle Palaeolithic of western Europe: history, perspectives and a new interpretation. In *The Middle Palaeolithic: Adaptation, Behaviour and Variability*, eds., H.L. Dibble & P. Mellars, pp. 1–28. Philadelphia: The University Museum, University of Pennsylvania.

Dillehay, T.D. 1989. *Monte Verde: A Late Pleistocene Settlement in Chile*. Washington DC: Smithsonian Institute.

Dillehay, T.D. & Collins, M.B. 1988. Early cultural evidence from Monte Verde in Chile. *Nature* 332, 150–52.

Dillehay, T.D., Calderón, C.A., Politis, G. & Beltrao, M.C.M.C. 1992. The earliest hunter-gatherers of South America. *Journal of World Prehistory* 6, 145–203.

Donald, M. 1991. *Origins of the Modern Mind*. Cambridge MA: Harvard University Press.

Donald, M. 1994. Précis of 'Origins of the Modern Mind'. *Behavioral and Brain Sciences* 16, 737–91.

Douglas, M. 1990. The pangolin revisited: a new approach to animal symbolism. In *Signifying Animals: Human Meaning in the Natural World*, ed., R.G. Willis, pp. 25–42. London: Unwin Hyman.

Duhard, J-P. 1993. Upper Palaeolithic figures as a reflection of human morphology and social organization. *Antiquity* 67, 83–91.

Dunbar, R.I.M. 1988. *Primate Societies*. London: Chapman & Hall.

Dunbar, R.I.M. 1991. Functional significance of social grooming in primates. *Folia Primatologica* 57, 121–31.

Dunbar, R.I.M. 1992. Neocortex size as a constraint on group size in primates. *Journal of Human Evolution* 20, 469–93.

Dunbar, R.I.M. 1993. Coevolution of neocortical size, group size and language in humans. *Behavioral and Brain Sciences* 16, 681–735.

Dunbar, R.I.M. 1995. *The Trouble with Science*. London: Faber & Faber.

Eastham, M. & Eastham, A. 1991. Palaeolithic parietal art and its topographic context. *Proceedings of the Prehistoric Society* 51 (i), 115–28.

Eccles, J. 1989. *Evolution of the Brain: Creation of the Self.* London: Routledge.

Eisenberg, J. 1981. *The Mammalian Radiations: An Analysis of Trends in Evolution, Adaptation and Behaviour*. London: Athlone Press.

Enloe, J.G. 1993. Subsistence organization in the Early Upper Palaeolithic: reindeer hunters of the Abri du Flageolet, Couche V. In *Before Lascaux: The Complex Record of the Early Upper Palaeolithic*, eds., H. Knecht, A. Pike-Tay & R. White, pp. 101–15. Boca Raton: CRC Press.

D'Errico, F. 1989a. Palaeolithic lunar calendars: a case of wishful thinking. *Current Anthropology* 30, 117–18.
D'Errico, F. 1989b. A reply to Alexander Marshack. *Current Anthropology* 30, 495–500.
D'Errico, F. 1991. Microscopic and statistical criteria for the identification of prehistoric systems of notation. *Rock Art Research* 8, 83–93.
D'Errico, F. 1992. A reply to Alexander Marshack. *Rock Art Research* 9, 59–64.
D'Errico, F. 1995. A new model and its implications for the origin of writing: the La Marche antler revisited. *Cambridge Archaeological Journal* 5, 163–206.
D'Errico, F. & Cacho, C. 1994. Notation versus decoration in the Upper Palaeolithic: a case study from Tossal de la Roca, Alicante, Spain. *Journal of Archaeological Science* 21, 185–200.
Falk, D. 1983. Cerebral cortices of East African early hominids. *Science* 221, 1072–74.
Falk, D. 1990. Brain evolution in *Homo*. The 'radiator theory'. *Behavioral and Brain Sciences* 13, 333–81.
Falk, D. 1992. *Braindance: New Discoveries about Human Brain Evolution*. New York: Henry Holt.
Farizy, C. 1990. The transition from the Middle to Upper Palaeolithic at Arcy-sur-Cure (Yonne, France): technological, economic and social aspects. In *The Emergence of Modern Humans*, ed., P. Mellars, pp. 303–26. Edinburgh: Edinburgh University Press.
Farizy, C. & David, F. 1992. Subsistence and behavioral patterns of some Middle Palaeolithic local groups. In *The Middle Palaeolithic, Adaptation, Behaviour and Variability*, eds., H.L. Dibble & P. Mellars, pp. 87–96. Philadelphia: The University Museum, University of Pennsylvania.
Faulstich, P. 1992. Of earth and dreaming: abstraction and naturalism in Walpiri art. In *Rock Art and Ethnography*, eds., M.J. Morwood & D.R. Hobbs, pp. 19–23. Melbourne: Occasional AURA Publication No. 5.
Féblot-Augustins, J. 1993. Mobility strategies in the late Middle Palaeolithic of Central Europe and Western Europe: elements of stability and variability. *Journal of Anthropological Archaeology* 12, 211–65.
Fischer, A. 1990. On being a pupil of a flintknapper of 11,000 years ago. A preliminary analysis of settlement organization and flint technology based on conjoined flint artifacts from the Trollesgave site. In *The Big Puzzle: International Symposium on Refitting Stone Artifacts*, eds., E. Cziesla, S. Eickhoff, N. Arts & D. Winter, pp. 447–64. Bonn: Holos.
Flood, J. 1983. *Archaeology of the Dreamtime*. London: Collins.
Fodor, J. 1983. *The Modularity of Mind*. Cambridge MA: MIT Press.
Fodor, J. 1985. Précis of 'The Modularity of Mind'. *The Behavioral and Brain Sciences* 8, 1–42.
Fodor, J. 1987. Modules, frames and fridgeons, sleeping dogs and the music of the spheres. In *Modularity in Knowledge Representation and Natural Language Understanding*, ed., J.L. Garfield, pp. 25–36. Cambridge MA: MIT Press.
Foley, R. 1987. *Another Unique Species*. Harlow: Longman.
Frayer, D.W. 1992. Cranial base flattening in Europe: Neanderthals and recent *Homo sapiens*. *American Journal of Physical Anthropology* (supplement) 14, 77.
Frayer, D.W., Wolpoff, M.H., Thorne, A.G., Smith, F.H. & Pope, G. 1993. Theories of modern human origins: the paleontological test. *American Anthropologist* 95, 14–50.
Frayer, D.W., Wolpoff, M.H., Thorne, A.G., Smith, F.H. & Pope, G. 1994. Getting it straight. *American Anthropologist* 96, 424–38.
Fremlen, J. 1975. Letter to the editor. *Science* 187, 600.
Frith, U. 1989. *Autism: Explaining the Enigma*. Oxford:Blackwell.
Gallistel, C.R. & Cheng, K. 1985. A modular sense of place? *The Behavioral and Brain Sciences* 8, 11–12.
Galef, B.G. 1988. Imitation in animals: history, definition and interpretation of data from the psychological laboratory. In *Social Learning: A Comparative Approach*, eds., T.R. Zentall & B.G. Galef pp. 3–28. Hillsdale NJ: Erlbaum.
Galef, B.G. 1990. Tradition in animals: field observations and laboratory analysis. In *Methods, Inferences, Interpretations and Explanations in the Study of Behavior*, eds., M. Bekoff & D. Jamieson pp. 74–95. Boulder: Westview Press.
Gamble, C. 1982. Interaction and alliance in Palaeolithic society. *Man* 17, 92–107.
Gamble, C. 1986. *The Palaeolithic Settlement of Europe*. Cambridge: Cambridge University Press.
Gamble, C. 1987. Man the shoveler: alternative models for Middle Pleistocene colonization and occupation in northern latitudes. In *The Pleistocene Old World*, ed., O. Soffer, pp. 81–98. New York: Plenum Press.
Gamble, C. 1989. Comment on 'Grave shortcomings: the evidence for Neanderthal burial by R. Gargett', *Current Anthropology* 30, 181–82.
Gamble, C. 1991. The social context for European Palaeolithic art. *Proceedings of the Prehistoric Society* 57 (i), 3–15.
Gamble, C. 1992. Comment on 'Dense forests, cold steppes, and the Palaeolithic settlement of Northern Europe' by W. Roebroeks, N.J. Conrad & T. van Kolfschoten. *Current Anthropology* 33, 569–72.
Gamble, C. 1993. *Timewalkers: The Prehistory of Global Colonization*. Stroud: Alan Sutton.
Gamble, C. 1994. The peopling of Europe, 700,000–40,000 years before the present. In *The Oxford Illustrated Prehistory of Europe*, ed., B. Cunliffe, pp. 5–41. Oxford: Oxford University Press.

Gamble, C. & Soffer, O. 1990. *The World at 18,000 B.P.* (2 vols). London: Unwin Hyman.

Gannon, P.J. & Laitman, J.T. 1993. Can we see language areas on hominid brain endocasts? *American Journal of Physical Anthropology* (supplement) 16, 91.

Gardner, R.A., Garner, B.T. & van Cantfort, T.E. 1989. *Teaching Sign Language to Chimpanzees.* New York: State University of New York Press.

Gardner, H. 1983. *Frames of Mind: The Theory of Multiple Intelligences.* New York: Basic Books.

Gardner, H. 1993. *Multiple Intelligences: The Theory in Practice.* New York: Basic Books.

Gargett, R. 1989. Grave shortcomings: the evidence for Neanderthal burial. *Current Anthropology* 30, 157–90.

Gazzaniga, M. 1985. *The Social Brain: Discovering the Networks of the Mind.* New York: Basic Books.

Gazzaniga, M. & Ledoux, J. 1978. *The Interpreted Mind.* New York: Plenum Press.

Geary, D.C. 1995. Reflections of evolution and culture in children's cognition: implications for mathematical development and instruction. *American Psychologist* 50, 24–37.

Geertz, C. 1973. *The Interpretation of Cultures.* New York: Basic Books.

Gellner, E. 1988. *Plough, Sword and Book: The Structure of Human History.* London: Collins Harvill.

Geneste, J-M. 1985. *Analyse lithique d'Industries Moustériennes du Perigord: une approche technologique du comportement des groupes humaines au Paléolithique moyen.* Thèse Univérsite Bordeaux I.

Geneste, J-M. & Plisson, H. 1993. Hunting technologies and human behavior: lithic analysis of Solutrean shouldered points. In *Before Lascaux: The Complex Record of the Early Upper Palaeolithic*, eds., H. Knecht, A. Pike-Tay & R. White, pp. 117–35. Boca Raton: CRC Press.

Gibson, K.R. 1986. Cognition, brain size and the extraction of embedded food resources. In *Primate Ontogeny, Cognition and Social Behaviour*, eds., J.G. Else & P.C. Lee, pp. 93–103. Cambridge: Cambridge University Press.

Gibson, K.R. 1990. New perspectives on instincts and intelligence: brain size and the emergence of hierarchical construction skills. In *'Language' and Intelligence in Monkeys and Apes: Comparative Developmental Perspectives*, eds., S.T. Parker & K.R. Gibson, pp. 97–128. Cambridge: Cambridge University Press.

Gibson, K.R. & Ingold, T. (eds.) 1993. *Tools, Language and Cognition in Human Evolution.* Cambridge: Cambridge University Press.

Gilead, I. 1991. The Upper Palaeolithic period in the Levant. *Journal of World Prehistory* 5, 105–54.

Gilead, I. & Bar-Yosef, O. 1993. Early Upper Palaeolithic sites on the Qadesh Barnea area, N.E. Sinai. *Journal of Field Archaeology* 20, 265–80.

Gillies, D. 1993. *Philosophy in the Twentieth Century: Four Central Themes.* Oxford: Blackwell.

Girard, C. & David, F. 1982. A propos de la chase spécialisée au Paléolithique moyen: l'exemple de Mauran (Haute-Garonne). *Bulletin de la Société Préhistorique Française* 79, 11–12.

Goodale, J.C. 1971. *Tiwi Wives: A Study of the Women of Melville Island, North Australia.* Seattle: University of Washington Press.

Goodall, J. 1986. *The Chimpanzees of Gombe.* Cambridge MA: Harvard University Press

Goodall, J. 1990. *Through a Window: Thirty Years with the Chimpanzees of Gombe.* London: Weidenfeld & Nicolson.

Gopnik, A. & Wellman, H.M. 1994. The theory theory. In *Mapping the Mind: Domain Specificity in Cognition and Culture*, eds., L.A. Hirschfeld & S.A. Gelman, pp. 257–93. Cambridge: Cambridge University Press.

Goren-Inbar, N. 1992. The Acheulian site of Gesher Benot Ya'aqov: an African or Asian entity. In *The Evolution and Dispersal of Modern Humans in Asia*, eds., T. Akazawa, K. Aoki & T. Kimura, pp. 67–82. Tokyo: Hokusen-Sha.

Gould, S. J. 1977. *Ontogeny and Phylogeny.* Cambridge MA: Harvard University Press.

Gould, S. J. 1981. *The Mismeasure of Man.* New York: W.W. Norton.

Gould, S. J. 1990. *Wonderful Life.* London: Hutchinson Radius.

Gould, S.J. & Lewontin, R.C. 1979. The spandrels of San Marco and the Panglossian paradigm: a critique of the adaptationist programme. *Proceedings of the Royal Society of London B* 205, 581–98.

Gowlett, J. 1984. Mental abilities of early man: a look at some hard evidence. In *Hominid Evolution and Community Ecology*, ed., R. Foley, pp. 167–92. London: Academic Press.

Green, H.S. (ed.) 1984. *Pontnewydd Cave: A Lower Palaeolithic Hominid Site in Wales. The First Report.* Cardiff: National Museum of Wales.

Greenberg, J.H., Turner, C.G. II. & Zegura, S.L. 1986. The settlement of the Americas: a comparative study of the linguistic, dental and genetic evidence. *Current Anthropology* 27, 477–97.

Greenfield, P.M. 1991. Language, tools and brain: the ontogeny and phylogeny of hierarchically organized sequential behavior. *Behavioral and Brain Sciences* 14, 531–95.

Greenfield, P.M. & Savage-Rumbaugh, E.S. 1990. Grammatical combination in *Pan paniscus*: processes of learning and invention in the evolution and development of language. In *'Language' and Intelligence in Monkeys and Apes: Comparative Developmental Perspectives*, eds., S.T. Parker & K.R. Gibson, pp. 540–74. Cambridge: Cambridge University Press.

Grønnow, R. 1987. Meiendorf and Stellmoor revisited: an analysis of Late Palaeolithic

reindeer exploitation. *Acta Archaeologica* 56, 131–66.
Groube, L., Chappell, J., Muke, J. & Price, D. 1986. A 40,000-year-old human occupation site at Huon Peninsula, Papua New Guinea. *Nature* 324, 453–55.
Grün, R., Beaumont, P. & Stringer, C. 1990. ESR dating evidence for early modern humans at Border Cave in South Africa. *Nature* 344, 537–39.
Grün, R. & Stringer, C. 1991. Electron spin resonance dating and the evolution of modern humans. *Archaeometry* 33, 153–99.
Gubser, N.J. 1965. *The Nunamiut Eskimos: Hunters of Caribou*. New Haven: Yale University Press.
Guidon, N., Parenti, F., Da Luz, M., Guérin, C. & Faure, M. 1994. Le plus ancien peuplement de l'Amérique: le Paléolithique du Nordeste Brésilien. *Bulletin de la Société Prehistorique Française* 91, 246–50.
Guthrie, D. 1984. Mosaics, allelochemicals and nutrients: an ecological theory of late Pleistocene extinctions. In *Quaternary Extinctions: A Prehistoric Revolution*, eds., P.S. Martin & R.G. Klein, pp. 259–98. Tucson: University of Arizona Press.
Guthrie, R.D. 1990. *Frozen Fauna of the Mammoth Steppe*. Chicago: Chicago University Press.
Gvozdover, M.D. 1989. The typology of female figurines of the Kostenki Palaeolithic culture. *Soviet Anthropology and Archaeology* 27, 32–94.
Hallam, S.J. 1989. Plant usage and management in Southwest Australian Aboriginal societies. In *Foraging and Farming: The Evolution of Plant Exploitation*, eds., D.R. Harris & G.C. Hillman, pp. 136–51. London: Unwin Hyman.
Halverson, J. 1987. Art for art's sake in the Palaeolithic. *Current Anthropology* 28, 65–89.
Hahn, J. 1972. Aurignacian signs, pendants, and art objects in Central and Eastern Europe. *World Archaeology* 3, 252–66.
Hahn, J. 1984. Recherches sur l'art Paléolithique depuis 1976. In *Aurignacian et Gravettien en Europe*, Vol. 1, eds., J.K. Kozlowski & B. Klima, pp. 157–71. Etudes et Recherches Archéologiques de l'Universite de Liège.
Hahn, J. 1993. Aurignacian art in Central Europe. In *Before Lascaux: The Complex Record of the Early Upper Palaeolithic*, eds., H. Knecht, A. Pike-Tay & R. White, pp. 229–41. Boca Raton: CRC Press.
Hankoff, L.D. 1980. Body-mind concepts in the Ancient Near East: a comparison of Egypt and Israel in the second millennium B.C. In *Body and Mind, Past, Present and Future*, ed., R.W. Rieber, pp. 3–31. New York: Academic Press.
Hatley, T. & Kappelman, J. 1980. Bears, pigs and Plio-Pleistocene hominids: a case for the exploitation of below-ground food resources. *Human Ecology* 8, 371–87.
Harris, J.W.K. & Capaldo, S.D. 1993. The earliest stone tools: their implications for an understanding of the activities and behaviour of late Pliocene hominids. In *The Use of Tools by Human and Non-human Primates*, eds., A. Berthelet & J. Chavaillon, pp. 196–220. Oxford: Clarendon Press.
Harrold, F. 1989. Mousterian, Chatelperronian and early Aurignacian in western Europe: continuity or discontinuity? In *The Human Revolution*, eds., P. Mellars & C. Stringer, pp. 677–713. Edinburgh: Edinburgh University Press.
Hay, R. 1976. *Geology of Olduvai Gorge*. Berkeley: University of California Press.
Hayden, B. 1990. Nimrods, piscators, pluckers and planters: the emergence of food production. *Journal of Anthropological Archaeology* 9, 31–69.
Hayden, B. 1993. The cultural capacities of Neanderthals: a review and re-evaluation. *Journal of Human Evolution* 24, 113–46.
Haynes, C.V. 1980. The Clovis culture. *Canadian Journal of Anthropology* 1, 115–21.
Haynes, G. 1991. *Mammoths, Mastodents and Elephants: Biology, Behaviour and the Fossil Record*. Cambridge: Cambridge University Press.
Hedges, R.E.M., Housley, R.A., Bronk Ramsey, C. & Van Klinken, G.J. 1994. Radiocarbon dates from the Oxford AMS system: archaeometry datelist 18. *Archaeometry* 36, 337–74.
Hewes, G. 1986. Comment on 'The origins of image making, by W. Davis'. *Current Anthropology* 27, 193–215.
Hewes, G. 1989. Comment on 'The archaeology of perception. Traces of depiction and language, by I. Davidson & W. Noble'. *Current Anthropology* 30, 145–46.
Heyes, C.M. 1993. Anecdotes, training and triangulating: do animals attribute mental states? *Animal Behavior* 46, 177–88.
Higgs, E. (ed.) 1972. *Papers in Economic Prehistory*. Cambridge: Cambridge University Press.
Higgs, E. & Jarman M.R. 1969. The origins of agriculture: a reconsideration. *Antiquity* 43, 31–41.
Hill, A. 1994. Early hominid behavioural ecology: a personal postscript. *Journal of Human Ecology* 27, 321–28.
Hill, K. & Hawkes, K. 1983. Neotropical hunting among the Ache of Eastern Paraguay. In *Adaptive Responses of Native American Indians*, eds., R. Hames & W. Vickers, pp. 139–88. New York: Academic Press.
Hillman, G.C. 1989. Late Palaeolithic plant foods from Wadi Kubbaniya in Upper Egypt: dietary diversity, infant weaning and seasonality in a riverine environment. In *Foraging and Farming: The Evolution of Plant Exploitation*, eds., D.R. Harris & G.C. Hillman, pp. 207–39. London: Unwin Hyman.
Hillman, G.C., Colledge, S.M. & Harris, D.R. 1989. Plant food economy during the Epipalaeolithic period at Tell Abu Hureya, Syria: dietary diversity, seasonality and modes of

exploitation. In *Foraging and Farming: The Evolution of Plant Exploitation*, eds., D.R. Harris & G.C. Hillman, pp. 240–68. London: Unwin Hyman.

Hirschfeld, L.A. 1995. Do children have a theory of race? *Cognition* 54, 209–52.

Hodder, I. 1985. *Symbols in Action*. Cambridge: Cambridge University Press.

Hodder, I. 1991. *Reading the Past* (2nd edition). Cambridge: Cambridge University Press.

Hodges, R. & Mithen, S. 1993. The 'South Church': a late Roman funerary church (San Vincenzo Minore) and hall for distinguished guests (with contributions by Shiela Gibson and John Mitchell). In *San Vincenzo al Volturno I*, ed., R. Hodges, pp. 123–90. London: British School at Rome.

Hoffecker, J.F., Powers, W.R. & Goebel, T. 1993. The colonization of Beringia and the peopling of the New World. *Science* 259, 46–53.

Hole, F. 1992. Origins of agriculture. In *The Cambridge Encyclopedia of Human Evolution*, eds., S, Jones, R. Martin & D. Pilbeam, pp. 373–79. Cambridge: Cambridge University Press.

Holloway, R.L. 1969. Culture, a human domain. *Current Anthropology* 20, 395–412.

Holloway, R.L. 1981a. Culture, symbols and human brain evolution. *Dialectical Anthropology* 5, 287–303.

Holloway, R.L. 1981b. Volumetric and asymmetry determinations on recent hominid endocasts: Spy I and II, Djebel Irhoud I, and Sale *Homo erectus* specimens, with some notes on Neanderthal brain size. *American Journal of Physical Anthropology* 55, 385–93.

Holloway, R.L. 1985. The poor brain of *Homo sapiens neanderthalensis*: see what you please. In *Ancestors: The Hard Evidence*, ed., E. Delson, pp. 319–24. New York: Alan R. Liss.

Holloway, R.L. & de La Coste-Lareymondie, M.C. 1982. Brain endocast assymetry in pongids and hominids: some preliminary findings on the paleontology of cerebral dominance. *American Journal of Physical Anthropology* 58, 101–10.

Houghton, P. 1993. Neanderthal supralaryngeal vocal tract. *American Journal of Physical Anthropology* 90, 139–46.

Howell, F.C. 1961. Isimila: a Palaeolithic site in Africa. *Scientific American* 205, 118–29.

Howell, F.C. 1965. *Early Man*. New York: Time-Life Books.

Hublin, J.J. 1992. Recent human evolution in northwestern Africa. *Philosophical Transactions of the Royal Society*, Series 13, 337, 185–91.

Humphrey, N. 1976. The social function of intellect. In *Growing Points in Ethology*, eds., P.P.G. Bateson & R.A. Hinde, pp. 303–17. Cambridge: Cambridge University Press.

Humphrey, N. 1984. *Consciousness Regained.* Oxford: Oxford University Press.

Humphrey, N. 1992. *A History of the Mind.* London: Chatto & Windus.

Humphrey, N. 1993. *The Inner Eye*. London: Vintage (first published by Faber & Faber in 1986).

Hyndman, D. 1990. Back to the future: trophy arrays as mental maps in the Wopkaimin's culture of place. In *Signifying Animals: Human Meaning in the Natural World*, ed., R.G. Willis, pp. 63–73. London: Unwin Hyman.

Ingold, T. 1992. Comment on 'Beyond the original affluent society' by N. Bird-David. *Current Anthropology* 33, 34–47.

Ingold, T. 1993. Tool-use, sociality and intelligence. In *Tools, Language and Cognition in Human Evolution*, eds., K.R. Gibson & T. Ingold, pp. 429–45. Cambridge: Cambridge University Press.

Inizan, M-L., Roche, H. & Tixier, J. 1992. *Technology of Knapped Stone*. Paris: Cercle de Recherches et d'Etudes Préhistorique, CNRS.

Isaac, B. 1989. *The Archaeology of Human Origins: Papers by Glynn Isaac*. Cambridge: Cambridge University Press.

Isaac, G. 1977. *Olorgesailie*. Chicago: University of Chicago Press.

Isaac, G. 1978. The food-sharing behaviour of proto-human hominids. *Scientific American* 238 (April), 90–108.

Isaac, G. 1981. Stone age visiting cards: approaches to the study of early land-use patterns. In *Pattern of the Past*, eds., I. Hodder, G. Isaac & N. Hammond, pp. 131–55. Cambridge: Cambridge University Press.

Isaac, G. 1982. The earliest archaeological traces. In *The Cambridge History of Africa, Volume 1, From the Earliest Times to c. 500 BC*, ed., J.D. Clark, pp. 157–247. Cambridge: Cambridge University Press.

Isaac, G. 1983a. Bones in contention: competing explanations for the juxtaposition of Early Pleistocene artifacts and faunal remains. In *Animals and Archaeology: Hunters and their Prey*, eds., J. Clutton-Brock & C. Grigson, pp. 3–19. Oxford: British Archaeological Reports, International Series 163.

Isaac, G. 1983b. Review of bones: ancient men and modern myths. *American Antiquity* 48, 416–19.

Isaac, G. 1984. The archaeology of human origins: studies of the Lower Pleistocene in East Africa 1971–1981. *Advances in World Archaeology* 3, 1–87.

Isaac, G. 1986. Foundation stones: early artifacts as indicators of activities and abilities. In *Stone Age Prehistory*, eds., G.N. Bailey & P. Callow, pp. 221–41. Cambridge: Cambridge University Press.

Isbell, L.A., Cheney, D.L. & Seyfarth, R.M. 1991 Group fusions and minimum group sizes in Vervet monkeys (*Cercopithecus aethiopus*). *American Journal of Primatology* 25, 57–65.

Jelenik, A. 1982. The Tabūn cave and Palaeolithic man in the Levant. *Science* 216, 1369–75.

Jennes, D. 1977. *The Indians of Canada* (7th edition). Ottawa: University of Toronto Press.

Jerison, H.J. 1973. *Evolution of Brain and*

Intelligence. New York: Academic Press.
Jochim, M. 1983. Palaeolithic cave art in ecological perspective. In *Hunter-Gatherer Economy in Prehistory*, ed., G.N. Bailey, pp. 212–19. Cambridge: Cambridge University Press.
Johanson, D.C. & Eddy, M.A. 1980. *Lucy: The Beginnings of Human Kind*. New York: Simon & Schuster.
Johnsen, S.J., Clausen, H.B., Dansgaard, W., Fuhrer, K., Gundestrup, N., Hammer, C.U., Iversen, P., Jouzel, J., Stauffer, B. & Steffensen, J.P. 1992. Irregular glacial interstadials recorded in a new Greenland ice core. *Nature* 359, 311–13.
Jones, J.S. 1993 *The Language of the Genes*. London: HarperCollins.
Jones, J.S., Martin, R. & Pilbeam, D. (eds.) 1992. *The Cambridge Encyclopedia of Human Evolution*. Cambridge: Cambridge University Press.
Jones, J.S. & Rouhani, S. 1986. How small was the bottleneck? *Nature* 319, 449–50.
Jones, P. 1980. Experimental butchery with modern stone tools and its relevance for Palaeolithic archaeology. *World Archaeology* 12, 153–65.
Jones, P. 1981. Experimental implement manufacture and use: a case study from Olduvai Gorge. *Philosophical Transactions of the Royal Society of London* B 292, 189–95.
Jones, R. & Meehan, B. 1989. Plant foods of the Gidjingali: ethnographic and archaeological perspectives from northern Australia on tuber and seed exploitation. In *Foraging and Farming: The Evolution of Plant Exploitation*, eds., D.R. Harris & G.C. Hillman, pp. 120–35. London: Unwin Hyman.
Kaplan, H. & Hill, K. 1985. Hunting ability and reproductive success among male Ache foragers: preliminary results. *Current Anthropology* 26, 131–33.
Karmiloff-Smith, A. 1992. *Beyond Modularity: A Developmental Perspective on Cognitive Science*. Cambridge MA: MIT Press.
Karmiloff-Smith, A. 1994. Précis of 'Beyond Modularity: A Developmental Perspective on Cognitive Science'. *Behavioral and Brain Sciences* 17, 693–745.
Keeley, L. 1980. *Experimental Determination of Stone Tool Uses: A Microwear Analysis*. Chicago: Chicago University Press.
Keeley, L. & Toth, N. 1981. Microwear polishes on early stone tools from Koobi Fora, Kenya. *Nature* 203, 464–65.
Keil, F.C. 1994. The birth and nurturance of concepts by domains: the origins of concepts of living things. In *Mapping the Mind: Domain Specificity in Cognition and Culture*, eds., L.A. Hirschfeld & S.A. Gelman, pp. 234–54. Cambridge: Cambridge University Press.
Kennedy, J.S. 1992. *The New Anthropomorphism*. Cambridge: Cambridge University Press.
Khalfa, J. (ed.) 1994. *What is Intelligence?* Cambridge: Cambridge University Press.
Kibunjia, M. 1994. Pliocene archaeological occurrences in the Lake Turkana basin. *Journal of Human Evolution* 27, 159–71.
Kibunjia, M., Roche, H., Bown, F.H. & Leakey, R.E. 1992. Pliocene and Pleistocene archaeological sites west of Lake Turkana, Kenya. *Journal of Human Evolution* 23, 431–38.
Kilma, B. 1988. A triple burial from the Upper Palaeolithic of Dolni Vestonice, Czechoslovakia. *Journal of Human Evolution* 16, 831–35.
Klein, R.G. 1989. Biological and behavioural perspectives on modern human origins in Southern Africa. In *The Human Revolution*, eds., P. Mellars & C. Stringer, pp. 530–46. Edinburgh: Edinburgh University Press.
Knecht, H. 1993a. Early Upper Paleolithic approaches to bone and antler projectile technology. In *Hunting and Animal Exploitation in the Later Palaeolithic and Mesolithic of Eurasia*, eds., G.L. Peterkin, H.M. Bricker & P. Mellars, pp. 33–47. Archaeological Papers of the American Anthropological Association, No. 4.
Knecht, H. 1993b. Splits and wedges: the techniques and technology of Early Aurignacian antler working. In *Before Lascaux: The Complex Record of the Early Upper Palaeolithic*, eds., H. Knecht, A. Pike-Tay & R. White, pp. 137–61. Boca Raton: CRC Press.
Knecht, H. 1994. Projectile points of bone, antler and stone: experimental explorations of manufacture and function. Paper presented at the 59th annual meeting of the Society for American Archaeology, Anaheim, California.
Knight, C. 1991. *Blood Relations: Menstruation and the Origins of Culture*. New Haven: Yale University Press.
Knight, C., Powers, C. & Watts, I. 1995. The human symbolic revolution: a Darwinian account. *Cambridge Archaeological Journal* 5, 75–114.
Koestler, A. 1975. *The Act of Creation*. London: Picador.
Kozlowski, J.K. (ed.) 1982. *Excavation in the Bacho Kiro Cave, Bulgaria (Final Report)*. Warsaw: Paristwowe Wydarunictwo, Naukowe.
Kroll, E.M. 1994. Behavioral implications of Plio-Pleistocene archaeological site structure. *Journal of Human Ecology* 27, 107–38.
Kroll, E.M. & Isaac, G.I. 1984. Configurations of artifacts and bones at early Pleistocene sites in East Africa. In *Intrasite Spatial Analysis in Archaeology*, ed., H.J. Hietela, pp. 4–31. Cambridge: Cambridge University Press.
Kuhn, S. 1993. Mousterian technology as adaptive response. In *Hunting and Animal Exploitation in the Later Palaeolithic and Mesolithic of Eurasia*, eds., G.L. Peterkin, H.M. Bricker & P. Mellars, pp. 25–31. Archaeological Papers of the American Anthropological Association, No. 4.
Kuhn, S. 1995. *Mousterian Lithic Technology*. Princeton: Princeton University Press.
Kuhn, T. 1979. Metaphor in science. In *Metaphor and Thought*, ed., A. Ortony, pp. 409–19.

Cambridge: Cambridge University Press.
Kuman, K. 1994. The archaeology of Sterkfontein: preliminary findings on site formation and cultural change. *South African Journal of Science* 90, 215–19.
Laitman, J.T. & Heimbuch, R.C. 1982. The basicranium of Plio-Pleistocene hominids as an indicator of their upper respiratory system. *American Journal of Physical Anthropology* 59, 323–44.
Laitman, J.T., Heimbuch, R.C. & Crelin, E.C. 1979. The basicranium of fossil hominids as an indicator of their upper respiratory systems. *American Journal of Physical Anthropology* 51, 15–34.
Laitman, J.T., Reidenberg, J.S., Gannon, P.J., Johanson, B., Landahl, K. & Lieberman, P. 1990. The Kebara hyoid: what can it tell us about the evolution of the hominid vocal tract? *American Journal of Physical Anthropology* 18, 254.
Laitman, J.T., Reidenberg, J.S., Friedland, D.R. & Gannon, P.J. 1991. What sayeth thou Neanderthal? A look at the evolution of their vocal tract and speech. *American Journal of Physical Anthropology* (supplement) 12, 109.
Laitman, J.T., Reidenberg, J.S., Friedland, D.R., Reidenberg, B.E. & Gannon, P.J. 1993. Neanderthal upper respiratory specializations and their effect upon respiration and speech. *American Journal of Physical Anthropology* (supplement) 16, 129.
Lake, M. 1992. Evolving thought (review of M. Donald's 'Origin of the Modern Mind'). *Cambridge Archaeological Journal* 2, 267–70.
Lake, M. 1995. Computer simulation of Early Hominid subsistence activities. Unpublished Ph.D. thesis, University of Cambridge.
Larichev, V., Khol'ushkin, V. & Laricheva, I. 1988. The Upper Palaeolithic of Northern Asia: achievements, problems and perspectives. I: Western Siberia. *Journal of World Prehistory* 2, 359–97.
Larichev, V., Khol'ushkin, V. & Laricheva, I. 1990. The Upper Palaeolithic of Northern Asia: achievements, problems and perspectives. II: Central and Eastern Siberia. *Journal of World Prehistory* 4, 347–85.
Larichev, V., Khol'ushkin, V. & Laricheva, I. 1992. The Upper Palaeolithic of Northern Asia: achievements, problems and perspectives. III: Northeastern Siberia and the Russian far east. *Journal of World Prehistory* 6, 441–76.
Larsson, L. 1983. The Skateholm Project – A Late Mesolithic Settlement and Cemetery complex at a southern Swedish bay. *Meddelånden från Lunds Universitets Historiska Museum* 1983–84, 4–38.
Laville, H., Rigaud, J-P. & Sackett, J.R. 1980. *Rockshelters of the Périgord*. New York: Academic Press.
Layton, R. 1985. The cultural context of hunter-gatherer rock art. *Man* (N.S.) 20, 434–53.
Layton, R. 1994. *Australian Rock Art: A New Synthesis*. Cambridge: Cambridge University Press.
Leakey, M. 1971. *Olduvai Gorge. Volume 3. Excavations in Beds I and II, 1960–1963*. Cambridge: Cambridge University Press.
Leakey, M., Feibel, C.S., McDougall, I. & Walker, A. 1995. New four million-year-old hominid species from Kanapoi and Allia Bay, Kenya. *Nature* 376, 565–71.
Leakey, R.E. & Walker, A. 1976. Australopithecines, *H. erectus* and the single species hypothesis. *Nature* 222, 1132–38.
Lee, R.B. 1976. !Kung spatial organisation. In *Kalahari Hunter-Gatherers: Studies of the !Kung San and their Neighbors*, eds., R.B. Lee & I. DeVore, pp. 73–98. Cambridge MA: Harvard University Press.
Lee, R.B. 1979. *The !Kung San: Men, Women and Work in a Foraging Society*. Cambridge: Cambridge University Press.
Lee, R.B. & DeVore, I. (eds.) 1976. *Kalahari Hunter-Gatherers: Studies of the !Kung San and their Neighbours*. Cambridge MA: Harvard University Press.
Legge, A.J. & Rowley-Conwy, P. 1987. Gazelle killing in Stone Age Syria. *Scientific American* 255, 88–95.
LeMay, M. 1975. The language capability of Neanderthal man. *American Journal of Physical Anthropology* 49, 9–14.
LeMay, M. 1976. Morphological cerebral asymmetries of modern man, fossil man and nonhuman primates. In *Origins and Evolution of Language and Speech*, eds., S.R. Harnard, H.D. Steklis & J. Lancaster, pp. 349–66. New York: Annals of the New York Academy of Sciences, Vol. 280.
Leroi-Gourhan, A. 1968. *The Art of Prehistoric Man in Western Europe*. London: Thames & Hudson.
Leslie, A. 1991. The theory of mind impairment in autism: evidence for a modular mechanism of development. In *Natural Theories of Mind: Evolution, Development and Simulation of Everyday Mindreading*, ed., A. Whiten, pp. 63–78. Oxford: Blackwell.
Leslie, A. 1994. ToMM, ToBY, and agency: core architecture and domain specificity. In *Mapping the Mind: Domain Specificity in Cognition and Culture*, eds., L.A. Hirschfield & S. Gellman, pp. 119–48. Cambridge: Cambridge University Press.
Levine, M. 1983. Mortality models and interpretation of horse population structure. In *Hunter-Gatherer Economy in Prehistory: A European Perspective*, ed., G.N. Bailey, pp. 23–46. Cambridge: Cambridge University Press.
Levitt, D. 1981. *Plants and People: Aboriginal Uses of Plants on Groote Eylandt*. Canberra: Australian Institute of Aboriginal Studies.
Lewis-Williams, J.D. 1982. The economic and social context of southern San rock art. *Current Anthropology* 23, 429–49.
Lewis-Williams, J.D. 1983. *The Rock Art of*

Southern Africa. Cambridge: Cambridge University Press.
Lewis-Williams, J.D. 1987. A dream of eland: an unexplored component of San shamanism and rock art. *World Archaeology* 19, 165–77.
Lewis-Williams, J.D. 1991. Wrestling with analogy: a methodological dilemma in Upper Palaeolithic art research. *Proceedings of the Prehistoric Society* 57 (i), 149–62.
Lewis-Williams, J.D. 1995. Seeing and construing: the making and meaning of a southern African rock art motif. *Cambridge Archaeological Journal* (in press).
Lewis-Williams, J.D. & Dowson, T.A. 1988. The signs of all times: entoptic phenomena in Upper Palaeolithic art. *Current Anthropology* 24, 201–45.
Lieberman, P. 1984. *The Biology and Evolution of Language*. Cambridge MA: Harvard University Press.
Lieberman, P. 1993. On the Kebara KMH 2 hyoid and Neanderthal speech. *Current Anthropology* 34, 172–75.
Lieberman, P. & Crelin, E.S. 1971. On the speech of Neanderthal man. *Linguistic Enquiry* 2, 203–22.
Lieberman, D.E. & Shea, J.J. 1994. Behavioral differences between Archaic and Modern Humans in the Levantine Mousterian. *American Anthropologist* 96, 330–32.
Lindly, J. & Clark, G. 1990. Symbolism and modern human origins. *Current Anthropology* 31, 233–61.
Lock, A. 1993. Human language development and object manipulation: their relation in ontogeny and its possible relevance for phylogenetic questions. In *Tools, Language and Cognition in Human Evolution*, eds., K.R. Gibson & T. Ingold, pp. 279–99. Cambridge: Cambridge University Press.
Lockhart, R.S. 1989. Consciousness and the function of remembered episodes: comments on the fourth section. In *Varieties of Memory and Consciousness: Essays in Honour of Endel Tulving*, eds., H.L. Roedinger & F.I.M. Craik, pp. 423–29. Hillsdale NJ: Erlbaum.
Lorblanchet, M. 1989. From man to animal and sign in Palaeolithic art. In *Animals into Art*, ed., H. Morphy, pp. 109–43. London: Unwin Hyman.
MacDonald, C. 1991. *Mind-Body Identity Theories*. London: Routledge.
Mackintosh, N. 1983. *Conditioning and Associative Learning*. Oxford: Oxford University Press.
Mackintosh, N. 1994. Intelligence in evolution. In *What is Intelligence?*, ed., J. Khalfa, pp. 27–48. Cambridge: Cambridge University Press.
Marks, S.A. 1976. *Large Mammals and a Brave People: Subsistence Hunters in Zambia*. Seattle: University of Washington Press.
Marler, P. 1970. Birdsong and human speech: can there be parallels? *American Scientist* 58, 669–74.
Marshack, A. 1972a. *The Roots of Civilization*. London: McGraw Hill.
Marshack, A. 1972b. Upper Palaeolithic notation and symbol. *Science* 178, 817–28.
Marshack, A. 1985. A lunar solar year calendar stick from North America. *American Antiquity* 50, 27–51.
Marshack, A. 1989. On wishful thinking and lunar 'calendars'. A reply to Francesco d'Errico. *Current Anthropology* 30, 491–95.
Marshack, A. 1990. Early hominid symbolism and the evolution of human capacity. In *The Emergence of Modern Humans*, ed., P. Mellars, pp. 457–98. Edinburgh: Edinburgh University Press.
Marshack, A. 1991. The Täi plaque and calendrical notation in the Upper Palaeolithic. *Cambridge Archaeological Journal* 1, 25–61.
Marshall, L. 1976. *The !Kung of Nyae Nyae*. Cambridge MA: Harvard University Press.
Martin, R.S. 1981. Relative brain size and basal metabolic rates in terrestrial vertebrates. *Nature* 293, 57–60.
Martin, R.S. 1990. *Primate Origins and Evolution*. London: Chapman & Hall.
Martin, P.S. & Klein, R.C. (eds.) 1984. *Quaternary Extinctions: A Prehistoric Revolution*. Tucson: University of Arizona Press.
Matsuzawa, T. 1991. Nesting cups and metatools in chimpanzees. *Behavioral and Brain Sciences* 14, 570–71.
McBrearty, S. 1988. The Sangoan-Lupemban and Middle Stone Age sequence at the Muguruk Site, Western Kenya. *World Archaeology* 19, 388–420.
McBurney, C.B.M. 1967. *The Haua Fteah (Cyrenaica)*. Cambridge: Cambridge University Press.
McCown, T. 1937. Mugharet es-Skhūl: description and excavation. In *The Stone Age of Mount Carmel*, eds., D. Garrod & D. Bate, pp. 91–107. Oxford: Clarendon Press.
McFarland, D. (ed.) 1987. *The Oxford Companion to Animal Behaviour*. Oxford: Oxford University Press.
McGrew, W.C. 1987. Tools to get food: the subsistants of Tasmanian Aborigines and Tanzanian chimpanzees compared. *Journal of Anthropological Research* 43, 247–58.
McNabb, J. & Ashton, N. 1995. Thoughtful flakers. *Cambridge Archaeological Journal* 5, 289–301.
McGrew, W.C. 1992. *Chimpanzee Material Culture*. Cambridge: Cambridge University Press.
Meehan, B. 1982. *From Shell Bed to Shell Midden*. Canberra: Australian Institute of Australian Studies.
Mellars, P. 1973. The character of the Middle-Upper transition in southwest France. In *The Explanation of Culture Change*, ed., C. Renfrew, pp. 255–76. London: Duckworth.
Mellars, P. 1989a. Major issues in the emergence of modern humans. *Current Anthropology* 30, 349–85.
Mellars, P. 1989b. Technological changes at the

Middle-Upper Palaeolithic transition: economic, social and cognitive perspectives. In *The Human Revolution*, eds., P. Mellars & C. Stringer, pp. 338–65. Edinburgh: Edinburgh University Press.
Mellars, P. 1992. Technological change in the Mousterian of southwest France. In *The Middle Palaeolithic: Adaptation, Behaviour and Variability*, eds., H.L. Dibble & P. Mellars, pp. 29–44. Philadelphia: The University Museum, University of Pennsylvania.
Mellars, P. & Stringer, C. (eds.) 1989. *The Human Revolution: Behavioural and Biological Perspectives in the Origins of Modern Humans.* Edinburgh: Edinburgh University Press.
Meltzer, D., Adovasio, J.M. & Dillehay, T. 1994. On a Pleistocene human occupation at Pedra Furada, Brazil. *Antiquity* 68, 695–714.
Menzel, E. 1973. Chimpanzee spatial memory organization. *Science* 182, 943–45.
Menzel, E. 1978. Cognitive mapping in chimpanzees. In *Cognitive Processes in Animal Behavior*, eds., S. Hulse, H. Fowler & W. Honig, pp. 375–422. Hillsdale NJ: Erlbaum.
Merrick, H.V. & Merrick J.P.S. 1976. Archaeological occurrences of earlier Pleistocene age from the Shungura Formation. In *Earliest Man and Environments in the Lake Rudolf Basin: Stratigraphy, Paleoecology and Evolution*, eds., Y. Coppens, F.C. Howell, G. Isaac & R.E.F. Leakey, pp. 574–84. Chicago: Chicago University Press.
Milton, K. 1988. Foraging behaviour and the evolution of primate intelligence. In *Machiavellian Intelligence: Social Expertise and the Evolution of Intellect in Monkeys, Apes and Humans*, eds., R.W. Byrne & A. Whiten, pp. 285–305. Oxford: Clarendon Press.
Mithen, S. 1988. Looking and learning: Upper Palaeolithic art and information gathering. *World Archaeology* 19, 297–327.
Mithen, S. 1989. To hunt or to paint? Animals and art in the Upper Palaeolithic. *Man* 23, 671–95.
Mithen, S. 1990. *Thoughtful Foragers: A Study of Prehistoric Decision Making.* Cambridge: Cambridge University Press.
Mithen, S. 1993. Individuals, groups and the Palaeolithic record: a reply to Clark. *Proceedings of the Prehistoric Society* 59, 393–98.
Mithen, S. 1994. Technology and society during the Middle Pleistocene. *Cambridge Archaeological Journal* 4 (1), 3–33.
Mithen, S. 1995. Reply to Ashton & McNabb. *Cambridge Archaeological Journal* 5, 298–302.
Mithen, S. 1996. Social learning and cultural traditions: interpreting Early Palaeolithic technology. In *The Archaeology of Human Ancestry: Power, Sex and Tradition*, eds., J. Steele & S. Shennon, pp. 207–29. London: Routledge.
Moore, A.M.T. & Hillman, G.C. 1992. The Pleistocene-Holocene transition and human economy in southwest Asia: the impact of the Younger Dryas. *American Antiquity* 57, 482–94.
Morphy, H. (ed.) 1989a. *Animals into Art*, London: Unwin Hyman.
Morphy, H. 1989b. On representing Ancestral Beings. In *Animals into Art*, ed., H. Morphy, pp. 144–60. London: Unwin Hyman.
Morris, D. 1962. *The Biology of Art.* London: Methuen.
Mosiman, J.E. & Martin, P.S. 1976. Simulating overkill by Paleoindians. *American Scientist* 63, 304–13.
Movius, H. 1950. A wooden spear of third interglacial age from Lower Saxony. *Southwestern Journal of Anthropology* 6, 139–42.
Moyà-Solà, S. & Köhler, M. 1996. A *Dryopithecus* skeleton and the origins of great ape locomotion. *Nature* 379, 156–59.
Nagel, T. 1974. What is it like to be a bat? *Philosophical Review* 83, 435–50.
Naroll, R.S. 1962. Floor area and settlement population. *American Antiquity* 27, 587–89.
Nelson, R.K. 1973. *Hunters of the Northern Forest: Designs for Survival among the Alaskan Kutchin.* Chicago: University of Chicago Press.
Nelson, R.K. 1983. *Make Prayers to the Raven: A Koyukon View of the Northern Forest.* Chicago: Chicago University Press.
Nishida, T. 1987. Local traditions and cultural transmission. In *Primate Societies*, eds., B.B. Smuts, R.W. Wrangham & T.T. Struhsaker, pp. 462–74. Chicago: Chicago University Press.
Nitecki, M.H. & Nitecki, D.V. (eds.) 1994. *Origins of Anatomically Modern Humans.* New York: Plenum Press.
Oakley, K.P., Andrews, P., Keeley, L.H. & Clark, J.D. 1977. A reappraisal of the Clacton spear point. *Proceedings of the Prehistoric Society* 43, 13–30.
O'Connell, J. 1987. Alyawara site structure and its archaeological implications. *American Antiquity* 52, 74–108.
Oliver, J.S. 1994. Estimates of hominid and carnivore involvement in the FLK Zinjanthropus fossil assemblages: some sociological implications. *Journal of Human Evolution* 27, 267–94.
Olszewski, D.I. & Dibble, H.L. 1994. The Zagros Aurignacian. *Current Anthropology* 35, 68–75.
Oring, E. 1992. *Jokes and their Relations.* Lexington: University of Kentucky Press.
Orquera, L.A. 1984. Specialization and the Middle/Upper Palaeolithic transition. *Current Anthropology* 25, 73–98.
O'Shea, J. & Zvelebil, M. 1984. Oleneostrovski Mogilnik: reconstructing the social and economic organisation of prehistoric foragers in northern Russia. *Journal of Anthropological Archaeology* 3, 1–40.
Oswalt, W.H. 1973. *Habitat and Technology.* New York: Holt, Rinehart & Winston.
Oswalt, W.H. 1976. *An Anthropological Analysis of Food-Getting Technology.* New York: John Wiley.
Otte, M. 1992. The significance of variability in the European Mousterian. In *The Middle*

Palaeolithic, Adaptation, Behaviour and Variability, eds., H. Dibble & P. Mellars, pp. 45–52. Philadelphia: The University Museum, University of Pennsylvania.

Parés, J.M. & Pérez-González, A. 1995. Paleomagnetic age for hominid fossils of Atapuerca archaeological site, Spain. *Science* 269, 830–32.

Parker, S.T. & Gibson, K.R. 1979. A developmental model for the evolution of language and intelligence in early hominids. *Behavioral and Brain Sciences* 3, 367–408.

Parker, S.T. & Gibson, K.R. (eds.) 1990. *'Language' and Intelligence in Monkeys and Apes.* Cambridge: Cambridge University Press.

Parkin, R.A., Rowley-Conwy, P. & Serjeantson, D. 1986. Late Palaeolithic exploitation of horse and red deer at Gough's Cave, Cheddar, Somerset. *Proceedings of the University of Bristol Speleological Society* 17, 311–30.

Parkington, J.E. 1986. Stone tool assemblages, raw material distributions and prehistoric subsistence activities: the Late Stone Age of South Africa. In *Stone Age Prehistory*, eds., G.N. Bailey & P. Callow, pp. 181–94. Cambridge: Cambridge University Press.

Parkington, J.E. 1990. A critique of the consensus view on the age of Howieson's Poort assemblages in South Africa. In *The Emergence of Modern Humans*, ed., P. Mellars, pp. 34–55. Edinburgh: Edinburgh University Press.

Pelcin, A. 1994. A geological explanation for the Berekhat Ram figurine. *Current Anthropology* 35, 674–75.

Pelegrin, J. 1993. A framework for analysing prehistoric stone tool manufacture and a tentative application to some early stone industries. In *The Use of Tools by Human and Non-human Primates*, eds., A. Berthelet & J. Chavaillon, pp. 302–14. Oxford: Clarendon Press.

Penfield, W. 1975. *The Mystery of the Mind: A Critical Study of Consciousness and the Human Brain.* Princeton: Princeton University Press.

Pepperberg, I. 1990. Conceptual abilities of some non-primate species, with an emphasis on an African Grey parrot. In *'Language' and Intelligence in Monkeys and Apes,* eds., S.T. Parker & K.R. Gibson, pp. 469–507. Cambridge: Cambridge University Press.

Peterkin, G.L. 1993. Lithic and organic hunting technology in the French Upper Palaeolithic. In *Hunting and Animal Exploitation in the Later Palaeolithic and Mesolithic of Eurasia*, eds., G.L. Peterkin, H.M. Bricker & P. Mellars, pp. 49–67. Archaeological Papers of the American Anthropological Association, No. 4.

Pfeiffer, J. 1982. *The Creative Explosion.* New York: Harper & Row.

Phillipson. D.W. 1985. *African Archaeology.* Cambridge: Cambridge University Press.

Piaget, J. 1971. *Biology and Knowledge.* Edinburgh: Edinburgh University Press.

Piette, E. 1906. Le chevêtre et la semi-domestication des animaux aux temps pléistocènes. *L'Anthropologie* 17, 27–53.

Pigeot, N. 1990. Technical and social actors: flint knapping specialists and apprentices at Magdalenian Etiolles. *Archaeological Review from Cambridge* 9, 126–41.

Pike-Tay, A. 1991. *Red Deer Hunting in the Upper Palaeolithic of Southwest France.* Oxford: British Archaeological Reports, International Series 569.

Pike-Tay, A. 1993. Hunting in the Upper Périgordian: a matter of strategy or expediency. In *Before Lascaux: The Complex Record of the Early Upper Palaeolithic*, eds., H. Knecht, A. Pike-Tay & R. White, pp. 85–99. Boca Raton: CRC Press.

Pike-Tay, A. & Bricker, H.M. 1993. Hunting in the Gravettian: an examination of the evidence from southwestern France. In *Hunting and Animal Exploitation in the Later Palaeolithic and Mesolithic of Eurasia*, eds. G.L. Peterkin, H.M. Bricker & P. Mellars, pp. 127–43. Archaeological Papers of the American Anthropological Association, No. 4.

Pinker, S. 1989. *Learnability and Cognition.* Cambridge MA: MIT Press.

Pinker, S. 1994. *The Language Instinct.* New York: William Morrow.

Plummer, T.W. & Bishop, L.C. 1994. Hominid paleoecology at Olduvai Gorge, Tanzania as indicated by antelope remains. *Journal of Human Evolution* 27, 47–75.

Pope, G. 1985. Taxonomy, dating and palaeoenvironments: the Palaeoecology of early far eastern hominids. *Modern Quaternary Research in Southeast Asia* 5, 65–80.

Pope, G. 1989. Bamboo and human evolution. *Natural History* 10, 49–56.

Potts, R. 1986. Temporal span of bone accumulations at Olduvai Gorge and implications for early hominid foraging behavior. *Paleobiology* 12, 25–31.

Potts, R. 1988. *Early Hominid Activities at Olduvai Gorge.* New York: Aldine de Gruyter.

Potts, R. 1989. Olorgesailie: new excavations and findings in Early and Middle Pleistocene contexts, southern Kenya rift valley. *Journal of Human Evolution* 18, 269–76.

Potts, R. 1994. Variables versus models of early Pleistocene hominid land use. *Journal of Human Evolution* 27, 7–24.

Potts, R. & Shipman, P. 1981. Cutmarks made by stone tools on bones from Olduvai Gorge, Tanzania. *Nature* 29, 577–80.

Povenelli, D.J. 1993. Reconstructing the evolution of the mind. *American Psychologist* 48, 493–509.

Premack, A.J. & Premack, D. 1972. Teaching language to an ape. *Scientific American* 227, 92–9.

Premack, D. 1988. 'Does the chimpanzee have a theory of mind?' revisited. In *Machiavellian Intelligence: Social Expertise and the Evolution of Intellect in Monkeys, Apes and Humans*, eds., R.W. Byrne & A. Whiten, pp. 160–79. Oxford: Clarendon Press.

Premack, D. & Woodruff, G. 1978. Does the

chimpanzee have a theory of mind? *The Behavioral and Brain Sciences* 1, 515–26.
Pulliam, H.R. & Dunford, C. 1980. *Programmed to Learn: An Essay on the Evolution of Culture.* New York: Basic Books.
Rae, A. 1986. *Quantum Physics: Illusion or Reality?* Cambridge: Cambridge University Press.
Renfrew, C. 1983. *Towards an Archaeology of Mind.* Cambridge: Cambridge University Press.
Renfrew, C. 1993. What is cognitive archaeology? *Cambridge Archaeological Journal* 3 (2), 248–50.
Reynolds, T.D. & Barnes, G. 1984. The Japanese Palaeolithic: a review. *Proceedings of the Prehistoric Society* 50, 49–62.
Riddington, R. 1982. Technology, world view and adaptive strategy in a northern hunting society. *Canadian Review of Sociology and Anthropology* 19, 469–81.
Rightmire, G.P. 1990. *The Evolution of H. erectus: Comparative Anatomical Studies of an Extinct Species.* Cambridge: Cambridge University Press.
Rice, P. 1981. Prehistoric venuses: symbols of motherhood or womenhood? *Journal of Anthropological Research* 37, 402–14.
Roberts, M.B. 1986. Excavation of the Lower Palaeolithic site at Amey's Eartham Pit, Boxgrove, West Sussex: a preliminary report. *Proceedings of the Prehistoric Society* 52, 215–46.
Roberts, M.B. 1994. Paper presented at Conference on the English Lower Palaeolithic, London, October 1994.
Roberts, M.B., Stringer, C.B. & Parfitt, S.A. 1994. A hominid tibia from Middle Pleistocene sediments at Boxgrove, UK. *Nature* 369, 311–13.
Roberts, R.G., Jones, R. & Smith, M.A. 1990. Thermoluminescence dating of a 50,000-year-old human occupation site in northern Australia. *Nature* 345, 153–56.
Roberts, R.G., Jones, R. & Smith, M.A. 1993. Optical dating at Deaf Adder Gorge, Northern Territory, indicates human occupation between 53,000 and 60,000 years ago. *Australian Archaeology* 37, 58–9.
Roberts, R.G., Jones, R. & Smith, M.A. 1994. Beyond the radiocarbon barrier in Australian prehistory. *Antiquity* 68, 611–16.
Robinson, J. 1992. Not counting on Marshack: a reassessment of the work of Alexander Marshack on notation in the Upper Palaeolithic. *Journal of Mediterranean Studies* 2, 1–16.
Roche, H. 1989. Technological evolution in the early hominids. *OSSA, International Journal of Skeletal Research* 14, 97–8.
Roche, H. & Tiercelin, J.J. 1977. Découverte d'une industrie lithique ancienne in situ dans la formation d'Hadar, Afar central, Ethiopia. *Competes Rendus de l'Académie des Sciences* 284-D, 1871–74.
Roe, D. 1981. *The Lower and Middle Palaeolithic Periods in Britain.* London: Routledge & Kegan Paul.
Roebroeks, W. 1988. From flint scatters to early hominid behaviour: a study of Middle Palaeolithic riverside settlements at Maastrict-Belvedere. *Analecta Praehistorica Leidensai* 1988.
Roebroeks, W., Conrad, N.J. & van Kolfschoten, T. 1992. Dense forests, cold steppes, and the Palaeolithic settlement of Northern Europe. *Current Anthropology* 33, 551–86.
Roebroeks, W., Kolen, J. & Rensink, E. 1988. Planning depth, anticipation and the organization of Middle Palaeolithic technology: the 'archaic natives' meet Eve's descendants. *Helinium* 28, 17–34.
Roebroeks, W. & van Kolfschoten, T. 1994. The earliest occupation of Europe: a short chronology. *Antiquity* 68, 489–503.
Rogers, M.J., Harris, J.W.K. & Feibel, C.S. 1994. Changing patterns of land use by Plio-Pleistocene hominids in the Lake Turkana Basin. *Journal of Human Evolution* 27, 139–58.
Rolland, N. & Dibble, H.L. 1990. A new synthesis of Middle Palaeolithic variability. *American Antiquity* 55, 480–99.
Ronen, A. 1992. The emergence of blade technology: cultural affinities. In *The Evolution and Dispersal of Modern Humans in Asia*, eds., T. Akazawa, K. Aoki & T. Kimura, pp. 217–28. Tokyo: Hokusen-Sha.
Rozin, P. 1976. The evolution of intelligence and access to the cognitive unconscious. In *Progress in Psychobiology and Physiological Psychology*, eds., J.M. Sprague & A.N. Epstein, pp. 245–77. New York: Academic Press.
Rozin, P. & Schull, J. 1988. The adaptive-evolutionary point of view in experimental psychology. In *Steven's Handbook of Experimental Psychology, Vol 1: Perception and Motivation*, eds., R.C. Atkinson, R.J. Hernstein, G. Lindzey & R.D. Luce, pp. 503–46. New York: John Wiley & Sons.
Sackett, J.R. 1981. From de Mortillet to Bordes: a century of French Palaeolithic research. In *Towards a History of Archaeology*, ed., G. Daniel, pp. 85–99. London: Thames & Hudson.
Sackett, J. 1982. Approaches to style in lithic archaeology. *Journal of Anthropological Archaeology* 1, 59–112.
Sacks, O. 1995. *An Anthropologist on Mars.* New York: Knopf.
Saladin D'Anglure, B. 1990. Nanook, super-male: the polar bear in the imaginary space and social time of the Inuit of the Canadian Arctic. In *Signifying Animals: Human Meaning in the Natural World*, ed., R.G. Willis, pp. 173–95. London: Unwin Hyman.
Santonja, M. & Villa, P. 1990. The Lower Palaeolithic of Spain and Portugal. *Journal of World Prehistory* 4, 45–94.
Savage-Rumbaugh, E.S. & Rumbaugh, D.M. 1993. The emergence of language. In *Tools, Language and Cognition in Human Evolution*, eds., K.R. Gibson & T. Ingold, pp. 86–108. Cambridge: Cambridge University Press.
Schacter, D. 1989. On the relation between memory and consciousness: dissociable

interactions and conscious experience. In *Varieties of Memory and Consciousness: Essays in Honour of Endel Tulving*, eds., H.L. Roedinger & F.I.M. Craik, pp. 355–90. Hillsdale NJ: Erlbaum.

Schepartz, L.A. 1993. Language and modern human origins. *Yearbook of Physical Anthropology* 36, 91–126.

Schick, K. & Toth, N. 1993. *Making Silent Stones Speak: Human Evolution and the Dawn of Technology*. New York: Simon & Schuster.

Schick, K. & Zhuan, D. 1993. Early Paleolithic of China and Eastern Asia. *Evolutionary Anthropology* 2, 22–35.

Schlanger, N. 1996. Understanding levallois: lithic technology and cognitive archaeology. *Cambridge Archaeological Journal* 6 (in press).

Scott, K. 1980. Two hunting episodes of Middle Palaeolithic age at La Cotte de Saint-Brelade, Jersey (Channel Islands). *World Archaeology* 12, 137–52.

Searle, J. 1990. Consciousness, explanatory inversion and cognitive science. *Behavioral and Brain Sciences* 13, 585–95.

Searle, J. 1992. *The Rediscovery of the Mind*. Cambridge MA: MIT Press.

Sémah, F., Sémah, A-H., Djubiantono, T. & Simanjuntak, H.T. 1992. Did they also make stone tools? *Journal of Human Evolution* 23, 439–46.

Sept, J.M. 1994. Beyond bones: archaeological sites, early hominid subsistence, and the costs and benefits of exploiting wild plant foods in east African riverine landscapes. *Journal of Human Evolution* 27, 295–320.

Shackleton, N.J. 1987. Oxygen isotopes, ice volume and sea level. *Quaternary Science Reviews* 6, 183–90.

Shackleton, N.J. & Opdyke, N.D. 1973. Oxygen isotope and palaeomagnetic stratigraphy of equatorial Pacific core V28-238. *Quaternary Research* 3, 39–55.

Shea, J.J. 1988. Spear points from the Middle Palaeolithic of the Levant. *Journal of Field Archaeology* 15, 441–50.

Shea, J.J. 1989. A functional study of the lithic industries associated with hominid fossils in the Kebara and Qafzeh caves, Israel. In *The Human Revolution*, eds., P. Mellars & C. Stringer, pp. 611–25. Edinburgh: Edinburgh University Press.

Shipman, P. 1983. Early hominid lifestyle: hunting and gathering or foraging and scavenging? In *Animals and Archaeology: 1. Hunters and their Prey*, eds., J. Clutton-Brock and C. Grigson, pp. 31–49. Oxford: British Archaeological Reports, International Series 163.

Shipman, P. 1986. Scavenging or hunting in the early hominids. Theoretical framework and tests. *American Anthropologist* 88, 27–43.

Shipman, P., Bosler, W. & Davis, K.L. 1981. Butchering of giant geladas at an Acheulian site. *Current Anthropology* 22, 257–68.

Shipman, P., Bosler, W. & Davis, K.L. 1982. Reply to Binford & Todd 'On arguments for the butchering of giant geladas'. *Current Anthropology* 23, 110–11.

Sieveking, A. 1984. Palaeolithic art and animal behaviour. In *La Contribution de la Zoologie et de l'ethologie à l'Interprétation de l'Art des Peuples Chasseurs Préhistoriques*, eds., H. Bandi *et al*, pp. 99–109. Fribourg: Editions Universitaires.

Sikes, N.E. 1994. Early hominid habitat preferences in East Africa: paleosol carbon isotopic evidence. *Journal of Human Evolution* 27, 25–45.

Silberbauer, G. 1981. *Hunter and Habitat in the Central Kalahari Desert*. Cambridge: Cambridge University Press.

Simons, E. 1992. The fossil history of primates. In *The Cambridge Encyclopedia of Human Evolution*, eds., J.S. Jones, R. Martin & D. Pilbeam, pp. 373–79. Cambridge: Cambridge University Press.

Sinclair, A. 1995. The technique as symbol in late glacial Europe. *World Archaeology* 27, 50–62.

Singer, R. & Wymer, J. 1982. *The Middle Stone Age at Klasies River Mouth in South Africa*. Chicago: Chicago University Press.

Smith, B.H. 1993. The physiological age of KNM-WT 15000. In *The Nariokotome Homo erectus Skeleton*, eds., A. Walker & R. Leakey, pp. 195–220. Berlin: Springer Verlag.

Smith, N. & Tsimpli, I-M. 1995. *The Mind of a Savant: Language Learning and Modularity*. Oxford: Clarendon Press.

Smith, P.E. 1982. The Late Palaeolithic and Epi-Palaeolithic of northern Africa. In *The Cambridge History of Africa, Volume 1, From the Earliest Times to c. 500 BC*, ed., J.D. Clark, pp. 342–409. Cambridge: Cambridge University Press.

Smith, R.J., Gannon, P.J. & Smith, B.H. 1995. Ontogeny of australopithecines and early *Homo*: evidence from cranial capacity and dental eruption. *Journal of Human Evolution* 29, 155–68.

Soffer, O. 1985. *The Upper Palaeolithic of the Central Russian Plain*. New York: Academic Press.

Soffer, O. 1987. Upper Palaeolithic connubia, refugia and the archaeological record from Eastern Europe. In *The Pleistocene Old World: Regional Perspectives*, ed., O. Soffer, pp. 333–48. New York: Plenum Press.

Soffer, O. 1989a. The Middle to Upper Palaeolithic transition on the Russian Plain. In *The Human Revolution*, eds., P. Mellars & C. Stringer, pp. 714–42. Edinburgh: Edinburgh University Press.

Soffer, O. 1989b. Storage, sedentism and the Eurasian Palaeolithic record. *Antiquity* 63, 719–32.

Soffer, O. 1994. Ancestral lifeways in Eurasia – The Middle and Upper Palaeolithic records. In *Origins of Anatomically Modern Humans*, eds., M.H. Nitecki & D.V. Nitecki, pp. 101–20. New York: Plenum Press.

Solecki, R. 1971. *Shanidar: The First Flower*

People. New York: Knopf.
Spelke, E.S. 1991. Physical knowledge in infancy: reflections on Piaget's theory. In *Epigenesis of Mind: Studies in Biology and Culture*, eds., S. Carey & R. Gelman, pp. 133–69. Hillsdale NJ: Erlbaum.
Spelke, E.S., Breinlinger, K., Macomber, J. & Jacobsen, K. 1992. Origins of knowledge. *Psychological Review*, 99, 605–32.
Sperber, D. 1994. The modularity of thought and the epidemiology of representations. In *Mapping the Mind: Domain Specificity in Cognition and Culture*, eds., L.A. Hirschfeld & S.A. Gelman, pp. 39–67. Cambridge: Cambridge University Press.
Spiess, A. E. 1979. *Reindeer and Caribou Hunters*. New York: Academic Press.
Srejovic, D. 1972. *Lepenski Vir*. London: Thames & Hudson.
Stepanchuk, V.N. 1993. Prolom II, a Middle Palaeolithic cave site in the eastern Crimea with non-utilitarian bone artifacts. *Proceedings of the Prehistoric Society* 59, 17–37.
Stern, N. 1993. The structure of the Lower Pleistocene archaeological record: a case study from the Koobi Fora formation. *Current Anthropology* 34, 201–25.
Stern, N. 1994. The implications of time averaging for reconstructing the land-use patterns of early tool-using hominids. *Journal of Human Evolution* 27, 89–105.
Sternberg, R. 1988. *The Triarchic Mind: A New Theory of Human Intelligence*. New York: Viking Press.
Stiles, D.N. 1991. Early hominid behaviour and culture tradition: raw material studies in Bed II, Olduvai Gorge. *The African Archaeological Review* 9, 1–19.
Stiles, D.N., Hay, R.L. & O'Neil, J.R. 1974. The MNK chert factory site, Olduvai Gorge, Tanzania. *World Archaeology* 5, 285–308.
Stiner, M. 1991. A taphonomic perspective on the origins of the faunal remains of Grotta Guattari (Latium, Italy). *Current Anthropology* 32, 103–17.
Stiner, M. & Kuhn, S. 1992. Subsistence, technology and adaptive variation in Middle Palaeolithic Italy. *American Anthropologist* 94, 12–46.
Stopp, M. 1988. A taphonomic analysis of the Hoxne site faunal assemblages. Unpublished M.Phil thesis, University of Cambridge.
Straus, L.G. 1982. Carnivores and cave sites in Cantabrian Spain. *Journal of Anthropological Research* 38, 75–96.
Straus, L.G. 1987b. Upper Palaeolithic ibex hunting is SW Europe. *Journal of Archaeological Science* 14, 149–63.
Straus, L.G. 1990a. The original arms race: Iberian perspectives on the Solutrean phenomenon. In *Feuilles de Pierre: Les Industries Foliacées du Paléolithique Supérieur Européen*, ed., J. Kozlowski, pp. 425–47. Liège, Belgium: ERAUL 42.
Straus, L.G. 1990b. On the emergence of modern humans. *Current Anthropology* 31, 63–4.
Straus, L.G. 1991. Southwestern Europe at the last glacial maximum. *Current Anthropology* 32, 189–99.
Straus, L.G. 1992. *Iberia Before the Iberians*. Albuquerque: University of New Mexico Press.
Straus, L.G. 1993. Upper Palaeolithic hunting tactics and weapons in western Europe. In *Hunting and Animal Exploitation in the Later Palaeolithic and Mesolithic of Eurasia*, eds., G.L. Peterkin, H.M. Bricker & P. Mellars, pp. 83–93. Archaeological Papers of the American Anthropological Association, No. 4.
Stringer, C. 1993. Secrets of the pit of the bones. *Nature* 362, 501–02.
Stringer, C. & Bräuer, G. 1994. Methods, misreading and bias. *American Anthropologist* 96, 416–24.
Stringer, C. & Gamble, C. 1993. *In Search of the Neanderthals*. London & New York: Thames & Hudson.
Stuart, A.J. 1982. *Pleistocene Vertebrates in the British Isles*. New York: Longman.
Sugiyama, Y. 1993. Local variation of tools and tool use among wild chimpanzee populations. In *The Use of Tools by Human and Non-human Primates*, eds., A. Berthelet & J. Chavaillon, pp. 175–90. Oxford: Clarendon Press.
Sullivan, R.J. 1942. *The Ten'a Food Quest*. Washington: The Catholic University of America Press.
Susman, R.L. 1991. Who made the Oldowan tools? Fossil evidence for tool behaviour in Plio-Pleistocene hominids. *Journal of Anthropological Research* 47, 129–51.
Svoboda, J. 1987. Lithic industries of the Arago, Vértesszöllös and Bilzingsleben hominids: comparisons and evolutionary interpretations. *Current Anthropology* 28, 219–27.
Svoboda, J. 1988. A new male burial from Dolni Vestonice. *Journal of Human Evolution* 16, 827–30.
Svoboda, J. 1992. Comment on 'Dense forests, cold steppes, and the Palaeolithic settlement of Northern Europe by W. Roebroeks, N.J. Conrad & T. van Kolfschoten'. *Current Anthropology* 33, 569–72.
Swisher, C.C. III., Curtis, G.H., Jacob, T., Getty, A.G., Suprijo, A. & Widiasmoro. 1994. Age of the earliest known hominids in Java, Indonesia. *Science* 263, 1118–21.
Tacon, P.S.C. 1989. Art and the essence of being: symbolic and economic aspects of fish among the peoples of western Arnhem Land, Australia. In *Animals into Art*, ed., H. Morphy, pp. 236–50. London: Unwin Hyman.
Talmy, L. 1988. Force dynamics in language and cognition. *Cognitive Science* 12, 49–100.
Tanner, A. 1979. *Bringing Home Animals: Religious Ideology and Mode of Production of the Mistassini Cree Hunters*. London: C. Hurst.
Tatton-Brown, T. 1989. *Great Cathedrals of Britain*. London: BBC Books.

Taylor, K.C., Lamorey, G.W., Doyle, G.A., Alley, R.B., Grootes, P.M., Mayewski, P.A., White, J.W.C. & Barlow, L.K. 1993. The 'flickering switch' of late Pleistocene climate change. *Nature* 361, 432–35.
Taylor, L. 1989. Seeing the 'inside': Kunwinjku paintings and the symbol of the divided body. In *Animals into Art*, ed., H. Morphy, pp. 371–89. London: Unwin Hyman.
Templeton, A.R. 1993. The 'Eve' hypothesis: a genetic critique and reanalysis. *American Anthropologist* 95, 51–72.
Terrace, H.S. 1979. *Nim*. New York: Knopf.
Terrace, H.S., Pettito, L.A., Saunders, R.J. & Bever, T.G. 1979. Can an ape create a sentence? *Science* 206, 891–902.
Thackeray, A.I. 1989. Changing fashions in the Middle Stone Age: the stone artefact sequence from Klasies River main site, South Africa. *African Archaeological Review* 7, 33–57.
Tobias, P.V. 1987. The brain of *Homo habilis*: a new level of organisation in cerebral evolution. *Journal of Human Evolution* 16, 741–61.
Tobias, P.V. 1991. *Olduvai Gorge, Volume 4*. Cambridge: Cambridge University Press.
Tomasello, M. 1990. Cultural transmission in the tool use and communicatory signaling of chimpanzees? In *'Language' and Intelligence in Monkeys and Apes: Comparative Developmental Perspectives*, eds., S.T. Parker & K.R. Gibson, pp. 274–311. Cambridge: Cambridge University Press.
Tomasello, M., Davis-Dasilva, M., Camak, L. & Bard, K. 1987. Observational learning of tool use by young chimpanzees. *Human Evolution* 2, 175–83.
Tomasello, M., Kruger, A.C. & Ratner, H.H. 1993. Cultural learning. *Behavioral and Brain Sciences* 16, 495–552.
Tooby, J. & Cosmides, L. 1989. Evolutionary psychology and the generation of culture, part I. Theoretical considerations. *Ethology and Sociobiology* 10, 29–49.
Tooby, J. & Cosmides, L. 1992. The psychological foundations of culture. In *The Adapted Mind*, eds., J.H. Barkow, L. Cosmides & J. Tooby, pp. 19–136. New York: Oxford University Press.
Torrence, R. 1983. Time budgeting and hunter-gatherer technology. In *Hunter-Gatherer Economy in Prehistory*, ed., G.N.B. Bailey, pp. 11–22. Cambridge: Cambridge University Press.
Toth, N. 1985. The Oldowan reassessed: a close look at early stone artifacts. *Journal of Archaeological Science* 12, 101–20.
Toth, N. & Schick, K.D. 1993. Early stone industries and inferences regarding language and cognition. In *Tools, Language and Cognition in Human Evolution*, eds., K.R. Gibson & T. Ingold, pp. 346–62. Cambridge: Cambridge University Press.
Toth, N., Schick, K.D., Savage-Rumbaugh, E.S., Sevcik, R.A. & Rumbaugh, D.M. 1993. *Pan* the tool-maker: investigations into the stone tool-making and tool-using capabilities of a bonobo (*Pan paniscus*). *Journal of Archaeological Science* 20, 81–91.
Torrence, R. 1983. Time budgeting and hunter-gatherer technology. In *Hunter-Gatherer Economy in Prehistory*, ed., G.N.B. Bailey, pp. 57–66. Cambridge: Cambridge University Press.
Trinkaus, E. 1983. *The Shanidar Neandertals*. New York: Academic Press.
Trinkaus, E. 1985. Pathology and posture of the La Chapelle-aux-Saints Neandertal. *American Journal of Physical Anthropology* 67, 19–41.
Trinkaus, E. 1985. Cannibalism and burial at Krapina. *Journal of Human Evolution* 14, 203–16.
Trinkaus, E. 1987. Bodies, brawn, brains and noses: human ancestors and human predation. In *The Evolution of Human Hunting*, eds., M.H. Nitecki & D.V. Nitecki, pp. 107–45. New York: Plenum Press.
Trinkaus, E. 1992. Morphological contrasts between the Near Eastern Qafzeh-Skhūl and Late Archaic human samples: grounds for a behavioral difference. In *The Evolution and Dispersal of Modern Humans in Asia*, eds., T. Akazawa, K. Aoki & T. Kimura, pp. 277–94. Tokyo: Hokusen-Sha.
Trinkaus, E. 1995. Neandertal mortality patterns. *Journal of Archaeological Science* 22, 121–42.
Trinkaus, E. & Shipman, P. 1992. *The Neandertals*. New York: Knopf.
Tuffreau, A. 1992. Middle Palaeolithic settlement in Northern France. In *The Middle Palaeolithic: Adaptation, Behaviour and Variability*, eds., H.L. Dibble & P. Mellars, pp. 59–73. Philadelphia: The University Museum, University of Pennsylvania.
Tulving, E. 1983. *Elements of Episodic Memory*. Oxford: Clarendon Press.
Turq, A. 1992. Raw material and technological studies of the Quina Mousterian in Perigord. In *The Middle Palaeolithic: Adaptation, Behaviour and Variability*, eds., H.L. Dibble & P. Mellars, pp. 75–85. Philadelphia: The University Museum, University of Pennsylvania.
Tuttle, R.H. 1987. Kinesiological inferences and evolutionary implications from Laetoli bipedal trails G-1, G-2/3 and A. In *Laetoli, a Pliocene Site in Northern Tanzania*, eds., M.D. Leakey & J.M. Harris, pp. 503–23. Oxford: Clarendon Press.
Tyldesley, J. 1986. *The Wolvercote Channel Handaxe Assemblage: A Comparative Study*. Oxford: British Archaeological Reports, British Series 152.
Valladas, H., Cachier, H., Maurice, P., Bernaldo de Quiros, F., Clottes, J., Cabrera Valdés, V., Uzquiano, P. & Arnold, M. 1992. Direct radiocarbon dates for prehistoric paintings at the Altamira, El Castillo and Niaux caves. *Nature* 357, 68–70.
Valoch, K. 1984. Le Taubachien, sa géochronologie, paléoécologie et sa paléoethnologie. *L'Anthropologie* 88, 193–208.

Vandermeersch, B. 1970. Une sépulture moustérienne avec offrandes découverte dans la grotte de Qafzeh. *Comptes Rendus Hebdomadaires des Séances de l'Académie des Sciences* 270, 298–301.

Vandermeersch, B. 1989. The evolution of modern humans, recent evidence from Southwest Asia. In *The Human Revolution*, eds., P. Mellars & C. Stringer, pp. 155–63. Edinburgh: Edinburgh University Press.

van Schaik, C.P. 1983. Why are diurnal primates living in large groups? *Behaviour* 87, 120–44.

Vértes, L. 1975. The Lower Palaeolithic site of Vértesszöllös, Hungary. In *Recent Archaeological Excavations in Europe*, ed., R. Bruce-Mitford, pp. 287–301. London: Routledge and Kegan Paul.

Villa, P. 1983. *Terra Amata and the Middle Pleistocene Archaeological Record from Southern France*. Berkeley: University of California Press.

Villa, P. 1990. Torralba and Aridos: elephant exploitation in Middle Pleistocene Spain. *Journal of Human Evolution* 19, 299–309.

Villa, P. 1991. Middle Pleistocene prehistory in southwestern Europe: the state of our knowledge and ignorance. *Journal of Anthropological Research* 47, 193–217.

Visalberghi, E. & Fragaszy, D.M. 1990. Do monkeys ape? In *'Language' and Intelligence in Monkeys and Apes: Comparative Developmental Perspectives*, eds., S.T. Parker & K.R. Gibson, pp. 247–73. Cambridge: Cambridge University Press.

de Waal, F. 1982. *Chimpanzee Politics: Power and Sex among Apes*. London: Jonathan Cape.

Wadley, L. 1993. The Pleistocene Late Stone Age south of the Limpopo River. *Journal of World Prehistory* 7, 243–96.

Walker, A. & Leakey, R. (eds.) 1993. *The Nariokotome Homo erectus Skeleton*. Berlin: Springer Verlag.

Wanpo, H., Ciochon, R., Yumin, G., Larick, R., Qiren, F., Schwarcz, H., Yonge, C., de Vos, J. & Rink, W. 1995. Early *Homo* and associated artifacts from China. *Nature* 378, 275–78.

Wellman, H.M. 1991. From desires to beliefs: acquisition of a theory of mind. In *Natural Theories of Mind: Evolution, Development and Simulation of Everyday Mindreading*, ed., A. Whiten, pp. 19–38. Oxford: Blackwell.

Wendorf, F., Schild, R. & Close, A. (eds.) 1980. *Loaves and Fishes: The Prehistory of Wadi Kubbaniya*. Dallas: Southern Methodist University Press.

Westergaard, G.C. 1995. The stone tool technology of capuchin monkeys: possible implications for the evolution of symbolic communication in hominids. *World Archaeology* 27, 1–24.

Weyer, E.M. 1932. *The Eskimos*. New Haven: York University Press.

Whallon, R. 1989. Elements of culture change in the Later Palaeolithic. In *The Human Revolution*, eds., P. Mellars & C. Stringer, pp. 433–54. Edinburgh: Edinburgh University Press.

Wheeler, P. 1984. The evolution of bipedality and the loss of functional body hair in hominids. *Journal of Human Evolution* 13, 91–8.

Wheeler, P. 1988. Stand tall and stay cool. *New Scientist* 12, 60–5.

Wheeler, P. 1991. The influence of bipedalism on the energy and water budgets of early hominids. *Journal of Human Evolution* 21, 107–36.

Wheeler, P. 1994. The thermoregulatory advantages of heat storage and shade seeking behaviour to hominids foraging in equatorial savannah environments. *Journal of Human Evolution* 26, 339–50.

White, R. 1982. Rethinking the Middle/Upper Paleolithic transition. *Current Anthropology* 23, 169–92.

White, R. 1989a. Production complexity and standardization in early Aurignacian bead and pendant manufacture: evolutionary implications. In *The Human Revolution*, eds., P. Mellars & C. Stringer, pp. 366–90. Edinburgh: Edinburgh University Press.

White, R. 1989b. Husbandry and herd control in the Upper Palaeolithic. *Current Anthropology* 30, 609–31.

White, R. 1992. Beyond art: toward an understanding of the origins of material representation in Europe. *Annual Review of Anthropology* 21, 537–64.

White, R. 1993a. A social and technological view of Aurignacian and Castelperronian personal ornaments in S.W. Europe. in *El Origin del Hombre Moderno en el Suroeste de Europa*, ed., V. Cabrera Valdés, pp. 327–57. Madrid: Ministerio des Educacion y Ciencia.

White, R. 1993b. Technological and social dimensions of 'Aurignacian-Age' body ornaments across Europe. In *Before Lascaux: The Complex Record of the Early Upper Palaeolithic*, eds., H. Knecht, A. Pike-Tay & R. White, pp. 247–99. Boca Raton: CRC Press.

White, T.D., Suwa, G. & Asfaw, B. 1994. *Australopithecus ramidus*, a new species of early hominid from Aramis, Ethiopia. *Nature* 371, 306–12.

White, T.D. & Toth, N. 1991. The question of ritual cannibalism at Grotta Guattari. *Current Anthropology* 32, 118–38.

Whitelaw, T. 1991. Some dimensions of variability in the social organisation of community space among foragers. In *Ethnoarchaeological Approaches to Mobile Campsites*, eds., C. Gamble & W. Boismier, pp. 139–88. Ann Arbor: International Monographs in Prehistory.

Whiten, A. 1989. Transmission mechanisms in primate cultural evolution. *Trends in Ecology and Evolution* 4, 61–2.

Whiten, A. 1990. Causes and consequences in the evolution of hominid brain size. *Behavioral and Brain Sciences* 13, 367.

Whiten, A. (ed.) 1991. *Natural Theories of Mind: Evolution, Development and Simulation of*

Everyday Mindreading. Oxford: Blackwell.
Whiten, A. & Perner, J. 1991. Fundamental issues in the multidisciplinary study of mindreading. In *Natural Theories of Mind: Evolution, Development and Simulation of Everyday Mindreading*, ed., A. Whiten, pp. 1–18. Oxford: Blackwell.
Wiessner, P. 1983. Style and social information in Kalahari San projectile points. *American Antiquity* 48, 253–57.
Willis, R.G. (ed.) 1990. *Signifying Animals: Human Meaning in the Natural World*. London: Unwin Hyman.
Wills, C. 1994. *The Runaway Brain*. London: HarperCollins.
Winterhalder, B. 1981. Foraging strategies in the boreal environment: an analysis of Cree hunting and gathering. In *Hunter-Gatherer Foraging Strategies: Ethnographic and Archaeological Analyses*, eds., B. Winterhalder & B. Smith, pp. 66–98. Chicago: Chicago University Press.
Wobst, H.M. 1977. Stylistic behavior and information exchange. In *Papers for the Director: Research Essays in Honour of James B. Griffin*, ed., C.E. Cleland, pp. 317–42. Anthropological Papers no. 61, Museum of Anthropology, University of Michigan.
WoldeGabriel, G., White, T.D., Suwa, G., Renne, P., de Heinzelin, J., Hart, W.K. & Heiken, G. 1994. Ecological and temporal placement of early Pliocene hominids at Aramis, Ethiopia. *Nature* 371, 330–33.
Wolpoff, M.H. 1989. The place of Neanderthals in human evolution. In *The Emergence of Modern Humans*, ed., E. Trinkaus, pp. 97–141. Cambridge: Cambridge University Press.
Wolpoff, M.H., Wu, Xinzhi & Thorne, A.G. 1984. Modern *Homo sapien* origins: a general theory of hominid evolution involving the fossil evidence from East Asia. In *Origins of Modern Humans: A World Survey of the Fossil Evidence*, eds., F.H. Smith & F. Spencer, pp. 411–83. New York: Alan R. Liss.
Wood, B. 1992. Origin and evolution of the genus *Homo*. *Nature* 355, 783–90.
Wood, B. 1994. The oldest hominid yet. *Nature* 371, 280–81.
Wood, B. & Turner, A. 1995. Out of Africa and into Asia. *Nature* 378, 239–40.
Wrangham, R.W. 1977. Feeding behaviour of chimpanzees in Gombe National Park, Tanzania. In *Primate Ecology: Studies of Feedings and Ranging Behaviour in Lemurs, Monkeys and Apes*, ed., T.H. Clutton-Brock, pp. 503–78. London: Academic Press.
Wrangham, R.W. 1987. Evolution of social structure. In *Primate Societies*, eds., B.B. Smuts, D.L. Cheney, R.M. Seyfarth, R.W. Wrangham & T.T. Struhsaker. Chicago: Chicago University Press, pp. 342–57.
Wu, Rukang & Lin, Shenglong 1983. Peking Man. *Scientific American* 248, 86–94.
Wymer, J. 1974. Clactonian and Acheulian industries from Britain: their character and significance. *Proceedings of the Geological Association* 85, 391–421.
Wymer, J. 1988. Palaeolithic archaeology and the British Quaternary sequence. *Quaternary Science Reviews* 7, 79–98.
Wynn, T. 1979. The intelligence of later Acheulian hominids. *Man* 14, 371–91.
Wynn, T. 1981. The intelligence of Oldowan hominids. *Journal of Human Evolution* 10, 529–41.
Wynn, T. 1989. *The Evolution of Spatial Competence*. Urbana: University of Illinois Press.
Wynn, T. 1991. Tools, grammar and the archaeology of cognition. *Cambridge Archaeological Journal* 1, 191–206.
Wynn, T. 1993. Two developments in the mind of early *Homo*. *Journal of Anthropological Archaeology* 12, 299–322.
Wynn, T. 1995. Handaxe enigmas. *World Archaeology* 27, 10–23.
Wynn, T. & McGrew, W.C. 1989. An ape's view of the Oldowan. *Man* 24, 383–98.
Wynn, T. & Tierson, F. 1990. Regional comparison of the shapes of later Acheulean handaxes. *American Anthropologist* 92, 73–84.
Yellen, J.E. 1977. *Archaeological Approaches to the Present*. New York: Academic Press.
Yellen, J.E., Brooks, A.S., Cornelissen, E., Mehlman, M.J. & Steward, K. 1995. A Middle Stone Age worked bone industry from Katanda, Upper Semliki Valley, Zaire. *Science* 268, 553–56.
Yen, D.E. 1989. The domestication of the environment. In *Foraging and Farming: The Evolution of Plant Exploitation*, eds., D.R. Harris & G.C. Hillman, pp. 55–78. London: Unwin Hyman.
Yi, S. & Clark, G. 1983. Observations on the Lower Palaeolithic of Northeast Asia. *Current Anthropology* 24, 181–203.
Yost, J.A. & Kelley, P.M. 1983. Shotguns, blowguns and spears: the analysis of technological efficiency. In *Adaptive Responses of Native Amazonians*, eds., R. Hames & W. Vickers, pp. 189–224. New York: Academic Press.
Zhonglong, Q. 1992. The stone industries of *H. sapiens* from China. In *The Evolution and Dispersal of Modern Humans in Asia*, eds., T. Akazawa, K. Aoki & T. Kimura, pp. 363–72. Tokyo: Hokusen-Sha.
Zollikofer, C.P.E., Ponce de Leon, M.S., Martin, R.D. & Stucki, P. 1995. Neanderthal computer skulls. *Nature* 375, 283–84.
Zvelebil, M. 1984. Clues to recent human evolution from specialised technology. *Nature* 307, 314–15.
Zvelebil, M. 1986. Postglacial foraging in the forests of Europe. *Scientific American* (May), 86–93.
Zvelebil, M. 1994. Plant use in the Mesolithic and the transition to farming. *Proceedings of the Prehistoric Society* 60, 35–74.

Illustration credits

Figures

1. Illustration by Steven Mithen using data from Aiello & Dunbar (1993); upper figure modified from Aiello (1996b).
2. Drawing by Margaret Mathews, after Saladin D'Angular (1990).
3. Drawing by Margaret Mathews, after McGrew (1992).
4. Illustration by Margaret Mathews and Steven Mithen.
5. Drawing by Margaret Mathews, modified from Schick & Toth (1993).
6. Illustration by Steven Mithen.
7. Drawing by Aaron Watson.
8. Drawing by Aaron Watson.
9. Drawing by Margaret Mathews, after Jones *et al* (1992).
10. Illustration by Margaret Mathews and Steven Mithen.
11. Drawing by Margaret Mathews.
12. Drawing by Margaret Mathews.
13. Drawing by Aaron Watson.
14. Drawing by Aaron Watson.
15. Illustration by Margaret Mathews and Steven Mithen.
16. Illustration by Margaret Mathews and Steven Mithen.
17. Illustration by Margaret Mathews and Steven Mithen.
18. Drawing by Margaret Mathews, based on a photograph by A. Marshack in *National Geographic* 174 (1988).
19. Drawing by Margaret Mathews, after Delluc & Delluc (1978).
20. Drawing by Margaret Mathews, after Mania, D. & Mania, U. (1988). Deliberate engravings on bone artefacts by *Homo erectus*, *Rock Art Research* 5: 91–107.
21. Drawing by Margaret Mathews, after Breuil (1952).
22. Drawing by Simon S. S. Driver, in Fagan, B. (1990) *Journey from Eden* (London & New York: Thames and Hudson).
23. Drawing by Margaret Mathews, after Bahn & Vertut (1989).
24. Drawing by Margaret Mathews, after Marshack (1991).
25. Illustration by Margaret Mathews and Steven Mithen.
26. Illustration by Margaret Mathews and Steven Mithen.
27. Illustration by Margaret Mathews and Steven Mithen.
28. Drawing by Margaret Mathews, modified from Schick & Toth (1993).
29. Drawing by Margaret Mathews, after Jones *et al* (1992).
30. Drawing by Margaret Mathews, after Jones *et al* (1992).
31. Drawing by Margaret Mathews, after Jones *et al* (1992).
32. Drawing by Margaret Mathews, after Jones *et al* (1992).
33. Illustration by Margaret Mathews and Steven Mithen.
34. Drawing by Margaret Mathews, after Wendorf *et al* (1980).
35. Drawing by Aaron Watson.
36. Drawing by Margaret Mathews, after Piette (1906).

Boxes

p. 14. Illustration by Steven Mithen.
pp. 24–5. Drawings by Margaret Mathews, after Jones *et al* (1992).
pp. 26–7. Drawings by Margaret Mathews, (from top to bottom) quartz flake, after Merrick & Merrick (1976); chopper, after Bordes (1968); pointed handaxe, after Roe (1981); Levallois flake and core, after Bordes (1968); the Clacton-on-Sea 'Spear', after Oakley, K. (1949) *Man the Tool-maker* (London: Trustees of the British Museum (Natural History)); blade core, after Bordes (1968); bone harpoon, after Bordes (1968); the 'Willendorf Venus', after Marshack (1991).
p. 28. Drawing by Margaret Mathews.
p. 29. Drawing by Margaret Mathews.
p. 30. Drawing by Margaret Mathews.
p. 31. Illustration by Steven Mithen, modified from Wood (1993).
p. 32. Illustration by Steven Mithen, after Stringer & Gamble (1993).
p. 67. Illustration by Steven Mithen.
p. 127. Drawings by Margaret Mathews, after Shea (1988) and Oswalt (1973).
p. 158. Drawings by Margaret Mathews, after Morphy (1989) and Leroi-Gourhan (1968).
p. 163. Illustration by Steven Mithen.
p. 166. Illustration by Steven Mithen.
p. 175. Drawing by Margaret Mathews, after Cunliffe (1994).
Box pp. 196–97. Illustration by Steven Mithen.
Box p 198. Illustration by Steven Mithen.

Index

Numerals in italics refer to pages with illustrations

Fridtjof
Nansen Land
Spitsbergen
ARCTIC OCEAN
New Siberian
Islands
Greenland
Sea
Novaya
Zemlya
Kara Sea
North Cape
Barents
Sea
CIRCLE
Iceland
Siberia
Lena
Dvina R.
URAL MTS.
R. Ob
Yenisei River
River
North
Sea
Baltic Sea
EUROPE
Dnieper R.
Volga R.
River
ASIA
Sea of
Okhotsk
Lake
Baikal
Sakhalin
Irtish
R. Danube
ALPS
Black Sea
Caspian Sea
Aral
Sea
Lake Balkhash
Amur
River
Mediterranean Sea
Amu Darya R.
HIMALAYA
MTS.
Hwang-ho
(Yellow R.)
Sea of
Japan
JAPAN
Yangtze Kiang
Brahmaputra
R.
Euphrates R.
Suez
Canal
Indus R.
Ganges R.
Sahara
Desert
Nile
Red Sea
Arabian
Sea
Mekong
Salween R.
South
China
Sea
PACIFIC
Philippine
Islands
Guam
L. Chad
Niger R.
R.
Bay of
Bengal
Irrawaddy River
AFRICA
OCEAN
Ceylon
Gulf of
Guinea
L. Victoria
Sumatra
Borneo
Celebes
New
Guinea
Ascension I.
River
Congo
L. Tanganyika
Lake
Nyasa
INDIAN
Java
Zambesi R.
Madagascar
OCEAN
AUSTRALIA
Orange R.
Cape of Good Hope
Murray R.
Tasmania
ANTARCTIC OCEAN
ANTARCTICA

Lands and Peoples

THE WORLD IN COLOR

VOLUME III

THE GROLIER SOCIETY

NEW YORK TORONTO

M

Volume III

TABLE OF CONTENTS

UNATIONS

SHEPHERD OF CENTRAL GREECE

Only about one-fifth of the soil of Greece can be planted to crops, but the arable land is farmed with skill. Large areas, however, are better suited to the raising of sheep and goats, and there are more sheep and goats in Greece than people. This shepherd with his staff wears the traditional tunic, tight trousers and turned-up slippers with pompons.

THE GREEKS OF TO-DAY

Modern People in a Land of Ancient Culture

The Greek people have the oldest recorded history of the European nations, and the Greek language to-day, though its form has changed in many ways, is obviously the tongue used by Homer, who lived about 1000 B.C. The Greeks, or Hellenes, besides being unequaled in art and literature, were also clever and brave warriors. They were not, however, a united nation, but merely a collection of city-states which combined only in times of stress. It was not until 1832 that, for the first time, this race of ancient culture [illegible]me a united nation. To-day it is a monarchy. Here we shall learn something of modern Greece, with the exception of Athens, which is so important historically as to deserve a separate chapter.

THE very mention of the name Greece brings to our minds that country of long ago in which the best in art and literature was produced. Most of us know little of the Greece of to-day and were we to go there, we should probably neglect the present in order to reconstruct those scenes of long ago.

A map would show us that Greece is a peninsula extending into the Mediterranean at its easternmost end. While the Mediterranean forms its southern boundary, two upraised arms of that great sea, the Ionian Sea and the Ægean Sea, determine its western and eastern limits. To the north are the Balkan countries of Albania, Yugoslavia and Bulgaria.

One will notice that the Grecian peninsula is in two parts and that the southern portion seems to dangle from the mainland by a mere thread of territory, the Isthmus of Corinth. It has really been severed entirely for a canal has been cut through to give trade ships a shorter route.

Although the west coast consists of high mountains with no harbors, the east coast is full of bays and havens for ships. Nearly all the large towns—Athens, the capital and most important city, Piræus, the chief port, and Thessaloniki (Salonica), a thriving town in Macedonia—are on the eastern side of the country. In this respect Greece differs from Italy, whose principal cities, with the exception of Venice, lie on the western coast. The mountain barriers to the west and north and the fine natural harbors on the east made Greece from the very beginning a maritime country. Trade was carried on in the earliest days with the Ægean Islands, with Africa and with Asia, and the contacts thus made with older and more civilized countries had no little influence on the civilization of Greece.

The approach by water to the eastern side of Greece is through the Ægean Archipelago, and the scenery which it presents is unmatched in any other part of the world, for the sea is studded with many islands and groups of islands, varied in shape and size and color, rising out of the purple-blue waters. In ancient days, some of these islands were separate states and commerce as well as warfare was carried on among them.

When the history of Greece opens, many centuries before the birth of Christ, this land was known as Hellas and the people were called Hellenes. Their own explanation of their origin is not unlike our story of Noah and the Ark. Zeus, "father of gods and men," had brought about a flood in order to destroy wicked mankind, but Deucalion and Pyrrha, who had been forewarned, survived this catastrophe. In order to repeople the earth Deucalion and Pyrrha were commanded to throw stones behind them and for each stone Deucalion threw, there sprang up a son and for each one that Pyrrha threw, a daughter. One of the sons was called Hellen and it was from him that the Hellenes or Greeks were descended. Historians believe, however, that tribes of Indo-European origin came down from the north and the east and made this land their home.

These Hellenes did not exist as a nation, but were split up into many little states

BILDARCHIV FOTO MARBURG

RUINS OF THE GREAT AMPHITHEATER AT EPIDAURUS

The ruins above, unearthed by the Greek Archaeological Society, are the outstanding example in existence today of a Greek theater. Although the actors performed on the circular stage that we see far below, this huge theater, built by the famous architect Polyclitus, was so constructed that all the 16,000 spectators, even those seated farthest away, could hear every word of the plays. On the plain beyond the theater is the ruined temple of Esculapius, the god of healing. Invalids flocked here during the yearly festivals in his honor to beseech him for a divine cure.

GREEK INFORMATION OFFICE

THE WHITE TOWER NEAR THE HARBOR OF SALONIKA

Probably dating back two thousand years, the ancient tower still guards the modern port of the second largest city of Greece. Salonika (Thessalonike), in Macedonia, was founded during the fourth century B.C., and St. Paul later found Christian converts there. Today it is an important trading center and seaport of the Aegean and Mediterranean seas.

usually with a city as a centre. The geography of Greece partly explains this lack of unity, since it is divided into small sections by the great mountain ranges, and each of the sections had a ruler, laws and customs of its own. There was little sympathy between the city-states, as we call them, and the record of their relations with each other is one of jealousy, quarrels and wars.

In the fifth century B.C., the Persians, who at that time made up the most powerful nation in all Asia, came to Greece with a mighty army to subject these people. Even the danger of conquest failed to unite the Greeks, for they became allies only to defeat the enemy and immediately after, again went to war among themselves.

The greatest of the city-states was Athens, capital of Attica, which at its zenith was a great sea-power, and the home of literature, of art and of learning—that wonderful culture which we associate with ancient Greece. The story of Athens, however, we shall reserve for the following chapter.

West of Athens was Bœotia with Thebes as its capital and in the extreme south, known as the Peloponnesus, was Sparta, noted for its courageous warriors. So great was the Spartan desire for supremacy that they killed all the babies who did not measure up to their standard of physical fitness and trained the surviving male children in hardship and endurance in preparation for military life. Thus Sparta became a powerful state. These three were the most important although there were over 150 in all, counting the many island states.

Alexander the Great succeeded in conquering the city-states, but even he failed to weld them into a nation. They fought for him and helped him to conquer all the parts of Asia and Africa that were then known. At his death, however, in 323 B.C., his vast empire was broken up and about 200 years later Greece was taken by the mighty Roman Empire. Greece later became a part of the Byzantine or Eastern Roman Empire, whose capital was at Constantinople. This might be called a Greek Empire, for so great was the influence of

BLACK STAR

A GIRL OF THE GREEK VINEYARDS SHOULDERS A LUSCIOUS BURDEN

The most valuable grape of Greece is the currant—not the currant of jams and jellies, but a kind of raisin that takes its name from the Corinth region where it grows in abundance.

ECA

A BUMPER RICE HARVEST WHERE ONCE THERE WERE SALT FLATS

Marshall Plan aid has turned a wasteland into fertile fields near the mouth of the Spercheios south of Lamia. The modern reaper cuts the stalks, husks the kernels and sacks the rice.

UNATIONS

THE TRUSTY MULE, A FAMILY TREASURE IN A MOUNTAINOUS LAND

To market, to church or to the fields, the Greek farmer packs his mule and is off. His slow ride is bumpy, to be sure, but is a safe one without a worry about engine or tires.

SPENDER

SPARTA was once the chief city of the Peloponnese, and its inhabitants were famous throughout Greece as warriors of great fortitude. Even to-day when we wish to pay great tribute to a man's endurance we say that it is Spartan. There are, however, very few traces left of the grandeur of ancient times, and on the hillsides, where stood the greater part of old Sparta, are modern houses, many tall cypress trees and rich orchards. Modern Sparta, built in the early nineteenth century, occupies the southern hills within the walls of the old city.

© UNDERWOOD & UNDERWOOD

THE METEORA MONASTERIES in Thessaly are all perched on the summits of high pillar-like rocks such as this one. They were built in the Middle Ages, when their impregnable positions ensured the safety of the monks, and visitors and provisions were drawn up in a basket lifted by a windlass. At the present, most of them have been abandoned.

BLACK STAR

THE SEVERELY SIMPLE GRAY LIMESTONE PALACE AT ATHENS

The Royal Palace, completed in 1838, is not a beautiful building. But it marks an important turning point in the history of Greece. In 1833, when Athens was selected by the newly established Greek kingdom as the site for its capital, there was nothing here but a few fishermen's huts which stood around the base of the Acropolis with its remnants of ancient glory.

larly on market days, we may still see the native dress—the men in their full short linen kilts, or fustanellas, the women in their beautiful dresses with richly decorated bodices and aprons. It is very pleasant to pay a visit to these people for they are most hospitable and kind and take a great interest in foreigners.

They are, perhaps, seen at their best when at their daily work or enjoying their simple pastimes. How simple their pleasures are is indicated by an ancient custom which still survives at Tenos. This is known as the "evening sitting" and is nothing more than a meeting of groups of people after the day's work is done to listen to the older folk telling stories, which they relate night after night with a gusto that makes them sufficiently exciting to hold the attention of their audience.

The Greeks are very fond of their old customs, and of none more than their ancient dances. These are danced both by the peasants and by the more educated people at the balls in the large towns. In order to preserve these dances at least one or two are performed at the beginning or end of every ball, and in the army and navy only these national dances are permitted.

Birthdays, as we know them here, have little significance in Greece. Their place is taken by what are termed "name days." Most Greeks are called after some patron saint, and when a saint's day comes round all people bearing his name take occasion to celebrate. Friends call and offer presents of flowers and cakes just as we receive presents on our birthdays.

It is interesting to know that the many

TRANS WORLD AIRLINES

COLORFUL GREEK EVZONES GUARD THE ROYAL PALACE IN ATHENS

In a strictly military sense, the evzones are simply riflemen. But their history is as colorful as their uniforms. Traditionally, the members were recruited from the mountains and trained from an early age to be fierce, valiant fighters. They are famous for their heroism and wear with pride the full circular skirts and tufted shoes of their regiment.

© E. N. A

RUINS OF ANCIENT CORINTH, which in olden days was the most prosperous and one of the fairest of Greek cities, dot the slopes beneath the rock of the Acrocorinth or citadel. The seven columns that we see in the centre of the photograph are all that remain of the once splendid temple of Apollo, now surrounded by other ruins. A few miles away there has sprung up a new city of Corinth which, although its trade brings it considerable prosperity, does not enjoy the commercial greatness that belonged to the ancient city visited by St. Paul.

AUTOTYPE CO.

THE TEMPLE OF APOLLO at Corinth, which we saw in the distance on the page opposite, is the most impressive ruin now standing among the remains of that ancient city. Even these seven battered columns, each of which is carved from a solid block of stone, enable us to imagine the splendor of the temple as it originally stood. Situated on the narrow isthmus that joins the Peloponnese peninsula to the Greek mainland, ancient Corinth was the most convenient centre in the Mediterranean for trade from the east and the west.

GREEK WAR RELIEF ASSN., INC.

FARMING—HEARTBREAK STYLE

Agriculture is the principal occupation in Greece, although only about one-fifth of the land is arable, and the civil war reduced even that area temporarily. Modern methods of irrigation will undoubtedly be an important factor in increasing production. The farmer shown above is engaged in the backbreaking task of operating his old-fashioned irrigating apparatus by hand.

THREE LIONS

WOOL MUST BE DRIED GENTLY IF THE YARN IS TO BE STRONG

Modern equipment is difficult to get in Greece, even for those who can afford to buy it. So many farm women dry wool for their homespun clothing in the open air and sunshine.

customs concerning weddings are quite different from those which exist in this country.

A marriage in Greece is often an elaborate affair. The wedding ceremony generally takes place in the home instead of at a church and, in the country districts, it is often preceded and followed by a long series of formalities, which vary in different parts of the country. For instance, in some districts the bride has to observe various customs with regard to the gathering together of the articles required for her future home, and then she retires to the house of her parents, pretends she does not want to be married and resists the efforts of her friends to bring her to a more reasonable frame of mind. She maintains this attitude for as long as is the custom of the district, until finally the bridegroom comes with his relatives and carries her away by "force." Even when she arrives in her own home she is obliged to spend several days performing various ceremonies and giving presents to the relatives and friends who throng around her till the proper time arrives for them to leave her alone with her husband.

BOISSONNAS

VILLAGERS OF ZEMENON, led by priests, walk slowly homewards over the winding hill path in the calm evening. All the women and children are dressed in their holiday clothes—brightly colored dresses and hoods—and one of the men wears the white fustanella or short linen kilt of the Greeks. The bearded priests, who are of peasant stock, are permitted to marry. The curious, tall hat with the brim at the top instead of round the head, worn by the one who is second from the right, is part of the conventional garb of the Greek priests.

BOISSONNAS

NEMEAN PEASANTS drive a team of horses and mules yoked together over the wheat to separate the grain from the ears. Behind them are three pillars, all that remain standing of the famous old temple of Zeus, "ruler of the universe." These peasants may not have heard the legend, but a story runs that a ferocious lion once ravaged the Nemean valley until it was slain by Hercules, who afterwards wore its skin. In ancient times, famous games were held every two years at Nemea, and athletes came from all over Greece to compete in them.

KOSTICH

MENDING NETS IN A SUNNY HARBOR ON RHODES

Sponge divers are mending their nets, while the boats ride high in harbor. In ancient days the trading ships of the Rhodians freely roamed the Mediterranean; and Rhodians founded colonies in Asia Minor, in Sicily, Italy and as far away as Spain. Almost 2,000 years ago the people of Rhodes set up a maritime code that has influenced maritime law down to the present day.

BLACK STAR

A NEW VILLAGE, NEA ARACHOVA, COVERS THE SCARS OF WAR

Marshall Plan aid helped to build the sturdy brick homes of Nea (New) Arachova. The old village, badly damaged during World War II, lies in the shadow of Mount Parnassus, sacred shrine of the Muses, nine goddesses of song and poetry and of the arts and sciences. Farther along the slope of Parnassus are the ruins of Delphi, ancient home of a famous oracle.

The position of women in Greece has, in the past, been an inferior one. Women did most of the work but were limited in their freedom and, even among the upper classes, conversed only among themselves. During recent years this has completely changed, and, although they still maintain control of the home, they have now entered various professions formerly reserved only for men. Today they even compete with men for national office.

In spite of having been a part of the Moslem Turkish Empire for 400 years, the Greeks are Christians but they have many strange customs in connection with their religious festivals. Christmas and New Year's Eve are observed in a quiet manner, but at Epiphany the ceremony of blessing the waters is most unusual. This is especially true at Syra.

The night before the festival boys parade the streets with lanterns, singing

POPOFF

MACEDONIAN WOMEN, appareled in the beautiful dress of their district, suggest the barbaric splendor of Asia rather than the costume of the oldest state in Europe. Heavy embroidery in colors and a profusion of gold thread needlework represent many hours of painstaking effort, but what matters it, if the effect is such as these two women have produced.

CROOK

A WEDDING in Macedonia, a district in northern Greece, is an occasion for much festivity. Both the bride and bridegroom wear gay national costumes and, as a usual thing, the bride waits on the guests at the wedding breakfast as though she were a servant. In this case, she has presented the company with an embroidered handkerchief like the one she is carrying.

religious songs appropriate to the occasion, and early the following morning a service is held in the Church of the Transfiguration. At the conclusion of the service a procession is formed of priests accompanied by men bearing a cross tied with ribbons. They proceed down to the harbor and after the water has been blessed, one of the priests throws the cross into the sea, then numbers of men dive in and struggle for it. The one who secures the cross is regarded as being peculiarly lucky, especially if in the struggle the ribbons have been torn off. A similar ceremony is held at Athens, but, as the cross is only thrown into a reservoir, it naturally lacks the picturesqueness of the scene at Syra.

Easter is a great festival for then besides religious services, there are processions through the streets, houses are illuminated, and in country districts dancing takes place. On Easter Tuesday ancient dances performed by people in national costume are a great feature at Megara, and one of the peculiarities of the festival is that the women decorate themselves with old Turkish coins.

Interesting, indeed, are the monasteries —the Meteora in Thessaly, shown on page 13, and those at Mount Athos occupying the eastern prong of the Chalcidice Peninsula. Women and even female animals are not allowed there, and the monks (numbering nearly 5,000) manage the affairs of the community so efficiently that they have been granted an autonomous government.

We have often heard people describe a place as being "a perfect Arcadia," by which they meant, of course, that it was extremely lovely and quite unspoiled by man. Yet Arcadia is composed of rugged mountains, gloomy defiles and has a severe climate. This is how it came about.

The worship of the god Pan began in Arcadia, and from the hymn which was composed to him we learn that the piping and dancing, the nymphs and rustic gods and the country scene were really connected with early pagan ceremonies. It would appear, then, that the stern mountaineers of Arcadia, who had to fight hard for their living, imagined this beautiful land, and in their worship of Pan sang about the Arcadia for which they longed.

GREECE: FACTS AND FIGURES

THE COUNTRY

A peninsula lying south of the Balkan States; bounded on the north by Albania, Yugoslavia and Bulgaria, on the east by Turkey and the Ægean Sea, on the south by the Mediterranean Sea and on the west by the Ionian Sea. It includes about 220 islands, the largest of which is Crete. The mainland area is 42,427 square miles and the total estimated population is about 7,600,000, including the Dodecanese Islands ceded by Italy.

GOVERNMENT AND CONSTITUTION

A constitutional monarchy headed by King Paul I, who succeeded his brother, George II, in 1947. The years immediately following the end of World War II were followed by turbulent strife as extreme leftists carried on guerrilla warfare to upset the government.

COMMERCE AND INDUSTRIES

Agriculture is the chief industry and the land is largely in the hands of peasant proprietors. The total area, only one-fifth cultivable, is covered with mountains and occupied by lakes and wastelands. The chief crops are tobacco, currants, wheat, corn, barley, oats, olives, grapes, figs and cotton. The leading industrial products are flour, olive oil, textiles. cigarettes, leather, machinery, chemicals and building material. Mineral deposits include lead, salt, lignite, emery and crude magnesite. The chief exports are tobacco, currants, wine and raisins, and the imports are cotton goods, woolens, coal, iron and steel, and machinery.

COMMUNICATIONS

There are 1,668 miles of railway. A canal 4 miles in length has been cut across the Isthmus of Corinth. Telegraph lines are 15,065 miles in length; telephone lines, 36,914 miles.

RELIGION AND EDUCATION

Greek Orthodox is the state religion but liberty is granted other sects. Education is compulsory between 7 and 12 years but attendance is not well enforced in the country. There are trade, agricultural and technical schools. Athens is well supplied with schools and has six of university rank, including the National University. There is also a university at Thessaloniki. The Ministry of Education has charge of the Service of Antiquities.

CHIEF TOWNS

Athens, capital, 1,130,591; Piraeus, 184,980; Thessaloniki (Salonika), 216,838; Patras, 88,-414; Rhodos, 55,181; Kavalla, 42,250.

WHERE BEAUTY REIGNS IN RUINS

Athens and Its Vestiges of a Glorious Past

In ancient times Athens was the most famous of the cities of Greece. To-day it is the capital of the modern state that bears the ancient name of Greece, but its glory lies mainly in the past. From the marble ruins of the Parthenon, which crowns the Acropolis hill, we look down upon the buildings of the modern city and sigh for the beauty that has been lost to the world in the destruction of the ancient buildings of Athens. Yet lovers of art and students of history will find in the city a source of endless joy. Even the ordinary visitor can hardly fail to be fascinated by this pleasant city and its fine situation, which has been said to rival that of Naples.

WE could, if we so desired, approach Athens by train. We should jolt into a vast modern station at the end of our journey in so commonplace a manner that it would be exceedingly difficult to believe ourselves actually in the famous city whose history is as glorious as that of the greatest empire. But let us rather make part of the journey in a steamer, which we shall imagine is now churning through the bright blue waters of the Saronic Gulf. We pass a tiny green islet crowned with the ruins of an ancient temple. Beyond is Mount Hymettus whence, long ago, honey was brought to the Athenian market—honey so fragrant that poets wrote in praise of it.

Let us keep our eyes fixed on the land for presently we see in the distance, across dull green trees, the ivory-tinted pillars of the Parthenon standing on the huge flat rock of the Acropolis. At its base are the white buildings of the modern city of Athens. Before long, our ship is in the harbor of the Piræus, the port of Athens, and we are ready to disembark.

Much that we see is modern and familiar. There are steamboats and tugs, wharves and warehouses, for the Piræus is itself a large and bustling town. Many of the ships moored to the quays are small, gaudily painted boats with large sails. These remind us that, in about 500 B.C., ships of much the same type traded with the Piræus, for even at that time it was the port of Athens.

But we cannot delay any longer by the waterside, for a train is waiting to take us to Athens—a distance of about five miles. In the ancient days, these two cities were connected by massive walls, 16 feet wide and 30 feet high, running along each side of the road. Portions of them could now be seen if we were to go by motor or carriage along the beautiful boulevard lined with pepper trees, but if we did so we might be smothered in the dust that lies thick everywhere. Before we have been many days in Athens we shall have had enough experience of dust, and shall realize why there are so many prosperous bootblacks plying their trade in the streets.

The modern Athenians are not very different in appearance from the inhabitants of any other great city of western or southern Europe. Their clothes are lighter, of course, and their hats are generally broad-brimmed. But the short, voluminous kilts that constitute the Greek national dress (see page 42) are not commonly worn by the Athenian men, except perhaps on feast days and by some soldiers, for whom they are part of the regimental uniform. A fez may be seen occasionally and serves to remind us that we are on the threshold of the Near East. So do the many street merchants who try to sell us sweetmeats, flowers and an endless variety of cheap wares.

This Oriental atmosphere is especially noticeable in the meaner streets. Here we may see tinsmiths, cobblers and blacksmiths at work in their booths or in the open air. Cookshops abound, and we see that the food is often prepared in the streets. These establishments are very popular, and when a Greek from some country district visits Athens, he does not

© E. N. A.

HADRIAN'S ARCH stands close to Amalia Boulevard and was built by the Roman Emperor Hadrian, who did much to beautify Athens. He added a new quarter to the city which was named Hadrianapolis (City of Hadrian) and at the entrance stood this arch. The second story or "attica" was formerly filled with thin marble slabs which have long since disappeared.

© E. N. A.

GRACEFUL FIGURES support the roof of a portico on the south wall of the Erechtheum, a building constructed in the 5th century before Christ, which contained among other things the shrine of the guardian goddess of Athens—Athena Polias. The Erechtheum has since been put to many and varied uses, including a Christian church and a Turkish harem.

EUROPEAN

MODERN ATHENS AND LOFTY LYCABETTUS FROM THE STADIUM

The white marble stadium and its colonnade, built in the classical style in the nineteenth century, add a touch of old Athens to a panorama of the new city's parks and buildings.

TRANS WORLD AIRLINES

THE LIGHT BOATS OF FISHERMEN IN THE HARBOR OF PIRAEUS

Five miles from Athens is the ancient port of Piraeus, the capital's outlet to the sea. Precious little of the classical past remains in this thriving center of industry and trade.

THREE LIONS

FOR THE ENRICHMENT OF THE PRESENT—THE ART OF THE PAST

The Academy of Art and Science in Athens is a re-creation of ancient building styles. Its marble is from the same source—the Pentelic quarries—as the stones of the Parthenon.

THE ACROPOLIS, or Citadel Hill, dominating the surrounding plain made an ideal spot to the early Greeks for building temples to their deities. In the centre background is the Parthenon, dedicated to Athena with Mount Lycabettus at its right, while to the left is the Temple of Erechtheus. Farther to the left is the Propylæa, which was the ceremonial approach

© E. N. A.

to these temples. Beneath the Acropolis are the ruins of the Odeum, or Concert Hall, where Athenian playgoers gathered to witness dramatic performances. In the building, erected by Herodes Atticus, a wealthy Athenian, the seats rose in semi-circles up the side of the Acropolis, giving accommodation to 5,000 spectators.

BLACK STAR

ATHENS, MOTHER CITY OF GREECE, REFLECTS A GLORIOUS PAST

Modern Athens spreads out in a jumble between the Acropolis, heart of the ancient city, and Lycabettus, the nine-hundred-foot summit that looms up in the background.

EWING GALLOWAY

GENNADIUS LIBRARY, AT THE CENTER FOR AMERICAN STUDIES OF GREEK ARCHAEOLOGY AND CIVILIZATION

At the foot of Mount Lycabettus and facing Speusippus Street, in Athens, is the library of the American School for Classical Studies. The ground on which the beautiful building stands was donated by the Greek Government. Completed in 1926, the gracious structure was made possible by contributions from America. Its most striking feature is the slender columns with Ionic capitals. Within the library there is a valuable collection of rare manuscripts relating to the Byzantine Empire and to ancient and modern Greece, the gift of Dr. and Mrs. Johannes Gennadius.

© E. N. A.

THE PROPYLÆA, viewed from the northwest, seem to command the Acropolis. On the right, standing on a bastion flanking these imposing and stately ruins, is the temple of Athena Nike. Its date is uncertain but it was reconstructed in 1835 with the fragments of the original building. Like the Propylæa it is of Pentelic marble, and the sculptured frieze depicts a council of the gods. The Propylæa were begun in 437 B. C. on the foundations of an older gateway and are composed of a series of vestibules and doorways, which gave entrance to the Acropolis.

© E. N. A.

AROUND THE PARTHENON, lie shattered columns and weather-worn stones, each of which could tell a romantic story of the vanished glory of ancient Athens. In the central aisle of the Parthenon is a space paved with dark-colored stone, on which formerly stood a famous gold and ivory statue of Athena of colossal proportions, probably designed by Phidias.

usually stay at a hotel, but at a rooming house that supplies him only with sleeping accommodation, for he prefers to buy his meals at the eating place that looks the most attractive.

In the more prosperous districts there are splendid stores and handsome offices, apartments and mansions. The streets are lined with trees unfamiliar to us, and there is an abundance of excellent cafés. To them the Athenians flock to discuss the latest political news and to argue interminably over affairs of state. It is this love of arguing and freedom of speech that has much to do with the political unrest in Greece.

As might be expected in a city so full of remains of the past, there are exceedingly interesting collections of antiquities in Athens. Many glorious works of art are to be seen in the Acropolis Museum, which has a collection of sculptures found on the Acropolis, and the National Archæological Museum is a vast treasure-house of all that throws light upon the ancient history of Greece. These ancient monuments are kept in repair by a special department of the Greek government while institutions supported by the French, Americans, British, Italians, Germans and Austrians aid in archæological research so that we are coming to know more and more about the ancient Greeks and their culture.

It must not be thought that where learning is concerned Athens is always looking back to vanished glories. It is not only the capital of Greece and the seat of government, but it is also the national center of learning. There are six schools of university standing which provide for advanced education and there are numerous schools for special training. A walk along University Street will soon

EWING GALLOWAY

IMPRESSIVE REMAINS OF THE SHRINE OF THE DELPHIC ORACLE

In a grotto nearby the oracle sat upon her tripod stool. When asked for advice, she stroked a laurel branch, inhaled a vapor and chanted messages inspired by the god Apollo.

EWING GALLOWAY

THE THESEION, STAINED BY WEATHER AND AGE TO A GOLDEN HUE

On a small rise north of the Areopagus, meeting place of the ancient court of Athens, the Theseion stands out as a reminder of the architectural genius of the Greeks. Like the Parthenon, it is in the Doric style and its beautiful marble is from the Pentelic quarries.

convince us that the modern Athenians have a love for culture and are certainly progressive.

Their good taste, too, is shown in the architecture of the Academy of Science—a really noble building of classical plan, faced with gleaming white Pentelic marble such as was used in the ancient buildings. This institution does all in its power to encourage scientific studies in Greece. Another imposing building, constructed on the same lines, is the well-equipped National Library which has a very fine reading-room. Very different in outward appearance, however, is the University, which is gaudy in the bright sunlight and not at all in harmony with its surroundings.

Some of the schoolboys are educated for the Church, and these we easily recognize, for they look very like young monks. Their hair is long but is usually bunched under their hats.

As we stroll past the schools and colleges of modern Athens, we remember that the city was famous for its learning more than four hundred years before Christ. Here the great philosopher, Socrates, taught. Here, too, his most famous pupil, Plato, also a teacher of philosophy and one of the most profound thinkers that the world has known, established his school, the Academy, early in the fourth century B.C.

But the history of Athens is not altogether a record of peace and the advance of enlightenment. Time has not been the only destroyer of the splendors of ancient days. The Persians took and sacked the city in 479 B.C., but they were driven out, never to return to Greek soil. As a protection from further invasions, the Athenians built strong walls about the city and then proceeded to construct new buildings. Many of the fine temples, which we can see in ruins to-day, were erected. Pericles was then the head of the Athenian state and this period (445 B.C. to 431 B.C.) has come to be known as the Golden Age, for he did all in his power to make Athens

© E. N. A.

FROM THE PARTHENON, the Temple of Athena, which is situated upon the summit of the Acropolis, we can look down upon modern Athens. The temple was built between 447 and 438 B. C., and is the most perfect monument of ancient Greek art. It remained almost intact until 1687, when it was seriously damaged by the explosion of a powder magazine.

the intellectual leader of the city-states. The other states were jealous and this brought about the Peloponnesian Wars which resulted in the defeat of Athens. Although Athens was occupied by the Romans after their conquest of Greece in 146 B.C., they did not prove destructive. It was after the capture of the city by the Turks in 1458 that most damage was done, much of it, regrettably, by Greek guns. In 1833, when Athens became the capital of united Greece it was little more than a hamlet standing amid glorious ruins. Despite all that has been done in modern times to make Athens a great city, these remains are still its most impressive feature. Let us climb the Acropolis to the Parthenon, a ruined temple of the goddess Athena. We can easily imagine how majestic it must have been when it was unstained by the weather and gleamed with painted decorations, when all its carvings were perfect and its pillars of marble were white and unchipped and when, above all, the huge ivory and gold statue of the goddess stood in its place.

Marvels of Artistic Craftsmanship

But the statue is gone. Much of the sculpture has been broken or removed to museums, and the pillars have suffered from bombardments. Yet even to-day the plan of the building, the height and symmetry of its columns and the power and beauty of such of its reliefs as remain, convey an impression of incomparable magnificence. It is a most inspiring illustration of the spirit of ancient Athens.

The Parthenon was the holiest shrine in the city, but not by any means the only splendid one. On the Acropolis are also the remains of the Erechtheum, a very wonderful temple containing beautiful statuary; and to the south of the Propylæa, which was the ceremonial approach to the Acropolis, is an exquisite ruined temple to Athena Nike.

From the hill we can see the Theseum, which is probably the best preserved ancient temple in all Greece. Its form shows that the Theseum was planned by an architect of great genius whose every thought was concentrated upon making the building a masterpiece of art. Great sculptors executed the vivid carvings that adorn it, and each one of the craftsmen, too, who labored on its marble pillars, now shining like gold in the sunlight, must have been something of an artist. Altogether, if we are willing to learn, the Theseum can teach us more about Greek art in a day than all the textbooks that were ever written, for it is the result of an endeavor to erect a temple whose every detail should be ideally beautiful.

Remains That Tell of Greek Life

From the Acropolis we also notice the fifteen tall columns of the temple of the Olympian Zeus that are still standing. It is later in date than the Parthenon or the Theseum, which are almost contemporary, and it was one of the largest Greek temples ever built. According to a legend, it stands on the spot where the waters of the Flood disappeared into the earth.

Other remains tell us something of the different aspects of ancient Athenian life. There is the Stadium, for example, in which athletic contests were held. It is interesting to remember that it was here that the Olympic games were held when they were revived in 1896. But, however popular the sports in the Stadium might be with the people of Athens, they were not nearly so important as the performances in the theatres.

Two Theatres of Ancient Athens

The modern Athenian, like most other people, goes to see plays mainly for amusement; in ancient Athens, however, as in all Greek states, the drama had a religious significance. Plays were acted in honor of the god Dionysus, and this explains why the greatest theatre of ancient Athens is named the Dionysiac.

It lies at the base of the Acropolis and we can still survey the ruined stage and vast, semicircular "orchestra" from one of the many tiers of seats, although these date from Roman times. They are of limestone—except the seats of honor, which are of marble, richly carved. Here throngs of eager citizens watched the famous tragedies of Æschylus, Sophocles

THREE LIONS

TANGERINES SPREAD UPON PALM LEAVES TO TEMPT THE PASSER-BY

A wrinkled fruit vendor of Greece waits patiently at the edge of the curb for customers to purchase his freshly picked and juicy merchandise. Tangerines are also called mandarins.

TRANS WORLD AIRLINES

THE ANCIENT TEMPLE OF ATHENA STILL RISES ABOVE ATHENS

The marble columns of the beautiful Parthenon high on the Acropolis once sheltered a huge statue of the mythical goddess. Modern Athens has widened out from the base of its famous hill.

and Euripides, now enjoyed throughout the civilized world, when they were performed for the first time. We may visit another immense theater, too, the marble-built Odeum. This was erected at a much later period (160 A.D.) by a wealthy friend of Hadrian, Herodes Atticus, in memory of his wife.

As we walk about the city we pass the Tower of the Winds, where observations of the weather were made in ancient days. Not far away is the site of the Inner Kerameikos, or Agora, where Athenian municipal affairs and much business were transacted. Beyond it, again, is the Street of the Tombs, once lined from end to end with monuments to the dead. Some magnificent examples still stand today, but alas! how few. Here we will leave Athens with the thought that if these commemorate private individuals, the city itself might be considered as one vast monument commemorating all the forgotten Athenians, by whose aid so much beauty was created. Modern Athens, with a situation that rivals even that of Naples on its famous bay, is truly charming. We cannot fail to enjoy, too, the unaffected manners and real hospitality of the true Athenian, but when we think of this Greek city it is to the wonderful Athens of old and to its people that our thoughts turn.

THREE LIONS

PRESENT-DAY GREECE IS ACUTELY INTERESTED IN ITS OWN PAST

Broken fragments of statues and buildings, excavated from the surrounding countryside, are brought to a workshop in Athens to be carefully studied and, if possible, restored.

ALBANIA AND ITS MOUNTAINEERS

The Land of the Eagle People

Albania is a rocky country with narrow valleys, volcanic mountains in the south and coastal plains in the west. The rivers are short and the roads are few and poor. The Mediterranean climate and the soil are suitable for farming but modern methods are unknown and production is low and uncertain. Poor transportation and ancient methods have also prevented the profitable use of Albania's mineral wealth. Only through outside help has the little country been able to make anything at all approaching a decent livelihood from her resources. But this foreign aid—from Italy before World War II and from the Soviet Union since—has meant more profit to the outsider than to the Albanians and has led to a loss of independence.

SUPPOSE we plan to take a trip to Albania—the little slice of country that occupies a portion of the territory along the eastern coast of the Adriatic Sea. We shall find it interesting especially if we like to explore places little known, for Albania is not a mecca for tourists. Lack of railroads, lack of conveniences and the many mountain feuds scarcely make it attractive to those bent on sight-seeing, but we shall suppose that its difficulties make it all the more alluring to us and we set sail from Italy across the blue Adriatic.

Albania, or Shqypnië, as the map will show us, is an oblong country with many rugged mountains, especially in the northern part. Some of the peaks of the Prokletia, or Accursed Mountains, reach over 7,000 feet in height, and the scenery is equal in beauty to any in Europe. These, as well as the mountains of the east, form a natural frontier between Albania and its neighbors, Yugoslavia and Greece. There are mountains, too, in the south, though not so high or so continuous as those of the north. In the centre is a plain, while the coast is bare and rocky alternating with marshy plains. Rivers, few in number, rise in the mountains and flow toward the sea, but of these the only one navigable is the Boyana (or Bojana) which connects Lake Scutari with the Adriatic.

Dividing Albania almost in two parts is the river Shqumb which seems to separate it also in climate and people. North of it, the winters are colder and the land less cultivable. The people have become hardier, sterner, and different in temperament from those in the south. They call themselves Ghegs. The climate of southern Albania resembles that of the south of Italy, and the people living there, called Tosks, are lively, talkative and affable. These people differ too in the manner of dress for the Tosks still wear the fusta-

COUNTRY HOUSE BUILT FOR DEFENSE

Albania has ever been a land of brigands, and these and the inconveniences of the family feud have made it necessary that remote houses among the hills shall resemble fortresses.

Black Star

A DASHING YOUNG MAN OF ALBANIA

With his ornaments, braid-trimmed vest and plaid sash, he is ready to make merry at a wedding festival. Albanian men used to wear red fezzes; but since being freed from Turkish rule, they wear white ones.

nella, or pleated white linen skirt, while the Ghegs usually wear trousers. Both, however, are seen wearing the Moslem fez.

Except for Durrës (Durazzo), which is being fully equipped, the harbors of Albania have been little developed. There is one railroad, twenty-two miles long, which connects Tirana, the capital, with Durrës. Passable roads link the few towns. However, in many places transportation is still by means of pack ponies and donkeys, especially in the mountains to the north. There are ten regular air routes in service.

It is, indeed, strange that the Albanians, or Eagle People, as they like to call themselves, should be more backward than any other Europeans, for they are one of the oldest peoples on that continent. So early was their beginning that history and even legend does not tell when they arrived in the Balkan Peninsula. They are thought to be descendants of the earliest Aryan immigrants whom the ancient Greeks described as barbarous since they were non-Hellenic. They were a tribal people, and the succession of invaders who swept over the land subdued some, while other tribes, taking protection in the mountains, were able to resist.

This territory was part of the Roman Empire when in the fourth century A.D. that great empire was divided. Albania was then assigned to the Eastern or Byzantine Empire, the capital of which was in far-away Constantinople. There followed a period of invasions during which Goths, Slavs, Bulgars and Sicilians came but left few marks of their influence. Through it all, the Albanian people have remained Albanians and have retained their own language, customs and manners. In the fifteenth century, there was a brief period of native rule under Scanderbeg (George Castriota) who became lord of Albania and who to this day is their national hero. When he died, there was no one to take his place, and his country was bequeathed to the Venetians who, it was hoped, would hold back the Turks then pushing further and further into Europe. The Venetians failed. Albania was conquered by the Turks and was held until 1912 as a province of the Ottoman Empire. Because of its distance from Constantinople and the fact that most of the people accepted (at least in name) the Mohammedan religion, Turkey paid little attention to the Albanians. As a mark of favor, many of them were taken into the Turkish army and a few of them, such as Mehemet Ali who became famous as a

BLACK STAR

WEATHER-WORN CHURCH OF THE GREEK ORTHODOX FAITH

The tile roof and heavy stone walls, so typical of the Mediterranean region, offer protection against the hot summer sun; and the interior offers comfort to the followers of the Eastern Greek Church. The building has a look of repose and quiet endurance though it shows the scars of centuries. A rather unusual feature is the many-sided tower that crowns the top.

Black Star

WHERE OLD AND NEW MINGLE, IN ALBANIA'S CAPITAL

Looking down this street in Tirana, the telegraph poles almost hide the old mosque, but you can see its slender minaret from which faithful Moslems are called to prayer. In many ways Tirana has the appearance of an ancient Moslem city. However, the street is well paved; and the buildings at the left, with their graceful, decorative balconies, are new.

viceroy of Egypt, made places for themselves in the history of Turkey or of Turkey's vast dominions.

During this period of Turkish domination the people were slowly developing a national feeling which did not make itself felt very strongly until the whole northern part of the country blazed out in revolt. For three years, from 1909–12, they fought for their freedom, and finally proclaimed their independence. They were recognized by the European powers. Having no outstanding person for a ruler, the place was offered to Prince William of Wied who had held his regal position for a few months only when World War I broke out and he was forced to take refuge in another country. Albania, then, with no one at its head, fell into a state of anarchy, and at the same time several contending armies were making use of the land as a battleground. The Albanians fought on both sides with equal enthusiasm, for they were concerned more with the actual fighting than with the interests involved. The end of the war saw them with an independent country but it also saw their land desolated. The process of reconstructing their villages and endeavoring to make the soil produce sufficient food

THREE LIONS

TAKING A MOMENT OF REST OUT OF LONG HOURS OF TOIL

Workmen relax on top of a load of produce they have been handling. In the background forest-clad mountains come down to meet the waters of Valona harbor, on the Adriatic Sea.

BLACK STAR

CARRYING THE DAY'S PURCHASES HOME FROM THE MARKET

The sure-footed donkey is a highly valuable means of transportation in Mediterranean countries where streets are roughly paved and often too steep or narrow for any wheeled vehicle.

for their needs is occupying them even today.

The people have never produced a surplus of food. In fact, each family usually looks after its own needs, as most of them are engaged in agriculture of a primitive sort. It is the women who do most of the work, such as getting the firewood, carrying water, weaving, cooking and taking the small surplus to market.

The regard for women is higher than in most Mohammedan countries. A woman is safe in every way from the clans with which her family may be at feud, and safety is even accorded a man who may be accompanying her. In the country districts they often go unveiled, and some of them are very good to look upon. They are also much brighter and quicker witted than most Moslem women. Those who can afford it adorn themselves with embroidery and gold braid. Their apparel, like that of the women in most Mohammedan countries, consists of pantaloons (of silk if possible), which are gathered in at the ankles with gold-embroidered ankle bands. With these is worn a blouse made with wide flowing sleeves, and this costume is further embellished by a jacket or bolero richly embroidered in gold thread and studded with imitation stones. Some of the embroidery which comes from Albania is very fine. Most of it is used at home, however, and very little ever reaches the world's markets.

A marriage in Albania is an interesting event. Children are betrothed when very young and marry as early as thirteen years. On the day of the wedding the bride, in apparent protest, is taken screaming and struggling from her father's house, and is carried by her brothers to the husband's family, who come to meet them at a place between the lands of the two tribes.

SOVFOTO

ALBANIAN FARM GIRLS GATHER A CROP OF WARM-CLIMATE MELONS

The mountains in the background show how rough and rugged the terrain of the little Mediterranean country is. Only a small portion of Albania's land can be used for crops and pasturage.

BLACK STAR

REFRESHING PAUSE IN THE DAY'S OCCUPATIONS

A street vendor gives two Albanian workmen an opportunity for a brief respite. From his rough cart, he is dispensing what appears to be milk and bread—energy-giving foods anywhere.

It is not the custom for two people within the tribe to marry. On arriving at her husband's house, she takes a place in the corner and stands for three days and nights with her hands folded on her breast, her eyes downcast and without food or drink. In this way, the bride is a suppliant for the gift of fire, of life and of the mystery that continues the race. For six months, she must obey the commands of her elders and speak only when addressed and then some day when it is convenient she and her husband will go to the priest to be married.

A birth is none the less interesting for some ancient customs are still in use—customs that may be two thousand years old. When a child is born, cakes made of a mixture of flour, water and olive oil are fried and sent to the relatives and friends. Then etiquette requires that the relatives must call within three days. On the third day a banquet is given and presents are brought to the mother. According to a legend, on the third night after the child is born, three fairies appear carrying with them the skein of fate. The first spins the thread, the second measures it off on the spinning-wheel and the third cuts the thread with the scissors. Thus the destiny of the child is determined.

Due to the influence of the Turks, many of the Albanians, as we have said, became Moslems. Now about two-thirds of them call themselves Moslems, although they are not very strict about their religion, and have a tolerance for the Christians, as the Christians have for them, that is not found elsewhere—certainly not in the Near East. One will find the Christians using a prayer rug, and Moslems observing Roman Catholic feast days. But the Albanian is first of all an Albanian and no religion interferes with his own standard of right and wrong. Taking revenge when revenge is due is a matter of necessity to an Albanian,

SOVFOTO

"LIQUID GOLD" GUSHES FROM A PIPE IN AN OIL FIELD

The mountainous little Balkan country has been able to produce enough petroleum for its own use in recent years. There is a pipeline from its principal fields to the seaport of Valona.

and this has often brought about feuds among the various tribes.

In the old days Albania had a peculiar legal system called "the law of Lek." Lek was a fifteenth-century tribal chieftain who wrote down the unwritten laws of his people. The law of Lek placed great emphasis on the virtues of hospitality and of keeping one's promised word. Most of the law, however, was concerned with rules for conducting the feuds. By a certain kind of pledge, for instance, some persons were granted protection during the quarrels. This applied especially to boys under sixteen years of age and to women. A man accompanied by a woman would be safe.

Up until the early 1900's, the beys (Turkish governors) were the aristocrats of Albania. They lived in the hills in feudal splendor. King Zog, who reigned from 1928 until 1939, was the only Albanian monarch the country ever had.

The Albanian language, which has survived so many centuries, has ever been a puzzle to philologists. Unlike the Greek or Slav of the neighboring countries, it is thought to have come from the primitive Illyrian, the language of Macedonia in the time of Alexander the Great. All attempts of the Serb, Greek and Turk have failed to destroy the Albanians' love for it. Once, in southern Albania, where some of the people are Greek Orthodox Christians, the priests taught that it was useless to pray in Albanian for God could not understand it. The Turks forbade giving instruction or printing books in the language but books were printed abroad and smuggled in.

What education the people had was chiefly gained in the schools started by the

SOVFOTO

A JEEPLIKE TRUCK RECEIVES CARGO FROM A COASTAL STEAMER

The ship is docked at Durazzo, Albania's chief port, which is on the north shore of the Gulf of Durazzo, a little arm of the Adriatic. Most of the city's trade is with ports of other Balkan countries—offering olive oil, grains and tobacco in exchange for manufactured articles. Durazzo has a beautiful location, on a rocky promontory just south of Mount Durazzo.

BLACK STAR

ON A COBBLE-STONED SQUARE IN TIRANA

Once the red fez was the national headdress of the Turks and some other Moslem peoples. Since the 1920's its use has declined, but it is still to be seen in Albania. This family group (both husband and wife in baggy trousers) is perhaps from the country, spending a day in Tirana, the capital. At the right of the picture are arches of a famous old covered well.

Austrians and the Italians, each of whom had an eye to annexing the territory. Students who could afford it were sent away to Vienna or Paris or to the American School in Constantinople for advanced training but a vast majority of the people were totally illiterate. In the few years following her independence Albania set up several hundred primary and a few secondary schools. Primary education was free and compulsory, but there were not enough schools for the people within the age limits and the law was not enforced.

Albania's industries are little developed, each family generally providing for its own needs. Cattle-raising is the most important activity, and receives special attention. In the mountain pastures, goats and sheep graze. The chief dairy product is cheese. It is a staple of diet and an item of export. Tobacco is grown in sufficient quantity for shipment abroad.

Mineral resources, excepting oil, have been largely neglected. But Albanian crude-oil production was the sixth highest in Europe before 1940.

Between the two world wars, Italy had a strong influence on affairs in Albania. Italian businessmen built up the petroleum industry and financed other plans. But Italy wanted mostly to rule the Balkans. In 1939 she invaded Albania as a first step in this direction. For five years thereafter Albania was occupied by either the Italian or the German army.

After liberation in 1944, the new Communist Government turned to Yugoslavia for the help that Albania once had received from Italy. In 1948, however, when Yugoslavia broke with the Cominform (Stalin's international propaganda organization), Albania chose to side with Russia and abandon her treaties with Yugoslavia. As a result, Albania has been in a precarious position. Though dominated by Russia, she is outside the iron curtain and cut off from sources of food and raw materials.

ALBANIA: FACTS AND FIGURES

THE COUNTRY

A communist republic since the end of World War II, Albania is bounded on the north and east by Yugoslavia, on the east and south by Greece and on the west by the Strait of Otranto, the Adriatic Sea and Yugoslavia. The area of the country is 10,629 square miles, and the latest estimate of the population is 1,175,000.

GOVERNMENT

For centuries a semifeudal state under Turkish rule, Albania proclaimed its independence in 1913 and was a principality or aristocratic republic from then until 1928, when the President made himself King Zog I. His government included an elected chamber and a Cabinet. Zog was driven out by Italian invasion in 1939, when the King of Italy became King of Albania. German occupation replaced Italian in 1943, and a regency was set up. Albania was proclaimed a republic in 1946, and an all-communist Government fashioned a Soviet-type Constitution.

COMMERCE AND INDUSTRIES

Before World War II, the country had but 10% of its land under cultivation; animal husbandry was the principal industry. Number of livestock—mostly sheep and goats—is nearly 3,000,000. Principal crops are corn and wheat. Like other East European communist countries Albania has emphasized the development of manufacturing. The Government claims large postwar increases in the production of food, textiles, leather footwear, building materials, tobacco, chemicals and electric power. Considerable mineral resources include deposits of copper, oil, chromite, bitumen and salt. Trade with Italy, Yugoslavia and Great Britain, once considerable, has virtually stopped as a result of Albania's close ties with the Soviet Union.

COMMUNICATIONS

There are motor roads connecting all the principal towns, and three railroads have been built since the end of World War II. Communications in the mountainous interior are primitive. Principal and most modern port is Durrës (Durazzo). There are 7 radio transmitters (state owned) and 12 daily newspapers.

RELIGION AND EDUCATION

About 70% of the people are Moslems, 20% Orthodox Catholic and 10% Roman Catholic. Clergy and church leaders have been forced to submit to state control. Adult education is encouraged as part of state effort to reduce illiteracy; 10% to 20% of the people are now literate. There are about 2,200 elementary schools as well as secondary, teacher training, medical, trade, agricultural, art and technical schools.

CHIEF TOWNS

Tirana, the capital, has a population of 64,000; Scutari, 35,000; Koritsa, 25,000; Elbasan, 17,000; Durazzo, 16,000; Valona, 16,000; Berat, 13,000; Argyrokastron, 12,000.

THE FOLK OF YUGOSLAVIA

Among the Serbs, Croats and Slovenes

Yugoslavia (sometimes spelled Jugo-Slavia) is a Balkan state that was created at the end of World War I by uniting Montenegro and portions of the old Austro-Hungarian Empire with the kingdom of Serbia. Most of the inhabitants of this mountainous region are Southern Slavs, but in the northern regions there is a large number of Germans and Hungarians. Perhaps the most interesting people are the inhabitants of Montenegro, the Black Mountain. Montenegrins are Serbian highlanders who successfully resisted the Turks for five centuries while peoples around them were subdued by the fierce conqueror. In this chapter we shall read about these proud mountaineers and the other inhabitants of Yugoslavia and of this country which faces the Adriatic, stretching from Albania to the Alps.

YUGOSLAVIA, the land of the Southern Slavs, is made up of several countries and peoples. It includes Croatia, a part of the region known as Macedonia and also Slavonia, Bosnia, Herzegovina, Dalmatia, Slovenia, Serbia and Montenegro. This varied country was formerly called the kingdom of the Serbs, Croats and Slovenes, all of whom, racially, are Slavs, and it was created at the end of World War I by uniting Montenegro and part of the former Austro-Hungarian Empire with the old kingdom of Serbia.

Montenegro, formerly an independent kingdom, is the most interesting part of Yugoslavia, and its people are renowned for their bravery and love of independence throughout the whole world. Surrounded by powerful enemies, only the excessively mountainous nature of their country and their own courage have preserved the independence of the Montenegrins.

Let us imagine a land consisting almost entirely of naked rock with rugged mountains stretching as far as it is possible to see, a land hot in summer and bitterly cold in winter—that is Montenegro, the Black Mountain. It is difficult to believe that people can dwell amid such desolation, yet a splendid and freedom loving race has made this barren land its home.

After the Turks had defeated the Serbians at Kossovo, 1389, the Montenegrins retired to the mountains and became an independent people. The Mohammedan Turks at that time had a vast empire in Asia, but not content with this, they sought to conquer Europe. They swept through what is now Albania, Bulgaria, Rumania and Serbia, and then, confident of victory, sent an army to conquer the people of the Black Mountain.

The Montenegrins had to withdraw from the fertile land about Lake Scutari and, retreating into the mountains, founded their capital on the plain of Cetigne, or Cetinje. The Turks soon marched after them, but behind every rock stood a Montenegrin ready to shed his blood for his country. Charge after charge was repulsed, and regiment after regiment of Turks had to admit humiliating defeat.

There were large numbers of Turks to every Montenegrin but in spite of overwhelming odds, Montenegro was never conquered. For five centuries these two nations fought till at last the gallant and undefeated Montenegrins were protected from Turkey by the principal European powers. Thus, this little nation came about, and so it is no wonder that to-day the men walk with the proud step of conquerors. They are fine looking, too, as many of them are very tall, often exceeding six feet.

The Montenegrin gentleman wears a gorgeous and picturesque costume. A brightly colored coat hangs from shoulder to knee, and is open in front to display a beautifully embroidered waistcoat and baggy breeches tucked into high, Russian boots. A scarf encircles his waist, and in it are stuck a revolver and a whole armory of knives. Upon his head is worn a "kapa," or cap, of black with a crimson

HOLBACH

THE NARENTA VALLEY is one of Bosnia's most beautiful districts. Sometimes it narrows to a deep gloomy ravine, but often, as here, near Jablonica, green fields, fruitful orchards and groves of chestnut-trees line the banks of the river. As the whole course of the river is through mountainous country, the valley is usually narrow and is hemmed in by rugged peaks. For only ten miles, near its mouth, is the Narenta navigable, but the pathway it has cut through the mountains enables Serajevo to communicate with the Adriatic coast.

HOLBACH

THE SHEEP MARKET of Jezero is not held in the village, but in a pleasant meadow beside the River Pliva. There, the Mohammedan villagers—for the inhabitants of Jezero, like many other Bosnians, adopted the religion of their former conquerors, the Turks—drive their horned and long-fleeced flocks. The Pliva, just below Jezero, widens into a chain of small lakes and at Jajce, six miles below the point that we see here, falls over ninety feet into the River Vrbas, forming a beautiful cascade which is considered one of the finest in all Europe.

THE REPUBLIC OF YUGOSLAVIA

top, symbolic of the blood shed for freedom. The peasants dress similarly, only the materials are much coarser.

The Montenegrin is seldom to be seen without his gun, the symbol of his hard-won freedom. The late King Nicholas of Montenegro often used to stop one of his subjects in the street in order to examine his rifle, and if it were dirty, which was very seldom, the punishment would be severe. When a Montenegrin is happy or excited he discharges his gun into the air, which is naturally rather alarming.

Cetigne, the capital of Montenegro, has no port of its own, but does its shipping through Cattaro, on the coast, a town which possesses a wonderful natural harbor of indescribable beauty. The harbor is land-locked except for a narrow opening into the Adriatic Sea. There are several of these beautiful lake-like inlets along the coast, and they have been compared with the fjords of Norway.

The port of Cattaro itself is full of interest. It is so closely ringed by the mountains that it can scarcely find room beside the waters of the gulf. In the streets we may see Montenegrin peasants who have brought their market produce down the long zigzags of the "Stairs of Cattaro," a road carved out of the face of a mountain and the only way into Montenegro from the west.

Cetigne is really not very interesting, except from an historical point of view. There are no imposing buildings and we see no crowds in the streets. The market square is a feature of Cetigne, as it is of all Montenegrin towns, but there are no shops as we know them—in fact there is not a large glass window in the whole town. One sees many cafés and everywhere the colorful clothes that the people love to wear.

A characteristic of the Montenegrins is their absolute honesty. To be called a thief is a terrible insult, second only to being called a coward. They are a strong and hardy people, although they exist on a frugal diet of salted fish, called scoranze, potatoes, heavy bread made of rye or corn, and cheese.

On this simple fare, however, the Montenegrins perform wonderful feats of endurance and never show fatigue. Unfortunately, however, the men despise all manual labor and are content to sit about and dream of their victories. We may see old women and young girls toiling up a rocky path with buckets of water—which is sometimes more precious than wine for the spring may be a two hours' journey away—while near by may be sitting two handsome warriors who will never attempt to help these tired women, not even if they be their own sisters or mothers.

Christmas is a great festival in Montenegro. On Christmas Eve ivy branches are hung over the doors in order to bring good luck. Everyone is gay, songs are sung and revolver shots fired all day long. Easter is also a great festival all over Yugoslavia, and there is much rejoicing and feasting.

The Montenegrins are fond of family life and are devoted to their children, who are brought up very strictly and are taught to be brave and manly. Girl babies are counted as a misfortune because they are unable to fight. Once women were not counted in the census, which included only those able to bear arms for their country.

The Serbians, unlike the Montenegrins, were unable to hold out against the Turks, and for 345 years, they formed a pashalik, or province, of the Ottoman Empire. However, they had not given up their dream of a nation of Southern Slavs and they were frequently at battle with their oppressors until about 1830 when they became an autonomous state. Their history from then on did not run smoothly for there were constant upsets due to internal politics and there were wars with Turkey

Woods

IN CETIGNE, CAPITAL OF THE LAND OF THE BLACK MOUNTAIN

In Montenegro, which means Black Mountain, the men are warriors—excellent warriors—and the women do the work. That is why the men always carry guns and knives, and why the women are rarely seen except at church and on market days. They have to work very hard to wrest a living out of the mountain soil and then must take the produce to market.

© E. N. A.

ABOVE JAJCE, the capital of medieval Bosnia, the River Pliva is a rushing torrent interrupted by many rapids. The people who dwell in its fair, green valley realize the strength and usefulness of the swift stream, and so it has many a mill-wheel to turn before it reaches Jajce, a steep-roofed hill-top town which looks down on the river valley.

BUSHBY

"HALF ORIENTAL, half Italian and wholly Herzegovinian" is a phrase that has been used to describe Mostar with its many minarets and red-roofed white-walled houses. It lies in a beautiful and fertile valley between the hills of Hum and Podvelez, towards the latter of which we are looking. In the right background is the Greek cathedral.

BLACK STAR

ARGOSIES OF OLD SET OUT FROM THE HARBOR OF DUBROVNIK

Broad beaches and architectural riches attract tourists from all over the world to this loveliest of spots on the Dalmatian coast of the Adriatic. Known through most of its history as Ragusa, Dubrovnik was long a republic and the port for overland trade to and from Constantinople. Modern docking facilities make it one of Yugoslavia's busiest ports.

again, resulting in complete independence in 1878. Wars with their neighbors, the Bulgarians, followed, then came the Balkan wars and the murder of the Archduke Francis Ferdinand at Serajevo, which touched off the World War of 1914-18. After these years of struggle, Serbia finally came to realize the "Great Serbian Idea" upon the establishment of the new state of Yugoslavia, land of the southern Slavs.

The population of Yugoslavia has increased at one of the fastest rates in Europe. And about three out of four persons live on small farms, working with very crude implements. Indeed, farmers in some of the remote parts of the country have never used anything more modern than a wooden plow.

Less than one-fifth of the land is really fertile, and the good farming region—the north and east—is the most densely populated section of the country. Consequently, Yugoslavia is always dangerously close to famine. When crops fail, people go hungry.

Yugoslavia has been a communist state since World War II. The Yugoslav Government now invests large sums of money to build heavy industries in the cities. It feels that industry can, first of all, supply the tractors and trucks that are needed so badly on the farms. In fact, Yugoslavia has need of modern machinery in every field of manufacture. Increased production in industry will call for more workers; many young men and women will leave the farms and villages and go to the cities to earn the high wages that are promised them there.

These changes have undoubtedly affected the daily lives of the Serbs, Croats, Slovenes and others who make up the Yugoslav nation. In the old days these groups fought among each other bitterly, but city life has a tendency to break down barriers of prejudice. Though it is at odds with the Soviet Union, Yugoslavia is still a communist country and controls every facet of the lives of its people.

When a young Serbian goes to ask a girl to marry him he takes two friends and brings a flat cake made of wheat and a bunch of flowers. One of his friends

THREE LIONS

MACEDONIAN MOSLEMS GATHER ROUND THE FOUNTAIN OF A MOSQUE

At the entrance to a mosque in Skoplje, capital of Yugoslav Macedonia, several fezzed loungers pass the quiet time of day. More than one Yugoslav in ten is of the Mohammedan faith.

BUSHBY

THE RIVER NARENTA divides Mostar into two parts, but most of the chief buildings are on the left, or east, bank. The several minarets that over-top the houses show that Islam has here a strong hold—indeed half the population are Mohammedans. This is not surprising as the town was the Turkish headquarters in Herzegovina. Nevertheless, Mostar is also the seat of a Roman Catholic and of a Greek Bishop. The town dates from Roman days and commands the principal pass between the interior and the sea.

HOLBACH

AN OLD BRIDGE with a single, graceful arch spans the River Narenta and has provided Mostar with its name—"most" meaning "a bridge" and "star" meaning "old." Like the two gate-towers that guard its approach, it is said to be of Roman origin, but it really dates from the fifteenth century. A new bridge is used by vehicles in crossing the river

BLACK STAR

THE HORNS AND DRUMS OF THE GIPSY BAND SERENADE A BRIDE

A wedding party is not a wedding party in the western Macedonian village of Galicnik without the gay music of the gipsy bandsmen who are ever willing to lend their talents. Galicnik is on the Radika River in the high cattle-raising country near the border of Albania. The principal occupation of the villagers, aside from herding, is the making of cheese.

carries a pistol, for any joyful event is announced by the firing of rifles or pistols. After every convention has been carefully observed, the young man is encouraged by the father of the girl to come and ask for his bride. If he is successful, he pays a sum of money to show that he has bought her.

The marriage service usually takes place on a Sunday, but the celebrations often begin as early as the preceding Thursday, when special wedding cakes are prepared in the bride's and bridegroom's houses.

On Saturday the dowry is taken to the bridegroom's house. On Sunday the bride is decked with orange blossoms, and a coin is hidden in her hair, to prevent her ever wanting money in after life. The couple are presented with crowns of flowers or metal; they then walk with the priest three times round the altar, while the guests sprinkle them with raisins, sweets and nuts. Although the Serbs, Croats and Slovenes are not rich, there is always plenty of food at the wedding feast.

The costumes of the peasants are picturesque although in most parts of Serbia they do not display the desire for color seen throughout the Near East. White or gray linen clothes are worn by both men and women, and during the cold weather, they put on tweeds or woolen clothes and thick sheepskin coats with the fleece inside. The national costumes vary according to religion and locality. The Mohammedan men, for instance, wear a fez and the women wear baggy trousers.

There is beautiful scenery in Serbia, especially along the Danube, and a large part of the land is covered with splendid forests. We may sometimes come upon a gipsy camp, but though the gipsies occasionally settle down, forming separate camps or villages, they usually prefer a wandering life. They are generally admirable musicians, and almost every town possesses a gipsy band.

Croatia and Slavonia were freed from the Turkish rule in 1718 by the Austrians and, except for a brief period during which they were under French rule due to Napoleon's conquest, they remained as Austrian possessions until the end of World War I.

La Voy

"ALL THE FUN OF THE FAIR" IN A LITTLE SERBIAN TOWN

This is the Serbian version of a Ferris Wheel, but to us it has every appearance of being too ramshackle and too unsafe for use. However, to the young inhabitants of this Moslem village—there are many Mohammedan people in Serbia, especially in the south—a trip in one of these wooden boxes is a great adventure.

© E. N. A.

CROATIAN LOVERS are seen here wearing their holiday best to celebrate a feast day. Then both men and women array themselves in bright-colored clothes, often of silk, on which much hand-work has been lavished. The Croats, like the Serbs, are mostly Slavs by race, but differ in their modes of living and in their religious beliefs.

© E. N. A.

THIS YUGOSLAVIAN GIRL is posing in a gaily colored peasant costume typical of those which were once worn in her native Serbia, today a part of the Federation of Yugoslavia. After posing for this picture she returned to her work in the fields. There is still little industrialization in Yugoslavia, and farm women must work hard, raising crops by primitive methods.

THREE LIONS

SERBIAN WOMEN DRAW WATER FROM AN OLD VILLAGE FOUNTAIN

Serbian housewives fill earthen jugs, metal pots and a sprinkling can at the village fountain. It is their chief source of water for all washing, cooking and drinking needs.

THREE LIONS

LUMBER WAITING TO BE PUT ABOARD SHIP AT SENJ

The small harbor town is on the Adriatic Sea in western Croatia. Senj is said to be the oldest town in the region, dating back to the Romans, and was once a hiding place for pirates.

BLACK STAR

HOUSEWIVES STOP FOR A MOMENT OF GOSSIP IN A SERBIAN TOWN

The houses of Galicnik follow the road that winds up the side of a steep hill. There is good pasturage on the slopes; and the making of cheese is a profitable occupation in the town.

Racially, they are the same as the Serbs but most of them are Roman Catholic by religion, while in other parts of Yugoslavia, the larger number are Greek Orthodox or Mohammedan. The peasants occupying Croatia and Slavonia are perhaps less prosperous than those of Serbia as the climate is more severe. Among the Karst Mountains they have sudden and violent climatic changes, and at times the "bora," a fierce northeasterly wind, sweeps over the land. The riverside districts are barren, monotonous steppes which are somewhat unhealthy, especially beside the River Sava, where marsh fevers are prevalent.

The Croatian homes are more primitive than those of the Montenegrins and Serbians, for many of them are merely rough huts of wood with thatched roofs. As in Serbia proper, there is no middle class between the peasants and the very few educated people, and those who do the little trading that there is are mostly foreigners—Germans, Italians or Jews. Numerous gipsies wander from village to village, selling and buying horses.

The Croatian farmers produce corn in abundance and also cultivate wheat, oats, rye and barley, but much of the land is not fit for cultivation. The plum orchards of Slavonia are wonderfully beautiful when in blossom. Most of the fruit is dried, but some of it is made into a kind of homemade brandy which the peasants love. Many of the estates are planted with mulberry trees for feeding silkworms. Parts of both Croatia and Slavonia are covered by forests, and herds of swine feed in the oak and beech woods.

Dairy-farming and bee-keeping are other occupations, and horse-breeding is a flourishing industry. The farmers are constantly trying to improve their livestock by importing purer breeds.

KOSTICH

A SUNNY HARVEST MORNING IN A FIELD OF FLAX

The mist is rising in wispy clouds from the mountains beyond the meadow as the morning sun warms the ground. These women are at work early, gathering the flax and tying the stems in bundles. Flax plants must be harvested carefully by hand, for the fibers lose something of their spinning value if they are cut by a sharp instrument.

KOSTICH

GOTHIC SPIRES OF THE CATHEDRAL OF ST. STEFAN IN ZAGREB

The magnificent fifteenth-century edifice, which stands in the Main Square, is viewed from the Strossmayer Promenade in the old part of the city. Zagreb is the capital and cultural center of Croatia and is the second largest city in Yugoslavia. It is a trading and manufacturing town located on the abundant agricultural plains of the Sava River.

BLACK STAR

WHITE GEESE PLAY "FOLLOW THE LEADER" IN A SERBIAN FARMYARD

The geese furnish eggs, down and feathers as well as meat. High above the waddling fowl is an oddly shaped bird house or roost to entice small feathered visitors. For a time the Yugoslavian Government tried to collectivize farms on the Soviet model. In 1953, however, it gave up this plan and announced that Western types of agricultural co-operatives would be formed.

KOSTICH

TROUT-FISHERMAN'S DELIGHT

Lake Ochrida (or Ohrid), in southern Yugoslavia and eastern Albania, is twenty-five miles long and as much as 938 feet deep in some portions. Nestled high in the mountains, this lake is breathtaking in its scenic beauty. Its waters abound with rare fish, notably salmon trout. Fishing nets can be seen hanging to dry from the poles on the beach at the right.

North of Croatia, parts of the former Austrian territory of Carniola, Corinthia and Styria have been united to form Slovenia, so named because it is inhabited by Slovenes. Here, these Slavonic people have lived since the seventh century and have retained a language quite distinct from that of their neighbors although it is related. They are mostly peasants, but they produce some tannin, and bentwood furniture is manufactured to a considerable extent.

Dalmatia, the most beautiful province of Yugoslavia, consists of a strip of coastland running down most of the eastern shore of the Adriatic Sea. No part of the Mediterranean shore, except the coast of Greece, is so deeply indented as the Dalmatian coastline, with its multitude of rockbound bays and inlets sheltered from the open sea by a barrier of beautiful rugged islands.

In calm weather the channels between the islands and the mainland resemble a chain of lakes. All along the cliffs are half-ruined castles and monasteries, which seem to cling to the rugged rocks and add to the beauty of a scene not easily forgotten. Although it is not so rocky as Montenegro, the country is everywhere mountainous.

The highlands of Dalmatia are composed of dry, barren limestone which is honeycombed with caverns and underground watercourses, into which all the rain immediately goes. Even the few surface rivers often suddenly disappear underground and do not reappear for many miles. Owing to this strange geological formation the peasants are only able to cultivate about one-tenth of their land.

The once famous forests of Dalmatia were either burned by pirates or were cut down to provide timber for shipbuilding, and all attempts to replant them have failed owing to the lack of soil and rain. The peasants rival those of Montenegro in courage and stature and are like them, too, in having an olive skin with dark hair and eyes, although sometimes

Three Lions

QUEUING UP AT A BUS STOP IN MODERN BELGRADE

The bus is an up-to-date one as are the apartment houses in the background. Though Belgrade is an old city, it has been transformed in the years since 1866, when it was finally freed from the Turks. Outside of Yugoslavia, it is still usually called Belgrade, but its official name since 1929 has been Beograd. It was once the capital of the Kingdom of Serbia.

one sees the fair type with blue eyes.

The people of Dalmatia are hardy fishermen, their fleets taking in large catches of tunny, lobsters and sardines. Dalmatia's coastal waters are also rich in coral and sponges.

Across the Dinaric Alps from Dalmatia stretch the rugged limestone plateaus that form the region of Bosnia and Herzegovina, two states with long histories of subjection to a number of countries. They were finally united as one province by Austria-Hungary in 1878 and became a part of Yugoslavia in 1918.

The Hard Lot of the Farmer

Herzegovina and western Bosnia are poor farming lands. The valleys cut out by the Bosna and Vrbas rivers are fertile, but the yield of crops is low. Methods of cultivation are ancient. The poor mountain roads have kept the peasants from contact with the outside, and very near starvation year after year.

The northern and eastern parts of Bosnia are more fortunate. Here broad plains watered by the Sava and the Drina make farming easier and more productive.

There are also large mineral deposits scattered throughout the highlands of Bosnia-Herzegovina, and the tumbling mountain streams are great potential sources of hydroelectric power.

The greatest city of Yugoslavia is Belgrade—often called the northern gateway to the Balkans. Situated at the junction of the Danube and Sava rivers and commanding a rising bluff, it has been the center of trade for a rich region and a strategic site for military installations.

Building and Rebuilding

During World War I the city was occupied by Austrian troops. At the end of that war it became the capital of the new state of Yugoslavia. In the next twenty years the city was transformed and its population increased more than three times. Belgrade received a terrific bombing when the Germans occupied Yugoslavia in 1941; many buildings, such as the national library and the state theater, were destroyed or damaged. Most of them have been restored since or replaced with parks and houses.

We have seen that Yugoslavia has many problems. A high rate of farm production, for example, is a persistent requirement that is seldom met. Farm regions are overpopulated, and poor transportation makes the introduction of scientific methods and the distribution of goods extremely difficult.

During the 1920's improvement was hampered by hostility between the Croats and Serbs, who could not seem to work together in Parliament. Strong measures were taken by the King to control the situation. He closed Parliament and imposed military rule, which forbade the printing and reading of pamphlets likely to inflame regional ill will. Eventually the King restored order and brought the Croats and Serbs together. A period of recovery at the close of the decade was the result of this co-operation.

The Effects of Depression

Yet prosperity was cut short by the great depression of the 1930's. Yugoslavia, like all the countries of Europe, could find no markets for the products of industry. There was widespread want and unrest. In order to keep the country from complete collapse, the Government was forced to borrow money from Germany.

Later, however, Germany made Yugoslavia pay heavily for this indebtedness. In 1941 the Germans needed to send troops and materials to Africa, and demanded passage through Yugoslavia. When the Yugoslavs refused, Hitler ordered the invasion of the country and air raids on Belgrade. The entire country was occupied within ten days.

During the four-year occupation that followed, two groups—one led by the Serbian patriot Mihailovitch; the other by Josip Broz, or Tito, a Croatian Communist—waged telling warfare against German and Italian troops. Yet because the resistance groups differed in political ideals they could not present a united front to the enemy. Indeed, part of their time was spent in attacks upon each other. In 1944 the Allied governments openly supported Tito rather than Mihailovitch, upon the assumption that Tito waged more effective resistance to Hitler's troops.

Tito fought alongside Russian troops when they invaded Serbia in 1944 and also helped repulse the forces of Mihailovitch. When the war ended Tito set up a communist government. In 1946 he enacted a constitution modeled after the Soviet pattern. Mihailovitch was executed for collaboration with the Germans, and church leaders were imprisoned.

As time went on, Tito balked at Russian leadership. In 1948, his Government was banned from membership in the Cominform, the Soviet propaganda agency. From then on Yugoslavia was forced to make her way without the help of her former allies. She was shut off from trade on the Danube and was constantly fearful of attacks on her borders. The Government, therefore, eased its early hostility toward the West. Loans were obtained from the United States and a trade agreement was made with Britain.

Tito's tight grasp on the affairs of the entire population relaxed. Drought in 1949 and 1950 prevented further collectivization of farms. The Government continued to watch its large investments closely, but it gave local governments more authority than before in the regulation of social as well as industrial affairs. Elected representatives of labor began to take part in settling disputes and in planning production.

YUGOSLAVIA: FACTS AND FIGURES

THE COUNTRY

Yugoslavia has been both a monarchy and a republic since its formation at the end of World War I. At the end of World War II, it became the Federal Peoples Republic, composed of the 6 republics of Serbia, Croatia, Slovenia, Montenegro, Macedonia and Bosnia-Herzegovina, and the 2 autonomous provinces of Vojvodina and Kosovo-Metohija. It is bounded by Austria and Hungary on the north, by Rumania and Bulgaria on the east, by Greece on the southeast, by Albania on the south and the Adriatic Sea and Italy on the west. During World War II, the country was overrun by the Germans and partitioned among Germany, Italy, Hungary and Bulgaria. The Germans were driven out by the Russian Army in 1944. Its area is 99,069 square miles and the population is 16,338,500.

GOVERNMENT

The constitution provides for an elected parliament which elects a Presidium for 4 years. The Presidium elects two houses, the Federal Assembly and the House of the Peoples, for 4 years each. The president of the Presidium is the head of the state. The Government is communist though anti-Russian.

COMMERCE AND INDUSTRIES

Agriculture occupies about 70% of the population. Besides corn, wheat, oats, barley and rye, there are grown large quantities of grapes, plums, apples, pears, olives, sugar-beet and tobacco. Cocoon production is important. Fishing and the raising of livestock are carried on extensively. There is a large forest area. Minerals including lignite, iron, copper ore, gold, lead, chrome, antimony and cement are abundant but little developed. Oil is found to some extent. The chief industries are flour milling, brewing and distilling, cotton-spinning and weaving, tanning, boot-making, pottery and iron-working. Carpet-weaving (notably at Pirot) is an old industry. Meat-packing is a growing industry as is also cardboard- and paper-making.

The chief exports are wheat, timber, livestock, animal products, corn and eggs, and the imports are cotton and cotton goods, metals, machinery, chemicals and mineral oil.

COMMUNICATIONS

Total railway mileage, 7,010, mainly state-owned. Roads aggregate about 25,000 and are largely in an indifferent state. There is a navigation syndicate controlling the rivers Danube and Sava. The total length of navigable waterway is 1,200 miles. There are 12,000 miles of telegraph and 150,000 miles of telephone line. Air service connects Belgrade, Zagreb, and Skoplje.

RELIGION AND EDUCATION

About 48% of the population belong to Greek Orthodox Church, 37% are Roman Catholics, 2% Protestants and 13% Mohammedans. All ecclesiastical officials are controlled by a Minister of Public Worship. There is complete freedom of conscience. Primary education free and compulsory, under Ministry of Education. There are veterinary, law and engineering schools and universities in Belgrade, Ljubljana, Skoplje, Subotica and Zagreb.

CHIEF TOWNS

Belgrade, capital, 450,000; Zagreb, 325,000; Ljubljana, 130,000; Sarajevo, 125,000; Subotica, 115,000; Skoplje, 95,000; Novi Sad, 80,000; and Rijeka, 75,000.

THE BULGARS AT HOME

A Peasant People and Their Historic Land

The story of the Bulgarians is one of centuries of almost continuous warfare. It began almost as soon as the original Bulgars (they later mixed with Slavs) arrived from Asia in 679 A.D. and occupied part of the Balkan Peninsula. After enduring Turkish misrule from 1396 to 1878, the Bulgarians at last won independence in 1908. Then they were caught up in the terrible conflicts of World Wars I and II. Both of these wars ended, for them, in disaster and defeat. World War II was scarcely over when, in September 1946, the Bulgarians ousted their nine-year-old King, Simeon II, and established a republic. They drew up a constitution modeled after that of the Soviet Union, and their Government is now controlled by the Bulgarian Communist Party.

IF we glance at a map of Europe we shall see that Bulgaria forms a part of the Balkan Peninsula. It is wedged between Greece and Turkey on the south, and Rumania on the north, the republic of Yugoslavia on the west. The eastern boundary is formed by the Black Sea.

Sofia, the capital and largest city, lies between two mountain ranges in the heart of the Balkans. It has a population of about half a million people. Sofia is the major center of transportation, manufacturing and commerce. Its educational facilities include a university, a polytechnique institute and schools of various types ranging from academies of science and art to schools of physical education and military tactics. These, together with an opera house, theaters, a library, an astronomical observatory and museums, make the capital also a cultural center of Bulgaria.

Among its architectural masterpieces are the cathedral of St. Alexander Nevski, the hero-saint of Bulgaria, built by subscription of the peasants at a cost of $5,000,000, and the chapel of St. George, the oldest building in Sofia. There are several mosques, the only remnants of the days when Bulgaria was the Turkish province of Roumelia. These include the Banya-Bashi mosque, a minaret still used for Moslem worship, and the Black Mosque that was converted into a church. Sofia was rebuilt in 1880, and today it bears little resemblance to the Turkish town which it replaced. It has broad, tree-bordered avenues, public parks and modern buildings.

Yet despite its prosperous appearance, it gives unmistakable evidence of being the capital of a war-weary country that has been twice defeated. It is no longer the spruce capital of the early twentieth century. Its shops and restaurants have lost their sparkle; its air of buoyancy is gone.

In 1912 Bulgaria, flushed with successes in the first Balkan War, was at the height of her power. She had united with Greece, Serbia, Rumania and Montenegro to throw off the Turkish yoke but, after their victory, they were not able to come to any agreement about the division of the territory newly acquired from Turkey. War broke out among the countries so recently allied—that is, Bulgaria attacked the Serbs and the Greeks, and the second Balkan War in 1913 ended in utter defeat for Bulgaria.

Then, in 1914, came the World War and her ruler, King Ferdinand, again failed to justify himself as one of the wisest of the Balkan sovereigns for, after a year's hesitation and intrigue, he suddenly threw in his lot with the Germans and Austrians. The Bulgarian people paid heavily for the two errors of royal judgment. Not only did they lose several thousand square miles of their fertile lands but they were faced with a crushing war debt which would take years of hard work to lift.

Unable to cope with the rising discontent, Ferdinand gave up his crown, and was succeeded by his eldest son, as King Boris III, who assumed the powers of a dictator. But whether they had king or dictator was of little concern to

A LAKE SCENE IN THE BRACING AIR OF THE RHODOPE MOUNTAINS

The picturesque Rhodope range, with its evergreen forests and peaks more than nine thousand feet high, starts in southern Bulgaria and extends into the northeastern corner of Greece.

PHOTOS, WIDE WORLD

CURIOUSLY FASHIONED ROCKS NEAR BELOGRADCHIK IN BULGARIA

High in the Balkan Mountains of northwestern Bulgaria, not far from the Yugoslavian border, eroded rocks like grim giants watch over the ruins of an old fortress.

most of his subjects. Boris died under somewhat mysterious circumstances in 1943, after a conference with Adolf Hitler. Since the war's end Bulgaria has been governed according to the Soviet pattern.

In Sofia there is a Bulgarian National Museum which contains what will one day be a complete record of Bulgarian history. Let us stroll round the rooms and reconstruct from the coins, weapons and pottery, the story of this ancient people. The Bulgarians are the descendants of certain Mongol tribes, who originally came from Asia. They reached Europe during the seventh century and united with a large number of Slavs already living in the Balkans. They seized upon lands to the north of the Danube, the great river of Central Europe. Soon they spread southward, and their turbans, decorated with fluttering horse tails, caused terror wherever they appeared.

Their history consists of a succession of wars against and in alliance with that last outpost of ancient civilization—the Byzantine Empire whose emperors, taking shelter behind the mighty walls of Constantinople, trembled at the sound of the Bulgar war horns. The Emperor Nicephorus was slain in 809 by their Tsar Krum who, so it is said, fashioned his enemy's skull into a drinking-cup.

A later ruler, Simeon, seems to have been just such a man as King Alfred, so famous in English history. He wrote books in the Slav language, and his skill as a statesman and his valor as a warrior have passed into legend. Three times the silver armor of his bodyguard appeared before the walls of Byzantium, or Constantinople, and he took toll of all the merchandise passing from Europe into Asia. This was no small bit, for in the words of a contemporary writer: "Greece sends her silks, her wines, and her fruits; Asia her dyes and her perfumes, her precious stones, her white peacocks with gilded feet; Bohemia her swan-necked steeds; Russia her furs and her wax, her honey and her slaves."

In 1018, however, Bulgaria was occupied by the Byzantine Emperor Basil II, a cruel man who received, owing to his massacres, the nickname of the "Bulgarian Slayer." The Balkans have been the scene of much cruelty but none more terrible than one act of Basil's. Having captured an entire army of 15,000 men, he blinded them all and sent them back to their leader, King Samuel. The unfortunate king fell into a swoon and died.

European

CLEARING SOFIA OF WARTIME RUBBLE

The story of the next three hundred years is one of continual warfare with the Serbs and with the dying Byzantine Empire. A great change, however, was taking place. The Turks were spreading over Southeastern Europe, and Bulgaria, because of its position, was the first country to be conquered.

In 1396, it became the Turkish Province of Roumelia, and its position remained unchanged until toward the end of the nineteenth century, when Russia appeared as the champion of the oppressed Slavs in Europe. Then in 1878 after a short but decisive war, the Bulgars were free once again after nearly five hundred years of Moslem misrule.

Hereafter the story is one of steady progress, though there is little love lost

BLACK STAR

IT WAS ROSES, ROSES, ALL THE WAY

The rose garden in which this girl stands probably covers many acres. From the petals of the blossoms is distilled the oil, or attar, of roses that is exported to perfume makers. Formerly, many billions of roses were produced each year in Bulgaria, but the industry has declined since synthetic perfumes have largely replaced flower scents.

THREE LIONS

INTO THE BOILING KETTLE GO MILLIONS OF ROSE PETALS

Making attar of roses is an important industry in the Sofia region of Bulgaria, and thousands are employed on the rose plantations. Attar, a fragrant oil that comes to the surface when the petals are boiled in water, is a costly ingredient of perfumes and cosmetics. More than two hundred pounds of petals may be used to produce only an ounce of the attar.

BLACK STAR

CATHEDRAL COMMEMORATES RUSSIAN HERO-SAINT

Sofia is the site of the new Cathedral of St. Alexander Nevski, consecrated in 1924. The Russian hero received his surname to commemorate his victory on the Neva in 1240. The Russian church canonized him. Peter the Great honored his patron saint, in the 18th century, by building a monastery on the battle site and by creating the order of the Knights of St. Alexander Nevski.

between the various Balkan nations. In both World Wars these countries have neither aligned themselves against a common enemy nor remained neutral, but have fought among themselves. Border territory is likely to change hands during periods of international crisis, and the Balkan map does not remain fixed for very long.

Through all this welter of fighting and fear of war the Bulgar peasant has gone on driving his team of slow oxen or buffaloes across his fields. He, like the Dane, is a small holder, as most of the farms are from one to six acres.

The Bulgarian farmer has all the peasant virtues and defects. Though he and his forefathers have worked on the land for centuries, he has taken a long time to discover that the old ways are not always the best. Until quite recently his farming methods were as primitive as his great-grandfather's, but, nevertheless, he has always raised fine crops of wheat, corn, barley and oats. Tobacco, too, is cultivated to a great extent and forms a most important article of export. Around Sofia, where there are sugar refineries, the sugar-beet is grown.

The Bulgar, though he is quite a picturesque person, has not such a lovable nature as have others of the Balkan peoples. Frugal and taciturn, he has not the cheerful air of the Rumanian nor the expansive hospitality of the Serb.

As someone has said: "Put a Bulgar and a Montenegrin in a palace, and the Bulgar will look the peasant he is, while the Montenegrin, who has never bowed his neck to a conqueror, will look like a nobleman." But put them in a desert and the Bulgar will make it a garden of roses, while the other watches him work.

Elementary education in Bulgaria is free and obligatory for the youth but two-thirds of the population are peasants, who mostly live far away from the towns and are too much occupied with work to send the children to school regularly. Nevertheless, these hard-working farmers are the backbone of the Bulgar republic.

BLACK STAR

THE IMPOSING HOME OF OPERA IN BULGARIA'S CAPITAL CITY

Late in the nineteenth century, Sofia was rebuilt almost completely and the opera house dates from that period. It is a copy of the ancient classical style, with Ionic columns and a triangular pediment above the entablature. The building is embellished, however, in accordance with the rather fussy taste that frequently prevailed in the 1800's.

SOVFOTO

AN EQUESTRIAN STATUE DOMINATES A SQUARE IN SOFIA

To the right of the statue is the Moscow Cinema, which features Russian films. There is a star near the roof and the upper stories are probably offices for Soviet Union representatives.

THREE LIONS

AN ORNATE PUBLIC BATH IN SOFIA IN THE MIDST OF A PARK

Public baths are quite common in cities and towns of Europe, a custom left over from the days of ancient Rome. The conveniences of modern plumbing are lacking in many old buildings.

EWING GALLOWAY

MOHAMMEDAN ARCHITECTURE AT ITS SIMPLEST—SOFIA'S MOSQUE

Recalling the long rule of the Ottoman Turks over the Bulgarians is the Banya Bashi mosque at Sofia. The single minaret has a dramatic effect, lending distinction to a simple design.

© E. N. A.

MONKS OF BULGARIA are known as the "Black Clergy," because they wear long robes and tall caps of dead black. Those we see here dwell in a beautiful flower-decked monastery near Tirnovo, the ancient capital of the kingdom. Most Bulgarians are. by religion, members of a national form of the Orthodox Eastern Church.

© E. N. A

THE ISKER VALLEY is for a considerable distance a dark and gloomy gorge througn the mountains. At other parts it is wider and in the north, near the junction of the Isker River and the Danube, it is about two miles broad. The surrounding hills afford pasture for many sheep, whose wool is converted by the peasants into brightly-dyed cloth.

BLACK STAR

FASHION NOTE IN MILLINERY

The holiday costume in northern Bulgaria features a hat made from a kerchief smartly draped and tied and wreathed with flowers. Blouse and jacket are richly embroidered.

If we go on a railway journey through the Rhodope Mountains, which lie to the south of the Balkan Range, we shall see some magnificent scenery. These Rhodope Mountains are extremely beautiful and thrust their peaks above the forests and the vineyards that grow on their slopes. There are great gorges through which the rivers dash headlong to the sea, and in the dark pine forests that cover the hillsides we might expect to find those lost princes and green-winged dragons that figure so largely in the romantic old folk tales and ballads the Bulgarian shares with the Serbs and other Slavic neighbors.

Harvest Songs and Dances

In the autumn, when the grain has ripened, the Bulgarian peasant and his whole family almost live in the fields until the harvest is in. Then the harvest songs and dances enliven the villages. Young and old join in the fun. Dances are of various kinds, but the chief one is the *hora,* the national dance of Bulgaria. Any number of people can take part in this. Dancers join hands, or else each dancer places a hand upon the shoulder of his neighbor in front. A step is taken to the left and then three to the right. To the drone of a *gaida,* or bagpipe, the mass of dancers assumes the form of a serpent that coils and uncoils.

It is interesting to note that the bagpipe is a very ancient instrument, known to the Greeks and Romans. It has long been a favorite of Balkan peasants for whom it renders plaintive notes or stirring military airs or wildly gay melodies.

When the winter winds howl about the little lonely mountain cottages, the Bulgar peasant, snug by the fire, whiles away the long evenings telling old tales to amuse his children. Some of these stories are about peasants who marry beautiful fairies, only to see their brides vanish up the chimney on the wedding night. Others are of princes who fly as eagles and of women who are changed into swallows.

Prince Marko, Superman of the Slavs

Many wonderful tales are told about Prince Marko, son of a Serbian King. Marko actually lived in the fourteenth century; but the Serbs and Bulgarians and other Slavs have made him a legendary figure. In the stories, he resembles King Arthur, the English hero, or, perhaps, more exactly Paul Bunyan, early American Superman. Marko, in story and poem, lives for three hundred years; he rides a horse that is a hundred and fifty years old; his feats of strength and valor are prodigious if not supernatural; and he always uses his powers to comfort the sorrowful and free the oppressed. His great enemies are the Turks, and many of Marko's storied exploits are against Turks trying to bring Slavs under their yoke.

In spite of all the glamour that surrounds him, Marko is always a sad figure, a prince cheated of his throne.

There is not sufficient space here to tell

THREE LIONS

BULGARIAN WOMEN PLANTING FLOWERS ALONG THE PUBLIC STREET

In Bulgaria, it is up to the women to keep their towns beautified. This picture, taken in Karlovo, shows a group hard at work cultivating beds of flowers in the public square.

BALKAN NEWS AGENCY

THE FOUNTAIN used to play an important part in many customs of Bulgarian village life. Into it, for instance, a bride would throw a coin as an offering to the water nymphs. But such quaint customs, like the peasant costumes of the past, are gradually being discarded under the changes imposed by the communist-dominated Bulgarian Government.

BALKAN NEWS AGENCY

THIS FRUIT-GATHERER is returning home with her baskets full to overflowing. There are many types of Bulgarian national dress. This is the one that is worn round Kostenetz, a village in the south-west, at the foot of the Rila Mountains. The two young girls, whom we see on the opposite page drawing water are near neighbors of this girl.

SOVFOTO

THREE R'S IN BULGARIA

These girls are attending school in Ustove village in the Bulgarian countryside. The Government has reorganized the educational system along the same lines as those of the Soviet Union. Education is free, and children between the ages of seven and fifteen must attend school. There are schools at all levels, from kindergarten through the university.

of his many feats of daring against the Turkish invaders, but the story of his passing is well worth the retelling. In his castle the aged Prince Marko lay on his couch of hides, dreaming of old wars and of the brave days of his youth. To him there came an old friend, Philip the Hungarian, fresh from the Turkish wars. He told Marko that the way of fighting had changed.

"Old Marko," he cried, "do you know what has befallen the world? Men are making little tubes of iron. In that tube they put a black powder and a little ball. Out it flies. It strikes a man and away flies his soul."

But old Prince Marko laughed. "How can a little tube kill a man? Why, then a coward could slay a hero! With this right hand I have slain three sultans! Bring me a tube and I will catch the ball and throw it back to you." One of Philip's soldiers fired his rude matchlock and Marko's right hand was shattered.

Then seeing that the times were changed and being weary of the world, the old warrior mounted his horse and rode away into the mountains where, to this day, the peasants believe he sleeps till his country has need of him.

The national religion of the Bulgarians is Eastern Greek Orthodox. The small remaining minority comprises Moslems, Roman Catholics and Protestants.

The constitution "guarantees" freedom of worship, but in this respect it is honored more in the breach than in the observance. In 1949, fifteen Protestant clergymen were tried, convicted and sentenced to fines and imprisonment on the grounds of allegedly conspiring and conniving with the United States and Great Britain against the state. In the same year, it was decided to outlaw Catholic missions and missionaries, and their properties were forfeit to the state. And in 1950, the Turks accused the Bulgarians of the mass expulsion of Moslems. A law was introduced to provide for the prosecution of clergy found guilty of activities against "public order and morality" and against "democratic" institutions.

Churches may no longer maintain schools, hospitals or social agencies, which are now operated exclusively by the state.

Education is compulsory for children from seven to fifteen years of age. Reorganized on socialist lines in 1950, it follows the Soviet line. A census taken in 1934 showed roughly 63 per cent of the population to be illiterate. It is claimed that under the present system of schooling, the number is being sharply reduced. There are schools at all levels, from kindergarten through the university.

To increase the number of "intellectuals" among the people, a group of workers were permitted, in 1950, to enroll in the universities on the basis of preparatory courses arranged especially for them. Factory workers have not been overlooked in the state educational program, and short courses have also been introduced into the various factories.

APARTMENTS FOR BULGARIA'S WORKERS

Below are new apartments built for Bulgarian workers. In 1946, Bulgaria became a Soviet-type republic, and production was reorganized under the familiar Five Year Plan arrangement. One phase of the planning calls for improved living standards under which the people would receive a larger share of the total goods produced than in the past.

SOVFOTO

© E. N. A.

GABROVO ON THE YANTRA, a tributary of the Danube, is not really the poverty-stricken, tumbledown place that it appears to be in this photograph, for it has turned its poorest, though perhaps most picturesque, side to the camera. It is a thriving little town of ten thousand inhabitants, most of whom are engaged in the manufacture of woolens, cutlery, pottery or gold embroidery. It possesses six bridges over the river, more if we count such flimsy, wooden structures as the one across which these men are walking.

© E. N. A.

THE RILA MONASTERY, though most of its buildings are only a century old, is of ancient origin. In the ninth century a hermit, Ivan Rilski, dwelt among the Rila Planina, or Rila Mountains. He was venerated as a saint, and a monastery was later erected over his cell. That monastery has been rebuilt and enlarged until it has grown into the great building we see here, which includes within its high walls a church—building with domes on the left—a tower and an ancient armory. It is considered very holy by the Bulgarians.

WIDE WORLD

AT TROYAN, QUAINT APARTMENTS OVERLOOK THE GENTLE OSAM

Ducks waddle in the rocky headwaters of the Osam as it flows beneath the bracketed tenements of Troyan, a health resort and woodworking center on the slopes of the Troyan range.

SOVFOTO

A SUNNY PAVILION AT STALIN (VARNA), A SEASIDE RESORT

On a narrow sandy stretch between the Stalin Gulf and the Black Sea is the busy port of Stalin. Its mineral baths and pleasant beaches make it a Mecca for Russians on holiday.

© E. N. A.

THIS RIVER-CARVED GORGE made by the Elli Dere through the Rhodope Mountains of Bulgaria offered man a grade upon which he constructed a good roadway, while the river serves as a means of transporting the timber from the forest-clad slopes. The scene too is one of great beauty and grandeur, which one may contemplate as one drives along.

POPOFF

THE DUPNITSA GATE of the famous Rila Monastery is curiously painted in bright colors and frames a delightful view of the steep, beech-clad slopes of the Rila Mountains. The monastery, the religious centre of Bulgaria, is in a valley nearly 3,900 feet above the sea. It shelters a community of about 200, but can accommodate about 2,000.

Another important production is silk. There is considerable mineral wealth, but it is little exploited. Industry also is not highly developed, largely because of lack of capital. Among the more important industries are the weaving of textiles, flour-milling and the making of pottery, wines and cigarettes.

We have already told how the defeat of Bulgaria in the second Balkan War and in World War I left the state impoverished. World War II proved to be no less disastrous to the Bulgarians. Though neutral at first they soon joined Germany in the fight against the United States and Britain. When Russia declared war on Bulgaria in 1944, Bulgarians immediately begged for an armistice, which was granted in September of 1944.

After the defeat of Germany, the Communists in Bulgaria began their drive to control the country by gaining a hold on the Fatherland Front, the leading political coalition in the country. Parties outside the coalition were at first represented in Parliament, but in very small numbers. They had no Cabinet positions. In 1945 the Western Allies demanded that democratic elections be held before they would make a peace treaty.

But Bulgaria ignored the demand. A plebiscite in 1946 abolished the monarchy, and, in the elections for Parliament that followed, the Communists gained virtual control of the government. Yet there was a semblance of democracy; the opposition was allowed a few seats in Parliament. Britain and America signed the peace treaty in September 1947. The Communists then held trials and executions of opposition-party leaders. Finally, at the close of 1947, a Soviet-type constitution was drawn up. The Communist assembly soon passed laws taking over banking, industry and agriculture.

It can be seen that the story of Bulgaria since World War II has been much like that of other iron-curtain countries.

BULGARIA: FACTS AND FIGURES

THE COUNTRY

Became a republic by popular vote in 1946. It is bounded on the north by Rumania, on the east by the Black Sea, on the south by Greece and Turkey and on the west by Yugoslavia. As a result of the treaty of Craiova, signed with Rumania on September 8, 1940, Bulgaria gained Southern Dobruja, increasing both her population and area. The total area now is 42,796 square miles; population 7,022,206.

GOVERNMENT

Bulgaria declared war on the United States and Great Britain (but not on Russia) in 1941. In 1944 she declared war on Germany and signed an armistice agreement with Russia, the United States and Great Britain in the same year. The monarchy was abolished and a republic was established in 1946. However, in the following elections, the Communists gained control. At the end of 1947, a constitution modeled on that of the Soviet Union was drawn up.

COMMERCE AND INDUSTRIES

More than two-thirds of the population are engaged in agriculture. Most are peasant proprietors holding small farms from one to six acres. Wheat and corn are the principal crops but fruit, wine, cotton, tobacco, sugar-beet, roses and sunflowers are also important. Stock-raising is carried on extensively. Industries are not much developed. They include flour-milling, sugar-refining and the manufacture of woolen goods. Coal and iron are found in quantities, but there are deposits of copper, lead, iron, zinc and silver which are little worked. Exports are tobacco, wines, iron, wheat, hides and attar of roses; the imports are textiles, metals, machinery, hardware, chemicals, motor vehicles, mineral oils and cereals.

COMMUNICATIONS

Railways (2,211 miles) are owned and operated by the state. There are 372 miles of telegraph line, excluding that owned by railroads, and 13,208 miles of telephone line.

RELIGION AND EDUCATION

Most of the people belong to the Greek Orthodox Church. There are some Mohammedans and Roman Catholics. Elementary education is compulsory and free between the ages of 7 and 14. There are special factory schools and vocational courses and 11 universities and colleges, including the University of Sofia. Education is patterned along Soviet lines.

ESTIMATED POPULATION OF CHIEF TOWNS

Sofia, capital, 434,888; Plovdiv, 125,440; Varna (renamed Stalin in 1949), 77,792; Russe, 53,420; Burgas, 43,684; Pleven, 38,997; Stara Zagora, 37,057; Sliven, 35,553; Shumen, 31,169; Yambol, 30,311; Pazardjik, 30,430.

THE REPUBLIC OF RUMANIA

Modern Life in a Province of Ancient Rome

For centuries Rumania was practically unknown to the peoples of western Europe, and the country became an independent kingdom only in 1877, after having suffered Turkish misrule for many years. Though their country was laid waste during the World War of 1914–18, the Rumanians acquired much new territory and they strove earnestly to make a united kingdom of it. The second World War, in which Rumania was a more or less unwilling Axis partner, brought the Rumanians nothing but woe. At the war's end they had to give up considerable territory to Bulgaria and Hungary. Soon afterwards Russia extended her sphere of influence across Rumania.

THE beginning of Old Rumania (many Rumanians still speak affectionately of the Old Kingdom) appears to date from the expeditions made by the Emperor Trajan against the Dacians about 106 A.D. Trajan celebrated his victories over them by erecting a column, at Adam Klissi in the Dobruja territory, similar to the well-known Trajan's column in Rome. Many Roman colonists came to settle in the newly conquered fertile country, and thus it quickly became one of the most prosperous of all the Roman colonies. It was then known as "Dacia Felix."

It suffered terribly under the hordes of Goths who swept down upon the land in the third century. Some historians believe that the Daco-Romans retired to the Carpathian Mountains and, as the Goths did not pursue them, they lived there almost forgotten. There they formed themselves into a permanent nation with a language and a civilization that was far above that of the barbarians which later surged in from all sides. Others think that the main part of the population retired south of the Danube, but later returned to re-occupy the land. The territory between the Carpathians and the Danube has passed from one invader to another, but none succeeded in wiping out the people as a national body. Their own proverb exactly describes their national experience: "The water passes, but the stones remain."

There developed in this territory two large principalities, Wallachia and Moldavia, each of which tried separately to free itself from its oppressors, the Turks, who had conquered the country in the fifteenth and sixteenth centuries. It was not until 1859, however, that they united and gave the present name to the country. The people declared their independence from Turkey in 1877.

About the middle of the nineteenth century, Rumania was powerfully influenced by France. The educated classes sent their children to French schools, and French became the official language which was used in international negotiations. Napoleon III spoke of Rumania as "France's Latin sister" and encouraged the Rumanians to repel Turkish and Russian attempts to acquire political influence. Members of the younger generation who had gone to Paris came back with many French ideas, especially about education. An education act, passed in 1864, made education free and elementary education compulsory. But because there were few schools and not nearly enough teachers, the majority of the peasants remained illiterate, as they are even to this day, in spite of the act.

A slight knowledge of Latin will, however, be quite sufficient to prove how right the Rumanians are in claiming their language to be of Roman origin. There are many Latin terms and words in their language, although there is a larger percentage of Slavic with numbers of Turkish, Greek and Magyar words. The sound of it is not unlike Italian, and in poetry it is exceedingly musical.

There are two distinct and opposite types even among pure Rumanians. One is fair and blue-eyed, and the other is as

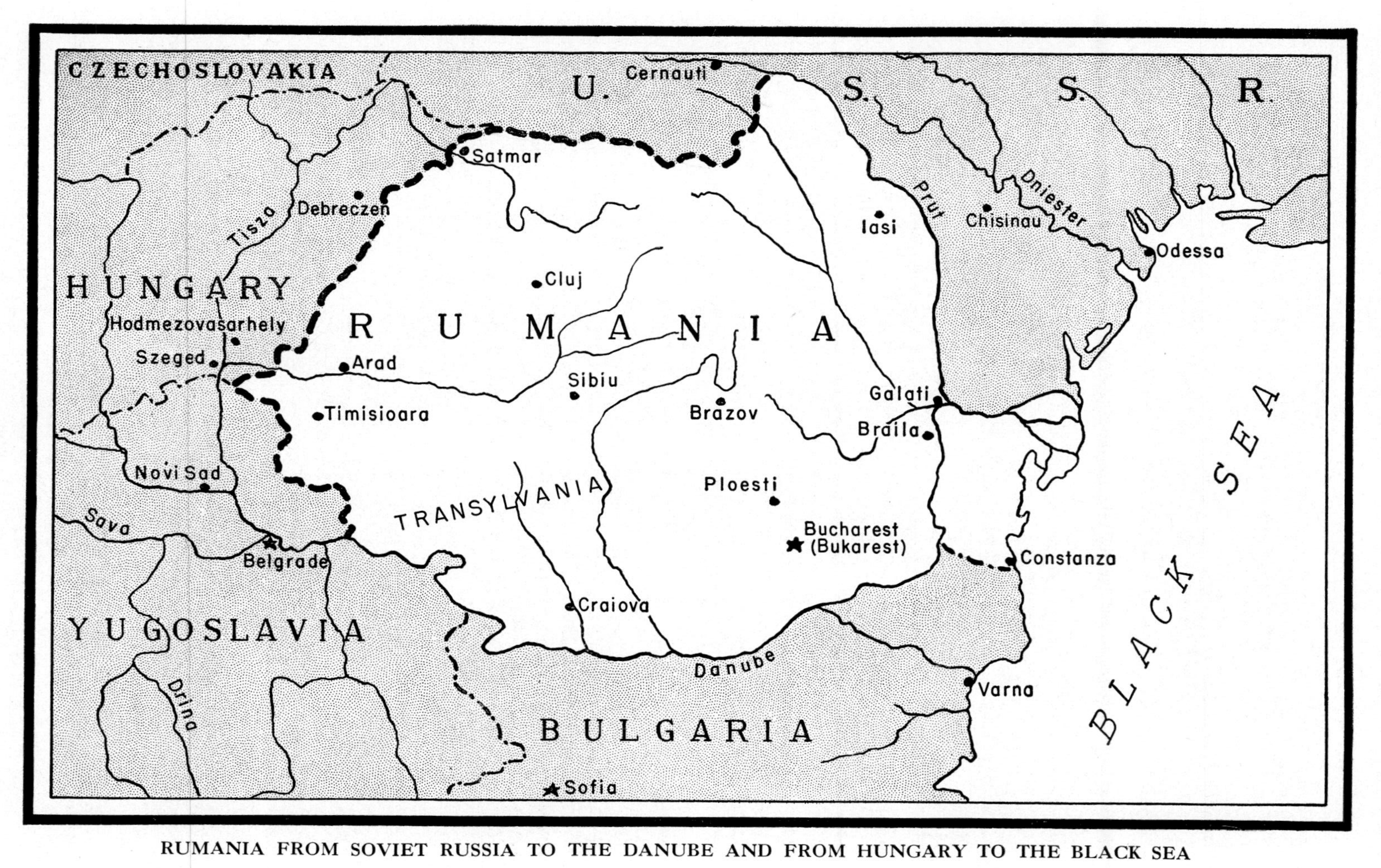

RUMANIA FROM SOVIET RUSSIA TO THE DANUBE AND FROM HUNGARY TO THE BLACK SEA

MONKMEYER

THRESHING TIME IN TRANSYLVANIA

The great Transylvanian plain is a rich, well-watered area; but the people have been backward in adopting modern farming methods. The scene above is typical—the grain is hauled by a team of slow-going oxen to an old-fashioned thresher in the field. The Rumanian Government has promised to mechanize the country's agriculture.

BLACK STAR

TIMBER FROM THE CARPATHIAN SLOPES

Though agriculture is the mainstay of the country, Rumania has many other fine resources. There are wide forests, rich oil and gas deposits, gold, silver, copper, iron, lignite and salt. Since Rumania became a satellite nation of the Soviet Union (in 1948), the people of the Western world have not been able to learn very much about her.

EASTFOTO

BRINGING TO THE SURFACE THE RICHES THAT LIE UNDER RUMANIAN SOIL: AN OIL FIELD AT PLOESTI

Rumania's most important source of mineral wealth is oil, although production has slackened in recent years. Ploesti, second city of Rumania, is an important center of the oil industry. During the early years of World War II, the rich Ploesti oil fields fueled the German war machine.

dark as the Italian people. Both types are tall, hardy, and proud of their race, and have a very keen sense of nationality, for every child is taught that he is a descendant of the ancient Roman colonists. The size of Rumania, however, has changed several times during the twentieth century. When it had the largest territory, after 1919, the population included many Magyars, Russians, Germans and Bulgarians.

A Land of Varied Resources

Rich in timber, rich in minerals and especially so in petroleum, Rumania is also one of the greatest grain-producing regions in Europe. The soil is fertile and there is plenty of rainfall. Even though agricultural methods are still rather primitive and the yield per acre is low, large quantities of wheat and corn are grown. The chief food of the poorer farmers is a corn-meal pudding called *mamaliga.* Plums are a special crop, from which a drink called *tuica* is made.

The main artery of trade is the Danube River, by which cargoes—mostly petroleum, grains and timber—are brought down to be loaded on sea-going vessels at Brăila and Galati, the two most important river ports. The Danube has one serious disadvantage for trade, however; it is either frozen or in danger of freezing during most of the winter. Then transportation must rely on the network of railroads and highways, which was greatly enlarged and improved in the years between the two world wars.

Rumania's only port on the Black Sea is Constanta. It has a modern harbor that can accommodate the largest ocean vessels. It is also the end of a pipe line that brings petroleum from the oil fields, which center about Ploesti, about 140 miles northeast of Constanta. Near the port are two seacoast summer resorts, Mamaia and Eforia, as well as the famous mud baths of Takir-Ghiol.

Rumania's Changing Shape

In the early 1900's the shape of Rumania on maps was somewhat like a crescent with a deep hollow and blunted ends. It became almost a perfect oval with the territorial gains made in the first World War, which more than doubled its size. The Old Kingdom consisted of the provinces of Wallachia, Moldavia and the Dobruja. Greater Rumania included Bessarabia (from Russia), Southern Dobruja (from Bulgaria) and Bukovina, Transylvania and other large sections from Austria-Hungary.

The Rumania of today is still an oval, but a smaller one. The Southern Dobruja has been returned to Bulgaria; and Bessarabia is a part of the Soviet Union. The loss of these two regions cost Rumania almost half its coastline on the Black Sea, though neither the wide mouth of the Danube River nor the port of Constanta. Toward the west, however, Rumania has kept the southern part of Bukovina, and Transylvania, a high, fertile plain. Almost all the people of Transylvania are Rumanian, and Rumanians everywhere consider it the cradle of their stock. The country's present-day neighbors, therefore, are the Soviet Union, on the north and northeast; Hungary, on the west; Yugoslavia, on the southwest; and Bulgaria, on the south.

The Pride of the Rumanian People

The Danube is the joy and pride of the people, although they can claim only its lower course. It is truly a marvelous river. It is said to take its rise "in the courtyard of a gentleman's house in Germany," and it receives many tributaries as it flows through other countries before it reaches the Kazan Pass, where it passes through the Iron Gates and then comes into Rumania. It is at its narrowest and deepest in this pass. The submerged rocks that gave rise to the name of the Iron Gates have been cleared by dynamite to make a safe channel through which ships may go. When this great engineering feat was accomplished, it was made a ceremonial occasion, and its opening was attended by the emperor of Austria (Francis Joseph), who was then reigning, and the kings of Rumania and Serbia.

Although the Danube is not "blue," as the song describes it, it is far more mag-

BLACK STAR

SUNDAY AFTERNOON IN TRANSYLVANIA

Tidy main street in Rucar, a village in the Transylvanian Alps. The Sunday costume has a white kilt over tight trousers, a bell-sleeved blouse and sleeveless overjacket. Since the second century, when the Emperor Trajan conquered it, Transylvania has had a checkered career. Invading Romans, Slavs, Magyars, Saxons and others have left their imprint.

nificent and imposing than even the Rhine because of its stillness and breadth. It expands to a width of between two and three miles near Belgrade, and has islands and lovely reaches that give variety to it. The most famous bridge over the Danube in Rumanian territory is that at Cernavoda, which was completed in 1905. It carries the railway line from Bukarest, or Bucharest, to the Black Sea port, Constantza. The bridge is itself over twelve miles long, as it has to cross vast tracts of marshy land as well as water. Three arches of it were blown up by Rumanian soldiers in 1916 to prevent the advance of the enemy. We can imagine the grief they felt at having to destroy it. The restoration took five years. Work is underway on a Danube–Black Sea canal.

But let us leave the Danube to carry its huge burdens of timber and grain at its own dignified, if rather lazy, pace and fly northward. We shall pass over the capital, Bucuresti, which is also spelled Bucharest and Bukarest.

The city's favorite drive crosses Kisilev Park, which is styled after the Champs Elysées in Paris. It is typical of the

SOVFOTO

POSING IN FRONT OF AN OLD CHURCH IN A TRANSYLVANIAN TOWN

The church's roof of straw is the kind found on peasant houses in villages of the Rumanian province, and the gaily colored embroidery of the man's blouse is a sample of the needlework for which Rumanian women are noted. On the garments of men, women and children, even on sheepskin coats, they like to work rich, intricate patterns in red, gold, blue and black.

© E. N. A.

GAY GARB OF A YEOMAN FAMILY OF RUMANIA

The national costume of Rumania is very distinctive. The women usually wear a long, full-sleeved, embroidered dress of white linen, with a brightly colored double apron hanging down back and front. Kerchiefs or transparent veils cover their heads. The tunic and wide trousers of the men are also of linen. This man's waistcoat is of sheepskin embroidered.

EASTFOTO

A RUMANIAN GIRL DISPLAYS THE COTTON SHE HAS BEEN PICKING

She stands knee-deep in the midst of the ripened cotton plants to gather the valuable fiber fluffs. The field she has helped to tend is not far from Bucharest, in the flat, fertile lowlands of southern Rumania below the Transylvanian Alps. When the cotton has been carefully picked by hand it will be shipped to the city's textile mills to be processed into cloth.

SOVFOTO

TENDING A BUSY TEXTILE LOOM WITH SKILLFUL HANDS AND EYES

Textile mills are among the important enterprises in Bucharest, a manufacturing city as well as a capital. Extensive Rumanian farmlands furnish the mills with cotton, flax and wool.

TRIANGLE

THE SUN MUST DO ITS SHARE IN BLEACHING NEWLY WOVEN LINEN

In Rumania, where a vast majority of the people are engaged in agriculture, flax is one of the profitable crops, and processing and weaving its fibers into cloth is a gainful industry.

EASTFOTO

A TALENTED PLAYER OF RUMANIA'S FOLK MUSIC

Wearing the hand-embroidered blouse of his Transylvanian village, he is eager to interpret the traditional songs of his country. Rumanians are devoted music lovers.

wide boulevards crossing the city. The principal one is the Calea Victorei. Most of the streets would look familiar to Westerners, but here and there are curious little byways lined with bazaars which point up how close Rumania is to the Middle East.

Before World War II, Bucharest was a gay, cosmopolitan capital, with many theaters, motion-picture houses and cafés. Its gaiety and luxury vanished with the rise of the Communists, of course. Nevertheless, it remains one of the most important cities in this part of the world behind the iron curtain. It is the center of a network of at least eight railroads and the chief terminal of the Rumanian air lines.

Burcharest lies in the midst of a vast plain, which swelters in the heat of summer and is lashed by bitter winds in winter. It is a fertile region, however—three-fourths of the Rumanians live on farms—and today maize (corn) has taken the place of wheat as the principal crop.

As far back as 1918, large land holdings were slowly being broken up and redistributed among the peasants. This process was speeded up after 1945, when the Communists gained control, and by 1949 all the great estates had disappeared. The Government then began to organize "Centers for Agricultural Machines and Equipment," similar to the machine-tractor stations of the Soviet Union. (The plain lends itself to large-scale farming, for which modern farm implements are necessary.) It is thought, however, that this plan has not been entirely successful and that production has suffered. Every phase of agriculture is subject to strict control under Rumania's masters, who work in close co-operation with the U.S.S.R.

On the small farms and in the little villages, the families usually occupy houses of a simple and hardy construction.

Upon four posts driven into the ground the builder places the roof. The walls are of clay and straw, and whitewashed when dry. Walls are brightened by gay bands of red or blue. The mud floor is as hard and smooth as timber. The cabin is divided into rooms. There will be a veranda gay with creepers, so that the home is quite picturesque outside and in.

The interior is bright with gay rugs and painted furniture and often with homemade embroideries and polished metals. It is only the better cottages, however, which are so charming for there are others so poor as to be hardly fit to live in. Each village has a church and school and post office, and a well, which is the meeting place of the gossips and of sweethearts.

There is a great love for children in Rumania. An old proverb says: "A child is a blessing to any man's roof," and a large family is the pride of the parents. Children are useful, of course, as they start to work in the fields at a very early age—the girls gather the flax and fetch wool and the boys help with the plowing and reaping. Attendance at school is, however, steadily increasing.

Young and old are very fond of dancing. The young people will walk miles to a dance in a neighboring village, and the public dancing ground is of earth beaten smooth and hard and clean as a board. The girls wear ribbons, flowers and a smart though home-made dress. The young men a long, snow-white blouse, with a border richly worked in color, a sash of scarlet or embroidered leather and a sleeveless coat. They keep on their hats while they dance. All wear heel-less sandals. There is invariably a master of ceremonies, whose duty it is to see that the girls have partners—and no "sitting-out" is allowed. Music is usually furnished by the gipsies, or *tzigani,* of whom there are a large number in Rumania. They are quite distinct in race from the other people and although some live in settlements, they are mostly nomadic. The haunting strains of their melodies have an immense popularity with the Rumanians both in the country and in the towns.

The Rumanian peasant has no fear of having his house robbed. When he goes out he props a stick against the door to show he is not at home. It would be a serious breach of good taste to disregard this and enter. On the other hand it is not a crime to help yourself to his fruit or his grain, provided you do not take more than you need for yourself. It is

©E. N. A.

EVERYDAY LIFE IN ONE OF THE PRINCIPAL SQUARES OF TIMISIOARA

Timisioara lies in a plain on the Bega Canal and is an important collecting and distributing center for the fertile Banat district. Timisioara was a Hungarian city until 1918, when it became Rumanian. In 1940 it returned again to Hungarian rule, but, following the end of the second World War, once again became a Rumanian city.

Monkmeyer

HARVESTING GRAIN IN TRANSYLVANIA

Late in summer, when the grain ripens, the plain of Transylvania is alive from dawn until sunset with men and women reapers. That season of the year is very warm on the plain, and this farmer wears light clothing, and a high straw hat to protect his head from the hot sun. In many parts of Rumania, the farmers still use old-fashioned, rather clumsy tools.

recognized as the right of the hungry to be fed, whether the host is at home or not.

The Rumanian woman has a busy life, especially after she is married. In addition to her housework, she has to collect and prepare all the material for spinning flax or wool. She spins and then weaves it on a hand loom, making the most beautiful materials in both light and heavy textures. The articles are also dyed and embroidered. The native love of color and design is clearly shown in this work. Many of the best pieces are taken to the towns for sale, but every home will be abundantly supplied with rugs and hangings, and the people are very fond of elaborately embroidered clothes. Everything, even pottery, is most lavishly decorated.

As we go north and cross the Carpathians, we come into quite a different type of country and to a people of quite an opposite character. On the farther side of the range the land is pastoral, of wild beauty and great charm. It is German, judging by the buildings, which are of stone and set in walled courtyards, and all as like one another as peas in a pod. The people are all alike, too, sturdy, stolid, not given to speech, but thrifty and most industrious. This is quite a contrast in disposition to the lively Rumanians we have left behind. It is a stretch of country surrounded by mountain peaks, called the Siebenburgen—the land of seven burgs or forts, or Transylvania, the land across the forest—that we come to now.

EASTFOTO

SEARCHING THE HORIZON FROM ATOP THE CARPATHIAN MOUNTAINS

Mountain-climbing vacationers in the southern Carpathians of Rumania examine the faraway valley with their field glasses. Their ascent was made easier by the cable chair that carried them up into the bracing air. This picturesque range of mountains is frequently called the Transylvanian Alps; some of its peaks are more than eight thousand feet in height.

BLACK STAR

EVERY RUMANIAN VILLAGE HAS ITS TRADITIONAL DRESS

Saliste, a Transylvanian village, was once well known for its elaborate costumes, its folklore and handicrafts. In times past needle arts and hand spinning took up much of the time of the women who created intricate embroidery designs and wove exquisite fabrics. The trousers of these men are of sheep wool; and the women's aprons, a fine black broadcloth.

Popoff

GIRLS OF RUMANIA IN DRESSES THAT ARE WORKS OF ART

A Rumanian will go with little food rather than lack a holiday costume, and that of even the poorest peasant is of rare beauty, covered, as it is, with hand embroidery of intricate design, in scarlet, blue and gold thread. There are some villages in Transylvania, however, where the women avoid all colors and wear elaborate dresses of only black and white

E. O. HOPPE

THE GREAT DANUBE collects the drainage of an immense region, and flows in hollows between the Alps and the Jura, the Alps and Bohemia, the Alps and the Carpathians, and the Carpathians and the Balkan range. Between the two last is that famous section of the river known as the Iron Gates. The Danube has also created land where once was sea, for it has a wide delta, formed by the deposition at its mouth of sediment—the stones and soil it carried away when cutting through the mountains—picked up during its course of nearly 1,800 miles.

© E. N. A.

A RUMANIAN PEASANT FAMILY in the doorway of its thatched, wooden cottage. Changes in government mean little in the daily lives of farming people such as these. They live close to the soil in a yearly rhythm of sowing and harvesting. Flocks of sheep provide them with wool and sheepskin coats for the bitter cold of winter.

BLACK STAR

MODERN ARCHITECTURE IN BUCHAREST

Bucharest, nicknamed "City of Delight," used to be a gay city, full of color and life. Its people loved to be called "Little Parisians." Today such innocent frivolities are frowned upon. The modern street we show here, Calea Victorei, Street of Victory, received its name after the Battle of Plevna, in 1877, by which Rumania freed itself from Turkish rule.

Many of these settlers are Saxons, although where they came from is a mystery. In fact, it is so mysterious that legend has it that the founders of this "tribe," if we may so call them, were those children whom the Pied Piper decoyed from Hamelin town, and who, you will remember, entered the mountain after him and were seen no more by their parents and townsfolk. It is said that they came through the tunnel out into this fertile plain and have remained here ever since, self-supporting, producing everything they want, from nails to embroideries. They are their own carpenters and shoesmiths and tailors, their own weavers and potters and farmers. Truly, the Pied Piper did not leave them helpless if those children from Hamelin town grew up and founded a colony as prosperous as Transylvania is now!

This "land of a thousand beauties and a hundred hopes," as someone has styled Rumania, is a country full of the quaintest superstitions. Many of the peasants live in dread of "The Little People," or, as some call them, "The Good People." Many spells and incantations are practiced to induce these spirits to be merciful.

It would seem that "The Little People" have not lent kindly ears recently to the inducements of the Rumanian people, for their country has been beset with many difficulties both in war and peace. Forced to enter World War II on the side of the Axis, the Rumanians suffered heavy losses. After the war's end the country came under the domination of the Communists and today forms a part of the Soviet bloc of nations.

In times of national joy and national sorrow, too, the mountains are dear to the country folk of Rumania. They know and deeply love the passes, the mountain pastures, the secluded valleys and the defensible gateways to the plain.

RUMANIA: FACTS AND FIGURES

THE COUNTRY

Lies in southeastern Europe on the Black Sea. It is bounded on the north by Soviet Russia; on the east by Russia and the Black Sea; on the south by Bulgaria; and on the west by Yugoslavia and Hungary. Under the terms of the United Nations armistice Rumania agreed to restore Bessarabia and Northern Bukovina to Russia and they are now recognized as part of Soviet Russia. Southern Dobruja was ceded to Bulgaria. Area, 91,671; population, 15,873,000.

GOVERNMENT

With the abdication of King Michael (Mihai) in December, 1947, Parliament voted to abolish the monarchy and have a Constituent Assembly draw up a People's Republic constitution. It created a Soviet-like Presidium of 5 men. The National Assembly adopted a republican constitution, modeled on that of the Soviet Union, in 1948.

COMMERCE AND INDUSTRIES

Agriculture is the chief occupation, and the main crops are corn, wheat, barley, oats, rye, beets and tobacco. Forestry is carried on extensively especially in the Carpathians. There is much livestock. Petroleum wells and salt mines are worked, and other minerals include lignite, iron and copper ores, lead and antimony. Salt-mining is a state monopoly. Other industries are flour-milling, brewing and distilling. The chief exports are cereals, petroleum, timber, hides, wool, vegetable oils, wood manufactures, and the imports are manufactured goods (mostly textiles), machinery, automobiles, vehicles and chemicals.

COMMUNICATIONS

There are 5,962 miles of state-owned main rail lines; 94,189 miles of telegraph wire and cable; 91,327 miles of telephone wires. Airlines connect with European cities. Both the Black Sea and the Danube are important for commercial navigation.

RELIGION AND EDUCATION

Most of the population belong to the state church, namely Greek Orthodox with liturgy conducted in Rumanian language. There are also Roman Catholics, Protestants, Armenians, Jews and Mohammedans. Education is free and compulsory. There are special schools, including commercial, agricultural and polytechnic institutes, and 5 universities located at Bucharest (Bucuresti), Iasi (Jassy), 2 at Cluj, and Timisoara.

CHIEF TOWNS

Bucharest (Bucuresti), capital, population 1,041,807; (others estimated): Iasi (Jassy), 108,987; Galati, 93,229; Timisoara, 108,296; Cluj, 110,956; Ploesti, 105,114; Arad, 82,882; Braila, 97,293; Brasov, 85,192; Constanza, 79,716.

RUMANIAN LEGATION

A PEASANT GIRL of Rumania returning from the well with a jar filled with water, greets with a smile any chance wayfarer she may meet for she believes she will bring him good luck. But should she meet anyone as she carries an empty jar to be filled, she is sad and ashamed for then it is ill-luck that she brings. Such is the old superstition.

THE CALUSARE, one of the national dances of Rumania, is usually performed by men. In gay costumes, decorated with fringe and tinkling bells at their knees, they dance in the open air at fairs and festivals to the music of the flute, the lute and the violin, played by ragged gypsy musicians. In another dance, the Hora, women also take part.

Florence Farmborough

THE LOVELY SHORES OF THE CRIMEA, THE RIVIERA OF RUSSIA

The Crimean peninsula is one of the beauty spots of Europe, with exquisite scenery, favorable climate, and fertile soil. The Greeks founded colonies in Crimea which formed into the Kingdom of the Bosporus. This region was the scene of the 1945 Yalta Conference of Roosevelt, Churchill and Stalin.

RUSSIANS OF EUROPE AND OF ASIA

The People of the Steppes and Frozen Tundra

The old Russia, with its tsars, princes and peasants, disappeared in 1917 in one of the greatest political upheavals of modern times. In its place is the Union of Soviet Socialist Republics, with its bureaucrats and workers. Though the exchange promised much and brought some benefits to the Russian people, it has been at the terrible cost of even less freedom than they had before. Work, recreation, home life, the upbringing of children, the arts, thought itself—all are subject to rigid control. The individual counts for nothing; the state is all. This has happened in spite of the fact that the country is vast and there is enormous variety among its millions of people, from Slavs to Mongolians. Abundant man power, fertile soil and a wealth of mineral resources, including iron and petroleum, have helped to make the Soviet Union strong—though just how strong today the Western world can only guess.

RUSSIA is a strange blend of East and West. Now and then it splashes the pages of both European and Asiatic history with barbaric splendor. Scythians appeared beside the Black Sea in the days of ancient Rome; and later came men who rode like the wind—Mongols, Tatars, Cossacks.

To mention but a few of the many stocks who live today in the European part of Russia, there are the Karelians, or Eastern Finns, who inhabit the cold northwest; the Samoyedes, nomads of the northeast, who dwell also in Siberia; the Great Russians of the north, east and centre; the Little Russians of the south; the White Russians of the west; the Cossacks, a race of warriors who now dwell in Caucasia, that mountainous district of the south between the Black and Caspian seas; and the Tatars who also inhabit Caucasia, the banks of the Volga River and the beautiful, fruitful land north of the Black Sea. For generations Russia, at the cost of great suffering to herself, served as a buffer state, protecting the people of western Europe from the invasion of barbaric Asiatic hordes, Mongols and others, many of whom have now become part of Russia.

Russia in Europe is mostly plain. It has, of course, ranges of hills, but they are never very high. Its only mountains are those on its frontiers and those of rugged Caucasia. In the north, it reaches beyond the Arctic Circle; in the south it is in the same latitude as Italy. This southernmost part, especially the Crimea, which has been called the Little Paradise or the Russian Riviera, has quite a mild climate; but Russia, on the whole, being so far removed from any large stretch of water, has a very rigorous climate.

Little is known of the early history of the vast land we now call Russia. We are told that about the year 862 certain barbarous tribes sent to the Norsemen (whom they called the "Men of Rus") asking them to come and rule them. They came and established numerous independent principalities and built Kiev, Moscow and other cities. After about 350 years the land was invaded by hordes of yellow men from the East called Tatars, or Mongols, who ruled for more than two hundred years. During this period the Russian princes paid tribute to the Great Khan somewhere in Siberia.

The Mongol power weakened and the Russians under the leadership of the princes of Moscow threw off the Tatar yoke. Gradually the rule of Moscow became absolute, the boundaries of the kingdom were much extended, and serfdom was established, but the country remained a half barbarous, Oriental despotism far behind the remainder of Europe. Finally the royal line of Moscow ran out and there was a period of disorder. Then Michael Romanov was elected tsar, but it is with his grandson, known as Peter the Great, that modern Russia begins.

HUGHES

THIS RUSSIAN OF THE NORTH is both woodman and hunter, and thoroughly familiar with the habits of all the beasts and birds that live in the forest. Here we see him on the alert, as though he had heard a suspicious sound. Russia can, roughly speaking, be divided into two areas—the area of the woods and that of the plains. The woods extend from the north to the centre, and the plains from the centre to the south. The Russians are very fond of their forests and often used to build houses among the trees where they lived during the summer.

UKRAINIAN GIRLS not only are accustomed to work in their homes, but also must help the men in the fields for there is much farm work to be done in this rich agricultural land. Grain, vegetables and fruit grow here in such great abundance that it is often referred to as the granary of Eastern Europe.

Sovfoto

HARVEST TIME ON A RUSSIAN COLLECTIVE FARM

In Russia to-day nearly all agricultural work is done on collective farms, that is where the farmers pool their labor and share a part of the crop. Here are shown two of the women harvesters who have paused to read the field newspaper posted where all may read.

Sovfoto

KOSTROMICHKA CATTLE ON A STATE FARM

The Kostromichka is a breed of milch cattle raised in the upper Volga region northeast of Moscow. State farms such as this usually have several hundred head of cows. Under a program begun around 1950, agricultural "towns," with 500 to a few thousand families, are taking the place of the old collective farms, which had 10 to 30 families.

This energetic ruler extended the boundaries, moved the capital from Moscow to the new city of St. Petersburg (which he built on land taken from Sweden), and attempted to make Russia a European rather than an Oriental state. It was a difficult task and success was not complete, but, at least, Russia never fell back to its former condition. Some of his successors were strong men and women and the power of Russia increased as time passed. The empire joined in the division of Poland, and also took much land from the Turk in the south, besides moving into Asia.

With the spread of education discontent with autocratic rule grew stronger during the nineteenth century. Many who were suspected of plotting against the government were exiled to Siberia, but riots and assassinations continued. Finally Tsar Nicholas announced the establishment of a legislative body known as the Duma, which met for the first time in 1906, but was soon dissolved. A second Duma was also dissolved, but the third and fourth Dumas were less radical, and managed to escape dissolution.

The story of Russia in World War I is sad. Though the soldiers fought bravely, they were often badly led, and usually lacked the most necessary supplies.

THIS FAMILY OF KARELIANS is enjoying a picnic on the bank of a river not far from the town of Archangel. Near the man on the right is a copper samovar—the Russian hot-water urn that is used in making tea. The Russians drink enormous quantities of tea, usually without milk or sugar, but often with a slice of lemon. The Karelians are confronted by more unusual problems of position and natural environment than most civilized peoples. Karelia was annexed to Russia by Peter the Great in 1721. The people are one of the eastern divisions of the Baltic Finns.

© E. N. A.

IN THE DAYS of the tsars there were only about 3,000 miles of paved roads in all Russia. Rough and narrow tracks like the one above were common, and are still to be seen in some of the very remote districts. However, fine, modern highways are rapidly being constructed and motor vehicles are taking the place of these simple home-made sleighs.

Sovfoto

KERCHIEFED HEADS ARE STILL THE FASHION

The girl might almost be a model for the array of round little dolls, all exactly alike. Hand-painted in bright colors, the vases and other articles as well as the dolls are made of wood. A factory of this kind is probably rather rare. The Government controls all industry and pays scant attention to products designed for amusement or decoration.

Finally in 1917 both people and army had become war-weary, and revolution broke out. The tsar abdicated but the provisional government was unable to maintain order and later the control was taken over by the Soviet of Workmen, Peasants and Soldiers, which declared for peace and the abolition of private property. Under Nicolai Lenin and Leon Trotsky, the new government was set up. Lenin died in 1924 and was succeeded by Josef Stalin. Trotsky was exiled and was assassinated in Mexico in 1940.

At first, the new Russia in Europe was considerably smaller than the old. However, the Russia of today, called the Union of Soviet Socialist Republics is a huge country which has expanded and extended its influence until it now covers more than half of Europe and an immense portion of Asia. Since World War II, many smaller countries of Europe have become parts of the Union, including Latvia, Lithuania and Estonia.

When the monarchy was overthrown and the Soviet government was established, naturally great changes took place. All power was placed in the hands of the workers and the property of the former business and professional classes was confiscated, and many of them fled the country. The cities, particularly, were

Sovfoto

A TRAVELING SHOP FOR BUSY HOUSEWIVES

The truck is fitted out as a regular store, with display windows at the rear. Halted in a near-by park, this shop serves people in Dnepropetrovsk, a large city in the east-central part of the Ukraine. Dnepropetrovsk is at the rapids of the Dnieper River, above the Dneprostroi Dam, one of the largest sources of electric power in the Soviet Union.

SOVFOTO

A MAIN STREET IN KIEV, CAPITAL OF THE UKRAINE

Kiev, on the Dnieper, is known in Russia as the "Mother of Cities," because of its great age. It was settled before the fifth century; by the thirteenth century it had become rich and powerful, and it was long the religious center of the Empire. Today Kiev is a bustling industrial town and a shipping port on the Dnieper, which flows into the Black Sea.

transformed, though the changes on the land have been hardly less striking Never before, perhaps, in the entire history of the world has so complete a transformation of an entire people taken place in so short a time.

For several years after the revolution Russia was engaged in wars with her enemies at home and abroad. When the Soviets had finally established their rule they found themselves masters of a country in ruins. Millions had been killed or had starved to death. The government controlled the country's resources, but commerce and industry were at a standstill.

During the first years food, clothing, and other goods were very scarce, and not until 1928, with the inauguration of the first "five year plan," did the real turning-point come. This plan and those that followed it were something new in national policy. Every detail of industry and agriculture—even of cultural life—was planned in advance. It was laid down just how many factories should be increased, what crops should be sown. The whole population was put to work with a will to transform a huge but backward country into a modern industrial nation. Since the Russians lacked technical skill and experience, many foreign engineers and experts—among them many Ameri-

Sovfoto

A TROIKA IS STILL USEFUL IN DEEP SNOW

Russians call any kind of vehicle drawn by three horses abreast a "troika." It may be a sleigh or a carriage. Automobiles have taken the place of the old-time carriages; but when the heavy snows of the bitter winters come, sleighs still glide over country roads. This troika is coming through an evergreen forest in the Ivanovo region, northeast of Moscow.

cans—were imported during the early years. As time went on, the Russians gradually took over the work of designing and operating their own machinery.

Though in many respects the plans fell short of the mark set, the results on the whole were astonishing. Entire new industries were created. A network of electric power began to cover the land. Much-needed canals and other important public works were constructed, often with the labor of political prisoners. In some fields of production the improvement was very great. A tremendously powerful, mechanized Red Army was developed. Education was greatly extended. Where formerly the vast majority of the people had been unable to read and write, to-day illiteracy has been much reduced.

The People Tighten Their Belts

In order to make these things possible, the Soviet Government, dominated by the Communist Party, ruled the country with an iron hand. For many years the people had to tighten their belts and endure many hardships. All enemies of the regime were ruthlessly punished; but the Russian people had undergone centuries of oppression and poverty. Now they were made to believe that the sacrifices demanded of them were in their own interest, for the purpose of building up a better order of things.

There were several five-year plans, with goals set for industry, transportation and so on. However, the planning was interrupted by World War II, in which Russia suffered great damage. After the war, the Soviet Union threw all its efforts into restoring the shattered areas. When the United Nations was set up, Russia became a member with a permanent seat on the Security Council. Unhappily for the world, it has not been a co-operative partner. Disputes and deadlocks have been the rule, aggravating international tension. Even as the carefully selected spokesmen of the Soviet Union have talked "peace" loud, Communists have seemed bent on making any real peace impossible. The most flagrant example, of course, is Korea, where the Chinese Communists have prolonged the conflict—evidently with the approval of the Soviet Union.

Though Russia has become a highly industrialized country, agriculture is as vital as ever it was under the tsars. For a long time, the peasants were the weak link in Soviet economy and not until after 1932 was there any real improvement in the agricultural problem.

The revolution gave land to the peasants, but farming was carried on by individual small land-holders, according to age-old, primitive and generally inefficient methods. Moreover the peasants could not sell their crops to the highest bidder. The government collected the entire surplus, often by forceful methods, paying far below the real value. As a result many peasants refused to raise anything beyond their needs, thus seriously endangering the country's food supply.

The Soviet plan for applying the revolution to the land was called the "collectivization of agriculture." It met with tremendous opposition, especially on the part of the moderately prosperous peasants called "kulaks." Not until there had been bloodshed and hundreds of thousands of these kulaks had been exiled did success begin to come.

Agricultural "Towns"

By the 1940's more than 90 per cent of Russian agriculture was being carried on in "collective" farms, where 10 to 30 families would work about 600 acres of land. Around 1950, however, the Government launched an even more extreme plan. Agricultural "towns" are being created, containing several thousand persons, to be run by a bureaucratic caste. It is believed that this plan will ultimately impoverish the peasants just as the kulaks were once liquidated.

Life on these vast farms is far from easy. Food is simple—mostly black bread made from rye flour, cabbage soup and, occasionally, mutton or pork. There is also a dish called "kasha," made from buckwheat and milk, with perhaps a few raisins. This is comparatively nourishing fare, but quite monotonous.

SOVFOTO

A SHEPHERD FONDLY PETS A PRIZE-WINNING ANIMAL

The shepherd's warm cap is no less fleecy than the coats of his charges. These sheep are a special breed developed in Russia and produce a semifine wool needed for some kinds of cloth.

Sovfoto

APARTMENT HOUSES ON THE OKTYABRSKAYA, A STREET IN STALINGRAD

This view of Stalingrad, taken since the second World War, gives little indication that the city was reduced to a heap of smoking ruins in one of the most prolonged and fierce battles of all time. Stalingrad is on the lower Volga River, where it bends to the west; and the Germans hoped to cut the vital supply artery of the river at this point. The battle lasted from August 1942 until February 1943. Defeat of the Germans here marked the beginning of their decline in military power. The Russians took pride in rebuilding Stalingrad as quickly as possible.

Under the agricultural-town plan, the workers who must leave the old collectives must give up their little private plots of land, a last vestige of capitalism, which each collective farmer was allowed. The peasant class was the last large element in the population that had demonstrated any capability of resisting the Government, at least by passive means.

However, as the towns have a centralized administration in the hands of Communist party bureaucrats, farm workers are supervised more closely than ever.

At the same time the towns are being created, a tremendous effort is being made to speed up the mechanization of agriculture. Consequently, more young men are being trained to handle machinery and tractors and would be readily available as reserves for mechanized armies.

One result of all this will be that in time villages and hamlets will disappear altogether. In fact, the Government has announced that the system will achieve "liquidation of the contrast between town and country." One can only guess what it must mean in terms of personal hardship

Sovfoto

WHERE NEVSKY PROSPECT CROSSES ANICHKOV BRIDGE, IN LENINGRAD

Nevsky Prospect is one of the principal thoroughfares in Leningrad and the most famous. For a time after the Revolution it was called October 25 Prospect. Some of the most imposing buildings of the days of the tsars still stand along this street, among them the baroque Stroganov Palace, and the Anichkov Palace. The latter is now called the Young Pioneers Palace.

RIVER-BOAT PIER ON THE VOLGA AT KUIBYSHEV

At this point in its course—called the Samara Bend—the Volga is joined by the Samara River and is very broad. Along the water front of the city there are many wharves and extensive shipyards. Traffic on the river is heavy, and Kuibyshev has a large share in this activity. River boats leave its docks laden with grain, livestock and many kinds of manufactured goods.

PHOTOS, SOVFOTO

HOUSES FROM TSARIST DAYS FACE REVOLUTION SQUARE

Like many other Russian cities, Kuibyshev (formerly called Samara) was made over in some ways and given a new name after the Communists came to power. Its modern development, beginning around 1900, was due to the fact that it was on the line of the railroads then being built into Asia. Today it is a center of heavy industry, with aircraft, locomotive and tractor factories.

© Ewing Galloway

GORKI (NIJNI NOVGOROD), CITY ON THE VOLGA

Gorki, formerly known as Nijni Novgorod, was once famous for the great fair that was held there each year. To it came traders not only from all over Russia but from many foreign lands as well. The fair was held on a huge plain where a temporary town was erected for the occasion. Gorki is a busy city of more than 450,000 inhabitants.

to the workers being shifted.

Outsiders believe that the vast program cannot be accomplished without economic turmoil, a reduction in the planned agricultural output and a social upheaval so great as to keep the Soviet authorities fully occupied for some time.

For years Russia paid little attention to foreign affairs. In August 1939, however, a non-aggression pact with Germany was signed. When Germany broke down resistance in Poland, Russia annexed over half of that state, and compelled the three little Baltic States, Latvia, Estonia and Lithuania, to allow the establishment of naval bases in their harbors. Next it was claimed that Finland was a danger to Russia and cession of territory was demanded. The Finns refused and for over a hundred days resisted the might of Russia, but in the end lost considerable territory. In 1940 Russia took complete control of the Baltic States and also took over Bessarabia and part of Bukovina from Rumania.

In spite of the non-aggression pact, Germany launched a sudden attack against Russia, in June 1941, which brought the Soviet Union into World War II on the side of the Allies. The high-water mark of the German invasion was the Battle of Stalingrad, where the Nazis were turned back after a fierce struggle. Eventually, in the closing days of the war in Europe, Red Army soldiers met Western Allied troops in Berlin. Germany was divided into four zones, with Soviet troops occupying the eastern zone. Here Communist influence became dominant. In Poland, Bulgaria, Rumania, Hungary and Czechoslovakia, the Communists also gained.

Before the Bolshevik revolution of 1917, religion played a great part in the life of the Russian people. The prevailing creed was that of the Russian Orthodox Church. Almost every cottage or house contained a corner with a small sacred picture or image, usually of the Virgin Mary or of one of the saints. Churches and chapels dotted the land.

SOVFOTO

REINDEER EAT LICHENS THAT GROW BENEATH THE SNOW

Reindeer can live where the land is always frozen, and in arctic places like northern Russia they are of great worth. They can draw sleds for long distances and can carry men or heavy loads on their backs, their sharp, cleft hoofs giving them firm footing on ice or in snow drifts. They also provide milk, meat, wool and leather for the people of these northern lands.

SOVFOTO

THEATER IN ARCHANGEL, NEAR THE WHITE SEA

Just below the great port city of Archangel the River Dvina empties into the White Sea. The Arctic Circle is only one hundred and fifty miles to the north, and the harbor at Archangel is frozen for a good half of the year; but it handles a great volume of traffic during the months when it is ice-free. Above is the Civic Theater, at the river's edge.

After 1918, the Communists separated the church from the state and the school from the church, and appropriated most of the church property. Freedom of worship was guaranteed in the constitution of 1936, but no church member may have a part in the Government. Atheism is taught in the schools. Among churchgoers the Russian Orthodox Church has the largest following. Its two branches have headquarters at Moscow.

Peter the Great began to build his city in 1703 upon land taken from the Swedes. The ground was marshy and it was necessary to build the houses upon piles. Thousands of people from all parts of Russia were brought to the spot and forced to labor. So many died that there is an old saying that the city was really built upon bones. Under the succeeding tsars the city grew until the population was about a million and a half at the beginning of the first World War. The name was then changed to the Russian form Petrograd instead of the German St. Petersburg.

In 1918 the Soviet Government transferred the government to Moscow, and the former capital declined. In 1924 the name was changed to Leningrad, after Nikolai Lenin, founder of the U.S.S.R.

There was a general exodus from the city after 1918, and the population was at one time estimated as hardly more than half a million. However, between the two World Wars, the tide turned, and Leningrad is now the second largest city of the Soviet Union, with well over 3,000,000 population. It is a busy port and shipbuilding center.

A number of railroads converge at Leningrad, and the city is connected with Kronstadt, a port on the Gulf of Finland, by a sixteen-mile canal. Another canal system connects Leningrad with the White Sea, 141 miles away.

Russia is full of museums of every sort. In some, are works of art. In others, the life, customs and dress of every era are shown. There are exhibits of industrial processes and methods. All works of art in private hands all through Russia have been confiscated and placed in museums already existing or in others founded since the establishment of the communist regime. One of the most famous of Russia's museums is the Hermitage, in Leningrad; it contains a magnificent art and archaeological collection.

Originally built by Catherine II, it was reconstructed in 1840–50.

Moscow is connected by rail with Leningrad, the old capital of Russia, first known as St. Petersburg, then as Petrograd. We are told that this particular railway affords an example of the autocratic rule of the tsars. The railway was under construction when Nicholas I was on the throne. Difficulties arose as to the line it should follow; marshes were in the way and thick forest had to be penetrated, so that a very winding route seemed necessary. As the engineers were unable to agree upon the best route, the matter was referred to the Tsar who, it is said, called for a map, a pencil and a ruler. Taking the map, he drew a line from Moscow to Leningrad and stated that that was the route to be followed. This is why the railway runs so very straight.

Eastern Domes and Western Subway

During its history Russia has had five capitals, and Moscow has had that honor again since 1918. However, it is a very different city from what it was in the days of the tsars, though still a curious mixture of East and West. The onion-shaped domes of the old churches have a Moorish look; and at the other extreme is a modern subway, one of the Communists' showpieces, with marble stations decorated in stainless steel.

Just when Moscow was founded is uncertain. However, its 800th birthday was celebrated in 1947. It is first mentioned in the Russian Chronicles in 1147. It grew up on the main trade routes that led from Europe to the Orient and from the Baltic to the Caspian Sea. Mongolian hordes sacked it again and again. The Russians themselves set fire to their beloved city—"Little Mother Moscow"—in 1812 in order to prevent Napoleon from setting up winter quarters there, after his capture of the city.

Moscow is in the center of the great Russian plain, and is situated on seven low hills, rising in terraces from the high banks of the Moscow River, which winds across the city. The main part is on the north bank. Overlooking the river from Borovitzky Hill, in the very center of the city, is the vast Kremlin, or "Fortress." Wide streets radiate from it to the city's suburbs.

The ground on which the Kremlin stands is an irregular triangle, surrounded by a wall about 1¼ miles in circumference and from 14 to 20 feet thick and from 30 to 70 feet high. In the wall are 5 gates, and 19 towers, each one in a different style though all are generally pyramids in shape. The eastern and main entrance to the Kremlin, from Red Square, is the fifteenth-century Spasskiya Gate (Gate of the Redeemer), 205 feet high. Atop this gate is a belfry. For many years after the Revolution, the bells pealed forth the INTERNATIONAL at regular intervals. Napoleon entered from the Borovitzkiya Gate (Gate of the Woods), 62 feet high. Inside the walls are a bewildering number of buildings, including a vast palace, in a variety of styles—Byzantine, Renaissance, Baroque. Towering over all is the high dome of the Cathedral of the Assumption, begun in 1393. There is one thoroughfare, Communist Street.

Red Square, 900 yards long and 175 yards broad, is the center of political life. In front of the Kremlin gleams the polished red and black marble tomb of Lenin, a communist shrine. On the other side from the Kremlin is the many-domed St. Basil's Cathedral, now a museum. Red Square frequently echoes to the sound of marching feet in the huge parades staged by the Government.

The Soviet Union in Asia

A train goes from Moscow east to Siberia, actually a rich and fertile territory, with vast natural wealth in minerals, furbearing animals and timber. Formerly Siberia was looked upon as a land of ice, but the Russians have discovered what a wonderful wheat-producing land it is as well as its other possibilities. There are a number of manufacturing towns east of the Urals today.

In the old days the only means of communication were the roads and rivers, and even the imperial mail took many months to reach its destination. Convicts

SOVFOTO

A STEAMER AND GREAT LOG RAFTS BREAST THE MIGHTY VOLGA

Though most of the timber is destined for sawmills, some of the rafts are permanent and have houses on them. They provide shelter for the men who must keep the unwieldy logs in order.

BURIAT SHEPHERD AND HIS STEED

The Buriats live in north-central Asia, on either side of Lake Baikal. They are of Mongol origin, with high cheek bones, slanting eyes and sturdy frame. They gain a living chiefly by stock-raising, their occupation now being under strict Soviet supervision. The land of the Buriats is rugged and beautiful. Lake Baikal contains seals, as well as many kinds of fish.

PHOTOS, SOVFOTO

WAREHOUSE FOR FURS IN THE FAR NORTH

Just across the Bering Strait from Alaska is the Chukotsky Peninsula, Russia's northeastern outpost. It is a chill region, bisected by the Arctic Circle and inhabited mostly by foxes, wolves and bears, and their trappers. Here a quantity of precious skins—polar fox and others—are sorted and processed. Furs are one of the Soviet Union's articles of export.

SOVFOTO

IN KHABAROVSK, EMBROIDERY IS A WORK OF ART

The women of Khabarovsk, in far eastern Asia, adorn their tunics, coats, gloves and even their fur footwear with lavish embroidery. Khabarovsk, on a cliff above the Amur River, has a cosmopolitan population, with Russians, Chinese, Koreans and others mingling on the streets. The city is cold for much of the year and clothing must be warmly padded.

took two years to reach the penal settlements situated to the north of what is now the Trans-Siberian Railway, and only the hardiest of them survived the terrible march. Until recently, Siberia was a convict colony, as Australia once was—a place to which all the political prisoners and many of the worst criminals of Russia could be sent. The opening of the Trans-Siberian Railway (1891-1905) caused a stream of voluntary colonists to flow into Siberia from all parts of Russia. These sturdy peasants began to develop the land, and the wealth of the forests was tapped. When the large estates in European Russia were confiscated and divided among the peasants, the movement to Siberia almost ceased for a time, but has begun again. The migration is encouraged by the government at Moscow, which sends technical experts to aid the colonists and plans to extend the mileage of the railways.

Siberia in the Winter

If we travel across Siberia by train, we shall see a varied landscape—vast plains, like the prairies in North America, valleys and hills covered with birch trees, and extensive forests of pine and fir. During the winter, communication between villages and towns that are far from the railway is maintained by means of sledges. Three horses are usually harnessed to a sledge, and the driver has to be so muffled up in furs that, when seated, he looks like a huge barrel. The thermometer often drops to fifty degrees below zero, and on leaving a house to get into a sledge the change from the warm air to the cold is so great that for the moment it takes away one's breath.

A Story of the Old Days

Irkutsk and Tomsk are two important cities of Siberia. The latter is in the western part of the country, fifty-four miles north of the railway. There is a story which illustrates the corruption under the tsars. When the line was being built the engineers suggested that they should receive the sum of one hundred thousand rubles (then about $50,000) as a reward for running the line through the city. The people of Tomsk refused to pay the bribe, and said that the city was so important that the railway must pass through it. To have given in would have made it difficult for the engineers to obtain money from the inhabitants of the other towns situated along the proposed route of the line, and they said they could not lay the line through Tomsk owing to natural obstacles. That is why Tomsk is not on the Trans-Siberian Railway, though it is now connected by a branch line.

Primitive Siberian Peoples

The Siberians are hardy, as they must needs be to exist in such a severe climate. In the market places everything is frozen during the winter months. Milk is sold in chunks, and fish and meat must be chopped up with an ax. North central Siberia is colder than the North Pole, but the summers are short and very hot.

Of the native Siberian peoples, the Samoyedes are the most primitive. There are several groups scattered over a wide area. Some of them build rude huts of stone. Others live a part of the year within the Arctic Circle in tents of reindeer skin, of which they also make their clothes. They gain a living by hunting and fishing, and at the beginning of winter they move south with their herds of reindeer to the forest districts, returning to the north in the spring. They pass about one-third of the year on the march, because in the summer they cannot remain in the south owing to the plague of flies and mosquitoes.

They have many strange beliefs and customs. For instance, they worship enormous stones weighing many thousands of tons which were probably deposited by glaciers in the early Ice Age. The Samoyedes regard these stones with great reverence, for they believe that the Creator himself brought them there. A wife is purchased with so many reindeer, the number varying between one and a hundred according to her beauty and the social position of her family. Her dowry consists of furs and a reindeer for driving, and if the husband finds that she is lazy he can send her back to her parents, though he cannot recover the price he

WITHIN THE VAST KREMLIN at Moscow are chapels, palaces, barracks, offices and two cathedrals. A battlemented brick wall, more than a mile and a quarter in circumference, strengthened with towers, encloses the group of buildings. The structures are of all sizes, styles and ages, for each tsar seems to have added a church or a palace. The Kremlin was the ancient residence of the tsars. The Great Kremlin Palace occupies the site on which stood the old wooden and stone palaces of the tsars. It is now the seat of a government far different from the old.

A ROW OF SMALL HOMES IN A WORKERS' VILLAGE NEAR KAKHOVKA

Kakhovka is the center of a hydroelectric project on the Dnieper River in southern Ukraine. The region is a steppe, rich in the production of wheat, cotton, grapes and vegetables.

PHOTOS, SOVFOTO

A MOSCOW FAMILY AT BREAKFAST IN A MODEST NEW APARTMENT

This family is indeed fortunate to have a new home. There is a continuing shortage of housing in the crowded capital and the growing industrial centers of the Soviet Union.

paid for her. This often suits the parents, as they can sell her again and so get more money. The Samoyedes are a hospitable race and are kind and generous to travelers, doing everything in their power to make them comfortable.

In northern Siberia we find another race—the Chukchi, who are remarkable as being one of the few tribes on the earth's surface who have remained unconquered. They have successfully resisted all efforts to annex their country. Some years ago the Russians did send a small force which was more an exploring expedition than an army of invasion, but not a man returned. Their fate still remains a complete mystery.

The Chukchi gain a living by spearing seals and walrus, from their skin canoes, and by tracking the polar bear, which is a dangerous task in the spring when the ice breaks up into bergs and floes. Many of the floes are several square miles in area, and on them the hunters are sometimes carried away, never to return. The Chukchi dwelling is a semi-circular tent of walrus and seal hide, seal oil being used to provide light. Both the men and the women dress alike in suits made from seal, walrus and reindeer skins.

The Chukchi religion is a queer mixture of Christianity, spirit worship and Shamanism. They believe that only those who die a violent death have a future life, and have a custom of killing the aged, the sick and the infirm. The sentence of death is accepted without question; indeed, those condemned will even give a feast before their execution, and at the end of it readily submit to being speared or to being strangled with a walrus thong.

The chief occupation of the people is preparing seal and walrus hides. This is done by the women, who chew the tough skins for hours at a stretch, with the result that within a few years the teeth are worn down to the gums, like those of the Eskimo women.

Farther east, in the province of Transbaikalia, which is said to be the most attractive in Siberia, we meet the Buriats. The province has many mountains and valleys. In it is Lake Baikal, one of the largest lakes in the world and by far the deepest. The natives there look upon it as a holy lake.

The Buriats are a race of Mongolian origin, with square faces, flat foreheads and rather high cheek-bones. The most numerous of all the native Siberian races, they are found on both sides of the immense lake. They gain a living chiefly by cattle-breeding, but this pastoral occupation is of comparatively recent origin. Culturally, they are the most advanced among all native tribes. In general they are Buddhists in religion, though some are Shamanists and others are Christians of a sort. They have some queer superstitions. They believe that the sky has a door, through which the good look to see how the affairs of the world are progressing.

If the gods consider that anyone is deserving of help they will send their children to perform the good work, and should anyone happen to be looking upward when the door in the sky is opened he will have good luck.

Far to the northeast of Transbaikalia is the province of Yakutsk, which is said to be the coldest region on the earth's surface. The thermometer in winter goes to 80° below zero, and the ground is frozen many feet deep. The Yakuts have many quaint customs, especially in connection with marriages. Two riders, one each from the bride's and the bridegroom's household, are chosen at a wedding to ride a race. The loser has to wait upon the guests at the marriage feast.

Before this feast a sacrifice is made in the future home of the bride. She walks from the north toward the fire on the hearth and throws into it three specially prepared sticks which she has brought from her parents' home. With the sticks is a piece of butter, and as they burn she declares that she has come to rule over the hearth—meaning that she will do all that a good wife should in the household. She then makes a bow to her husband's mother and father, and the actual ceremony is at an end.

All diseases among the Yakuts are treated by the shamans, or medicine men, who drive away sicknesses somewhat in

BECKETT

THE CATHEDRAL OF ST. BASIL (Vasili the Beatified) stands at the southeast end of the Krasnaya, or Red Square, in Moscow, presenting an extraordinary appearance with its twelve fantastic colored domes. It was begun in the reign of Ivan the Terrible, and there is a legend that he had the architects blinded when the work was done. It is now a Soviet museum.

"LITTLE MOTHER MOSCOW," as the city is sometimes called by Russians, is again the capital of Russia. It lies on both banks of the River Moskva. The outer city is called the White City, and is encircled by broad boulevards, intersected by wide thoroughfares radiating from the Kremlin which is seen in the distance. Moscow is one of the oldest cities of Russia.

PALATIAL ARCHED STAIRWAY OF THE METRO, MOSCOW'S SUBWAY

Polished marble walls, domed plaster ceilings, floral moldings and decorative wrought-metal chandeliers complete the picture of opulence in the Komsomolskaya-Koltsevaya Station.

PHOTOS, SOVFOTO

IZMAILOVSKAYA STATION, A SHOW PIECE OF THE SOVIETS

Supplementing the surface means of transportation—streetcars and busses—the Metro branches out in four lines though it is not very long. It is meant for show.

SOVFOTO

THE SOVIET IDEA OF WHAT MODERN ARCHITECTURE SHOULD BE

A blend of the old and the new in a Smolensk Square, Moscow, building—an example of skyscraper art in the Soviet Union. Massive stone piers seem to brace the gigantic tower and sweep the eye upward to the timid, ornate spire. Symmetrical wings, some of them with pinnacles, others without, flank the tower. There are two thousand air-conditioned offices in all.

FROM THE IVAN VELIKY TOWER within the Kremlin, we can look down upon the vast city that has grown up around this inner fortress-city. The huge bell-tower was completed in 1600 and rises in five stories to a height of three hundred and eighteen feet. From it Napoleon is said to have watched the city burn in 1812. The Church of the Redeemer,

BECKETT

seen in the distance, with its golden domes and its marble walls, has been destroyed to make room for the Palace of Soviets. There were about four hundred and fifty churches in Moscow, many of them having golden cupolas, so that on sunny days, they caught the eye, no matter in what direction we looked. To Western eyes the city seemed unreal.

the manner of the devil dancers of Ceylon —by frightening them, by spitting and blowing or by the making of hideous noises on drums and other instruments.

In southern Siberia there is yet another interesting tribe—the Kalmuks, who live in the Altai region, where the finest forests in Siberia are found. The Kalmuks are Buddhists. They wear their hair in short pigtails; their habitations are semicircular felt tents; and their general mode of living is similar to that of the Buriats.

UNION OF SOVIET SOCIALIST REPUBLICS: FACTS AND FIGURES

THE COUNTRY

Occupies the eastern half of Europe and the northern part of Asia. On the north the boundary is the Arctic Ocean, on the east the Pacific Ocean, on the south is China, Afghanistan, Persia (Iran), Caspian Sea, Turkey and the Black Sea; on the west, Rumania, Hungary, Czechoslovakia, Poland, the Baltic Sea and Finland. The Soviet includes the Russian Soviet Federal Socialist Republic (area, 6,609,000 square miles), Ukrainian Soviet Socialist Republic (225,200), White Russian or Bielorussian S.S.R. (81,090), Azerbaijan S.S.R. (33,460), Georgian S.S.R. (37,570), Armenian S.S.R. (11,640), Turkoman S.S.R. (189,370), Uzbek S.S.R. (159,170), Tadzhik S.S.R. (55,700), Kazakh S.S.R. (1,072,000), Kirghiz S.S.R. (76,900), Karelo-Finnish S.S.R. (69,720), Moldavian S.S.R. (13,200), Estonia S.S.R. (17,610), Latvia S.S.R. (24,840), Lithuania S.S.R. (31,600). Total population, 193,200,000; total area, 8,708,070 square miles.

GOVERNMENT

By constitution of 1936, the U.S.S.R. is a "socialist state of peasants and workers." The highest organ is the Supreme Council made up of two chambers—the Council of Union, elected by proportional representation, and the Council of Nationalities consisting of representatives from each constituent republic, autonomous republic, autonomous province and autonomous district. Executive and administrative power is vested in the Council of People's Commissars, responsible to the Supreme Council.

Greater decentralization in the internal political structure was adopted in 1944 as a means of facilitating admission of new republics into the Soviet Union through the assurance of autonomy in foreign and military affairs. All citizens of either sex over 18 years of age are granted the franchise. A "dictatorship of the proletariat" is maintained through the agency of the Communist Party.

COMMERCE AND INDUSTRIES

Formerly a strictly agricultural country Soviet Russia has become an industrial agrarian country, second only to the United States in its industrial output. Industrial production is organized under a planning system and conducted by state trusts and combines, operated under the supervision of appropriate governmental departments. There are great numbers of industrial establishments for the production of pig iron, steel, coal, oil, etc. Ninety-five per cent of the agricultural output, which includes wheat, rye, barley, oats, corn, cotton, sugar beets, flax, sunflower seeds, and tobacco, is produced on collective and state farms that have been highly mechanized. Mineral resources include coal, peat, oil, iron ore, manganese, copper, zinc and lead. The forests are important. Principal exports are sawn timber, furs, oil, cotton fabrics, pulpwood, grain, and manganese ore; the principal imports, industrial machinery and tools, sheet iron and steel, ferro-alloys, motor vehicles and parts.

COMMUNICATIONS

There are 66,000 miles of railways and about 68,365 miles of navigable waterways. In May 1952 a 63-mile canal was opened to join the Don and Volga rivers and so link the Baltic and White seas with the Caspian and Azov seas. There are some 1,200,000 miles of roadways (highways and local roads). The length of telegraph wires, about 600,000 miles; telephone wire, about 1,300,000. This does not include mileages in territory added after 1938.

RELIGION AND EDUCATION

Officially, according to the constitution, there is religious freedom in the U.S.S.R. However, the state is supreme in all things and even where a faith is tolerated (such as the Russian Orthodox Church, which was the largest denomination under the tsars), it is controlled rigidly by the Communist Government and, in fact, is far from free.

Education is compulsory and entirely state-controlled. There are special schools with emphasis on trade schools, classes and schools for adult education and various universities.

CHIEF TOWNS

Moscow, the capital, population, 4,137,018; Leningrad, 3,191,304; Baku, 809,347; Kharkov, 833,432; Kiev, 846,293; Rostov-on-Don, 510,253; Odessa, 604,223; Tashkent, 585,505; Gorki, (Nijni Novgorod), 644,116; Tiflis, 519,175; Sverdlovsk, 425,544; Stalingrad, 445,576; Dnieperpetrovsk, 500,662; Saratov, 375,860; Stalino, 462,395; Novosibirsk, 405,589; Kuibishev (Samara), 390,267; Kazan, 401,665; Omsk, 227,000; Voronezh, 326,836; Yaroslavl, 298,065; Astrakhan, 254,000.

A GLIMPSE OF TURKESTAN

And Its Crumbling Cities of Old Renown

Once the home of barbaric conquerors and their fierce, savage hordes, Turkestan sprawled across the ancient trade routes from Europe to the fabulous East. Through the noisy, crowded marts of "Golden Samarkand" passed untold wealth in rich silks, brocades and jade. In their caravans, traders brought from Bokhara (or Bukhara) fine carpets, the likes of which had never been seen in medieval Europe. Turkestan was a land that stirred the imagination. Today the old glamour and feeling of romance have disappeared from Turkestan, but the inhabitants remain strange and picturesque, as our photographs show. As part of the Soviet Union, Western Turkestan is strategically important in the modern world, with its wealth of mineral resources, potential hydroelectric power and growing industrial expansion.

STRETCHING far away from the Caspian Sea and Persia on the west to the borders of China in the east is the vast country of Turkestan (or Turkistan). Eastern Turkestan is a part of the Chinese province of Sin-Kiang (Sinkiang) of which we speak elsewhere. Here we shall tell of the larger Western, or Russian, Turkestan.

It is a large slice of Asia with an area of over a million square miles, and with a history that goes back thousands of years before Christ. The Huns, centuries previous to the time we hear of them in Europe, had an empire in this territory. They were broken up and driven out by the Chinese who were in turn succeeded by a people later known as Tatars. The Arabs, converting to Islamism as they came, overran it, as also did the Turks and Mongol hordes.

Turkestan, like many another part of Asia, has been a fierce battleground for the wild tribesmen of that region. Emir and khan, one after another, rose in power and held sway until a stronger leader came to wrest supremacy from their hands. Jenghiz Khan was one of these Asiatic kings who became one of the greatest conquerors known to history but greater even than he was Tamerlane who led his plundering hordes from the Volga to the Persian Gulf, from the Hellespont to the Ganges, and was actually on his way to invade China with his victorious armies when death overtook him.

It was at Samarkand, the "Golden Samarkand" of the Oriental poet, that Tamerlane held his court. Magnificent though it had been before, the city attained greater fame and glory under this mighty ruler.

What have the changing centuries brought to this old Asiatic empire? As Tamerlane's kingdom crumbled away it was parceled out among lesser kings and khans. One race and then another won independence and set up a khanate, or kingdom, of its own. We find the Turcomans had gathered in the country between the great river, Amu Daria (the Oxus of the ancients), and the Caspian Sea, and elsewhere were established the petty kingdoms of Bokhara and Khiva.

The greater part of this western portion of Turkestan is desert, but here and there oases occur and the land has become extraordinarily fertile. At Merv, for instance, in the heart of the Turcoman's country, there is the largest area of cultivated land in the whole province. The climate is well suited for cotton-growing and many thousands of acres are given up to this industry.

Never a single nation, the name Turkestan means simply the place of Turkish peoples. In this strange land of Turkestan the surface of the earth is constantly changing, rivers are shifting their courses or wandering off to be swallowed up by the desert sands, lakes are drying up and earthquakes sometimes occur.

Uzbek is sprinkled with ancient and very famous cities planted centuries ago on the oases of this semi-desert land. The mere mention of the name—Bukhara—

D. CARRUTHERS

SAMARKAND, a city in the Uzbek Republic, is a most ancient town. We first hear of it 329 B.C., under the name of Marcanda, at which time it was destroyed by Alexander the Great. It lies by the Zarafshan River, about 160 miles north of the Afghan border. No other city has by its name alone so stirred the imaginations of men as has Samarkand ever since the days of its magnificence in the fourteenth century under Tamarlane. It has since been overshadowed by Bokhara. In 1868 it was taken by the Russians and a modern town was built beside the old one.

D. CARRUTHERS

BOKHARA, the province, bounds Samarkand on the south. The several native States over which Uzbek dynasties formerly ruled were founded in the fifteenth century upon the ruins of Tamerlane's empire. Bokhara, the famous capital, lies in the northwest. The ancient Eastern city is an expanse of flat, gray-brown roofs relieved by towers of mosques.

© E. N. A.

TOBACCO BOUGHT BY THE PUFF

In Khiva, one need not be encumbered with smoking supplies. A tobacco dealer wanders about with a lighted water-pipe, which allows the smoke to bubble through water, and sells his wares to passers-by at so much a puff!

brings memory of gorgeous oriental rugs which have been named after the cities where they have so long been marketed.

But Turkestan is known not only for its rugs but also for its eagles. For the Mohammedans love to train hawks and eagles for hunting. Their eagles will attack even wolves.

Across this country people have sifted through the centuries like sand over a desert. To understand modern Turkestan a brief historical sketch is necessary. The country has altered little since the time when Tatar, Turk and Mongol ranged over its mountains and plains, when "Sultan after Sultan, with his pomp, abode his hour or two and went his way." And in some respects the peoples themselves have undergone but little change. Large numbers of them live by raising horses, camels, cattle and sheep, by growing cotton and wheat and fruit, or by working the rich mineral deposits of the country.

Among the peoples in the western part of this group of present-day Soviet Republics the Turcomans are the most important. Mohammedans by religion, they are akin to the Beduins in the nature of their life, for they have regular camping places and move from one pasturage to another according to the season. Turcomans were always nomads, and because of their fierceness they were always dreaded by their neighbors. They plundered ruthlessly, waylaying the rich caravans of the Persian traders and looting greedily. Out of this arose a great trade in slaves, but the Turcoman's activities in this direction have been checked by the Russians.

The Turcoman is rather a striking figure dressed in his baggy trousers and coarse shirt, which is mostly concealed by an outer garment of colored material somewhat like a dressing-gown. To complete his costume, he wears high-heeled boots, a shaggy high hat made of sheep's wool and a gaudy scarlet sash. This is the ordinary tribesman of the plains. In the case of the better class Turcomans, those who are counted wealthy in flocks and herds, the common garments give place to richly embroidered robes, while the trappings of their horses and camels are splendidly adorned with gold and silver and precious stones.

Their womenfolk like to wear quantities of jewelry and display many bracelets and anklets. In place of the sheepskin or felt hats of the men they cover their heads with cotton cloths, much in the form of a turban, and these headdresses, too, will be plentifully decorated with silver ornaments and coins. It is said that one judges the wealth of a Turcoman by the amount of silver worn by his wife. Like the Beduins to whom they have been compared, this people leave a great deal of manual work to the women for which reason the latter age quickly. The women go unveiled, like the Beduins again, but unlike the women of nearly all other Mohammedan countries.

There are Turcomans who settle in towns and villages, in which the houses are simply built of mud and stone. But the majority, true desert wanderers, live in tents—"kibitkas" they are called—which are made of braided willows and covered with felt. If we look into one of these tents we shall see that the furniture consists of a carpet on the floor and several brilliantly colored rugs hanging on the walls, together with cloaks, embroidered garments, saddlebags, bridles and other articles. In one corner is a wooden chest, which contains the women's clothing and other gear. During the winter time a fire burns in the middle of the tent, and as there is no chimney and the smoke has to find its way out as best it can, the atmosphere is none of the pleasantest.

Summer time on these western "steppes," or plains, is endurable, though often very hot. In the winter, especially when the weather is severe, the conditions of life are very hard. Terrible blizzards storm across the desert, often destroying flocks and herds and human beings as well. In January the temperature may go down to 40° below zero. We can get some idea of the intensity of the cold from the description given by Colonel Burnaby in his famous Ride to Khiva. The nostrils of the horses, he says, became blocked with ice, and cabbage soup froze solid when it was made. It had to be carried on camelback and broken off as it was wanted.

EWING GALLOWAY

TOWNSMEN AT EASE BEFORE A MOSQUE OF ANCIENT BUKHARA

A water seller sits behind his jugs; a melon peddler is at the foot of the steps to the mosque, a center of social as well as religious life in the Islamic city. Most of the people of Bukhara are Uzbeks, nomadic herdsmen of Turkestan who long ago drove the Persians and Turks from the Kyzyl Kum, the arid region between the Amu and Syr Darya (rivers).

LIEUT.-COL. P. J. ETHERTON

THE ROOF OF THE WORLD is the picturesque name man has given to that huge, bleak knot of mountains known as the Pamirs, lying in Central Asia between Afghanistan, Turkestan and Sin-kiang (Chinese Turkestan).

Himalayas, the Karakoram range and the Hindu Kush. "Pamir" means valley between two ridges. These valleys are nowhere less than 10,000 feet above the sea and the highest peak is over 26,000 above the sea. Through

It is desert country, this western region, as has been said, but it is made habitable by the presence of oases. A Turkestan oasis consists of wide fields of wheat, barley, cotton and grass, well watered by streams from a near-by river or by wells and irrigation ditches, and broken by groves of locust trees, with their sweet-smelling blossom, and orchards and vineyards. It is a paradise set in a stony wilderness. The soil here is usually very rich and it can be made to produce—as at Merv—fine crops of wheat and cotton. At one time Turkestan was quite a large wheat-growing country. Nowadays cotton is cultivated as yielding greater profit.

Peoples of Mongolian Origin

Two other peoples of the original Turki race go to make up the population of Turkestan. These are the Kirghiz and the Uzbegs. The first-named are themselves divided into the Kazaks, or Kirghiz-Kazaks, and the Kara-Kirghiz. Both tribes dwell in the eastern portion of Turkestan. Their features show plainly their Mongolian origin. They are a short people, with round, dark faces and small, keen, black eyes which look at one from beneath tightly drawn, slanting eyelids. The Kazaks are the lowlanders, the dwellers in the northern and eastern steppes, and are shepherds and herdsmen. The Kara-Kirghiz are the mountaineers, the highlanders, and their home is in the Pamirs and in the huge Tian Shan range, the Celestial Mountains.

By religion the Kirghiz, like other Turkestan peoples, are Mohammedans but shave their heads and allow their beards to grow. Their costume resembles that of the Turcomans, except that the baggy breeches are of leather. A coarsely made shirt with a wide-striped collar and an over-tunic of the dressing-gown pattern are worn, together with the usual tall hat of sheepskin.

The Persian name Kirghiz, it may be noted, means "forty daughters." In the tradition of the tribesmen, it was a son of Noah who settled in Turkestan after the Flood, and this son was the father of forty daughters. From these the Kirghiz believe themselves to be descended, and hence their name.

Turkestan's Fair-skinned Inhabitants

The Uzbegs, who, with a race known as Tajiks, are found in most parts of the country, are a people of light complexion. The men wear turbans of white linen, and their principal garment is the "khalet," a long flowing coat dyed in brilliant colors. With the Uzbegs, it is the custom for the women to wear a veil and no one but a husband, a son, or a very close relative is permitted to look upon their faces.

With a brief mention of the Tajiks, who lay claim to Arab descent, we may conclude this description of Turkestan's principal peoples. Actually they originally hailed from Persia; apart from physical characteristics and similarities in language, this is shown by their typical Persian aptitude for trade. They are the merchants of the province, and their reputation is one for cunning and greed. The intellectual superiors of the Uzbegs, the Tajiks congregate in the towns, while the majority of the former follow agriculture and kindred industries.

A Glimpse of Ancient Cities

And now, what of the cities of Turkestan, those strongholds of other days, which have witnessed such stirring events in the whirligig of time? First of all, let us take a peep at Tashkent. As a map shows, it lies on a branch of the River Syr Daria, with great mountains at its back. There are two cities actually—the old native city, inhabited by a people known as Sarts, a term used to designate the nomadic Uzbegs who have become settled, and there is the modern Russian quarter. Thanks to the care exercised by the Russian conquerors Tashkent has been beautified by many groves of trees and large gardens. One special feature of the capital is the market. The bazaars of Tashkent are declared to be the finest in the world, rivaling even those of Cairo. To its shops come all the treasures of the East, the beautiful carpets, the richly em-

EWING GALLOWAY

BUKHARA STUDENTS TAKE TIME OUT FOR A JOKE IN THE SUN

The young men are Mohammedans who are studying the Koran. Their setting is appropriate for the niche is in the Moslem style of architecture. Above the grill is a lovely mosaic.

EWING GALLOWAY

A SHOULDER MAKES A FINE PLACE TO DISPLAY A RUG

The fringed rug, in an interesting geometric design, is the product of a factory in Mary, Turkmenistan. Once called Merv, the city has long been a center of carpet manufacturing.

EWING GALLOWAY

IN THE BROILING SUN OF THE DESERT, AT TEKKE OASIS, A CARAVAN PAUSES FOR REST AND WATER

So much of Russian Turkestan is desert that caravans of camels are still the chief means of transportation. Most caravans move on regular schedules, and there are inns (the Eastern word is "caravansary") at several oases for the convenience of travelers and their beasts of burden.

BLACK STAR

A KAZAKH TRIBESMAN, HIS FACE ETCHED BY TIME AND WEATHER

On his native plains he has endured withering heat in summertime and intense cold in the winter. For Kazakhstan is deep within Asia and has the extremes of a continental climate.

BLACK STAR

A UZBEK COBBLER GRINS CHEERFULLY OVER A WORN BOOT

The soles must be of tough leather for the boots of Uzbek horsemen get hard wear. Instead of settling down permanently in a shop, the shoemaker follows his roving customers.

Sovfoto

STREET IN ASHKHABAD, A THRIVING COMMERCIAL TOWN ON THE TRANSCASPIAN RAILWAY

The town of Ashkhabad, the capital of Turkmenistan, owes its importance to its position on the Transcaspian railway, which connects Samarkand with Krasnovodsk on the Caspian Sea. It lies some 345 miles by rail southeast of Krasnovodsk at the northern base of the chain of hills known as Kopet Dagh. Since the Russian conquest of the province in 1881, the town has grown into a commercial centre, with flourishing industries, including tanning, brick-making, and minor manufactures. The huge statue dominating the square is of Lenin.

Miss Hunter

MARKETING HORSES BEFORE THE COLLEGE OF BIBI KHANYM

Samarkand is mostly a maze of dirty narrow streets, but unlike cities in other parts of the East it has open squares, of which the Righistan is one and this, where the great horse market is held, is another. The domed college behind was built by Bibi Khanym, Tamerlane's Chinese wife, in 1388. Horses and asses form a large part of Samarkand's trade.

broidered cloths and the delicate silver and brass ware of the skilled workers in metal. Among the frequenters of the bazaars a familiar figure is the sherbet-seller, who goes about in the crowd with a tank on his back and glasses in his hands. He makes his approach known by rattling the glasses together.

If Bokhara is not so large and important as Tashkent, it is, nevertheless, a great commercial centre. Into this old-world city pour the camel caravans from China, India, Afghanistan and Persia, loaded with their precious freights of tea, silk, furs, dyestuffs and other goods. These are the caravans which, in past years, were pounced upon by the rapacious Turcoman. From Bokhara they go out again with cotton, ironmongery, sugar, coffee and other commodities, which have been mostly obtained from Russia.

As a leading trading centre Bokhara is noted for its carpets. The finest in the world are exhibited here. Another particular feature of its market is "caracul," a fur, which comes from the prepared skin of the Persian lamb, or sometimes kid. We are also familiar with it under the name of astrakhan.

But Bokhara has another claim to distinction besides that of commerce. It is a university town, a home of learning, and has been so for more than a thousand years. At one time the city could boast of 197 mosques and 167 "madrasahs," or Moslem theological colleges, most of which have fallen into decay. There are, however, many state controlled educational buildings in Bokhara that are still in use.

The most famous mosque is the Masjid Kalian, dating back to the tenth century. It was into this mosque that Jenghiz Khan, the great Asiatic conqueror, rode in defiance of the mullahs, or priests. He dismounted, went up into the pulpit, and threw the Koran on the floor, shouting to his followers as he did so: "The hay is cut! Give your horses fodder!" This was the signal for the savage Mongolian soldiery to begin a dreadful massacre and to loot the city.

The chief college of Bokhara is the Mir Arab. Here are to be seen types of the two leading races of people, the bearded Tajiks and the Uzbegs with their more Mongolian cast of features. In these colleges are educated the mullahs, who are trained to their calling from early youth. Each one has a cell assigned to him in a "madrasah," and each has a certain class of pupils to instruct in the Uzbeg language, or it may be in Arabic, in the Koran, in astronomy and in other languages and sciences.

As has been told, Khiva has been joined up with Bokhara to form a Soviet Republican State. It is an ancient province of Turkestan, for it dates back to the first and second Persian empires and to the days of Alexander the Great whose armies were in the country more than two thousand years ago.

In the town of Khiva are several "madrasahs," for so important a place cannot be without its colleges. Khiva was the capital of the province of Khiva, a distinction which previously belonged to Urgenj, in the markets of which were sold the corn, cotton, rice, tobacco and other products of the rich province, as well as the splendid breed of horses for which it was famed.

Ferghana is another province of Turkestan, and its chief town is Khokan. It

Miss Hunter

IN THE RIGHISTAN OF SAMARKAND

Turquoise blue predominates the peacock colors of the tiles decorating the three colleges that stand round Samarkand's "Righistan," or square. Mosque colleges, such as these, are called "madrasahs," and are still famous for their schools of science. This is the college of Shir-dar. The other two are Ulug-beg and Tilla-kari.

SOVFOTO

POLO ON THE ROOF OF THE WORLD

The Pamir Plateau is a lofty tableland north of the Hindu Kush range. Much of it is mountainous, but there are flat areas that make good pasture land. The region is sometimes known as "the roof of the world," for its average elevation is about 13,000 feet. Polo is a favorite sport among the Kirghiz who live there and who raise fleet, intelligent ponies.

lies in a fork of the great Tian Shan mountain range and is a very fertile and fair country. Of all places in Turkestan, there is none that appeals more to the imagination than does Samarkand. The town of this name was in olden time the capital of Asia, and its splendors were unsurpassed and were extolled by historian and poet alike.

"Golden Samarkand" could not attain to such a height of glory without paying the usual penalty of those times. It was attacked, destroyed and rebuilt over and over again, and in the course of years much of its beauty and greatness passed. Today it is a city of considerable size, with a trade in horses and asses; but, except for a few open squares, it is composed of narrow, ill-kept streets. Prominent among its buildings are the three "madrasahs," seats of learning, which are still famous throughout the province.

Apart from these survivals of the past, the "madrasahs" and mosques, Samarkand has scarcely anything to show of its former splendor. In the city where Alexander the Great and Tamerlane in turn held sway are mean-looking houses, some of mud, and the rich trains of merchandise that once found their way thither by horse, mule and camel have long since turned their steps to Bokhara, to Tashkent and to the other newer cities.

These interesting cities with such a long and colorful past are all within the limits of the Uzbek Soviet Republic. In the Turcoman Republic, Merv, situated in an oasis renowned for its fertility, is considered in Hindu, Parsi and Arab tradition as the ancient Paradise. Like Samarkand and Bokhara, it became a rich and splendid city and at one time was the center of learning, but all its glory has passed away and in the nineteenth century, the old town was abandoned for a new site on the Transcaspian railway on which its carpets, long famous, and its agricultural products may be exported.

Ashkhabad, the capital, owes its growing importance as a commercial center to its situation on the Transcaspian railway, the western terminus of which is Krasnovodsk, on the Caspian Sea. Krasnovodsk is the port for the Republic. Cotton and dried fruits are the chief exports.

The people of Ashkhabad cannot look back on the glorious past of their city, for it has none, but they are already taking steps to insure for it a prosperous future. We should not be surprised, indeed, to find that they have a gardening school with a model garden and mulberry plantation, and that for years they have been reforesting the surrounding land.

One last feature of Turkestan—not the least notable—remains to be mentioned. This is the great mountain range known as the Pamirs, or "the Roof of the World." From this bleak, craggy tableland run some of the mightiest mountain chains on earth, such as the Himalayas, the Hindu Kush, the Karakoram, the Tian Shan and the Trans-Altai.

It is as wild a region as can be found anywhere, and the fascination of it has drawn many famous travelers thither since Marco Polo crossed it on his way to the court of Kublai Khan. Here is to be found the great-horned mountain sheep, the "Ovis Poli," whose head is reckoned as one of the finest of sportsmen's trophies. And on these mountain slopes and in the valleys the Kirghiz hillmen pasture their flocks. For many years past the Pamirs have been occupied by Russia, and the present borders of Russia and Afghanistan have been settled to run across "the Roof of the World."

EWING GALLOWAY

MELON VENDOR IN THE ANCIENT CITY OF SAMARKAND, UZBEKISTAN

From the days when Samarkand was a stronghold of Tamerlane, the people of the dry area in which the city is situated have prized melons with their refreshing juice. Today the desert is being transformed. Irrigation is bringing water to the parched earth and it is beginning to yield bountiful crops. Two-thirds of Russia's cotton production is grown in Uzbekistan.

EWING GALLOWAY

NOMADS OF THE DESERT IN RUSSIAN (OR WESTERN) TURKESTAN

Crossing the hot, shifting desert sands would be well-nigh impossible but for camels, those ships of the desert, which can do without water for long periods as well as detect it from afar.

TURKESTAN: FACTS AND FIGURES

THE COUNTRY

The territory east of the Caspian Sea, known as Western, or Russian, Turkestan, is divided into five Soviet Socialist Republics:—Turkmenistan, Uzbekistan, Tadzhikistan, Kazakhstan, Kirghizstan, and one autonomous republic.

TURKMENISTAN (*Turkmen Soviet Socialist Republic*)

Became a Soviet Republic in 1925. The area is 189,370 square miles and the population, 1,254,000, mostly Sunni Mohammedan. Agriculture is the main occupation of the people. Products include cotton, wool, and astrakhan fur. The region is famous for its carpets and special breed of horses. There are rich mineral deposits. A railway, air line and motor communication serve the country. The chief towns are Ashkhabad, the capital, Mary, Krasnovodsk, Kerki and Tashauz.

UZBEKISTAN (*Uzbek Soviet Socialist Republic*)

Became a Soviet Republic in May, 1925. The area is 159,170 square miles and the population 6,300,000, mostly Sunni Mohammedans. Agriculture, based on artificial irrigation, is the chief occupation, cotton the main product. There is a railway and air service. The chief towns are Tashkent, the capital, population, 585,000, Samarkand, Bokhara, Khiva and Andijan.

TADZHIKISTAN (*Tadzhik Soviet Socialist Republic*)

Became a Soviet Republic in October, 1929. The area is 55,545 square miles and the population, 1,500,000. Principal occuaption is farming and cattle-breeding, and there are rich mineral deposits. Capital, Stalinabad.

KAZAKHSTAN (*Kazakh Soviet Socialist Republic*)

Became a Soviet Republic in December, 1936. The area is 1,072,797 square miles and the population, 6,200,000. There are rich mineral deposits but the majority of the people farm and breed cattle. Capital, Alma-Ata.

KIRGHIZSTAN (*Kirghiz Soviet Socialist Republic*)

Became a Soviet Republic in December, 1936. The area is 76,042 square miles, population, 1,500,000. Capital, Frunze.

RUSSIA'S REPUBLICS IN THE CAUCASUS

Ancient Countries of Armenia, Georgia and Azerbaijan

During 1920 and 1921 these three little countries formed Soviet republics and the next year became a part of the new Soviet Union. Each has had a desire for independence but their position between large and often warring nations has prevented success. Armenia, the oldest Christian country, has suffered throughout the ages by the constant tyranny of foreign domination. Her people have been massacred or scattered, but they have clung to their religious belief and at last secured a bit of territory, Russian Armenia, where a weak national life is barely possible under Soviet domination.

TWO Mohammedan and one Christian country combined to form a republic! Georgia and Azerbaijan, converted to Islam by the Arabs in the seventh century, and Armenia, said to be the oldest Christian nation, were united as the Transcaucasian Federation, a member of the Union of Soviet Socialist Republics.

For ages their people have been at swords' points, for they were not tolerant of one another's religious beliefs. Massacre and destruction of property, encouraged and often initiated by near-by countries for political reasons, and also foreign invasions have kept them from any material progress. Now they are again separated, and each of the republics is now a member of the Union of Soviet Socialist Republics. Let us see where this region lies.

A glance at the map will show us that these three little countries occupy a bridge of territory which connects Russia, in the north, with Iran (Persia) in the south. It is separated from Asia, on the east, by the Caspian Sea and from Europe, on the west, by the Black Sea. Forming a natural frontier on the north are the snow-topped Caucasus Mountains, the scenery of which rivals even that of the Alps, a fact not generally known, for it is not so easy to travel in this country as in Switzerland. Although the land is almost treeless and presents a bleak, rugged appearance travelers are usually fascinated by its wild aspect and by the ever-changing color of the mountains, and are loath to leave. Highest of the mountain peaks are Mount Elburz and Mount Kazbek. On the latter, according to mythology, Prometheus was chained as a punishment for giving fire to mankind.

Just over the border to the southeast, completely isolated from the Caucasus range, is the lofty and inspiring Mount Ararat, which rises from the surrounding plains to a height of 16,916 feet. On Mount Ararat, Noah is supposed to have landed after the Deluge, and the inhabitants claim to be able to show evidence that this is true. They will point out the site of the burial place of Noah's wife and the location of his vineyard, and they will even show you pieces of the Ark itself.

It was on Mount Ararat also that the donkey learned to bray, so it is said. The story goes that Noah, when assembling his companions for a sojourn in the Ark, issued an invitation to a donkey. The donkey was very stubborn, however, and refused Noah's kindness. Then the flood came and the water began to rise; the donkey kept going higher and higher to avoid it. Finally he reached the summit of Mount Ararat but still the waters rose, until they reached the neck of the poor animal. Thoroughly frightened, then, he raised his head toward the heavens and bawled, "No-ah-h-h! No-ah-h-h!" Noah went to his aid and donkeys from that time on have always called the name of their benefactor.

Mount Ararat was formerly in Armenia, which occupies the southwestern portion of Transcaucasia, while Azerbaijan occupies the southeast and Georgia the north. Travel here we should find very difficult indeed, for there are few railroads, and those connect only the largest cities and ports. Horseback and motor are the favor-

SOVFOTO

YEREVAN, AT THE FOOT OF MOUNT ARARAT

From Yerevan (or Erivan), capital of Armenia, you can look up to glacier-crowned Mount Ararat, the mountain that tradition makes the resting place of Noah's ark. Yerevan is an industrial city of 200,000 inhabitants, and the cultural center of Armenia. It has a university, an opera, a number of scientific institutes and a branch of the Academy of Sciences of the U.S.S.R.

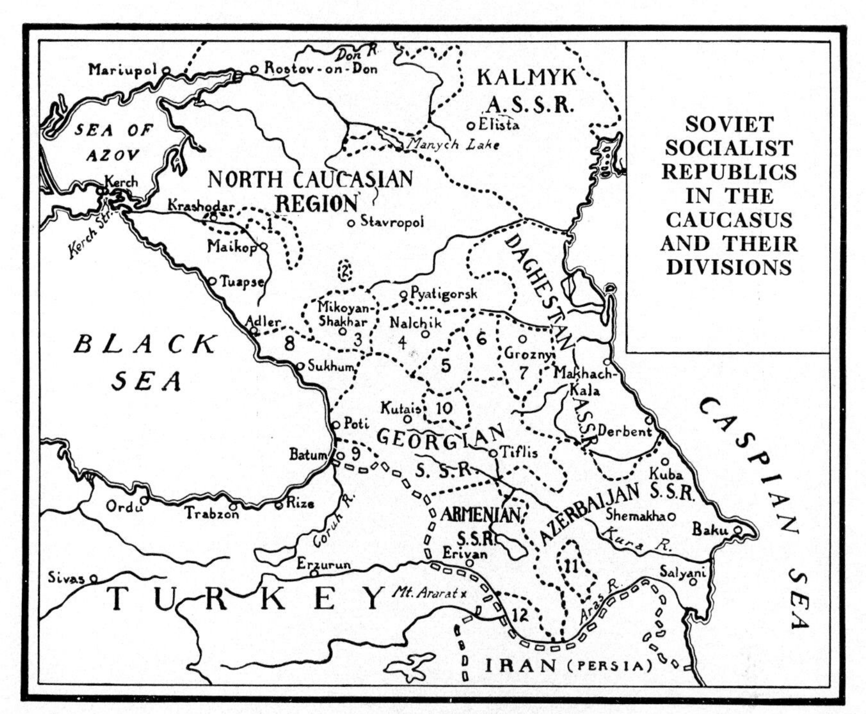

The northern part of the Caucasus and the divisions marked 1, 2, 3, 4, 5, 6, 7, are included in the R.S.F.S.R. (Russia Proper). Georgian S.S.R. includes the Abkhazian (8), the Adzharian (9) Autonomous Republics and the South Ossetian Autonomous Region (10). Armenian S.S.R. has no divisions. Azerbaijan S.S.R. included Nakhichevan Autonomous Republic (12) and the Nagorno-Karabakh Autonomous Province (11).

ite methods of getting about, but some of the districts are almost impossible to reach, so much so that the people living there are politically semi-independent.

Armenia, the oldest of these countries historically, was formerly a great kingdom and held extensive territories to the south. Armenia! The very name brings to our minds a picture of wretched and starving people, but let us look for a bit at its past, in order that we may understand some of the more recent events which come within our memory.

Like most countries, it was first inhabited by tribes who are thought to have come from the east and settled around the foot of Mount Ararat. These nomadic peoples were conquered about the sixth century before Christ by the Medes and Persians and then the territory was divided into two satrapies, or provinces, of the great Persian Empire. Eastern and Western Armenia, as they were known, became powerful in time and overthrew their overlord. This was accomplished mainly by Tigranes the Great who welded Armenia into one strong kingdom. Although it did not last long, it brought the Armenian people together and gave them a feeling of unity which has lasted through the ages.

Armenia has had an unfortunate situation. From its beginning, it has been a buffer state between more powerful and warring nations, between Asia and Europe, between the East and the West. In addition it has been a lone Christian nation among states of other religions whose followers sought to convert their neighbors by force.

The Armenians were converted to Christianity early in the fourth century under Gregory the Illuminator, and became most ardent in their faith. When Persia, their overlord, tried to make them adopt fire worship, they replied: "No one can move us from our belief, neither angels nor men, fire nor sword." So they have felt always even though it has meant massacre and the scattering of their people. Their faith

SOVFOTO

GRAPE-PICKING TIME IN ARMENIA

Irrigation has made nearly half a million acres of soil in Armenia suitable for agriculture. All but 2 per cent of the agricultural workers belong to collective farms that produce cotton (long-fibered variety), grapes and other fruit.

has withstood invasions of the Persians, Arabs, Seljuks, Mongols and Turks, but their territory has been conquered time and again. Now and then they had a brief period of independence, as that which began in 571, under the leadership of Vartan, but which lasted only seven years. Since then Vartan has been a favored Christian name for Armenian boys and Vartan's Day is celebrated even now as a national holiday.

The Turkish conquest was completed about 1514, when Selim I set out toward the East on a campaign against Persia. Turkey was then at the zenith of her power but she was in time to be checked in the north by a nation whose strength in Europe had been greatly increasing. That was Russia. In the wars between them, during the nineteenth century, Russia advanced her Caucasus boundary well into Armenia, and since then Armenia, divided, has belonged partly to Russia and partly to Turkey.

Russia found her Armenian subjects intelligent and industrious, and able to help in the development of the country. She therefore encouraged emigration from Turkish Armenia into the provinces she owned. The Armenians on their part felt better protected in Russia. They accumulated property, became more progressive, and the land itself was noticeably better cultivated than on the other side of the line. Except for feuds with their Moslem neighbors the people were better off than they had been in centuries.

During the struggle between Russia and Turkey, there had been growing secretly a party called the Dashnacks, who sought to secure the independence of Armenia. Although it represented only the more

Sovfoto

MOUNTAIN CLIMBING AMONG THE PEAKS OF RUSSIAN ARMENIA

The ancient country of Armenia, divided today among Iran, Russia and Turkey, is on the southern edge of the breath-takingly beautiful Caucasus Mountains. They mark a land boundary between Europe and Asia. In the Russian part, there are many peaks above 10,000 feet; the highest, Alagöz, is 13,435 feet. These climbers are ascending the summits of the Aragats range.

radical element of the people, it brought about local warfare which served to arouse the Turks and as a result, during the years 1895 and 1896, thousands of the Christian inhabitants were exterminated in a series of massacres so atrocious that the story is almost unbelievable. Foreign nations were horrified and attempted to interfere, but as they could not agree to go to war with Turkey, their concern did little to help.

When World War I broke out the Turks again took occasion to rid themselves of their Christian subjects. Claiming that the Armenians were taking up arms against them, they slaughtered men, women and children with savage brutality and forced others toward Mesopotamia and the Syrian deserts to almost certain death. American and British missionaries helped to relieve the suffering by giving

SOVFOTO

MUSICIANS ENTERTAIN COLLECTIVE FARMERS AT HARVEST TIME

Armenia has undergone many changes since it became a Soviet Socialist Republic in 1920. A State Song and Dance Ensemble is the official musical group of the country. Some of its performers are shown here on a collective farm. Part of the Soviet program to encourage greater agricultural production is to supply on-the-spot entertainment for the workers at harvest time.

out food and first aid treatments, but in spite of their aid many thousands perished.

Russian Armenia quite naturally allied herself with Russia at the beginning of World War I, but the Russian Revolution three years later left her only partially able to protect herself. Caught between the advancing Turkish armies and the unorganized armies of the Bolsheviki who had control of Russia, she had a most difficult time. In addition the country became flooded with starving and disease-stricken refugees who had been able to escape from Turkey, and had trekked across Northwestern Persia to what seemed to be their only refuge. Unable to retain the independence which the Dashnacks had hastened to declare, Armenia finally decided to cast her lot with the Soviet Government which had succeeded the Bolshevists, and in 1920 became a republic of the Soviet Union under Russia. About 85 per cent of the people in the territory are Armenians.

The question of the Armenian people and Armenia was considered by the League of Nations. It was hoped that in time a national home could be established in Armenia where those refugees who had reached other lands in safety might be repatriated. Armenians were especially interested in the plan as they had long desired a land of their own where they could live by themselves and could develop it into one of great prosperity.

Until the Soviet Government took the land over, it had been badly in need of development. In most of the region it was hard indeed for the peasant to make even a meager living. In the valley of the Araxes River, which girds Mount Ararat, there is rich and fertile soil, and tobacco, rice and cotton are grown as well as many varieties of fruits and vegetables. There are vineyards, but the vines must be buried during winter frosts. In the hilly districts, forestry is important and cattle are raised.

Agriculture is the main occupation of the people, and, as one might suspect, their methods have been quite primitive. Homemade wooden plows, drawn by oxen or water buffaloes, still serve some Armenian farmers. However, several large canals have been completed for irrigation purposes, and more than half the land is in large collective farms worked by modern machinery. Much of the irrigated land is devoted to the cultivation of cotton.

The houses of the peasants are usually built against the side of a hill or a mountain which saves the material necessary to make a back wall. Then, too, it gives protection from the wintry winds and thus saves fuel which is a very scarce article in this unforested region. The roofs are flat and are sometimes covered with earth, so that grass will grow and serve as pasture for the family cow or sheep. Inside the houses are almost bare of furniture—a few simple chairs and possibly a fireplace where the cooking is done. In the winter the cow and sheep are given a place in the house, for their body heat is needed to bring the temperature of the room a bit higher.

Accustomed to living in this mountainous region where the winters are long and severe, the Armenians are strong and energetic and not unused to hard work. They are usually dark and the women are noted for their beauty. Many Persians, Kurds and Turks have fallen under the spell of the beautiful black eyes of Armenian maidens, and have taken them back to their own countries as their wives. The women have won a reputation too for their beautiful handwork, which they do at home in order to help out the family income. Fine Armenian lace, lovely embroidery and Oriental rugs are made with painstaking effort, often at the cost of their eyesight

The Armenian farmer gets his real enjoyment out of a trip to market, for he likes to talk and argue, and the sale of a cow or sheep will give him a great opportunity. Like all buying and selling in Near Eastern countries, it will take hours, perhaps all day, to arrive at a price which each knew at first would have been perfectly satisfactory.

A birth or wedding also gives cause for a celebration. In the olden days a wedding in a prosperous Armenian home was a gala event. It would probably last all night and from start to finish, the tables would be piled with food and drink while the guests made speeches and danced, sometimes singly, sometimes together. The bride would be decked with jewelry—a headdress draped with coins, bracelets and necklaces, for, aside from their liking for decoration, the Armenians thought it safer to have their wealth in a form which would be easy to carry.

Suppose we had been invited to the home of a well-to-do Armenian and were pressed to stay to dinner. What interesting food we should have had! There would have been a meat dish consisting of tender bits of lamb combined with vegetables, in some appetizing way; there would have been pilaf, which is rice cooked in oil, and eggplant, probably, for the Armenians know many ways of preparing that vegetable—ways of which Western people have never heard. Then for dessert there would have been paklava, for that is, indeed, a delectable sweet—a light crusty pastry with nuts and honey. Of course, we should have wines to drink and small cups of sweet Turkish coffee, and we should all have agreed that we had had a delicious meal most bountifully served.

Armenians who have migrated to Europe or America have proved to be

Near East Relief

ARMENIAN WOMAN COOKING

In Armenia, cooking and baking are done on the front of the house in a leisurely way as we may see here. The large hole in the foreground is an underground oven.

BLUE MOSQUE

In Erivan is the beautiful mosque of Hussein Ali Khan, familiarly known as the Blue Mosque because of the blue tiles that are used to decorate its exterior. Armenians, Persians, Tatars, Russians and Greeks have worshiped in Yerevan (or Erivan); and the city has many old churches and mosques, survivals of a happier time.

Near East Relief

valuable citizens. They are shrewd and energetic, qualities that make them successful in business.

Most of the cities of Armenia are small, in fact hardly more than towns. However, Yerevan (or Erivan), the capital and largest city, has a population of about 200,000. It was almost completely rebuilt during the 1920's and made quite modern in appearance. The city reflects the communist emphasis on education—though *what* is taught, of course, must follow the dictates of the state. The Armenian State University is here, as well as several colleges, a library and a Tropical Institute. There is also a branch of the Academy of Sciences of the U.S.S.R. Imposing buildings house the government offices and the state theater of opera and ballet. One of the most interesting old structures remaining is the Blue Mosque.

Yerevan is on the Zanga River. Since a hydroelectric station was built here in 1926, the city has developed numerous industries. Machinery, furniture, brick, leather goods, silk, glycerin, wine and brandy are among the many products.

A few miles west of Yerevan is the ancient monastery of Echmiadzin, the seat of the Armenian, or Gregorian, Church. The monastery is the residence of the Catholicus, or head of the church. Reports indicate that the Soviet Union has not attacked the church directly, knowing how deeply the Armenians are attached to it. Instead, it has been made an instrument of the state. Armenians outside of Russia consider the Catholicus a communist puppet.

At Leninakan (once called Aleksandropol), which is on a branch of the Araks River, is another hydroelectric station. The waters of Lake Sevan have also been harnessed. Altogether there are more than fifty hydroelectric stations in Soviet Armenia, for both power and irrigation purposes. Under the Soviets, the region has become an important industrial center. More than 80 per cent of its products are manufactured goods.

Mining has kept equal pace. Armenia has rich stores of copper, zinc, aluminum, molybdenum and other metals. These are

NEAR EAST RELIEF

LIBRARY OF ARMENIAN LITERATURE

The monastery, Echmiadzin, includes the ancient and valuable library shown above. Though not beautiful architecturally, it contains a large collection of Armenian literature.

essential raw materials for heavy industry, which is one of the chief concerns of the communist planners. There is also a wealth of building materials.

Georgia is almost as old historically as Armenia and has suffered almost as many invasions. The Georgians, however, after their country had been devastated for nearly two centuries by the Arabs, finally succumbed to Mohammedanism and since then have not suffered persecution.

Tradition has it that the inhabitants of Georgia are descended from Japheth, son of Noah, but we cannot trace their history from that early time. We know of them first in the fourth century before Christ when Alexander the Great sent one of his generals to annex the territory then known as Iberia. The people were able to free themselves from the Macedonians after the death of Alexander and then enjoyed independence for over a hundred years. However, Georgia was not to be left alone. The great Persian Empire, always eager for more territory, was to the East what the Turks and the Byzantine Greeks later were to the West. Georgia had some friendly connection with the Byzantine Empire, for Constantine, the first Byzantine emperor, had sent Christian missionaries who had converted the Georgians. Therefore, when Persia's strength had somewhat weakened, Georgia took the opportunity to appeal to the Byzantine

Near East Relief

CHURCH OF ST. HRIPSIME, AN EARLY CHRISTIAN MARTYR

Legend tells us that Hripsime, a beautiful Christian nun, who lived in Rome, fled to Armenia to escape the attentions of Emperor Diocletian, a pagan. The Armenian king, Tiridates, on beholding her beauty, fell in love with her, too, and because she repulsed him ordered her slain. Her body is said to have been placed in a vault buried deep beneath this church.

Empire for a king. She was granted a viceroy, and the Bagratid dynasty which was then founded ruled from 571 to 1803.

In the seventh century came the Arabs and for 180 years the country was overrun until the people finally accepted Islam. Georgia then enjoyed a period of relief during which the boundaries were extended from the Black to the Caspian Sea and at one time included part of Armenia. She had successfully repulsed the Seljuks and the Persians, but was not able to withstand the Mongol hordes who came west led by Jenghiz Khan. Again the land was overrun by the Mongols under Tamerlane who set fire to the entire country. Wars between the Persians and the Turks during the seventeenth century caused Georgia to seek the help of Russia and in 1801 she became a Russian province.

Since then Georgia has been independent for two short periods—from 1904 to 1906, when Russia was at war with Japan, and from 1918 to 1921. The latter period of freedom came immediately following the Russian Revolution, when Georgia felt she had an opportunity to break off, but she was finally forced to join the Soviets and to become a republic.

Like Armenia, Georgia is an agricultural country, but it is much more fertile owing to the fact that the melting snow from its many mountains and an irrigation system provides water in plenty for those who live in the valleys. However, those living in the mountains are wretchedly poor and have a hard time making a living from the barren soil. Rye bread, cattle and sheep is their principal diet, and a traveler will sometimes find that the village inn or rest-house cannot provide a speck of food.

In the valleys, one may see fruit of many varieties, both tropical and subtropical, corn, grown for food by nearly every valley peasant, wheat, barley, cotton, tobacco, tea and rice. A great variety indeed! Mulberry trees are seen, too, for silkworm culture is one of the oldest occupations of the people. Grapes grow in great luxuriance, sometimes wild, and so the making of wine has become the industry for which Georgia is most noted.

In a few areas, the workers still use a primitive press for squeezing the grapes, and when the wine is ready it is put into tarred buffalo skins and then piled on wooden carts which joggle along the rough mountain roads until they reach the city. In 1930, the Soviet Union made plans for a great expansion of the industry. One of the most important points in the plan was for the development of champagne!

Because of the mountains, Georgia has rich mineral deposits, chief of which is a fine quality of manganese, but there is also copper and iron and there are numerous mineral springs, both hot and cold, containing sulphur, iron and radium.

So much for Georgia's products. Let us now see what the people are like. The majority are Georgians, although there are a goodly number of Armenians, Tatars and Russians. The Georgians speak a language that is supposed to have been connected with the Sumerian-Babylonian and so difficult has it proved that very little has been translated into other languages.

The Georgians are fine looking people and very intelligent and they delight in colorful costumes. The women, even though poorly dressed, usually seem gay with many colors. The well-to-do women wear a long coatlike garment of silk covering loose trousers which are caught at the ankles. On their heads they wear scarlet velvet caps decorated with pearls. The men usually wear a tall cap made of astrakhan which is called a papahk, and a shaggy wool coat. Part of the male costume is a dagger or sword for Daghestan,

Near East Relief

ANCIENT CHRISTIAN CHURCH OF ECHMIADZIN

The monastery of Echmiadzin, west of Erivan, was the seat of the Catholicus or primate of the Armenian church. Among the buildings is an ancient Christian church which is thought to have been founded by St. Gregory the Illuminator in 302, and is said to be the oldest Christian church. The Church of the Nativity in Bethlehem also claims this distinction.

SOVFOTO

A SHEPHERD AND HIS FLOCKS IN THE GRASSLANDS OF GEORGIA

A shepherd watches over his sheep as they graze on the rolling Shiraki Steppe of southern Georgia. In the summer the flocks trek more than a hundred miles to mountain pasture.

that province of Georgia which borders on the Caspian, is famous for its fine artistry in silver and steel.

In the mountainous districts, the houses are built on terraces, but in the more prosperous places they are made of rough stone or baked mud and often have large wooden balconies around the first floor, and roofs of undulating red tiles. The houses of the rich are often very beautiful, especially those which are decorated with colored glazed tiles, indicating the Persian influence.

Now and then there is a neat, orderly village inhabited by German people. Early in the tenth century, the founders of these villages started toward the Holy Land because they thought the end of the world was near. They made their way slowly until agents sent in advance returned to report that all was not as they believed in Jerusalem and so they stayed where they were. They farmed as they had done in Germany, built villages on the German plan and retained their German language until recently. Since World War II, German place names have been changed to Russian, and the people speak Russian.

One may see also villages where the Molokans reside. These people belong to a sect of the Russian Church comparable to our Quakers. They derive their name from the custom of living on milk (*moloko,* in Russian) on fast days. The Molokans have no organized priesthood.

Tbilisi (Tiflis, in Russian) is the capital. It is the largest and one of the oldest cities in Georgia. The old section has an Asiatic air. A tangle of narrow, crooked alleys and primitive architecture, it is in the center of the city. To the north and to the south extend modern industrial and residential areas where the buildings are European in style. Tbilisi has many scientific and technical institutions, among them the Georgian Academy of Science.

The people of Azerbaijan are mostly

SOVFOTO

A DANGEROUS CURVE ON A MOUNTAIN HIGHWAY IN GEORGIA

A gigantic cliff leans menacingly over the road from the right, and on the left is the deep Kheva Gorge. The narrow highway through the mountains is a masterpiece of engineering skill.

Tatars, or Tartars, a people related to both the Turks and the Mongols. The Tatars (also called Azerbaijanians) follow the Mohammedan faith, but just how this religion has fared under the Soviet Government is hard to determine.

A Divided Land

Since 1920 the ancient country of Azerbaijan has been divided between Russia and Iran, with Russia holding the smaller but richer part to the north. In 1936, this was organized into the Azerbaidzhan Soviet Socialist Republic (A.S.S.R.). The republic also includes two other sections—with jawbreaking names—the Nakhichevan Autonomous Soviet Socialist Republic and the Nagorno-Karabakh Autonomous Region. Nakhichevan is a high plateau, on the Iranian border, separated from the rest of the A.S.S.R. by a narrow strip of Soviet Armenia. The forest-clad mountains of Nagorno-Karabakh, also on the Iranian border, form a continuous part of the A.S.S.R.

Only about three-fifths of the population of Soviet Azerbaijan is now of Tatar stock. The balance is made up of Armenians, Georgians and Russians. Too, national groups such as the Tatars have been disappearing. In 1949 a mass deportation, probably to somewhere deep in the interior of the Soviet Union, was carried out, mainly against people of the Caucasus border. At the time, Soviet officials said that this was necessary to guard against "enemy agents, diversionists, spies, saboteurs and all doubtful and suspicious people." All of which would seem to indicate that the Tatars, among other minority groups in the Caucasus, have never been completely reconciled to communist rule.

The central part of the A.S.S.R. is a plain, naturally arid, through which the Kura River and its tributaries flow to the Caspian and empty into that vast inland sea south of Baku. North of the plain are the moist, cool slopes of the eastern end of the Caucasus Mountains, and to the south are the eastern peaks of the mountains of Armenia.

In former years, Azerbaijan was a pastoral country, remote from the world's bustle, where the Tatars wandered with their flocks of sheep. Like many other people who live in mountainous lands, they were proud and independent. They could also be fierce fighters on occasion. Indeed, to English-speaking people the name of "Tartar" calls up a fellow with a violent temper—whether or not the Tatars really deserved this reputation. Hospitable to a fault, they would kill a sheep in a stranger's honor. After it was cooked whole in a huge pot, the host would fish out delectable morsels and pop them, willy-nilly, into his guest's mouth. The mutton would be washed down with kumiss—fermented mare's or camel's milk—poured into a bowl from which all drank.

Where the shepherds once roved there now are vast state farms with irrigated fields and numbers of drab little workers' settlements. The greatest change of all is represented by the oil derricks that bristle the land along the coast of the Caspian Sea. Here is one of the world's largest petroleum fields, which supplies the Soviet Union with about 75 per cent of its oil. Baku—center of the industry, seaport and capital of the A.S.S.R.—commands a bay on the south shore of the Apsheron Peninsula, which juts out on the southwest coast of the Caspian. There are oil wells on the peninsula, on off-shore islands and even in the bed of the sea itself, near the shore.

Baku, the Petroleum City

Baku is one of the largest cities in the Soviet Union, with a population of around 800,000. The old part of the city, to the west, dates back to at least the ninth century A.D. Here the streets are narrow and crooked, with a decidedly Oriental atmosphere. In their midst a medieval mosque still stands. Most of Baku, however, which has grown with the oil industry, is modern, with tall buildings and boulevards. It has a university and technical schools. Baku is connected with the Black Sea by two railroads; and it handles more tonnage—mostly oil, as one would expect—than any other port in the Soviet Union. Much of the crude oil is treated on the spot, and there are large refineries. The

SOVFOTO

A FOUR-HUNDRED-ACRE TEA PLANTATION, PART OF A COLLECTIVE

In Georgia, on the subtropical coast of the Black Sea, tea is one of the most important crops of the collective farms. The worker is removing the ripest leaves from the shrubs.

city also has chemical plants for processing fertilizer and rubber. This rubber is made from kok-sagyz—the Russian dandelion—which is being cultivated extensively in southern Russia.

From very ancient times it was known that the area around Baku was rich in oil, but it was not until 1871 that the first scientifically drilled wells were sunk. In 1901, Baku supplied half the world output of oil, although, of course, the total was quite small in comparison with production today. Development of this tremendous resource leaped forward after the U.S.S.R. came into existence. Some of the wells have now been drilled to a depth of more than 8,500 feet.

Pipe Lines and Tankers

Nevertheless, the Baku field is only part of a great petroleum area that spreads north beyond the boundary of Azerbaijan. Grozny, to the northwest, is second only to Baku in Russian oil production; and the Maikop field, still farther west, is almost equally important. From Baku to Batum, on the Black Sea just north of the Turkish border, there is a double pipe line, one pipe for crude oil and one for refined. However, much of the Baku oil is shipped by Caspian tankers to the Volga River—which empties into the Caspian some distance north of Baku—and thence distributed throughout the Soviet Union. Other pipe lines carry the "black gold" from the Grozny and Maikop fields to Tuapse, also on the Black Sea, or to Trudovanya, in the eastern Ukraine. All of the oil fields are electrified and connected with Baku. Altogether they yield at least 175,000,000 barrels of petroleum a year.

As we indicated earlier, Azerbaijan has also been transformed by means of irrigation, large-scale machine-farming methods and hydroelectric power. Three huge pumping stations alone on the Kura River, powered by hydroelectric installations, are said to irrigate about 75,000 acres. In fact, the A.S.S.R. has become a center of subtropical agriculture. Excellent Egyptian and Sea-Island cottons (long-fibered) are being grown in the one-time semidesert of the central plain. Too, at various seasons of the year, the irrigated tracts may be golden with ripe wheat, grayish green with alfalfa or show the pale jade of rice seedlings.

In the mountain valleys, in addition to walnut orchards and vineyards, silk culture has become important. It is claimed that Soviet scientists have bred a new kind of silkworm, one which gives twice as much silk as the older Bagdad variety. For the silkworms, mulberries are raised in the north.

On the Caspian coast, where malaria used to be rife, the marshlands are being drained, and there are thriving tea and tobacco plantations and groves of tangerines, pomegranates and figs.

Few travelers from the West have ever visited this Caucasian region, even before it was organized into three Soviet republics. Until the days of the airplane, Caucasia was a long journey from Western centers of civilization, although those who made the difficult trip were rewarded by some of the most magnificent rugged mountain scenery to be found anywhere.

Today, the Caucasian republics are of critical importance to the Soviet Union. They contribute a large share to the state's wealth. Soviet economy and industry—not to speak of Russia's fighting forces—are at least partly dependent on the petroleum of this region.

Caucasia—Question Mark

Even more important, perhaps, is the fact that this is a border region where the Soviet Union has no buffer satellite countries to take the brunt in the event of war. Across the mountains lie a strong Turkey, closely allied with the Western community of nations, and an unpredictable Iran. The oil wells of Baku are only a brief flying distance from either of these countries. From another point of view, it is through Caucasia that Russia could reach the fabulous petroleum wealth of all the Middle East and the long-coveted water route of the Persian Gulf. One may be certain that all these possibilities have entered into the calculations of the councils both of the Western powers and of the Soviet Politburo.

SHOTA RUST'HAVELI, AN IMPRESSIVE THOROUGHFARE IN TBILISI

Cutting a broad, decorative swath through the center of the capital city is the impressive boulevard that has been named for the greatest of Georgian poets, Shota Rust'haveli.

PHOTOS, SOVFOTO

A CHORUS AND FIVE KHORUMI DANCERS IN THE ADZHAR REPUBLIC

Adzhar stalwarts kick out fiercely in the spirited Khorumi to the accompaniment of a folk song. The Adzhar Republic is a political subdivision on the Black Sea coast of Georgia.

SOVFOTO

RICH OIL FIELD IN BAKU

In the seventies of the last century, Baku, on the Caspian Sea, was a sleepy village of some 1,500 inhabitants. Today it has a population of more than 800,000. The increase has been due to the discovery of rich oil deposits in the neighborhood. The forest of derricks photographed here from offshore is in the Ilyich oil field. Baku is in the Azerbaidzhan Republic.

TRANSCAUCASIA: FACTS AND FIGURES

THE COUNTRY

Region south of the Caucasus Mountains and north of Iran and Turkey between the Black and Caspian seas; was known as the Transcaucasian Federation. Armenia, Azerbaijan and Georgia, the members of the federation, have, since 1936, been administered as separate republics within the Union of Soviet Socialist Republics.

ARMENIA

In southern Transcaucasia; area, 11,500 square miles, and population, 1,345,000. Soil is fertile and major industry is agriculture. Chief crops are grain, cotton, tobacco, sugar beets, grapes and other fruits. Irrigation and hydroelectric works and projects have been built. Livestock, 1,600,000 head. Mining of copper, zinc, aluminum and molybdenum is important. Other industries include production of synthetic rubber, fertilizers, building materials and textiles. In 1950 there were 300,000 pupils in primary and secondary schools, technical and special colleges and the Armenian branch of the Soviet Academy of Science. Population of chief cities: Yerevan (capital), 255,000; Leninakan, 75,000.

AZERBAIJAN

In eastern Transcaucasia, it includes Nakhichevan Autonomous Republic, an enclave within Armenia, and Nagorno-Karabakh Autonomous Region, within Azerbaijanian borders. Total area, 33,100 square miles, and population, 3,100,000. Oil production, centered on the Caspian coast around Baku, and agriculture are the leading industries. Chief farm products are grain, cotton, rice, fruits, vegetables, tobacco and silk. Other products include copper, chemicals, building materials, food, timber, salt, textiles and fish. Over 500,000 pupils in primary and secondary schools; also technical and special colleges, Baku University and a branch of the Academy of Science. Population of chief cities: Baku (capital), 800,000; Kirovabad, 110,000.

GEORGIA

In northwest Transcaucasia, it includes Abkhazian and Adzhar autonomous republics and South Ossetian Autonomous Region. Total area, 29,400 square miles; population, 3,555,000. Chief crops are tea; citrus fruits; tung, eucalyptus and bamboo trees; tobacco, and grapes. Livestock, 4,100,000 head. Mountain streams afford immense electrical power. Chief minerals are manganese and coal. There are large iron and steel works and auto plants. Batumi is the terminus of an oil pipe line from Baku. Nearly 750,000 pupils attend about 4,800 primary and secondary schools; also technical schools and colleges, a branch of the Academy of Science and 80 research institutes. Population of chief cities: Tbilisi (capital), 540,000; Kutaisi, 90,000; Batumi, 75,000.

A LAND OF ANCIENT GRANDEUR

The Iranians and Their Rugged Home

Under Cyrus the Great and his immediate successors, the Persian Empire became a powerful state but was conquered by the Greeks. Again, it rose to power under the Sassanians who were finally overthrown by the Arabs and, although it has retained its independence, it never regained its former position. In the early part of the twentieth century, it could have been called a land of the Middle Ages ruled by an official class that was both lazy and dishonest. Government appointments were bought and the purchasers in order to get their money back extorted large sums from the people. In 1925, the Shah Ahmed was deposed and a man of humble birth, Riza Khan, who was possessed of energy and enlightened ideas, ascended the Peacock Throne. This man of the people did much to restore law and order in Persia, now called Iran. In 1941, however, he was forced to abdicate and his son, Muhammed Riza Pahlevi came to the throne.

PERSIA, one of the most interesting and historical countries of the Middle East, consists mainly of a vast plateau between Afghanistan and Pakistan on the east and Iraq, or Mesopotamia, on the west. To the north lies the Caspian Sea and on each side of this stretch of water the Persian frontier adjoins that of Russia; to the south lies the torrid Persian Gulf.

The Persians call their country Iran and themselves Irani (a form of the word Aryan). Their beginning is legendary, but it is thought that as nomadic tribes they wandered from parts further east and, attracted by the Caspian Sea, settled near its shores. In about 550 B.C. Cyrus the Great made himself known to history for he conquered all the neighboring tribes and formed the Persian Empire, the first great Aryan empire. His successors extended the boundaries from the Punjab in India to beyond the desert in Egypt and sought to conquer Greece, but were defeated by Alexander the Great, who in 334 B.C. made it a Greek province.

The next great period in Persian history began about six hundred years later under Sassanian rulers, who again brought to Persia the glory and splendor of her earlier period. This empire endured until it was overrun by the Arabs in the seventh century A.D.

Up to the time of the Arab invasion, the Persians were followers of Zoroaster and worshiped the sun and fire, but after the Arab conquest, they were converted to Mohammedanism, which is their religion still, although they belong to a division known as Shiite or Separatist.

Arab rule, however, fell before the warring Mongols under Jenghis Khan, which in turn gave way to Tamerlane the Tatar and his hordes who swept over the country on their way westward. In the sixteenth century, a strong leader, Ismail, came to power and founded the Safavid Dynasty. Under the first Safavid rulers, the boundaries were extended and Persian art, especially miniature painting and hand-woven carpets, reached a height of perfection that has never been surpassed.

Weak rulers followed, and the next centuries saw the territory reduced to its present boundaries. In the twentieth century, the country fell into a sad state of political corruption under the Kajars who were ousted in 1925 by a man of the people, Riza Khan, who became Shah.

The climate of Persia is one of extremes, for while frost is common enough in the winter season, the heat in the summer months is intense, especially in the low-lying provinces bordering on the Persian Gulf. As a rule the heat is a dry one and the climate on the plateau is delightful, but the storms are terrible.

The present population of Persia is about fifteen millions, and, as the area of the country is about three times that of France, it is very widely scattered. Owing to the scanty rainfall, there is a lack of water except in the Caspian provinces and there are huge uninhabit-

THE ANCIENT LAND BETWEEN THE CASPIAN AND ARABIAN SEAS

able areas. The country may be described as a desert with a few towns and villages dotted about in it, wherever water happens to be available.

The Elburz Mountains run across the north of Persia, south of the Caspian Sea, and contain the superb cone of Demavend, which rises to a height of 19,400 feet—the loftiest mountain of Asia west of the Himalayas.

Elsewhere in Persia the ranges generally run from southeast to northwest, a fact that has made the country difficult of access, especially from the Persian Gulf and from Iraq. If we look at a map we shall see that the chief cities, such as Teheran (or Tehran), Meshed, the sacred city of Persia, and Tabriz, its chief trade centre, are situated close to the mountains. It might be said that the size of a city mainly depends on the height of the neighboring ranges and the amount of water obtained from them. The country relies for its water on the snow on the mountains which melts in the spring and fills the irrigation channels.

The most important feature of Persia, which has impressed itself forcibly on the life and character of the people and on its government, is the Great Desert. This desert occupies the centre of the country and separates one province from another more effectually than any mountain barrier.

The southern part of this vast area was described by Marco Polo, the great Venetian traveler of the thirteenth century, as "a desert of surpassing aridity . . .; here are neither fruits nor trees to be seen and what water there is, is bitter and bad, so that you have to carry both food and water." Government and trade are both rendered very difficult by this desert, which is a refuge for rebels and brigands who can only be caught with extreme difficulty.

Owing to the meagre rainfall and the high ranges surrounding the plateau, there is not a single river of importance in the many hundreds of miles of coast which lie between the mouths of the Indus and the Shat-el-Arab. One of the tributaries of the latter river is the Karun, which flows through what was, in ancient times, the kingdom of Elam. Its modern importance consists mainly in its being the only navigable river in the whole of the huge Persian Empire.

The Persian Gulf, which washes the southwest and south coasts of Iran, is an almost completely land-locked body of water 700 miles in length, with an average width of about 120 miles. It is shallow and receives the waters of the Tigris and Euphrates, which are united in the broad stream of the Shat-el-Arab. If we are fortunate, we shall pass into the gulf through the Straits of Hormuz by moonlight, with the black cliffs of Cape Musandam rising to the south.

People of southwestern United States can well imagine a country so dry that

W. P. Rodd

WESTERN BUSTLE DOES NOT APPEAL TO THIS METAL-WORKER

Early in the morning he spreads a mat outside his house, arranges his tools about him and begins his daily work. Every now and then he stops to take a comforting puff or two at his kalian, or water-pipe. The Persians are very skillful metal-workers, and they take great pride in fashioning beautiful articles of steel inlaid with gold and silver.

U. S. ARMY

WANDERING TRIBESMEN OF LURISTAN

About a fifth of the inhabitants of Iran are nomads, wandering tribesmen who drive their flocks and herds from place to place seeking fresh pasture. They set up rough, temporary shelters as they go. On crude looms the women weave tent cloth, blankets and other textiles. The tribesmen in this picture are Luris, of Luristan, in the west-central part of Iran.

THREE LIONS

BATHHOUSES, NOT IGLOOS

In the towns of northern Iran, the village bathhouses are the cleanest structures in the section. Their mortar surfaces are painstakingly scrubbed to a dazzling perfection. Elsewhere cleanliness is less evident. Bad sewage, inadequate medical facilities and the lack of pure water are responsible for the prevalence of diseases that thrive in unsanitary surroundings.

trees and crops can be grown only where the land is well irrigated. The vegetation consists of bushes, generally of a thorny nature and only two or three feet high, with a little grass which shows green for a month in the spring and then disappears.

Where there is water, crops of wheat and barley (which is the staple horse food), millet, cotton, opium, lucerne (known here as alfalfa), clover and tobacco are grown. Rice and corn flourish in the moist Caspian provinces. Persia is rich in fruits, which grow well in spite of the lack of scientific cultivation. Pears, apples, quinces, apricots, black and yellow plums, peaches, nectarines and cherries are produced in great abundance. Figs, pomegranates and the famous almonds and pistachio nuts grow best in the warmer districts, and the date-palm, orange and lime are confined to the low-lying "Hot Country." The grapes and melons of Persia are famous. We owe to Persia the peach, the pistachio nut, spinach, the narcissus and lilac, all of which have retained their Persian names.

Persia has long been famous also for her carpets and rugs, and a trip to the rug dealer's shop is a very interesting experience for the proprietor will probably serve coffee and cigarettes while lengthy discussion takes place. Bargaining is quite the order of the day, and one must never seem in haste for then the dealer will surely get the better of it. Among the Persians themselves, it sometimes takes days to conclude a transaction satisfactorily.

Persia's Industries

With the exception of rug-weaving and the manufacture of silk and cotton textiles, pottery and some leather goods, Persia has few industries. Most of the manufactured goods used by the Persians must be imported.

Persia's chief wealth is in her oil fields, which cover about five-sixths of the country. The richest single oil field in the world is in the southern region. At Abadan, a town near the head of the Persian Gulf, is the world's largest oil refinery.

Oil and the British

For many years the fields were operated by a British company. Persia could not run them herself, at least partly because there were few Persians with the necessary technical training. This arrangement began in 1901, when Persia granted a monopoly in the exploitation of the oil fields to an Englishman, William Knox D'Arcy. His venture eventually became the Anglo-Iranian Oil Company—53 per cent British-owned. Then in 1919 Persia agreed to a convention by which British advisers were placed in various departments of the Persian Government, military as well as civil. This made Persia practically a British protectorate.

As the years went by, resentment against British domination grew more open and bitter in Iran (Persia changed its name to Iran in 1935). After World War II, the unrest came to a boil, particularly over the oil situation. It was heated still further by a growing spirit of nationalism—Iran for the Iranians—the same spirit that has been emerging in so many other parts of Asia since the war.

The climax came in the spring of 1951. Under the leadership of Mohammed Mossadegh, who was Prime Minister of Iran at the time, Iran suddenly nationalized the oil industry. This meant the end of British control. It also brought the industry, Iran's chief source of income, to a standstill. The British technicians departed and there were few trained Iranians to take their places. Regardless of Iranian feelings, it was obvious that the industry could not be operated without outside help of some kind.

An International Problem

The Western world was alarmed. Here was one of its chief sources of oil idle. What is more, there was a threat that communism might gain headway in Iran just as it has thrived on turmoil elsewhere. The specific dispute between Britain and Iran was carried all the way to the UN Security Council, but that body failed to settle it.

When the oil industry came to a halt, its Iranian labor force of about 65,000 was thrown out of work. These men received unemployment compensation, a drain on the Iranian treasury. On the whole, however, the stoppage affected the great mass of the Iranians much less than one might expect. Actually, very little of the wealth from the oil fields had ever trickled down to them. Their standard of living had always been low. As they had received little of the industry's benefits, they would be the last to feel the pinch.

If, however, operation of the industry were not resumed soon, other Iranian businesses would be affected. This could lead to a serious political upheaval.

Solution to Come?

In the winter of 1951–52, great efforts were being made by the International Bank for Reconstruction and Development to work out a plan that Iran would accept for operating the fields. It was possible that a foreigner, neither British nor Iranian, might be put in charge of the industry. He, in turn, would employ an international staff of technicians. The largest number of these, however, would probably be British. After so many years of experience in Iran, Britain is the only country in the world that has oil experts to spare.

In ancient times, the Persians obtained valuable pearls from the Persian Gulf and even now pearl fishing is carried on to some extent. The principal exports, however, are oil, opium, carpets and rugs and dates which are brought from the interior by caravan to either the gulf or Caspian Sea ports for shipment.

Until recently, the means of communication were the caravan routes that have been in use for many centuries. In the last few years, however, under an ambitious programme projected by the government, new roads are being constructed and old ones improved. Several hundred miles of railways have been opened with more under way, and telegraph, telephone and wireless systems have been installed. Aeroplanes fly regularly from the capital, Tehran, and Kermanshah to Bagdad, where there are plane connections with European cities.

© Gorbold

VEILED WOMAN ON HER WAY TO MESHED

This woman must find it uncomfortable to ride without stirrups and to be muffled up in a veil and cloak, especially in hot weather. Discomfort is a small matter, however, for she will soon reach her goal—the shrine of Imam Reza.

Although Persia is slowly awakening to her need of improvements, there are obstacles which stand in the way of progress. The greatest, perhaps, is the clergy who resent actively the institution of modern customs which is taking from them the great power and influence they formerly enjoyed.

The peasant is the backbone of the country. His village is sometimes enclosed within a high mud wall, in which case the houses are small and squalid and the open space in the centre of the village, whither cattle are driven at night, is usually dirty. When the houses are scattered about each occupies a good deal of space, having one courtyard around which the living-rooms are grouped and a second courtyard for the cattle. Adjoining many of the houses are orchards, surrounded by mud walls. The peasants are still practically serfs under a real feudal system but the landlords are not unkind to them owing to the fact that the land is so sparsely settled that labor is scarce. The most primitive methods of agriculture are still in use as one might expect in a country that has been unprogressive in other ways. The ruling classes may be divided into the landowners and the religious groups, who have a great deal of wealth, and of course, in the towns and villages, there are large numbers of merchants who have their little shops or cafés.

Besides these, Persia has many nomad tribes, who live in tents of goats' hair and

A BAS-RELIEF FROM THE DAYS OF THE SASSANIAN KINGS

At Taq-i-Bustan, near Kermanshah, there are arched recesses cut into the rocks containing bas-reliefs. In this one King Ardashir II appears to be presenting a trophy to the victor of a battle. The sculptures date from the Sassanidae, a dynasty of Persian kings who ruled from the third century A.D. and were finally overthrown by the Arabs in the seventh century.

PHOTOS, EWING GALLOWAY

TRIBUTE-BEARERS ON THEIR WAY TO A PERSIAN CONQUEROR

The sculpture is from a building wall still standing among the ruins of Persepolis, the dazzling capital founded by Darius the Great around 500 B.C. Under Darius and his successor, Xerxes, the Persian Empire was at the height of its power. The story of its vanished glory may still be read from the sculptures at Persepolis, though the city has long been dust.

BLACK STAR

CHILD WORKERS IN IRAN

Children are shown weaving carpets in Hamadan, a district where famed Persian rugs are produced. Rug-making ranks among the top native industries in Iran, and in normal times about $3,000,000 worth of carpets are exported to the United States alone. The law of 1943 calling for the gradual establishment of compulsory education has lagged in enforcement.

THREE LIONS

PEACE WITHIN THE SHELTERED GARDEN OF A MOSQUE IN TEHERAN

Students reflect on the Koran by a serene pool, where their eyes may rest on exquisite mosaic tile. The teeming, noisy city just outside their retreat seems far away.

EWING GALLOWAY

STREAMLINED MODERN ARCHITECTURE FOR THE SHAH OF IRAN

The Shah's palace in Teheran is in vivid contrast to the delicate design of the guarded gateway. The appearance of Iran's capital has been undergoing rapid changes in recent years.

U. S. ARMY

A YOUNG IRANIAN PRACTICES AN OLD ART WITH A SKILLED HAND

The boy is painting a graceful design on the kind of pottery for which Qum is well known. The shelf above is stacked with bowls, and there are lids in the hole behind him.

move about with their flocks and herds in search of fresh grazing-grounds. They spend the summer months in the mountains and move down to the plains at the approach of winter. They follow the same route year after year. Physically, they are splendid people, but they are very fond of raiding villages and of plundering caravans. When they are on the march the old men, the women and children look after the sheep, goats, cattle, camels and donkeys, while the fighting men act as scouts and try to rob any villages that may be in the vicinity.

In Persia the position of the men is far better than that of the women. When a boy is born the father receives congratulations, whereas the birth of a girl passes almost without notice. The baby will have amulets to avert the evil eye hung around its neck; no glass may be brought into the room lest its rays might cause the child to squint and indeed the very word glass may not be mentioned. Moreover, no one wearing black clothes is permitted to enter.

The baby is swaddled tightly and, when taken out for an airing, is dressed in coarse clothes—this again being to avert the evil eye. Friends may admire the child without causing him ill-luck provided they exclaim "Mashallah!" (that which Allah wished).

In former times, upon reaching the age of eight, the boy was placed in charge of a manservant, and a mullah, or priest, undertook his education, which consisted mainly of learning to read and write. The textbook was the Koran (the Moslem scriptures) and the unfortunate pupil was forced to learn sentence after sentence in the original Arabic with its meaning in Persian. He repeated it exactly as a parrot so he learned neither Arabic nor Persian. Little else was studied under private instruction or in the numerous religious schools.

EWING GALLOWAY

WOMEN THRESHING GRAIN BY A CENTURIES-OLD METHOD

When the sieve is shaken vigorously, the grain falls through to the rug spread to catch it and the chaff is left behind. It is a tedious method that yields little in proportion to the effort.

COURTHOUSE OF BANDAR SHAH VIEWED ACROSS A PUBLIC GARDEN

The attractive building is one of many modern structures in the port on the southeast coast of the Caspian Sea. Bandar Shah is the northern terminus of the Trans-Iranian Railway.

PHOTOS, EWING GALLOWAY

THE SIMPLEST OF SCALES SUFFICES THIS MERCHANT

The stones in one pan determine the weight as the scales are held aloft and filled with raisins or nuts. The technique is old, but no one questions its accuracy.

EWING GALLOWAY

MASJED-I-SHAH (SHAH'S MOSQUE) ON THE ROYAL COURT IN ISFAHAN

Covered with glazed tiles and ornamented with gold and silver, the Masjed-i-Shah is a dazzling sight. The court—the Maidan-i-Shah—is an enormous rectangle 1,680 feet by 522 feet.

If a boy was idle, his feet were tied to a pole and beaten by canes. This punishment of the bastinado is known as "eating the sticks." All exhibitions of high spirits were discouraged and it was impressed on the young pupil that it was undignified to run or to jump.

The result was that a boy soon became a miniature man. He wore a long coat much kilted at the waist and the same kind of "kulla" or astrakhan headdress as his father. His manners, too, tended to become artificial and when greeted by a friend, he would reply, "May your nose be fat," "May your shadow never grow less," and other similar compliments that formed an important part of Persian etiquette.

When a boy reached the age of sixteen, his mother arranged a marriage with a cousin, whom, perhaps, the boy had not seen since he was a child, for women were kept strictly secluded and were always veiled in public.

The bride and bridegroom then met and gazed intently at one another's faces which were reflected in a mirror at which they both looked together. Finally the bride was taken, with rejoicings, to her future home, where the young couple partook of bread, cheese and salt that had been brought by the bride, and were left by their relatives to settle down.

This plan of selecting a wife and the marriage customs are still practiced in some parts of Persia, but as girls are now admitted to the public schools, this, as well as other old customs, is dying out in the face of rapid Westernization.

Great progress has been made in education. Modern schools have been established, which, in the lower grades, are attended by boys and girls together. Hundreds of students have been sent abroad to study so that they may return to teach in the schools or become leaders. A university in Teheran gives higher education in all branches of sciences and arts.

We have said that the position of women is lower than that of men. This is true in any Mohammedan country. The Koran, by which the followers of Mohammed model their lives, makes no provision for the education of women and puts many restrictions on them. Nevertheless, the number of both women and men who cannot read or write is decreasing, and women without veils are seen more and more. In wealthy families, women are given

Weston

GREAT PALACE OF SHAH ABBAS IN ISFAHAN, ONCE THE CAPITAL OF PERSIA

Under the great Shah Abbas I, who died about 1628, Isfahan was made the capital of Persia and became a city of splendid palaces. This magnificent palace still looks much the same as it did then even to the upper porch-pavilion from which the Shah and his court watched the Persian nobility at their favorite game now known as polo. Isfahan is a city of many ruins. There are heaps of debris and fallen houses everywhere, and a man could be buried in some of the large holes in the streets. Even the palaces are made of mud bricks instead of stone.

ANGLO-IRANIAN OIL COMPANY

ABADAN, OIL-FAMOUS HARBOR

From the harbor of Abadan, oil refineries may be seen in the background. The tanker at the right rides high in the water as she awaits her cargo of the flowing wealth of Iran. In the foreground is a native sailing craft. Abadan became a familiar name overnight as a result of the nationalization of the oil industry and the expulsion of the Anglo-Iranian Oil Company in 1951.

special quarters, called in Persia the anderun, in which no man except a relative may enter. Turkey was the first to throw off these customs and Persia is following slowly. To-day, Persian women may attend the theater and movies unveiled and are encouraged by the government to adopt the dress and the manners of Western women.

The new order which is gradually taking the place of the old in Persia is due to a large extent to the efforts of Riza Khan, who was Shah from 1925 to 1941. His story is a fascinating one. A man of humble birth, he began his career as a trooper in the Persian Cossack Brigade. He gradually rose in rank through sheer energy and ability and at last assumed command of the brigade. In February, 1921, being then in command of more than 2,000 Cossacks, he overthrew the Persian Cabinet. He became Minister of War in the new cabinet formed by the Shah.

In this Middle East land of Omar Khayyam the Allies had a land bridge. In Iran's capital, Tehran, was held the historic conference of November, 1943, at which the leaders of the United States, Great Britain and the Union of Soviet Socialist Republics, among other statements of policy, pledged the independence of Iran.

Iran presents a medley of East and West, ancient ways and modern magic of the machine age. The single-track Trans-Iranian Railway streaks by baked-mud villages whose outlines were old a thousand years ago. On its way it ducks into more than 200 tunnels, crosses thousands of bridges, and in some places winds so sharply it can be seen at three different levels. Yet Iran still holds the flavor of the old East, from the lonely shepherd on the mountainside to the crowded, covered bazaars where bearded merchants bargain over products of Oriental handicraft. As planes fly over, a nomad with a hawk on his wrist looks up respectfully. Strange to us are many Iranian customs—the still sheltered lives of women, the Moslem taboo against drinks and dogs; their particular rituals of prayer and fasting.

IRAN (PERSIA): FACTS AND FIGURES

THE COUNTRY

An independent kingdom which occupies the western and larger half of the Iranian plateau. It is bounded on the north by Transcaucasia, the Caspian Sea and Turkestan, on the east by Afghanistan and the Dominion of Pakistan, on the south by the Arabian Sea and the Persian Gulf, and on the west by Iraq and Turkey. The total area is about 628,000 square miles, and the population is about 20,000,000, of whom about 3,000,000 are nomads.

GOVERNMENT

Legislative government consists of a National Assembly called Majlis, elected every two years. The shah, or king, appoints a prime minister who selects a Cabinet agreeable to the Majlis.

COMMERCE AND INDUSTRIES

Food products include wheat, barley, rice and fruits. The production of gums, tobacco, cotton, silk, wool and opium is important. Sheep-raising is carried on to some extent. The minerals, though numerous, are, except in the case of oil, undeveloped. They include deposits of iron ore, coal, copper, lead and manganese; there are turquoise mines in Khorasan worked by primitive methods. Weaving of rugs and carpets is by far the most important industry. Chief exports include petroleum, carpets, raw cotton, and wool, and the imports are cotton piece goods, sugar, tea, machinery and automobiles.

COMMUNICATIONS

About 1181 miles of railway. Much of the country's commerce is carried on over the great trade routes. There are over 11,436 miles of telegraph line. There is a regular air service.

RELIGION AND EDUCATION

Bulk of population belong to the Shiite sect of Mohammedanism, and there is a large minority of adherents to the Sunni persuasion. Besides these Mohammedans, there are about 10,000 Parsees, 50,000 Armenians, and 40,000 Jews. By Government order the foreign schools have been liquidated by the Ministry of Education. Primary education compulsory since 1943. There are 8,381 schools with 457,236 pupils. Primary school for children of Soviet nationality is run by the Soviet Government. Religious schools maintained from endowments.

CHIEF TOWNS

Teheran, capital, has a population of 1,000,000; Tabriz, 250,000; Isfahan, 225,000; Meshed, 185,000; Shiraz, 140,000; Hamadan, 120,000; Resht, 115,000; and Kermanshah, 100,000.

In the Garden of Eden

Modern Iraq, Cradle of Ancient Empires

Some believe that the site of the Garden of Eden lay between the Tigris and Euphrates rivers in the land once called Mesopotamia, and known today as Iraq. Certainly the land is very ancient, and the earliest civilizations may have risen there. There is little in modern Iraq, however, that resembles a paradise, although in the days of the Sumerian, Babylonian and Assyrian empires it was one of the world's most fertile regions. Decay had set in before it came under Turkish rule in the sixteenth century, and it became a desolate tract. Iraq's present rulers are attempting to restore the country's rich soil to its fertile state so that it can once again be cultivated. Because Iraq is one of the world's great oil-producing countries it holds a position of great strategic importance in the struggle between free nations and the communist powers. Its vital oil has more than once in recent years been the cause of serious international disagreements.

MESOPOTAMIA, now known as Iraq, has been called the "cradle of civilization" because here the human race is thought to have had its beginning and it has also been termed the "dust heap of the nations," because the ruins of mighty empires of ancient times are buried under its sun-baked soil. This tract of country, which was before World War I the Turkish provinces of Mosul, Bagdad and Basra, stretches in a southeasterly direction from Kurdistan to the Persian Gulf. Two mighty rivers, the Euphrates and Tigris, flow through the land and finally unite to form the Shatt-al-Arab, which discharges its waters into the Persian Gulf over one hundred miles farther to the south.

Tradition says that the Garden of Eden lay somewhere in this land, and modern excavation has shown that there once existed here what is believed to be one of the oldest civilizations on earth—the Sumerian. The Sumerians, who were probably of Indo-European origin, were the first known astronomers. It was they who divided the day into twelve double hours and who gave us the first writing. They had laws and learning and they practiced medicine. After long years, they were overrun by the Semite invaders, nomadic peoples of Arabic origin, who adopted the writing, laws and customs of the Sumerians.

From this fusion of Sumerians and Semites rose the Babylonians and Assyrians. The first Babylonian Empire was founded about 2100 B.C. Its chief city was the Biblical Babylon. Centuries later the Assyrian nation arose in the north and there was a long struggle for supremacy between the two kindred nations. Babylon and Lower Egypt, for a time, fell under the sway of the bold Assyrian conquerors, and then Nineveh, its capital

PHILIP GENDREAU

AN AGED SHEPHERD OF IRAQ

An Iraqi's face, furrowed and wrinkled, tells of lifetime toil against desert wind and sun.

RODD

THE TOMB OF EZRA, blue-domed and surrounded by palm trees, stands on a bend of the Tigris near Kurna. It is known that Ezra was buried on the banks of the Tigris many centuries ago, so this cannot really be his burial place, as the river has changed its course since that time. However, bands of pilgrims pause here as they do at other Biblical sites of Mesopotamia although, like this one, they are probably legendary. On the Euphrates below Baghdad is the supposed tomb of the great Jewish prophet, Ezekiel, revered as a shrine by both Jews and Christians.

RODD

SAMARRA, with its gold-domed mosque and minarets of richly colored tiles, is considered a very holy place by the Shiah Mohammedans. They believe that the Mahdi, the savior who is expected by all Mohammedans, actually appeared long ago, and vanished in a cave near Samarra. Here, they think, he will reappear at the end of the world.

BLACK STAR

THE GATE OF ISHTAR, THE BABYLONIAN GODDESS OF LOVE

Bulls and goats molded from glazed bricks decorate the Ishtar Gate in Babylon. Nearby is E-Sagila, the great temple of the god Marduk and the site of the Biblical Tower of Babel.

—the ruins of which are found on the bank of the Tigris opposite Mosul—was the premier city of the world. With the destruction of Nineveh in the seventh century B.C., Babylon again rose to power. Nebuchadnezzar rebuilt the city, enclosing it with mighty walls which, with the "hanging gardens," formed one of the Seven Wonders of the World. The ruins of Babylon lie to the south of Bagdad (Baghdad)..

But Babylon, as recorded in the Bible, was taken by Cyrus, king of the Medes and Persians. The Persians in turn fell before the Greeks under Alexander the Great. The Greeks were followed by Parthians, Romans and then Persians again. After the death of Mohammed in 632 A.D. his Arab followers overran the Persian Empire. At Ctesiphon, the Parthian and Persian capital, they found great treasure and the materials of its wonderful buildings were used for the construction of Bagdad in 762. Under the famous Harun-al-Rashid, Bagdad became the centre of the wit, learning and art of Islam. Then in 1516 A.D. the country finally passed to the Turks, under whose misrule it remained for about four hundred years.

KEYSTONE

A WINGED GUARD OF KHORSABAD

A minister to a sacred winged bull flanks a gate to the palace of King Sargon II of Assyria.

And so, during the centuries, the greatness of Babylon and Assyria passed away. Their magnificent cities were used to supply the bricks for succeeding towns and villages, and such ruins as the barbarians left fell into decay until they became shapeless mounds whose very names were forgotten. The peoples of these cities had used a curious writing called "cuneiform," which they had developed from the script of their Sumerian ancestors. They scratched figures with a triangular pointed instrument on soft tablets of clay which they afterward baked. The knowledge of this writing also passed away.

That old phrase "the changeless East" is obsolete. Change is resistless. Following the expulsion of the Turks, Mesopotamia was left under British control. In 1921 Emir Feisal was crowned King of Iraq under a British Mandate. Then Iraq became independent in 1932. Governmental shifts, plus oil, speeded up far-reaching changes.

The "Mosul question," involving rich oil areas, caused international rivalry and dispute. Mosul, city of northern Iraq,

RODD

AN ARAB WOMAN loves jewelry. This one is adorned with rings, bangles, necklaces, brooches and a pendant from her head-dress. Although her head is amply covered, her feet are quite unaccustomed to shoes or stockings. Arab people are of marked character and intelligence and usually are possessed of self-confident manners and a great sense of dignity.

MUDD

CLIMBING A DATE PALM is no great difficulty to this Arab. He first girds the tree with a rope which he fastens to his sash so that when leaning back, he is held securely. He is further aided by the leaf-scarred trunk which makes a good foothold. Dates fresh from the tree are much different from the dried fruit we know.

OPEN-AIR FERRY ON THE TIGRIS

The glorified raft, or kelek, as it is called, is made of alternating layers of planks and logs supported on the inflated skins of sheep or goats. This one is ready to float its load of passengers comfortably down the Tigris from Diarbekr, Turkey, to Mosul, Iraq. Keleks are as familiar on the Tigris as ferryboats are on the Hudson River and the St. Lawrence.

PHOTOS, UNDERWOOD AND UNDERWOOD

ROOFS OF REED BY THE EUPHRATES

An old-time Arab village by the Euphrates, of a type rarely seen nowadays. The houses, or huts, are made of reeds and are roofed with reed matting. The Tigris and Euphrates once emptied into the Persian Gulf through separate mouths. Now they meet, on land which they themselves have laid down bit by bit through long centuries, and flow into the gulf as one.

KEYSTONE

OUTSIDE THE WALLS OF OLD BAGDAD—THE TOMB OF ZOBEIDE

Herdsmen lead their flocks near the base of the strange building outside Bagdad where Zobeide, wife of Harun-al-Rashid, is buried. He was the great caliph who ruled over Bagdad at the height of the city's power, when it dominated most of the Arabian world. The roof of the tomb, a pyramid of small overlapping domes, surmounts a bold octagonal base.

MOSUL, the chief town in an oil-bearing province, stands on the Tigris opposite Nineveh, the ruined capital of ancient Assyria. The streets of Mosul are narrow, undrained and filthy, so the town is always evil-smelling. A treeless city, its monotony is relieved only by towers, domes and minarets. Great Mosque, formerly dedicated to St. Paul, has leaning minarets which help to give the city its untidy appearance. Of the two bridges that span the Tigris at Mosul, the unstable looking one, which we see in this photograph, is made of boats placed side by side.

RODD

THE ARCH OF CTESIPHON was once a part of the royal palace in Ctesiphon, the capital of the great Persian Empire when it extended over Mesopotamia, or Iraq as it is called at present. It became an important city and in 550 A. D., Chosroes I built this magnificent palace there. Beneath the arch, which was the roof of the audience chamber, there was once a blue ceiling set with gold stars to imitate the sky. The ruins are very important from an architectural standpoint for they are among the few existing examples of construction in the Sassanid or Persian period.

EWING GALLOWAY

THE ROUND BARGES OF THE TIGRIS, LADEN WITH WATERMELONS

On the Tigris at Bagdad, Iraqi boatmen guard their striped, delicious cargo. For perhaps as long as man has been transporting goods on the waterways of Mesopotamia, the unwieldy, almost unsinkable gufa has been bounding its useful way from farm to market. The gufa is made of reeds, covered with hides and plastered inside and out with pitch for waterproofing.

is on the west bank of the Tigris. Each large house is built round an open courtyard. The houses are of burnt brick faced with slabs of a kind of gray marble, quarried nearby. The same marble serves for paving and for wall panels in the interiors. There is a fine mosque, the cupolas and minarets of which are of turquoise blue tiles. The summers are very hot, and for three or four months the inhabitants are glad to sleep on the flat roofs. The winters are rainy, and frost is sometimes experienced.

Although there is a railway line, considerable trade on the upper Tigris is by means of native craft. As some parts of the river are very shallow, use is made of rafts of saplings lashed together and packed underneath with inflated goatskins. These are floated and paddled down the river, but the return journey has to be made by road for at Bagdad the raft is pulled to pieces and sold.

Iraq is not a well wooded country. Much of the north is undulating pasture land, but wheat, barley, linseed and flax are grown and, if the rainfall be sufficient, yield good crops. A little distance to the north of Bagdad we find an alluvial plain formed of the mud which the two rivers have deposited. This was once the most fertile and thickly populated spot on earth. Here we meet the first palm trees in the narrow strips of cultivated land beside the rivers. Wherever the land is irrigated it responds readily to cultivation. The growing of wheat is increasing and the cotton crop shows a yearly gain. But the land under cultivation is only a small proportion of the entire country, and that is the reason why Iraq is so sparsely settled.

The clay of the plain, mixed with chopped reeds and grass, can be baked into a hard substance by the sun alone, and of this the single-storied dwellings of the villages are built. We find also huts made of reeds, which in some of the swamps grow to a height of 20 feet. The larger canes, placed side by side, are bent over in a half loop for the framework and are then covered with mats made of rushes. The end walls are of reed straw bound together, and the entrance is covered with a hanging mat. These huts can be put up in a day and can be taken down and moved elsewhere whenever the owner wishes.

The nomadic tribes who wander about with their flocks and herds use tents made of goat hair. The houses in the towns are mainly strong, two-story buildings. In order to lessen the terrific summer heat, screens made either of camel thorn or of licorice twigs, are hung before the windows and kept moist by having water thrown over them.

The Tigris is navigable by steamers as far as Bagdad, and though the passage of "the Narrows," just beyond Ezra's Tomb, is difficult for large craft, the river is crowded with boats of all descriptions, carrying passengers and merchandise. The famous round basket which is known as the "gufa" was in use in the days of Nineveh's glory. Below Sheikh Saad the gufa gives place to the canoe-shaped "bellum."

The Euphrates, which is navigated by native craft only, is much better wooded than the Tigris. In its lower reaches it passes through marsh land which by draining is becoming rich and fertile. At Kurna the rivers unite and form the Shat-el-Arab, and the cultivated land near this

Cox

DRAWING DRINKING WATER FROM THE TIGRIS AT BAGDAD

The inhabitants of Iraq are not at all particular about the cleanliness of the water that they drink. This man stands in the Tigris River while he fills his goatskin with the dirty water that he will shortly sell in the streets. On the bank two women wait to draw their supply. Into the Tigris goes much of the sewage and rubbish of Bagdad.

RUDD

KERBELA is a very holy city to the Shiah Mohammedans, or Shiites, since here is the tomb of Hussein, grandson of the prophet Mohammed. Hussein was killed at Kerbela, and is regarded as a martyr. Thousands of pilgrims visit his tomb every year, and seem so grief-stricken by Hussein's death that it would be easy to imagine that he had died recently and not years ago.

RODD

THE PORT OF BASRA, which is the port of Iraq (Mesopotamia), is situated seventy miles up the Shatt-el-Arab at the head of the Persian Gulf. Eighty per cent of the world's production of dates passes out of this seaport. There is also a fine export trade in barley, wheat and other crops.

EWING GALLOWAY

IRAQI FARMERS AND THEIR CRUDE HORSE-DRAWN THRESHING SLED

The sled-like contraption separates the grain from the stalks. It is by no means the crudest of implements in a land where tractors and other farm machines are seldom seen. In fact, the design of the contraption, rough as it is, shows a considerable amount of ingenuity.

estuary is one of the largest date-producing centers of the world. Nearly 200 varieties of dates are grown, and they are a staple article of food and a big item of export.

In the midst of this fertile strip, and 70 miles from the Persian Gulf, stands Basra, the principal port of the country. During World War II, Basra's trade and importance greatly increased. The modern city has up-to-date shipping facilities and is a road, rail and air terminal. Basra has been called the Venice of the East for all through and about the city are numberless waterways and creeks.

The majority of the population of Iraq is Arab. There are Arabs of all types and ranks with a large admixture of Persians. These people are Mohammedans and are divided mainly into the Shiah and Sunni sects. In this country are some of the most famous places of pilgrimage in the Moslem world.

The holy city of Nejef, which lies to the west of the Euphrates, stands on a cliff overlooking the desert. The golden dome of the mosque which covers the tomb of Ali, the murdered saint, makes a most conspicuous landmark. The city is walled, and consists of very narrow streets where tall houses shut out most of the light and air. Some of these houses stand on as many as three, four or even five floors of cellars hewn out of the rock, which form a cool retreat from the stifling heat of the crowded city above. A broad bazaar, a quarter of a mile long, leads up to the mosque. This small city of devout citizens during certain feasts has as many as 120,000 pilgrims pass through its gates.

Everything required in the city has to be brought from without and water has to be carried in skins a distance of three-quarters of a mile.

The Jews, who today number only a few thousand—we remember the captivity of their race in Babylon and the fact that Abraham their founder came from Ur of the Chaldees, which was near the junction of the canal Shat-el-Hai with the

KEYSTONE

BUYING POLISHED COPPERWARE AT A SIDEWALK SHOP IN BAGDAD

The robes might have been worn in Harun-al-Rashid's day, but the merchandise comes from modern factories in the capital. Present-day Bagdad is a manufacturing and trading city.

EWING GALLOWAY

COOLING OFF IN THE WATERS OF THE TIGRIS RIVER, NEAR MOSUL

There is very little rainfall in Iraq, and river water is doubly precious. Iraqis wash and bathe in the Tigris, finding surcease from the heat when the sun is high.

Euphrates—have also their holy places of pilgrimage here. The Jews are chiefly men of the towns, traders, shopkeepers and sometimes bankers.

The Christians, who are more in number than the Jews, are found around Mosul and are mainly Assyrians. Being better educated than the rest of the natives they form for the most part the professional class. In addition to these people there are wild Kurds from the north, nominally Mohammedans, and representatives of many other nationalities and religions. Among the latter are two communities that call for notice, the Sabæans and the Yezidis.

The Sabæans, or Subbis, get their name of Star-Worshipers from the fact that they turn to the polar star when praying, under the belief that the supreme deity has his residence beyond that star. Sunday is their holy day, they practice baptism once a week and they have a ceremony in which bread and wine are used. They are not Christians, but they have great veneration for John the Baptist. They are a very handsome people. Living among the marshlands in the south, their chief industry was the making of canoes until the war made their wonderful inlaid silver work known to the British troops. When the latter captured Amara the Sabæans migrated thither, and their silver work has brought them increasing prosperity.

The Yezidis are often called Devil-Worshipers. Although they believe in God the

BLACK STAR

SCREENED WINDOWS THROUGH WHICH SECLUDED WOMEN MAY PEER

In many places in Iraq, such as Mosul where this picture was taken, the Mohammedan way of life is still followed strictly. Women have little freedom; on the street they must wear veils.

PHILIP GENDREAU

A CROWDED CANAL JOINS BASRA WITH THE SHATT-AL-ARAB RIVER

Mosques and their minarets rise above simple dwellings and the activity of the canal. Basra is only seventy miles from the Persian Gulf, whence the Shatt-al-Arab (Tigris and Euphrates) flows.

Creator, they hold that the devil is very powerful and treat him with deference.

Although the red fez, formerly worn in Turkey, is much in evidence, the characteristic headgear of Iraq is the shafiyah. This is a piece of material, usually cotton, which covers the head and falls down over the shoulders, and is often crowned by a thick loop of wool. Worn with the flowing robes it is always associated with the Arabs. There is a great variety of costume here. We meet the poorer classes of the country and the desert dressed in a single long shirt and a shafiyah. Then we see the costume so frequently affected by the wealthy young Arab of Bagdad or Basra—that of a European gentleman save for the hat, which is replaced as a rule by the red fez.

The women when they appear out of doors are usually enveloped in a shawl-like outer garment, and even when they adopt European clothes they generally wear a shawl over the head to protect them from unwelcome glances.

All classes rise early, and rest during the afternoon heat. Coffee is taken many times a day, and much of the leisure time is spent in the coffee-shop, which is the meeting place for recreation and social intercourse so far as the men are concerned. The women, especially those of the upper classes, usually follow the custom of the East and lead secluded lives.

Within recent years there has been truly a marvelous change in many respects. A great deal of money has been expended, and the results are to be seen in all directions. Education—elementary, secondary and technical—is advancing; sanitation, to which no attention was ever paid before, has been introduced, and the streets of the cities have been paved and lighted with electricity.

Hospitals and dispensaries have been established, railways extended and motor roads constructed; bridges have been built over rivers where only rickety bridges of boats existed before, and, strange to say, taxicabs are to be seen in the streets of Bagdad. The traffic is controlled by an efficient police force and aeroplanes are to be seen flying all over the country. Two miles outside the old city of Bagdad a new town has sprung up where the Europeans and officials reside—for Bagdad is the capital and seat of government. The story of this city of Harun-al-Rashid and the Arabian Nights is reserved for another chapter.

The future of the new Iraq is full of promise, but its realization will depend on the way in which its people adapt themselves to the new conditions.

IRAQ: FACTS AND FIGURES

THE COUNTRY

Consists of the former Turkish vilayets of Baghdad, Basra and Mosul, which are bounded on the north by Turkey, on the east by Iran, on the south by the Persian Gulf and Kuweit, on the southwest by Arabia and on the west by Jordan and Syria. The total area is 116,600 square miles and the population is more than 5,100,000.

GOVERNMENT

A limited monarchy ruled by a king and Cabinet. Legislative body consists of a Senate of 29 elder statesmen, nominated for 8 years, and a Lower House made up of 138 deputies, who are elected.

COMMERCE AND INDUSTRIES

Chief product is oil. The rich soil is now being developed by irrigation. Cotton, wheat, barley, oats, linseed and flax are produced though mostly in the experimental stage. Dates are grown. Principal exports are barley, wheat, wool and dates, and the imports are textiles, sugar, carpets and tea.

COMMUNICATIONS

Railway length is 1,027 miles, and the telegraph line mileage, 6,493; telephone line, 73,876 miles. There is a regular air service.

RELIGION AND EDUCATION

Bulk of the population is Mohammedan of both Shiah and Sunni sects. There are primary schools, secondary schools and several colleges and technical schools.

CHIEF TOWNS

Bagdad, the capital, has a population of about 550,000; Mosul, 230,000; Basra, 110,000; Kirkuk, 80,000; and Amara, 60,000.

THE CITY OF THE ARABIAN NIGHTS

Bagdad (or Baghdad) the Historic City

Bagdad! At the mention of this magic word our thoughts turn to the wonderful stories of the Thousand and One Nights, to the great Caliph Harun-al-Rashid, during whose reign the city reached the zenith of its splendor. It was then the capital of the Saracenic Empire, a vast centre for the trade of all Asia, a home of romance, of mystery and of learning. Unfortunately the Bagdad of to-day is not the Bagdad of the Arabian Nights. The palaces, gardens and courtiers have gone with most of the splendid buildings of the vanished city, on the site of which is a suburb—a collection of mud hovels—of the modern Bagdad. Bagdad, as we shall read in this chapter, is gradually being transformed into a city of the West and in due time it may regain some of its bygone splendor and commercial importance.

WHEN speaking of Bagdad we conjure up visions of the genii and of the Forty Thieves, for the glamour of romance hangs over this city from its associations with the Caliph Harun-al-Rashid and the Arabian Nights. We think of the palms, the splendid cities, wealthy merchants, mighty princes and beautiful princesses—all the glory of the East, as pictured in the greatest story-book of all times.

Not much is known of the town of Bagdad previous to the period of Islam. In 762 A.D., Caliph Mansur decided to transfer his residence from Damascus, which was then the seat of the Caliphate, and was looking about for a place for the new seat of government. The Arabs themselves say that a Christian monastery stood on the site and that a Christian monk very obligingly pointed out to Mansur the great advantages of its position. However that may be, Mansur built a mosque and a palace as the centre, and the city was laid out around them in concentric circles with three strong walls. The townspeople and the bazaars occupied the space between the first and second walls but, for purposes of defense, the space between the second and the third was left entirely empty.

In the days of Harun-al-Rashid about twenty-five years later, Bagdad was the capital of a large empire. It comprised not only Mesopotamia and Arabia, but also Persia, Egypt, Syria, North Africa and all the Caucasian countries such as Georgia and Circassia near the Black Sea.

The court of the Caliph was the most magnificent the world has ever seen; more than eighty thousand servants lived within the palace. There were ornaments of gold and silver and in the Hall of Audience stood the famous golden tree upon which, so tradition says, birds of gold and silver, studded with precious stones, fluttered mechanical wings and poured forth delightful songs. Everything was agleam with precious gems and some say that one street was even paved with silver.

Under Harun-al-Rashid, it became also the golden age of commerce, of science, of literature and of art. It was no wonder then that its fame reached far and wide and that it was coveted by ambitious nations. Constant warfare followed the death of Harun-al-Rashid, and it was not many years before the fine buildings were all destroyed. Although it was rebuilt, it never regained its former splendor.

The city changed hands many times—Turks, Mongols, Persians fought for it and held it for a time until finally the Turks conquered it again in 1638 and retained it until World War I. But the Bagdad of to-day is not that of long ago as we shall soon see.

From the south we approach it by the River Tigris, sailing through a flat and desolate country of sand, upon which we may see an occasional encampment of wandering Arab tribes. Within a few miles of Bagdad the land begins to assume a different aspect. Native boats are plying along the river, and the paddle-steamer

PHILIP GENDREAU

RADISHES GROW AS BIG AS PARSNIPS IN THE WARM SUN OF IRAQ

A bumper crop of the edible root is being washed in a trench before being taken to market. Radishes are thought to be native to Asia, but they can no longer be found in the wild state.

that has brought us from the Persian Gulf threads its way through a maze of craft of all descriptions, and berths at one of the rough wooden jetties. We are in the center of the land of the Caliphs, of Sindbad the Sailor, and the peris and genii of which we have read in the Thousand and One Nights.

We shall be disappointed to learn that the present site of Bagdad is not the one of the Caliphs. They had their city on the west bank and now almost all that remains of their glory are some of the royal tombs and the shrine of Zobeide, the favorite wife of Harun-al-Rashid. We see a group of mud hovels, a new railway station, trim bungalows with English gardens where the railway people live, and we turn away disturbed indeed by the fact that we cannot see Bagdad as it was.

Two pontoon bridges connect the old city with the present city which is situated on the east bank of the Tigris. Here the buildings straggle along about two miles of the shore and each end is marked by the North and South Gates which were used formerly when the city was protected by a wall. Bright-colored domes and minarets greet our eyes, for Bagdad is still one of the centers of the Shiite sect of Mohammedans and the Faithful come from afar to worship at its holy places. Of the difference between the Shiite and the Sunni sects, we shall read in the article on Arabia.

Connecting North and South Gates, a distance of about three miles, is a broad thoroughfare called New Street. This was started by the Turks in 1916 for transporting artillery and many buildings were torn down to make way for it. When the British captured the city in March, 1917, they continued the building of the street.

Bagdad is now the capital of Iraq which

TENDING THE VALUABLE SKINS OF KARAKUL LAMBS NEAR BAGDAD

The karakul is a hardy breed of broadtail sheep that thrives in dry regions. Newborn lambs have a tightly curled, glossy fur, sometimes called astrakhan, that is widely used in clothing.

PHOTOS, PHILIP GENDREAU

HOW COTTON IS SPUN IN THE LAND OF DATE PALMS AND TURBANS

The climate of Bagdad is so dry that some kinds of factories may be rigged up out-of-doors in a shady spot. Cotton is an important crop in Iraq, and its production employs many people.

Parfit

ARAB CROWDS ON THE BANK OF THE TIGRIS WHERE GUFAS DISCHARGE THEIR MOTLEY CARGOES

Bagdad is a very busy commercial centre, and great quantities of all kinds of merchandise are brought to its markets in the queer, round, native boats, known as gufas. The scene by the Tigris at Bagdad where these craft, about which we have spoken on page 228, are being unloaded, is one of noisy bustle. Arabs, in gay flowing robes, carry vegetables and poultry, sacks of grain and dates up the bank. Often they have to land a pair of kicking donkeys or a few goats, and in this photograph we see a horse stepping carefully from an especially large gufa.

was formerly under British mandate. In 1932 the mandate ended and Iraq became independent. Iraq took an active part in founding the Arab League and has been a member of the United Nations since the signing of the UN Charter in 1945. British influence in Iraq, as in most Middle East countries, declined after World War II, though British and American firms still held large interests in Iraqi oil.

New Street Becomes Arab

Toward North Gate the city becomes Arab in character and just beyond the Gate is the residence occupied by King Feisal whom the British selected as the native ruler of Iraq. He died in 1933, and was succeeded by his son Ghazi. He died in 1939, and his infant son succeeded as Feisal II.

We must go through the narrow cross streets, which lead from New Street to the river, to find the real atmosphere of Bagdad. Here are the bazaars and the coffee-houses and the many types of people that form an interesting part of the city.

A large number of the population is Arab but as we go wandering about we shall see also Syrians, Armenians, Indians, Persians, Turks—members of all the tribes and races of the Near and Middle East. The languages used mostly are Arabic and Turkish, and the principal religion is, of course, Mohammedanism.

Let us take a walk through the bazaars, where we shall see the life of Bagdad. On market days they are crowded with town and country-folk who come in from the surrounding districts laden with the produce of the field and looms and with various articles made at their homes. All classes are represented, from the rich merchant to the beggar who clamors for alms amidst the din of bargainings.

Importance of the Letter-writer

Here and there in the narrow streets, we may see a fortune-teller who for a small sum promises life-long prosperity to his patrons; and the professional letter-writer is also a common sight. He sits cross-legged with paper spread out upon his lap. Clients gather round him and recite documents and letters and the scribe writes it all down. Education is not so universal as in the West, so the professional letter-writer is kept very busy on market day, when the terms of the bargains have to be recorded and deeds of sale drawn up.

The medical profession is often popular amongst Orientals, since it affords a ready means of acquiring wealth and influence, for among these simple people anyone may pose as a healer of all the ills to which flesh is heir. I remember once discharging a groom for inefficiency who shortly afterward set up as a medical man. As I passed through the market place one day, I saw my former groom presiding over a stall, which was well stocked with herbs and potions. Quite a crowd was assembled at his consulting room, and before dealing out the medicines he felt the patient's pulse and looked at his tongue, as he had probably seen European doctors do. Then he glanced through a book in his hand, following this up by selecting some medicines, as if in accordance with the instructions in the book. I was curious to see that book, and on inspection it proved to be a copy of a novel that had formerly been in my library!

Houses Built for Extremes of Climate

The houses in Bagdad are interesting because they are built to meet extremes of climate. From the end of April until the beginning of October the heat is excessive, so the houses are constructed partly underground with windows high enough to admit light and air. The occupants sleep on the roof in summer, retiring to the cellar at sunrise for soon after that time the temperature will rise to as much as 110° Fahrenheit in the shade. During the winter the weather is cold and there are often ice and snow.

Primary and secondary education is free and compulsory. However, there are less than a thousand elementary schools. Iraq has no university, but there are a number of vocational and technical schools, and about twelve colleges for training teachers, doctors, lawyers, engineers and so on.

MONUMENT TO A KING

King Feisal I Bridge spans the colorful Tigris at Bagdad. Feisal was chosen King of Iraq by a referendum in 1921, receiving 96 per cent of the votes cast. He remained on the throne until his death in 1933. His grandson, Feisal II, who has ruled through his uncle, the prince-regent, since 1939, will take over in his own right in 1953 on his eighteenth birthday.

PHOTOS, BLACK STAR

KING FEISAL SQUARE

This view of still another monument to a beloved monarch is taken from a department store roof. The buildings under construction and the state-owned Iraqi Airways office add a modern touch. In contrast, the domes of some ancient mosques may be seen in the background. These, together with other buildings of historic importance, make Bagdad a tourists' paradise.

KEYSTONE

THE ICE-CREAM VENDOR IS A POPULAR FELLOW, EAST AND WEST

Arab children in a street in Bagdad gather eagerly to clamor for a portion of the cooling sweet. Hundreds of years ago ice cream was such a rare delicacy that only kings and emperors could enjoy it, but today it is for everyone. These youngsters would probably enjoy it in cones. Instead, they are eating it from little flat dishes, and the hot sun says, "Hurry."

The schools tend to be nationalistic, that is, they teach the rich history of Iraq's past and try to stimulate the pupils to think about the future of their country. In the campaign against illiteracy nearly 150 tribal schools have been opened and free books are distributed to those students who cannot afford to buy texts.

Many children do not attend the more progressive government schools, but are taught by comparatively ignorant teachers in badly organized, primitive classes. The pupils in such poor schools must sit on the ground at desks made of rough-hewn logs. Some sing their lessons aloud, in an ancient Oriental belief that the mind

Rodd

CITIZENS OF BAGDAD STROLL BY THE PALM-FRINGED TIGRIS

On the river banks below Bagdad the townspeople walk in the cool of evening. They are of all classes—the camel-driver, with a great kerchief as a headdress and flowing garments, as well as the merchant in his fez, his white gown and dark voluminous abas, or cloak. Most of the women wear their robes over their heads and many have masks of black horsehair.

absorbs knowledge through the ears rather than by the eyes.

There is one thing that we do not meet with in Bagdad, that is caste—the distinction between the different classes which is such a handicap to the people of India. Here any means of livelihood may be adopted, and no one will sneer at a man because of his trade.

Market day reveals the national costumes in all their many colors. The under-garment is usually a long shirt, over which is a close-fitting coat of colored cloth fastened at the waist by a girdle. Above this is a cloak of camel's hair, often with black-and-white stripes. Perhaps the most practical part of the costume for this hot climate is the scarf which is arranged over the head in a form of turban so that the long ends hang from the shoulders and can be used as a protection against the rays of the sun.

The food of the people consists of wheat, barley, corn and mutton, and the date is also an important article of diet. It is, in fact, the staff of life of the Arab, and the Prophet Mohammed directed all his followers to honor it as they would their parents. Coffee is another thing of which the people are very fond, and the first thing an Arab does in the morning, after he has said the early prayers ordered by his religion, is to take a cup. It is said that coffee was first discovered by an Arab near Bagdad, who one day lighted a fire beneath a wild shrub. A most uncommon and pleasing smell resulted which led to the discovery of the famous beverage. At first it was considered an intoxicant and was forbidden by the Mohammedan religion but its popularity was so great that it seemed impossible to prevent it and so it became the favorite drink of Near Eastern people.

KEYSTONE

A BAGDAD STREETCAR TRAVELS LEISURELY

The car may not move faster than a boy can walk, but it offers some shade on the way. The roof is a popular spot since it affords the best view of the passing scene.

Music of a kind peculiar to the Orient is played in the bazaars and at entertainments, but the tunes are a monotonous repetition and mainly of a dull and plaintive character. Indeed, there is no accounting for taste in that direction. Some years ago a party of desert tribesmen were taken to Leningrad, in Russia, where they witnessed a performance at the Opera House. At the fall of the curtain they unanimously agreed that the finest part of the entertainment had been the tuning-up of the violins!

The coffee-house, a form of open-air café, is a feature of Bagdad. There the gossips congregate to discuss the news of the day and a great deal of business is accomplished over the cups. As the Bagdadis are strict Mohammedans they observe the fast of the Ramadan, the foremost religious observance of the Moslem faith, and it is then that the coffee-shops are most crowded.

The Ramadan is chosen as the period of fasting, because the Koran is believed by the Mohammedans to have been revealed to Mohammed during this month. While the fast lasts no food whatever may be taken between dawn and nightfall; there can be no eating, drinking, nor any form of material pleasure, and the fast is considered to have been broken if perfumes are smelled.

During the hours of complete darkness eating is permitted, and so the coffee-shops remain open all night and are gay with lights and other attractions until the coming of dawn, when the fast begins again. While the rich may lessen the severity of the ordeal by turning night into day, its hardships fall heavily upon the poor and industrial classes, who must continue their daily labors.

All through Bagdad we shall find evidence of the historic past, and, with the advance of civilization and under the great influence of Western ideas it is being gradually developed into a great and prosperous city. Vast distances in this land are now covered by aeroplane in a few hours, where formerly all transport was by camels, which averaged but fifty miles per day. Now double as much is done in an hour, and soon this once magnificent city, with its quaint streets, its cafés, mosques and market places, will be within reach of the traveler, who can, if he has the imagination, then feel himself really in touch with the Orient.

KEYSTONE

WISE CARE FOR PERISHABLES WHERE REFRIGERATORS ARE SCARCE

The Arab woman is carrying milk straight home from the cow. The man walking on the left holds a squawking chicken, which will not be killed until it is time to cook it.

THE CHANGING EAST

The Turks in Europe and in Asia Minor

It is probable that the people who founded the Turkish Empire came westward from central Asia. They waxed in power as the Byzantine Empire, last remnant of the Roman Empire, waned. The long struggle between Byzantium and the Turks lasted for several hundred years and was finally resolved when the Turks conquered Constantinople in 1453. Thereafter the Turks made deep inroads into eastern Europe. Gradually, however, they lost most of this territory. Modern Turkey covers only a few square miles of European soil; most of its territory is in Asia. Turkey became a republic a few years after World War I. Under the leadership of Kemal Atatürk, president from 1923 until his death in 1938, the country was made over along Western lines, with a democratic constitution. Today Turkey is the strongest and the most advanced of any nation in the Middle East. It is a member of the United Nations and also of the North Atlantic Treaty Organization.

TURKEY and the customs of its inhabitants are changing so rapidly that many people who knew it a few years ago would scarcely believe it to be the same land if they returned to-day. The people are adopting new ways and every day they are becoming more and more like the nations of Europe.

Turkey was formerly one of the great empires of the world although its beginning was small indeed. It is thought that a horde of about 2,000 to 4,000 people driven by enemy forces came west from Central Asia about 1200 A.D. At that time the Seljuk Empire was very powerful and held extensive territories in Western Asia. This small band of Turks applied to the Seljuks for a place to live and were granted territory near the present site of Ankara in Asia Minor. For a long time they fought for the Seljuks but Othman, who was head of the tribe, was ambitious. He increased his lands and grew so powerful that finally the Seljuk Empire itself was absorbed by the tribe it had befriended.

The Seljuks and the conquering Turks were Moslems or followers of the Mohammedan religion. As we may read in the chapter on Arabia, it was the aim of the Moslems to force their religion on all the world. Accordingly, when Othman and his successors wished to expand the Ottoman Empire, it was natural to turn toward the West where was the Christian Greek Empire of the East with its seat at Constantinople. Efforts to take Constantinople were unsuccessful but all Asia Minor and Palestine were conquered and then they broke into Europe. Finally in 1453 Constantinople fell to them as we shall see in another chapter.

The great empire they created extended along the coast of North Africa as far as Morocco so that the Ottoman Empire at its height held considerable portions of three continents. But this was not due to last, for Turkey's rulers were not always great warriors. In 1683 the Turkish army was put to rout in an attempt to take Vienna in Austria, and from that time Turkey gradually lost much of what she had, for so many centuries, been successfully acquiring.

Turkey as an ally of Germany in the first World War lost territory but regained a little in the Greco-Turkish War that followed. All there is now of the former great empire is Asia Minor and a portion of Thrace in Europe up to the Maritza River, including, however, the city of Constantinople.

The Asian territory, which is a peninsula, covers a large area stretching from the borders of Russia, Persia, Iraq and Syria on the east to the Mediterranean Sea on the west. It is separated from Europe by the Dardanelles, the Sea of Marmora and the Bosporus. Turkey, or Anatolia, a name used very often to refer to this territory, is really a great plateau which rises in the south and east to form the Taurus and Anti-Taurus ranges.

TURKEY WITH NEW NAMES FOR OLD CITIES AND TOWNS

There are two kinds of climate—that in the interior which is one of extremes with cold winters and hot summers, and that of the coastal regions which is milder and more comfortable. Rivers are few in number and run so sluggishly that they are of no commercial value. On the whole the land is very fertile and a great variety of products is grown.

Let us look at Turkey as it was years ago. We should see signs of neglect and dirt on every side. Instead of cleaning the towns and carrying away all rubbish, the Turks allowed large numbers of wild dogs to roam the streets. These dogs lived by eating up all the waste that the people threw out of their houses into the dirty and ill-paved roadways. Their numbers increased to such an extent that at one time the country was almost overrun. Moslem law, however, forbids the killing of animals so they must find another way of ridding themselves of the dogs. They solved the problem by loading the poor beasts on boats and sending them to one of the islands near by where they all starved to death. To a Mohammedan that is not a cruel way to dispose of pests, for is it not cruel and also wicked to kill them?

In spite of an attitude quite different from ours, we should have found the Turkish gentlemen very agreeable persons. They had athletic figures and dark complexions which, combined with polished manners and a culture acquired in European schools, made them interesting people to know. Dressed always in black clothes and wearing the gay tasseled fez they were also attractive in appearance.

Turkish ladies were very carefully guarded. All the female members of the family, which included aunts and cousins, lived together in an apartment of the house especially set aside for them. This was called a harem and no men except relatives were allowed in to see them. Here they spent their time looking after the home, although there were plenty of slaves to do the actual work. In a sheltered garden, they would cultivate beautiful flowers. Many of them liked to read, especially French books, and they had music and dancing. They might go visiting too at the houses of friends, but before going outside the house, it was necessary to veil themselves in a "charchaf," leaving only the eyes exposed. Usually they drove in carriages but should they walk it was necessary to have a male attendant march behind.

Turkish boys and girls received very good treatment for the Turks are naturally fond of children. Before they were many years old, however, they were separated, and the boys were sent to school while the girls remained in the women's quarters. If the family could afford it, the daughters of the household would have a French governess, and were taught music, but while they were still young their father would have selected a husband for them. Then they would go to live in another home and would spend their days as their mothers had done before them. A Turkish man was allowed more than one wife, so the young bride often had these other wives as her companions.

The houses of the rich were simply furnished. Usually a low divan ran along the wall or perhaps along three of them and was covered with velvets or heavy silks richly embroidered. The walls were highly ornamented which made up for the lack of furniture. A beautiful Persian or Turkish rug covered the floor and there might be a small low table on which smoking articles were placed. Strangely enough, the Turks have liked European furniture and have imported it so that at the present time, their homes are a mixture of the two types

BLACK STAR

LEADING A FLOCK OF SHEEP TO NEW PASTURE IN THE MOUNTAINS

Dressed in an embroidered felt cape that keeps him both dry and warm, the Turkish shepherd is taking his sheep from the Cilician Plains near the Mediterranean, where they have passed the winter, up to the plateau of the Taurus Mountains for spring pasturage. In addition to the sale of wool and mutton, he will make a profit from the ewes' milk and its products.

BLACK STAR

HOUSES OF PUMICE DUG FROM THE LAVA PLATEAU OF CAPPADOCIA

The volcanic cone in the background is one of thousands left by erosion of deposits of extinct Mount Argaeus, in central Turkey. Early Christians dug out refuges in the cones.

BLACK STAR

KEEPING THE GROUNDS TIDY IN A MODEL VILLAGE IN TURKEY

The tile roofs and thick walls of stone and stucco have been wisely planned to shield residents against the hot sun of southern Turkey. The dusty ground shows the lack of rainfall.

EWING GALLOWAY

TURKISH FARMERS CHEERFULLY POSE BEFORE THEIR NEW TRACTOR

Knowing that modern machinery will make their land more productive, they look forward to a bumper crop. It will be shipped to the nearby city of Adana, where farm produce is traded.

Courtesy, Turkish Consulate, N. Y.

THE DARDANELLES, GATEWAY BETWEEN THE EAST AND WEST

The Dardanelles, on which this city is located, is a strait separating Europe from Asia. It is the ancient Hellespont of the Greeks. Since earliest times it has been of great strategic importance. To-day, with its banks protected by modern fortifications, it protects the city of Istanbul, which lies beyond the straits and the Sea of Marmara.

of decoration and the effect is far from pleasing

But Turkey was then and is to-day mostly an agricultural country and it is the peasant or small farmer who forms the greater part of the population. Their homes are very simple, usually consisting of two rooms with very little furniture in them. In one room there may be a slightly raised platform with some simple cushions on it, for here the family sleeps at night without undressing.

The men have a very picturesque costume—a blue coat, a red sash, a pair of dark loose breeches, and a cloth wound around the head to form a turban. They must work very hard to make a living. Using primitive implements and with no knowledge of improved methods, they are able only to eke out enough to live on. What extra they have has to go to pay the heavy taxes. Formerly, when they could not pay they were punished severely.

The women work in the fields too and so the Turkish peasant in times past availed himself of the privilege of having more than one wife in order that he might have that many more unpaid laborers. Children also are put to work at a very early age and consequently have little chance of going to school. Many of them are illiterate and when they grow up they

Courtesy, Turkish Consulate, N. Y.

A TYPICAL STREET SCENE IN A POOR TURKISH VILLAGE

Frequently the second stories of the mud-washed homes of rural Turkey project out over the bottom story, as we can see here. When this occurs on both sides of the street, the sky is seen only as a narrow ribbon between the overhanging balconies. The roofs of these country houses are often occupied by storks who have built nests there.

Courtesy, Turkish Consulate, N. Y.

COTTON, ONE OF TURKEY'S NATURAL TREASURES

A cotton picker in Anatolia, Asiatic Turkey. Cotton is one of Turkey's chief export materials. Under an intense four-year plan for cultivation instituted by the government, cotton is expected to show a further increase in production in the future. This plan is another indication of progressive trends at work within the country.

Courtesy, Turkish Consulate, N. Y.

TURKISH GIRLS NO LONGER HIDE THEIR FACES

Turkish girls at work in a cigar factory. Until recently girls in factories were unheard of in Turkey. They kept to the seclusion of their homes, and when they ventured out even for a few moments, their faces were heavily veiled. To-day, however, the veil has almost disappeared from Turkey, a sign of the country's westernization.

have to depend on the "letter-writer" to read, write and transact business for them.

They have many things to eat in Turkey that we do not usually get here. In the country districts, huge dishes are prepared and are served in bowls on a stand upon the floor. Everyone sits around it on cushions and each helps himself with a horn spoon. In other parts, even where there is a tablecloth, the tablecloth is often put underneath the little tables and on to it the diners throw the bones they have picked. The well-to-do people, however, have very fine tableware.

The favorite meat of the Turks, and of all Near Eastern people, is lamb, and the Turkish lamb which comes from the mountain parts is as tender as any chicken. There are a number of appetizing ways of preparing it, but the most common way is to cook small bits of it with rice and oil, a dish which they call "pilaf." They have many kinds of vegetables and fruits, but the fruits they like best in preserved form. Turks are very fond of sweets and eat large quantities, especially the kind known as "Turkish delight." The Turks are not supposed to drink alcohol because the Mohammedan religion forbids it, but they drink much coffee and sometimes the sour milk, known as Yaghoort, which is said to keep people healthy.

BURSA, NEAR THE SEA OF MARMARA

Bursa (or Brusa) is a city of semitropical gardens and groves, at the foot of a mountain called the Mysian Olympus. Bursa was the residence of many Turkish sultans, who loved to adorn it; and here and there all over the city the slender white minarets of mosques lift their spires above the tree tops. The Sea of Marmara is only twenty miles away.

PHOTOS, TURKISH INFORMATION OFFICE

CROESUS NEVER HAD A PALACE LIKE THIS

Elegant and luxurious in the contemporary manner is this hotel, the Çelikpalas, in Bursa. The city is on the site of ancient Prusa, capital of Bithynia, which was conquered by Croesus and made part of his empire. Hannibal of Carthage is said to have fled to Prusa after his defeat by Rome, and to have committed suicide there. Bursa is a modern, well-kept city.

Turkey is truly a land of contrasts. The visitor sees this quickly as he goes from the minarets and mosques of Istanbul to the capital, Ankara, with its twentieth-century look.

The Modern Capital

Ankara, nonetheless, is really a very old town. It was founded three thousand years ago by the Phrygians, and it has known the tread of many conquerors. Today this past history is practically obliterated. There are broad tree-lined avenues, along which up-to-date busses lumber, buildings in the most advanced architectural styles, a soccer stadium, a national theater and an opera house.

Yet only a few miles outside Ankara one comes upon villages where time seems to have stood still. Most of the people still live in mud-brick huts—generally sleeping on the floor—and follow many of their old ways.

There is also a great contrast between the Turkish people as one meets them in their homeland and the reputation they achieved in centuries of conflict between Moslems and Christians. If the visitor takes time to make their acquaintance, he will find that the citizens of modern Turkey are friendly toward strangers and most courteous. Yet the quiet, mild-mannered folk of today still have fierce fighting qualities.

Turkish Troops in Korea

In the Korean conflict, the Turkish brigade quickly won the respect and admiration of their allies. But they were known as courageous fighters long before then.

After World War I, the Turks rebelled against the terms of peace. Allied armies occupied much of the land, and Allied fleets patrolled the Turkish straits. In 1919, the Greek army landed at Smyrna. This occupation was a bloody one. Atrocities were committed by both sides. The incidents aroused Turkish feeling to fever pitch and the Turks determined to resist occupation to the last, even if it meant total disintegration of their country.

The Allies became alarmed at the new nationalism in Turkey and permitted the Greeks to spread into the area beyond Smyrna in order to keep the Turks down. But the desperate Turkish patriots organized a terrific offensive. They drove the Greeks back from Ashak to Smyrna; and as they recovered this land, they burned to the ground many of the more prosperous towns in western Turkey. They left millions homeless in their fiery onslaught; and when they approached Smyrna, the occupants fled in terror.

It should be remembered that the Turkish army was greatly outnumbered by its enemies; but the Turks were fighting for their fatherland which, they considered, the Allies had no right to hand over to another nation.

The government and future of Turkey had been unstable for some time. During

BLACK STAR

HAIR-DO FOR A YOUNG GIRL

Braids are the custom in several southern provinces. A scarf covers them after marriage.

TURKISH INFORMATION OFFICE

SPONGE DIVER IN TURKISH WATERS

The finest sponges are found in Turkish waters. The season for gathering them runs from May to about October. Many Mediterranean divers, like the one above, now use diving equipment, but until comparatively recently they employed no gear. They submerged by means of a rope weighted with a stone, tore the sponges from the rocks and brought them up in a net.

BLACK STAR

AN OLD COVERED WAGON SERVES FOR A HOLIDAY RIDE

To a village in the suburbs have come city dwellers of Istanbul, taking advantage of a national holiday to explore the countryside and enjoy the fresh country air. Istanbul, on the Bosporus, is not far from many picturesque and historic villages and towns that are sprinkled along both shores of the Bosporus northward almost as far as the Black Sea.

these years, however, many of the Turks were beginning to realize that their old ways of living and governing could be improved. They had always been ruled by a sultan who was most despotic and gave them very little liberty. In 1922, as the time seemed ripe, a number of these people, who called themselves Nationalists, deposed the sultan and later established a republic with their leader, Mustapha Kemal, as president. (In 1934, by act of Parliament, Kemal received the family name of Atatürk—"chief Turk.")

Numerous reforms were instituted but

Ewing Galloway, N. Y.

HOME OF THE TURKISH MINISTRY OF FINANCE IN ANGORA (ANKARA) THE CAPITAL

After the World War, when Turkey in Europe was so reduced in size, Constantinople was no longer considered a fitting capital. The seat of government was then moved to Angora, almost in the centre of Turkey in Asia. Angora was a flourishing town before the Christian era, but in the centuries that had elapsed it had become of little importance though known for its special breed of goats. Since becoming the capital, its growth has been amazing. Many fine government buildings, foreign embassies and residences have been erected. Here is shown the Ministry of Finance Building.

BLACK STAR

THE ANCIENT POTTER'S WHEEL STILL SPINS IN MODERN KUTAHYA

Kutahya in western Turkey is noted for its decorative ceramics and tiles. Though these vessels are being made by hand, they are perfectly symmetrical. Notice the fluted rims.

probably none were more startling than freeing the women from harem life. Many of the women had been contented in the old life but others were anxious to do as the women in Europe were doing. If we were to go to Constantinople today we should see Turkish husbands going about freely in the streets with their wives and children. The men no longer wear the fez, or red cap, for the government has forbidden its use. The Turkish women dress in the European manner without a veil and a great many of them now earn their own living by working in shops or offices. In the country districts, however, changes are not made so quickly and there we should see the women still unaccustomed to exposing their faces.

No less startling was the transfer of the seat of government from Constantinople, where it had been since 1453, to Angora, now called Ankara, a small town in the interior. Angora was a commercial center renowned for the export of mohair made from the hair of the Angora goat. It was a city without improvements so that it has had to be entirely rebuilt in order to accommodate the government offices as well as the official residences. Since becoming the capital, its population has grown enormously.

The name, Angora, has been changed, as we have mentioned above, and so have most geographical names for the government has latinized the Turkish alphabet. While, in this article, we have used the old familiar names for the cities, the reader who wishes to acquaint himself with the new ones will find them given below with the old names in parentheses following.

TURKEY: FACTS AND FIGURES

THE COUNTRY

Occupies the greater portion of Asia Minor and a small part of the Balkan Peninsula. It is bounded on the north by the Black Sea, on the northeast by Transcaucasia (Union of Soviet Socialist Republics), on the east by Iran, on the south by Iraq, Syria and the Mediterranean and on the west by the Aegean Sea, Greece and Bulgaria. Area, 296,300 square miles; population, 20,902,628, including the Sanjak of Alexandretta (Iskanderoun) incorporated in the Turkish territory in 1939.

GOVERNMENT

In 1921 the Grand National Assembly at Ankara proclaimed a Fundamental Law which declared that all sovereignty belonged to the people and that the legislative and executive power was vested in the hands of this Assembly representing the people. The term "Ottoman Empire" was abolished and the country officially designated Turkey. A republic was proclaimed in 1923, and Kemal Pasha became first president. In 1924 a new constitution provided for election of the Assembly every four years. Executive power is exercised by the president and a Council of Ministers appointed by him. In 1937 the Assembly agreed to recognize only one party and established a form of state socialism. Other parties have since been allowed.

COMMERCE AND INDUSTRIES

Agriculture, though carried on by primitive methods, is the chief occupation of the people. Modern methods are replacing the old. A Land Reform Bill, passed in 1945, distributed large tracts of agricultural lands among peasants who had none. The chief products are tobacco, cereals, figs, silk, olives and olive-oil, dried fruits, hazelnuts, mohair, cotton, wool and hides. There are said to be rich deposits of minerals but they are little worked. Industrial production is increasing. Principal exports are leaf tobacco, cotton, raisins, hazelnuts, livestock, chrome and hides. Imports are machines, cottons and woolens, iron and steel products, petroleum, cereals, lumber, motor vehicles and railway equipment.

RELIGION AND EDUCATION

Most of the people are Mohammedans, though Mohammedanism has been abolished as a state religion. Primary education is compulsory. State schools, which include primary, secondary and preparatory schools, are all under the Ministry of Public Instruction. There are teachers' colleges and other advanced schools, as well as the universities of Istanbul and Ankara, attendance at which is free and optional. In 17,000 primary schools there are about 1,625,500 pupils and 34,000 teachers; in 380 secondaries, 69,225 pupils and 3,500 teachers; in special schools, 80,100 pupils and 6,700 teachers; and in colleges and universities, 26,625 students and 1,500 teachers.

COMMUNICATIONS

Length of federal roads, 14,300 miles; provincial roads, 6,000 miles; railways, 4,800 miles; telegraph lines, 19,690 miles. State-owned shipping numbered 57 vessels with tonnage over 200,000. Flights by state air line, 8,700.

CHIEF TOWNS

Ankara (Angora), capital, 226,712; Istanbul (Constantinople), 860,588; Izmir (Smyrna), 198,396; Seyhan (Adana), 100,780; Bursa (Brusa), 85,030.

DEVOUT TURKS MAKING THEMSELVES FIT TO ENTER THE MOSQUE

No matter where a Mohammedan may be he turns to face Mecca when he hears the voice of the muezzin giving the call to prayer, and bows to the earth. Whenever he wishes to enter a mosque he must first make himself "abtest," or "legally pure," by washing hands, forearms, face and feet in running water provided by every mosque.

ISTANBUL THE COVETED CITY

Turkey's Last Foothold on European Soil

THE approach to Constantinople (Istanbul) by sea hints at the beauty of that city. Passing up the Dardanelles into the little Sea of Marmora, our ship, after a few hours, comes within sight of the domes and minarets that rise fairy-like from the many hills on which Constantinople is built.

As we draw nearer the city we see the rugged walls and battlements which at one time defended it from invaders. We follow the city's lines of sea-washed walls until we come to the old ruins and pavilions of Eski Serai, the Old Seraglio, which was at one time the palace where the Turkish sultans dwelt in the greatest splendor.

The Seraglio is passed and we steam at last into Constantinople's harbor, which is called the Golden Horn. It is one of the most fascinating ports in the world. A thousand boats sway gently at their moorings or bear out to sea on some distant errand. Narrow cushioned boats cut swiftly through the shadows cast on the water by huge liners. Gaily painted "caiques," or Turkish sailing boats, pass and repass. Swift motor boats dart like dragon-flies among the maze of other craft and heavy barges lumber along like oxen of the sea.

In front of us a host of modern buildings straggle up a hillside to form the European quarter. To the left are the domes and minarets of Stamboul, the Turkish heart of Constantinople. In the opposite direction are the cool green hills that rise from the shores of the Bosporus, while behind us, on the other side of the water is Scutari, that portion of Constantinople built on Asiatic soil, where the most fanatical Turks make their homes.

Constantinople is one of the most interesting cities in the world. Its age alone is enough to make us wonder. We look upon London, Paris and Berlin as very old cities, but they were nothing more than villages when Constantinople was one of the fairest cities the world had ever seen. Other places like Athens or Rome are really older, but they had long periods in which they were unimportant, almost uninhabited and half-forgotten.

Byzantium Is Given a New Name

That was not the case with Constantinople. From the very beginning the city was of great importance. Its natural position on a wonderful land-locked harbor, later called the Golden Horn, made it seem to Byzas and his Greek colonists, who came there about 657 B.C., that this was the place where they would find the success promised them by the oracle of Delphi in Greece.

The city became prosperous and beautiful and consequently envious invaders were always attacking it, but usually without success. The Romans, however, were successful in the fourth century B.C., and Byzantium, as it was then known, became part of the great Roman Empire.

Later, Constantine, the first Christian emperor of the Roman Empire, decided to move his court to the Bosporus and there to establish a new capital. He built his city, an enlargement of the ancient Byzantium, on seven hills because Rome was built on seven hills and he called it Nova Roma or New Rome. But the people gradually began to call it Constantinople, in his honor, and Constantinople it remained, though the Turks called it Stamboul or Istamboul. The new Turkish Republic has officially named it Istanbul, but the old name will most likely continue to the outside world.

The Capture of Constantinople

A later emperor, Theodosius the Great, having two sons, made a final division of the great Roman Empire between them. He gave to his one son the Western Empire with Rome as its capital, and to the other the Eastern Empire with Constantinople as its seat of government. The Western Empire did not long withstand the attacks of the barbarians but the Byzantine Empire resisted for many centuries. In 1453, Constantinople fell to the Mohammedan Turks who, as we may read in the chapter on Turkey, overran this whole region.

The story of the capture of Constantinople is very thrilling. Unable to take it in earlier attacks, the Turks had conquered all Asiatic territory surrounding it and had crossed into Europe. Reaching the environs of Constantinople on the European side, they bided their time. One night their plans being ready, they placed greased logs side by side over the land and by pushing their boats over these, were able to land in the Golden Horn. So great was the number of Turks that it was all accomplished in one night. Then the sultan, Mohammed II, led an army, frantic with victory, through the gates of the city and planted the green flag of Islam where before had been the cross of the Christians. Since then, Constantinople has belonged to the Turks and was the capital of the Ottoman Empire until 1923.

The Ancient City at Our Feet

So much for the history of Constantinople. It is always good to know something of a city's history. It helps us to understand many of the things we see, and we are better able to cast our minds back hundreds of years and to imagine what things were like in olden days. In the case of Constantinople it enables us to see a city which, in early Greek times, was called "the Dwelling of the Gods"; then to become, under Constantine the Great and those emperors who followed him, the Queen City of Christendom; and, until recent times, the heart of the most powerful Moslem country the world has known.

THE GOLDEN HORN can be seen in its entire length from the cemetery of the Mosque of Eyub. The narrow inlet of the Bosporus gives Istanbul a magnificent land-locked harbor. Notice that the thoughtful young Turks surveying the scene are wearing fezzes. These caps were once the national Turkish headdress, but now they can be worn only in places of worship.

EWING GALLOWAY

A PANORAMA OF ISTANBUL, LOOKING OUT OVER THE HARBOR

The view southwestward from Galata Tower takes in an ancient section that leads down to the harbor of the great crossroads city. In Stamboul, across the Golden Horn, is the terminus of the Orient Express, famous train through the Balkans from Paris. Across the Bosporus, on the Asiatic side, is Haydarpasa Station, starting point of the Bagdad Railway.

BLACK STAR

RUSH-HOUR CROWDS CLOG GALATA BRIDGE AND THE FERRY PIERS

Bumper-to-bumper lanes of cars and trolleys inch across Galata Bridge between Stamboul and the northern suburbs. Ferry boats shoulder their clumsy way in and out of the piers to take city workers to towns on both sides of the Bosporus. Modern freighters line the far shore and Hagia Sophia, above all the bustle, seems to rest patiently.

Courtesy, Commercial Attaché, Turkish Embassy, N. Y.

THE MOSQUE OF ST. SOPHIA, WHICH HAS BECOME A MUSEUM

This great mosque is very remarkable in having been founded as a Christian church, the Church of the Divine Wisdom, by Constantine the Great. The present building dates from 538, but it was not until 1453 that it became a Mohammedan mosque. The minarets at the four corners were built then and Christian symbols were effaced from the beautiful interior.

Let us now get a bird's-eye view of Constantinople. For this we can do no better than to go to the Stamboul section and climb up the Seraskerat Tower, which stands in the gardens of the former Turkish War Office. We shall have 220 steps to climb, but what is that when at the end of it we have all Constantinople at our feet?

Below us lies Stamboul, the oldest and most interesting part of the city, a mass of weather stained ruins, red tiled houses with latticed windows, great colored domes rising from clusters of smaller domes, a forest of minarets, like the masts of many ships, and streets beflagged with red bunting ornamented by the familiar white crescent of the Turks. In these streets we shall see priests of many Near Eastern religious sects, peasants from the country, officials from the public offices, and all classes of Turkish, Greek, Armenian and Jewish people.

If we look southwestward we see the buildings of the city straggle out to little lonely groups and come at last to a broken line of walls which used to defend the city. These walls were pierced by four gates, the most important of which was called the "Sublime Gate" because it was used solely by triumphant sovereigns on their return to the city. From this comes the term "Sublime Porte" by which the Turkish government was formerly known

© E. N. A.

THE GALATA TOWER, 148 feet high, stands on the wall that was built round Galata in the fifteenth century by the Genoese settlers. The walls have now crumbled into ruin and the tower would have met the same fate had not the Turks reconstructed it and, as it overlooked the harbor and town, made it into a fire signal tower. Galata, which is the centre of Constantinople's commerce and foreign trade, is mostly modernized with wide streets and handsome buildings, but there are still many narrow Eastern-looking streets such as this. The red fez has been abolished in Turkey.

© E. N. A.

CROSS THE GALATA BRIDGE from Istanbul and you are in Scutari (Uskudar). The sight that first catches the eye in this city is the dense green forest of cypress trees that covers the enormous Moslem cemetery of Biyuk Mezaristan. This cemetery occupies over three square miles and contains literally millions of graves. Through the trees in this picture you can see some of the grave markers, tall slim headstones carved so that the tops resemble turbans. The trees also serve as markers. One cypress is planted at the head and one at the foot of each grave.

TURKISH INFORMATION OFFICE

ANCIENT TOWER IN ISTANBUL

The mosque of Sultan Bayezit is one of the sights of Istanbul, set off by a spacious courtyard. Outside the gates is this tall tower where fire guards once kept watchful eyes on the mosque. Bayezit II, who built the mosque, was the son of the Ottoman Turk Mohammed II who captured Constantinople in 1453. Bayezit was a patron of the arts. He built several mosques.

to other nations. Now turning westward, we see a few mosques, far apart, and then an ancient aqueduct which is a relic of the Roman emperors. If we look north to the Golden Horn and let our gaze pass over masses of buildings and groups of ships to the western end, we shall see where slender minarets soar heavenward from the Mosque of Eyub, the city's most sacred mosque.

On the other side of the Golden Horn we see a number of small suburbs, and behind these are green fields and then hills. Following along that shore of the Golden Horn, we come presently to a tottering old bridge with rusty barges underneath it and all kinds of small craft tied alongside. A stone's throw away is the new bridge, thickly crowded with people of all nationalities and as colorful as a garden. Behind this are the modern white buildings of Galata, the commercial centre of Constantinople, rising up a steep hill to the European quarter of Pera where are the hotels and big shops.

Now look northeast to the Bosporus. All the way along its shore, as far as we can see are white mosques with their tall minarets, and green wooded hills and little clusters of pink and white houses.

Turning southeast we can make out the great white railway station of Haidar Pasha, where the train starts for the interior of Asia Minor; and just alongside are the cypress groves of Scutari guarding a large Turkish cemetery.

Punishment for Evil Doers

There is a story that has a connection with these cypress trees. As we approached Constantinople we could not but notice the many little birds, like thrushes, skimming the surface of the water. All day and apparently all night, they may be seen darting swiftly within a few inches of the sea, but never will you see them at rest. The story is that these birds are the souls of dead Turks who had done some evil in their lifetime and this ceaseless flying is the punishment they have received. Once a year they all meet among these cypress trees when they welcome new souls to their ranks.

Now that we have glanced over Constantinople let us take a stroll through its streets. Close by the Seraskerat Tower, which we have just descended, is the Old Seraglio, formerly the palace of the sultans. It is now ruined and neglected, but it has a pleasant park that is a cool place to rest in. The Stamboul quarter is the site of the ancient city built by Constantine the Great, but there are very few traces of it left. When the Turks came they made it their headquarters and in the centre of it was a beautiful garden in which were situated the sultan's pavilion, the Seraglio Mosque, some magnificent Turkish baths and the Imperial Treasury.

Ancient Splendors of the Seraglio

One can imagine the barbaric splendor in which the early Turkish sultans lived, with their wonderful gardens, and their pavilions made of dazzling cloth-of-gold embroidered with precious stones.

There is nothing left of that splendor All that we may do is to stand within the crumbling walls of the Seraglio and imagine the spectacle we might have seen had we stood there two hundred years ago. It is a place to dream in, but the dreams are not always pleasant ones. They so frightened the gentle Sultan Abdul-Mejid that about 1855 he left its grim walls and fearful memories for a brighter palace on the Bosporus.

The City's Beautiful Mosques

To see the real splendor of Constantinople we must go to some of its great mosques, for these beautiful edifices are there in order that all the Faithful may pray. A follower of the Mohammedan religion must pray five times a day and as the muezzin calls, he drops his work or whatever he may be doing and hastens to comply with the requirements of his faith. If he goes to a mosque, he first removes his shoes and washes his feet, hands and forearms in running water which is provided in every mosque courtyard. Then he enters the mosque and kneels facing Mecca, the Holy City, and touches his bare forehead to the floor. As he must not remove his hat, it has been

MOSQUES AND MINARETS of dazzling marble are found in great numbers in Istanbul. The Mosque on the left is the great Hagia Sophia, the other is the Mosque of Sultan Ahmed I, the only one of Istanbul's many temples with six minarets. In the foreground is the Atmeidan or Place of Horses, the site of an old Roman hippodrome where chariot races

© E. N. A.

were held. The nearer of the obelisks is called the monument of Constantine but it is not known which of the Constantines it commemorates. Traces of bronze nails in the masonry show that it was once covered with plates of gilded bronze. The other obelisk was erected in Egypt to Thothmes III, but was renamed for Theodosius I who brought it from Egypt.

BLACK STAR

HAMMERED COPPERWARE FOR THE BUSY BAZAARS OF ISTANBUL

A coppersmith makes decorative hammer marks on strangely shaped pots. They are sold by the hundreds in the bazaars. Metalworking is but one of the many skills of Turkish artisans.

BLACK STAR

MEERSCHAUM, BROCADE, TAPESTRY—ALL AT THE GRAND BAZAAR

A vacationer shops for a meerschaum pipe at one of the innumerable stalls in the Grand Bazaar. Most of the world's meerschaum is mined in Turkey, near the city of Eskisehir.

THE CASTLES OF EUROPE AND ASIA are two historic and ancient fortresses built a few miles northeast of Istanbul. They face each other across the narrowest point of the Bosporus, here known, from the swiftness of the current, as the Devil's Stream. Anatoli Hissar stands on the Asiatic shore and Rumeli Hissar upon the European. Rumeli Hissar is said to have been built in forty days by Mohammed II, who put six thousand men to work on it. The ground plan forms the characters of his name. There are four towers, the highest of which is the Janissaries' Tower.

UCHTER KNOX

THE BIYUK JAMI, or Great Mosque, is one of the eight mosques that make the suburb of Scutari so beautiful from the sea. Their marble walls and slender minarets gleam against the dark green of the cypress trees. Scutari, the part of Istanbul that is built on Asiatic soil, used to be called Chrysopolis, which means the Golden City.

BLACK STAR

AN ISTANBUL MARKET, FRESH FRUIT AND VEGETABLES FOR SALE

On a jumble of crates, boxes and tables and on the cobbled alleyway, shopkeepers display the varied produce—figs and dates, oranges, lemons and succulent greens—of the Turkish farmland.

the custom in Moslem countries to wear a head covering without a brim, like the turban or the red fez. The fez, however, has been abolished in Turkey since the country has become a republic. Recently, a visitor curious as to how the question of praying in a cap or a derby might be solved, was interested to find that a derby may be pushed back on the head far enough for the purpose and that a cap can be adjusted equally well by wearing the vizor on the back.

As one may imagine, in any Moslem country, there are many, many mosques and Constantinople is no exception. They are specially interesting, too, in that some of them were originally built for Christian churches in the days before the Turks came and no expense was spared to make them the most magnificent buildings on earth. After the fall of Constantinople, these were changed into mosques. Succeeding sultans have erected additional ones until the city is dotted with large white domes and minarets.

Let us enter the greatest of all mosques, the St. Sophia. It was built as a Christian cathedral by Constantine the Great in 326 A.D. and was named by him St. Sophia, or the Church of Divine Wisdom. It was destroyed by fire in the reign of Justinian about 532, and he resolved to rebuild it sparing no expense in order that he might outdo the Temple of Solomon. Architects were summoned from other countries and it is said that he put them to death afterward so that they could never build another that would surpass it in grandeur and magnificence. Mohammed II converted it into a mosque when he took the city.

The interior was changed very little and we see magnificent pillars of porphyry; columns of split marble in which are natural patterns in blood-red and white; green marble of Laconia; blue marble of Libya; black marble veined with white; white marble veined with blue; lovely mosaics and dazzling pillars which support a dome with delicate arcades beneath it.

In 1935 the great structure was made over into a museum of Byzantine art. When the plaster was carefully scraped from the walls, priceless mosaics were revealed. They had been covered by Mohammed II because they were symbols of the Christian faith. The building itself is a splendid example of sixth-century Byzantine art.

Now let us go out into the courtyard. All the big mosques have one courtyard or more, a gathering-place, where people sit at tables smoking their water-pipes and drinking coffee. The courtyard of the Mosque of Eyub is one of the most pleasant in the city. It has trees and splashing

H. H. KREIDER

BEFORE MORNING CLASSES AT THE AMERICAN COLLEGE FOR GIRLS

Students from Turkey and many other lands stroll to morning classes. American College for Girls and Robert College, both founded by Americans, share a campus on the Bosporus.

ST. SOPHIA'S interior is enriched with rare marbles which were brought from all over the then known world and made into one of the most beautiful creations of art in the world. Lavish use was made also of gold, silver and precious jewels. Here it is shown as a mosque with inscriptions from the Koran, the Moslem bible, on the huge shield.

fountains, and stalls filled with beads, perfumes and silk, and is always crowded with people.

Medley of Races on Galata Bridge

But if we want to see a throng of people we must go to the great bridge which spans the Golden Horn, connecting the European quarters of Galata and Pera with the Turkish quarter of Stamboul, and having tne Mosque of Yeni Valideh—or "of the Sultan's Mother"—at the Stamboul end. If we stand there half an hour, representatives of almost every race in the world will pass by—Turks, Egyptians, Persians, Indians, Europeans of all nations, people from cities, forests and deserts, and from countries known and unknown.

The bazaar is always the centre of life in an Oriental city, and always of interest to a European. To enter this one of Constantinople we pass through a stone door into the courtyard of a mosque. On our right and left are sellers of nuts, candy, figs and flowers. Squatting by the wall will probably be two old women telling fortunes to peasants.

An Arabian Nights' Bazaar

A few steps farther on we enter the bazaar proper. It is like a maze of vaulted or roofed-in lanes, and seems to be almost a separate town, with every shop like a cell within a honeycomb. If there were not so much color and such a babble of voices, we might think we stood in the aisle of some old cathedral, lighted by dim, stained glass windows. But filled with the thousand-colored merchandise of Asia it is like a scene from a fairy tale. Shafts of sunlight come down from the roof and fall on rich piles of silks, carpets, red slippers, harness studded with beaten brass, vessels of silver, brass, gold and bronze, heaps of precious jewels, carved daggers, fantastic water-pipes, swords, guitars, filigree necklaces and a thousand other quaint things.

We are a little bewildered as we come out of the bazaars into the sunlit streets. But as the noise dies away, and our eyes again become accustomed to the scenes of the streets, we begin to notice some of the curious characters of the city. One of the first we observe is the "hamal," or porter. He is really a human beast of burden, and carries enormous loads on his back. Boys, whose fathers and forefathers have done this before them, are trained as early as eight or ten years of age for this work. Consequently, they are very strong and carry loads which would seem humanly impossible.

Curious Characters of the Streets

Another frequent character is the "saraf," or money-changer, whom we see at every street corner. Then there is the "beskjies," who goes about at night banging the stones of the street with a thick staff and calling out to all and sundry. He is a sort of night watchman. Another quaint character is the "kapudji." Every building has a "kapudji" to guard its doors. Beggars and hawkers we shall find everywhere.

Now let us give a few minutes to the European quarters, Galata and Pera. Galata spreads itself along the north shore of the Golden Horn. It is the centre of Constantinople's shipping and banking, and has all the principal quays of the city, where vessels of every nationality may be seen. But it is not very interesting, though there is a fine old tower, which we illustrate on page 268.

Pera is more interesting because it contains all the good shops, hotels and restaurants of the city. It is rather French in appearance. The names of the hotels and shops are nearly always in French and even the streets are given French names. Here also are the shops selling Paris clothes where the Turkish woman of to-day gowns herself like the woman of Europe and very effectively too. Almost every language is spoken in this section and members of almost every race are met.

Formerly, the embassies of foreign nations were located in Pera, but in 1923, after the Nationalist Government had made Turkey a republic, the capital was moved to Angora in Asia. Members of the diplomatic circles were loath to give up their residences, for Angora was hardly

NEAR EAST SOCIETY

TRAVELING SALESMAN, OLD STYLE, BRINGS PRODUCE TO THE DOOR

A common sight in old towns of many Mediterranean countries is the huckster with his stock of fresh fruit and vegetables, traveling from door to door. His sturdy, sure-footed burro can pick its way with ease over the uneven paving stones and through the narrow, winding streets. The baskets, or panniers, on its back are not too heavily laden.

PRIVATE HOUSE IN THE TURKISH QUARTER OF CONSTANTINOPLE

Turkish houses are usually of two stories. Those of the middle class are often surrounded on three sides by a garden and courtyard and the fourth side abuts on the street. The rooms on the ground floor include reception rooms, kitchen, and offices; those above, with latticed windows, are the private apartments of the women.

more than a village. The transfer has been made gradually, and, as Angora increased in population, Constantinople decreased. Constantinople is still the largest and most important city in Turkey and as one of the most interesting cities in the world, it is visited yearly by thousands, eager to see the many historical places.

A trip up the Bosporus will give us a final idea of the beauty and variety of Constantinople. The Bosporus is one of the most picturesque waterways of the world. Along its shores are hills and valleys with marble palaces and villages dotting the greenery. We exclaim over a beautiful white marble palace and learn

Haekel

STEEP THOROUGHFARES LEAD FROM GALATA TO PERA

Constantinople is built on hills and this makes many of the thoroughfares extremely steep. Some of those that connect Galata with Pera, where formerly the embassies were situated, rise so abruptly that they are made in wide shallow steps and have houses and shops built on each side. Wheeled traffic is quite impossible on this kind of street.

Courtesy, Turkish Consulate, N. Y.

A MUSEUM IN WHICH ISTANBUL'S PAST IS PRESERVED

An interesting storehouse of the wonders of the past is the Archeological Museum in Istanbul. There are two buildings. In the one shown here, you will find priceless Chinese porcelains, in the other, remains of Greek, Roman and Byzantine life. It is believed by some that here is preserved the true sarcophagus of Alexander the Great.

that it is the Dolma Bagtche where the last sultan lived until he was deposed and that afterwards it became the Constantinople residence of the first president of the republic, Kemal Ataturk. Another palace, or group of them, surrounded by a wall, is the Yildiz Kiosk which housed one of the sultans with his immense household and numerous wives.

Then we come in sight of a group of modern looking buildings which proves to be Constantinople Woman's College, started by an American missionary society as a high school but which has now become a college for Moslem girls as well as Christians, while Robert College founded by Mr. C. R. Robert of New York offers advanced education to men of all religions and we find Christians, Moslems and Jews mingling in a friendly relationship heretofore unknown.

We shall pass many beautiful summer residences especially at Therapia where formerly the diplomatic colony spent their summers but suppose we stop here at a very modern hotel for tea. People from many nations come here for sociability and we must not be surprised at the sound of jazz for that is, indeed, a final touch to the variety of Constantinople.

EWING GALLOWAY

MINARET AND ROWS OF ARCHES—THE GREAT MOSQUE, DAMASCUS

One of the greatest examples of Mohammedan architecture, the mosque was built under the Omayyad caliphs who reigned from 661 to 750, not long after the Prophet's own time.

THE TROUBLED LAND OF SYRIA

Trade Center of the Ancient World

Syria is a country that is rich in the remains of vanished empires. There are ruins of what were once splendid cities, such as Palmyra; and the strongholds of the Crusaders stand gaunt and crumbling on lonely crags. The land has echoed to the war cries of conquerors—Alexander the Great, the armies of Rome, Tamerlane and his Mongol hordes, the Turks and many others. Today, as we shall see, Syria is still a country of violent changes and its unsettled present makes its future unpredictable. In order to understand the problems of modern Syria, we must first understand the people who inhabit the land.

SYRIA is a land with a rich yet stormy history. The tapestry of its past is embroidered with scenes of bloodshed, upheaval and Eastern splendor. Like its past, the country's present is turbulent and unsettled. Even independence and home rule have not succeeded in bringing peace to the ancient land and its people.

Syria's boundaries once embraced not only the area of the present-day Republic but also Lebanon, most of Israel and Jordan and parts of Saudi Arabia. Since this area lies at the strategic crossroads of three continents, it formed the highway along which trading caravans and armies from Europe, Asia and Africa had to pass. As a result, Syria grew rich on the trade of the ancient world, but it also shook to the thunderous tread of many invading conquerors and existed under foreign rule for the better part of its history.

Modern Syria, formed out of the old, stretches from Turkey on the north to Jordan on the south. It is bordered on the west by the Mediterranean Sea, Lebanon and northern Israel. To the east and southeast lies Iraq.

In northwestern Syria, an extension of the Lebanon mountain chain parallels the country's short Mediterranean coastline. Its western slope dips gently to the sea. The eastern slope falls away sharply for some 3,000 feet to the marshy, malaria-infested Ghab Valley and the rich valley of the Orontes River. Farther to the east the land rises to a plateau. The well-watered and relatively productive valley of the Euphrates River lies in northeastern Syria and forms part of the Fertile Crescent, which extends inland from the Mediterranean, along the mountains of southern Turkey and then down the Tigris-Euphrates basin to the Persian Gulf.

Along the Lebanese border are the main peaks of the Anti-Lebanon Mountains, which are arid and largely uninhabited. The chain is continued southward in the equally inhospitable and uninhabited Hermon range and reaches its high point of more than nine thousand feet at Mount Hermon.

Southern Syria, below Damascus, is a plateau region of long-extinct volcanoes. Some of the cones reach a height of three thousand feet. The lava-enriched soil of the Plain of Hauran in the southwest has long been cultivated. In ancient times this section was a main source of grain for the Roman Empire, but its modern output is on a much smaller scale. The volcanic plateau reaches its highest level in the Jebel Druse region of the southwest, where one cone rises almost five thousand feet above sea level. This area is unsuitable for cultivation and is a refuge for outlaws and bandits. The central and southeastern parts of Syria are the arid wastelands of the Syrian desert.

The country's climate ranges from the cold winters and very hot summers of the desert to the mild Mediterranean climate of the western coast. Sufficient rain falls only in the western mountains and droughts are frequent in steppe and desert regions. Strong winds, some of great force and violence, blow the hot, dust-filled air from the deserts across the face

WIDE WORLD

SALT ENOUGH TO MAKE A HOST OF GIANTS THIRSTY

The mineral has been extracted from salty rivers and seas; and the usual beasts of burden in this part of the world are used to transport it. The "salt mountain" is near Aleppo.

of the country, leaving a parched path.

Because of the land's varied geography, the ancient Syrians, who were of Semitic stock, never developed a single, strong and politically united civilization such as those existing on the great river plains of Egypt and Mesopotamia. Instead, a group of small city-states sprang up, each one jealous of the others. As the early civilizations of Egypt and Mesopotamia grew and spread, their merchants established trading routes across Syria, and the city-states came to depend on the rich commerce of the larger empires. It was from the Lebanon Mountains, for instance, that Egypt obtained lumber and also the rare oils used in embalming its pharaohs. As the city-states grew in wealth, outsiders began to envy their prosperity.

The first known invaders came down from the north and included the Hyksos, or Shepherd Kings, the Kassites, the Mitanni and the Hittites, all vigorous and ingenious peoples. They brought with them the horse and the chariot, and the Hittites introduced their discovery of iron which was later to replace the bronze then in common use. Invaders also moved in from the southern desert regions and settled around some well-watered areas. In this way a number of communities grew up and gained in power and cultural influence. Prominent among them were communities of the Philistines, Canaanites, Israelites and Phoenicians.

Syria fell in turn under the rule of the Egyptians, Assyrians, Babylonians, Persians and Macedonians. The Persians, in their attempt to unite all the Middle East under a single ruler, spread a common language (Aramaic) throughout Syria and introduced the Semitic culture of the west to the great Indo-Aryan culture of the east. The Macedonians found that they could exercise their power in Syria more readily through the townspeople than through the farmers. Therefore they established a number of new cities, and Syria became a center of Greek life, with Antioch (now Antayka in Turkey) as its capital.

The legions of Rome conquered Syria in 64 B.C., and Roman engineers built a chain of fortifications along the old trade route across Syria to the East. The bases reached from the Hauran and Jebel Druse in the southwest, through Damascus, and then across the desert by way of Palmyra to the mountains near Nisibini in the extreme northeast. A Roman fleet occupied the country's coastal harbors.

Under Roman rule, Syria reached heights of prosperity probably not equalled since. The land was intensively cultivated for grain to supply the growing needs of the Roman homeland. New industries flourished, notably textile production, glass blowing, and metalworking. Antioch was the center of Rome's rule and was said to have had a population of three-quarters of a million people. Most Syrians, however, continued to live in the country.

When the Roman Empire was divided into two parts, East and West, Syria came under the domain of the Eastern, or Byzantine, Empire. In 636 the Arabs wrested the country from the weakened Empire, and ever since Syria has remained an important part of the Moslem world. In the eleventh century the Seljuk Turks overran the land.

For about a century, beginning in 1096, Crusaders from Europe established strongholds in Syria and tried to take the holy places from infidel hands. They were eventually driven out of the country by the brilliant Moslem warrior Saladin and his Saracen armies. It was about this time that savage Mongol hordes from the wilds of central Asia began to terrorize the Middle East. They ravaged the countryside and destroyed cities, massacring the inhabitants. Tamerlane (Timur), a Mongol leader, pushed on into Syria where his armies looted and burned the cities of Aleppo, Homs and Damascus.

The barbaric Mongols were finally checked by the Ottoman Turks who rose

EWING GALLOWAY

A WATER WHEEL NINETY FEET IN DIAMETER AT HAMA

Hama has breath-taking gardens, irrigated by means of huge water wheels. The water comes through aqueducts from the Orontes River. Outside of Hama, in western Syria, is a desert.

ALL THAT REMAINS OF THE BIBLICAL "CITY OF PALMS"

The Bible refers to this site as Tadmor, meaning the "city of palms." It is supposed that it was built by Solomon. The present-day village near these ruins is called Palmyra.

PHOTOS, EWING GALLOWAY

HITTITE SCULPTURES CARVED PERHAPS 3,500 YEARS AGO

Though the sculpture of the Hittites was crude, it had force and imagination. The Hittites were vigorous fighters, and these carvings represent archers and warriors armed with shields.

to power rapidly after they had captured Constantinople in 1453. These fanatical Moslems ruled all Syria by 1516. Their control was maintained through a highly trained military police force known as Janissaries. It was during the period of Turkish rule that Syria began to decline economically and politically.

The discovery in 1498 of a new overseas trade route around the Cape of Good Hope to the markets of the Orient spelled out doom for the affairs of Syria. The difficult overland trade route across the country fell into neglect and Syria's decline was rapid. From the sixteenth century until trade began to flow through the newly opened Suez Canal in 1869, Syria and other countries of the region held an unimportant place in world affairs.

The Era of French Control

The weakened Ottoman Empire controlled Syria until World War I. In 1920 the country was placed under French protection by a mandate from the League of Nations. A French-controlled government was set up, but internal unrest plagued Syria and several times disturbances had to be subdued by armed force.

With the outbreak of World War II, Syria was still a part of the French colonial empire. After France surrendered to Germany, the pro-Vichy government collaborated with the Germans in Syria. Consequently British and Free French forces, after some fighting, occupied the country in 1941. By the end of 1946 occupying troops were withdrawn, the French mandate was formally ended, and Syria was declared a sovereign republic.

The course of Syrian politics continued to be one of violent change. King Abdullah of Jordan was ambitious to unite under his rule a Greater Syria, to be made up of Syria, Lebanon, Iraq, Jordan and Palestine. His plan had the support of important political groups within Syria but was opposed by the military and by the Arab League nations of Egypt and Saudi Arabia. In a single year Syria was rocked by three military-led revolts to establish new governments, and plans for a Greater Syria were put aside.

BLACK STAR

ORCHARDS ON WALLED TERRACES

Apricots, figs, almonds and pomegranates grow on the narrow plots to the top of the hill.

EWING GALLOWAY

A SYRIAN FARMER GLOWS WITH PRIDE OVER HIS NEW TRACTOR

Though few Syrians who work the land have such up-to-date equipment as this, modern agricultural methods are slowly making headway. There is good soil, which could give greater yields.

FREDERIC LEWIS

PRECARIOUS WORK—SPLITTING A LONG LOG LENGTHWISE

The saw is rigged to move up and down, and as the man wields it he must also keep his balance as he steps backward. This ancient way of cutting logs seems awkward in the extreme.

WIDE WORLD

FROWNING LANDMARK IN ALEPPO—THE ANCIENT CITADEL

Built in the late fourth century B.C., the Citadel has witnessed the rise and fall of empires. Aleppo is on a plateau in northwest Syria, and the Citadel is on a still higher hill.

EWING GALLOWAY

TROLLEY TRACKS GUIDE A COUNTRY FAMILY THROUGH THE CITY

Riding donkeys, this family has come from a remote district and it is probably their first sight of a city. All their worldly goods are stowed on the backs of the patient animals.

PIX

WHO'LL BUY MY COFFEE—HOT, SWEET AND THICK?

Most people of the Middle East love coffee, and vendors are a common sight on city streets. The beverage is usually made in the Turkish way, so sweet and thick it is almost a sirup.

EWING GALLOWAY

"THE STREET WHICH IS CALLED STRAIGHT" IN DAMASCUS

The famous byway, mentioned in the New Testament in connection with Paul's conversion, is really crooked. It runs from the eastern to the western gate, flanked by bazaars.

The people of Syria are mostly of Arab origin. Arabic is the principal language although some Armenian, Turkish, Kurdish and Syriac is spoken. The large majority of the people are Moslems and most of them follow the Sunni branch of Islam. The rest of the population is divided between Christians and Jews.

Around the volcanic plateau of Hauran in the southwest live the Druses, a proud people famed for their fierce fighting qualities. More is told about them and their customs in the chapter on Lebanon.

Many tribes inhabit Syria, particularly the Bedouins of the desert region. In northwestern Syria dwells a group known as the Ismaili, or Assassins. They are the remainder of a once-powerful secret order of religious fanatics who flourished during the eleventh and twelfth centuries. From his stronghold in the wild Syrian mountains, Sheik el Jebel (the Old Man of the Mountain), leader of the sect, dispatched young men to assassinate enemies of the order. So that the killers would be unafraid, they were first drugged with hashish. Because of this practice, these religious murderers became known as *hashashin,* from which comes the English word "assassin." Today the production of hashish is a concession of the Syrian Government and is an important source of revenue.

Another group of the northwest is the Alawi who live in the Jebel Ansariyeh, a part of the Lebanon mountain range. Though they are considered Moslems, they have taken over the celebration of Christmas from the Christians and also practice certain ceremonies of pagan origin.

The Yezidi, a small group, live in northeast Syria. The largest body of them is in neighboring Iraq. These people still possess a strange pagan religion and believe that evil powers dominate the world. Their rites to ward off the evil spirits have led outsiders to call them devil-worshipers.

The life of the nomadic Bedouins has

EWING GALLOWAY

THE MODERN FACE OF PERHAPS THE WORLD'S OLDEST CITY

Twentieth-century shops and apartment houses line a street in a section rebuilt within the old walls of Damascus. Most other parts of the city, however, have an Oriental atmosphere.

BLACK STAR

A MODEL OF ISTANBUL'S HAGIA SOPHIA HIGH ON A PEDESTAL

The attractive square, laid out with formal flower beds, is in the center of Damascus. Its most curious feature is the replica of the celebrated Byzantine structure in Istanbul.

PIX

PICNICKING ALONG THE BANKS OF A RIVER IN DAMASCUS

In the cool of the evening families come to enjoy a meal beneath the trees. Two rivers flow through the city—the Barada and the A'waj—called the "waters of Damascus" in the Bible.

NEAR EAST FOUNDATION

A CUP, A BOWL, A COFFEE URN—BRASS DAZZLING IN THE SUN

The Syrians have always excelled in metal work. In the days of chivalry a blade of Damascus steel was prized above all others. That craft has vanished but not the skill with metals.

EWING GALLOWAY

A MARKET SQUARE—OPEN-AIR DEPARTMENT STORE AND GROCERY

Whatever a Syrian needs for his house or his person he is likely to find in the market square. Bargaining is the order of the day, a game of wits that both buyer and seller relish.

changed but little down through the centuries. Their life and customs are described in detail in the chapter entitled The Desert Rangers. It has been said that if Abraham were to return today to a Bedouin encampment in the Syrian desert, he would feel quite at home, noting few changes since his time.

Bedouin tribes rarely combine with one another. If some strong leader does accomplish a union of a number of tribes, it proves to be a temporary arrangement that falls apart at his death. There is an almost perpetual state of warfare and feuding between tribes. Warfare is conducted according to strict rules. It is through warfare that a young Bedouin proves himself a worthy member of the tribe. Tribal territorial limits are carefully drawn. Some tribes remain in a relatively small area; others travel great distances in their search for pasture for their livestock.

Despite the numerical importance of the Bedouin and the farmer, or Hadhar, the dominant element of Syria's life centers about the cities. Here live the great landowners or feudal lords, owners of most of the nation's arable land. The landowners and traders or bazaar merchants guide the political career of the country. In recent years, however, as we have seen, the better-educated military class has begun to wield considerable political power.

The principal cities are all in the western part of the country and near the foothills of the mountains where there is an ample water supply. Damascus and Aleppo are the two main cities, followed by Homs, Hama and Latakia.

Damascus, the capital, is sometimes called the Pearl of the Desert because of the beauty of its surroundings. It is said to be the world's most ancient city, and it appears to have been a notable place as early as 1913 B.C. At one time Damascus was a thriving center for the trade between Europe and the Orient and its bazaars and markets overflowed with goods from the Eastern and Western worlds.

EWING GALLOWAY

A PURCHASE OF FRUIT CALLS FOR SERIOUS CONSIDERATION

The vendor of the fruit appears indifferent to the outcome and ready for a nap alfresco. Meanwhile his unhurried customers examine the fruit and discuss its possible merits.

FRENCH EMBASSY—INFORMATION DIVISION

A HAWKER CRIES HIS WARES—HEAPS OF LUSCIOUS FRUIT

What passer-by would not be tempted by the fragrance and colors of downy apricots, pomegranates bursting with red pulp or ripe, purplish figs with the morning dew still on them?

The plain on which the capital is situated is watered by the Barada River and is rich with orchards of figs, apricots, almonds, pomegranates, lemons, oranges, plums, pears and apples.

The modern city is still very Oriental in character and has preserved most of its Eastern flavor. The Moslem section is considered the best and wealthiest quarter of Damascus and has wider streets, better houses and a more abundant water supply than other parts of the city. Elsewhere the streets are narrow and crooked and often extremely dirty. The house fronts are generally prisonlike in appearance, with a few small grated windows piercing their mud walls. Sometimes, however, a drab and forbidding front conceals a luxurious interior.

The trade and commercial life of a Middle Eastern city centers about the bazaar section, an area where the merchants buy and sell almost everything under the sun. In Damascus the bazaars and khans (inns housing men and pack animals) are very large affairs. To the noisy, bustling bazaars come the Bedouins to exchange wool, leather and other products for cereals and the few manufactured things they need. The varied products of field and orchard are brought there, and cargoes from overseas find their way to the bazaars. Although the city no longer makes and sells the famous Damascus steel, fine handmade metalwork can be bought in the bazaars. There are tea merchants, sellers of beautiful textiles, dealers in fine leatherwork and furniture, jewelers and merchants who handle imports from other countries. If you should wish to buy a radio or a typewriter, they, too, can be found in the colorful bazaars of Damascus.

Damascus is linked by railway with Amman, the capital of Jordan, and with Aleppo in the north. There is a connecting railway line with Beirut and Cairo, and a huge bus runs across the desert country to Bagdad. At the Damascus airfield one can board a plane for Bagdad and other Eastern cities, or for Cairo.

Aleppo, on the ancient main caravan

FREDERIC LEWIS

A SIDEWALK IS AS GOOD A PLACE AS ANY FOR A SHAVE

A Syrian barber is ready to set up shop wherever he finds a customer. Instead of a red-and-white pole, he hangs up a towel on the wall to mark the place as his for the time being.

route across Syria, is a typical Oriental city of darkened, narrow streets. Parts of it, however, are modern and possess great charm. Aleppo is the junction for railroads serving the upper Tigris-Euphrates valley, Hama, Homs, the Damascus region and the Mediterranean coastal plain. Rail lines meeting in Aleppo connect with Cairo, Ankara and Bagdad.

About two-thirds of Syria's people live in villages and depend upon agriculture for their livelihood. The mountain slopes and other arable areas are farmed to produce all kinds of cereals, fruits and vegetables. Cotton and tobacco are grown in the warmer regions, such as that about the Mediterranean port of Latakia. The villages themselves are parts of large estates of the landlords. The small farmers live in poverty, for the city-dwelling landlords contribute nothing to the development of the land, yet they claim up to half of all crops. When a harvest is made, an agent of the landlord is present to collect the landlord's share.

The life of the farmer, like that of the Bedouin, is a very hard one. He must always be on guard against Bedouin raids. His agricultural implements are primitive and he plows with wooden sticks that are pulled by long-horned oxen, camels, donkeys or by the farmer himself. He lives in a mud hut that consists of only one or two rooms which he shares with his animals. Landless laborers are even worse off than the farmers. They get enough to eat only at harvest time. In winter they subsist on grain, bread and grass.

Education is quite limited and the great bulk of Syria's people cannot read or write. Except for the small educated class, the people sign a document by inking their thumb and making an imprint on the paper. There are elementary schools, largely private, and a university in Damascus. Health standards are low.

Western nations have tried to bring about improvements in Syria, and there are many Syrian leaders who well understand the difficulties that must be overcome if their country is to have order and stability and democracy approaching that of Western lands.

By E. S. Ferguson

SYRIA: FACTS AND FIGURES

THE COUNTRY

Formerly a mandate of France and situated in Asia Minor, the Republic of Syria became a completely independent state in 1946. It is bounded on the west by the Mediterranean and the Lebanese Republic, Israel and Jordan on the south, Iraq on the east and by Turkey on the north. It is composed of nine administrative Sanjaks (districts): Aleppo, Damascus, Euphrates, Hama, Hauran, Homs, Jebel de Druz, Jezire and Latakia. Area, 66,046 square miles; population about 3,253,000.

GOVERNMENT AND CONSTITUTION

Since gaining her complete independence, Syria's government has changed hands several times through military coups. Normally, the government consists of a president, premier and a parliament, all popularly elected. However, Parliament was dissolved in 1951, and all political parties in 1952. Syria is a member of the UN and of the Arab League.

COMMERCE AND INDUSTRIES

Agriculture and cattle-raising are the leading occupations. About half of the cultivable land, some 7,000 square miles, is normally under crops; the chief crops are wheat, barley, oats, maize, sesame, hemp, sugar cane, lentils and chick-peas; fruit trees cultivated are banana, orange, lemon, olive and the white mulberry for feeding silkworms. Cotton cultivation has increased during recent years; cotton and its products, raw wool and silk are exported. Cereals and manufactured goods constitute the bulk of the imports. The mineral deposits, although largely undeveloped, include iron, lignite, gypsum, marble and building stone.

COMMUNICATIONS

The means of communication in Syria are being steadily improved. The total mileage of improved roads exceeds 3,000; the railway mileage is 890 miles. Steamers give regular service to ports and there are air services to Marseilles and Bagdad from Damascus.

RELIGION AND EDUCATION

Over half of the inhabitants of Syria are Moslems, chiefly of the Sunni sect. Over 1,612 public elementary schools have been established. The elementary schools are still largely private. There is a Syrian university in Damascus and an Arab academy. There are also two agricultural colleges.

CHIEF TOWNS

Damascus, the capital, has a population of 335,060; Aleppo, 362,541; Homs, 244,094; Hama, 146,564; and Latakia, 100,462.

NEW AND OLD LEBANON

From Snow-capped Peaks to Sunny Shores

As a separate state Lebanon is very young, but its story reaches far back into the mists of time. Tyre, on the coast, was the chief city of the daring Phoenician sailors and merchants; and in the Old Testament the prized cedars of Lebanon are mentioned time and again. Through the passes of the Lebanese Mountains strode conquerors and traders. There is a footway, between Beirut and Baalbek, that has been in existence since 1500 B.C. Modern Lebanon is on a bridge between old and new, weighed down on one end by customs that are centuries old, while at the other end twentieth-century ideas beckon.

AT the dawn of history a civilization already existed in Lebanon. Archaeologists have established that at Gebal, or Jebeil—today a village of about a thousand people, about twenty miles north of Beirut—there existed a city named Byblos around 3000 B.C. Because of its export of papyrus for making books, the ancient Greeks used the name of Byblos for the word "book," from which came "Bible" and many words containing "biblio." At this early date Byblos ranked above Tyre and Sidon and other flourishing centers of Phoenician culture.

Tripoli and Aradus also existed as coastal ports during this early period. A large maritime trade had been built by the Phoenicians. As shipbuilders they were without peer, and their vessels carried lumber and pine products to Egypt and other parts of the Mediterranean. It is supposed that Phoenician seamen sailed as far as Cornwall, England, where tin was mined.

The timber from the forests of Lebanon was a great source of wealth to the coastal cities, and they were not lacking in other industries. Glass-making was developed to a high degree. From a small shellfish (murex) they made a purple dye—the Tyrian purple beloved of the Romans centuries later.

Our alphabet is sometimes said to have been invented by the Phoenicians, but this is only partially true. There is no doubt that these people did evolve one of the earliest alphabets but they were probably helped by their knowledge of the alphabets of other peoples, gained through their activities as traders. However, it was because of the widespread commercial relations of the Phoenicians that languages using an alphabet, such as Aramaic, were transmitted to other peoples throughout the Middle East and as far as Persia.

Because of their riches and their location on the highway from the north to Egypt (they were also the terminal points of the long caravan route from India and China), the Phoenician cities came under the rule of a long line of conquerors. Around 3000 B.C. they were under the protection of Egypt, and then, in turn, they were subdued by the Assyrians, the Persians and Alexander the Great. At times, nevertheless, the cities were able to break away from outside rulers. One instance of this is when Tyre allied herself with Israel during the reign of Solomon, exchanging timber for grain and olive oil. Later the cities became part of the Roman Empire and the Romans built great temples in them. A famous one was to Jupiter, at Baalbek. With the break-up of the Empire, the region became part of the Byzantine realm, though by this time most of the greatness of the past had faded.

In the seventh century the Arabs gained power and later the area passed under Ottoman control, which lasted until the end of World War I. Lebanon was then made a French mandate. The country was declared a republic in 1926 under the mandate but was a republic in little more than name. During World War II the Free French forces ousted the Vichy Government in Lebanon and again pro-

KEYSTONE

ALL THE FAMILY WATCHES AS DAUGHTER MAKES BREAD

Pieces of dough are spread flat and then baked over a fire of twigs set between stones. Instead of loaves, the finished product in the tray (right) looks more like crisp pancakes.

claimed Lebanon a free republic. This became a reality on January 1, 1944. Even then French troops remained stationed in Lebanon and were not withdrawn until 1946.

The tiny Republic of Lebanon is almost squeezed into the eastern end of the Mediterranean Sea by its much larger neighbor, Syria. On the south Lebanon shares a short boundary line with the Republic of Israel.

Much of Lebanon is mountainous. The Lebanon Mountains parallel the coast for more than a hundred miles. In Biblical days they were covered with cedars. The highest peak in this range—Dahr el Qadib—near Tripoli in the north, is more than 10,000 feet high, and one near Beirut—Qurnet es Sauda—is only a little lower. The eastern border is rimmed by the Anti-Lebanon Mountains. Between these chains lies the narrow Bekaa, or Biqa', valley, watered by two rivers, the Orontes and the Litani (called Leontes in ancient days). The Orontes flows north for about 250 miles, entering Turkey and finally emptying into the Mediterranean. The Litani begins close by the Orontes, in the center of the valley, and flows south through deep gorges toward the upper Jordan. Because of the deep ravines, this river is of little use for irrigation.

PHOTOS, BLACK STAR

A SHAWL INSTEAD OF AN OVERCOAT

On a chilly day this man of Beirut wears a camel's-hair shawl over his Western suit.

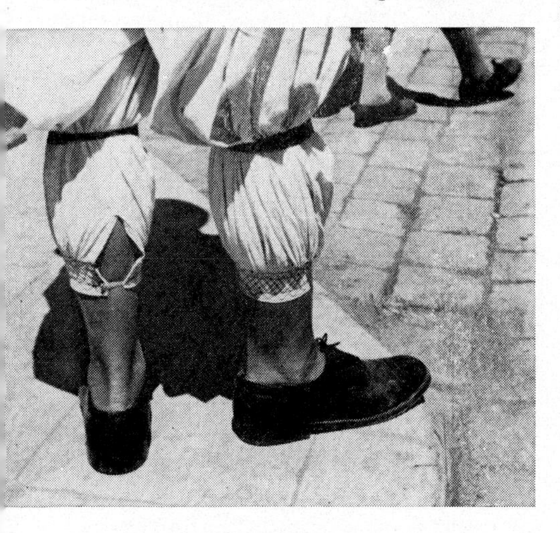

BLEND OF EAST AND WEST

Lebanese mix Eastern and Western dress with unconcern—old-time trousers and oxfords.

On the watershed of the rivers, at a height of about 3,600 feet above sea level, is the site of the ancient town of Baalbek (which the Greeks called Heliopolis, city of the sun) where Baal, the sun-god, was worshiped. There now remain only the ruins of its once huge temples. Baalbek was destroyed by an earthquake about the middle of the eighteenth century. The Arabs believe that it is the oldest city in the world and that Adam lived there.

Along the narrow coastal plains the climate is subtropical. Winters are mild, summers are moderately hot and there is plenty of rainfall. But in the mountains

BLACK STAR

A CRUSADERS' CASTLE WEATHERED BY WIND AND WATER

The castle is in the harbor of Sidon, where some Crusaders landed. Deserted and crumbling for long years, the site was later used for a mosque. Its dome is visible in the center.

there is a great change even within as short a distance as five miles from the coastal plains. Here we find snow and cold winters. Snow stays unmelted on the Lebanon range about three months, and the peaks are usually covered with snow from December to June. It is said that the name "Lebanon" comes from a word *Leben* (whiteness) used in the old Aramaic language (spoken by Jesus) and refers to the view of the glistening mountains.

An average of forty-five inches of snow falls in the Lebanon Mountains each year. The Beirut-Damascus railway, which crosses the range, is covered with permanent snowsheds for several miles. The railway rises five thousand feet above sea level so steeply (in some places it was necessary to lay ten miles of winding track to advance two miles) that a cog rail is used for a quarter of the way.

In the Bekaa valley, winters are cool, and summers hot and dry. The rainy season starts in October, and the Bible refers to these autumn rains as the "former rains." The spring rains of April and May are termed the "latter rains." It is from December to March that the downfall is most heavy.

On the western slopes of the Lebanon Mountains, Mediterranean plants are found. Near sea level along the coast there are locust trees and stone pine. Wide areas are covered with brush. Farther up the mountains begin the woodlands, dominated by dwarf hardwood oaks. Still higher on the slopes is a belt of tall pines. At about four thousand feet the famous Lebanon cypress and cedar appear. There are also oaks and other leaf-bearing trees together with coniferous trees, including the rare Cilician silver fir. Extending nearly to the summits, stunted oak, juniper and barberry grow. The Lebanon cedars, you remember, were

BLACK STAR

THE STILL GRACEFUL COLUMNS OF THE TEMPLES AT BAALBEK

Though chipped and eroded, the stones have an impressive dignity. Baalbek is in the Bekaa Valley and strange gods have been worshiped there: Baal, the sun-god, and later Jupiter.

MONKMEYER

TURKEYS PEER ABOUT CURIOUSLY ON THE WAY TO MARKET

The big birds stroll to market at an amiable pace. They are probably destined for the dinner tables of luxury hotels; for they are hardly the usual diet in a Lebanese home.

used in building Solomon's Temple and palace. Only a few of these cedars are left, in groves considered sacred. Some of the cedars are extremely old and are nearly one hundred feet high and over fourteen feet in diameter.

Beirut, the capital of Lebanon, is the country's only modern seaport. In fact, it is one of the main ports of entry in the Arab world. Close by, in Khalde, is the Middle East's largest airport. Mountains rise almost directly behind the harbor, one of the most beautiful in the world. With its fine beaches, promenades and pine-studded backdrop, Beirut is also a popular resort. In the modern hotel lobbies one finds sheiks on holiday, rich merchants from other lands, cosmopolitan

BLACK STAR

SIGNS IN ARABIC AND FRENCH IN A BEIRUT ARCADE

There are fine shops in Beirut which sell exquisite imported goods. A French atmosphere lingers in the city and the French language is likely to be heard as often as Arabic.

diplomats, tourists, secret agents, adventurers and promoters. Political intrigue is rife. The atmosphere is French but a great many languages are heard. Many of the city's old streets are steep, winding alleys; but alley or avenue, Lebanese drivers ignore all hazards. Traffic moves at a terrific pace, made possible only by the drivers' lightning alertness. With what seems a natural bent for mechanics, the Lebanese love automobiles, the more powerful the better.

A mountain highway connects Beirut with Damascus, about sixty miles to the east. It is an exciting and sometimes hair-raising experience to motor around the hairpin curves, in the shadow of peaks or on the very edge of deep gorges. If one dares to look up from the road there are wide views of wild mountain scenery.

The people of Lebanon are about equally divided into Moslems and Christians. For this reason the president is usually a Christian, and the prime minister a Sunni (orthodox) Mohammedan. Chief of the Moslem group is the Sunni sect, although the Shiite sect is almost as large. The Druses may also be considered as a Moslem group.

However, the Druses seem to believe in a mixture of both Christian and Moslem ideas. Unlike Mohammedans, who do not believe in incarnation, the Druses believe that seventy incarnations of God

FISHING BOATS AT A QUAY ON ONE SIDE OF BEIRUT HARBOR

Ships from all over the world anchor in the harbor, and its shores are a semitropical playground. Behind the beaches and shore hotels rears a verdant backdrop of mountains clad with pines.

FREDERIC LEWIS

have occurred, the last one about 1000 A.D.; and Druses say there will be no more until the rest of the world is converted to the beliefs of the Druses, the "true children of God." These people are spread over much of the Lebanon and Anti-Lebanon mountains as well as through Syria. Among the most fierce fighters to be found anywhere, the Druses keep very much apart from their neighbors. They are jealous of their own customs and are especially hostile to Lebanese Christians, particularly the Maronites. In contrast with most other Mohammedans, the Druses are respectful of women. Women are allowed to join the men in religious services. They may also bring suit for divorce, an action unheard-of among orthodox Moslems. Having more than one wife is forbidden. Women must wear a veil but their sober black dress is relieved by scarlet slippers. Men wear a black robe with a white girdle. As a distinguishing mark from other Mohammedans, a white roll encircles the red fez. Druses are a tall people, with a fairer complexion than is usually found in the Levant.

KEYSTONE

A BEDOUIN FAMILY COMES TO TOWN

Almost everywhere in the Middle East one will find Bedouins, the wanderers of the deserts.

Like the Druses, the swarthy Maronites are also mountaineers. They make up about a third of the population and form a distinct sect within the Roman Catholic Church. Their religious leader, under the pope, is called the patriarch of Antioch, which is in Turkey. He lives, however, in Lebanon. It is thought that some of the mountain folk were converted to Christianity about the seventh century and became followers of Saint John Maroun, from whom they derive their name. Like many people of a rugged land, the Maronites once engaged in bloody feuds but as a result of their relations with the Western world, their barbarous ways are vanishing. A national festival is held on September 14. The night before, bonfires are lighted and Maronite men and boys

KEYSTONE

A YOUNG GIRL OF THE DRUSES

The clothes she is wearing are light in color and have gay embroidery. When she is grown up, however, among her own people she will wear a black dress, crimson slippers and a veil.

show their bravery by leaping over the flames. At the same time there is an uproar of shouts and gunfire.

In Beirut and the larger towns living conditions are similar to those found in Europe; but village life is quite different. In most parts of the country the huts of the peasants are made of wattle or mud-brick or in part of stone. Interiors are bare of all but the merest necessities. In the far north and south poverty is severe. Villagers cannot afford to buy even rice, but live on lentils, bread and curdled milk.

Most of the villages are owned by a landlord and the people work for him. These landlords are the most important and influential groups in all Middle Eastern countries. There are, however, more freeholders in Lebanon than elsewhere. Possibly as many as one-half of the rural communities are freeholding peasants with small plots of land. Some of them spend part of the year tending to their crops and the balance working in factories. Methods of tilling the soil are still primitive but better results are obtained than elsewhere in this part of the world. It is not only the heavier rainfall but also a better-informed people that account for this. For instance, in places the western slopes are terraced to keep the soil from being washed away and to hold water. Though the land is cultivated intensively, not enough is grown to supply the country's needs and some grain is imported from Syria. Crops are diversified and include, in addition to various grains, olives, bananas and citrus fruits.

A Gateway for Trade

Despite the fact that two-thirds of the population is engaged in agriculture, trading is the most important economic activity. From the time of the Phoenicians to the present this seems to have been true. It is largely because Lebanon is one of the important gateways to the Far East. Today the country is a major center of foreign exchange and a place where goods are traded that never enter Lebanese territory. Beirut itself is the biggest gold market between Tangiers and Bombay.

The Lebanese factory worker is the best to be found in the Middle East, not excluding Turkey. After the fall of the Ottoman Empire, Lebanon gained rapidly in new factories. Unlike the experience of its neighbors, construction of new plants in Lebanon was due entirely to private enterprise and not to aid from the Government. A large number of small factories now produce various beverages, foodstuffs, cloth, razor blades, cement, soap, matches and other items. The silk industry, which had been a source of considerable wealth, was hurt by the invention of nylon, but is now reviving.

Electric power output is nearly 50 per cent greater than that of Syria, a much larger country. With mountain rivers such as the Litani, the possibilities for greater power generation are enormous. However, the country's known mineral resources are of no consequence. Since the country is already the most densely populated in the Middle East, further expansion appears quite limited. In fact, one of the reasons for the present relatively high living standard is that large amounts of money are sent back to relatives by those who have emigrated, especially to the United States (chiefly Detroit). Since the late 1890's, with little else to export, Lebanon has been exporting its population. It is said that almost every adult Lebanese has lived abroad or intends to; but they come home to retire—and usually bring with them the fastest, shiniest cars they can.

Pipelines from Iraq and Arabia

Two oil pipelines terminate on the Lebanon coast. One line originates in the Kirkuk oil fields of Iraq, with a branch going to Haifa in Israel and another branch ending at Tripoli. There are small refineries at both places. Another pipeline starts on the Persian Gulf, near the Bahrein Islands, crosses Saudi Arabia and ends at Sidon.

Schools and Colleges

Though the Government spends much more on national defense and internal police than it does on such matters as health and education, educational facilities in Lebanon are well above Middle Eastern standards. French Jesuits and American Presbyterians deserve a large part of the credit for this development. The Jesuits staffed numerous schools and founded the University of St. Joseph in Beirut in 1875. Earlier, in 1820, the Americans established several schools and a printing press. The Syrian Protestant College was chartered in 1863, under the laws of the State of New York, from where most of the money for its founding came. Eventually this college became the present internationally known American University of Beirut. For a campus, it has seventy acres of semitropical gardens, all overlooking the blue Mediterranean. No at-

KEYSTONE

A PRIEST OF THE MARONITE SECT

Most Christian Lebanese are Maronites, a distinct sect within the Roman Catholic Church. The priest's vestments include a chasuble, the beautifully embroidered outer garment.

EWING GALLOWAY

DRAWING WATER FROM A WELL DUG BY THE CRUSADERS

Walled in by rough stones, the little well is on the summit of a mountain in a dry region where water is scarce. These women must make a long climb and clamber down heavily laden.

tempt is made to "Americanize" the students, which in a recent year were drawn from forty nations and twenty-one religious groups.

Lebanon has the framework of an educational system from the elementary grades through college. Almost 80 per cent of the Lebanese can read and write, compared with about 10 per cent in the rest of the Arab world.

Health standards are also higher. However, diet is hardly above the subsistence level for many of the people. Bread, milk, olive oil and fruits when in season are the basic foods. Sanitation is poor and disease prevalent. Malaria, typhoid, trachoma and other diseases are chronic. There are few doctors. Some headway in this field is being made, however. An antimalaria campaign has begun, there are a few classes for public-health nurses, and an effort is being made to improve water supplies and other sanitary facilities.

In Lebanon the conflict between the cultures of the East and West is especially sharp. It emerged with the end of the Ottoman Empire and the beginning of French influence. The attempts of the French to bring about a more orderly government, to improve education and health and to correct bad economic conditions met with great opposition from age-long traditions among the illiterate populace led by selfish landlords. Externals were changed but the basic social structure of semifeudalism held. This old order is breaking up and many serious problems arise in the process. To a considerable extent the valuable aspects of the traditional culture are lost while only material things are taken from the West. The forward-looking leaders of Lebanon are keenly aware of this problem. One such leader, Charles Malik—widely admired as Lebanon's delegate to the United Nations—has said that four developments are

PIX

LOOKING OUT OVER TRIPOLI TOWARD THE MEDITERRANEAN

Little of ancient Tripoli survives but the present-day city is thriving as the terminus of an oil pipeline from Iraq. This provides work and income for the city's people.

MULBERRY LEAVES FOR SILKWORMS

To add to the returns from their land, many farmers raise silkworms as a side line.

necessary within Lebanon and the rest of the Middle East: land reform, eliminating the present semifeudal system; replacement of bureaucratic administration with an efficient government; a high order of national leadership; and economic and political freedom for all.

It is interesting to note that one of the elements that has speeded the process of change has been the motion picture.

Another factor, mentioned earlier, is the number of Lebanese who emigrate and then return long years after. Though they remain loyal to their homeland, they cannot help but bring back new ideas.

Today the patriarchal family system—in which the father is all-powerful—is declining. At the same time the country is affected by the deep underlying ferment of Arab nationalism and by the challenge of its modern neighbor, Israel. Thus the peoples of Lebanon are not likely to find an easy solution to their difficulties.

By E. S. Ferguson

PHOTOS, PIX

FOOD FOR THE VORACIOUS APPETITES OF YOUNG SILKWORMS

The squirming caterpillars are kept on large, flat baskets in a dark room at a cool temperature. To keep up with their tremendous appetites, they must be fed every six hours.

KEYSTONE

ZAHLE, WHICH CLINGS TO A HILLSIDE IN THE BEKAA VALLEY

The delightfully cool summers of the valley make Zahle a refuge for people from the warmer coast. They can reach the town easily for it is on the railway between Beirut and Damascus.

BLACK STAR

HIGH IN THE LEBANON MOUNTAINS A SKIER TRIES THE SNOW

Though Lebanon is usually thought of as a warm country, snow stays unmelted toward the tops of the ranges during the three winter months. Skiing on the firm crust is a popular sport.

BLACK STAR

TERRACED SLOPES ON THE EMERALD COAST OF LEBANON

The Emerald Coast—verdant with vegetation—is the narrow strip between the sea and the mountains. So that every bit of the fertile soil may be used, the slopes are terraced.

EWING GALLOWAY

CEDARS OF LEBANON, TREES FAMOUS IN BIBLICAL DAYS

Few of the cedars, which King Solomon valued so highly, are left and the remaining groves are considered sacred. They grow in the mountains about four thousand feet above sea level.

THE COUNTRY

A republic in Asia, on the eastern shore of the Mediterranean, which was formed from five Turkish districts in 1920, administrated under a French mandate until 1941 and was finally given its full independence in 1944. The country is bounded on the north and east by Syria and on the south by Israel. It has an area of about 4,000 square miles and a population estimated at 1,300,000.

GOVERNMENT

Lebanon is governed by a president, a prime minister, and a Parliament having 77 seats which are distributed according to religious sects and not parties. The country is a member of the United Nations and of the Arab League.

COMMERCE AND INDUSTRIES

Although less than a quarter of its total area is under cultivation, Lebanon is primarily an agricultural state. Its chief food products, ranked according to the weight of their yield, are grapes, citrus fruits, wheat, onions, barley, potatoes, tomatoes, watermelons, maize, apples, pears and olives. Tobacco and cotton are also important crops. Besides processing crude oil piped in from Iraq, the country manufactures matches, soap, cigarettes, shoes and cotton goods—and weaves silk and woolen materials from imported yarn. There is a little mining of lignite. Tripoli is the terminus of an oil pipeline from Kirkuk, Iraq; and Sidon is the terminus of another pipeline from Abqaiq, Saudi Arabia.

COMMUNICATIONS

There are less than 500 miles of railway but the highways and secondary roads are good. Most of the passenger and freight traffic is handled by the hundreds of inexpensive bus and truck companies. Lebanon also has two national airlines and an international airport which is used by a number of foreign lines whose planes offer direct service to and from the Far East, European capitals, London and the U. S. A.

RELIGION AND EDUCATION

Various sects of Christians make up about half of the population, while the rest of the people belong to various Moslem sects. The Government maintains more than 1,000 primary and technical schools; and there are some 850 private and foreign schools. The country has two outstanding universities, the University of St. Joseph and the American University, both located in Beirut.

CHIEF TOWNS

Beirut, the capital, has a population of about 350,000; Tripoli, 65,000; Zahle, 26,000; and Saida, 20,000.

INTERNATIONAL BECHTEL

PLOWING IN THE OLD WAY BESIDE OIL STORAGE TANKS

The crude implement drawn by oxen and the tanks are symbolic of present-day Lebanon. It is at a crossroads in its history where ancient customs and modern ideas are meeting head-on.

IN PALESTINE TO-DAY

Its Sacred Places and Medley of Races

Palestine, the Canaan of the Old Testament, the Holy Land of the Crusaders, sacred alike to Christians, Jews and Mohammedans, has had a long and turbulent history. After World War I, it was made a British mandate. Though the Jews always regarded Palestine as their homeland, the idea of a modern Hebrew nation did not take root until the late 1800's. It bore fruit, in spite of bitter opposition by the Arabs of the Levant, when the state of Israel came into existence in 1948, after the United Nations divided Palestine between the Jews and the Arabs. The Kingdom of Jordan has taken over still another part of Palestine.

BETWEEN the lofty mountains of Lebanon on the north and Egypt on the south, between the Mediterranean on the west and the River Jordan and the Dead Sea on the east, lies the hilly country of Palestine proper. The territory of Trans-Jordan lies, as its name implies, beyond the Dead Sea and the River Jordan.

Although it is only a small strip of territory, Palestine is the most famous land on earth and one of the oldest. Indeed, excavations show us that it was inhabited probably as early as 10,000 B.C. by cave dwellers; but that is all prehistoric and we really know little about it until about 3000 B.C. when these cave dwellers were driven out by a Semitic people. The country was called Canaan. History tells us that it was occupied by the Babylonians and later by the Egyptians, and we shall see that it has been used as a highway by most of the great nations of the world for it was the connecting link between the great Mesopotamian empires and those of Egypt, Greece and Rome. Obliged to side with one or the other, the people of Palestine were continually being despoiled by the combatants. Their homes were often destroyed, and they themselves were killed or made captive.

When the Romans destroyed Jerusalem and the Jews were dispersed, the great nations of the ancient world were no longer vigorous fighting peoples. But another trouble was to arise for Palestine, for the interests of three of the great religions of the world became centred there. The Jews regarded Palestine as theirs by right (their "Promised Land"); the Christians regarded as holy the ground whereon the Founder of Christianity lived and taught and died; the Mohammedans, revering the Jewish patriarchs almost as much as did the Jews themselves, considered that they had a right to the land they had conquered. Thus, Jew, Mohammedan and Christian fought each other, and the Christians fought among themselves, for the holy places of Palestine.

Many Christian churches arose in the land after the emperor, Constantine the Great, early in the fourth century, made Christianity the state religion of the Roman Empire, but in the seventh century Palestine was overrun by the Mohammedan Arabs. At first the Christians met with kindly treatment, but there came a time when the churches were turned into mosques and the Christians were persecuted, especially those bands of pilgrims who have journeyed to Palestine throughout the ages.

These persecutions led to the Crusades, and for a time Palestine was under Christian rule, and a Christian king reigned in Jerusalem. Huge churches and castles were built, but the new kingdom did not last long. Gradually the Saracens, or Arabs, won back the land, until in 1291 Acre, the last Christian stronghold, fell to Egypt. More than two centuries later Palestine passed to the Turks, in whose possession it remained until December 9, 1917, when the Mayor of Jerusalem surrendered the city to Lord Allenby. Two days later the general entered the city at

Photo from Three Lions

PALESTINIAN SHEPHERDS TENDING THEIR FLOCKS OUTSIDE THE ANCIENT TOWN OF BETHLEHEM

Flocks of sheep and herds of goats have always been the chief wealth of the people of Palestine. Recently, however, more and more of the settled inhabitants have taken up agriculture, and so many, if not most, of the sheep are now owned by nomadic Beduin tribes, who wander with their flocks from pasture to pasture. This shepherd, dressed, with a turban on his head and sandals on his feet, just as his forefathers were in the days of the Old Testament, leads his flock of horned, lop-eared sheep from the hills beyond Jordan to market on the coast.

McLeish

VILLAGERS DRAWING WATER FROM THE WELL IN CANA OF GALILEE

Kefr Kenna is, according to tradition, the Cana of the Bible, where Christ wrought His first miracle—that of changing the water into wine. Another hamlet, Kana el Jelil, also claims to represent the ancient village. This photograph was taken in the evening, when the men water their animals and the women replenish their household supplies.

CHURCH OF THE NATIVITY IN THE VILLAGE OF BETHLEHEM

The Church of the Nativity is one of the oldest churches in the world and was built over the grotto which is believed to be the site of Christ's birth. The modern name of the village is Beit Lahm, and it is five miles southwest of Jerusalem. Most of the inhabitants are Christians, but many Beduins come hither on market day to barter their goods.

American Colony

Near East Relief

IN THE GROTTO IN THE CHURCH OF THE NATIVITY AT BETHLEHEM

Under the Church of the Nativity, shown on page 325, is the grotto where it is believed Christ was born. It is difficult, indeed, to try to reconstruct in one's imagination the scene in the comfortless, cattle manger for now when one descends to this marble-floored room by the winding staircase, one finds decorative mosaics and numerous lights kept burning day and night. A star has been placed to mark the sacred spot. It is most unfortunate that the Christian sects quarrel bitterly over the right to care for this revered place.

Horsfield

LOOKING ALONG A JERUSALEM STREET OF HALLOWED MEMORY

This narrow cobbled way, looking so quiet and restful in the morning sunlight, is called the Via Dolorosa, "the street of pain," for it is said to be the one along which Jesus Christ carried the cross to Golgotha. This cannot, unfortunately, be definitely proven, for, although the fourteen Stations of the Cross are marked by tablets on the walls, it is known that the sites of these stations have often been changed. Near this graceful arch is the sixth station, where, so the legend runs, the miracle of St. Veronica's handkerchief took place.

the head of his victorious troops.

From 1923 until May of 1948, Palestine was governed by the British under mandate of the League of Nations. The twenty-five years of her mandate, however, were marked by almost continuous unrest as Britain unsuccessfully tried to placate both Jewish and Arab inhabitants and bring peace to the Holy Land.

Until about a century ago, there were few Jews in Palestine, but after the Balfour Declaration of 1917, which favored the establishment of a Jewish homeland, thousands of Jews came to the little country. Some entered as pioneers to drain the swamps and to terrace the stony hillsides. Today nearly 300 agricultural colonies dot the land as a result of their efforts. Industry, too, has flourished. Industrial establishments of many kinds have been set up—glass, wood and metal works; food and drug supplies; a great cement factory; electrical and machine shops. The waters of the River Jordan have been harnessed, giving the entire country the benefits of electric light and power. A giant plant extracts the potash, bromine and other chemicals that lie dissolved in the waters of the Dead Sea. In the Jewish districts of Palestine great improvements have been made in education, in sanitation and other public services. The Arabs have benefited directly or indirectly by many of these outstanding improvements.

World War II Aftermath

The second World War brought a temporary lull in the unrest; but its end proved to be only the beginning of even greater strife. Thousands of displaced persons in Europe sought to begin life anew in Palestine—to settle as farmers or to work in the towns and industries. Many were skilled craftsmen.

Meanwhile, Arab resentment increased steadily because of what they considered unlawful occupation of their country. The crisis came in 1947. British attempts to limit immigration were met with open defiance by Jewish underground organizations. There were outbreaks of violence between Arabs and Jews. Many soldiers and civilians were killed. Finally, Britain decided that she had had enough of Palestine. She decided to give up her mandate.

End of Mandate

The problem of Palestine then became the immediate concern of the United Nations General Assembly which, after much debate, ordered the division of Palestine into separate Jewish and Arab states late in 1947. The decision was joyfully received by the Jews and bitterly opposed by the seven states of the Arab League. By May 1948, England had evacuated all of her troops from Palestine.

The British evacuation was the signal for the beginning of a full-scale war between the new Jewish state of Israel and the Arab League states (an alliance of Arab countries including Saudi Arabia, Yemen, Egypt, Iraq, Trans-Jordan, Lebanon and Syria). The Arabs attacked, led by the Arab Legion of King Abdullah of Trans-Jordan. The Jewish army, Haganah, rallied to the defense of its new homeland.

The war continued, despite efforts of the United Nations to halt it. However, as the Jewish forces proved so much stronger than those of the Arab League, the conflict eventually died out. The new state of Israel was firmly established, and won recognition by every important country in the world.

The little country of 10,460 square miles has more than a million Moslems and slightly more than a half-million Jews, plus almost 150,000 persons of other denominations. Under terms of the partition, the Holy City of Jerusalem was to become a neutral territory with a governor appointed by the United Nations. The governor was to be from a neutral nation. The first governor to be appointed was from the United States.

Jerusalem, the Holy City

Jerusalem is a city set on a hill. Its name is supposed to mean "vision," or "abode of peace," but it has known less

MC LEISH

THE KUBBET ES SAKHRA, or the Dome of the Rock, which was built by the Arabs in the seventh century, is commonly but incorrectly referred to as the Mosque of Omar. Mohammedans believe that here the souls of sinners will be weighed on Judgment Day.

© THE MATSON PHOTO SERVICE

ORANGE MARKET BEFORE THE DAMASCUS GATE

The walls of Jerusalem about which we read in the Bible have long since disappeared, and the thick, battlemented walls that now stand were built in the Middle Ages. The city may be entered by means of many gates. The Damascus Gate above is one of the most important. In the foreground are orange vendors piling high their golden wares to tempt the customer.

of peace than has almost any other city on earth. It has been destroyed and rebuilt again and again. The foundations of one city were set on top of another, so that to see the real Via Dolorosa of Christ's time it is necessary to go down into a cellar where, thirty feet below the present road, lie the Roman pavements.

Since the British occupation, the streets of Jerusalem have been kept clean; flowers have been planted in the waste places; the walls have been repaired; and within the walls the city has been provided with a proper water supply. Apart from this, Jerusalem has changed but little. Its streets are filled with a bewildering mass of humanity—Greek priests in black robes and tall hats, peasant women in cotton draperies, dark-eyed, stately Arabs in flowing robes, Jews in gabardines with a curl hanging down each side of the face, Jews in European dress, Mohammedan ladies in silken garments and semi-transparent veils and European tourists in sun-helmets.

The southeastern quarter of the city is the place where once rose the magnificent Jewish Temple, with its Holy of Holies, and which, to the Jews, is the most sacred spot on earth. On this site the Saracens raised a beautiful round building, the Dome of the Rock. Under the dome is a bare rock, the summit of Mt. Moriah, where, it is said, Mohammed came to pray, declaring that one prayer here was worth a thousand elsewhere. The Crusaders who turned this building into a church mistook it for the Temple of Solomon.

To-day this Dome of the Rock and other Mohammedan buildings stand in a beautiful courtyard adorned with fountains and praying-places. The Mohammedans call the whole of this area Haram el-Sherif and regard it as a holy place, second only in importance to Mecca. No infidel may enter without a permit. No Jew will ever enter it, lest by accident he might tread on the spot where once was the Holy of Holies.

A portion of the wall of the Haram el-Sherif is believed to be part of the ancient Temple wall. It is called "the Wailing Place of the Jews." Here every Friday afternoon the Jews assemble, press their foreheads against the stone blocks and chant their lamentations for the departed glories of their nation. On page 217 of Volume VII, this wall is shown in color.

The Christian quarter of the city lies to the northwest, and here stands the Church of the Holy Sepulchre, which is a mass of buildings covering the traditional sites of the crucifixion and burial of Jesus. Here, in a large round building known as the Rotunda, is a small chapel containing the sepulchre. This chapel belongs to the Greek Church, as does the large church adjoining, but Syrians, Copts and other Christian communities have each their own chapel under its roof.

Here, on the eve of the Greek Easter Sunday, is held the Festival of the Holy Fire. Every part of the buildings and their precincts is thronged with people, all holding bundles of candles. Presently the Greek Patriarch enters at the head of a procession. He then goes into the Chapel of the Sepulchre, where, so it is claimed, a fire, sent direct from heaven, appears on the altar. The fire is passed out through two openings in the wall of an ante-chamber and instantly there is a mad rush, as everyone wishes to light his candles at the sacred fire. Lights are passed from hand to hand, and outside horsemen are waiting to snatch the sacred flame and carry it to Bethlehem and Naz-

Donald McLeish

MONKISH CURATOR OF THE GARDEN OF GETHSEMANE

By the side of the highway that leads to the Mount of Olives may still be seen this garden, now surrounded by a wall and tended by Franciscan monks, who present the visitor with a bunch of flowers as a souvenir of the visit. Some of the olive trees are said to date from the beginning of the Christian era and are shored up with stones.

MC LEISH

ACROSS THE SEA OF GALILEE glides this boat with a bright blue sail. Its progress is assisted by the crew bending to their blue-and-white oars. Formerly the sea, which is thirteen miles long and eight miles wide, was crowded with shipping, for on its shore were several important cities, but of these only Tiberias remains today, so that usually only a few fishing boats are now to be seen upon its surface. The Lake of Tiberias is another name for this sheet of water, which, though deep set among steep hills, is often swept by sudden and violent storms.

BY THIS ANCIENT BRIDGE Roman legions crossed the River Jordan in the days of long ago. The bridge spans the river at a point about seven miles south of the Sea of Galilee, and was constructed by Roman engineers. The exact date of its construction is unknown. To the south of this ancient structure is a modern railway bridge, sixty-five yards in length, over which pass trains from Haifa, a port on the Bay of Acre, to El Hamme, a town in southern Syria. In Hebrew times the Jordan valley was regarded as a "wilderness." Only in Roman times was it at all populous.

© American Colony

CUSTOMERS AT A STREET RESTAURANT IN THE CITY OF JERUSALEM

As in most Eastern countries, we may see restaurants set up in the thoroughfares of the Holy City. On the box are many skewers upon which are choice morsels of roasted meat and to the right is a pile of flat loaves of bread. Customers can also take a puff or two at a nargileh, or water-pipe. Dust, heat and flies do not affect Eastern appetites.

Manley

YOUTHFUL PEDDLER OF JAFFA'S GOLDEN FRUIT

This Syrian boy is offering his basketful of refreshing, juicy fruit in the hot streets of Jaffa, which was an important seaport of Palestine in ancient times as it is to-day. Jaffa's chief trade is in the exceptionally fine oranges which are grown in the neighborhood and are exported to Egypt and Europe. Olives are grown also, and the oil is exported.

MC LEISH

NEAR THE JAFFA GATE, the western portal of Jerusalem, two turbaned Moslems loiter to watch the bustling crowd of travelers, pilgrims and traders that gathers round this spot. Jerusalem is a Holy City to Mohammedans as well as to Christians and Jews; and each group has sacred places. There are mosques, churches and synagogues.

THESE THREE OLD JEWS, who are taking their leisure beneath the ramparts of Jerusalem, have seen the population of that city change considerably since they were young. Among the Jews who are citizens of Israel are some whose families have lived in Palestine for generations; but many more Jews have immigrated to their homeland.

© Underwood & Underwood

SOLEMN YOUNG BRIDE AND BRIDEGROOM OF PALESTINE

Parents arrange the marriages of their children in Palestine, and often the bride and bridegroom are quite young. A dowry must be provided for the girl, but this is not always necessary if she happens to be beautiful. The bridegroom is holding a scimitar as a token that he has the right to exact obedience from his modest-appearing wife.

areth and other places, to kindle the lights on the altars of the Greek churches for another year.

At about the same time of the year takes place the Mohammedan festival of Neby Musa, "Tomb of Moses." The festivities start with the assembling of pilgrims at Jerusalem. Through the Jaffa Gate come the men of Hebron, carrying variously colored flags embroidered with texts from the Koran. Each flagstaff is hung with handkerchiefs given by women to be placed on Musa's shrine to ensure a blessing. The pilgrims come singing and shouting, sometimes holding hands and dancing along in a circle, while in the centre others play on cymbals and drums. Last of all comes the Green Banner of Hebron, guarded by wiry swordsmen.

Meanwhile, through the Damascus Gate, a similar procession is arriving from Nablus. Pilgrims go by, representatives of each village bearing their own banner, but all assemble in the Haram el-Sherif for an opening service. Next day a vast procession leaves the city, carrying a holy banner from Jerusalem to the hilltop on which stands the shrine of Neby Musa.

Hebron and Nablus are almost entirely Mohammedan, but in Nablus there lives a tiny community, the Samaritans, which claims descent from the remnant of the Ten Tribes left behind at the time of the Captivity. They regard only the Pentateuch and the Book of Joshua as sacred. At the time of the Passover the whole community climbs Mt. Gerizim, where tents are pitched, and at sunset lambs are slaughtered. Part of the flesh is burned as a sacrifice, and the rest is put in ovens. Three hours later the people stand and eat the Passover feast.

The Jordan is Palestine's only river of note. Rising at the foot of Mt. Hermon,

McLeish

CHEERFUL YOUNG PEOPLE FROM THE TENTS OF THE BEDUINS

Arabs form a large proportion of the varied population of Palestine, but not all of them are wanderers over the face of the desert, for there are many Arab villages in the country. The Beduins, the nomadic Arabs, were a source of annoyance to the inhabitants when the Turks were in Palestine, as they raided villages and attacked small caravans.

© E. N. A.

IN BETHLEHEM the birthplace of Christ and of King David, the girls carry their jars of water balanced upon their heads, as is the custom among many Eastern races. The head-dress of this girl is decorated with overlapping coins, and her head-shawl and gown are embellished with delicate colored embroidery that she has worked herself.

MC LEISH

MARRIED WOMEN of Bethlehem wear a white veil draped over a tarboosh, or fez. Rows of coins ornament the hat, and from it are suspended silver chains. It is the custom for them to pull the veil over the tarboosh and also to secure it under the chin when they go out of doors. Over the richly colored dress, a short embroidered jacket is worn.

© United Palestine Appeal

THESE PLOWMEN FROM POLAND HAVE COME TO PALESTINE

Although Palestine is not a land flowing with milk and honey as recorded in the book of Exodus, it does respond to new methods. The Zionist movement, which advocates a national home for the Jews, is bringing many of the scattered race back to Palestine and to their original occupation of farming.

© United Palestine Appeal

TEL AVIV, THE SECOND PORT OF PALESTINE

So great has been the influx of Jews into this boom town that houses cannot be built fast enough. Tel Aviv has mushroomed from empty sands. This Miracle City of Palestine has become the centre of her intellectual life just as Jerusalem is the political hub. The port of Tel Aviv exports much fruit.

© United Palestine Appeal

A STREET IN TEL AVIV, INTELLECTUAL CENTRE OF PALESTINE

Fine shops and modern apartment buildings line a broad Tel Aviv street. Not so many years ago the city was a small residential suburb. But during the 1930's and 1940's Jewish immigrants from eastern Europe settled there and the growth was rapid. Modern Tel Aviv soon surpassed its ancient neighbor, Jaffa. The two cities together now form the metropolis of Israel.

© United Palestine Appeal

CHEMISTRY BUILDING OF THE HEBREW UNIVERSITY

Development along educational lines has kept pace with other improvements in "New Palestine." Jewish organizations have established over 600 schools which include secondary schools, teachers' training colleges, agricultural schools, technical schools, and schools of music. In 1925 the Hebrew University on Mount Scopus, near Jerusalem, was opened.

© EWING GALLOWAY

IN JORDAN, the country lying east of the Dead Sea and the River Jordan and bounded by the Syrian desert, we may often see a shepherd leading his flock of sheep and black goats. Parts of Jordan, such as the arid plateau of Moab, are absolutely desolate. The climate of Palestine proper is a healthful one, but here the heat is almost unbearable during the summer months. Between the two world wars, Jordan was a British mandate; but in 1946 a treaty was signed by which Britain recognized the kingdom as a sovereign independent state.

MC LEISH

IN ACRE is this mosque, built by a Turk named Jezzar Pasha, who brought columns for its ornamentation from the ruins at Caesarea. Caesarea was the capital of Roman Palestine, but is now only a small village. Acre, a seaport situated on a promontory at the base of Mount Carmel, was regarded as the "Key of Palestine" in the time of the Crusades.

it flows through the Sea of Galilee and then, winding and twisting its way through a deep valley, sinks lower and lower till it flows into the Dead Sea nearly thirteen hundred feet below sea level.

The Dead Sea is a deep lake, but it is so salty that no fish can live in it and no green thing can grow on its banks, hence its name. Among the many enterprises undertaken on this most remarkable lake is one to utilize the waters of Jordan for generating electric power, and a further scheme is in contemplation by which the hitherto useless Dead Sea shall be exploited for its salts, of which it is said to contain thirty thousand million tons. In South Palestine, especially around the southern end of the Dead Sea, oil is known to exist, and, it is thought, might be worked profitably.

The district east of the river, now known as Jordan, was originally part of the League of Nations mandate for Palestine. For a time it was governed by a local Arab administration with the advice of a representative of the British High Commissioner for Palestine. By a treaty signed on March 22, 1946, Britain recognized the independence of Jordan, and Abdullah ibn-Husein became king. Jordan has played an important part in the Arab League, formed to promote the interests of the Arab peoples dwelling in the Near East.

ISRAEL AND JORDAN: FACTS AND FIGURES

ISRAEL—THE COUNTRY

The area known as Palestine was formerly administered by Great Britain under mandate from the League of Nations. In 1947, it was partitioned into Jewish and Arab states. The Jewish portion became the State of Israel and the Arab portions were absorbed by the Kingdom of Jordan. Israel is bounded on the north by Syria and Lebanon, on the west by Egypt and the Mediterranean and on the east by Jordan. The area is about 7,978 square miles and its estimated population is 1,170,000 Jews, Arabs and Christians.

GOVERNMENT

The Republic of Israel was officially proclaimed in May 1948. A provisional government was formed and a constituent assembly, called the First Knesset, was elected in January 1949. A month later, the Knesset passed its first law—known as the Transition Law—which laid the foundations for the permanent departments of government. In June 1950, the Knesset voted to delay the adoption of a constitution. Rather, it was decided to let one grow with the republic.

COMMERCE AND INDUSTRIES

Agriculture is the chief occupation in regions where rainfall is sufficient. Barley, wheat, millet, grapes, oranges, melons, olives, figs, sorghum and lentils are raised, with limited quantities of tobacco and cotton. There is pasturage for sheep, goats and camels and some progress has been made in bee-keeping. Many trees have been planted. Mineral resources include limestone, sandstone, gypsum, rock salt, some sulphur and traces of petroleum. The principal manufactures are olive oil, soap and wine. Oil refineries and tanks have been constructed in Haifa to process petroleum from the Mosul oil fields.

COMMUNICATIONS

There are 438 miles of railway; 1,453 miles of metalled roads and in addition, many hundreds of miles of tracks passable in dry weather. Telephone and telegraph wire, over 78,959 miles. Jaffa and Haifa are the chief ports with regular steamer service.

RELIGION AND EDUCATION

The religious affairs of Israel are supervised by a special government ministry. The Sephardic and Ashkenasic chief rabbis are the principal religious authorities of the Jews; the heads of the various communities serve the Christians, and the Kadi, the Moslems. Education is directed by the Ministry of Education and is free in the primary and kindergarten grades. There are separate schools for Jewish and Arab students, with Jewish and Arab teachers. There are schools of music, teachers training colleges, trade schools, the Hebrew University in Jerusalem, and the Haifa Technical Institute for engineering and architectural studies.

CHIEF TOWNS

Populations (estimated): Jerusalem, capital (Israeli part only), 110,000; Tel Aviv and Jaffa, 300,000; Haifa, 145,000; Gaza, 37,820; Hebron, 26,390; Nablus, 24,660.

JORDAN

Formerly governed by Britain under the Palestine mandate. Became an independent state in 1946 now known as the Hashimite Kingdom of Jordan. It is governed by King Abdullah and a legislature consisting of a council, ministers and 16 elected members. Agriculture is promising; and phosphate deposits are being developed. Passable roads total 360 miles; the Cairo-Bagdad air route crosses the country. The area is 34,750 square miles; estimated population, about 450,000.

THE DESERT RANGERS

The Beduins as They Are in Reality

The Beduin is a man of many countries. A pastoral nomad, he wanders from one oasis to another in search of good grassland and water for his flocks. Beduins are found throughout the deserts of North Africa, Arabia and Syria. They live as simply as the most primitive peoples on earth, yet many have an intelligence as quick and subtle as the most civilized men of the West. Outsiders find it hard to understand the changeable nature of the Beduin. At one moment hostile and the next a generous host, he earns respect at all times for his ability to wrest a living from the unyielding desert.

IN song and story the Beduin is often pictured as a picturesque fellow, leading a roving life much as gipsies do. This portrait is false. The Beduin's life is as monotonous as his diet of dates, camel's milk and camel flesh. Living in the hostile desert, his wandering is a matter of necessity, for he must constantly seek pasture, wherever a bit of grass grows, for his sheep and goats.

Camels, however, are his chief source of food, his beasts of burden and his medium of exchange. Without them, he could not live in the desert at all. If he is wealthy, by Beduin standards, he may own one or more horses, and lavishes great care on them.

The desert man's mental horizons are severely limited. He is bound by strict allegiance to his clan and his tribe. Yet through his nature there runs a rich vein of poetry. His intelligence is naturally quick; and it has been shown that when he is placed in a totally different environment, he can adjust himself to it with surprising ease.

© CRÉTÉ

TRINKETS OF A DESERT WOMAN

Her ornaments are usually a number of necklaces of metal chains and glass beads with numerous bracelets and armlets, but rarely does she wear earrings.

In the northern area of the great deserts of the Nile one may find here and there Beduins who have at least an idea of modern ways of life. These are the wealthier tribesmen who, perhaps, have been successful in breeding and trading camels and horses. Some live in villages and differ greatly from their poorer desert brothers, who pitch their tents in the wilderness and lead a wandering life.

For many centuries the Beduin has been one of the best-known features of the East. His very name in Arabic means "man of the desert," and his range is a wide one. From Arabia and Syria, his original home, he spread over Mesopotamia and Egypt, and all along the northern coasts of Africa. At the present day he has wandered even as far afield as Persia and Turkestan. In all it is reckoned that there are about 1,500,000 of these desert gipsies, of whom those in Arabia and Egypt are perhaps the most widely known. Those of the former country com-

DESERT TWILIGHT shows a glory of color which does not last beyond a few seconds. Soon after, the day's fierce heat is radiated away through the clear dry air and the warmth of a fire is grateful. It is through such country as this that the Beduins wander with their flocks and herds from camp to camp, for the pasturage is scant and often gives out in twelve days. Indeed, the hard life of the desert is to-day driving many of them coastward to the cities where unfortunately they soon lose their good qualities and mingle with the lower classes of the population.

© LEHNERT & LANDROCK

BEDUIN WOMEN, when they go upon a journey, are usually shut within a litter fixed upon the back of a camel. It is a Moslem practice that women shall be hidden from the public gaze, so they must travel swaying giddily to and fro on their unwieldy covered platform, which is fastened upon the camel's hump, and how uncomfortably hot and stuffy it must be inside.

INSIDE THE SHEIK'S TENT: A VISIT TO A TRIBE LIVING NEAR THE DEAD SEA

Coffee is always offered to a guest in token of friendship. In the middle of the floor is a charcoal fire, and to the left a man is grinding the coffee in a beautifully made mortar. After roasting the crushed berries on the fire the coffee is boiled and handed round in the little white cups. Much of this coffee is imported from Brazil as the native kind, being of superior quality, is all needed for export. The sheik, who is the one on the extreme right, is smoking a hookah, a sort of pipe in which the tobacco smoke is inhaled through scented water.

prise about one-fifth of the whole population, including in this estimate the territories of Iraq, Palestine and Syria. How this figure is arrived at one cannot say, for all attempts to get the nomadic tribesmen into a recent census were unsuccessful. The Beduins saw behind the census papers the threatening figure of the tax collector, and as they have never paid tribute to any government they refused to have their heads counted.

Of the higher class Beduins, most live in communities each of which, as has been said, is ruled over by a sheik. It is among such that the more picturesque features of desert life are to be seen. Here are larger and better equipped tents. The sheik himself will be garbed in clothes of fine quality while his tribesmen, in their parti-colored robes, will make a brave show. The national dress consists of the "abba," or camel's-hair cloak—striped gaily with colors or black and white—beneath which is a closely fitting tunic that may be of silk or cotton, according to the owner's means. This is gathered in by a leather girdle or a colored sash, in which a pistol or dagger can be stuck.

How the Desert Men Dress

As headdress is worn a square of cloth —again cotton or silk—brightly hued and striped. This is doubled over the head, the two long ends falling down upon the shoulders. A notable feature of this headgear is the twisted band of camel's hair, which is worn round the top of the head and helps to keep the cloth in position when the front part is pulled forward as a shade for the eyes.

Women's garments among the more settled tribes may also be brightly colored. A blue, red or yellow handkerchief serves for head-covering while the loose robe, fastening with a girdle, is striped or of a striking pattern. But out in the desert the women are drably clothed compared with their husbands. Unlike her Arabian sisters, the Beduin woman does not wear a face veil. Her custom is to cover the lower portion of her face with a corner of her shawl at the approach of a stranger. But she has a feminine weakness for necklaces and other trinkets especially for bangles round arm and ankle. Most likely too she will wear a talisman in her headdress, a small transparent stone set in beads, which is supposed to act as a charm against the "evil eye."

With her brown skin, her dark flashing eyes gazing at one from below a well-draped headdress, and with the pleasant jingle of her metal chain necklaces and ornaments, this daughter of the East is quite charming in her youth. But she ages too quickly for her life is one of constant toil with little pleasures.

Workaday Life of the Womenfolk

The Beduin man leaves all the domestic duties to his womenfolk. They grind the wheat in the handmill or pound it in the mortar. It is they who knead and bake the bread, make butter, carry water from the wells, work at the loom and mend the tent covering. To the women also usually falls the task of rolling up the tents when camp is broken and the tribe is moving on to some fresh pasturage.

One of our pictures shows a Beduin mother carrying her baby in the manner usual among this people. The youngster, wrapped in garments of bright colors, is swung over the mother's back in a shawl. At other times it may be set astride her shoulder. As a rule the little ones are strong and healthy for in their babyhood they are left to roll naked in the sun. As they grow up, however, numbers of them suffer from ophthalmia and other eye troubles brought on by dirt and inflammation from the sand or by the sun's glare. In some cases total blindness follows, and then they drift into the towns to join the ranks of the beggars who are so common there.

The Beduin at Close Quarters

If he be less presentable than his more prosperous brothers of the village, the Beduin of the desert, the true nomad who shifts continually from place to place, is even more truly a descendant of Ishmael in the Bible story. Romance and color fall away from this type the closer we get to him. Below middle stature, lean and wiry

© LEHNERT & LANDROCK

BEDUIN GIRLS, like this attractive nomad maid of Tunisia who is shown here with her mother, are as fond of dolls as any young ladies of the same age in our country. It was the Arab conquests of the eighth century which took her forefathers from their original home in the wilder parts of Syria and Arabia along the coast of North Africa as far as Morocco.

© LEHNERT & LANDROCK

BABY BEDUINS, carried pickaback in a shawl, soon get tanned a rich clear brown by the desert sun. So too do their mothers, for the Beduins are an independent folk and their womenkind do not always wear the face-veil. They cover the lower part of the features with a corner of their cloak when a man not of their own household is seen approaching.

in physique, he is clad in coarse garments; his tents are of poor quality, and his horses and camels are underfed and shamefully ill-used. With the poorest of these desert gipsies a few wretched goats are often their only livestock.

The Bedouin's treatment of his camel is far from what the "Ship of the Desert" deserves at his hands. It is true that the animal has few good points in his nature; he cannot be described as lovable. He is sulky and refractory and appears to be incapable of affection for his master—though this may only be the result of the treatment he receives. He is made to flop down for loading and unloading pur-

STANDARD OIL CO. (N. J.)

AN ARABIAN BEDOUIN AND HIS FAMILY RELAX BEFORE THEIR TENT

In Abqaiq, Arabia, a Bedouin employed as a watchman in the nearby oil fields builds his tent and clothes his family in the manner of his nomadic tribesmen. The large metal food can the boy to the right holds and the burlap sacking that has been used for the tent are typical of many objects from the modern West that have found a place in Arab life. The women are closely veiled.

STANDARD OIL CO. (N. J.)

THE BEDOUIN IS NO LESS MANLY FOR HIS LONG BRAIDS OF HAIR

A Bedouin of Al Kharj in the Nejd region of Saudi Arabia seems fiercely proud of his distinctive hair style. Al Kharj is one of the best farm regions of the Arabian peninsula. Modern irrigation waters date groves and fields of wheat, alfalfa and millet. Because of the abundance of feed, Bedouins have settled with their herds on the lands about Al Kharj.

poses by blows on the knees; there is no word of command, such as other draught animals learn to obey. When resting with heavy loads on his back, and when taking his food, the ill-fitting framework on which his burden is piled is not removed.

On the other hand he is quite indispensable to his master for he can travel far in a waterless region and can feed on the thorny plants that grow in the sand. His eyes are well protected from the sun by the thick upper eyelids with which he is provided, and when the fierce simoon wind rages across the waste he can close his nostrils to it and the blown sand particles.

A sand storm in the desert is one of the terrors of the nomad's life. When it breaks, the camels crouch down with their backs to it, the travelers seek shelter within

ARAB CHILDHOOD does not last very long, and for the girls it ends even earlier than for the boys. At the age of thirteen or fourteen the Beduin girl shown above will be considered to be grown up and a husband will have been found for her. But while she is yet in the playtime of her life she makes the very utmost of it as her cheerful smile suggests.

© LEHNERT & LANDROCK

BEDUIN MOTHERS, though they usually have bright wrappings for their babies, often leave them entirely unclothed. It is a common sight in an encampment to see dusky-skinned infants left on their bare backs in the sand to kick in the sun. Notice the chains of metal trinkets that clash at every movement, and the number of different colors and patterns worn.

tent or other covering and the women who are fortunate enough to be in litters draw the cloth screens tightly around these for protection. To face the rushing wind, which brings along with it minute grains of sand, is a terrible experience. The Beduin's skin, hardened by exposure and screened by his cloak from the full force of the blast, enables him to bear it; but a foreigner, less accustomed to the elements, will come through the ordeal with his face badly cut and bleeding.

Shepherd and Robber by Turns

From time immemorial the Beduin has been a herdsman and a shepherd. It is the necessity of finding fresh pasturage for his flock that compels him to move from one spot to another. He will pitch his tent in some oasis in the desert with its water wells, until the scanty herbage has been exhausted, then the camp is broken and the journey onward is continued.

But such a peaceable existence as this has never satisfied the restless wanderer. The stern struggle for existence and ever-ready opportunity have made him an outlaw, a highwayman of the desert. To how many travelers and caravans has not the sudden cry of "Beduins" brought terror! The plundering of a caravan is a fierce joy to the Beduin. With rifle, lance and yataghan he descends upon his victims, and woe betide the trader who is not strong enough to beat off the marauders.

Why Caravans Are Looted

The Beduin on a foray is an enemy to be feared. He is merciless in the treatment of his captives and the ransom he extorts is heavy. The Arabs have a proverb which runs: "Entertain a Beduin and he will steal your clothes." So powerful are these marauding bands that they will levy toll even on the safe conduct of pilgrimages to Mecca. They regard the looting of caravans and travelers, indeed, in an original light—namely as the equivalent to the taxes and customs that are exacted in civilized countries. "The land is ours," they argue, "and if you trespass on it you must pay us compensation."

If, however, traveler or trader can show anything in the nature of a permit to enter the territory dominated by a tribe, such a document is generally recognized and respected. A permit of this kind can be purchased from a sheik, who will place some of his followers at the disposal of the travelers and thus pass them on from tribe to tribe across the desert.

Side by side with this lawlessness among Beduins there runs a regard for the laws of hospitality that is almost sacred. They are Mohammedans by religion, and the stranger who has eaten of their salt is safe from molestation. It might be well to amend the statement that they are followers of Mohammed for they are only nominally so. The tribes vary greatly in their religious customs and most of them disregard entirely the Prophet's command to pray five times daily and to make the pilgrimage to Mecca.

Supper in the Tent of a Sheik

Suppose now that we try to picture a sheik who is entertaining some guests. The Beduin camp has been pitched at an oasis. Outside the tent of their chief a little courtyard has been railed off with a hedge of brushwood. A fire blazes in the centre of this enclosure, partly for illumination as the tent is open on this side, and partly for boiling the water. Several of the womenfolk hasten to and fro, busy on the preparation of the coming meal. On the other side of the hedge are to be seen the dark figures of the kneeling camels.

The company gathered in the tent squats upon the mats and begins the meal, a mixture of meat, flour and hot oil, the bowl in which it is served being passed from hand to hand. An earthenware goblet of water makes the circuit of the tent in the same way. Rice is a favorite dish and of course there are dates and some sweetmeats, for the host is a man of position.

As an accompaniment to the feasting, one of the sheik's retinue who enjoys a reputation as a flute-player performs on his instrument. The chief guest—we will assume that he is a newcomer in this country—does his best to converse with his host, and is conscious occasionally of subdued laughter from the screened-off

EWING GALLOWAY

A BEDOUIN CHILD TAKES A DRINK FROM A GOATSKIN WATER BAG

In a Bedouin camp at an Algerian oasis children take their turns at the goatskin water bag. In the desert water is not easily come by. Everyone must be careful not to waste a drop or to take more than his share, especially when the family is on the move, far from the next well. The Southern Territories of Algeria make up one vast desert broken by few oases.

portion of the tent in which the women have been placed. The more curious of these cannot be restrained from peeping at times over the screen to gaze upon the stranger.

Then, while hookahs and cigarettes are being lighted, coffee is served as a special token of friendship. During the evening, to add to the general comfort, a bowl is handed round in which are some live coals sprinkled with fragrant incense. Each of the company takes a good sniff at this as he passes it on.

With more pleasant converse and entertainment the evening slips away. The various guests make their salutations and depart; blankets are spread upon the tent floors, and soon the whole encampment, except for the watchers posted on the outskirts, is wrapped in sleep.

© LEHNERT & LANDROCK

BEDUINS. Desert life, in spite of what is said in the imaginative stories of Arab chiefs, is not very healthful, nor are the desert folk overly clean. Opthalmia and other affections of the eyes are common, and this blind Beduin is only one of the many who wander into the towns to beg with a child as guide. He is in a market-place of Tunis in Africa.

ARABIA THE MYSTERIOUS

Its Arabs of the Desert and Its Holy Cities

The peninsula that we know as Arabia, the land of the Arabs, extends between the Red Sea and the Persian Gulf, somewhat in the shape of a baby's boot. Saudi Arabia, a kingdom that came into existence in 1932, occupies much the larger part of the peninsula. Yemen, whose present independence dates from 1934, is a mountainous triangle in the southwest corner. Along the southern edge is the Aden Protectorate, under British protection. In the southeast corner is Oman (officially the Sultanate of Masqat and Oman). Oman, as well as several sheikdoms along the Persian Gulf—Trucial Oman, Qatar and Kuwait—all have close ties with Great Britain. Much of Arabia is a desert, but there are many fertile valleys and beautiful oases.

THE peninsula of Arabia is familiar to us as being the birthplace of the Mohammedan religion and the home of many of its followers. In romantic stories, Arabia is sometimes pictured as a land of sandy wastes where bold sheiks, their robes streaming in the wind, dash across the desert on fleet Arabian horses. It all sounds very exciting, but the true picture is a little more prosaic.

Arabia has indeed many vast stretches of sand but there are arid wastes of stone and gravel with only occasional patches of grass and stunted bush—a desert of another kind. It is extremely dry and excessively hot so that only about one-third of its area is inhabited by settled people. The whole of Arabia, however, is not a desolate waste. There are oases of palm trees and expanses of green fertility amid the general desolation. Here and there, one may see broad green valleys dotted with bushes, where the Arabs and wandering tribes of Beduins graze their herds of cattle, sheep and camels.

The history of Arabia dates from the Creation, for Jidda (Jeddah) on the shores of the Red Sea and one of the principal Arabian ports, is said by the Arabs to have been the birthplace of Eve. In early times, Arabia was inhabited by many tribes who did not unite until the time of Mohammed in the seventh century A.D. Mohammed believed that there is but one God and he finally persuaded the people to give up their pagan gods, to accept his belief and to look to him as God's Prophet. At times, he fell into trances during which he said he was in communication with God, and the messages, eagerly taken down by his listeners, form their Bible, known as the Koran. Among other things it commands a Mohammedan to be temperate, to pray five times a day—just before sunrise, just before noon, before and after sunset and when the day is closed—to fast from sunrise to sunset during the month of Ramadan, to give alms to the poor, and to make the pilgrimage to Mecca at least once during his lifetime.

At first, Mohammed did not have a large following but the numbers increased when he allowed the new religion to be promoted by means of the sword. The Arabs, or Saracens as they were then known, gathered under the green flag of Islam and determined to carry it throughout the world. Mohammed died in 653 A.D. but his successors carried out his plans and this vast empire at its zenith extended through Western Asia across North Africa and even into Spain.

However, as time went on, Arabia broke up again, and although the Turks conquered the territory in 1517 and held it until the War of 1914-18, some of the nomadic people were never subdued.

In the middle of the eighteenth century, there began what was known as the Wahhabi movement. It was named for its founder, Wahhab, who sought to purge the Moslem faith of its evils and to return to the true simplicity of the original Mohammedanism. In recent times, under the leadership of Ibn Saud, its object has changed from religious reform to nationalism and an increasing number of Arabians have been attracted to this cause.

© LEHNERT & LANDROCK

THE GREAT DESERT in the centre of Arabia is well named the Dahna, which means "empty quarter," for it is a waterless stretch of sand and rock that has only twice been crossed by white men, and rarely by an Arab. Here, on its western edge, where it is known as El Ahkaf, we see an Arab citadel, built, probably, to protect the oasis nearby from predatory Beduins. That there is water we can see from the scrub and few palm-trees. There may even be a stream, but if so it will be dry for most of the year, for that is the fate of all Arabian rivers.

CAMEL CARAVANS must serve the purpose of both freight and passenger trains between Medina and its port of Yembo, for there is no railway line, only a rough track crossing about 130 miles of sun-scorched steppe. It is a frequently used road, however, for Yembo is known, with reason, as the "Gate of the Holy City." Thousands of Mohammedan pilgrims arrive there every year bound for Mecca, the birthplace of Mohammed, and Medina, his burial place. A large escort was needed for every caravan until quite recently, for nomad tribes waylaid and robbed all ill-protected travelers.

BLACK STAR

A SAUDI ARABIAN CHIEFTAIN CLINGS TO HIS ANCIENT FASHIONS

The flowing robes of the desert people are still worn in Jidda, Saudi Arabia's Red Sea port. Light covering, especially of neck and head, is needed for protection from the desert sun.

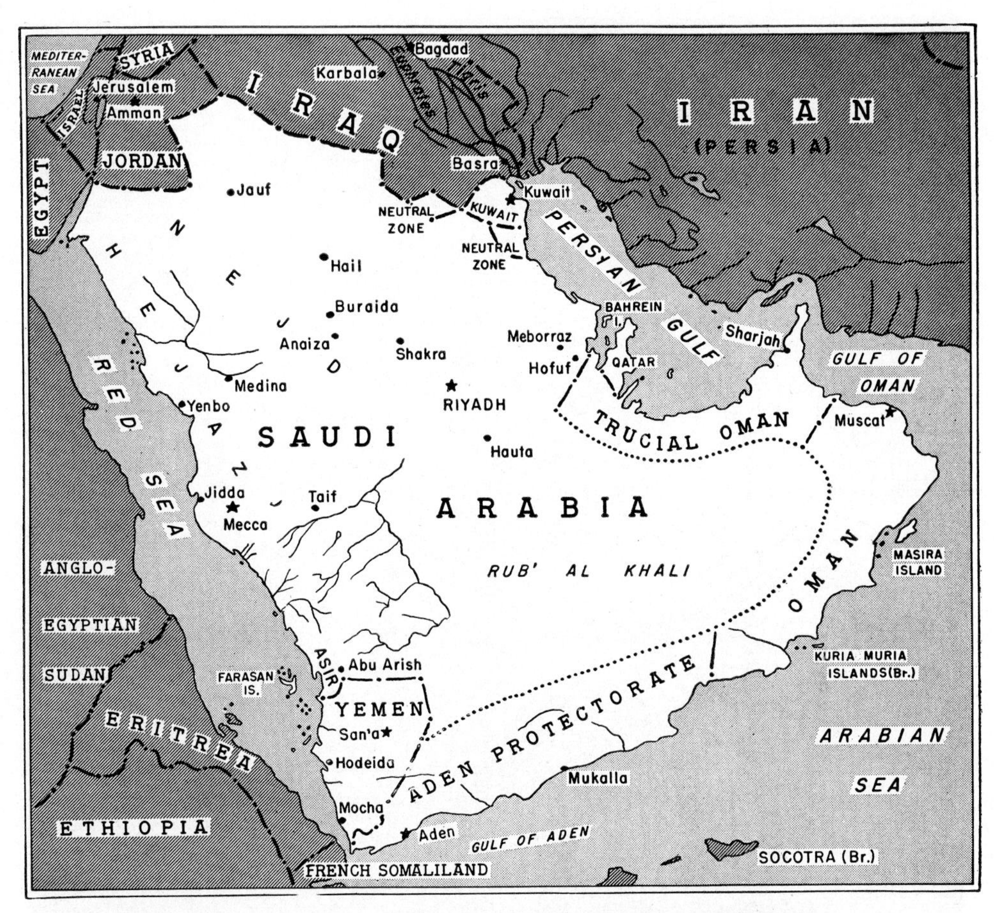

THE STATES OF THE GREAT ARABIAN PENINSULA

Ibn Saud took advantage of the first World War to free his domains from Turkish rule. Later he conquered Hejaz, extended his authority over the larger part of the peninsula, and renamed his kingdom Saudi Arabia. Colonel T. E. Lawrence, a British officer, who sympathized with the cause, did much at that time to develop a spirit of nationality among the Arabs.

Besides Saudi Arabia there are several smaller states, some of them under special treaty arrangements with Britain. In the southwest is the sultanate Yemen and the British colony and Protectorate of Aden. The sultanate of Oman and Muscat is on the Gulf of Oman. On the Persian Gulf are the Trucial Coast sheikdoms and Qatar, the Bahrein Islands and Kuwait.

Mecca and Medina are the two most important towns in Arabia from a religious and political standpoint. Mohammed, the founder of the Moslem faith, was born in Mecca, and to that city as many as 200,000 devotees make the annual pilgrimage to do honor to the Prophet. Medina, his burial place, is also a place of worship to which unbelievers are denied entrance. It is interesting to note that the religion is divided into two main factions, the Sunnis and the Shiites. The division arose from the fact that Mohammed died without leaving a successor as the temporal and spiritual head of the faith. For twenty-two years after his death Arabia was ruled by three successive Caliphs.

It was then that the two rival factions rose. The Sunnis claimed the right to nominate the Prophet's successor, while the Shiites contended that the divine right of succession lay with Ali, Mohammed's son-in-law, and his descendants. Arising thus, the dispute assumed such proportions that the rival sects still have an undisguised dislike for each other. Cer-

FORBES

THIS WILD RAVINE, the Wadi Musa, on a ledge of which these men are standing, leads to the valley in which are the ruins of the rock-city of Petra. In ancient times this city was extremely prosperous, and controlled the trade route through it, although often captured and sacked by invading armies. To-day little remains except a few temples and tombs cut in the rock.

© E. N. A.

AN ANCIENT TRADE-ROUTE between Palestine and Arabia runs through this dark narrow gorge of the Wadi Musa near Petra. Although caravans are not so frequent to-day as they were before the Hejaz railway was built, many old-fashioned merchants and pilgrims still prefer to travel by foot or on horse or camel and robbers as in olden times still lie in wait for them.

LEVELING SANDY TUFTS TO MAKE WAY FOR IRRIGATED FARMS

A road grader, ungainly master of ruts and tufts, chugs across a bare field near an oasis in the Nejd. Next, plows will turn the soil, and water will pour from irrigation wells, pumps and pipes. Crops will be sown and harvested. Once again science and technology in the hands of an eager people will have pushed farther back the wasted, dry frontiers of the desert.

PHOTOS, STANDARD OIL CO. (N. J.)

MORE PLENTIFUL, LESS EXPENSIVE, THE IRREPLACEABLE OXEN

Arabs walk behind yokes of oxen, guiding primitive leveling tools. It is a long, hard day of work, but the effort brings the reward of a smooth field and a fine, porous soil. Though more and more tractors and other farm machines are being brought into Arabia for the development of the irrigated areas, draft animals still must shoulder much of the burden.

STANDARD OIL CO. (N. J.)

MELONS, STOREHOUSES OF WATER FOR DRY DESERT JOURNEYS

An Arab farmer and an American technical expert admire a harvest of watermelons, one of many crops grown on the model farms of Khafs Dhaghra. Nearby are the limestone pits, dug in the 1940's, that irrigate the vast Al Kharj oasis in the Nejd. Because they contain a great amount of water, melons are highly prized by desert travelers of the Middle East.

CARVED BALCONIES, many of them beautifully painted and decorated with Arabic scrolls, overhang the winding streets of Jidda (Jeddah), a Red Sea port. Mohammedan pilgrims on their way to the holy city of Mecca, come here by boat and then, in recent years, make use of the motor bus service to reach their destination. There are several foreign legations in Jidda.

MC LEISH

THIS RED STONE TEMPLE of El-Deir at Petra was not built up of separate blocks of stone but was hewn from the solid cliff. To-day it is the most splendid of the remains that tell of the city's vanished glory. It was fashioned by the Romans when they captured Petra in the hope of securing for themselves the wealth and commerce of its inhabitants.

DHOWS AT ANCHOR IN THE HARBOR OF MANAMA, BAHREIN ISLANDS

Bahrein Islands fishermen spend much of their time in the dhow, the heavy craft with the leaning mast and the swinging yard from which is hung a large lateen, or triangular, sail. From Manama, capital of the islands, the fleets go out into the Persian Gulf, where they brave the hottest of suns, and come back laden to the gunwales with pearl oysters and fish.

PHOTOS, STANDARD OIL CO. (N. J.)

IN THE MANAMA BAZAAR, MARKETING CENTER OF THE BAHREINS

A ragged canopy of burlap cools a street in the bazaar of Manama. People walk the sun- and shadow-striped way at a summer's pace, haggling at the shops and stalls for a comb, a gem, a watch—perhaps a typewriter or a phonograph. Sometimes the rarest, least expected goods can be produced from shelf or trunk. Then buyer and seller bargain on the price.

© E. N. A.

ARAB WOMAN TRANSPORTING WATER

Like their sisters in many other Eastern lands, the women of Arabia carry their water-jars to and from the wells balanced carefully upon their heads. They usually wear clothes of sombre hue, and seldom appear unveiled.

tain sects of the Shiites say that they doubt the divine character of the Koran, stating that it was given to the Angel Gabriel for transmission to Ali, the Prophet's son-in-law, but that by mistake he handed it on to Mohammed.

The population is more or less divided into the semi-permanent inhabitants of the coast and of the cities and towns, and the wandering tribes of the interior. The latter are constantly migrating for their life is a pastoral one and they must move their encampments in order to find fresh pastures for their flocks and herds.

The dress of the men and women is very much the same. It is designed to give both ease and dignity, and consists of a long linen shirt, baggy trousers of linen that are fastened at the waist with a cord, and a cloak with ample sleeves. In the cold weather the sleeves can be used as gloves by being drawn over the hands. Over this cloak is worn a mantle of bright-colored cloth with, perhaps, a collar of gold or silver work.

A colored handkerchief covers the head and is secured by a woolen band worn in a double circle round the head. For footwear the Arab uses sandals. An Arab when mounted is an imposing sight, with his cartridge belt round his waist, his rifle slung across his shoulder or over the back part of the camel saddle, with his dagger stuck in a belt and his cloak thrown back. Thus arrayed he looks the picture of romance and wild freedom. He has some curious customs regarding the cloak. When entering a town or village it must be worn properly and not thrown back, but when approaching a camp or caravan out in the open plains he waves it as a sign that he has no hostile intentions and that none need fear for life or property.

HEADLEY

MECCA'S GREAT MOSQUE is the holiest place on earth to a Mohammedan. He turns towards it when he prays, no matter in what part of the world he may be. The black cube-shaped structure in the centre of the courtyard of the mosque is the Ka'ba, or Holy House, the chief sanctuary of the town of Mecca even long before Mohammed. It is covered with silk. Pilgrims must, as their first duty, walk or run around the Ka'ba seven times murmuring prayers the while. In the courtyard, it can be seen, is a well in which pious Mohammedans dip linen that is later made into shrouds.

HEADLEY

THIS PILGRIM CARAVAN is on its way to the hill of Arafat which Mohammedans hold in the greatest reverence. It lies about thirteen miles east of Mecca. All those who make the pilgrimage to the Holy City go to Arafat. They travel on foot, donkeys, horses and camels. This Caravan has two files of camels; those on the right carry the baggage and provisions, those on the left bear "shugdufs," tents of carpets and curtains which protect the riders from the sun. Every Moslem, financially able, is bound to go to Mecca once in his lifetime, or provide a substitute.

Ewing Galloway, N. Y.

MUSCAT, INDIAN OCEAN PORT AND CAPITAL OF THE SULTANATE OF OMAN

Glimmering in the hot sun, the white buildings of the town nestle beneath an old Portuguese citadel. It dates from the days when Muscat was in Portuguese hands, during the sixteenth century. White buildings reflect heat and are a necessity in a land where the temperature seldom goes below 90 degrees in the shade and often reaches 110 degrees. Muscat is the only port for steamships in the region, although the town itself is a rather quiet, sleepy place. Ships that stop there load dates, Arabian horses and wheat, the most valuable products of the region.

The houses vary according to the district. There are camps of tents and houses of limestone blocks quarried in the vicinity. Let us pay a visit to an ordinary city or town. It is a curious mixture of architecture. There are the dwellings of the rich, with solid walls and exquisite woodwork tracery and carving; houses of mud with flat roofs; reed huts and, upon the outskirts of the towns, the camps of those who have come in from outlying parts to barter and trade. Among the houses are mosques with tall white minarets, from the summits of which the "muezzin," or priest, will call the Faithful to prayer five times during the twenty-four hours.

We may best see the life of Arabia on a bazaar, or market day. Tents of matting are erected and are crowded with all kinds of marketable goods, from wool, cloth, reed mats, palm fibre and dates, to fruit of every description, cattle, sheep, implements and all that goes to make up commercial and pastoral existence in Arabia of to-day.

STANDARD OIL CO. (N. J.)

HAMMERING SILVER INTO USEFUL SHAPES

A silversmith of the Bahrein Islands follows the old ways of his craft in an open shop. With infinite patience he will beat the silver bar, held on the old-fashioned anvil, into a tray or dish or box.

Apart from the booths and tents, there are the permanent shops, which are roofed like arcades in our country. In them we may see tailors, potters, metal-workers, jewelers, dressmakers, carpet-sellers and members of most other trades and professions, with crowds of people always seeking bargains. Every now and then, donkeys heavily laden with merchandise or camels with loads sticking out at dangerous angles force a way through the crowd. They may often unceremoniously hurl passers-by into shop fronts, thereby upsetting the shopkeeper's goods, but no one seems to resent this treatment for it has all been a part of the bazaar for ages past.

In Arabia, religion plays an important part in the daily life of the people, and when the priest gives the call to prayer from the towering minaret all business ceases for the moment and everyone turns to wash their hands and feet before praying. At the conclusion of the prayer business is resumed and the clamor of buying and selling continued.

Marriage in Arabia is a simple affair for it demands no more than the presence of a priest and four witnesses. In the interior of the country it is still further shorn of ceremony, for the legal necessities of the occasion are satisfied by the presence of witnesses from both families, and, a feast having been given, the marriage festivities are over.

From the romantic aspect, the Arabs of the desert are the most interesting to us, for they are the riders of the plains and are forever on the move. The internal

Black Star

ONE OF THE FORTIFIED GATES TO THE WALLED CITY OF SAN'A, CAPITAL OF YEMEN

San'a lies high in the mountainous interior of Yemen, 7,250 feet above sea level. It is a walled city with eight gates, and within are forty-eight mosques. San'a has been a trading center since ancient times. Tradition has it that San'a was one of the chief cities of the kingdom of the Queen of Sheba (or Saba), whose visit to King Solomon is recorded in the Bible. Today camel caravans, laden with coffee, indigo, safflower, madder, frankincense and myrrh, still plod the road between San'a and its port Hodeida, on the Red Sea, forty miles away.

McLeish

WATER-CARRIER OF YEMEN WITH HIS WELL-LADEN CAMEL

The southern stretches of the great Tehama Desert lie in Yemen, and are occupied mainly by camel-breeders. There is little water in the Tehama, so that a water-carrier and his camel are important figures in any expedition, whether warlike or peaceful, made by the desert Arabs. This man has filled his earthenware water-jars from the well by the mosque.

decoration of an Arab tent is often carried out on artistic lines if the owner be moderately wealthy. The floor is covered with carpets, and on one side will be a divan formed of carpets and cushions for the host and his guests. The walls are hung with embroideries worked by the women, who are as clever with the needle as they are at rounding-up cattle and camels. Suspended along the walls will be guns, harness and clothes, and on the floor stand the numerous coffee-pots and cups.

The Arab diet is mainly mutton, rice and bread, with small cakes made from milk and a form of vermicelli. If the camp be near the coast, fish is included. Prawns served dry are very popular. Camels' milk is drunk, and the first thing a thirsty traveler does is to drain a bowl of it.

On the occasion of a big feast, such as the marriage of an important person or some political event, the meat and rice are cooked in a kind of steamer raised a few inches above the ground and are served with bread, cakes, fruit, dates, milk and sundry other dishes. The company disposes of the food without the aid of knives and forks, making use of the fingers as Nature intended. At the end of the repast brass and copper bowls are handed round, in which the guests wash their hands.

An Arab Tribe on the March

When on trek the Arabs have some interesting customs in connection with their camping grounds. They send one of their number ahead, and he reserves the site of the proposed camp by spreading a mantle over a bush in the centre of the chosen ground. Although there may be others moving in the same direction, no one will interfere with the selection, however good the pasturage or attractive its other qualities.

The tribe marches in a long cavalcade, with possibly several thousand head of camels, sheep, goats and cattle. The men are distributed along the convoy directing the line of march. The women and children and all the paraphernalia of the camp are on camels and donkeys, and at the head of the tribe rides the sheik, or chief.

The women are veiled and ride on camels in a sort of huge pannier—a basket-carriage placed on the camel's back —with two large wooden crescents at front and rear, the horns of which stand out on each side of the pannier. From them hang the long tassels and the gaudy embroidery of this queer carriage. These are its most attractive feature, for the pannier is very uncomfortable, and the unfortunate occupants are like hens cooped up in a form of rocking carriage, the motion of which varies in accordance with the ground over which the caravan is passing.

Camp Site Dependent on Water

The camp is always pitched by a well. Water is scarce in Arabia, and the site of a well is usually marked by cairns of stones erected on the surrounding heights, so that the weary traveler may know that water is at hand and he is near his goal. The camels are watered once in every four or five days, but they can exist much longer in cases of dire necessity. The loading and unloading are done by the women, while the men watch the process and drink coffee.

As an Arab caravan leaves its camp in the morning it is a sight that reminds us of the stories of biblical days. Even as the patriarchs and their followers marched across the desert, so in our time do the Arab tribes move across the deserts, their banner leading them on by day and a lamp at night.

Unchanging Ways of the Desert

Thus do the ways of the desert remain the same, for time has not changed the order of things that was in vogue three thousand years ago. Not only in this respect is the life unchanged, for even the drawing of water at the wells is done the same way as in the days of Abraham. A rope is attached to the leather bucket, which is lowered and drawn up by a camel descending and ascending an inclined plane. It is picturesque, but laborious, yet the Arab will not change it for any more modern and rapid system, for it is sanctified by time and a recognized institution of pastoral life.

Among the wild life of Arabia is the ostrich, but it is only met with in certain parts. There are also gazelles and hares and a variety of bustard. The cheetah, or hunting leopard, is found in those parts of the desert frequented by gazelles, its principal prey. Its speed is almost incredible when it gives chase. It covers the ground in a rush that must be seen to be realized. A cheetah that the writer

FRITZ HENLE

CANALS TO COLLECT RAIN WATER FOR THE DESERT TOWN OF ADEN

Aden has little fresh water, and these canals help to conserve the scanty rainfall. Drinking water is also obtained from artesian wells and by distilling sea water. The British-owned fortress town, built partly in the crater of an extinct volcano on a rocky peninsula, guards the southern entrance to the Red Sea. Its climate is normally hot and dry.

Dixon

MUZZLED OXEN TRAMPLING OUT GRAIN NEAR ADEN, ARABIA

In direct opposition to Mosaic law, the oxen of Arabia are muzzled so that they are unable to eat the grain while they are treading. The animals work in pairs, and are roped to a central stake around which the jowari, a grain grown near Aden, is piled. Oxen are specially suited to this work, since the more tired they become the more heavily they tread.

knew brought down an antelope in a run of six hundred yards, the quarry having a start of two hundred yards.

The Beduins, the true children of the desert, have changed least of all in Arabia. They are the wild freemen who harassed the caravans of pilgrims a thousand years ago and they still keep their old wild habits. As they ride along they note every fold in the ground, for it may serve them in case of an attack or a raid by other tribesmen, and they notice every tuft of grass and every bush as possible fodder for their herds or for some sign of foes in the neighborhood.

They guard their flocks and herds like the tribesmen of old. In the heat of the day they recline in the shade of a palm tree, if there be one, or beneath reed matting stuck up on poles. They know the ways of their sheep and goats, and during the noonday siesta we may see a mantle arranged upon sticks so that it resembles a man and serves as a substitute for the shepherd. From time immemorial the goats and sheep have grazed quite placidly round the dummy under the impression that it is their master, and so they do not stray, while the shepherd is enjoying his sleep in peace.

One of the chief occupations of the Arabs is that of camel-breeding and they understand this animal better than any other race. From its hair they make blankets, tents, ropes and even clothing. They drink its milk, eat its flesh and tan its hide for leather; but they have no affection for the beast that gives them so much. Without the camels the Arab would scarcely be able to live in the desert, but all his affection, if he has any, is lavished upon his horse, which is looked upon as a family pet.

The horse is, however, unsuited to life in the desert as is shown in the following story which is current among the Arabs: "The horse complained to Allah that he was not made for desert journeying. His hoofs sank into the sand, the saddle slipped off his back, he could not reach the

STANDARD OIL CO. (N. J.)

STRIPPING DATE-PALM STALKS IN THE FERTILE OASIS OF KHARJ

The date palm is by far the most important product of Kharj district and of the entire province of Nejd in central Saudi Arabia. Not only the fruit but every part of the date palm is valuable. Seeds are roasted for coffee or pressed for oil, leaves are woven into baskets or thatch, bark fiber is made into rope. These stalks will go into the roof of a new building.

scanty grass and small shrubs which grew by the roadside. So Allah designed an animal which had a long neck for reaching after food, cushioned feet which did not sink into the sand, a hump on which the load could be balanced. But when the horse saw this animal it started with horror, and knew how foolish it had been to complain. It still may be observed how horses shy at the sight of camels, and sometimes can hardly be induced to pass them."

There is much of interest throughout Arabia. There are tribes whose origin is veiled in the mists of antiquity and there are fertile corners that the Arabs tell us have yet to be explored. There are no rivers, only "wadis," or valleys that are dry during most of the year but are sometimes occupied by streams. There are high mountains, stretches of bleak, arid desert that become fresh green pastures in the months of spring, and wonderful ruins of ancient, deserted cities. It is a fascinating country, for there we seem to be back in early days and among biblical scenes that have altered little in many centuries.

THE ARABIAN PENINSULA: FACTS AND FIGURES

THE COUNTRY

A large eastern peninsula of Asia, bounded on the north by Iraq and Jordan, on the east by the Persian Gulf, on the south by the Arabian Sea, on the west by the Red Sea. Much of the land is desert, and some has never been crossed by Europeans. Includes several more or less independent states with boundaries ill-defined. Total area over 1,000,000 square miles; total population, probably about 12,000,000, but no census has ever been taken.

SAUDI ARABIA

The kingdom of Saudi Arabia is composed of two former kingdoms—Hejaz and Nejd—and their dependencies, and occupies the northwestern and central areas of the peninsula. The area is estimated to be 800,000 square miles, and the population about 6,000,000. Although ruled by one king, the country is dual in government, with two capitals—Mecca and Riyadh. In Nejd, the king rules in a patriarchal form of government. Hejaz has a constitutional government, with a president (ordinarily a son of the king) and council of ministers. A single constitution was proposed in 1932. The religious law of Islam is the common law of all the land and is administered by religious courts headed by a chief judge.

In the Nejd, the products are dates, wheat, barley, fruits, hides, clarified butter, wool and livestock. The export trade is of little significance. Imports are cotton piece-goods, tea, coffee, sugar and rice. The towns of Hufuf and Riyadh have populations of about 50,000.

Hejaz produces dates, honey and fruit. The Beduin products are hides, wool and butter. Foreign oil concessions are of great value to the country. The annual pilgrimage to Mecca is another source of revenue. There are few roads. Routes are made suitable for motor traffic especially for carrying the pilgrims. The population of the chief towns are: Mecca, 200,000; Jedda, 75,000; Medina, 50,000.

YEMEN

An independent imamate located in the southwest corner of the peninsula with a king or imam as its head. The area is about 75,000 sq. mi. and the population about 5,000,000. Agricultural products include barley, wheat, millet and especially coffee. Hides and coffee are exported. San'a, the capital, has a population of 30,000.

MUSCAT AND OMAN

An independent state located in the easterly corner of the peninsula with an area of about 82,000 sq. mi. and a population estimated at 550,000 chiefly Arabs though there are also negroes. It is governed by a sultan. Date cultivation and the breeding of camels are the chief occupations. Dates, pomegranates, limes, and dried fish are exported. Imports are rice and coffee. The capital, Muscat, has a population of 5,000.

KOWEIT (KUWEIT OR KUWAIT)

A state located on the northwestern coast of the Persian Gulf. It is governed by a native ruler. The population is about 180,000.

ADEN

A British colony (since 1937) on the southwest coast of the peninsula which is important as a bunkering station on the highway to the east. Its area is 75 sq. mi. and that of Perim Island 5 sq. mi. The total population is 80,876. A British governor and commander-in-chief have charge of the government which includes the Aden Protectorate and Hadhramaut (combined area, 112,000 sq. mi.). Attached for the purposes of government is Sokotra Island. The five Kuria Muria Islands, south of Oman, are also a part of the colony.

BAHREIN

The Bahrein Islands, in the Persian Gulf, are an independent state with a population of about 120,000. Oil and pearl-fishing are the chief industries.

Index for Volume III

Color Plates in Volume III

INDEX FOR VOLUME III

(General Index for entire work of 7 volumes may be found at the end of Volume 7)

A single star before a page number marks an illustration; two stars are placed before color-plates. The repetition of a page number, first without a star, and then with a star, shows that there is an illustration on the page, in addition to an important text reference.

PRINTED IN THE U. S. A.